Patrick B. Mahoney
Editor

Distance Learning Library Services: The Tenth Off-Campus Library Services Conference

Distance Learning Library Services: The Tenth Off-Campus Library Services Conference has been co-published simultaneously as *Journal of Library Administration*, Volume 37, Numbers 1/2 and 3/4 2002.

Pre-publication REVIEWS, COMMENTARIES, EVALUATIONS . . .

"INDISPENSABLE for librarians who have responsibility for off-campus programs . . . EXTREMELY USEFUL for administrators and others who realize that services offered to off-campus students need to come into the mainstream of the academic library's overall goals."

Michele D. Behr, MLS
Off-Campus Services Librarian
Western Michigan University

The Haworth Information Press
An Imprint of The Haworth Press, Inc.

Distance Learning Library Services: The Tenth Off-Campus Library Services Conference

Distance Learning Library Services: The Tenth Off-Campus Library Services Conference has been co-published simultaneously as *Journal of Library Administration*, Volume 37, Numbers 1/2 and 3/4 2002.

The *Journal of Library Administration* Monographic "Separates"

Below is a list of "separates," which in serials librarianship means a special issue simultaneously published as a special journal issue or double-issue *and* as a "separate" hardbound monograph. (This is a format which we also call a "DocuSerial.")

"Separates" are published because specialized libraries or professionals may wish to purchase a specific thematic issue by itself in a format which can be separately cataloged and shelved, as opposed to purchasing the journal on an on-going basis. Faculty members may also more easily consider a "separate" for classroom adoption.

"Separates" are carefully classified separately with the major book jobbers so that the journal tie-in can be noted on new book order slips to avoid duplicate purchasing.

You may wish to visit Haworth's Website at . . .

http://www.HaworthPress.com

. . . to search our online catalog for complete tables of contents of these separates and related publications.

You may also call 1-800-HAWORTH (outside US/Canada: 607-722-5857), or Fax 1-800-895-0582 (outside US/Canada: 607-771-0012), or e-mail at:

docdelivery@haworthpress.com

Distance Learning Library Services: The Tenth Off-Campus Library Services Conference, edited by Patrick B. Mahoney (Vol. 37, No. 1/2/3/4, 2002). *Explores the pitfalls of providing information services to distance students and suggests ways to avoid them.*

Electronic Resources and Collection Development, edited by Sul H. Lee (Vol. 36, No. 3, 2002). *Shows how electronic resources have impacted traditional collection development policies and practices.*

Information Literacy Programs: Successes and Challenges, edited by Patricia Durisin, MLIS (Vol. 36, No. 1/2, 2002). *Examines Web-based collaboration, teamwork with academic and administrative colleagues, evidence-based librarianship, and active learning strategies in library instruction programs.*

Evaluating the Twenty-First Century Library: The Association of Research Libraries New Measures Initiative, 1997-2001, edited by Donald L. DeWitt, PhD (Vol. 35, No. 4, 2001). *This collection of articles (thirteen of which previously appeared in ARL's bimonthly newsletter/report on research issues and actions) examines the Association of Research Libraries' "new measures" initiative.*

Impact of Digital Technology on Library Collections and Resource Sharing, edited by Sul H. Lee (vol. 35, No. 3, 2001). *Shows how digital resources have changed the traditional academic library.*

Libraries and Electronic Resources: New Partnerships, New Practices, New Perspectives, edited by Pamela L. Higgins (Vol. 35, No. 1/2, 2001). *An essential guide to the Internet's impact on electronic resources mangement–past, present, and future.*

Diversity Now: People, Collections, and Services in Academic Libraries, edited by Teresa Y. Neely, MLS, PhD, and Kuang-Hwei (Janet) Lee-Smeltzer, MS, MSLIS (Vol. 33, No. 1/2/3/4, 2001). *Examines multicultural trends in academic libraries' staff and users, types of collections, and services offered.*

Leadership in the Library and Information Science Professions: Theory and Practice, edited by Mark D. Winston, MLS, PhD (Vol. 32, No. 3/4, 2001). *Offers fresh ideas for developing and using leadership skills, including recruiting potential leaders, staff training and development, issues of gender and ethnic diversity, and budget strategies for success.*

Off-Campus Library Services, edited by Ann Marie Casey (Vol. 31, No. 3/4, 2001 and Vol. 32, No. 1/2, 2001). *This informative volume examines various aspects of off-campus, or distance learning. It explores training issues for library staff, Web site development, changing roles for librarians, the uses of conferencing software, library support for Web-based courses, library agreements and how to successfully negotiate them, and much more!*

Research Collections and Digital Information, edited by Sul H. Lee (Vol. 31, No. 2, 2000). *Offers new strategies for collecting, organizing, and accessing library materials in the digital age.*

Academic Research on the Internet: Options for Scholars & Libraries, edited by Helen Laurence, MLS, EdD, and William Miller, MLS, PhD (Vol. 30, No. 1/2/3/4, 2000). *"Emphasizes quality over quantity. . . . Presents the reader with the best research-oriented Web sites in the field. A state-of-the-art review of academic use of the Internet as well as a guide to the best Internet sites and services. . . . A useful addition for any academic library." (David A. Tyckoson, MLS, Head of Reference, California State University, Fresno)*

Management for Research Libraries Cooperation, edited by Sul H. Lee (Vol. 29, No. 3/4, 2000). *Delivers sound advice, models, and strategies for increasing sharing between institutions to maximize the amount of printed and electronic research material you can make available in your library while keeping costs under control.*

Integration in the Library Organization, edited by Christine E. Thompson, PhD (Vol. 29, No. 2, 1999). *Provides librarians with the necessary tools to help libraries balance and integrate public and technical services and to improve the capability of libraries to offer patrons quality services and large amounts of information.*

Library Training for Staff and Customers, edited by Sara Ramser Beck, MLS, MBA (Vol. 29, No. 1, 1999). *This comprehensive book is designed to assist library professionals involved in presenting or planning training for library staff members and customers. You will explore ideas for effective general reference training, training on automated systems, training in specialized subjects such as African American history and biography, and training for areas such as patents and trademarks, and business subjects.* Library Training for Staff and Customers *answers numerous training questions and is an excellent guide for planning staff development.*

Collection Development in the Electronic Environment: Shifting Priorities, edited by Sul H. Lee (Vol. 28, No. 4, 1999). *Through case studies and firsthand experiences, this volume discusses meeting the needs of scholars at universities, budgeting issues, user education, staffing in the electronic age, collaborating libraries and resources, and how vendors meet the needs of different customers.*

The Age Demographics of Academic Librarians: A Profession Apart, by Stanley J. Wilder (Vol. 28, No. 3, 1999). *The average age of librarians has been increasing dramatically since 1990. This unique book will provide insights on how this demographic issue can impact a library and what can be done to make the effects positive.*

Collection Development in a Digital Environment, edited by Sul H. Lee (Vol. 28, No. 1, 1999). *Explores ethical and technological dilemmas of collection development and gives several suggestions on how a library can successfully deal with these challenges and provide patrons with the information they need.*

Scholarship, Research Libraries, and Global Publishing, by Jutta Reed-Scott (Vol. 27, No. 3/4, 1999). *This book documents a research project in conjunction with the Association of Research Libraries (ARL) that explores the issue of foreign acquisition and how it affects collection in international studies, area studies, collection development, and practices of international research libraries.*

Managing Multicultural Diversity in the Library: Principles and Issues for Administrators, edited by Mark Winston (Vol. 27, No. 1/2, 1999). *Defines diversity, clarifies why it is important to address issues of diversity, and identifies goals related to diversity and how to go about achieving those goals.*

Information Technology Planning, edited by Lori A. Goetsch (Vol. 26, No. 3/4, 1999). *Offers innovative approaches and strategies useful in your library and provides some food for thought about information technology as we approach the millennium.*

The Economics of Information in the Networked Environment, edited by Meredith A. Butler, MLS, and Bruce R. Kingma, PhD (Vol. 26, No. 1/2, 1998). *"A book that should be read both by information professionals and by administrators, faculty and others who share a collective concern to provide the most information to the greatest number at the lowest cost in the networked environment." (Thomas J. Galvin, PhD, Professor of Information Science and Policy, University at Albany, State University of New York)*

OCLC 1967-1997: Thirty Years of Furthering Access to the World's Information, edited by K. Wayne Smith (Vol. 25, No. 2/3/4, 1998). *"A rich–and poignantly personal, at times–historical account of what is surely one of this century's most important developments in librarianship." (Deanna B. Marcum, PhD, President, Council on Library and Information Resources, Washington, DC)*

Management of Library and Archival Security: From the Outside Looking In, edited by Robert K. O'Neill, PhD (Vol. 25, No. 1, 1998). *"Provides useful advice and on-target insights for professionals caring for valuable documents and artifacts." (Menzi L. Behrnd-Klodt, JD, Attorney/Archivist, Klodt and Associates, Madison, WI)*

Economics of Digital Information: Collection, Storage, and Delivery, edited by Sul H. Lee (Vol. 24, No. 4, 1997). *Highlights key concepts and issues vital to a library's successful venture into the digital environment and helps you understand why the transition from the printed page to the digital packet has been problematic for both creators of proprietary materials and users of those materials.*

The Academic Library Director: Reflections on a Position in Transition, edited by Frank D'Andraia, MLS (Vol. 24, No. 3, 1997). *"A useful collection to have whether you are seeking a position as director or conducting a search for one." (College & Research Libraries News)*

Emerging Patterns of Collection Development in Expanding Resource Sharing, Electronic Information, and Network Environment, edited by Sul H. Lee (Vol. 24, No. 1/2, 1997). *"The issues it deals with are common to us all. We all need to make our funds go further and our resources work harder, and there are ideas here which we can all develop." (The Library Association Record)*

Interlibrary Loan/Document Delivery and Customer Satisfaction: Strategies for Redesigning Services, edited by Pat L. Weaver-Meyers, Wilbur A. Stolt, and Yem S. Fong (Vol. 23, No. 1/2, 1997). *"No interlibrary loan department supervisor at any mid-sized to large college or university library can afford not to read this book." (Gregg Sapp, MLS, MEd, Head of Access Services, University of Miami, Richter Library, Coral Gables, Florida)*

Access, Resource Sharing and Collection Development, edited by Sul H. Lee (Vol. 22, No. 4, 1996). *Features continuing investigation and discussion of important library issues, specifically the role of libraries in acquiring, storing, and disseminating information in different formats.*

Managing Change in Academic Libraries, edited by Joseph J. Branin (Vol. 22, No. 2/3, 1996). *"Touches on several aspects of academic library management, emphasizing the changes that are occurring at the present time. . . . Recommended this title for individuals or libraries interested in management aspects of academic libraries." (RQ American Library Association)*

Libraries and Student Assistants: Critical Links, edited by William K. Black, MLS (Vol. 21, No. 3/4, 1995). *"A handy reference work on many important aspects of managing student assistants. . . . Solid, useful information on basic management issues in this work and several chapters are useful for experienced managers." (The Journal of Academic Librarianship)*

The Future of Resource Sharing, edited by Shirley K. Baker and Mary E. Jackson, MLS (Vol. 21, No. 1/2, 1995). *"Recommended for library and information science schools because of its balanced presentation of the ILL/document delivery issues." (Library Acquisitions: Practice and Theory)*

The Future of Information Services, edited by Virginia Steel, MA, and C. Brigid Welch, MLS (Vol. 20, No. 3/4, 1995). *"The leadership discussions will be useful for library managers as will the discussions of how library structures and services might work in the next century." (Australian Special Libraries)*

The Dynamic Library Organizations in a Changing Environment, edited by Joan Giesecke, MLS, DPA (Vol. 20, No. 2, 1995). *"Provides a significant look at potential changes in the library world and presents its readers with possible ways to address the negative results of such changes. . . . Covers the key issues facing today's libraries . . . Two thumbs up!" (Marketing Library Resources)*

Monographic "Separates" list continued at the back

Distance Learning Library Services: The Tenth Off-Campus Library Services Conference

Patrick B. Mahoney
Editor

Distance Learning Library Services: The Tenth Off-Campus Library Services Conference has been co-published simultaneously as *Journal of Library Administration*, Volume 37, Numbers 1/2 and 3/4 2002.

The Haworth Information Press
An Imprint of
The Haworth Press, Inc.
New York • London • Oxford

Published by

The Haworth Information Press®, 10 Alice Street, Binghamton, NY 13904-1580 USA

The Haworth Information Press® is an imprint of The Haworth Press, Inc., 10 Alice Street, Binghamton, NY 13904-1580 USA.

Distance Learning Library Services: The Tenth Off-Campus Library Services Conference has been co-published simultaneously as *Journal of Library Administration,* Volume 37, Numbers 1/2 and 3/4 2002.

Cover design by Lora Wiggins.

Library of Congress Cataloging-in-Publication Data

Off-Campus Library Services Conference (10th : 2002 Cincinnati, Ohio)
Distance learning library services : the tenth Off-Campus Library Services Conference : [proceedings] / Patrick B. Mahoney, editor.
     p. cm.
     "Co-published simultaneously as Journal of Library Administration, Volume 37, Numbers 1/2 and 3/4, 2002."
     Includes bibliographical references and index.
     ISBN 0-7890-2074-2 (hard : alk. paper) – ISBN 0-7890-2075-0 (pbk. : alk. paper)
     1. Academic libraries–Off-campus services–Congresses. 2. Libraries and distance education–Congresses. 3. University extension–Congresses. 4. Libraries–Special collections–Electronic information resources. 5. Electronic reserve collections in libraries–Congresses. 6. Information literacy–Congresses. I. Mahoney, Patrick B. II. Journal of Library Administration. III. Title.
Z675.U5 O35 2002
025.5–dc21

2002154467

Indexing, Abstracting & Website/Internet Coverage

This section provides you with a list of major indexing & abstracting services. That is to say, each service began covering this periodical during the year noted in the right column. Most Websites which are listed below have indicated that they will either post, disseminate, compile, archive, cite or alert their own Website users with research-based content from this work. (This list is as current as the copyright date of this publication.)

Abstracting, Website/Indexing Coverage . . . . Year When Coverage Began

- *Academic Abstracts/CD-ROM* 1993
- *Academic Search: data base of 2,000 selected academic serials, updated monthly: EBSCO Publishing* 1995
- *Academic Search Elite (EBSCO)* 1993
- *Academic Search Premier (EBSCO)* 2001
- *AGRICOLA Database <www.natl.usda.gov/ag98>* 1991
- *Business ASAP* 1993
- *CNPIEC Reference Guide: Chinese National Directory of Foreign Periodicals* 1995
- *Current Articles on Library Literature and Services (CALLS)* 1992
- *Current Cites [Digital Libraries] [Electronic Publishing] [Multimedia & Hypermedia] [Networks & Networking] [General]* 2000
- *Current Index to Journals in Education* 1986
- *Educational Administration Abstracts (EAA)* 1991
- *FINDEX <www.publist.com>* 1999
- *FRANCIS. INIST/CNRS <www.inist.fr>* 1986
- *General BusinessFile ASAP <www.galegroup.com>* 1993
- *General Reference Center GOLD on InfoTrac Web* 1984
- *Higher Education Abstracts, providing the latest in research & theory in more than 140 major topics* 1991
- *IBZ International Bibliography of Periodical Literature <www.saur.de>* 1995
- *Index Guide to College Journals (core list compiled by integrating 48 indexes frequently used to support undergraduate programs in small to medium sized libraries)* 1999
- *Index to Periodical Articles Related to Law* 1989

(continued)

*Special Bibliographic Notes related to special journal issues
(separates) and indexing/abstracting:*

- indexing/abstracting services in this list will also cover material in any "separate" that is co-published simultaneously with Haworth's special thematic journal issue or DocuSerial. Indexing/abstracting usually covers material at the article/chapter level.
- monographic co-editions are intended for either non-subscribers or libraries which intend to purchase a second copy for their circulating collections.
- monographic co-editions are reported to all jobbers/wholesalers/approval plans. The source journal is listed as the "series" to assist the prevention of duplicate purchasing in the same manner utilized for books-in-series.
- to facilitate user/access services all indexing/abstracting services are encouraged to utilize the co-indexing entry note indicated at the bottom of the first page of each article/chapter/contribution.
- this is intended to assist a library user of any reference tool (whether print, electronic, online, or CD-ROM) to locate the monographic version if the library has purchased this version but not a subscription to the source journal.
- individual articles/chapters in any Haworth publication are also available through the Haworth Document Delivery Service (HDDS).

Distance Learning Library Services: The Tenth Off-Campus Library Services Conference

CONTENTS

ABOUT THE EDITOR

Patrick B. Mahoney, MBA, MLS, is an off-campus librarian with Central Michigan University. He works with the school's distance students in accessing information both online and in traditional print formats, and regularly teaches students to conduct research and use the school's databases. His professional interests include information use by nontraditional students and the implementation of assessment guidelines. Mr. Mahoney is active with several ALA committees, including the Instruction Committee within the Distance Learning Section and the Dun & Bradstreet Public Librarian Support Award Committee within the Business Reference Services Section. He also has conducted numerous presentations that pertain to information access for the Kansas City Metropolitan Library & Information Network. In addition, he has written numerous book reviews for *Library Journal* and various newsletters.

Foreword

One of the many changes the 1990s brought to librarianship has been a need to provide library resources to non-traditional students who rarely visit an institution's main campus. More and more, colleges and universities have made concentrated efforts to take their degree programs to off-campus students. As that trend developed, it soon became obvious that there was a student body who needed library resources, and, for a variety of reasons, was not able to travel to the distant campus library. As a result, libraries sought to accommodate this new user group and the concept of providing basic library services to distant learners has developed into a growing new field of librarianship.

Central Michigan University Libraries and Central Michigan University College of Extended Learning have evolved as leaders in the field of off-campus library services. For a decade, Central Michigan University has sponsored national conferences that examine the issues and challenges of providing library resources to distant learners. The 2002 conference was held in Cincinnati, Ohio, on April 17-22, 2002 and the papers presented there are published in this volume. They cover a broad spectrum of distant learning issues including the evaluation of Web resources for distance learners; changing librarian perspectives about serving distant learners; and the need for cooperation with public libraries in communities served by distant learning programs. The papers also include many valuable case studies that explore how colleges and university libraries are meeting distant learning needs.

The 2002 conference was an important venue for the exchange of ideas about, and practices for serving distant learning programs. We believe that the articles presented here will be of interest to a wide range of librarians. It is our hope that publishing them in the *Journal of Library Administration* will make them available to a large segment of the profession.

Sul H. Lee
Editor
Journal of Library Administration

[Haworth co-indexing entry note]: "Foreword." Lee, Sul H. Co-published simultaneously in *Journal of Library Administration* (The Haworth Information Press, an imprint of The Haworth Press, Inc.) Vol. 37, No. 1/2, 2002, p. xxi; and: *Distance Learning Library Services: The Tenth Off-Campus Library Services Conference* (ed: Patrick B. Mahoney) The Haworth Information Press, an imprint of The Haworth Press, Inc., 2002, p. xvii. Single or multiple copies of this article are available for a fee from The Haworth Document Delivery Service [1-800-HAWORTH, 9:00 a.m. - 5:00 p.m. (EST). E-mail address: docdelivery@haworthpress.com].

Preface

Welcome to the Tenth Off-Campus Library Services Conference Proceedings. Once again, the Central Michigan University Libraries and the Central Michigan University College of Extended Learning have provided generous support of both this conference and these Proceedings.

The papers included here were selected by a twenty-four member Program Advisory Board using a juried abstracts process. All of the contributed papers have been formatted consistent with the conference *Guidelines for Preparing Manuscripts* distributed to contributors. Typographical errors have been corrected and cited references have been formatted consistent with guidelines published in the *Publication Manual of the American Psychological Association* (5th ed.), *APA Publication Manual* Web site at http://www.apastyle.org/, and other reputable sources.

Patrick B. Mahoney
Editor

[Haworth co-indexing entry note]: "Preface." Mahoney, Patrick B. Co-published simultaneously in *Journal of Library Administration* (The Haworth Information Press, an imprint of The Haworth Press, Inc.) Vol. 37, No. 1/2, 2002, p. xxiii; and: *Distance Learning Library Services: The Tenth Off-Campus Library Services Conference* (ed: Patrick B. Mahoney) The Haworth Information Press, an imprint of The Haworth Press, Inc., 2002, p. xix. Single or multiple copies of this article are available for a fee from The Haworth Document Delivery Service [1-800-HAWORTH, 9:00 a.m. - 5:00 p.m. (EST). E-mail address: docdelivery@haworthpress.com].

Acknowledgments

As usual, I am thrilled to have the many presenters participate in this year's OCLS Conference. Their knowledge of unique information services to distant students, faculty, and others who are not able to utilize a traditional library has helped make the Conference a success.

Thanks go to Anne Marie Casey and P. Steven Thomas, whose advice based on past OCLS Conference experiences have been invaluable. Thanks also go to the Program Advisory Board for reviewing dozens of submitted Conference paper proposals. A special thanks goes to Connie Hildebrand, who again has served as Conference Coordinator. Without her wisdom and guidance these Proceedings would not be possible.

I would also like to recognize the support and encouragement from Thomas J. Moore, CMU Dean of Libraries and Marcia Bankirer, CMU Vice Provost/ Dean of the College of Extended Learning.

Program Advisory Board
and Executive Planning Committee*

Dr. Tom Abbott
Dean of Libraries and Instructional
Support and Dean of UMA's Lewiston-
Auburn Campus
University of Maine at Augusta

Robert K. Baker, Ed.D.
Community Campus Librarian
Pima Community College

Nancy E. Black
Regional Services Librarian
UNBC Library

Amy Brunvand
Marriott Library Circulation Department
University of Utah

Marissa Cachero*
Off-Campus Library Services
Central Michigan University

Hide Calvert
Head of Access Services
Ball State University

Patricia Cardenas
Academic Outreach Library
University of Illinois
at Urbana-Champaign

Anne Marie Casey*
Director, Off-Campus Library Services
Central Michigan University

Anthony Cavanagh
Document Delivery Librarian
Deakin University Library

Dr. Doug Cook
Reference and Instruction
Librarian
Shippensburg University

Monica Hines Craig*
Off-Campus Library Services
Central Michigan University

Trish Del Nero
Outreach Librarian
Loyola University

William Denny*
Off-Campus Library Services
Central Michigan University

Stephen Dew
Coordinator of Library Services
for Distance Education
University of Iowa Libraries

Daniel Gall*
Off-Campus Library Services
Central Michigan University

Connie Hildebrand*
Conference Coordinator
Off-Campus Library Services
Central Michigan University

Katherine Holmes
Assistant Director
Ludcke Library at Lesley University

Ann Jacobson
Reference and Instruction Librarian
Naval Postgraduate School

Doreen M. Keable, Ed.D.
Professor Emeritus
St. Cloud State

Jamie Kearley
Outreach Librarian
University of Wyoming Libraries

Robin Lockerby
Instructional Services Coordinator
National University Library

Patrick Mahoney*
Off-Campus Library Services
Central Michigan University

Stephanie Race
Assistant Director
Northeast Florida Library
Information Network

Joanne Smyth
Distance Education Services
University of New Brunswick
Libraries

Introduction

This year's contributed papers reflect the concerns of librarians specializing in providing services to an ever-growing segment of information seekers who do not have access to a traditional library. Several contributors grapple with issues dealing with using electronic resources, such as the World Wide Web, to effectively reach distant learners. Many other contributors discuss collaborating with faculty and academic departments in order to better coordinate efforts of distance learning programs.

As the needs of distance learners change thus expanding the duties and roles of off-campus librarians, guidelines are needed to provide a point of reference. This is reflected in the use of the *ACRL Guidelines for Distance Learning Library Services*, revised in 2000, in many papers. A hallmark of any profession is its growth by building on previous bodies of works. This year's papers reflect this building process by widely citing papers from earlier OCLS Conferences.

Perhaps the major strength of these papers rests in the practical applications of solutions to challenges facing off-campus librarians. If the goal of a conference is to provide papers that exchange ideas and offer solutions to tough problems, then these contributed papers have been highly successful.

Patrick B. Mahoney
Editor

[Haworth co-indexing entry note]: "Introduction." Mahoney, Patrick B. Co-published simultaneously in *Journal of Library Administration* (The Haworth Information Press, an imprint of The Haworth Press, Inc.) Vol. 37, No. 1/2, 2002, p. 1; and: *Distance Learning Library Services: The Tenth Off-Campus Library Services Conference* (ed: Patrick B. Mahoney) The Haworth Information Press, an imprint of The Haworth Press, Inc., 2002, p. 1.

http://www.haworthpress.com/store/product.asp?sku=J111
10.1300/J111v37n01_01

Content and Design
of Academic Library Web Sites
for Distance Learners:
An Analysis of ARL Libraries

Kate E. Adams
Mary Cassner

University of Nebraska-Lincoln

SUMMARY. College and university libraries use the Web to communicate with distance learners about library services. How easy is it for distance learners to determine which library services offered by their home institution are available to them? Do academic libraries provide a comprehensive Web page intended specifically for distance learners? This study evaluates the Web pages of Association of Research Libraries member libraries for content and design of pages intended for distance learners.

KEYWORDS. Academic libraries, distance learners, Web sites, design

Distance students expect to remotely access multiple services and resources from their academic institution's library. For nearly a decade college and university libraries have utilized available technology to develop a Web presence. Librarians are continuously refining library Web sites to make them more content-rich and navigable.

[Haworth co-indexing entry note]: "Content and Design of Academic Library Web Sites for Distance Learners: An Analysis of ARL Libraries." Adams, Kate E., and Mary Cassner. Co-published simultaneously in *Journal of Library Administration* (The Haworth Information Press, an imprint of The Haworth Press, Inc.) Vol. 37, No. 1/2, 2002, pp. 3-13; and: *Distance Learning Library Services: The Tenth Off-Campus Library Services Conference* (ed: Patrick B. Mahoney) The Haworth Information Press, an imprint of The Haworth Press, Inc., 2002, pp. 3-13.

The purpose of this research is to identify the content and design of library Web sites serving distance learners. Of particular interest to the researchers are libraries' distance education home pages, the beginning point for many distance learners interested in library resources and services. How easy is it for distance learners to determine which library services are available for them? Do academic libraries provide Web pages intended specifically for distance learners? Or, are programmatic services for distance learners blended with those for campus-based students? To ensure a Web presence for distance learners that communicates information clearly and with details (but not exhaustively), libraries need to examine the content and design of their Web sites. Findings from this study should be of interest to distance education coordinators, Web page developers, and libraries that provide services to distance learners.

The population studied is the Association of Research Libraries (ARL) member libraries, a not-for-profit membership organization with over 120 members from the United States and Canada. ARL libraries are geographically dispersed, and include both public and private institutions. Since they are large and complex institutions, it was expected there would be a variety of approaches in Web pages that present services to distance learners.

The research builds upon earlier studies that evaluate the design and content of university and academic library home pages, applying other researchers' methodologies and findings to distance education services. Among the design elements studied are institutional and library logos, graphics, colors, screen lengths, number and types of links, and link headings. Hypertext links have been analyzed for content of services and resources provided by each library for distance learners. Data collected from the distance education Web pages of each library have been tabulated in order to compare similarities and differences.

REVIEW OF THE LITERATURE

Academic library Web sites have become a significant topic of discussion in the literature. Stover and Zink (1996) studied forty academic library Web home pages to ascertain trends, patterns, and anomalies in both design and organization. They noted that "the home page has become an important navigational device in the organization of information at individual Web sites" (p. 16). King (1998) examined the home pages of ARL libraries to compare design similarities and differences. Cohen and Still (1999) identified core content common to academic library Web sites at research level universities and two-year colleges. They identified four major purposes of a library Web site:

informational, reference, research, and instructional. Medeiros (1999) observed that second generation Web design, with its flatter structures and common "look" predominating, is meant to assist users. McGillis and Toms (2001) and Battleson, Booth, and Weintrop (2001) reported on usability studies of academic library Web sites.

Some authors have looked at selected services as links on academic library Web sites. Dewey (1999) studied access, reference, information, and user education services as described on the Web pages of thirteen member libraries of the Committee on Institutional Cooperation (CIC). Dewey's emphasis was on the findability, or ease of locating services, on the libraries' Web pages. Bao (2000) looked at how academic libraries provide links to commercial databases and remote access to those resources. Coffta and Schoen (2000) examined Web sites from four- and five-year colleges and universities to find out about interlibrary loan policies, contact information, and holdings. Stacy-Bates (2000) examined design characteristics of ready reference and e-mail reference pages from ARL libraries. Stacy-Bates noted that "librarians must carefully plan the site content and design to serve patrons for whom the Web has become a central source of information" (p. 61).

Osorio (2001) studied Web sites of science-engineering libraries at forty-five universities, using a prototyping model to access content and design. A list of 66 elements was developed consisting of design features such as navigation bar, library photograph/logo, screen lengths, and colors, and content features such as "search this site," electronic resources, user education program, subject guides, and electronic reference. Osorio also identified predominant design features represented in the science-engineering libraries studied. This approach forms the starting point for the authors' methodology regarding distance education pages.

From the distance education literature, Linden (2000) recommended the type of content to include when designing Web sites for distance learners. Buckstead (2001) discussed the essential components of a Web site for off-campus library services, addressing both content and design features that should be included. The ACRL *Guidelines for Distance Learning Library Services* (rev. 2000) at http://www.ala.org/acrl/guides/distlrng.html briefly mentions Web pages as part of virtual communication with distance learners. The topic of Web pages specifically for distance learners is not well developed in the literature. This study analyzes the distance education home pages of ARL libraries and the relationship with their respective institutional home pages. The authors of this study analyzed current design features and assessed content of the distance education pages.

DEFINITIONS

For this study the terms *distance education* and *distance learning* are used synonymously. According to the ACRL *Guidelines for Distance Learning Library Services* (rev. 2000), *distance learning library services* refers to "those library services in support of college, university, or other post-secondary courses and programs offered away from a main campus, or in the absence of a traditional campus, and regardless of where credit is given" (Association of College & Research Libraries, 2000, para. 4).

Librarian-administrator, referred to in this study as *distance education coordinator*, is a "librarian, holding a master's degree from an ALA-accredited library school, who specializes in distance learning library services, and who is directly responsible for the administration and supervision of those services" (Association of College & Research Libraries, 2000, para. 8).

A *library home page* is a "Web page meant to serve as the primary gateway to a library Web site" (Stacy-Bates, 2000, para. 18). This welcome page is the first or "front" page of the library's Web site.

METHODOLOGY

The population considered for the study consisted of all 123 members of the Association of Research Libraries (ARL) as listed on the ARL Web site in September 2001. Criteria for final selection included that the institution be an academic library, and that the library Web site have links to distance education services for library users. Ten ARL members did not meet the first criterion and were eliminated from the study. These included Boston Public Library, Canada Institute for Scientific & Technical Information, Center for Research Libraries, Library of Congress, National Agricultural Library, National Library of Canada, National Library of Medicine, New York Public Library, New York State Library, and Smithsonian Institutions Libraries. Sixty-five other ARL libraries did not contain a distance education home page. The library Web sites of the remaining forty-eight ARL institutions were studied in depth.

The two aspects of data collection were design characteristics of the distance education home page and content of the distance education and main library home pages as reflected by hyperlinks. Design elements reflected the form and structure of the Web site, while content elements covered the subjects or topics. Evaluative criteria were not included in this study nor were measurement scales.

The authors adapted the list of 66 elements that Osorio (2001) presented in his study of science-engineering libraries' Web sites. Some elements were added to Osorio's list while others were deleted. The final list of 43 elements in this study was comprised of 15 design elements and 28 content elements (see Appendix).

A preliminary check of ARL libraries' Web sites was conducted in September 2001. The authors searched library home pages using site searches and site indexes as needed to locate the distance education pages. The list of elements was modified based on the preliminary searching. Final data collection occurred in November 2001.

A spreadsheet containing home page design and content elements was developed using an Excel program. As each home page was examined, the presence or absence of each element was noted with a "y" for yes or "n" for no. Selected elements, such as the number of colors found within the home page, were counted. Additional notes concerning the home pages were entered into a Word file. Printouts of library and distance education home pages were made for ease of use. Data for each library's Web site was entered into an Excel spreadsheet and manually compiled using raw numbers and percentages. Data were tabulated using simple averages (and medians in several instances).

RESULTS

The ARL libraries use various terms to refer to distance learners and to the services offered to them. The most frequently used term was distance learners. Other terms used included distance students, off-campus students, distance education students, extended-campus students, and off-grounds or continuing education students. The most frequent terms used by libraries to describe services to this population were distance learning, off-campus, or distance education services.

Design elements comprised one portion of the study. Two design elements consistently appeared on each of the 48 distance education pages analyzed–variation in font size and links present on the home page. A white or neutral-colored background was found on the majority of distance education home pages. Wallpaper was found on only two libraries' distance education home pages. Just 12% of distance education home pages contained a text only option. However, the text only feature was sometimes available at the library's home page.

Nearly all of the distance education home pages displayed at least one navigation bar with multiple links such as the library's home page. Thirty-one distance education home pages (65%) used a top navigational bar, 25 (52%) a side bar, and 20 (42%) a bottom navigational bar. Seventeen percent of the home pages used all three types of navigational bars.

Ninety percent of distance education home pages contained at least one graphic. The logo or banner from the library's home page was repeated in 75% of the distance education home pages. Oftentimes, graphics were small photographs or illustrations. At other times the graphics appeared to be completely unrelated to library or university logos. Ruffini (2001) stated that Web pages communicate effectively when visuals convey one basic idea; multiple visuals are confusing and lead to misinterpretation. Most of the libraries in the study have one small photograph or small illustration. This suggests that libraries are trying to give the page a visual identification with the library (Osorio, 2001).

The number of links available on distance education home pages ranged from 5 to 81 with an average of 28 links and a median of 23 links. This average is slightly lower than the 34 found in Osorio's (2001) study of engineering and science library home pages. The number of different colors on the distance education home pages ranged from 3 to 13 with an average of six and a median of five. Those distance education Web sites with graphics generally used more colors.

The Print Preview command was used to determine the length of the distance education home page. The screen length of the home pages was two pages in length for both average and median, although actual length varied from one to eight screens. A very short home page may not present essential links and information for distance users. A lengthy home page may lead to navigation problems and may cause users to lose interest (Osorio, 2001).

The number of screen levels from the library home page to the distance education home page was both an average and median of two, although the range varied from 1 to 4. This design element was measured by mouse clicks from the library's home page.

Of the distance education pages analyzed, few could be considered "one-stop" or standalone pages. For example, two distance education pages were very brief. One contained only proxy information, while the other presented only information regarding the distance library card. Many distance education pages contained links for services, with fuller descriptions of those services elsewhere on the library's Web site. Most distance education pages did not duplicate full descriptions of library services and resources. For this reason, the authors chose to combine counting the content elements as found on distance education pages with the libraries' home pages.

About one-third of the content elements studied related to the distance education home page while two-thirds related to elements found on the library's home page. Links to the library's home page were found on 96% (all but two) of the distance education home pages. Osorio (2001) found a much lower percentage of science-engineering libraries (17%) with links to their main library. Ninety-four percent of the distance education home pages contained links to the university Web site. However, a much lower figure, 60% of distance education home pages, contained a direct link to the university services for distance learners.

All distance education home pages in the ARL population provided links to the library's online catalog. Most distance education home pages (87%) listed a mission statement or explanation of services offered to distance learners.

Eighty-three percent of the ARL libraries' Web sites analyzed listed some kind of contact information for their library distance education services. Frequently, however, the description of library services lacked the name of a distance coordinator. The name of a coordinator librarian-administrator appeared on only 29 Web sites, or 60% of the sample. Contact information for generic library distance education services appeared on 40 of the sites, or 83% of the sample. The description of distance services often does not mention either a distance librarian or librarians at all.

One element had a surprisingly low ranking. Fewer than half (44%) of distance education home pages contained links to library services specific to distance faculty.

All 48 libraries provided links to journal indexes and to electronic journals. A smaller percentage of libraries (69%) provided access to electronic books. Links to electronic reference materials such as online encyclopedias were available from 90% of the library home pages. The same percentage of library home pages (90%) contained links to Web search engines. Ninety-four percent of library home pages had links to the online catalogs of other libraries or associations. Links to proxy instructions for remote access into licensed databases were found on 94% of library home pages.

A significant number of library home pages (85%) contained a search, site search, or site index feature. Cohen and Still (1999) noted the value of site search engines, which provide users with "the opportunity to locate materials of interest without needing to navigate through the site" (p. 278).

Ninety-two percent of the 48 libraries' home pages provided the library's address. A contact link for the Webmaster or Web committee was available on 90% of home pages.

Specific library resources or services available to distance students were also analyzed. The following resources or services were available from the library home pages studied: electronic reference assistance (98%); interlibrary loan forms (96%); library instruction (96%); lists of subject specialist librarians (92%); guides to using the Internet (87%); guides to conducting library research (81%); list of reciprocal borrowing institutions (73%); and electronic reserves (71%). The study found that 96% of ARL libraries with distance services have links to subject guides or pathfinders. This compares to Cohen and Still (1999) who found pathfinders on 60 percent of the 50 research libraries studied (p. 283).

DISCUSSION

The authors urge distance librarians to collaborate with Web developers to present distance learning services in a more accessible fashion. Design elements are crucial to the success of distance education home pages. Distance education Web pages should be reviewed to determine the degree to which they are visually appealing and well designed. These sites should contain "user friendly" design and content along with a current freshness date. Ruffini (2001) suggests that "the top vertical four inches are the most valuable real estate in your Web site [and] should be the densest area in your site." Good design is essential for effective presentation of content.

As more and more library users access the library remotely, the library Web site has become increasingly important as a communication tool. Library users "expect customization, interactivity, and customer support" (Library and Information Technology Association, 1999, para. 4). This is particularly important to distance learners, whose primary contact with libraries is through a Web page.

In order for distance learners to become aware of available library services and resources, it is essential that the distance education home page be easily accessible, or findable. This study showed that while the distance education home page on average was two screen levels below the top page, some were several levels down, and these pages were effectively hidden. Terminology is another barrier to findability. For the ARL libraries studied, there were half a dozen descriptors for distance education students and distance education services. While the terminology used to describe distance students is often institution-wide rather than library-driven, it is important for libraries to use terminology that distance students recognize.

A related findability issue is jargon. Distance students often are non-traditional students, who are returning to academic study after several years away from campus. They may not be familiar with new or enhanced library services with names that they may perceive as unfamiliar jargon. These services call for some explanation. Linden (2000) recommended spelling out the services and resources so that it is clear to distance students what is available. Also, Linden suggested creating multiple approaches to the same information, while keeping redundancy to a manageable amount.

Only twenty-one of the 48 distance education home pages provided information on services to distance faculty. The authors believe that services specific to distance faculty should be further developed on distance education pages. Faculty who are well informed about library services for distance learners and resources will likely refer their students more often to the library. Also, seventeen percent of the ARL member libraries studied lacked a direct link to the university's Web site for distance education services. This is another useful link for distance learners.

"It's time to put a human face on the virtual library. What do libraries emphasize on their Web sites? Resources, collections, facts with no human guidance or presence" (Library and Information Technology Association, 1999, para. 6). The authors of this study believe it is essential that the distance education librarian be identified, along with contact information for this individual.

CONCLUSION

Distance education home pages are a primary venue to reach distance learners. Librarian-administrators and Web developers should collaborate to make distance education pages easy to locate from the library's home page. The content of distance pages should be reviewed for inclusion of links useful to distance learners. These strategies will help ensure that distance students are able to navigate available library services and resources.

REFERENCES

Association of College & Research Libraries. (rev. 2000). *Guidelines for distance learning library services*. Retrieved December 3, 2001, from American Library Association, Association of College & Research Libraries: http://www.ala.org/acrl/guides/distlrng.html.

Bao, X. (2000). Academic library home pages: Link location and database provision. *The Journal of Academic Librarianship 26*, 191-195.

Batteleson, B., Booth, A., & Weintrop, J. (2001). Usability testing of an academic library Web site: A case study. *The Journal of Academic Librarianship 27*, 188-198.

Buckstead, J. R. (2001). Developing an effective off-campus library services Web page: Don't worry, be happy! *Journal of Library Administration 31*, 93-107.

Coffta, M., & Schoen, D. M. (2000). Academic library Web sites as a source of interlibrary loan lending information: A survey of four- and five-year colleges and universities. *Library Resources & Technical Services 44*, 196-200.

Cohen, L. B., & Still, J. M. (1999). A comparison of research university and two-year college library Web sites: Content, functionality, and form. *College & Research Libraries 60*, 275-289.

Dewey, B. I. (1999). In search of services: Analyzing the findability of links on CIC university libraries' Web pages. *Information Technology and Libraries 18*, 210-213.

King, D. L. (1998). Library home page design: A comparison of page layout for front-ends to ARL library Web sites. *College & Research Libraries 59*, 458-465.

Library and Information Technology Association. (1999, January). *Top tech trends*. Retrieved December 4, 2001 from American Library Association, Library and Information Technology Association: http://www.lita.org/committee/toptech/trendsmw99.htm.

Linden, J. (2000). The library's Web site *is* the library: Designing for distance learners. *College & Research Libraries 6*, 99-101.

McGillis, L., & Toms, E. G. (2001). Usability of the academic library Web site: Implications for design. *College & Research Libraries 62*, 355-367.

Medeiros, N. (1999). Academic library Web sites: From public relations to information gateway. *College & Research Libraries News 60*, 527-529+.

Osorio, N. L. (2001). Web sites of science-engineering libraries: An analysis of content and design. *Issues in Science and Technology Librarianship 29*, Retrieved December 3, 2001 from http://www.library.ucsb.edu/istl/01-winter/refereed.html.

Ruffini, M. F. (2001). Blueprint to develop a great Web site [Electronic version]. *T.H.E. Journal 28*(8), 64-73.

Stacy-Bates, K. K. (2000). Ready-reference resources and E-mail reference on academic ARL Web sites [Electronic version]. *Reference & User Services Quarterly 40*, 61-73.

Stover, M., & Zink, S. D. (1996). World Wide Web home page design: Patterns and anomalies of higher education library home pages. *Reference Services Review 24*(3), 7-20.

APPENDIX

Content and Design Elements Included in the Study of Library Web Sites for Distance Learners

Design Elements

The following elements related to the *Distance Education Home Page*:

Presence of a distance education home page
Text Only Option available on distance education home page
Links present on home page
Font variation
Top navigation bar
Bottom navigation bar
Side bar
Bar similar in appearance to library's home page
Presence of graphics
Library's logo or banner reflected on distance education home page
Presence of wallpaper
Number of links on the distance education home page
Number of colors on the distance education home page

Home page screen length–number of pages
Number of screen levels from library home page to distance education
   home page

Content Elements

The following elements related to the *Distance Education Home Page*:

Freshness date on distance education home page
Distance education coordinator's name
Contact information for library distance education services
Library services for distance faculty
Mission statement or explanation of services offered to distance students
   and/or distance faculty
Link to library home page
Link to the library online catalog
Link to university Web site
Link to university services for distance education

The following elements related to the *Library Home Page*:

Search, Site Search, or Site Index on library home page
Library (institution) address
Electronic journals
Journal indexes available electronically
Electronic books
Electronic references materials (such as encyclopedias)
Web search engines
Online catalogs of other institutions, associations, etc.
Proxy instructions
Lists of Subject Specialists or Liaison Librarians
Subject guides or pathfinders
Library instruction
Guides to library research
Guides to using the Internet
Electronic reference
Interlibrary loan forms
Electronic reserves
Reciprocal institutions
Contact link for Webmaster

The Virtual Reserve Room: Extending Library Services Off-Campus

Emilie R. Algenio

University of Massachusetts Amherst

SUMMARY. This paper explores the challenges of implementing an electronic reserves program which extends library services to off-campus distance education students. Using the University of Massachusetts Amherst as a case study, the paper briefly describes the project's context and history, with a focus on the practicalities, problems, and solutions in starting an electronic library reserves service. The discussion also covers issues integral to the service and which affect off-campus learners, including budgeting, staffing, partnering with affiliated campuses, addressing faculty concerns, managing copyright permissions, utilizing e-books and incorporating full-text databases.

KEYWORDS. Distance education, reserves, library service, distance learners

INTRODUCTION

At the W. E. B. Du Bois Library, the print Reserve collection totals 8,000 distinct readings, and the electronic reserve collection totals 268 electronic files, as of Fall 2001. Those electronic files had to be coordinated between the center of operations, the Du Bois Library, and three other Amherst University Libraries. Their locations are geographically distinct: the Music Reserve Lab, the Biological Sciences Library, and the Physical Sciences and Engineering

[Haworth co-indexing entry note]: "The Virtual Reserve Room: Extending Library Services Off-Campus." Algenio, Emilie R. Co-published simultaneously in *Journal of Library Administration* (The Haworth Information Press, an imprint of The Haworth Press, Inc.) Vol. 37, No. 1/2, 2002, pp. 15-25; and: *Distance Learning Library Services: The Tenth Off-Campus Library Services Conference* (ed: Patrick B. Mahoney) The Haworth Information Press, an imprint of The Haworth Press, Inc., 2002, pp. 15-25.

Library. These four facilities serve a total of 34,000 students and 1,400 faculty. The W. E. B. Du Bois Reserve staff totals one half-time professional, five full-time classified employees, two part-time classified employees, and 32 part-time student employees. Of this staff, one full-time employee and one part-time employee have the priority of servicing electronic reserves. This paper describes the research, development, and evaluation processes to start a pilot service, followed by a discussion of the lessons learned.

The impetus for an electronic reserves service came from the convergence of many different factors: (a) the burgeoning growth of distance education programs in higher education; (b) the individual University of Massachusetts Amherst campus and the University of Massachusetts five-campus system were developing an official distance education program; (c) the Library's enthusiasm to support services for distance learners; and (d) the Library's commitment to incorporate new technology within their traditional service points. A staffing opportunity also came into play; the Library proposed hiring a newly degreed librarian as a Research Library Resident. The Residency program entailed the use of emerging library technology, and this particular position would provide leadership in the process of conducting electronic reserve pilots and developing the new electronic reserves service. The Resident would have a term of two years and would serve as the Project Coordinator.

The initial objective was a migration in two different dimensions: from a physical space to a virtual space, and from print-only documents to virtually accessible electronic files. This project started in Fall 2000 with researching the three most important topics: copyright, faculty candidates, and the necessary equipment. Due to the immediate need for the latter two to be resolved, copyright concerns became a lower priority initially. The time frame was to begin the first pilot the following semester, Spring 2001. The three distinct phases of this project are research, implementation, and evaluation. That autumn was focused on research, and the project moved into implementation by December.

RESEARCH

This phase was devoted to: (a) the history and progress of the service within academic libraries; (b) the available hardware and software, including in-house, local, and commercial products, and their usability for physically challenged patrons; and (c) the identification of appropriate faculty participants. Meetings were held every two weeks with all four Reserve departments to provide updates and to gather input from the staff. Site visits were also conducted at other Massachusetts institutions, and afforded the chance to learn about their similar services. The Library Information Systems and Technology

Services (LISTS) department was consulted for their technical expertise. After thorough market research and a review of online clearinghouses, discussion groups, and the professional literature, the commercial vendor Docutek provided on-site demonstration.

The Library chose Docutek's ERes product for the following advantages: (a) the clear and comprehensive management of a copyright notification feature; (b) the copyright security features fell within the accepted limits of current digital copyright practices; (c) the readiness of the product to work with the pilot start date of January 2, 2001; (d) the affordable price; (e) the navigational ease of the GUI design; (f) the product, company, and technical support were highly recommended via the American Research Libraries' Electronic Reserves online discussion group; (g) the issues in relation to the American Disabilities Act were manageable; (h) it was a ready-made and Web-based product; and (i) Docutek, as a company, had established and well-known clients. The product's limitations were also apparent: (a) it cannot handle large-scale use; (b) it cannot recover from an invalid, failed, or incomplete transaction; and (c) and it did not have a built-in recovery system. Given the presence of the Library's Innovative Interfaces Inc. Release 2001 Web catalog, III's Electronic Reserve module was also considered. The disadvantages were many, and far outweighed the advantages. Hence, Docutek's ERes product was selected.

Apart from III's Electronic Reserve module and Docutek's ERes, six other commercial products were considered. Contec Data Systems' C3-CRS had a decent reporting engine, yet the company was located in New Zealand, its size was small, and it had few clients. Free Reserves, a joint effort by three individuals, was Unix-based, but the disadvantage was its high maintenance, which required a specialized skill set. Also, the program's design was questionable; only 50 hours of work were spent on its construction. Nousoft, Inc.'s product was unavailable and still in development. The advantages of Open Source Course Reserves were its zero cost, its scalability, its use of an Apache Web server, SQL (structure query language), and Unix, and it was a finished product. However, technical support was not an option, product maintenance raised the question of sufficient Library staff and training, and the creator did not indicate the number or identity of their clients. Sitebuilder had no advantages, and the disadvantages stemmed from ProQuest's sole support for their Direct customers and sole use of ProQuest Direct materials. Finally, Xerox is a solid company, its Digital Curriculum product was scalable, but the cost was prohibitive.

Many local resources were used in deciding which faculty were the best candidates for the upcoming pilots. Professors were selected based on two criteria: (a) their support for the Library, and (b) their support and use of new technology in the classroom. Consulting with the Education Librarian, the names of TEACHnology Fellows came to the fore. The list of potential candidates started with fifty-one faculty who had participated in a campus program involving the research and execution of new technology in their classroom. The goal was to support a total of five professors. Further consultation with subject librarians resulted in a working roster of candidates who fit both criteria mentioned previously. Ten were solicited, and seven were chosen.

In addition to the TEACHnology Fellows, the Library also hoped to support professors teaching distance education courses. This was a challenge; faculty were using a wide range of homegrown and commercial course management software products. The administration of these courses was disparate and decentralized: it was via either their own department, the new UMass Online distance education program, or under the auspices of other University programs. To identify appropriate pilot candidates, assistance was provided by the Library's Distance Learning Task Force (DLTF). They had developed a working roster of faculty teaching online, and this resource supplemented the above list.

This first phase was complete with the project proposal submitted to the Director of Libraries, the Coordinator of LISTS, and the Coordinator of User Support Services. The proposal summarized all research, and was a blueprint for the first year of the service as a whole. It included an explanation of the actual work process, a general timeline, the necessary equipment, a brief justification for a copyright policy, necessary staffing and staff training, defining the equipment choices and the relation to the American Disabilities Act, and a projected budget. The proposal was distributed to the other four University of Massachusetts Library Directors. Based upon this document, both the University of Massachusetts Dartmouth and Boston campuses joined Amherst to collectively purchase the Docutek software, with the intention of developing similar services.

IMPLEMENTATION

This period lasted from December until the start of the Spring 2001 semester. Contact was established with faculty participants in the upcoming pilot, the Reserve staff processed material, faculty concerns about copyright issues were addressed, and administrative forms were modified. Once the Library initiated its formal relationship with the Docutek vendor, the Reserve staff and LISTS prepared the equipment and customized the ERes software.

Throughout the year, the project's larger picture was also kept in perspective. For example, the Library had negotiated the purchase of electronic book titles with NetLibrary. These titles could be applied in an electronic reserve capacity. Also, the Head of the Acquisitions Department was consulted about the Library's Infotrac and JSTOR licenses, with the intention of using full-text databases to their greatest extent.

During the first pilot semester, the electronic reserves service was introduced in the actual classroom for seven courses. The rationale for this face-to-face contact was to market the Library's services beyond the Library's walls, and to introduce to faculty and students a new experiment at the Library. During the course of the semester, if a student needed assistance, an e-mail address was the only avenue to seek help with electronic reserves per se. The justification for this sole source was the level of staffing in LISTS and Reserve, in addition to the technical skill of the latter. For computer difficulties, the appropriate information for reaching the Office of Information Technology was also provided. As a measure of quality control, in-class student surveys were conducted. Again, the reasons for doing this were many: the desire for Electronic Reserves to be an excellent service, users' feedback (including the faculty) was crucial for determining the pilot's success, a physical presence in their classroom would emphasize both points and hopefully increase the survey return rate.

The electronic reserves service starting supporting a distance education course the following summer. The important details were conveyed via a "Help" Web page. The professor was strongly encouraged to add the URL on their own course Web site. Surveys were conducted by e-mail communications. The professor served as an intermediary, having the e-mail addresses of their online students, and returning their results to the Project Coordinator.

EVALUATION

Toward the end of April 2001, the process of Evaluation was ongoing. The success of the pilot was measured by a number of quantitative factors: frequency of electronic reserve use, frequency of print reserve use, and frequency of email assistance use. In addition, both students and faculty were asked open-ended questions to gain insight into the success of both the electronic reserves service as a whole and the software as a method of delivery. Given the fact that the pilots were in an experimental mode, both students and faculty needed to understand that the service was fallible, their feedback was critical, and that the Library was striving to offer high quality curriculum support.

Preliminary data indicates 86% of faculty who would use electronic reserves again, and 76% of students who would also use electronic reserves again.

Preliminary figures for the two pilots are in Table 1 and Table 2.

TABLE 1. General Service Figures for the Spring and Fall Pilots

	Spring 2001	Fall 2001
Number of faculty represented	7	3
Number of academic departments represented	6	3
Total number of students using electronic reserves	132	207 (approximation)
Total number of classes using electronic reserves	7	3
Total number of online reserve readings as indicated by number of files*	187	81

*Reserve readings that totaled more than ten print pages were broken down into specific increments and distinct electronic files. For example, if one reserve reading had twenty print pages, the document was scanned and saved as two different electronic files having no more than ten pages each. So, one print reserve reading could have an electronic accompaniment of one or more distinct files.

TABLE 2. Spring 2001 Pilot Figures, Total Times Students Accessed Reserve Readings by Month

	Document Web Page Hits
January	65
February	1123
March	606
April	299
May	177
Total	**2093**

The project's progress was continually monitored. Faculty guidelines were formulated, which included submission deadlines, document standards, and copyright parameters. Agendas were drafted for the newly formed University of Massachusetts Five Campus Copyright Task Force, and an Access database was constructed to streamline and centralize daily tasks for the Reserve staff.

ONGOING ISSUES

During the second pilot, Fall 2001, two significant changes occurred. New staff were hired for the Reserve department, one full-time employee and one part-time employee. Their first priority was to support electronic reserves, and to assist with print reserves as needed. Training sessions with ERes, JSTOR, Infotrac, and the Copyright Clearance Center commenced immediately. The second difference was the need, for the first time, to seek copyright permission. The working policy dictated that material available online in the first instance was fair use; the second instance required the copyright owner's permission. Practices that continued were in-class introductions, student and faculty surveys, and recruiting faculty.

In March 2001, the effort to research the legal components of electronic reserves, copyright issues, and distance education ensued. This research took the form of literature reviews, staff development workshops, individual faculty assistance, drafting a Library copyright policy, perusing undecided court cases, and updates to the Reserve staff regarding those cases. The University of Massachusetts Copyright Task Force was formed within the Libraries' system, and their goal was to draft a policy by Fall 2002. For this Task Force, the charge, agendas, and white papers were drafted. Two librarians were consulted, one for Integrated Library Systems and Staff Development, and another for Resource Access. Their previous experiences with electronic reserves corresponded well to render an informal and collective base of local expertise. Although a law librarian was on staff, intellectual property was not her specialty.

Library communication with faculty about copyright law called for a serious degree of diplomacy, tact, and education. Their awareness was expressed in a wide variety of responses; they ranged from unfamiliarity with the topic to well-informed opinions about intellectual property. For example, one professor in the Legal Studies department routinely searched the Web for his full name, in order to discern where his name was being used online, and whether or not he himself had authorized that use. Their primary concerns were the logistics for seeking and paying for permissions.

Throughout all three phases, the opportunities to promote the Library's new service were always used, both internally and beyond the Library community. The electronic reserves pilot was presented during the DLTF's mini-conferences for faculty and administrators supporting distance education, and for Five Campus librarians supporting digitization projects. Both the University of Massachusetts Boston and Dartmouth Electronic Reserve Project Coordinators consulted with the Amherst staff for assistance. As a gesture of appreciation and goodwill, a reception was held to thank the faculty and Library staff involved in the first pilot.

LESSONS LEARNED

Campus Environment

Take the pulse of your campus in a political sense. Are the conditions and timing ripe for this kind of service? What administrative support do you have?

Are there similar projects already happening? Can those be taken advantage of? What lessons do they have to offer?

Resources People

Draw upon any and many local resources: within your library, consortium, multi-campus institution, and nearby universities. Many different kinds of expertise and assistance will be needed: legal (copyright), vendor licenses, statistical evaluation, issues pertaining to the American Disabilities Act and technology, IT, database construction, publicity/marketing, Web authoring, subject librarians, and a distance education task force or committee.

Time

Do not underestimate the time and resources to plan, fund, staff, equip, implement, and maintain the service. Document time spent on all areas of activity as much as possible (see Table 3).

Money

Plan for the time to research, implement, evaluate, maintain, and staff this service. For University of Massachusetts Amherst figures, see the Appendix.

Copyright Faculty

Do not underestimate your faculty's level of expertise regarding the issue of copyright. An obvious example are those who have a doctorate of jurisprudence, and have a solid argument ready with case studies. On the other hand, it

TABLE 3. General Timeline for Implementing the University of Massachusetts Amherst Electronic Reserves Service, by Years

	Significant activity
2000	
August	Resident's term started
December	Docutek license signed
2001	
Spring	First pilot started
Summer	First distance education course supported
Fall	Second pilot started
	Two new electronic reserves staff started
2002	
Spring	Third pilot starts

is possible to overestimate their knowledge of the subject. Have copies of the classroom guidelines as primary material, and any campus policies, on hand.

Copyright Money

The money that you will spend on seeking permissions will not be any consistent nor comforting figure–entirely based upon the prerogative and whim of the copyright owner/author and/or publisher.

Copyright Policy

Have a policy in place prior to recruiting faculty. The policy itself might have two variations: one for campus counsel, and another, more practical one for the frontline staff. Have copies ready to distribute to professors.

Service General

Market the service within all contexts of the Library's services, including distance learning. This includes all appropriate Web pages, public events, networking with interested faculty and administrators.

Service Guidelines

Have guidelines for faculty in place as early as possible. Suggestions for content include any or all of the following elements: whether online reserve readings are required or optional, possible document length limitations, required document types (this might be dependent on your copyright policy, e.g., all material must either be previously published or the original work of, and copyright owned by, the professor), and submission deadlines.

Faculty Relations

Have guidelines for faculty in place as easy as possible–post necessary forms (with critical bibliographic fields required), project guidelines, and whatever help online. Their support for this service, whether it is mentioned in class, on their syllabus, on their course Web site, etc., is critical. Otherwise, it could be a waste of time and effort.

Students

Have at least an e-mail account for assisting students. Tailor the Web-based "Help" page into A Frequently Asked Questions format, and store as a draft within the e-mail account for quick reference.

FUTURE DEVELOPMENTS

The following are suggestions about the future of electronic reserves, including general predictions and ones specific to the University of Massachusetts Amherst:

1. The electronic reserve commercial market is still quite new; ProQuest, Xerox, Nousoft, and Adobe are developing products that could surpass the current selection.
2. Copyright law, like new technology, is a moving target. Many lawyers have suggested that libraries use the four factor test–economic impact, amount, nature, purpose and character–to judge fair use. Otherwise, fair use will be usurped as a justifiable defense.
3. The University of Massachusetts Amherst electronic reserves service itself is uncertain. The copyright issues can make relations with the faculty contentious and politically tenuous. The growing use of course management software, and its accompanying reserve features, is in direct competition to the Library's service. Many academic libraries are outsourcing entire services, and XanEdu's ready-made online course packs could appropriate the Library's target audience.
4. Monetary challenges may preclude a librarian administering this service in the long term. The electronic reserves staff will be trained to ensure the service's longevity. These sessions will include a copyright basics workshop, resources for current copyright cases, NetLibrary, Excel, Dreamweaver, and Access software.
5. Given the attendance at local and national copyright seminars and workshops, a working roster of potential speakers was generated. This could serve as the basis for a campus symposium series focused on new technology and the law.
6. Indiana University is using the University of Massachusetts Amherst Music department as a test site for a digital library system called Variations. It offers a searchable database of more than seven thousand compact discs accessible online. The results of their collaboration could work in conjunction with the electronic reserves service.
7. The University of Massachusetts Amherst Libraries are involved in the New England Research Libraries' project called Books You Teach Every Semester (BYTES). The objective is to compare the Reserve collections of various East Coast research university libraries, and to purchase common titles as electronic books. Once these titles become available, and depending on their corresponding licenses, they could be used in an electronic reserve capacity.

APPENDIX. Startup Costs for the University of Massachusetts Amherst Electronic Reserves Service

	Dollar amounts
Staffing	
Professional (8 months FTE)	$22,000
Classified (1 PTE)	$3,711
Equipment	
Docutek's ERes	$11,699
Copyright	$71
Total	**$37,481**

Bringing the Library to the Students: Using Technology to Deliver Instruction and Resources for Research

Judith Arnold
Jennifer Sias
Jingping Zhang

Marshall University Libraries

SUMMARY. To provide equitable services and access to off-campus students, librarians must meet the challenges of the digital divide and the geographic divide. Instruction and document delivery are key services that can determine how successful a library is in meeting its responsibility to distance learning. This session will focus on technological solutions to instruction, access, and document delivery in technology-challenged and remote environments.

KEYWORDS. Distance education, distance learners, technology, instruction

INTRODUCTION

Located in Huntington, West Virginia, Marshall University is a comprehensive, state-supported university with a student body of 16,000 and over 600 full-time faculty. The university offers 24 associate programs, 41 baccalaureate programs and 46 graduate programs. As one of the leading universities in

[Haworth co-indexing entry note]: "Bringing the Library to the Students: Using Technology to Deliver Instruction and Resources for Research." Arnold, Judith, Jennifer Sias, and Jingping Zhang. Co-published simultaneously in *Journal of Library Administration* (The Haworth Information Press, an imprint of The Haworth Press, Inc.) Vol. 37, No. 1/2, 2002, pp. 27-37; and: *Distance Learning Library Services: The Tenth Off-Campus Library Services Conference* (ed: Patrick B. Mahoney) The Haworth Information Press, an imprint of The Haworth Press, Inc., 2002, pp. 27-37.

http://www.haworthpress.com/store/product.asp?sku=J111
10.1300/J111v37n01_04

the state, Marshall University attracts students from all regions of West Virginia, as well as from the surrounding states of Ohio and Kentucky and throughout the Appalachian region. Primarily undergraduate courses are delivered through the School of Extended Education each year to nearly 5,000 students via ITV, WebCT, or as live classes at a series of extension locations including centers in Point Pleasant, Beckley, and Gilbert, and at other settings in the Teays Valley area, Logan, and Williamson. The Marshall University Graduate College (MUGC), located in South Charleston, offers additional extended education courses at the graduate level. The curriculum for off-campus courses is diverse, encompassing traditional baccalaureate courses, with many majors, such as computer science, nursing, education, business, counseling, and social work. In order to mesh with a developing information literacy program, instructional efforts are aimed at courses traditionally receiving instruction on campus, such as freshman orientation (UNI 101), English Composition (ENG 101/102), courses in the major, such as Introduction to Women's Studies (WS 101), and graduate research courses, such as EDF 621.

PART ONE:
DELIVERING INSTRUCTION TO DISTANCE STUDENTS

Ever-changing technology requires frequent training. With the ever-expanding array of online resources, instruction is an important corollary to insure effective use of information resources. Recent acquisitions of NetLibrary, the Synergy collection, and, during this same period, Marshall University's conversion to the ILLiad document delivery service are only a few examples of the numerous changes during the past academic year that have impacted library instruction.

Training is often controlled by the location of the audience. Students who take classes at the regional centers or in facilities such as high schools, vocational centers, or Chamber of Commerce offices do so because travel to the main campus is inconvenient or prohibitive due to conflicting or tight work or family schedules. Providing instruction sessions to off-campus students frequently means grappling with a vast range of teaching environments–from the state-of-the-art computer classroom to a room in a modular building offering only desks and chairs. As a consequence, a great deal of planning, imagination, and flexibility are required for those times when the setting is totally devoid of the technology that the students will be using to do their research.

TECHNOLOGICAL CHALLENGES AND SOLUTIONS

Without a live connection, instruction loses immediacy and effectiveness. Alternate methods of teaching how to access and search online resources need to be created to restore the feeling of interacting with an online resource. Past presentations at the Off-Campus Library Services Conference, as well as numerous articles, have explored a variety of methods of simulating this "live" instruction, from using video clips (Adams, 1998) to combining presentation software and WebWhacker (Barnes, Holmes, and Stahley, 1998) to designing Web tutorials (Caspers, 1999).

Furthermore, articles by MacDonald (1998) and Kenny (1997) suggest that there can be benefits to "canned" instruction as they describe their instructional solutions to simulate live searching. One method is a multimedia program housed on a computer hard drive, which can enable instruction that is independent of the frustrations of network downtime (Kenny). Kenny's software and hardware solution for creating these simulated searches uses a multimedia authoring program, Authorware, to hyperlink screenshots to simulate searching. The resulting multimedia program is then housed on the computer's hard drive. In this situation students can perform simulated searches within defined parameters, which gives them the experience of searching without a live connection (Kenny). MacDonald describes a "portable" instructional unit that serves as an additional method of delivering instruction onsite when instructional classrooms are in use, or even as a backup for live connectivity when the network is down (p. 130). MacDonald's method uses PowerPoint slides and a program such as Snappy 95 to capture static screens from the World Wide Web, online catalog, and online databases (p. 129). This "canned" presentation may even be more effective, MacDonald offers, because instructional text and graphic examples can be interspersed with demonstration slides (on Boolean searching, for example) and make instruction more clear than searches alone (p. 130).

Marshall University Libraries' solution to providing instruction in the barebones lecture setting is an enhancement of this latter method described by MacDonald. A CD-ROM based multimedia presentation that is customized and stand-alone simulates connectivity by using a variety of software, including SnagIt and PowerPoint. Such an approach has proved successful in providing research instruction for groups as diverse as freshman composition classes, graduate students in technology management, and new students beginning doctoral studies in education.

Microsoft PowerPoint is a presentation software that is widely available, which makes it a good choice because it is frequently loaded on most computers that will be used in classroom or office settings. Screen capture software, such as Techsmith's SnagIt, enables video capture of catalog, database and

Web searches. The video capture is replayed, using RealPlayer, within the framework of a PowerPoint slide show and replicates exactly the search that was executed. SnagIt is a relatively inexpensive program (around $80) that is easy to use. Presentation software surpasses overhead transparencies in visual impact and screen capture software simulates a live connection, adding to effectiveness. CD-ROM technology then provides the storage capacity and portability to travel with ease.

DEVELOPMENT STAGES

Planning the Presentation

Development of this multimedia presentation entails careful planning. First, it is important to determine the session objectives beforehand. Some examples might include: to teach users how to search the online catalog by author, title, subject; or to teach users how to locate articles in an online database, or to show users how to submit requests for document delivery of books and articles. An instructional segment might then be planned for each of these objectives.

Second, it is essential to assess the teaching environment to determine what tools are available. To utilize the PowerPoint slide show with video captures requires a projector, screen, and a computer equipped with RealPlayer and PowerPoint software. For best results, it is preferable to take a compatible projector and a computer loaded with the designated software.

Creating the Presentation

Following this careful planning comes the actual creation of the presentation, a series of steps that include (1) creating a PowerPoint show; (2) capturing the action with SnagIt; (3) integrating the information and action; and (4) saving the final version to CD using Adaptec's Easy CD Creator.

Creating the PowerPoint Show

Microsoft PowerPoint is a familiar presentation tool that appeals to visual and auditory learners. A presentation often begins with a Title Slide, which provides a template to list the presentation title and the presenter's name and title. Frequently that title slide is followed by a slide known as the bulleted list. For instance, this template might describe library services or provide detailed information about a database such as ERIC. Slides also effectively present visuals, such as pertinent photographs and clipart, to enhance a point. In order to incorporate a SnagIt video, insert a blank PowerPoint slide in the appropriate location to serve as a backdrop for captured video sequences.

Capturing the Action with SnagIt

SnagIt software creates a video of actual online searches, capturing a search from start to finish: from clicking on a link from the Marshall University Libraries' Web page; to the step-by-step process of logging into a database, such as ERIC in EbscoHost; to devising a search strategy and typing in subject terms; and, finally, to the results of that search. SnagIt captures mouse movements and screen changes. This software can capture actions that show students how to refine searches, and how to e-mail and cite articles.

Trial and error has yielded many important lessons and tips on using SnagIt. For instance, it is important to know what to capture before actually doing so. Practicing the entire search movement by movement before doing the real capture helps anticipate challenges and results in smooth and efficient movements. Experience has taught that shorter SnagIt videos are better, more efficient, and easier to follow than one long video. For instance, rather than taping methods of logging in to several databases in one long video sequence to demonstrate the concept of database searching, it is more effective to tape individual examples of database searching separately. This method allows the viewer to select and view only those videos that are relevant instead of sitting through several minutes of various database searches that may not be relevant to the user. Rehearsing and practicing the steps, the actual key strokes (Control, Shift, P) to begin and end taping, as well as doing a step-by-step rehearsal of each screen to be taped, is important for flawless and effective video demonstrations. It is also advantageous to think in advance about saving a SnagIt file. SnagIt files consume a great deal of disk space and often must be saved to the C drive, a zip disk, or burned to a CD. One also should think ahead about naming each file. Short file names that distinguish each step work well, such as ERIC, IDS (for Information Delivery Services), etc.

To create a SnagIt video, first open the program to be taped. For instance, to capture the steps of logging into a specific database, open Netscape Navigator or Internet Explorer and go to the Website that will serve as the starting point. Next, open the SnagIt program. Select the appropriate settings and start taping by pressing the Control, Shift, P keys. Next, methodically go through the steps of logging into a database and doing a search, which have been rehearsed prior to taping. To finish, press keys Control, Shift, P. Finally, save the SnagIt movie to a drive that has enough storage capacity and name the file something short and recognizable.

Integrating the Information and Action

To insert this or other SnagIt videos into the PowerPoint slideshow, while in Microsoft PowerPoint, use the Slide Sorter View to select the blank slide that will serve as the backdrop for a video capture. In this blank slide, use the Insert menu to select "Movies and Sounds" and then "Movie from File." Browse for the appropriate .avi file and insert it. For more effective viewing, re-size the inserted file to fill the entire slide. PowerPoint should display a prompt that will enable automatic play of the video in the slide show. Test the first video capture by trying the Slide Show View and use Page Down to advance slides. If the SnagIt file does not play automatically, click on the slide when it appears.

Creating the CD

When the PowerPoint slideshow with inserted SnagIt videos is flawless and needs no further revisions, it is ready to be burned to a CD, which can be used for a presentation and/or distributed to students, faculty and other interested parties. A simple CD-ROM duplication program called Easy CD Creator is provided by Computing Services at Marshall University. Prompting the user step-by-step, this program allows one to "burn" audio and data CDs. Prior to burning the CD, select the type of CD to be created. Experience has shown more success in using a CD-R rather than a CD-RW because the CD-R is more successfully recognized by other computers. When burning the CD, remember to select and copy both the PowerPoint slideshow as well as all appropriate SnagIt .avi files.

Sample Presentation

This process for producing a multimedia presentation was used to create CD-ROMs for new doctoral students in Education, who are also distance education students and who often do doctoral-level research from home or work. Because many of these students do not regularly use the main campus or the Marshall University Graduate College Library onsite, they must learn to become adept at doing literature searches, developing effective search strategies, retrieving full-text articles and documents, and knowing how to request books, dissertations and non-full-text articles. Each year, a librarian is invited to an orientation for these students, but unfortunately is given only 20 minutes to demonstrate these techniques. A CD-ROM, which these students could take home and view at their leisure, was created to provide them with the focused library instruction they needed.

On this CD-ROM, the first slide lists the title of the presentation and introduces the two librarians who produced the instructional CD. A table of contents slide is followed by bulleted slides describing services and resources. Inserted SnagIt .avi files demonstrate how to search the following databases: ERIC, E-Subscribe, Dissertation Abstracts, Digital Dissertations, PsycINFO, Academic Search Elite, Mental Measurements Yearbook, MILES (online catalog), and WorldCat. Another SnagIt .avi file shows students how to use Information Delivery Services to request items using IDS Express. The module ends with a slide listing contact information.

Revising this basic presentation is easy because the SnagIt .avi files were limited to single database searches. For instance, if drastic changes occur with regard to accessing and searching one database, revising that one SnagIt .avi video, not the entire cadre of SnagIt files, is easily managed by deleting the outdated SnagIt file and replacing it with a revised one. It is crucial to delete outdated SnagIt files because PowerPoint could divert to old SnagIt files.

Future plans include adding sound to explain and reinforce the action of the SnagIt videos, and also making these instructional modules available through the Marshall University Libraries' Website. Web-based access would allow continual updating without investing a great deal of time, effort, and money on producing CDs or even VHS versions of library instruction. Another benefit is that a wider audience could access these instructional materials.

PART TWO:
RESOURCES ACCESS AND INFORMATION DELIVERY SERVICES

In addition to enhancing and expanding instruction, technology has also bolstered efforts to make resources accessible to the off-campus user. In technology-challenged and remote environments libraries strive to provide services that offer anytime and anywhere access or delivery, driven by users. In order to provide users anywhere in the world with access to Marshall University's online full-text journals as well as to see print and microfilm journal holdings, Marshall University has developed a Web-based system that enables the user:

- To know if the libraries provide online access to a journal
- To find out if the libraries own a print copy or own a microfilm copy of a journal
- To use Information Delivery Services when needed.

PHASE/PROJECT I:
MARSHALL UNIVERSITY FULL-TEXT ONLINE JOURNALS
(http://www.marshall.edu/libtech/search/)

The rapid growth of aggregator databases has presented libraries with both new opportunities for collection enhancement and new challenges of bibliographic control and access management. Marshall University Libraries provide access to numerous aggregated databases, which contain 6,774 unique electronic full-text/image journal titles. It is important that the libraries find efficient ways to manage and provide access to these resources.

To answer this challenge the libraries developed a Web-based, searchable database for the online full-text journals that are contained in the libraries' subscription databases. It can be searched by title and subject and also can be browsed by journal title (A to Z) and vendor/aggregator. It provides a single interface for the user to search for the full-text online journals contained in EbscoHost, JSTOR, ABI-INFORM, Project MUSE, EbscoOnline, Wilson OmniFile, Kluwer, Synergy and other publishers.

In the database record, holdings are listed and a URL links to a journal title level whenever it is possible. Therefore, it identifies what issues are available and then with a click puts the user directly at the site of the requested resources instead of the vendor/aggregator provider site. For example, any titles in JSTOR, Project MUSE, Kluwer, Synergy and EbscoOnline are linked to the individual title.

The next step in providing "seamless" access for distance students is to implement EZProxy, which will allow authorized Marshall University users easy access to online collections without using individual passwords for each database.

PHASE/PROJECT II: MU JOURNALS
(http://www.marshall.edu/libtech/mujournals/)

An essential part of a library's function is to provide its users with an effective and efficient means of accessing print resources as well as electronic resources; however, it is not easy to search for all of the journals that the libraries own or have access to because there are many places to look and many clicks to navigate. A recent development is another Web-based database system for Marshall University journals, titled MU JOURNALS. It includes all formats of journals owned or accessible through all Marshall University libraries. For users it is simple and easy, and all journals, regardless of format, are there. Users can browse journal titles (A to Z) or search for journals by any of the following criteria:

- Journal title
- Subject
- ISSN
- Call number
- Vender/Aggregator
- Location
- Format

Users can view, on a single screen, all of their possible options for obtaining a given journal title with coverage in all different formats and in all different locations. When a user searches for a journal title that is not found in MU JOURNALS, the system directs the user to Information Delivery Services. The database also provides usage reports at the database level and title level. This database has greatly enhanced journal access and expanded the libraries' collection.

INFORMATION DELIVERY SERVICES
(http://muntids.marshall.edu/illiad/logon.html)

IDS Express

Once students have learned in instruction sessions how to access resources, they require a strong information delivery system to deliver the materials. A Web-based end-user interface system, IDS Express, using ILLiad software, provides automated interlibrary loan and document delivery service which allows users to submit (or cancel) requests and track the status of their request 24 hours a day, 7 days a week from around the world–anywhere they have access to the Internet. Through IDS Express, users can retrieve/view/print/save electronic photocopies on the same "anytime/anywhere" schedule via the Web. Users can view a list of checked out items and renew loans online and also can view their entire request history, including cancelled and completed items with all tracking and notes.

IDS Express provides convenient and fast delivery of materials to distance students. Distance students use it to request any materials needed regardless of the libraries' ownership. Their requests are filled either from the Marshall University Libraries' collection or from other libraries or institutions via interlibrary loan or document delivery. If a distance student chooses electronic delivery, journal articles owned by MU are scanned or any articles received electronically via Ariel can be delivered directly to the student in PDF format (Adobe's Portable Document Format) through the World Wide Web using capabilities built into ILLiad, IDS Express. The student can then log in to IDS Express to download/view or save the electronically delivered articles. Home delivery service is provided to a user registered with a patron status of distant student in his/her IDS Express profile.

With IDS Express there are no more labor-intensive paper files. Requests are handled more quickly, easily, and accurately by getting rid of the problems arising from hand-written requests. Using IDS Express has enabled the libraries to meet the increased demand for ILL and document delivery services. In 2000-2001 patron requests dramatically increased 87.45% over three years ago (1997-1998). IDS Express provides a responsive, user-friendly gateway to ILL and document delivery.

UNMEDIATED DOCUMENT DELIVERY

Marshall University Libraries give faculty, staff and graduate students unmediated access to document delivery service via the Marshall Ingenta Gateway (previously called Marshall UnCover Gateway). Ingenta is a multidisciplinary journal article database that covers approximately 20,000 journals (coverage 1988-present). The Gateway allows authorized users free ordering of articles. When a journal is not available from the libraries' collection, Marshall University faculty, graduate students and staff may order articles online directly from Ingenta and have these orders automatically charged to the libraries' account. The Libraries will cover the cost of articles from journals not held by the Libraries up to $40 per article for faculty and staff in MU Medical School and up to $30 per article for the rest of MU authorized users. The articles are available electronically (html or pdf) or via fax. Electronic articles are available for downloading and viewing immediately, and most faxed articles are delivered within 24 to 48 hours during the normal business week. Fax deliveries are sent to the number designated by the requester. A maximum of 30 articles per patron may be ordered in an academic year.

Unmediated document ordering and delivery offers a value-added service with expanded access, convenience, and faster speed of delivery. It is a cost-effective alternative to traditional interlibrary loans, and the range of titles ordered demonstrates the value of access over holdings because no title has been ordered significantly to justify purchase. Bringing the library resources and services to distance students continues to be very exciting and accompanied by lots of change, challenge, new technology and system implementation.

REFERENCES

Adams, C. (1998). A Web handbook for library research. In P. S. Thomas & M. Jones (Comp.), *The Eighth Off-Campus Library Services Conference Proceedings*, (pp. 183-195). Mt. Pleasant, MI: Central Michigan University.

Barnes, S., Holmes, K., & Stahley, M. (1998). Library instruction at a distance: The high tech/high touch mix. In P. S. Thomas & M. Jones (Comp.), *The Eighth Off-Campus Library Services Conference Proceedings*, (pp. 183-195). Mt. Pleasant, MI: Central Michigan University.

Brandsma, T. W. (2001, October). *Journal article access and the library Web: From frustration to integration.* Poster session presented at the annual meeting of EDUCAUSE, Indianapolis, IN.

Buehler, M., Dopp, E., Hughes, K. A., & Thompson, J. (2001). It takes a library to support distance learners. *Internet Reference Services Quarterly, 5*(3), 5-24.

Caspers, J. S. (1999). Hands-on instruction across the miles: Using a Web tutorial to teach the literature review process. *Research Strategies, 16,* 187-197.

Felts, Jr., J. W. & Frick, R. L. (2001). Creating an interactive web application for providing access to full-text electronic journals from any location. *The Serials Librarian, 40*(3/4), 277-290.

Kenny, D. (1997). Teaching the 'net without a net: Custom simulations boost freshmen's PC skills. *THE Journal, 24*(7), 87+. Retrieved October 12, 2001, from EBSCO*host* database (Academic Search Elite) on the World Wide Web: http://search.epnet.com.

MacDonald, B. (1998). Class act: Designing a portable approach to multimedia library instruction for the remote classroom. *Research Strategies, 16,* 127-133.

Thinking Outside the Library:
How to Develop, Implement and Promote
Library Services for Distance Learners

Meredith Ault

University of Texas TeleCampus

SUMMARY. Supporting distance learners requires a shift in the traditional "library" mindset. Librarians who serve distance learners must
come up with new and innovative ways to meet the needs of their unique
users. Librarians must attempt to define and identify who their distance
users are and what their needs are, and in turn, develop and implement a
set of library resources and services in support of these needs. Promotion
of the resources and services available is necessary in order to successfully provide library support; students and faculty must know what services are available and how to access them.

KEYWORDS. Distance learners, promotion, library services, development

Distance education is becoming a larger and more visible part of higher education institutions in this country. Distance learning is defined by the United
States Distance Learning Association as "the acquisition of knowledge and
skills through mediated information and instruction. Distance learning encompasses all technologies and supports the pursuit of life-long learning for all"
(2000, Resources-Reference Info & Statistics section, para. 1). The term dis-

[Haworth co-indexing entry note]: "Thinking Outside the Library: How to Develop, Implement and Promote Library Services for Distance Learners." Ault, Meredith. Co-published simultaneously in *Journal of Library Administration* (The Haworth Information Press, an imprint of The Haworth Press, Inc.) Vol. 37, No. 1/2,
2002, pp. 39-48; and: *Distance Learning Library Services: The Tenth Off-Campus Library Services Conference*
(ed: Patrick B. Mahoney) The Haworth Information Press, an imprint of The Haworth Press, Inc., 2002,
pp. 39-48.

http://www.haworthpress.com/store/product.asp?sku=J111
10.1300/J111v37n01_05

tance learning encompasses many different formats including, but not limited to, online courses, interactive broadcasts or videoconferencing to designated sites, live classes in remote locations, prerecorded programs broadcast locally or available for loan on videotape or correspondence courses.

According to the National Center for Education Statistics report *Distance Education at Postsecondary Education Institutions: 1997-1998*, "about one-third of the nation's 2-year and 4-year postsecondary education institutions offered any distance education courses during the 12-month 1997-98 academic year, and another one-fifth of the institutions planned to start offering such courses within the next 3 years" (Lewis, Farris, Snow, & Levin, 1999, p. iii). Thanks to the rapid growth and pervasiveness of the Internet, online learning has put a new and timely face on the concept of distance education. In the past, distance education meant correspondence courses or videotapes of talking heads. Online learning was the perfect marriage of technology and education and it helped to renew interest in the concept of distance education. So suddenly distance education, the "step child" of higher education, began to grow and expand and so did the numbers of students participating in distance learning. According to the *Distance Education at Postsecondary Education Institutions: 1997-1998*, "there were an estimated 1,661,100 enrollments in distance education courses in the 1997-98 academic year" (p. iv).

This resurgence in the popularity of distance education created a new population of library users, who in the past had been small in numbers and remote in location and therefore, were not considered when it came to the resources and services offered by the typical college or university library. Now that distance learners are increasing in both visibility and numbers, libraries are having to "think outside the library" and come up with new and innovative ways to meet the needs of these unique users.

Why should a library worry about providing quality library services to distance learners? According to the Association of College and Research Libraries' *Guidelines for Distance Learning Library Services*, "members of the distance learning communities are entitled to library services and resources equivalent to those provided for students and faculty in traditional campus settings" (Philosophy section, para. 1). It may eventually become an accreditation issue. One of the six regional accrediting bodies, Western Cooperative for Educational Telecommunications (WICHE), published *Best Practices for Electronically Offered Degree and Certificate Programs* (2000) in which they outlined some expectations in regards to library services in the Student Support section of the document:

> The institution recognizes that appropriate services must be available for students of electronically offered programs, using the working assumption

that these students will not be physically present on campus. With variations for specific situations and programs, these services, which are possibly coordinated, may include: library resources appropriate to the program, including, reference and research assistance; remote access to data bases, online journals and full-text resources; document delivery service; library user and information literacy instruction, reserve materials; and institutional agreements with local libraries. (Student Support section, para. 4c)

The process that librarians must go through in order to design effective library resources and services for distance learners involves defining who their distance learners are, identifying some of the needs and characteristics of this remote population, developing a resource and services plan to meet these needs, being aware of the potential barriers to resources and services, and implementing and promoting the resource/service plan. It is important for the library to have a written analysis of their current situation as well as a plan for which services and resources need to be developed and when they should be implemented. Having a written plan for these resources and services will help keep the library on target with the development and implementation.

DEFINE DISTANCE LEARNER

One of the first steps in creating a set of distance learning library resources and services is for the library to define who is considered a distance learner. The library may follow the institution's lead by defining distance learners as students enrolled in the classes designated "distance education" classes. This way of defining distance learners may become murky for some libraries if the student is enrolled in an online course as well as on-campus courses. Is this student considered an on-campus student or distance learner? Some libraries define their distance learners based on their geographic distance away from the campus and will set up a certain criterion (e.g., the student must live 100 miles from the campus) to define "distance" status. How a library defines who is considered a distance learner is a local decision that must be made by library administration and librarians. But this criterion must be in place prior to the development of resources and services.

Another consideration when developing library services in support of distance learning is whether the library will provide services and resources to both the students and the faculty involved with distance learning courses. This is an important distinction that needs to be made early on since some services and resources made available to the faculty are going to be different than those provided to students.

IDENTIFY DISTANCE LEARNERS AND THEIR NEEDS

Librarians must attempt to identify who their distance users are and what their needs are, keeping in mind the mode of distance education being offered may impact those needs.

It is important to try to get an idea of how many distance learners the library is going to need to support, as well as some information about who the distance learners are. Knowing something about this remote population will make the development and implementation of services easier. Some of the considerations to take into account when trying to profile distance learners are: distance learning format of classes in which they are enrolled, geographic location of student (especially if it involves international students), area of study and status (undergrad/grad) of students.

Knowing what type of distance education class a student is taking can have an impact on the types of services needed. Is the student enrolled in a fully online course or is the instruction provided via satellite, television or video conferencing software? Or is the class taught live in the classroom, just at a location remote from the college or university? Students who take completely online classes are the toughest to serve since they never meet together in one physical space, which can affect services, like the ability to provide hands-on instruction. Also, since online courses have asynchronous aspects, there may be more international students enrolled, which can effect hours and methods of service. Does the toll free number work outside the continental U.S.?

It is also helpful to know the geographic location of the distance learners. Are most of them located within the state, within the United States? What time zone are they in? Geographic location can affect many things like hours of service, method of contact and delivery of materials. Geographic location is an issue since many distance learners use local libraries and resources in addition to the service provided by the college or university sponsoring the course. Knowing where a distance learner lives and therefore, what resources he/she might have access to locally, is important.

The area of study and the status of the students can have an impact on the type and level of library services that need to be provided. Certain disciplines traditionally make greater use of the library and its resources; this should remain true in the online environment as well. Also, the type of services and resources needed by an undergrad are often quite different than those needed by a master's or doctoral level student. All these factors must be taken into account when developing services and purchasing resources.

Keep in mind that discovering how many distance learners there are at a university and any additional useful information about these students is often very difficult. Many universities do not have a centralized, administrative body through which distance learning classes are organized. At many colleges and universities distance learning classes are handled on a departmental level, leaving each department responsible for the administration of the classes. This decentralized model for administering distance education courses makes the library's job of getting to know its distance learners tougher since information must be obtained from multiple departments, instead of one centralized body.

Assessing the needs of these distance learners can be done by surveying the distance users directly and then creating services to respond to those needs. Librarians can also survey the distance learning faculty to find out how the faculty will be integrating library research into their course and therefore, what their students will need to access. Libraries can also create a set of distance learning library services and resources and then survey their distance users in order to discover if the user's needs and expectations are being met. Which assessment model a library chooses will depend on the information available to them about their distance learners and the lead time they have to create and implement the needed services and resources.

DEVELOPING RESOURCES AND SERVICES FOR DISTANCE LEARNERS

The development of resources for distance learners centers on off-campus access to the resources, technical support of the resources, and the purchasing of resources. Most libraries are spending larger amounts of their budgets on purchasing electronic resources, since they are accessible to more users than the print counterparts. So an important issue for off-campus students, especially distance learners, is getting access to these resources. Most libraries provide access to their electronic resources via IP-validation, which means off-campus users must have access to a proxy server in order to be authenticated by the resources. Most libraries have a technical support staff that could maintain the proxy server in addition to the library's other hardware. But maintaining a proxy server could be more of a challenge for smaller libraries with less staff and less technical support.

Libraries must be prepared not only to purchase, configure and maintain the proxy server, but they must also be prepared to provide the technical support the user will inevitably need. Most proxy servers require users to change configurations on their browser for use, and that often results in the users needing additional technical support. Librarians, as well as technical support personnel, must be prepared to provide this support.

Purchases of electronic resources may be affected by this new distance learning library program. The library may choose to put more of an emphasis and consequently more money towards the purchasing of full-text databases since these type of resources are especially critical since many remote users do not have a local option for finding materials.

Librarians who serve distance learners must identify which library services they can provide to their distance learning students and faculty. Once the services have been identified the library must deliver these "traditional" library services in a non-traditional way. Some of these library services may need to be adapted to the distance learning environment. These services include reference and technical assistance, document delivery/interlibrary loan, library instruction, and borrowing privileges at local libraries.

Reference and technical assistance, which traditionally takes place face to face, can be provided to distance learners by offering telephone and electronic reference. For many distance learners contacting the library for assistance would mean a long distance call. A toll-free telephone number is one of the simplest and most effective ways to provide library assistance to remote users. Toll-free numbers are a relatively inexpensive way to offer remote students a cost-free option for calling and receiving assistance. Keep in mind that toll-free numbers are often restricted to the continental United States, Canada and Mexico and therefore, will not be a solution for international learners.

Librarians can also offer reference services and technical support electronically via email, Web forms or chat software. Offering reference and technical assistance electronically is important because some users might only have one phone line through which they connect to the Internet and therefore, they aren't able to be online and on the phone at the same time. Electronic reference allows the users to obtain assistance while still maintaining their connection to the Internet; this is especially helpful when troubleshooting technical problems. Email reference is a popular way to provide reference assistance since email is such a prevalent and easily accessible technology for most students. One of the drawbacks to email reference is that there is no opportunity for the librarian to conduct a reference interview because of the unstructured nature of email. This usually results in dialogue between the librarian and the users asking questions.

One way to avoid the ambiguity associated with email reference is to provide Web forms for reference and technical assistance. Creating Web-based forms for use on a Website provides a bit more structure and allows the librarian to ask some reference interview or troubleshooting questions up front. The scripting on the Web form can have the results sent to numerous email addresses. The Web form question can then be answered with an email directly to the user.

Unlike the asynchronous electronic reference via email or Web forms, synchronous or "real time" reference and technical support can be provided electronically by using chat software. Chat software can be more expensive (depending on the software used) and it can also be more technologically challenging than email or Web forms. But the major advantage of using chat software to provide support is that users can get "real time" assistance. They can chat with a librarian live and get their question answered or their technical problem resolved right away. Some chat software programs also offer more sophisticated features like call center management and collaborative browsing. One issue to consider when offering real time reference assistance is that, in essence, the library is creating another service point that has to be staffed constantly during its hours of operation.

Document delivery/interlibrary loan is another important library service that can be provided to remote users. Remote users may identify library materials that they need, but cannot obtain full-text online. Librarians must decide what their policies and procedures will be for the request and delivery of library materials to remote users, since these procedures will be very different than the procedures for on-campus students. How the library is going to deliver articles (both owned and those obtained through interlibrary loan) must be decided (mail, fax or electronically?), and online forms for remote users to request these items must be created. Delivery of books is often a trickier decision for a library since it involves a "returnable item." Delivery of books obtained via interlibrary loan can complicate this issue more since the library does not own the "returnable item" they are sending. Although delivery of materials is often logistically complicated, it is an important part of providing equitable services to distance learners.

Library instruction to remote users can be quite challenging and librarians need to be prepared to offer instruction in non-traditional places or ways. For live remote distance education classes the librarian may need to travel to the location of the class so that a hands-on instruction session may be conducted. Librarians must also be prepared to provide either live or taped library instruction to learners via broadcast, satellite, or videoconferencing technology. Providing library instruction to online learners may be the most challenging since online learners are never in one physical space together. Reaching online learners may require the librarian to use chat software in order to conduct library instruction sessions virtually. The librarian can schedule chat sessions that are focused on teaching students how to use a certain resource or to develop specific research skills. When conducting library instruction sessions via chat it is important to remember to keep the student to instructor ratio low and offer multiple sessions to accommodate students' varied schedules.

Many state or university systems have created reciprocal borrowing privilege programs so that users at one library may check out items at other libraries. These types of arrangements often include access to both academic and public libraries. These reciprocal borrowing programs are beneficial to all library users, but they can be especially important for distance learners since it increases their access to local libraries. Access to local libraries and their resources may be critical, depending on the availability and convenience of the library services being provided by their educational institution's library. The library must create a way in which remote learners can request and receive the necessary authorization they need in order to take advantage of these borrowing privileges.

POTENTIAL BARRIERS TO ACCESS AND SERVICES

In a perfect world, libraries could offer all the above-mentioned services to all their distance learners in order to provide them with the equivalent, if not enhanced, library services. But the reality is that there are often barriers to providing all these library services. Some of these barriers can be geographical, technological, or budgetary and staffing in nature.

Geographic barriers may exist if learners are located in a foreign country or rural area. Learners in foreign countries or rural areas are sometimes at a disadvantage because, depending on their location, they might not have stable or quality Internet access and they might have limited local libraries or resources.

Technological barriers include not only unstable or slow access to the Internet, but the inherent bandwidth limitation of the Internet in its current state. Graphic-laden Web pages may be an effective instructional tool, but if the user cannot download the pages in a reasonable amount of time then the pages are useless. Libraries could use multimedia and conferencing software to assist and educate users, but the bandwidth limitations of the Internet make the application of these technologies less practical than they could be.

Budgetary and staffing restraints are familiar to all libraries and librarians, not just the ones who serve distance learners. It seems that libraries are constantly fighting stagnant or decreasing budgets. Library services for distance learners can be expensive since many of these services require an addition or revision to current services, which may require more money and/or more staff. Adding toll-free telephone numbers, buying chat software, staffing electronic reference services, mailing books and articles are going to be added costs to the operational budget of the library. Also, libraries may not currently have the staff to support these new programs and services, and may not have the money to hire additional staff.

All these potential barriers need to be considered when developing a set of library services for distance learners. The library must balance the need to offer equivalent access to library services with these restrictions. The library must develop innovative and cost-effective ways to deliver traditional services in a non-traditional way to non-traditional students.

IMPLEMENTATION OF RESOURCES AND SERVICES

Once the needs of the distance learners have been assessed and a set of resources and services have been developed to meet these needs, the next step is for the library to start implementing the new resources and services. Since there may be quite a few new resources and services being offered, it is important to prioritize the resources and services to be rolled out, since it is unlikely that the library will have enough money, staff, or sanity to roll out everything at once.

It is important to implement the bulk of the resource portion of the plan. It is imperative that students have remote access to electronic resources as soon as possible. So the library would want to make sure the proxy server was functional early on so that students have the ability to search for the research materials they need. Once the access is in place the library should concentrate on adding databases and electronic journals in order to increase the number of full-text resources available online. When the resource portion of the plan is in place the next thing to look at is the services aspect of the plan. The most needed services should be implemented first followed by the services that will immediately benefit the largest number of users.

PROMOTION OF RESOURCES AND SERVICES

Now that the library has developed these quality library resources and services for distance learners it is important that the students and the faculty involved with these classes find out what is available. The library should plan to market its services directly to the students and faculty. Marketing to the students is important because the library must reach the end user in order to be successful. But it is also important to market the library resources and services to the distance learning faculty so that they will integrate research assignments into their curriculum and stress to students the importance of what the library has to offer.

Marketing to students could include a prominent position on the "campus" Web site, posting information about the library to the courseware bulletin boards and student listservs. More direct marketing tactics could also be used, such as sending an email to all students via a distribution list or sending them promotional pieces in the mail. These promotional items should stress what the library has to offer (both in the way of resources and services), ways to contact the library, and how a librarian can help the student. If the students see the direct value of the library to their academic success they will be more likely to make use of the library.

Marketing to the faculty is also important because a recommendation from the faculty member can really drive students to the library for assistance. Another way to make sure students use the distance learning library services is to work with the faculty as they create their courses in order to get library resources and research skills fully integrated into the curriculum, so that using the library becomes less of an option and more of a necessity. Marketing to faculty could include emails and posting to faculty listservs. Presenting and taking part in faculty training sessions is another way to get in at the "ground floor" with faculty members. Faculty training opportunities usually occur throughout the development of the course, so offering up the library and its services during this crucial time may encourage faculty to include the library in the curriculum.

Working to provide library services for distance learners can seem to be a daunting proposition at first. Trying to identify and assess the needs of users who could be located across the country, or around the world, can be difficult. Providing traditional resources and services to the non-traditional clientele of distance learners requires librarians to think in new and innovative ways and to "think outside of the library." Library services for this unique population of users forces librarians to focus on creative solutions and to develop excellent customer service skills.

REFERENCES

Association for College and Research Libraries (1998, July). *Guidelines for distance learning library services*. Retrieved November 14, 2000 from the World Wide Web: http://www.ala.org/acrl/guides/distlrng.html.

Lewis, L., Farris, E., Snow, K., & Levin, D. (1999). *Distance education at postsecondary education institutions: 1997-98*. Retrieved November 27, 2001 from the World Wide Web: http://nces.ed.gov/pubsearch/pubsinfo.asp?pubid=2000013.

United States Distance Learning Association. Retrieved November 26, 2001 from World Wide Web: http://www.usdla.org/.

Western Cooperative for Educational Telecommunications (2000). *Best practices for electronically offered degree and certificate programs*. Retrieved November 27, 2000 from the World Wide Web: http://www.wiche.edu/telecom/article1.htm.

Distance Learning Librarian: Essential Team Member in Distance Learning Design

Constance M. Baird

Pat Wilson

University of Kentucky

SUMMARY. This presentation will explore the unique relationship of distance learning library services at the University of Kentucky to key academic and administrative units on the campus including the Distance Learning Technology Center (DLTC), the University Library System and academic colleges and departments. Through the distance learning librarian's dual role as library faculty and DLTC Director, unique services are developed, delivered and evaluated in a collaborative environment with Center administrators, instructional designers, key support personnel and a wide range of faculty.

KEYWORDS. Distance learners, design, library service, teamwork

A review of the current literature on distance learning library services highlights and emphasizes the changing role of distance learning librarians. More and more, these professionals are being asked to take highly active roles in the distance learning academic program development and delivery process. Spe-

[Haworth co-indexing entry note]: "Distance Learning Librarian: Essential Team Member in Distance Learning Design." Baird, Constance M., and Pat Wilson. Co-published simultaneously in *Journal of Library Administration* (The Haworth Information Press, an imprint of The Haworth Press, Inc.) Vol. 37, No. 1/2, 2002, pp. 49-57; and: *Distance Learning Library Services: The Tenth Off-Campus Library Services Conference* (ed: Patrick B. Mahoney) The Haworth Information Press, an imprint of The Haworth Press, Inc., 2002, pp. 49-57.

http://www.haworthpress.com/store/product.asp?sku=J111

10.1300/J111v37n01_06

cifically, librarians working in the field of distance learning are being challenged to:

- Be actively involved in the online/multimedia course design and development process
- Serve as members of instructional design teams at an institution
- Develop information literacy tools to respond to the new virtual learning environment
- Consult on course migration from a traditional classroom setting to the new electronic technological environment
- Assist faculty with obtaining necessary copyright permission for electronic reserves
- Create a collaborative environment for resource sharing among multiple institutions
- Work with faculty to emphasize lifelong learning through information access ("ACRL Standards & Guidelines," 2000).

The Association for College & Research Libraries (ACRL) recognized not only the changing role of distance learning librarian but the changing nature of higher education itself with the 2000 revision of the 1990 *Guidelines for Extended-Campus Library Services*–now entitled *Guidelines for Distance Learning Library Services*. The ACRL noted several critical factors leading to the guidelines revision including the:

- Rapid emergence of distance education
- Changing nature of information access
- Increase in the number of unique environments where educational opportunities are offered
- Increase in the recognition of need for library services beyond the main campus
- Concern and demand for equitable services for all students and faculty in higher education–particularly at remote locations
- Increase in technological innovations
- Rapid emergence of the virtual university (Cooper, Dempsey, Menon, & Millson-Martula, 1998).

In 1998, the University of Kentucky responded to these critical changes in the academy with the creation of the Distance Learning Technology Center (DLTC)–symbolically and physically housed in the William T. Young Library–the Commonwealth Library for all Kentuckians. This new organizational model encourages and facilitates the active involvement of valued library professionals by combining the various distance learning service units under one administrative umbrella to provide a one-stop service center for distance learning faculty and students.

Distance Learning Library Services is one of four primary units that comprise the Center. Each unit has its own Director and staff and provides a unique set of services creating a strong infrastructure for distance learning at the institution.

DISTANCE LEARNING PROGRAMS (DLP)

- Provides a host of distance learning student support services (registration/admissions/campus liaison; online course registration)
- Markets and schedules distance learning courses and programs
- Supports faculty in the development and delivery of distance learning courses and programs
- Provides the funding for development and teaching of online and multimedia courses
- Provides the funding for Distance Learning Library Services (DLLS) student personnel, marketing, travel and current expenses
- Provides the funding for copyright clearance fees for DL course electronic reserves
- Hires and supports part-time technical coordinators at 120+ interactive video sites statewide
- Operates in-state and out-of-state toll-free lines for distance learning students and faculty
- Designs, implements and analyzes data gathered from DL support services evaluation instrument
- Provides information for and actively engages in grant writing for distance learning programs
- Supports students and faculty involved in the Kentucky Virtual University (KyVU)

DISTANCE LEARNING LIBRARY SERVICES (DLLS)

- Serves as reference contact for the Kentucky Virtual Library (KyVL)
- Serves as a reference resource for the Distance Learning Technology Center
- Consults with faculty/academic departments on information resources needed for distance learning courses delivered via a variety of technologies
- Works with collaborative institutional programs
  - Information resources consultation/workshops
  - Electronic reserves

- Contributes to grant writing projects
- Provides bibliographic instruction
  - At remote sites via interactive video and in person
  - Via course specific guides
  - Via online tutorials for select electronic databases
  - Via subject-specific electronic modules for inclusion in online courses
- Collaborates with Media Design and Production personnel in development and production of online tutorials
- Serves as part of the instructional design team for development of online courses
- Heads copyright clearance efforts for online course electronic materials in collaboration with faculty and DLTC personnel
- Serves on the E-Courses Working Group
- Markets library/information support services in collaboration with Distance Learning Programs personnel
- Provides document delivery for students/faculty
- Provides electronic reserves/traditional reserves service
- Maintains home page specifically designed for distance learners

DISTANCE LEARNING NETWORKS (DLN)

- Coordinates scheduling and actual delivery of distance learning courses and programs through various technology networks
- Liaison to the Kentucky Telelinking Network (KTLN)–a "network of networks" using interactive video (2-way audio/2-way video) to deliver DL programming to 120+ Kentucky sites and link with regional, national and international interactive video sites as well
- Provides training for professional full-time and part-time staff in effective use of the technologies
- Provides training for distance learning faculty in effective use of the technologies
- Explores new technology options for academic program delivery such as desktop videoconferencing

MEDIA DESIGN AND PRODUCTION (MDP)

- Provides instructional design and course development support to faculty delivering in the online/multimedia course environment
- Provides training for faculty in the use of new course management systems for online delivery
- Provides system administrators to manage online course tools and systems

- Provides audio, video and graphics support for faculty developing course content for DL delivery
- Provides support for development of bibliographic instruction tools for use in the online/multimedia environment

The librarian who heads the Distance Learning Library Services unit holds dual roles as both a tenured library faculty member within the University Library System and as a Director in the Distance Learning Technology Center. Through this unique combination, critical library and information support services are developed, delivered and evaluated in a collaborative environment with Center administrators, instructional design staff, support personnel and a wide range of faculty across disciplines. The two Directors of Distance Learning Programs and Library Services work particularly close together to achieve a seamless and transparent educational experience for the distance learning student–ensuring that all library and academic support services available on the main University campus are replicated (and, on occasion improved upon) in the distance learning environment. These support services are reviewed and evaluated on a semester basis through unique instruments designed for students in the online and other distance learning environments–allowing the Directors to directly respond to student concerns and needs. The close working relationship among Center Directors also creates a solid foundation for regional and discipline-based accreditation reviews–a critical component in the evolution of distance learning as an integral part of the higher education environment.

The select projects described below are illustrative of the quality products and services that can emanate from a strong collaborative partnership among dedicated professionals.

INFORMATION LITERACY/BIBLIOGRAPHIC INSTRUCTION FOR DISTANCE LEARNERS

Creating increased awareness of the vast array of library services and resources available to our Distance Learning (DL) faculty and students has been a direct response to student concerns voiced on the annual DLTC online course support services evaluation. Various methods for expanding resource awareness and providing much needed skill-sets for use of those resources have been employed. Methods have included (a) Subject-specific electronic library resource modules embedded in online courses, (b) online tutorials for targeted electronic resources, (c) bibliographic instruction sessions delivered to remote DL sites using interactive video technology, (d) on-site visits by the DL Librarian to remote sites to deliver face-to-face bibliographic instruction and coordinate with local librarians and administrators, and (e) targeted brochures for DL students and faculty outlining specific services and resources. Each of these endeavors has required the collaboration of one or more units within and outside of the DLTC.

a. For the subject-specific electronic library resource modules, the DL Librarian has worked closely with faculty members, DLP, and MDP to develop modules for courses, taking into account course requirements and expectations for students. Preparation for such a module includes in-depth consultation with the faculty member so that the course goals and objectives are understood. It is essential that the course syllabus be perused for a further understanding of what is expected from the course participants. Using this information, the content of the module is developed addressing the specific information requirements for the course. Blackboard and PowerPoint are currently being used for course delivery. The focus of the module is on the students' information assignments, specifically, what resources they need to access and utilize in order to be successful in the course. The module is developed as a set of PowerPoint slides with audio, which is eventually posted on the Web and made available to students as part of the instructor's course in the Blackboard Learning Management System (LMS). The recording time, audio editing, slide preparation, and HTML work are all done on a charge-back basis with development funding provided by DLP.

b. Online tutorials for 10 databases have been developed and made available on the DLLS home page. The original suggestion for the tutorials was made by MDP after the DLLS Librarian recorded a bibliographic instruction session via streaming video. The idea was to create tutorials that could be used by all distance learning students and faculty. Together it was decided that screen images with an audio script would be the best way to deliver the product. MDP staff served as the "test subjects" for the prototype module. The first tutorial went through several edits as the script was developed for the screen prints. The DLLS Librarian chose databases such as the LEXIS-NEXIS Statistical Universe to feature. Sample tutorial development steps include:

- Preparation of PowerPoint slides (average 20-27 slides) and the script (Word document)
- Submission of the PowerPoint file and Word file to the tech editor
- Recording of the script by the DLLS librarian (average 20 minutes)
- Digital taping, editing and encoding of the presentation by the TV Engineer
- Submission of the RealMedia audio file to the tech editor
- Saving of PowerPoint as GIF files (PNG image files converted using Fireworks)

- File "tweaking" by tech editor
- Links and menu updating
- Review and corrections by DL Librarian

c. Interactive video (IV) technology is still a very effective and viable delivery medium used throughout Kentucky for distance learning courses and programs–particularly at the graduate level where faculty to student and student to student interaction is a critical part of the pedagogy. The DL Librarian, working with staff from Distance Learning Networks, has successfully used the technology to delivery synchronous bibliographic instruction sessions simultaneously to students in the on campus IV rooms and to students at remote DL sites. DLN personnel staff the IV rooms at the main campus sites as well as schedule the remote sites. They work closely with the DL Librarian, originating from one of the on-campus rooms, to effectively utilize the technology. DLP hires and funds the part-time staff at the remote sites to ensure smooth delivery of course content and materials.

d. The DL librarian also works closely with distance learning faculty, the DLP Director and local administrators to coordinate on-site visits to remote distance learning locations to participate in face-to-face orientations and deliver bibliographic instruction. On-site workshops require close coordination with local technical staff, particularly when demonstrating access to and effective use of online electronic resources. Distance Learning Programs makes all logistical arrangements for the on-site orientation sessions as well as funds the travel.

e. Marketing the extensive services and resources of the Distance Learning Library office to students and faculty involved in distance learning and teaching has been a main priority for the DLTC. The Directors of DLP and DLLS have worked closely to coordinate these efforts and have employed the services of the University Libraries graphics artist to create a design reflective of the innovative nature of the services. These marketing pieces have not only been sent to the primary targeted audiences but have been used to promote the DLLS office itself with other library professionals within and outside of the University of Kentucky Libraries System. In addition, the Directors have worked to expand the DLLS presence in the Distance Learning hard-copy semester catalogs that highlight courses and programs offered. Electronic marketing efforts have also been enhanced and expanded through an integrated design for the entire Distance Learning Technology Center Web site–featuring separate but well coordinated and connected pages for each DLTC unit. This tool was developed using content input from each Director as well as graphic artists and electronic resource staff from the DLTC and from University Libraries.

In addition to the ongoing efforts described above, the Directors of DLP and DLLS are actively involved in statewide, regional, national and international collaborative distance learning programming–coordinating services and resources for multiple faculty and multiple institutions over a wide range of disciplines. The DLP, DLLS and DLN are also taking a more active role with faculty and academic departments in the grant-writing process–proposing instructional, technological and administrative coordination of distance learning support services for developing technology-driven academic programming.

The productive working relationships described above among all units within and outside of the DLTC is aided and enhanced by the strong individual commitment of the professional faculty and staff involved, as well as the close physical proximity of the group housed in the Distance Learning Technology Center. The clear mission of service for distance learning faculty and students allows the DLTC unit teams to:

- Consult on and formulate new policies and procedures for distance learning support as needed
- Provide "quick fixes" for faculty and student problems related to DL services
- Provide more timely turn around on student and faculty requests for DL services
- Provide DLTC team members with updates on new distance learning programs, technologies and faculty
- Coordinate technology/computer training efforts
- Generate new ideas for approaches to problem areas

Distance learning is impacting higher education today in ways that are still evolving. What we do know is that this new virtual environment will reshape all institutions of higher education. Learners today want to be linked to global resources and learning opportunities anytime/anyplace/anywhere–without the inhibitions of physical structures such as classrooms, libraries or even technology-centered sites. We, as information and distance learning professionals, will be working with a new age of learners who have lived their entire lives in an electronically based/technologically linked world (Sorenson & Snider, 1998). Our challenge is not to just keep abreast of the advances in knowledge acquisition and dissemination through technology to better serve student and faculty clientele–but to insert the human element into the process–making the inevitable transition to the distance learning environment as painless, exciting and successful as possible. The faculty and staff of the UK Distance Learning Technology Center look forward to that challenge.

REFERENCES

ACRL standards & guidelines: Guidelines for distance learning library services. (2000, December). *C&RL News, 61*(11), 1023-1029.

Cooper, R., Dempsey, P.R., Menon, V., & Millson-Martula, C. (1998). Remote library users–Needs and expectations. *Library Trends, 47*(1), 42-64.

Sorensen, A.A. & Snider, J.C. (1998). Linking the university campus with the global village in the 21st century. *Journal of Continuing Higher Education, 46*(3), 2-7.

It's My Library, Too, Isn't It?

Rita Barsun

Indiana University-Bloomington

SUMMARY. Institutions that offer distance education courses are responsible for providing commensurate library services and resources. Whether or not they fulfill that responsibility, their students may opt to use local public or academic libraries in addition to or instead of the institution's library (i.e., the home library). Academic libraries may have policies that forbid or limit services and public libraries often do not have the resources necessary to support college students. Distance librarians have a responsibility and opportunity to assist their students in developing a Total Information Network that equitably uses both virtual and brick-and-mortar libraries. Distance librarians also have a responsibility and an opportunity to communicate with colleagues in other libraries regarding use of their facilities by online learners.

KEYWORDS. Distance education, resource sharing, responsibilities, library service

GUIDELINES, BENCHMARKS, AND REQUIREMENTS

Institutions that offer distance education courses are responsible for providing their students with adequate library services and resources. The *Guidelines for Distance Learning Library Services* (2000) of the Association of College and Research Libraries (ACRL) stipulate that services and resources "may dif-

---

[Haworth co-indexing entry note]: "It's My Library, Too, Isn't It?" Barsun, Rita. Co-published simultaneously in *Journal of Library Administration* (The Haworth Information Press, an imprint of The Haworth Press, Inc.) Vol. 37, No. 1/2, 2002, pp. 59-82; and: *Distance Learning Library Services: The Tenth Off-Campus Library Services Conference* (ed: Patrick B. Mahoney) The Haworth Information Press, an imprint of The Haworth Press, Inc., 2002, pp. 59-82.

http://www.haworthpress.com/store/product.asp?sku=J111
10.1300/J111v37n01_07

fer from, but must be equivalent to" (Philosophy section, para.10) those offered to on-campus students. In addition to the precepts presented in the
Philosophy section, the *Guidelines* list and define seven elements necessary
for meeting the library and information needs of distance learners, their faculty, and support staff. The seven are summarized below:

- Management: The originating institution bears responsibility for funding, staffing, and supporting library resources and services, but through
  the leadership of the library administration and as implemented by the librarian-administrator of the program (para. 11).
- Finances: Not only is the financial support to cover the needs of students,
  but it is also to enable librarians to provide innovative approaches to service and to permit arrangements with other libraries (para. 12).
- Personnel: Library staff should include a librarian-administrator as well
  as professional and support staff with training in identifying and meeting
  the needs of distance learners. The originating institution is also to provide opportunities for professional development of library personnel
  (para 13).
- Facilities: There is to be adequate physical space for both services and
  personnel. Communication links are essential, and agreements with
  other libraries may enhance access to resources (para. 15).
- Resources: Here "equivalent to those provided in traditional settings" is
  emphasized. Besides meeting the needs for course assignments, the access to materials is also to meet faculty needs for teaching and research,
  and to facilitate lifelong learning (para. 16).
- Services: Eleven are listed, with a comment that the list is not exhaustive.
  The combination and number depend on the needs of the specific institution (para. 19).
- Documentation: The intent here is to demonstrate how well the institution is meeting the *Guidelines*. Eighteen types of documents are listed,
  from user guides to position descriptions and details of the program budget (para. 20).

The *Guidelines* also call for schools of library and information science to offer
courses and course units in distance librarianship (para. 21).

Quality on the Line: Benchmarks for Success in Internet-Based Education
(April, 2000) includes library services and resources among the "Benchmarks
That Are Essential for Quality Internet-based Distance Education." Access to
sufficient library resources, which may include a virtual Web-accessed library,
is listed among the Course Structure Benchmarks. Hands-on bibliographic instruction is included among the Student Support Benchmarks. Assessment of

the validity of resources is one of the Teaching/Learning Benchmarks (p. 26). The report comments on the fact that library resources are given high ratings–4.7 of 5.0 points–as being essential for quality distance education and it notes that some respondents indicated interest in 24-hour reference assistance (p. 20).

Although informative and helpful for establishing or evaluating a distance library services program, neither the *Guidelines* nor the *Benchmarks* require an institution to conform to them. Only accreditation criteria have that power. The eight regional accrediting agencies in the United States have implemented the *Best Practices for Electronically Offered Degree and Certificate Programs* (2000), which list seven categories of "library services appropriate to the program":

- Reference and research assistance;
- Remote access to databases;
- Online journals and full-text resources;
- Document delivery services [underwritten by the institution];
- Library user and information literacy instruction;
- [Electronic] reserve materials;
- Institutional agreements with local libraries (p. 11).

The importance of and need for information literacy instruction are highlighted by its being mentioned a second time following the above list. In addition, institutions are to inform prospective students of "library and other learning services available to support learning and the skills necessary to access them" (p. 10).

PROVISION OF LIBRARY SERVICES FOR DISTANCE LEARNERS

Do distance education providers meet the above guidelines or standards and, if so, to what extent? The library literature offers anecdotal evidence about the failure of some institutions to meet the standards: "Library-less" students struggling to find research resources (Goodson, 1998, para. 3); courses that have no provision for library support (Jansen, 1993, p. 9); "little or no correlation between how innovatively an institution delivers distance courses and the way in which it provides library services to its distance students" (Lebowitz, 1997, para. 2); institutions that have not considered the need for library services when planning distance education courses (Stephens, Unwin, & Bolton, 1997, p. 31).

There is a need for research-based up-to-date information. Corrigan's study of library resources for external degree programs was conducted in 1993. Data indicated that administrators opted for services that merely "suffice" (p. 66). Course providers responding to a survey conducted in the United Kingdom between 1994 and 1996 stated that packets of materials supplied by the institution and purchased by students were adequate for their course work (Stephens & Unwin, 1997, p. 156). If library research was necessary, students were expected to use their local libraries (p. 157).

Distance Education in Higher Education Institutions, the most recent analysis by the National Center for Education Statistics, dates from the fall of 1995. The figures are disheartening, as shown by the services not available at that time to the students of 1,276 postsecondary institutions. Access to an electronic link with the institution's library was not offered in 40% of the cases. Half of the distance education providers did not have library staff to assist students, and only 30% had negotiated arrangements for students to use other libraries (Table 12).

The findings of a study of Association of Research Libraries (ARL) members are more encouraging. Among the 46 institutions that reported having distance education programs, more than 74% of their libraries circulated materials to distance learners and more than 81% granted them interlibrary loan services. Conversely, Extended Campus Librarians coordinated the off-campus library services in only six of the libraries (Snyder, Logue, & Preece, 1997, para. 3). The survey also found that "usually there is no difference in providing library services to parties on- or off-campus" (para. 5).

DISTANCE EDUCATION STUDENTS' USE OF NEARBY LIBRARIES

Even when off-campus library services and resources are very good, students may prefer nearby brick-and-mortar libraries to their home library, the library of the institution in which they are enrolled. In some cases, the students' choices reflect their perception that the home library is not adequate, or they may simply not be aware of what is available–despite efforts by distance librarians to contact students and promote library services. It may be a matter of feeling more comfortable in a familiar setting. Other possible reasons: a student may want to see a book before borrowing it or purchasing it; he does not want to wait for interlibrary loan; the library may have quicker access to the Internet than her home computer; or it may own databases, including some with full text, that the student's home library does not own. Anecdotal evidence and personal experience lend credence to many instances of the situations just described, as do the studies described below.

Distance education librarians at the State University of West Georgia (SUWG) have conducted three surveys of their off-campus students (Goodson, 1996).

Although the librarians make contact with almost every distance learner and publicize their program every quarter, the results of the surveys were disappointing. According to the 1991 study, only 8% of the off-campus students took advantage of the SUWG library services, while 35% used local public libraries and 51% frequented other nearby academic libraries. The 1995 survey showed improvement, with 17% students reporting that they used the home library services; i.e., the library services provided by SUWG. The figure for public libraries dropped to 31% and use of other academic libraries was reported to be 40%, down 11% from the previous survey (para. 16). The decrease in 1995 in use of other libraries may reflect the introduction of GALILEO, Georgia's statewide access to full-text databases. Data from a third survey, conducted in 1999, had not been compiled when this paper went to press, but the figures will be reported at the Off-Campus Library Services Conference (C. Goodson, personal communication, October 4, 2001).

The most extensive survey of distance learners to date was conducted between 1994 and 1996 in the United Kingdom. Usage figures for local libraries were high. Especially interesting was the finding that, although half the students lived less than ten miles from university libraries, public libraries appeared to be the preferred local resource (Stephens, Unwin, & Bolton, p. 29).

An unpublished survey was conducted by Jennifer Sutherland (2000), an MLS student at the University of Denver. She distributed the questionnaire to distance learners by e-mail. The 71 respondents represented 14 states, but the number of institutions was not indicated (p. 16). Her survey is perhaps the most relevant to date, as it specifically includes remote access to the home library. Only 32% of the students reported taking advantage of remote access to the library resources provided by their institutions (p. 23). Sutherland also found that, while 55% of the students had been encouraged to use the library of their distance education provider, 70% had been advised to find local resources (p. 18). Local public libraries were the preferred source for borrowing materials (p. 19).

Comments by students in the Sutherland survey are especially telling:

- "We did not have online access to the [home] library resources until the last two classes!" (p. 44).
- "I never learned how to access the [home] library. . . . " (p. 45).
- "The main campus library does not cater to distance students from other states. . . . " (p . 46).
- "Tried to access main campus library online several times for several semesters, could not access databases, never could get information from

anyone at the library that would help me to access the databases–finally gave up and stopped trying" (p. 47).

• " . . . we never got any 'orientation' type training [from the home library]" (p. 48).

The dearth of empirical studies calls for more surveys of the provision of library services to online learners and their choices regarding library resources, local versus home institution. Studies that make funding bodies aware of the impact on libraries by unaffiliated users may benefit those libraries. Such was the intent of the survey of state-supported academic libraries in New York (Judd & Scheele, 1984). An extensive survey of usage of United Kingdom libraries by "external researchers"–not necessarily distance education students–resulted in financial compensation for additional strain on staff and resources, with the highest amounts going to the libraries most heavily affected (Milne & Davenport, 1999). Similarly, hard facts and figures about services to distance education students may influence course providers to increase financial and staff support to overburdened off-campus library programs.

The complete report of another survey conducted in the United Kingdom was published in book form (Unwin, Stephens, & Bolton, 1998). In addition to responding to the questionnaire, 47 students enrolled in 12 universities kept detailed diaries of their library use for three months to one year (p. 167). Course providers were queried regarding their perspectives on the role of the library in distance education (p. 133). Responses from 134 public librarians agreed with information from students about their reliance on public libraries (p. 123). The appendices provide copies of each survey and suggestions for students' library logs (pp. 219-246). Because of its detail and comprehensiveness, this survey could well serve as a model for further research.

POLICIES OF ACADEMIC LIBRARIES TOWARD UNAFFILIATED USERS

"Unaffiliated users" are defined here as those who are not students, faculty, or staff of the library's parent institution. Examples of other terms that have appeared in the literature are outside users, secondary users or clientele, community users, and the general public.

If distance learners do opt to use local library resources–especially nearby academic libraries–what are they likely to find? Even entry to an academic library by the general public may be forbidden, limited to certain hours and/or days (Heath, 1992, p. 18; Landwirth, 1988, p. 209), or indirectly require a fee–disguised perhaps as paid membership in an alumni association or a donation to a friends of the library organization. Some academic libraries permit only primary clientele, those directly affiliated with the parent institution–students, present or emeritus faculty, and staff–to check out materials. One of the most common practices is to charge a borrowing or library card fee for secondary clientele, ranging from $5 to $500 a year (Jansen, 1993, p. 11). Those that do not charge for borrowing may restrict circulation in other ways. However, if borrowing is not permitted, unaffiliated users may often use materials on the premises. In-house access to electronic resources depends in large part on licensing restrictions.

College and university libraries opened their doors wide in the 1950s and early 1960s, but the information explosion and the growth of technology soon changed the situation. Besides trying to meet the needs of their own burgeoning student bodies, academic libraries were being overwhelmed by the general public and by students from "information-poor institutions" (Judd, 1984, p. 126). "It is high time that the academic library stop trying to be all things to all people" was a reflection of the times (Deale, 1964, p. 1697). Cutbacks in staff and resources in the 1970s were not accompanied by a corresponding decrease in use or expectations. The Association of College and Research Libraries (ACRL) Committee on Community Use issued the *Access Policy Guidelines* to assist libraries "in codifying their policies with respect to access by persons other than their respective primary clientele" (*C&RL News*, 1975, p. 322). A presentation to the Off-Campus Library Services Conference in the 1980s reflected the continuing adverse impact of outside users on academic libraries (Kelley, 1985, p. 147).

Numerous surveys have been noted in the literature since one commissioned by the ACRL in 1965 and distributed to 1,100 academic libraries (Josey, 1967). A summary of several conducted within the last 15 years follows. All the surveys queried libraries in the United States.

Results of a 1989 questionnaire mailed to 12 academic libraries in the Atlanta, Georgia, metropolitan area showed that "most" allowed members of the outside community to use their collection but few offered circulation privileges. The cost for borrowing materials ranged from $25 to $500 per year (Russell, Robison, & Prather, 1989, p. 136).

The same team conducted a study of 26 large urban research and doctorate-granting universities "with a self-declared urban mission" (Russell, Robison, & Prather, 1992, p. 29). Of the 18 libraries responding, only one had a closed collection. "Students in external degree programs" were granted circulation privileges by eight of the libraries; six charged fees ranging from $25 to $125 and one permitted borrowing with some limitations (p. 30). This report contained the first direct reference to use of and/or charges for access to

CD-ROM databases (p. 31). It is also the only one to mention distance learners as a class of unaffiliated users.

There were 49 respondents to a survey sent to directors of libraries in 68 public colleges and universities in major metropolitan areas in February 1990. Only one did not permit access, while 27 permitted borrowing by the general public and 35 granted circulation privileges to Friends of the Library (E. Mitchell, 1992, p. 36). Although one library charged $500 a year for borrowing, most fees were in the $10 to $50 range (p. 41).

Best-Nichols (1993) queried the 16 state-supported institutions in North Carolina. All ten respondents indicated that they permitted in-house use of their collections by unaffiliated users, but eight charged a fee for borrowing. The maximum cost was $15 per year (p. 123).

A questionnaire sent to private and public academic libraries in Louisiana in the late 1990s found that 31 of the 32 respondents opened their doors to the community and that 15 permitted community users to borrow materials (Hayes & Mendelsohn, p. 136). The highest fee for borrowing was $250 a year (p. 137).

The report of an informal telephone survey of 25 large public academic libraries throughout the United States indicated that access to electronic resources depended on licensing agreements. "Nearly all" gave unaffiliated users access to their collections, and approximately half charged a fee. The highest cost to unaffiliated users was $500 a year (Johnson, 1998, p. 10).

Walden University Library Liaison personnel searched the Web sites of 99 ARL academic libraries during the spring and fall of 2000 to identify their policies toward secondary users. The categories surveyed included access to the collection, circulation privileges, interlibrary loan services, and in-house or remote access to online databases. Fewer than half the library sites provided such information. Among the 35 sites that stated policies regarding access to the collections, 13 limited it in some way and four charged a fee. Only one site clearly noted that the library did not grant circulation privileges to unaffiliated users. Twelve of the library Web sites indicated that the general public may borrow materials, and 38 specified that one must be a resident (usually, of the State).

Because the populations surveyed differed, it is difficult to confirm a trend toward less openness to unaffiliated users, but a comparison of the ACRL's 1975 *Access Policy Guidelines* and the 1992 *Guidelines for the Preparation of Policies on Library Access* may shed some light. Both distinguish between a library's primary clientele (the students, faculty, and staff of the library's parent or sponsoring institution) and secondary clientele. The 1992 *Guidelines*, however, offer much more detail and repeatedly refer to the effect of "library-defined patron categories" on policies.

A more telling observation was made by a retired professor seeking access to private academic libraries in New York City. One senses that he had been away from the city, and perhaps out of the country, for an extended period. In his view, "Until recent years, the American approach [of academic libraries] contrasted through its openness; everyone in America was presumed worthy of access to the wisdom of the ages. Today, the situation is actually a good deal worse here than in Europe" (Cohn, 1993, p. 183).

DISTANCE LEARNERS AND NEARBY PUBLIC LIBRARIES

As noted earlier, studies of distance learners' use of local libraries have revealed a reliance on public libraries, because students may be most familiar with them and because they are often more accessible than academic libraries (Power & Keenan, 1991, p. 443). With the exception of large urban ARL public libraries, the collections of public libraries serve the community in which they are located, from pre-schoolers to senior citizens, and are not intended to support postsecondary course work. Yet the public library mission to "serve those individuals who seek to learn outside the realm of the organized educational process can cause philosophical conflict, resentment, and frustration as librarians attempt to meet the needs of their community's distance learners without adequate resources" (pp. 444-445). A letter from "Distantly Disturbed" to "Tech Talk" reflected such frustration (Peterson, 1997).

It is possible that some public librarians see distance learners as an annoyance, but others may view them as "the marketing opportunity of a lifetime" (Dority, 2000, p. 24). Some public librarians consider distance education students as one more facet of their service to their constituency. The Wilkinson Public Library in Telluride, Colorado, is a strong supporter of distance students in its community, whether undergraduates or doctoral candidates. A forthcoming article in *Colorado Libraries* will describe the efforts of the librarian to serve distance learners, in particular her sponsorship of a two-day Distance Learning Expo in May, 2001, in which six distance education providers participated (A. Russell, personal communication, October 5, 2001).

The former director of a public library in a small rural community in Washington State took such a proactive role in serving distance education students that a community college established a branch there. Her continuing interest in online education was evidenced by a challenge issued to colleagues at the 2001 Minnesota Library Association conference to make Minnesota public libraries the premier supporter in the country of distance learners (Reng, 2001). Copies of her handouts to conference attendees may be found in Appendix 1 and Appendix 2.

STATEWIDE INITIATIVES
FOR LIBRARY SERVICES AND RESOURCES

Supported by a consortium that may include academic libraries or by their state legislature through the state library, public libraries are often a gateway for on-site or remote access to electronic databases. A survey by the Alaska Statewide Database Licensing Committee resulted in a detailed document posted on a publicly accessible Web site, *Statewide Licensing of Information Resources: A 50-State Survey* (1999). The report included the electronic resources tested and selected, the sources of funding, and contact information for the projects. The writer is conducting an updated but less comprehensive survey, with completion anticipated by the end of the year.

Thirty public, high school, community/junior college, and university libraries comprise the Colorado Virtual Library Connection. The participating libraries use an electronic interlibrary loan service that enables students to receive materials within a maximum of two or three days after placing a request. Distance learners benefit from the agreement among the libraries to serve students in their particular regions even if the student's home institution is located elsewhere (Wessling, 1999).

Thanks to Florida's Distance Learning Library Initiative, online learners in that state have remote access to a suite of full-text and abstract databases, speedy document delivery through a statewide courier service, and telephone and e-mail access to reference librarians through the Reference and Referral Service (Smith, Race, & Ault, 2000).

Partnerships among public and private academic libraries, public libraries, and schools of nursing ensure that students throughout Louisiana, even in rural communities, have access to a broad range of electronic resources (Wittkopf, Orgeron, & Del Nero, 2000, p. 293). A reciprocal borrowing card enables students to check out materials at any academic library in the state, and interlibrary loan has been facilitated by the provision of Ariel software and scanning equipment to both private and public academic libraries (p. 294).

The services and resources of the Utah Academic Library Consortium include Pioneer, Utah's Online Library of licensed databases; reciprocal borrowing; Utah Article Delivery, a fax-based interlibrary loan system; and online information literacy instruction through the Internet Navigator, consisting of modules, courses, and tutorials to meet the needs of distance learners as well as resident students (Brunvand, Lee, McCloskey, Hansen, Kochan, & Morrison, 2000).

BENEFITS OF USING LOCAL ACADEMIC OR PUBLIC LIBRARIES

No matter how hard distance librarians try and how advanced the technology, the virtual library provides only part of what students need. There is little to compare with wandering the stacks in search of a particular book or journal, only to chance upon something that did not turn up in a database search but which is right on target. Face-to-face consultation with a reference librarian, even if the librarian is not familiar with the student's program of study, has advantages over remote communication. The librarian at a distance cannot read the body language that provides important clues to what a person is really saying or asking.

Another reason not to discourage the use of local libraries is that they are an important part of a student's *Total Information Network*, a term used by Walden librarians to help students understand the breadth of their opportunities. Once students graduate they often are not granted library privileges by their alma mater, especially not remote access to bibliographic databases. Thus, it is beneficial to learn what is available locally while they have their own institution's librarians to advise and assist them with the process. This is especially important for doctoral students of an institution like Walden University, as they are expected to continue in their role as scholar-practitioners after earning their degrees, without library support from the University.

DISTANCE LIBRARIANS' RESPONSIBILITY TO STUDENTS AND TO LOCAL LIBRARIES

How do librarians serving distance learners assist students who choose to use local libraries, whether academic or public? The basic principle underlying their efforts is that the home institution is responsible for providing adequate library services and resources. Thus, the first and most important steps are to inform students about what the home library can provide and instruct them in accessing and using its resources. It is also essential to disabuse them of false perceptions and unrealistic impressions of what they will be able to do in other libraries and how they may be regarded there. Butler (1999) noted that students often have expectations of "seamlessness and homogeneity" among all libraries and thus expect to receive the same services and access as a library's primary clientele (p. 10).

Efforts to explain reasons for limitations on service may not be well received, especially in the case of libraries in public state-supported universities. W. B. Mitchell (1982) suggested posing this question: "Since students (and/or their parents) are tax payers but are required to pay tuition fees before receiving academic library services, why shouldn't the noncollege patrons also be charged a fee that will contribute to covering the cost of library services?" (p. 13). More than 20 years ago R. Russell (1979) countered complaints about limitations on services to unaffiliated users with this logic: ". . . I remind the inquirer that they cannot freely use the university lawn mowers, motor pool vehicles, computer center, or athletic facilities" (p. 39). Martin (1998) noted that the majority of the institution's budget comes not only from tuition but also from endowments by alumni, and overhead on grants and contracts won by faculty (p. 469). Jansen (1993) would attempt to inform a disgruntled student that the amount of tax support for public academic libraries is not generous (p. 10). The relationship between the distance librarian and his or her student plays a large part in determining if any of the previous explanations could be offered and how they would be accepted by the student.

In cases where outsiders, such as distance learners, may use materials in a nearby academic library but not borrow them, stressing the importance and benefit of having access to a rich collection to complement the home library's resource is one possible tactic. Some distance education institutions reimburse their students for fees charged by local academic libraries for library cards. Explanations of the restrictions on database use imposed by vendors can do much to enlighten students and provide an opportunity to explain the differences between what is freely available on the World Wide Web and what can be found only via subscription databases.

Students must be made aware of policies toward unaffiliated users, including costs for access or use, and encouraged to respect such policies. When possible, information is presented to groups in face-to-face or online orientation sessions. If the distance librarian becomes aware of an individual student's interest in using local library resources, often there is an offer to assist the student in learning about its policies. Distance librarians have also developed Web sites that provide details about library policies, as well as locations and service hours of libraries in many geographic areas. Because of a reluctance to give the impression of encouraging students to use other libraries, some of the Web sites are pass code protected and shared with students only upon request. Distance librarians make every effort to avoid a scenario in which a student's local library becomes or feels like a "victim library" (Dugan, 1997). Providing local librarians with information about how to refer distance learners to their home library and/or establishing reciprocal agreements with them is essential (Caspers, 1999, p. 307).

AGREEMENTS WITH LOCAL LIBRARIES

When librarians are aware of clusters of students in particular geographic regions, they may negotiate contractual agreements with libraries in those areas. For example, the State University of West Georgia contracted with a public library and with the library of a community college at the sites of the University's two external degree programs (Goodson, 1996, para. 11). Nova Southeastern University has a "handful of agreements" with libraries in the United States (J. Tunon, personal communication, September 20, 2001).

Although the relationship between the University of Southern California and the County of Ventura has ceased, it enabled a group of students to earn graduate degrees with minimal cost and maximum benefit to both parties (Britton & Combe, 1991). Rochester Community College, Minnesota (now University Center–Rochester), contracted with three colleges offering off-campus courses in that city (Dollerschell, 1991). The partnership has evolved, but the basic framework is still in place (D. Pedersen, personal communication, October 5, 2001). Wing and Gauri (1991) explained how collaboration by Macomb Community College, near Detroit, with five other institutions provided full library services including reciprocal borrowing to residents of its county pursuing baccalaureate and graduate degrees through distance education. Austin (2000) described the process by which Moorhead State University, Kentucky, negotiated an agreement with five community colleges and one private academic college that allows its students to use their libraries. He noted that, because of accreditation requirements, the agreements must be reviewed annually (p. 13).

Clearly written and detailed contracts are essential to the success of cooperative agreements. Slade (1991) has carefully detailed each component of such a contract. The program joining Regis University and a public library was based on a written Memorandum of Understanding (Scrimgeour & Potter, 1991). The relationship is still in existence, albeit with a different partner library. Power and Keenan (1991) spoke of three steps that might lead to establishing a relationship with other libraries: assessing the need for resources, services, and facilities; evaluating the "most practical and effective means of delivering the needed library services in cooperation with local libraries"; and actually preparing and negotiating the contracts (p. 447). Distance students of Chattanooga State Technical Community College receive services from libraries close to home, thanks to well-planned contracts between its library and public or college libraries in four geographic areas [OFFCAMP POSTING]. The Memorandum of Understanding between the University of West Florida and Okaloosa-Walton Community College is based in large part upon the *Guidelines for Distance Learning Library Services* (Gilmer, 2000).

Jean Caspers, formerly a distance librarian at Oregon State University, prepared a Draft Worksheet for library services agreements with other libraries. The Draft in its entirety may be found in Appendix 3.

Appendix 4 contains a sample agreement between Chattanooga State Technical Community College and a local library. In developing such relationships, the librarian looks for something her library can do for the cooperating library that will benefit both the distance learners and the local library's "primary patrons" (V. Leather, posting to OFFCAMP electronic mailing list, January 12, 1999).

CONCLUSION

Despite guidelines and criteria for accreditation, institutions that offer distance education courses may fail to provide optimum library resources, and may expect students to turn to their nearby public or academic libraries for services and course materials. When distance library services and resources are available, students may still use local libraries, for various reasons: they are more comfortable there, they are unaware of what their home library offers, or they experience difficulty using the Internet for communication and library research. Distance librarians must walk a fine line in addressing the issue, as they interact with their institution's administrators, their students, and colleagues in brick-and-mortar libraries. This paper has attempted to present evidence of the challenges faced by distance librarians and students but has also attempted to demonstrate examples of how proactive and caring librarians–in both virtual and brick-and-mortar libraries–have turned the challenges into opportunities. It has also shown that there is a need for more empirical research that, in part, may be used to influence institutional support of a library program for distance learners.

REFERENCES

Association of College & Research Libraries. Access policy guidelines. (1975, November). *College & Research Libraries News, 10,* 322-323.

Association of College and Research Libraries. *Guidelines for distance learning library services.* (2000). Retrieved November 24, 2001, from http://www.ala.org/acrl/guides/distlrng.html.

Association of College & Research Libraries. *Guidelines for the preparation of policies on library access.* (1992) Retrieved November 24, 2001, from http://www.ala.org/acrl/guides/acrlaccs.html First published in *College & Research Libraries News, 53*(11), December, 1992. 709-717.

Austin, G. L. (2000). Using a 'summit meeting' to negotiate library agreements. *The Ninth Off-Campus Library Services Conference Proceedings.* Mount Pleasant, MI: Central Michigan University, 13-17. Also published in *Journal of Library Administration, 31*(3/4), 2001. 23-30.

Best-Nichols, B. (1993, Fall). Community use of tax-supported academic libraries in North Carolina: Is unlimited access a right? *North Carolina Libraries, 51,* 120-125.

Britton, R., & Combe, D. B. (1991). Providing off-campus library service using academic/public library cooperation and remote access to sophisticated online systems. *The Fifth Off-Campus Library Services Proceedings.* Mount Pleasant, MI: Central Michigan University, 55-63.

Brunvand, A., Lee, D. R., McCloskey, K. M., Hansen, C., Kochan, C. A., & Morrison, R. (2000). Consortium solutions to distance education problems: Utah academic libraries answer the challenge. *The Ninth Off-Campus Library Services Conference Proceedings.* Mount Pleasant, MI: Central Michigan University, 49-59. Also published in *Journal of Library Administration, 31*(3/4), 2001. 75-92.

Butler, J. T. (1999, March/April). The promise and challenge of distance learning. *MLA Newsletter, 20*(1), 10-11.

Caspers, J. (1999). Outreach to distance learners: When the distance education instructor sends students to the library, where do they go? *The Reference Librarian, 67/68,* 299-311.

Cohn, W. (1993, February). Private stacks, public funding: Private universities severely limit citizen access to collections. *American Libraries, 24*(2),182-183.

Corrigan, A. C. (1995). A national study of coordination between external degree programs and libraries. *The Seventh off-Campus Library Services Conferences Proceedings* (pp. 61-68). Mount Pleasant, MI: Central Michigan University.

Culpepper, J. (1998). Equivalent library support for distance learning: The key to staying in business in the new millennium. *Journal of Library Services for Distance Education, 1*(2). Retrieved November 24, 2001, from http://www.westga.edu/library/jlsde/vol2/1/JCulpepper.html.

Deale, H. V. (1964, April 15). Campus vs. community. *Library Journal, 89*(8), 1695-1697.

Dollerschell, Allen. (1991). Contracting with local libraries for off-campus library services. *The Fifth Off-Campus Library Services Proceedings.* Mount Pleasant, MI: Central Michigan University. 79-84.

Dority, K. (2000, Winter). Online learners and public libraries: Annoyance or opportunity? *Colorado Libraries, 26*(4), 23-26.

Dugan, R. E., & Hernon, P. (1997, July). Distance education: Provider and victim libraries. *The Journal of Academic Librarianship, 23*(4), 315-318.

Gilmer, L. (2000). Straddling multiple administrative relationships. *The Ninth Off-Campus Library Services Conference Proceedings.* Mount Pleasant, MI: Central Michigan University, 147-150. Also published in *Journal of Library Administration, 31*(3/4), 2001. 219-224.

Goodson, C. (Summer 1996). A continuing challenge for librarians. *MC Journal: The Journal of Academic Media Librarianship 4*(1). Accessed November 24, 2001, from http://wings.buffalo.edu/publications/mcjrnl/v4n1/goodson.html.

Hayes, C. W., & Mendelsohn, H. (1998, Winter). Community service in Louisiana academic libraries. *Louisiana Library Association, 60*(3),136-139.

Heath, F. (1992). Conflict of mission: The midsize private university in an urban environment. In Gerard B. McCabe (Ed.), *Academic libraries in urban and metropolitan areas: A management handbook* (pp. 15-23). New York: Greenwood Press.

Jansen, L. M. (1993, Spring). Welcome or not, here they come: Unaffiliated users of academic libraries. *Reference Services Review, 21*(1), 7-14.

Johnson, P. (1998, January). Serving unaffiliated users in publicly funded academic libraries. *Technicalities, 18*(1), 8-11.

Josey, E. J. (1969, July). Community use of academic libraries. *Library Trends, 18*(1), 66-74.

Josey, E. J. (May, 1967). Community use of academic libraries: A symposium. *College & Research Libraries, 28*(3), 184-202.

Judd, B., & Scheele, B. (1984, Winter). Community use of public academic libraries in New York State: A SUNY/CUNY survey. *THE BOOKMARK, 42*(11), 126-134.

Kelley, P. M. (1985). Library privileges for off-campus faculty and students: The view from an impacted library. *The Off-Campus Library Services Conference Proceedings.* 147-156.

Landwirth, T. K., Wilson, M. L., & Dorsch, J. (1988, July). Reference activity and the external users: Confluence of community needs at a medical school branch library. *Bulletin of the Medical Library Association, 76*(3), 205-212.

Leather, V. (1999, January 12). Formal agreements between academic libraries and non-academic sites (e.g., public libraries). Message posted to OFFCAMP electronic mailing list.

Lebowitz, G. (1997, July). Library services to distant students: An equity issue. *The Journal of Academic Librarianship, 23*(4), 303-308. Retrieved November 24, 2001, from Academic Search Premier database.

Library services for distance learners. (1998). Retrieved November 24, 2001, from NODE learning technologies Web site: http://node.on.ca/networking/june1998/feature1.html.

Martin, S. K. (1998, November). A new kind of audience. *The Journal of Academic Librarianship, 24*(6), 469.

Milne, R., & Davenport, G. (1999). The Research Support Libraries Programme access survey. *The New Review of Academic Librarianship 5*, 23-33.

Mitchell, E. S. (1992). General circulation policies for private citizens: The practices of publicly supported academic libraries. In Gerard B. McCabe (Ed.), *Academic libraries in urban and metropolitan areas: A management handbook* (pp. 33-44). New York: Greenwood Press.

Mitchell, W. B. (1982, Spring). Formulating a policy for academic library service to unaffiliated borrowers: Some problems and considerations. *PNLA Quarterly, 46*(3),10-17.

National Center for Education Statistics. *Statistical analysis report: Distance education in higher education institutions.* (1997). Retrieved November 24, 2001, from http://nces.ed.gov/pubs98/distance/.

North Central Association Commission on Institutions of Higher Education. *Best practices for electronically offered degree and certificate programs.* (2000) Retrieved November 24, 2001, from http://www.ncahigherlearningcommission.org/resources/electronic_degrees/Best_Pract_Ded.pdf.

Peterson, B. *LIRT News tech talk.* (1997). Retrieved November 24, 2001, from Library Instruction Round Table site: http://web.uflib.ufl.edu/instruct/LIRT/1997/mtechtalk.html.

Power, C., & Kennan, L. (1991, Spring). The new partnership: The role of the public library in extended campus services programs. *Library Trends, 39*(4), 441-453.

Quality on the line: Benchmarks for success in Internet-based education. (April 2000). Available as a PDF file from the National Education Association Institute for Higher Education Policy Web site: http://www.nea.org/he/abouthe/distance.html.

Reng, J., Browne, J., & Barsun, R. (2001). Distance learners: Who to they belong to? Panel presentation at the Minnesota Library Association Conference. Abstract published in the *MLA Newsletter 28*(6). Retrieved November 30, 2001, from http://www.mnlibraryassociation.org/NovDec.htm.

Russell, R. E., Robison, C. L., & Prather, J. E. (1989, Winter). External user access to academic libraries. *The Southeastern Librarian, 39*(4),135-138.

Russell, R. E., Robison C. L., Prather, J. E., & Carlson, C. E. (1992). External user access to academic libraries in urban/metropolitan areas. In Gerard B. McCabe (Ed.), *Academic libraries in urban and metropolitan areas: A management handbook* (pp. 27-32). New York: Greenwood Press.

Russell, R. E. (1979, Fall). Services for whom: A search for identity. *Tennessee Librarian, 31*(4), 36-40.

Scrimgeour, A. D., & S. Potter. (1991).The tie that binds: The role and evolution of contracts in interlibrary cooperation. *The Fifth Off-Campus Library Services Conference Proceedings.* Mount Pleasant, MI: Central Michigan University, 241-251.

Slade, Alexander L. (1991). A librarian-centered model for developing and implementing an off-campus library support system: Establishing a proactive process. (1991). *The Fifth Off-Campus Library Services Conference Proceedings.* Mount Pleasant, MI: Central Michigan. 255-272.

Smith, R. M., Race, S. F., & Ault, M. Virtual desk: Real reference. *The Ninth Off-Campus Library Services Conference Proceedings.* Mount Pleasant, MI: Central Michigan University. 2000, 245-252. Also published in *Journal of Library Administration, 32*(1/2), 2001. 371-382.

Snyder, C. A., Logue, S., & Preece, B. G. (1997). *Expanding the role of the library in teaching and learning: Distance learning initiatives.* Retrieved November 24, 3001, from the Web site of the American Library Association: http://www.ala.org/acrl/paperhtm/d28.html.

Statewide licensing of information resources: A 50-state survey. (1999.) Retrieved November 24, 2001, from http://www.lib.uaa.alaska.edu/database/survey.html.

Stephens, K., & Unwin, L. (1997). Postgraduate distance education and libraries: Educational principles versus pragmatic course design. *Teaching in Higher Education, 2*(2), 153-165.

Stephens, K., Unwin, L., & Bolton, N. (1997, November). The use of libraries by postgraduate distance learning students: A mismatch of expectations. *Open Learning, 12*(3), 25-33.

Sutherland, J. (November, 2000). Library use among adult distance learners: Its implications for local public and academic libraries. Unpublished capstone project, University College, University of Denver.

Unwin, L., Stephens, K., and Bolton, N. (1998). *The role of the library in distance learning: A study of postgraduate students, course providers and librarians in the UK.* London; New Providence, NJ: Bowker-Saur.

Wessling, J. (1999, Winter). Virtual library connections. *Colorado Libraries*, *25*(4), 48-53.

Wing, D., & Gauri, K. B. (1991). Extending boundaries of access: Library services in an educational consortium. *The Fifth Off-Campus Library Services Conference Proceedings*. Mount Pleasant, MI: Central Michigan University, 337-344.

Wittkopf, B., Orgeron, E., & Del Nero, T. (2000). Louisiana academic libraries: Partnering to enhance distance education services. *The Ninth Off-Campus Library Services Conference Proceedings*. Mount Pleasant, MI: Central Michigan University, 293-299. Also published in *Journal of Library Administration*, *32*(1/2), 2001. 439-446.

APPENDIX 1. How to Make Your Public Library into an Extension University

1. Adjust your priorities. Make higher education part of your mission.

2. Arrange for a quiet study area. Post information on various extension classes.

3. Become knowledgeable in the area of scholarships and financial aid. Hold workshops on How to Go Back to College, College for Adults, College for Mommies, or College for Senior Citizens.

4. Acquire extension catalogs from all colleges and universities in the state. If there are popular courses from out of state, get literature on those also.

5. Develop an Orientation for Non-Traditional Students. Include how to contact university libraries, use statewide access to library resources, and how to search the bibliographic and full-text databases available in your library. Publicize it at the beginning of each semester and/or quarter, depending on where you have students registered. You will find that there are more students than you thought.

6. Ask local colleges to send you registration materials. When students register for particular courses, ask for the syllabi and lists of required readings. If possible, acquire the textbooks and make them available for circulation.

7. Set aside a part of your hold shelf for "reserve" materials. Use cards to check out materials for short periods of in-house use.

8. Get to know the outreach librarian at the university or college where your students are enrolled. Ask for hints for working with particular professors or programs. Work collaboratively to serve your students.

9. Your attitude can make the difference between success and failure for the non-traditional student.

10. Keep statistics for your Board on how serving extension students increases your circulation, your computer usage, and your reference service.

11. Use the idea of "Extension University" for as much PR as you can.

12. Be sure to thank the outreach librarians for their cooperation in helping you to provide this unique service to your patrons.

Handout from "Distance learners: Who do they belong 'to'?" a presentation by the Distance Learning Round Table of the Minnesota Library Association at its annual conference, Saint Cloud, Minnesota, October 10, 2001.

Reproduced with permission from the author, Jodi Reng, Director, Plum Creek Library System, Minnesota.

APPENDIX 2. How to Help Your Public Library Help Your Extension Students

1. Take a look at the registration information for your extension students. Make a note of where they live and check to see if there is a public library in their community, or ask them which public library they usually use.

2. Call and get to know the public librarian in each community where you have extension students. Explain what you are trying to do. Let him or her know the parameters of the program. Be sure there is an understanding of how much of the work is to be done by the student and how much by the library staff. The public library staff is used to working with high school students; it is up to you to let them know the difference.

3. Let each public library know the names of the students whom they will be serving and which classes they are taking each semester or quarter. Fill them in on what kinds of requests to expect. If possible, furnish them with copies of the syllabi.

4. Include the phrase "or your public library" in instructional materials about using the library resources.

5. Don't assume that the public library doesn't have anything useful. Public libraries have come a long way in the past two decades.

6. If materials are on reserve for a given class, see if copies can be sent to the public library. Whenever possible, send a copy of required readings to the libraries, to be returned at the end of the semester.

7. Remember that not every public library will be dealing with every class. Keep paperwork to a minimum. Work with individual cases.

8. The public library will not be receiving funds to provide this service to your students. Try to make it easy for them to cover the additional workload.

9. Set up a toll-free number so library staff can contact you for more information.

10. Keep statistics of growth in your outreach program. Each satisfied student will sign up for more classes and will tell a friend about the opportunity.

11. Be sure to say "Thank you" to the public library staff members who are offering a new kind of service to help their patrons and your institutions.

Handout from "Distance learners: Who do they belong 'to'?" a presentation by the Distance Learning Round Table of the Minnesota Library Association at its annual conference, Saint Cloud, Minnesota, October 10, 2001.

Reproduced with permission from the author, Jodi Reng, Director, Plum Creek Library System, Minnesota.

APPENDIX 3

DRAFT WORKSHEET
Library Services Agreement Between OSU Libraries
and
_____ Community College Library ("Host Library")

This *draft* was compiled only as a guideline for informal discussions with cooperative libraries. To date, it has not been used to support any formal agreements. Rather, the agreements have been of an informal nature, sealed by a handshake.

The template reflects the spirit of the arrangements. OSU details what it offers and requests what it would like from the other library. The other library then responds according to what it is willing to offer OSU students. The open-endedness lends itself well to such informal arrangements as well as to reciprocal agreements.

The document is being used with the permission of its developer, Jean Caspers, Distance Education Librarian, Oregon State University.

Note: In this document, "OSU STUDENTS" refers only to OSU students registered for classes in distance education programs which the host institution has agreed to serve.

	OSU Libraries will provide the services described below:	**OSU's Requests of Host Library:** *Italics indicate services requested of host institution (subject to approval of host library).*	**Host Library's Response:** *Please indicate "yes" or "no" or a qualified "yes" with specifics. Attach extra sheet(s) if needed.*
Reserves at Host Institution	OSU library staff will facilitate delivery of materials from OSU library and/or teaching faculty to be placed on reserve at host library.	*Host will maintain reserves of print and non-print materials, including videotapes, for the use of OSU students.*	
Reference Assistance	OSU will provide via the toll free number 1-800-235-6559; and/or via email.	*Host will provide to OSU students equivalent to that provided to students enrolled at host's institution; and will refer to OSU reference staff if appropriate.*	
Access to Online Databases	OSU will provide passwords for access to its research databases to OSU students, and will provide the host reference staff with information needed to instruct students about such access. ------------------------ OSU reference staff will perform mediated searching for OSU students when needed.	*Host will provide access to OSU students to host's research databases from the host library's public reference area, as available.* ----------------------- *Host's reference staff will remind students about OSU's research databases and instruct them about access to them as appropriate; and/or refer students to OSU reference staff.*	·

	OSU Libraries will provide the services described below:	OSU's Requests of Host Library: *Italics indicate services requested of host institution (subject to approval of host library).*	Host Library's Response: *Please indicate "yes" or "no" or a qualified "yes" with specifics. Attach extra sheet(s) if needed.*
Access to the Internet	OSU provides access to the Internet for all OSU students; however, this may be via a long distance call for those outside either the Corvallis or Portland calling area.	*Host will provide students Internet access from the host library's public reference area, as available.*	
Interlibrary Loan Services	OSU will provide ILL services for students who use OSU materials delivery forms to request materials not owned by OSU libraries. The materials will be delivered directly to students' addresses.	*Host library will provide OSU students with interlibrary loan services -OR--------------------- Host library will provide OSU students with instructions and OSU's forms for submitting ILL requests to OSU for fulfillment.*	
Access to OSU Library Materials	OSU will provide materials delivery forms for OSU students to request materials to be delivered to them. The materials will be delivered directly to students' addresses.	*Host library will maintain copies of the OSU materials delivery forms and instructions for their use by OSU students.*	
Borrowing Privileges	OSU students may borrow directly from OSU using the materials delivery forms. OSSHE reciprocal borrowing will allow OSU to use any OSSHE libraries. *Future reciprocal agreements which may be established for OSU students will apply to those in distance education programs as well.*	*Host library will provide OSU students with borrowing privileges equivalent to those offered to students enrolled at the host institution.*	
Replacements of materials & payment of unpaid fines	OSU will pay for replacements for host library's materials if they are lost by OSU students; and will pay fines OSU students do not pay.	n/a	
Fax number for students to receive materials from OSU	When materials are sent to students via fax, OSU will send them to a fax number designated by the student.	*Host institution will provide a fax number for OSU students to send and receive materials from OSU libraries.*	

APPENDIX 3 (continued)

	OSU Libraries will provide the services described below:	OSU's Requests of Host Library: *Italics indicate services requested of host institution (subject to approval of host library).*	Host Library's Response: *Please indicate "yes" or "no" or a qualified "yes" with specifics. Attach extra sheet(s) if needed.*
Bibliographic instruction and Orientation to Library Services	A newsletter describing OSU's services for distance education students is delivered to students in each class each term. Copies will be sent to the host library each term. ----------------- A web site facilitating OSU's services for distance education students is maintained at http://www.orst.edu/ dept/library/distance_ed/ bridge.htm ----------------- As requested by the teaching faculty, OSU librarians will provide bibliographic instruction as needed. ----------------- A library research tutorial is available via OSU's library web site.	*OSU students may attend general or tailored bibliographic instruction and/or orientation sessions offered by the host institution library.* ----------------- *The host library will maintain a file with copies of the OSU newsletter describing services for distance education services to give to OSU students who appear to not have received it.* ----------------- *If the host library maintains a web page, it will provide a link from its web page to the OSU distance education library web page at http://www.orst.edu/dept/ library/distance_ed/ bridge.htm*	
Pony Express drop site for receiving &/or returning materials for OSU students	OSU library will include a return label and instructions to students for securing packages for return to OSU via Pony Express **if** the host library will agree to receive these packages from the students and facilitate their return to OSU.	*Host library will receive packaged and labelled materials from OSU students for return to OSU via Pony Express.*	
OTHER: *May vary from agreement to agreement.*			

Prepared by Jean Caspers, reference librarian at Linfield College, Oregon, formerly distance librarian at Oregon State University.

Used by permission from Ms. Caspers.

APPENDIX 4

AGREEMENT BETWEEN
CHATTANOOGA STATE TECHNICAL COMMUNITY COLLEGE
AND
_____ PUBLIC LIBRARY

This Agreement is made for the year beginning July 1, 2001, and ending June 30, 2002, by and between Chattanooga State Technical College, hereafter referred to as the "Institution," and _____ Public Library, hereinafter referred to as the "Contractor."

WITNESSETH:

In consideration of the mutual promises herein contained, the parties have agreed and do hereby enter into this agreement according to the provisions set out herein:

A. The Contractor agrees to perform the following services:

> Provide library services to the following Chattanooga State students:
> Students taking classes at the Chattanooga State Bledsoe/Sequatchie Center
> Students taking dual enrollment classes at Bledsoe County High School
> Students who live in Bledsoe County

Students will be referred to the Contractor to use Chattanooga State's book catalog and information databases available via the Internet. The library staff at the Contractor will be given passwords each semester for Chattanooga State students to access the databases. Students may check out 3 books at the Contractor library and use other databases and indexes available there. The Contractor library staff will provide reference service and fax requests for books and periodical articles to the CSTCC library. Those materials will be checked out at CSTCD to the students at Pikeville and mailed to the Contractor library. The Contractor may be asked by faculty to show a class how to find resources and use information databases. The Contractor will contact the Dean of Library Services or the Coordinator of Access Services if additional resources, reference assistant, or instruction is needed.

B. The Institution agrees to compensate the Contractor as follows:

1. $_____ per fiscal year.

2. Upon receipt of invoice and signed contract.

3. Payments to the contractor shall be made according to the schedule set out above, but only after receipt of invoice.

4. In no event shall the liability of the Institution under this contract exceed $_____.

C. The parties further agree that the following shall be essential terms and conditions of this Agreement.

1. The contractor warrants that no part of the total contract amount provided herein shall be paid directly or indirectly to any officer or employee of the State of Tennessee as wages, compensation, or gifts in exchange for acting as officer, agent employee, sub-Contractor, or consultant to the Contractor in connection with any work contemplated or performed relative to this agreement.

2. The parties agree to comply with Title VI and VII of the Civil Rights Act of 1964, Title IX of the Educational Amendments of 1972, Section 504 of the Rehabilitation Act of 1973, Executive Order 11,246, the Americans with Disabilities Act of 1990, and the related regulations to each. Each party assures that it will not discriminate against any individual including, but not limited to, employees or applicants for employment and/or students because of race, religion, creed, color, sex, age disability, veteran status, or national origin.

APPENDIX 4 (continued)

The parties also agree to take affirmative action to ensure that applicants are employed and their employees are treated during their employment without regard to their race, religion, creed, color, sex, disability, or national origin. Such action shall include, but not be limited to, the following: employment, upgrading, demotion or transfer, recruitment or recruitment advertising, layoff or termination, rates of pay or other forms of compensation, and selection available to employees and applicants for employment.

3. The Contractor, being an independent contractor and not an employee of this Institution, agrees to carry adequate public liability and other appropriate forms of insurance, to pay all taxes incident hereunto, and otherwise protect and hold the Institution harmless from any and all liability not specifically provided for in this agreement.

4. The term of this contract shall be for one year commencing July 1, 2001. This Agreement may be renewed annually with approval of all parties for four additional terms.

5. This agreement may be terminated by either party by giving written notice to the other, at least 30 days before the effective date of termination. In that event, the Contractor shall be entitled to receive just and equitable compensation for any satisfactory authorized work completed as of the termination date.

6. If the Contractor fails to fulfill in timely and proper manner its obligations under this agreement, or if the Contractor shall violate any of the terms of this agreement, the Institution shall have the right to immediately terminate this agreement.

Notwithstanding the above, the Contractor shall not be relieved of liability to the Institution for damages sustained by virtue of any breach of this agreement by the Contractor.

7. This agreement may be modified only by written amendment executed by all parties hereto.

8. This agreement shall be binding upon the parties until it is approved by the Institution's president or his designee.

In witness whereof, the parties by their duly authorized representatives set their signature.

CHATTANOOGA STATE TECHNICAL COMMUNITY COLLEGE

_____
James L. Catanzaro   President   Date

_____ PUBLIC LIBRARY

_____
Signature   Title   Date

Used with permission from Vicky Leather, Dean of Library Services, Chattanooga State Technical Community College.

Separate but Unequal?
Do Web-Based Services
Fulfill Their Promises?

Dianne Brownlee
Frances Ebbers

St. Edward's University

SUMMARY. As many universities seek to increase the number of off-campus programs as a source of revenue, librarians are challenged to provide a growing number of Web-based services to this population. Librarians must enhance these programs to ensure that distance education students are afforded adequate and equal services to those received by their on-campus counterparts. This program seeks to examine current Web-based services to distance education students. The ACRL guidelines as well as SACS guidelines will be used as evaluation tools for Web-based services to distance students.

KEYWORDS. Library services, distance education, design, Internet

Johannes Gutenberg's invention of the printing press in the 1450s marked the arrival of mass communication. Ideas and information could now be disseminated to a growing literate population from a single source–the printed book! (Jones). The next significant revolution known as the "Information Age" occurred around 1981 as TCP/IP technology led to the formation of the "Internet"–a connected set of networks. The information revolution for the li-

[Haworth co-indexing entry note]: "Separate but Unequal? Do Web-Based Services Fulfill Their Promises?" Brownlee, Dianne, and Frances Ebbers. Co-published simultaneously in *Journal of Library Administration* (The Haworth Information Press, an imprint of The Haworth Press, Inc.) Vol. 37, No. 1/2, 2002, pp. 83-91; and: *Distance Learning Library Services: The Tenth Off-Campus Library Services Conference* (ed: Patrick B. Mahoney) The Haworth Information Press, an imprint of The Haworth Press, Inc., 2002, pp. 83-91.

http://www.haworthpress.com/store/product.asp?sku=J111
10.1300/J111v37n01_08

brary world can be traced from the proliferation of the World Wide Web, from 130 sites in 1993 to over 31 million in 2001 (Zakon, 2001). The rapid growth in information available through the Internet has dramatically transformed the way in which libraries receive and disseminate information, and has changed the expectations of library patrons.

No longer are students and faculty "text-bound." Now Web-based services are not only available but also expected. Students in our universities today have grown up along with the Internet and the World Wide Web. A Nielsen survey in August 2001 indicates that 166.14 million adults over the age of 16 or 59.75% of the population of the United States are online (NUA Internet Surveys, August 2001). Gruenwald Associates estimates that more than 32 million parents and 25 million children ages 2-17 are online in America (2000). The NUA Internet survey dated November 26, 2001 documents the use of the Internet by teenagers: 62% visit news and information sites; 30% download music or software; and 15% shop. E-mail and chat are the most popular online activities ("US Teens").

The Nielsen/Net Ratings of the "Top 25 Web Properties" for the week ending November 18, 2001, list AOLTime Warner as number 1, Yahoo! as number 2, Disney as number 10, Ask Jeeves as number 17, with iVillage number 25. Our current students are lured by the promises of the Internet–quickly garnered information with minimum effort. Although no university or library site is among the top 25 Web properties, this has not deterred the proliferation of Web use by both universities and libraries.

Universities have responded to the growth of the Web with the increase in distance education programs, and there is no indication that this growth is slowing. In 1997-98, 44 percent of 2- and 4-year degree institutions offered distance education courses compared to 33 percent in fall 1995 (NCES 1998-1999). In 1997-98, an estimated 1,680 institutions offered distance education courses, with 28% of those institutions offering between 16-35 courses (NCES). The 1998 survey by the National Center for Educational Statistics indicated that "half to three-quarters of the institutions that currently offer or plan to offer distance education courses plan to start or increase their distance education course offerings to other types of remote sites." These institutions also plan to offer distance education courses through a variety of means: on-site instruction at a remote site which may include another branch of the institution, other college campuses, work sites, or other locations such as libraries, elementary/secondary schools, community schools, and students' homes.

St. Edward's University in Austin, Texas, a small, liberal arts institution with 3,800 full-time students, has recently grown from two long-established master's level programs, the MBA and MAHS (Master of Arts in Human Services) to five programs currently. St. Edward's University has had a program for adults returning to school called New College, which currently enrolls 1,050 students. Under the umbrella of New College is the PACE program, an accelerated program leading to a bachelor's degree in business administration. Five years ago, all classes at St. Edward's University were held at its campus location south of downtown Austin. A look at enrollment figures for three semesters in 2001 reveals a distinct change.

In Spring 2001, 78 classes were offered at three off-campus sites, with an enrollment of 783 students. In Summer 2001, 45 classes were offered at two off-campus sites, with an enrollment of 739 students. In Fall 2001, 53 classes were offered at three off-campus sites, with an enrollment of 718 students. This means that at any given time during the 2001 academic year, 20% of the university's enrolled student population attended classes at three off-campus locations within the metropolitan areas surrounding Austin.

The students who attend classes at off-campus locations are enrolled in the graduate programs, mainly MBA students; New College students (adults 25 years and older); and PACE students enrolled in an accelerated program (students must have 60 hours to enter the PACE program). Typically, these students work full-time at one and sometimes two jobs, have families, and generally carry from six to nine hours per semester.

An additional change is the current number of online courses offered. Five years ago, the online course structure was attempted by a few professors who mainly used discussion forums, which were posted to an intranet newsgroup. Rapid development in Web technology led to a decision two years ago to work toward an online MBA program. This program began with five online classes; currently there are twelve classes online. This push for a totally online environment for a large graduate program has resulted in rapid growth in full-time staff positions within the Instructional Technology Department. Two full-time positions were added in Web development and Web programming to support and develop the online program. The Instructional Technology Department also plans to add a position for an instructor who would be available to deal with any technology problems at the three off-campus locations. A Digital Campus Curriculum Committee, which includes members of the Instructional Technology staff, faculty who teach in the online environment, and students enrolled in online courses, will handle issues related to quality control development in the online environment. This committee will also look at the range of activities within a given course to determine those that work best online and those activities that are better completed offline or as a self-paced instruction unit. The department also plans to add a virtual teaching assistant who will visit online classes to determine the level of online support needed for the class. Future plans call for a live collaborative conferencing system to integrate with the current Blackboard system. The University has also upgraded its

Internet connection to enhance off-campus delivery of courses, and is in the process of upgrading the network to the desktops to support live Web casting.

A 1996 survey by the Association of Research Libraries confirmed that 62% of the 74 ARL members responding, participate in distance education programs. Also that year, the Executive Board of the Distance Learning Library Services Guidelines Committee of ACRL mandated the revision of the 1990 guidelines. The decision to update the guidelines was based on the following factors which the committee termed as "increasingly critical." ACRL's recognition of these factors reflects the proliferation of library services to an ever-increasing distant population of library users:

- Non-traditional study is becoming more commonplace in higher education.
- Educational opportunities and environments are becoming more diverse.
- The need for equitable library services for all students, faculty, and staff regardless of location is being recognized.
- Technological innovations in the transmittal of information and delivery of courses are increasing.
- The number of students enrolled at central campus sites is decreasing.
- The necessity to deliver post-secondary education in a more cost-effective way is increasing.
- The virtual university with no physical campus is a growing component of the educational system.

Libraries play a crucial supporting role for distance education programs. Most libraries, including the Scarborough-Phillips Library, have greatly enhanced services that are available to distance education students twenty-four hours a day, seven days a week. Many libraries provide remote access to library online catalogs, circulate library materials and provide interlibrary loan services to distance education students at remote sites. Patrons may request interlibrary loan materials through e-mail or forms available on library Web sites. Reference services are available by telephone, scheduled appointments, or Web requests. Many libraries also have resource sharing agreements with other in-state libraries.

While we can look at these initiatives as minimum requirements for basic services to patrons who visit the library and who access library services remotely, do these support activities meet the requirements of the ACRL *Guidelines for Distance Learning Library Services* and of the Southern Association of Colleges and Schools (SACS) reaccreditation guidelines?

The new guidelines, approved by the ACRL Board of Directors and the ALA Standards Committee in fall 2000 state that "Access to adequate library services and resources is essential for the attainment of superior academic skills in post-secondary education, regardless of where students, faculty, and programs are located. Members of the distance learning community are entitled to library services and resources equivalent to those provided for students and faculty in traditional library settings."

The term "adequate library services" used in the ACRL *Guidelines for Distance Learning Library Services* actually means services that are adequate to insure the attainment of a superior level of learning by the distance education population (Gover, 1999). In other words, universities should expect that library services provided to the traditional on-campus population will support the educational endeavors of their best and brightest students. According to the ACRL *Guidelines*, universities should expect no less support for their off-campus students. But are universities willing to support the necessary library initiatives needed to provide superior services to their remote community?

The ACRL *Guidelines* very clearly state expectations for university support of library services for off-campus students. "Traditional on-campus library services themselves cannot be stretched to meet the library needs of distance learning students and faculty who face distinct and different challenges involving library access and information delivery. Special funding arrangements, proactive planning, and promotion are necessary to deliver equivalent library services and to achieve equivalent results in teaching and learning, and generally to maintain quality in distance learning programs. Because students and faculty in distance learning programs frequently do not have direct access to a full range of library services and materials, equitable distance learning library services are more personalized than might be expected on campus."

For most libraries in universities with rapidly developing distance education programs, the fulfillment of this initiative would require additional staff, as well as added budget. The guidelines committee was "concerned that institutions would attempt to cover expansions into distance learning with existing funding levels. The term 'stretched' was used to characterize this process and to warn against its use . . . " (Gover, 1999, p. 51). According to a survey done by the Association of Research Libraries in 1996, most libraries responding coordinate off-campus library services through access services departments, extension library services departments, or distance education coordinators (ARL, 1996). However, only six of the 43 libraries responding had a permanent budget in place for distance education.

While it appears that large research libraries have hired additional staff and created new library departments specifically designed to support off-campus students, this is not the case for many small or private universities that may be unable to increase professional staff or reserve a budget line item to support distance education initiatives. However, many additional services have been added that enhance access for both on-campus and off-campus students. Many libraries, including the Scarborough-Phillips Library, have added these additional services in the last five or six years: online renewal of books, online re-quest forms for interlibrary loan items, e-mail notification when interlibrary loan materials have arrived, e-mail overdue notices, online access to reserve materials, Web access to library guides, pathfinders, online tutorials, and self-paced instruction. Add to this list the enhanced services available from the more than one hundred databases which offer both full-text and indexing ser-vices for thousands of journals, magazines, newspapers, government docu-ments, and statistical sources. Web access to JSTOR gives users complete coverage and document delivery to hundreds of journals, some of which in-clude historical runs of selected titles. Patrons have come to expect services such as this which formerly required a physical visit to the library.

Obviously, providing superior library services to a remote population re-quires a commitment from the library and the university to continually incorpo-rate emerging and existing technologies into distance education services. The ACRL guidelines require the originating institution to provide "facilities, equip-ment, and communication links sufficient in size, number, scope, accessibility, and timeliness to reach all students and to attain the objectives of the distance learning programs" (2000, Facilities section, para. 1). Facilities should include "virtual services, such as Web pages, Internet searching, using technology for electronic connectivity" (ACRL 2000). Effective use of technology is also im-portant for accreditation or reaccreditation. The accrediting body for St. Ed-ward's University is the Southern Association of Colleges and Schools (SACS). SACS guidelines require that "The institution's use of technology enhances student learning, is appropriate for meeting the objectives of its programs, and ensures that students have access to and training in the use of technology" (2001, Program section, p. 12). An interpretation of these guidelines would indicate that enhanced Web-based services fulfill the requirements as long as the institution ensures adequate connectivity and bandwidth. The ideal, of course, is a "failsafe" delivery system as well as "on-demand" technical support.

Objective measurement of Web-based services is inconsistent at best. Often libraries do not have the means to gather the statistics that will help in effective evaluation of these services. For example, are the usage statistics for Web-based services available and is that information disseminated to library staff? Can the library staff determine the number of on- and off-campus connections to the li-brary's Web page? Are usage statistics available for electronic reserves? Even vendor-generated usage statistics can be inexact. For example, some aggregated database vendors can provide the number of hits to a particular title, but does that "hit" mean that the student has actually viewed or printed the article?

Most universities give priority to the development of Web-based delivery of distance education programs as a cost-effective measure to increase revenue while controlling expenditures. As a result, many Instructional Technology departments continue to add staff to meet the demands of course development. This is certainly true of many smaller institutions, including St. Edward's University. While the Instructional Technology Department at St. Edward's University has added positions to deal with the growth in online courses, the library has added no new positions and assigned the title of "Distance Education Librarian" to a current staff member. Yet the expectations for library services for this significant population (20% of the total student body) challenges the library in several crucial areas. The library must deliver resources and services to these students who are pressed for time and frequently under a great deal of stress to succeed in programs where their employers may be paying the tuition fees! These students, especially, want technology-driven services and expect service anytime and anyplace. The prediction that "librarians will deal with users almost exclusively in a virtual environment" (qtd. in Harley) is certainly true with this population. Additionally, with the projected growth in online and off-campus courses, the library must maintain a proactive position to deliver services to these students.

Traditionally, distance education has only meant education provided to students at remote locations. The original use of the term was applied to students enrolled in correspondence courses. Most librarians would probably agree that the term today not only applies to students enrolled in online courses or those taking traditional classes at remote locations, but to any student, traditional or otherwise, who accesses information from an online source without the intervention of a professional librarian. As distance education courses and remote access to library databases become increasingly popular, the need for library instruction increases exponentially.

However, library instruction is one of the most difficult services to provide to remote students. The ACRL guidelines list as essential services "a program of library user instruction designed to instill independent and effective information literacy skills while specifically meeting the learner-support needs of the distance learning community," including "assistance with and instruction in the use of nonprint media and equipment." At St. Edward's University, as our student body has grown so has our library instruction program. Since 1996, we have greatly enhanced instruction services to our on-campus community, and have tripled the number of instruction sessions taught each year to this population. As our distance education program grows, our library instruction faculty is further challenged to support this new group of users in an equitable manner. We currently manage to reach our students at remote classes on a personal basis. Each semester library teaching faculty travel to university remote class sites throughout the city to provide the traditional "one shot" instruction sessions. Despite our best efforts, many on-campus and distance education students receive no library instruction at all. In addition, students who access online databases or search the Internet from remote sites, may or may not ask for help if they run into problems.

In an attempt to reach all students, the Scarborough-Phillips Library has become part of a university computer competency curriculum requirement. All undergraduate students who enroll in the university beginning with the fall 1999 semester must pass the Computer Competency Requirement test prior to graduation. The Basic Library Research module is one of six module tests included in the requirement. The library faculty has created a Web-based tutorial to support students completing the library portion of the computer competency requirement. Although 774 students have taken the test since it went online in Spring 2000, the library has not had many requests for assistance from those who have attempted the test. In order to evaluate the effectiveness of the online tutorial, it would be necessary to compare the number of students actually accessing the tutorial to prepare for the test. As with many other Web-based services accurate statistics are often not available.

Effective and equitable delivery of library instruction to remote populations will continue to be problematic for libraries. Johannes Gutenberg's invention of the printing press provided the literate population with access to information on, what was then, an unprecedented scale. Students today have access to an even larger body of information from an enormous array of sources, but often do not have the information literacy skills to effectively access and use the sources.

As more students access library services and other information resources from Web-based sources, evaluation will continue to be spotty at best and inadequate for most. Until libraries are able to utilize a full range of accurate statistical data on the use of Web-based services, it will be difficult to measure the growing use by off-campus or distance users. Traditionally, gate counts and other data indicating a physical presence in the library have been used for budget projections. It is especially important, then, for smaller universities that an equal commitment of resources be made available to libraries to comply with current ACRL and SACS standards.

REFERENCES

Association of College and Research Libraries (Fall 2000). *Guidelines for distance learning library services.* Retrieved from http://www.ala.org/acrl/guides/distlrng.html.

Association of Research Libraries (July 1996). *Role of libraries in distance education.* Retrieved from http://www.arl.org/spec/216fly.html.

Coffman, S. (2001, April). Distance education and virtual reference: Where are we headed? *Computers in Libraries, 21.* Retrieved November 27, 2001, from http://infotoday.com/cilmag/apr01/coffman.htm.

Demner, D. (2000 April). *Children on the Internet.* Retrieved from http://www.otal.umd.edu/UUPractice/children/.

Disability Rights Education Defense Fund Inc. (2001). *Children and technology.* Retrieved November 26, 2001, from http://civilrights.org/issues/communication/equity/access/children.html.

Gover, H. & Caspers J. (1999). Key concepts in the Association of College and Research Libraries (ACRL) guidelines for distance learning library services. *FD Review 1,* 50-52.

Grunwald Associates. (2000, July 7). *Children, families and the Internet.* Retrieved November 26, 2001, from http://grunwald.com/survey/survey_content.html.

Harley, B., Dreger, M., & Knoblock, P. (2001). The postmodern condition: Students, the web, and academic library services. *References Services Review 29,* 23-32.

Jones Telecommunications & Multimedia Encyclopedia. (n.d.). *Printing: History and development.* Retrieved from http://www.digitalcentury.com/encyclo/update/print.html.

Marsh, D. (n.d). *History of the Internet.* Retrieved November 27, 2001, from http://netvalley.com/archives/mirrors/davemarsh-timeline-1.htm.

National Center for Educational Statistics (1998). *Characteristics of distance education courses and programs.* Retrieved November 27, 2001 from http://nces.ed.gov/pubs98/distance/chap4.html.

National Center for Educational Statistics (1998). *Future plans for distance education course offerings.* Retrieved November 27, 2001, from http://nces.ed.gov/pubs98/distance/chap6.html.

National Center for Educational Statistics (1998-1999). *Survey on distance education at postsecondary education institutions.* Retrieved November 27, 2001, from http://nces.ed.gov/quicktables/Detail.asp.

Nielsen//Net Ratings. (2001, October). *October Internet universe.* Retrieved November 26, 2001, from http://www.nielsen-netratings.com/hot_off_the_net.jsp.

Nielsen//Net Ratings. (2001, November 18). *Top 25 Web properties.* Retrieved November 26, 2001, from http://pm.netratings.com/nnpm/owa/NRpublicreports.top properties weekly.

NUA Internet Surveys. (2001 August). *Total Western European IT security forecast and analysis 2000-2005.* Retrieved November 26, 2001, from http://www.nua.ie/surveys/how_many_online/index.html.

NUA Internet Surveys. (2001, November 26). *US teens visit news, music, shopping sites.* Retrieved November, 2001, from http://www.nua.ie/surveys/?f=VS&art_id=905357439&rel=true.

St. Edward's University. (2001). *Office of the Registrar Report: Online courses.* 13 November 2001.

St. Edward's University. (2001). *Office of the Registrar Report: Off-Campus courses.* 28 November 2001.

Southern Association of Colleges and Schools (2001). *Principles of accreditation.* Retrieved from http://www.sacscoc.org/accrrevproj.asp.

Zakon, R. H. (23 August 2001). *Hobbes' Internet timeline–the definitive ARPAnet & Internet history.* Retrieved from http://www.zakon.org/robert/internet/timeline/.

Collaboration for Program Enrichment: Exploring JSTOR and Nursing

Denise Burggraff
Mary Kraljic

South Dakota State University

SUMMARY. This paper describes a collaborative project funded by a grant through Project JSTOR and the Bush and Mellon Foundation. The project was designed to increase the depth of content in the Registered Nurse Upward Mobility Program at South Dakota State University, which recently completed its first year of online delivery. Through evaluation and assessment strategies, two goals were identified to increase the richness and depth of content in this curriculum. The first goal was to identify and include scholarly, research based, electronic resources in the six courses of this program. The second goal was to establish a uniform framework for insuring that students in the program attain the information literacy competencies outlined by the Association of College and Research Libraries. Collaboration between an experienced instructor in the RN Upward Mobility Program and the Distance/Interlibrary Loan Librarian at South Dakota State University was necessary to assist faculty to achieve these goals and to develop a partnership model that could be shared among nurse educators. A third collaborator, the instructional designer and expert in WebCT courseware, also made significant contributions to the project.

KEYWORDS. Collaboration, cooperation, distance education, design

[Haworth co-indexing entry note]: "Collaboration for Program Enrichment: Exploring JSTOR and Nursing." Burggraff, Denise, and Mary Kraljic. Co-published simultaneously in *Journal of Library Administration* (The Haworth Information Press, an imprint of The Haworth Press, Inc.) Vol. 37, No. 1/2, 2002, pp. 93-100; and: *Distance Learning Library Services: The Tenth Off-Campus Library Services Conference* (ed: Patrick B. Mahoney) The Haworth Information Press, an imprint of The Haworth Press, Inc., 2002, pp. 93-100.

http://www.haworthpress.com/store/product.asp?sku=J111
10.1300/J111v37n01_09

INTRODUCTION

The Registered Nurse Upward Mobility Program (RN Upward Mobility Program) in the College of Nursing at South Dakota State University (SDSU) provides an opportunity to serve the needs of Registered Nurses who wish to pursue a Bachelor of Science degree in nursing via a distance learning model. Over 97% of South Dakota is considered frontier, rural or reservation by federal definition. Over 83% of the counties in South Dakota are federally designated as health professional shortage areas and over 90% are medically underserved. Additionally, about one-third of the counties are designated nursing shortage areas. The RN Upward Mobility curriculum is designed to enable the adult learner to access distance learning via a Web-based course management system (WebCT) and to enable isolated rural nurses to continue their education. The program also accommodates the lifestyles of working nurses who have family commitments and want to continue their education with minimal interruption to work and family responsibilities.

This academic year, 69 students are enrolled in the RN Upward Mobility Program. This enrollment represents 12 states and 3 countries (U.S.A., Canada and Germany).

A close working relationship between the library and the College of Nursing has been established over the past several years. Along with her colleagues, the Distance/Interlibrary Loan Librarian has facilitated student use of library resources through face-to-face instruction, assistance by phone and e-mail, and user guides to help decrease frustration and increase student satisfaction and productivity. The librarian is also a vital source for accessing and retrieving information and data related to health care.

With online delivery of courses, the role of the librarian has changed. Several factors contribute to this new role. These factors are "accelerated and dramatic technological change, the altering expectations and behaviors of information users, and the enduring need for human connection, for the human touch in providing library services" (Lindell, 1999, p. 1).

As fewer online students come into the library to have their information needs met, the librarian must utilize new technologies to train, advise, consult, and alert them about library services and resources. This trend indicates the need for more collaboration among faculty, students, librarians, and other support personnel. In the summer of 2001, a faculty member from the College of Nursing and the Distance and Interlibrary Loan Librarian received a Project JSTOR Bush and Mellon Foundation grant to enhance the RN Upward Mobility Program by combining the technological and human components of library services needed to meet these dramatic changes in library research. The grant project was also meant to expand the librarian's role as a resource for teaching information literacy skills.

A cooperative effort among the following people was proposed:

- The Nursing Faculty member who is a health care nursing expert with experience teaching RN Upward Mobility courses online. She is a full-time faculty member in the College of Nursing.
- Other faculty members who teach in the RN Upward Mobility program.
- The Distance and Interlibrary Loan Librarian who is experienced in reference services and has worked with RN Upward Mobility students for over 10 years.
- The Instructional Designer from the Information Technologies Center at SDSU. He is also an expert in WebCT, the courseware used for the RN Upward Mobility online program.
- These professionals worked together to meet the goals stated below.

Goals

- To re-conceptualize the partnership between nursing faculty and librarians to strengthen program delivery and serve as a regional model for faculty/librarian collaboration.
- To identify and include JSTOR and other scholarly, research-based, electronic resources in the six courses of this program.
- To establish a uniform framework for insuring that information literacy competencies are attained.

The first step in this process was to construct a project activity plan and a timeline. (See Appendix A.)

INSTRUCTIONAL DEVELOPMENT WITH INFORMATION RESOURCES

Information Literacy Defined

The increasing amount of health-related information now available poses specific challenges to nursing especially as it relates to using the information effectively. With this in mind, the Project Faculty and Librarian utilized the Association of College and Research Libraries' (ACRL) *Information Literacy Competency Standards for Higher Education* as a source for insuring that students have the necessary competencies to use information effectively. ACRL

(2000) defines information literacy as the ability to "recognize when information is needed and have the ability to locate, evaluate, and use effectively the needed information" (Information Literacy Defined section, para. 1). The standards further state that the information literate student:

- Determines the nature and extent of the information needed.
- Accesses needed information effectively and efficiently.
- Evaluates information and its sources critically and incorporates selected information into his or her knowledge base and value system.
- Individually, or as a member of a group uses information effectively to accomplish a specific purpose.
- Understands many of the economic, legal, and social issues surrounding the use of information and accesses and uses information ethically and legally (para. 2).

The *Essentials of Baccalaureate Education for Professional Nursing Practice* (1998) outlines active learning strategies to effectively stimulate students to learn. The document stresses that overall goal achievement should be through active learning strategies. However, variances in methods will occur depending on content, students' needs and expertise of faculty. Additionally, the Boyer Commission on Educating Undergraduates (1998) addresses pedagogical strategies for optimal resource-based learning. These are active learning, inquiry-based learning, problem-based learning, project-based learning, and service learning. Utilizing these concepts as an underlying framework, learning experiences utilizing JSTOR and other electronic journal resources were developed in the six courses in the RN Upward Mobility Program:

- Nurs 222 Transition to BS in Nursing
- Nurs 381 Family & Communication
- Nurs 385 Health Assessment & Clinical Decision Making
- Nurs 416 Community Health
- Nurs 454 Leadership & Management
- Nurs 474 Nursing Research

Instructional Development Goals

- Insure inclusion of and methods for evaluating attainment of Information Literacy Standards in each RN Upward Mobility Course.
- Identify methods for using JSTOR (and other pertinent electronic resources) in new and existing learning experiences designed to enhance student inquiry.

- Develop an archive of health-related JSTOR articles within WebCT (through collaboration with an instructional designer) to be used by students as a research bank and by faculty for future assignment development.
- Design a learning tutorial within WebCT specific to searching the JSTOR database.
- Create and administer student information literacy assessments (pre- and post-tests) in the first and last courses of the program.

Student Learning Outcomes

- Students will achieve the outcomes defined by Information Literacy Standards for Higher Education.
- Students will exhibit increased inquiry, research and information evaluation skills as evidenced by knowledge and use of JSTOR and other electronic databases.

Professional Development Goals

- *Project faculty* will become increasingly familiar with JSTOR and its potential for use in nursing programs and will serve as a faculty resource for those who desire to enrich their research-based student learning experiences with this unique database. Project faculty will also more fully understand the role of the librarian and his/her capabilities in assisting faculty to identify resources used to develop learning experiences that enhance student inquiry, research and information evaluation skills.
- *Project librarian* will become increasingly familiar with RN Upward Mobility Program, which will promote new and innovative uses of library resources in each of the six courses.
- *Project faculty and librarian* will develop an innovative partnership model to be used by other faculty and librarians as future collaborative activities are investigated.

UTILIZATION OF JSTOR AND OTHER DATABASES

Most nursing faculty were already using some current articles from electronic resources in their courses even before this project began. To varying degrees, they were familiar with InfoTrac, ProQuest and IDEAL as useful sources for articles online. Although JSTOR is not typically used for nursing research, the project coordinators saw it as a valuable tool for examining historical influences in today's health care system, so they planned to emphasize its use in appropriate courses of the RN Upward Mobility program.

The first step in encouraging use of JSTOR among the target faculty was the creation of an archive in WebCT to include all articles related to nursing. The project librarian conducted a full-text search of all JSTOR journal categories using the keywords, NURSE, NURSES, NURSING. The search was limited to articles only. This search yielded over 11,000 hits, many of them false hits. So the search strategy was revised using the same keywords but searching only the titles and any available abstracts. The resulting list of 294 citations was reviewed to eliminate false hits. The instructional designer formatted the list using APA citation style, and the project faculty had the URL for the archive Web site posted to the appropriate WebCT courses.

RN Upward Mobility faculty attended face-to-face instruction sessions to learn about use of JSTOR. To help instruct students in the program, the project librarian drafted a JSTOR tutorial as a PowerPoint slide presentation. The instructional designer further developed the tutorial by improving the layout, adding graphics and audio, and creating two more versions of the tutorial, one to run on RealPlayer software and another published as a Web site. Two of the three tutorials were selected for testing with RN Upward Mobility students.

The URL for the PowerPoint tutorial was posted in each course of the RN Upward Mobility program as an instructional tool for students who choose to use it. In each of the six courses, students are assigned various learning experiences that build on that knowledge gained through the tutorial. Using articles within JSTOR, other databases, and the archive, students are expected to complete information searches and formal writing assignments, participate in online discussions, and identify usefulness of information through informal journaling. The project faculty member and her colleagues conduct on-going evaluation of student learning outcomes as the research databases and archived articles are utilized within each course.

INFORMATION LITERACY COURSE ASSESSMENTS

Preliminary course assessments indicate that the nursing faculty already incorporate a variety of assignments into their individual courses that are designed to enhance information literacy. The assessment results indicated much strength in ACRL information literacy standards one, two, and three. This illustrates that students are given opportunities to achieve competencies in "determining the nature and extent of information needed, to access information effectively and efficiently, and to evaluate information and its sources critically and incorporate the selected information into his or her knowledge base and value system" (ACRL, 2000). The assessment also showed weakness in addressing Information Literacy Standards four and five. This demonstrates that the students are given lesser opportunities for "acquiring the information literacy skills of using information effectively to accomplish a specific purpose, either individually or as a group, and understanding the economic, legal, and social issues surrounding the use of information" (ACRL, 2000). As part of the project goals, the project faculty is working with other nursing faculty to develop assignments designed to achieve these standards.

STUDENT INFORMATION LITERACY ASSESSMENT

An information literacy assessment (pre-test) totaling 15 questions was given in the first course of the RN Upward Mobility Program. The first round of assessments revealed that students were weakest on questions covering standard two, the ability to access information effectively and efficiently. They also did poorly, but not as poorly, in answering questions related to standards one (determining the nature and extent of information needed) and three (evaluating information). However, the 15 questions on the assessment are heavily directed towards standards one, two, three, and five. No questions cover standard four. This is partly due to limitations of the course software used to deliver the information literacy assessment, but it is also due to the difficulty in writing test questions that elicit a student's use of "information effectively to accomplish a specific purpose" (ACRL, 2000). Certainly, graded course assignments will complement the student assessment of information literacy, but more work is needed to refine this assessment and to test its validity and reliability.

COLLABORATION MODEL

As this project unfolds, the project coordinators are in the process of developing a collaborative model for nursing faculty and librarians who wish to investigate innovative partnerships. This model will strengthen diversity of teaching methodologies and improve learning outcomes. The model, focused on attaining information literacy among students, will outline the process of interactions between faculty, students, librarians and technical personnel. In addition, all regental institutions in South Dakota must now evaluate every undergraduate student's information literacy skills before graduation. So from a statewide perspective, faculty from other universities within our regental system, especially those with online programs, could use this model for their own programs.

REFERENCES

American Association of Colleges of Nursing. (1998). *Essentials of baccalaureate education for professional nursing practice.* Washington, DC: Author.

Association of College and Research Libraries. (2000). *Information literacy competency standards for higher education.* Retrieved April 1, 2001, from *http://www. ala.org/acrl/ilcomstan.html.*

Boyer Commission on Educating Undergraduates. (1998). *Reinventing undergraduate education: A blueprint for America's research universities.* Stony Brook, NY: State University of New York at Stony Brook.

Lindell, L. (1999). The library in 2010. *The Conspectus, 25,* 1-3.

APPENDIX

Project Activity Plan

Planning Phase	Target Dates
Assess 6 RN Upward Mobility courses for inclusion of information literacy standards.	July 1, 2001
Identify articles relevant to nursing in JSTOR and in other electronic databases.	Aug 1, 2001
Generate archives within WebCT of identified JSTOR journal articles and other pertinent electronic resources for each course.	Aug 15, 2001
Implementation Phase	
• Assist faculty to incorporate JSTOR and other identified electronic resources into teaching methodology and student learning experiences. • Train faculty in use of JSTOR and other identified electronic resources • Design PowerPoint presentation for JSTOR searching and publish to WebCT	Sept 30, 2001
Final Phase	
• *Conduct formative and summative evaluations* • *Presentation at JSTOR conference* • *Publication of results* • *Final Project Report*	2001-2002

Blackboard and XanEdu:
A New Model for an Old Service

Nancy J. Burich

University of Kansas

SUMMARY. This paper will discuss a limited partnership between the University of Kansas and XanEdu to evaluate their production of course packs and the acceptance of this product by faculty and students. This analysis will include project design and management information, identification of issues needing to be addressed, and an assessment of the project at its conclusion. The paper concludes with a model for providing broad access to Blackboard-based electronic reserve readings that is based on an evaluation of the pilot project.

KEYWORDS. Instruction, technology, Internet, design, cooperation

Faculty have been putting materials on reserve in libraries for years. The University of Kansas (KU) entered into a contract with Blackboard™ in August 2000 to become the only course management software package supported by the university. Instructional Development and Support (IDS) offered faculty orientation and support to develop Web-based and Web-enhanced courses. There is a specific part of Blackboard devoted to "Assignments" that made it possible for faculty to develop reserve collections on their own, and the "External Links" feature made it easy to import sources, including locally scanned materials. Some instructors were comfortable posting their own reserve read-

[Haworth co-indexing entry note]: "Blackboard and XanEdu: A New Model for an Old Service." Burich, Nancy J. Co-published simultaneously in *Journal of Library Administration* (The Haworth Information Press, an imprint of The Haworth Press, Inc.) Vol. 37, No. 1/2, 2002, pp. 101-116; and: *Distance Learning Library Services: The Tenth Off-Campus Library Services Conference* (ed: Patrick B. Mahoney) The Haworth Information Press, an imprint of The Haworth Press, Inc., 2002, pp. 101-116.

http://www.haworthpress.com/store/product.asp?sku=J111
10.1300/J111v37n01_10

ings to their Blackboard pages, but the few individuals who came to the library for help were told that we were not prepared to offer this service. This effectively removed the library from the process. However, the growing number of Blackboard courses (more than 1,200 by the Spring 2001 term) and their associated electronic reserve collections led to serious concerns by university officials. The library needed to provide leadership and guidance in making e-reserves available legally and effectively.

The challenge has been to provide a workable model for electronic reserve that is sustainable and scalable. Some of the issues in doing this have been ably outlined by others (Lowe and Rumery, 2000). John Butler's article (Butler, 1997) provides a very useful description of the development process used by the University of Minnesota to develop an electronic reserve service. With very limited resources and with little hope for their growth in the near future, it became clear that we needed to explore outsourcing our Blackboard-based reserve collections. Enter XanEdu.

On February 20, 2001, IDS hosted a demonstration of XanEdu for faculty. At the demo, I learned that XanEdu is a division of ProQuest with access to the vast archive that once was UMI. They provide copyright-cleared digital course packs. XanEdu has entered into a partnership with Blackboard to make it easy to attach the course packs to the "Assignments" page. In addition, those materials that an institution can legally include in electronic reserve collections will be added to the pack at no additional charge. Students buy the course packs; there is no charge to the institution or the instructor. The idea of charging the student is a departure from the traditional library philosophy; however, most students incur a charge by copying reserve readings rather than reading them in the library. In addition, experience shows that students prefer electronic versions of journal articles instead of paper. A faculty member from the School of Social Welfare attended this demo and reported on her experience in developing a course pack on her own. Though paper copies of her reading materials were placed on reserve in the library, at least half of her undergraduate students purchased the course pack. It appeared that the services that XanEdu could provide would address current needs. However, a serious look at actual course packs (and their cost to students) was essential before any decision could be made about their use on a large scale.

THE TRIAL OF XanEdu COURSEPACKS

During the next week, I worked on a proposal for a trial of XanEdu's CoursePacks. I needed to develop a process and a model to provide electronic reserves using current resources (i.e., very limited staff and budget). On February 27, 2001, the proposal was delivered to the Dean of Libraries for her consideration. She in turn discussed the matter with the Vice Chancellor for Information Services. The Campus Partners Agreement between the University of Kansas and XanEdu was signed on March 20, 2001. XanEdu agreed to produce a CoursePack for one class that would be held during the Summer 2001 term. KU agreed to promote the use of XanEdu's products and services during the trial. (Appendix A contains the text of the Campus Partners Agreement.)

Because the goal was to learn about all aspects of providing electronic reserve materials via a course pack, the pilot project required that I perform the work faculty usually do, working directly with XanEdu. I was fortunate to locate a faculty member who was willing to participate in the project, a professor and former chair of the department of Health Policy and Management. He was willing to serve as a guinea pig, knowing that there would be problems and unanswered questions. He also agreed to pass on students' comments and to fill out an evaluation form at the end of the term. (Appendix B contains the evaluation form and the instructor's comments.)

THE XanEdu COURSEPACK

The reading list consisted of thirty different journal articles, most in the sciences and medicine. KU had rights to use electronic versions of seven articles (five were in InfoTrac databases, one was available through JSTOR [databases to which we subscribe], and the other through the PubMedfree database). Seven articles were owned in paper by KU but not electronically; and one article was not owned by KU in any format. Most troubling were the sixteen articles that were available only at the KU Medical Center Dykes Library. By contract, they are available only to Medical Center students and staff; the greater university community has no access. University leadership has touted the concept of "one university," but these sixteen articles illustrate how far removed from that ideal we really are. These articles also illustrate what happens when faculty members use a library to compile a reading list to which students have no access. Thus, KU could provide access to seven articles, but XanEdu would need to provide access to the rest of them.

It became clear that providing such access would not be easy or inexpensive. XanEdu could not provide cost estimates for the use of articles in specific journal titles. Instead, they needed to request formal permissions for each. However, I discovered that the cost for articles within a title was constant. Therefore, I was able to compile a table of costs by journal title to help to guide the development of future packs. (Appendix C contains the table.) Costs to use articles fluctuated greatly. For instance, the *British Journal of Cancer* was available only by paying a flat $4,000 fee. *Executive Excellence* charges just

$1.33 per student. Readings in some journals were not available at all due to ongoing negotiations between XanEdu and the publisher for rights to use all their publications, and they were not willing to interrupt the process to negotiate rights for a single article. One publisher would not grant permission under any circumstances. Consequently, the XanEdu editorial staff in Louisville, KY suggested alternative readings for those that they were unable to provide. This service proved to be of limited value because the instructor wanted to select his own material. The cost per student to provide access to the initial list of journal articles (without the *British Journal of Cancer*) was $157.34, even though there was no charge for the seven articles KU could provide. But in discussions with the instructor, it became clear that he had built redundancy into his list. With traditional paper reserves, he had assumed that not all students would be able to obtain a copy of every article and so had included alternative readings. However, with the CoursePack, the redundant readings could be removed, since full access for all students was assured. The final CoursePack contained just fourteen articles, including five with free library links, and it cost students $73.02. The price was high but acceptable, since there was no textbook.

There were two issues that needed to be addressed almost immediately. In the first version of the pack, readings were not listed in the same order as on the syllabus, but were in alphabetical order by journal title. This was changed easily, because the XanEdu software permits re-ordering the readings. If the instructor had been building the pack, this would not have been an issue. Since XanEdu was doing the work, however, they needed to be told that this was important. The second challenge was that the order in which elements within a citation (author, article title, title of journal, etc.) were presented was not uniform, and this order could not be modified when the full-text was taken from the ProQuest database. Often the citation appeared as two lines of text with the elements separated by punctuation marks. The solution we used was to highlight the author's name in bold type so that it was easier to see.

Another challenge that was not so obvious concerned the free library links to materials in KU databases. The links were provided by cutting and pasting the URL's for each article from the database. When the links were tested from a KU terminal, they worked flawlessly. However, there was no way for the XanEdu staff to test them, because they were not using a KU sign-on. Consequently, once the pack was assembled, these links needed to be tested from within the KU network. If we pursue an institutional partnership with XanEdu, we may consider providing the editorial team in Kentucky with a KU sign-on so that they can test the links themselves.

Construction of this list led to another modification of the normal XanEdu process. As an instructor builds a CoursePack, the total cost to the student appears at the top of the screen. By de-selecting readings and refreshing the screen, the total cost changes. However, with a long list that included many suggested alternative readings, this was impractical. Instead we requested that XanEdu list a cost for each item. This made it much easier for the instructor to adjust the content of the list to a cost he thought reasonable for his class. Once the list is finalized, the instructor indicates his acceptance by "adopting" it for his class.

The purpose of the trial with XanEdu was to discover the limitations of their product as well as ways to make it meet the needs of the university. In this we were very fortunate to work with the excellent and responsive editorial team in Louisville. Not only did they listen to my concerns, they sought solutions with grace and good humor. Concerns were addressed promptly and their work was accurate. Even though my name appeared prominently on the CoursePack as the person to call with problems, I received none about the pack's content. Contacts with students were limited to problems with authentication and access through firewalls at offices outside the university.

At the conclusion of the term, the instructor completed an assessment of his use of the CoursePack for his class. The assessment tool was developed using elements from many sources. XanEdu provided the text of a student survey they use. Central Michigan University shared the text of their faculty assessment form. The KU Libraries Coordinator for Instruction provided comments on a draft of a hybrid document. The instructor returned the form with very useful comments. (See Appendix B.) He thought that the cost was too high, but recognized that there are limited options for a distance learning course. He also mentioned the numerous authentication problems students had in accessing library articles. This is not a XanEdu problem, but one that needs to be addressed no matter how we provide electronic reserve materials. He rated content options from XanEdu as a 5 (best) and his overall opinion of the product was a 4, due to software navigation concerns. He believed that he received sufficient assistance with the CoursePack from me and the Louisville crew. Most importantly, he indicated that he probably would use a XanEdu CoursePack again.

THE COURSEPACKS OUTSIDE OF THE TRIAL

As word spread about the first CoursePack, I was approached by three other faculty members to provide a similar service for them. One was in the same department (Health Policy and Management), another was in Public Administration (she is also an associate dean in the College of Liberal Arts and Sciences), and the third was on the faculty of the School of Business as well as being the Vice Chancellor of the Edwards campus where my office is based. Consequently, it was very clear that there is great interest in electronic reserves among faculty and an overwhelming potential to increase the number of requests for this service.

I prepared a CoursePack for each course during the summer of 2001, and useful feedback was received from the instructors. In each instance new material formats and other issues arose that needed to be addressed. This included the use of Study.Net to access *Harvard Business Review* articles, the inclusion of links to KU's Endeavor Online Catalog reserve readings lists, the use of XanEdu's ReSearch Engine to provide inexpensive access to current publications, and our first assertion of Fair Use under newly-adopted guidelines. (See Appendix E for additional information.) Clearly, these additional CoursePacks increased significantly what was learned during our association with XanEdu.

THE ISSUES RAISED DURING THE TRIAL

At the conclusion of the trial, a report was prepared for the Dean of Libraries. It contained a description of the trial, a list of issues raised, and several recommendations. Below is an expanded discussion of those issues. (See Appendix D for the "Report on the XanEdu Trial.")

Copyright issues must be addressed. All materials included in electronic reserve collections need to be copyright cleared and used legally. This means securing permissions and paying applicable fees. However, as we learned in this pilot project, some publishers will not permit use of their materials, while others permit use but at a prohibitive cost.

Fair Use was not applied during the trial but it needs to be asserted. The university must decide its policy in this regard in consultation with the General Counsel's office. At KU, it is especially important to feel secure in our policy, because our Provost, David Shulenberger, has a national reputation as a leader in the discussion about intellectual property and scholarly communication issues. The decision to assert Fair Use was made after the first three packs were prepared, but it was applied to the final one. If KU's Fair Use guidelines had been applied to the first reading list, it would have reduced costs significantly. (See Appendix F for "Impact of Fair Use Guidelines on Electronic Reserves.")

Including materials already acquired by the University is very important. The ability to include these materials in the XanEdu CoursePack at no charge to students was decisive in signing this agreement with them. It will guide any future partnership with a vendor to provide electronic reserve collections. The Provost feels strongly that student costs should be minimized to reflect university resources already spent. During fiscal year 2001, the Libraries committed more than $800,000 to purchase access to electronic information. We are in the process of contracting with Serials Solutions (a commercial firm) to provide a database that analyzes our access to journal titles contained in consolidators' databases (e.g., InfoTrac, SilverPlatter, FirstSearch, etc.).

Scalability must be addressed. Because preparing a pack using XanEdu is very labor intensive, there must be a process that encourages faculty to create electronic reserves on their own. It is one thing to provide individual assistance when demand is low, but quite another if all who use Blackboard want help. I have hoped to learn enough with the trial to create templates for faculty to use as they begin to assemble their electronic reserve collections. Each template or guide will have my contact information prominently displayed for assistance with answering questions or helping to solve problems.

Affordability is always an issue. Because my department has no budget to pay copyright fees or other expenses, the cost to the Libraries for early trials of models for providing the service must be minimal. For the purpose of the trial, we decided to pass costs along to students in a graduate course that had no textbook. But this model is not reasonable for undergraduates or for courses with textbooks. In the long run, some basic decisions must be made about who pays the higher cost of electronic reserve. I hope that many staff members representing various library departments will participate in the discussion. Using the old model for traditional paper reserves, the library purchases something and uses it repeatedly. Students copy the material at their own expense. But even if we assert Fair Use, once a faculty member exceeds the guidelines, fees must be paid. It is yet to be determined who pays these repeated fees: students, faculty, library subject funds, or a new general fund that is available to all faculty. There are no easy answers, because use of the service will not be spread evenly across disciplines or even within departments.

Alternative models must be considered beyond the use of XanEdu. As the trial progressed, it became clear that a mixed model might also be useful as faculty learn to assess the need for or appropriateness of readings in electronic form. Faculty will need training on the use of various technologies to compile reading lists, just as they are learning how to teach using them. This mixed model for providing reserve readings should include traditional paper reserves, reading lists on Blackboard or other Web pages that are linked to existing KU resources, use of a commercial firm to provide what the library cannot, or a combination of these options. The use of a combined model might also be the best way to address the needs of some courses, especially in those disciplines with limited access to electronic resources. XanEdu (or a similar product) cannot meet all of our needs for all courses.

CONCLUSIONS: THE LESSONS LEARNED

XanEdu deserves a place among various options for providing electronic reserves. KU will explore the idea of a developing a "container" on the Blackboard "Assignments" page to hold the options so that information about locating reserve readings for a course is provided in one place. In addition, such a container would provide a place for the library to list additional services. In compliance with university policy, it would also remove their commercial logo from the Blackboard page.

The model developed for the trial–that of CoursePacks prepared by the library for each instructor–cannot be scaled. Word of mouth spread quickly among faculty, and this created a much wider demand for the service than we were prepared to deliver. One course with a XanEdu CoursePack led to four, each with its own slightly different needs. These courses provided a great learning opportunity, which was the primary goal of the trial. However, by the end of the summer, it had become clear that the library needs to offer a variety of ways to create reserve collections so that the faculty and the Libraries have options. This will include the traditional paper reserve, scanned files attached to individual or Blackboard Web pages, and access to commercial electronic databases. This conclusion has led to the creation of a series of guides for faculty to assist them as they begin to work on assembling electronic reserve collections for their courses. The first guides have been added to the Distance Learning Information Services Web page.

NEXT STEPS

Early in 2001, the Vice Chancellor for Information Services created a Task Force on Electronic Reserves to unify policies and procedures that were being established by many offices across the campus. These include Instructional Development and Support (which administers Blackboard training and use), the Provost's Office (which provides guidelines to new faculty about intellectual property issues), the Edwards campus (where many of the distance learning courses originate), and the Libraries. This group looked for alternatives to XanEdu, but no other commercial firms could be located that provided copyright-cleared electronic reserve materials to meet our needs. Two firms that were identified initially (Booktech.com and NetPaper.com) could not deliver a product during the trial period. Later examination of the services offered by Docutek and Jones e-global library also failed to identify viable alternatives. However, we must continue to evaluate new services as they become available.

A final report of the Task Force is nearing completion and will be delivered to the Vice Chancellor in December 2001. The report probably will include a recommendation that the University investigate entering into a formal (non-exclusive) institutional partnership with XanEdu, if our concerns (as outlined above) can be addressed. If such an agreement can be reached, it will be evaluated at least annually. In addition, KU will continue to search for new models for delivering the service and will investigate them as they become available. The report also will suggest that an internal library working group begin to address library policies, procedures, and responsibilities for establishing a widely available electronic reserve service.

REFERENCES

Blackboard. (2001). *Welcome to Blackboard.* Available: http://www.blackboard.com (2001, November 27). For the KU Blackboard homepage see *Blackboard 5.* Available: http://courseware.ku.edu/ (2001, November 27).

Booktech.com. (n.d.). *BTC.* Available: http:booktech.com/ (Site was not operational on 2001 November 27).

Burich, Nancy J. (2001, May 16 last update). *Distance Learning Information Services.* Available: http://www2.lib.ku.edu/~public/distlearn/ (2001, November 27).

Butler, John. (1997). From the margins to the mainstream: Developing library support for distance learning. *Library Line,* 8(4), (7 pp.). Available: http://staff.lib.umn.edu/Library Line/Llvol18no4.htm (2000, March 21).

Docutek Information Systems, Inc. (2001). *Docuteck Information Systems, Inc.* Available: http://www.docutek.com (2001, November 27).

Harper, Georgia. (2001, August 10 last update). *Fair use of copyrighted materials.* Available: http://www.utsystem.edu/ogc/intellecltualproperty/copypol2.htm (2001, November 27).

Jones e-global library. (No date). *Jones e-globallibrary.* Available: http://www.egloballibrary.com (2001, November 27).

Lowe, Susan and Rumery, Joyce. (2000). Services to distance learners: Planning for e-reserves and copyright. In P. Steven Thomas (Comp.), *The Ninth Off-Campus Library Services Conference Proceedings, Portland, Oregon, April 26-28, 2000* (pp. 213-220). Mount Pleasant, MI: Central Michigan University.

NetPaper.com. (No date). *NetPaper.* Available: http://www.netpaper.com/ (2001, November 27).

Serials Solutions. (2000-2001). *Serials solutions.* Available: http://www.serialssolutions.com (2001, November 27).

Study.Net. (No date). *Welcome to Study.Net.* Available: http://www.study.net/ (2001, November 27).

XanEdu. (2001). *XanEdu: Utopia for the mind.* Available: http://www.xanedu.com/ (2001, November 27).

APPENDIX A

Campus Partners Agreement

XanEdu, A Division of Bell & Howell Information and Learning, headquartered in Ann Arbor, MI and the University of Kansas Libraries at the University of Kansas located in <u>Lawrence, Kansas</u> agree to the following terms and conditions as stated.

For the purpose of an evaluative pilot project with Nancy Burich of the University of Kansas Library for the Health Policy and Management Cost Effectiveness and Decision Analysis course, XanEdu will provide the following resources for the duration of the project:

- Copyright permission solicitation and digitization of 19 articles currently available from UMI as well as 2 articles not available in UMI's holdings (a small additional fee per article may result from the acquisition of content not currently in UMI/ProQuest holdings as well as for digitization of those articles).
- Nancy Burich will work with the XanEdu editorial team, based in Louisville, KY, as well as the XanEdu technical team, based in Ann Arbor, MI, to develop the finished product.
- Students will not be charged for access to the articles currently in University of Kansas Library databases other than ProQuest as these materials will be accessed via hyperlinks embedded in the CoursePacks.
- XanEdu will also provide ReSearch Engine access as specified by Nancy Burich.
- The deadline to have the work done is May 1, 2001.

In return the Library (or its designee) will provide the following:

- Raising of faculty awareness of XanEdu products and services through faculty listservs, email.
- Designated contact and champion to facilitate implementation of this project.

University Benefits

- Faculty receives free access to our research tools and CoursePack curriculum products in order to trial our offering and build materials for adoption in their courses.
- Copyright cleared content that assures institutions are in compliance.
- Worldwide online delivery to students.
- CoursePack remains accessible to faculty for two years after every session in CoursePack. Results in faster, easier Course preparation the next time it is taught because the CoursePack is being revised as it is being used.
- Students pay only for materials selected by faculty. Faculty controls the price.
- Technical support services provide the institution with seamless integration with existing learning management systems and platforms (e.g., Blackboard, WebCT, etc.)

Implementation

The XanEdu sales account team will arrange for a conference with the Campus partner and appropriate parties within 2 working days of this agreement to develop a mutual timeline of action items and next steps based upon the business needs of the institution.

Agreed to by:

_____Date:_____

Ron Stefanski, Vice President, Sales
XanEdu, A Bell & Howell Information and Learning Company

Agreed to by:

_____Date:_____

APPENDIX B

XanEdu CoursePack Evaluation

Thank you for trying this method of delivering electronic course reserves. Your evaluation of this service is very important to our use of XanEdu in the future.

Name: Robert H. Lee

Course: HP&M 872

Term: Summer 2001

Number of Students Enrolled: 12

1. What was the final price of your CoursePack? $83
    Do you think that this is a reasonable price?
    ___X__ yes   ___X__ no
    Please comment:
    For this group of students (older, all working, geographically dispersed), during this time frame and for a course with no text, it was ok. But, we had to do a substantial amount of traditional reserve to keep the cost down. The problem was largely with journals. Some were quite reasonable; others were ridiculous.

2. Did your students report trouble accessing the CoursePacks?
    ____ yes   _____ no
    Please comment:

    The articles to which KU offered access were a bit of a problem. Students and I needed to be at KUEC to get them.

3. What other issues did your students have with the CoursePacks?
    Please comment:
    None

4. What is your overall opinion of the <u>content</u> available from XanEdu? (5 = best)
    _____ 1   _____ 2   _____ 3   _____ 4   ___X__ 5
    Please comment:

5. What is your overall opinion of the CoursePacks? (5 = best)
    _____ 1   _____ 2   ___X__ 3   ___X__ 4   _____ 5
    Please comment:

APPENDIX B (continued)

The Xanedu interface is still pretty odd and user unfriendly. If I tried to come in through the main entrance, I found I could not get anywhere at times. I'm still apprehensive about building a CoursePack. Navigation at the XanEdu site remains a problem.

6. Did you get sufficient assistance in developing the CoursePack?
___X__ yes _____ no
Please comment:

7. Would you use XanEdu again?
_____ yes _____ no ___X__ probably
Please comment:

8. How would you improve this service?

XanEdu needs to improve navigation. The alternatives are traditional reserves, use of electronic materials to which KU can grant access, and digital reserves. I still need a clear sense of the legal status of digital reserves (scanned by the professor).

Thank you.

Please e-mail this completed survey to Nancy Burich nburich@ku.edu or mail it to her at KU Edwards Campus, 12600 Quivira Rd., Overland Park, KS 66213.

APPENDIX C

Journal Copyright Fees

Journal Title	Per Student Cost	Course Number
Academy of Management Journal	$1.33	BUS 895
American Behavioral Scientist	$1.33	BUS 895
American Journal of Knee Surgery	$2.08	HPM872(r)
American Journal of Public Health	$1.33	HPM872(r)
Annals of Internal Medicine	$3.72	HPM872(r)
Annual Review of Public Health	Highwire	HPM821
Annual Review of Sociology	EAI	HPM821
Archives of Internal Medicine	$15.83	HPM872
Australian & New Zealand Journal of Public Health	$1.33	HPM872(r)
British Journal of Cancer	$4,000	HPM872
British Journal of Dermatology	PubMed	HPM872
Educational & Psychological Measurement	$1.33	BUS 895
Executive Excellence	$1.33	BUS 895
Financial Times	$1.99	BUS 895
Formulary	$1.99	HPM872(r)
Group & Organization Management	$1.33	BUS 895
Harvard Business Review	$3.60 Study.Net	PUAD 845

Journal Title	Per Student Cost	Course Number
Health Care Financing Review	$1.33	HPM872(r)
Healthcare Financial Management	EAI	HPM872
Houston Chronicle	$1.33	BUS 895
JAMA	EAI ($15.82)	HPM872
Journal of Quality and Participation	$1.33	BUS 895
Journal of Business Ethics	$1.33	BUS 895
Journal of Epidemiology & Community Health	$1.33	HPM872(r)
Journal of Medical Ethics	$1.33	HPM872
Journal of the American Geriatrics Socy.	$1.33	HPM872(r)
Machine Design	$1.33	BUS 895
Management Review	$1.33	BUS 895
Medical Care	$15.82	HPM872(r)
Medical Decision Making	$9.31	HPM872
Nations Business	$1.33	BUS 895
Science	JSTOR	HPM872
Sloan Management Review	$1.33	BUS 895
Strategy and Leadership	$1.33	BUS 895
Stroke	$3.73	HPM872(r)
Wall Street Journal	$0.98	BUS 895

APPENDIX D

Report on the XanEdu Trial
Summer 2001

Trial
- Limited partnership signed in May between XanEdu and the University of Kansas for XanEdu to develop and deliver one CoursePack for use during the summer term
- Actual CoursePacks developed during the trial: 4
- Lee (Health Policy and Management) used during the summer term
- Zimmerman (Health Policy and Management) for the summer term (not adopted by instructor)
- Romzek (Public Administration) used during the summer term; included Study.Net for access to *Harvard Business Review* articles
- Clark (Business Administration) developed for fall term use; will include access to their ReSearch engine; will assert Fair Use under KU guidelines to provide those materials at no cost to students instead of using Study.Net for which a fee is charged
- Types of material included in CoursePacks:
- Basic course information (from the syllabus)
- Contact information for Library help (Nancy Burich)
- Journal articles they supplied for which students were charged
- Links to KU materials (InfoTrac and JSTOR) for which no fee was charged
- Electronic files supplied by KU for which no fee was charged

APPENDIX D (continued)

- Book chapters for which a fee was charged to students
- Links to Study.Net for access to *Harvard Business Review* articles which students accessed separately from within the CoursePack and for which a fee was charged to students
- Feedback from users
- Lee returned evaluation form (attached); Romzek has not
- All student requests for assistance that were received by the Coordinator concerned authentication and firewall issues

What was learned

- XanEdu editorial and technical staff responded quickly and with enthusiasm to suggested changes
  - The order citations appear in the CoursePack should correspond to the syllabus (instead of by author or by the title of the journal in which they appear)
  - The order of the elements appearing within citations was not always flexible (especially if coming from the ProQuest database); solution was to highlight the author's name
  - They supplied the fee charged for each item (previously only the total cost appeared) to help instructor adjust final cost
  - The value of alternative readings suggested by XanEdu staff was of limited value to faculty (though appreciated, most were not used)
- Permissions could not be secured for all items requested
  - XanEdu was not willing to interrupt ongoing negotiations with some publishers for access to all their publications in order to request permission to use the single items we needed for this CoursePack (e.g., Lippincott, Blackwell Science, *New England Journal of Medicine*); unable to get a list of firms, learn of limit only after requesting an item
  - Some firms refuse permissions (Elsevier Science, *Preventive Medicine, Current Issues in Public Health*)
  - One publication too costly to use (*British Journal of Cancer* charges a flat fee of $4,000 for use)
- How to link from CoursePack directly to reserve reading list in Voyager for a particular course (John Miller assisted in determining which parts of the URL for the lists included in Voyager needed to be included in the links to eliminate session information that would later make the link fail; XanEdu needed to modify the way their software used this data)
- Faculty include redundancy in readings lists to compensate for high demand and inaccessibility of readings (Lee's readings decreased from 31 items to 14 with the CoursePack)
- Costs for access can range from less than $1.00 (per student) to $4,000 (the total cost for use; to have been divided among the students enrolled in the course)
- Costs charged are based on use for one term (permissions received for longer periods are pro rated in the CoursePack)
- Multiple authentications are problematic and need to be eliminated (access to library databases from a remote location, XanEdu, Study.Net, Blackboard are all different)

Limits to broad use

- Process currently goes through one person (Coordinator) which limits scalability
- Must take full advantage of KU Library and other resources
- Must include faculty education on best use of XanEdu

Fair Use issues

- Address faculty responsibility for agreeing to use Guidelines with preliminary screen having a check box (?)
- Willingness to incorporate files provided by KU of copyrighted materials used under the Guidelines (preliminary discussions with Jeff Letson [sales rep.] were positive)
- Develop a process to reuse material beyond Fair Use (XanEdu might use our files of scanned images the first time but subsequent use might be for a fee with their CoursePack)

Conclusions

- Developed good working relationship with their teams (responsive and timely)
- Trials of similar products should be investigated whenever viable alternatives identified
- XanEdu should be among the options offered to faculty to meet electronic reserve needs

Recommendations

KU and XanEdu should enter into an institutional partnership for a period of one year (renewable by mutual agreement) **IF**
- We can ensure that students will not be charged for something KU has already purchased, regardless of how the CoursePack is submitted (directly by a faculty member or by the Coordinator for Distance Learning Information Services)
- Institutional partnership funds will be used by XanEdu to finance fully the automatic checking of all readings against a list of local holdings supplied by KU (i.e., the Serial Solutions database) AND
- They notify the Library and it supplies links to the full text of these readings
  - Materials can be used under the Fair Use Guidelines with no charge to students
    - XanEdu will accept files from KU containing copyrighted material used under Fair Use (a database of Fair Use agreement forms signed by faculty will be maintained by KU)
    - XanEdu will not re-use our scanned images for the same instructor for the same course but will supply the material in a CoursePack for a fee

APPENDIX E

Lessons Learned from Four CoursePacks

Types of Materials Included

- Book chapters
- Free library links to journal articles
- From KU databases
- From JSTOR
- From PubMed
- Journal articles supplied by XanEdu
- Links to other vendor's resources (Study.Net)
- Pamphlets
- Scanned files on KU's server (Fair Use)
- Scanned files on XanEdu's server
- Manuscript
- Book chapter to which KU department holds copyright
- XanEdu's ReSearch Engine

Major Issues

- Affordability
- Alternative models
- Copyright
- Fair Use
- Inclusion of library resources at no cost to students
- Scalability

Minor Issues

- Linking to Endeavor reserve list URL's
- Navigation within XanEdu
- Order of elements within a citation
- Order of readings in CoursePack mirrors reading list
- Restricted access to some publisher's materials due to ongoing negotiations with XanEdu
- Single place to locate all reserve readings, regardless of model used
- Typical copyright fees for particular journal titles
- Universal sign-on

APPENDIX F

Impact of Fair Use Guidelines on Electronic Reserves

HP&M 872

- 31 readings on original list, all journal articles
- Dykes only: 18
- KU: 12 (no dups per issue)
- No KU: 1
- With Guidelines, pay for 15 (1 JSTOR and 3 links to databases available)

HP&M 821

- 13 readings, 5 book chapters, 1 manuscript, 1 pamphlet
- KU owns 16 journal articles (no dups per issue)
- No KU: 1
- With Guidelines, pay for one journal article and 5 book chapters

PUAD 845

- 16 readings, 2 manuscripts and 14 journal articles
- KU owns 9 journal articles (no dups per issue)
- No KU: 5
- With Guidelines, pay for 5 articles

BUS 895 (fall)

- 10 readings, 6 book chapters and 4 journal articles
- KU owns all 4 journal articles (no dups per issue)
- With Guidelines, pay for 6 book chapters

Distance Education from a Collections Development Perspective

Hildegund M. Calvert

Ball State University

SUMMARY. Research has shown that distance learners are more suc-cessful in their courses and have a higher level of satisfaction with their programs when quality library resources and services are available to them. Despite such findings, universities often continue to plan the de-livery of distance education programs without consulting with the li-brary. The author shows how collaboration between librarians, faculty and administrators can lead to successful distance education programs. In addition, she also reports on studies and initiatives at Ball State Uni-versity Library to address these challenges.

KEYWORDS. Distance education, design, collections, library services

INTRODUCTION

The author had been interested in distance education issues for some time when she was appointed library liaison for distance education at the University Libraries and given responsibility for providing reference assistance to distance learners and for filling their document delivery requests. Membership on a uni-versity-wide distance education committee afforded many opportunities to pro-mote the precepts outlined in the ACRL Guidelines for Distance Education and

[Haworth co-indexing entry note]: "Distance Education from a Collections Development Perspective." Calvert, Hildegund M. Co-published simultaneously in *Journal of Library Administration* (The Haworth Infor-mation Press, an imprint of The Haworth Press, Inc.) Vol. 37, No. 1/2, 2002, pp. 117-126; and: *Distance Learning Library Services: The Tenth Off-Campus Library Services Conference* (ed: Patrick B. Mahoney) The Haworth Information Press, an imprint of The Haworth Press, Inc., 2002, pp. 117-126.

http://www.haworthpress.com/store/product.asp?sku=J111
10.1300/J111v37n01_11

helped with their implementation. Participation on that committee further demonstrated that cooperation between librarians, faculty who teach the distance education classes and administrators who conceive them is crucial for providing quality services to distance learners. In December of 2000, the author transferred to Collections Development where responsibilities for distance learners continued to be part of her duties, albeit of a very different nature. It soon became evident that existing electronic databases needed to be evaluated to determine their usefulness for supporting the research needs of the BSU community, including those of distance learners, and to establish a benchmark for future acquisitions. This realization and a number of events such as the University's decision to offer the Master's Degree in Nursing and the BS Completion Degree in Nursing exclusively over the Internet, and the appointment to a university committee charged with developing a strategic plan for distance education prompted the studies and initiatives discussed in this paper.

COLLECTION DEVELOPMENT ISSUES

There are no subject specialists at the BSU Libraries. The Head of Collections Development is responsible for overseeing selection of materials in all subject areas and for all formats acquired for the University Libraries. This includes coordinating the renewal of existing and the purchase of new electronic resources and databases, and ensuring that distance learners have access to these resources from wherever they are located. In order to bring organization to this task and to facilitate informed decisions, an inventory of existing electronic resources was prepared and a report of usage statistics was set up and updated monthly. The inventory lists electronic resources by title and gives details for aggregator databases such as the number of journals with full-text coverage, the number of abstracted titles, etc.

The rapid growth and the impact of digitization of information has changed users' expectations and has intensified the debate over access versus ownership of resources among librarians. Students and faculty, regardless of whether they are on campus or off campus, expect to find the material they need online, full-text, at the time they need it. These expectations have changed the thinking and activities of librarians and have placed new demands on those involved in collection development. In addition to selecting resources for their institutions, collectors now must be more involved in the organization and access of electronic resources.

Newman addresses issues of organization and access for different publication types and packaging for purchased and free electronic resources. He argues that libraries are not using their resources as fully as possible if they do not provide clear and easy access to all the titles available (Newman, 2000). Free and purchased electronic journals are cataloged at the University Libraries, and all electronic databases are listed on the electronic resources pages. There are links to the journals and the databases; however, individual titles included in the aggregator packages are not currently cataloged. Since hooks to holdings are not available for all aggregators, users do not have clearly defined access to all of the Libraries' resources. This shortcoming has been of concern to this author and to other librarians at the University Libraries. In order to gain a better understanding of how this lack of access affects users, the Head of Collections Development conducted a case study of interlibrary loan (ILL) requests from distance learners and a review of ILL requests for which copyright was paid. The results are discussed later in this paper.

Carrigan discusses the need to evaluate collections and argues that overselection is a costly problem that must be detected (Carrigan, 1996). While he primarily examines print materials, the danger of overselection and duplication also applies to electronic resources, particularly aggregator packages. Ferguson argues that selectors should become full-text Amazon.coms, and like Newman, he emphasizes that providing access to information is crucial. He advises collectors to concentrate on increasing the volume of information available to users and to include free and purchased information and not be overly concerned with selecting the best material. He discusses purchasing electronic information in packages, obtaining research and curricular support materials on demand and examines collaborative acquisition programs. He provides an introduction to the Scholarly Publishing and Academic Resources Coalition (SPARC) and concludes by stating that duties of selectors have changed and need to change even more by proactively pursuing the goals of SPARC (Ferguson, 2000).

Baldwin also addresses the impact of digitization on the work of collection development librarians. He advises them to keep abreast of new technologies, learn about emerging technologies and use these technologies to evaluate resources along with organizing them for ease of access (Baldwin, 2000). Peters argues that technological innovations, computers and computer networks are transforming collection development while the majority of librarians are slow to change and even refuse to change altogether. He advocates a patron-driven collection model to meet the immediate need of patrons instead of spending large amounts of money each year building collections. He believes that the purpose of collection development is not to develop a collection but to meet the actual information needs of real members of a defined community of potential users (Peters, 2000). This suggestion merits consideration, particularly in the selection of materials for disciplines in the sciences.

LIBRARY SERVICES FOR SCHOOL OF NURSING
DISTANCE LEARNERS

As a result of improved technology, a number of academic departments at Ball State University are now offering courses via the Internet. School of Nursing faculty have been leaders in using this new technology for some time now. They have Web-enhanced many of the basic nursing courses they teach on campus and have made instructional materials available to their students online. In order to enable practitioners to continue their education, courses required for the baccalaureate completion track and for the Master's Degree in Nursing are now taught exclusively via the Internet. Many of the students who enter these programs are working full time in addition to taking classes, often live in remote parts of the state of Indiana, and more recently, also come from other states across the country.

The University Libraries realized that this new delivery mode and the new population to be served made it necessary to review and reevaluate resources and services provided to distance learners in general and to School of Nursing students in particular. The ACRL Guidelines for Distance Education (http://www.ala.org/acrl/guides/distlrng.html) address the issue of access and state:

> Access to adequate library services and resources is essential for the attainment of superior academic skills in post-secondary education, regardless of where students, faculty, and programs are located. Members of the distance learning community are entitled to library services and resources equivalent to those provided for students and faculty in traditional campus settings. (Philosophy section, para. 1)

The School of Nursing had also become aware of a new section in the current policies of the National League for Nursing Accrediting Commission (NLNAC), which addresses resource accessibility for the distance learning population much in the same way the ACRL Guidelines do, requiring that resources on campus and at remote locations be comparable.

In order to deal with these issues and to begin discussing the specific needs of Internet courses, librarians from Instructional Services, Reference, Interlibrary Loan, Access Services and Collections Development began to meet with School of Nursing faculty. These joint discussions led to the acquisition of new online resources and to the introduction of a number of electronic library services. Some of the most popular ones are online renewal and recalls and electronic notification of due dates that help avoid overdue charges. Ultimately, these improved services benefited not only the distance learners, for whom they were originally designed, but also faculty and students on campus.

Librarians and faculty from the School of Nursing evaluated the University Libraries' existing print subscriptions to nursing journals and determined that coverage was adequate. Online access to index databases such as CINAHL and Medline as well as to a small number of full-text electronic journals was available to the on-campus population. The Indiana Spectrum of Information Resources (INSPIRE), a collection of databases including Health Source Plus and Academic Search Elite, is an additional online resource available to all Indiana residents, including on-campus and off-campus students. Coverage in INSPIRE extends from 1984 to the present, and many entries are full-text. One of the most urgent needs expressed by School of Nursing faculty was off-campus access to full-text peer reviewed nursing journals. INSPIRE was not seen as a viable option to satisfy this need. The database is not available to students who reside outside of Indiana and does not offer full-text access to the nursing literature that students in the newly designed Internet courses must have to satisfy their higher-level information needs.

In an effort to improve this situation, the University Libraries set up a trial for the Nursing Collection I of Journals@Ovid, a database aggregation of searchable, scientific, technical and medical full-text journals. Librarians and nursing faculty evaluated the resource, and their recommendation resulted in a one-year pilot project to test the usefulness of Journals@Ovid for the students enrolled in Internet courses, particularly out-of-state distance learners. This new database includes access to the bibliographic citations, abstracts and references of 362 journals indexed in Clinical Medicine, 65 in the Behavioral & Social Sciences, 58 in the Life Sciences, 47 in Nursing and eleven in Physical Science & Engineering. The Libraries' subscription to the Nursing Collection I includes full-text online access to 14 nursing journals. Titles for full-text coverage were selected by librarians and faculty based on students' perceived research needs. The Libraries also subscribe to nine of these 14 titles in print.

The Ovid pilot project was a success, and the University Libraries continue to subscribe despite the relatively high cost. The Libraries' Automation unit collaborated with University Computing Services and was finally able to set up a proxy server during the summer of 2001. The Electronic Resources Librarian reviewed licensing agreements to make sure they permitted off-campus access. When existing agreements were unclear or did not address off-campus access, he contacted vendors for clarification and/or permission. Completion of this project was an important milestone in the Libraries' quest to comply with the ACRL Guidelines and provide quality service to its distance learners. All registered students and current faculty now have access to the Libraries' electronic resources regardless as to whether they are on campus or off campus.

The Libraries ILL Office had web request forms (http://www.bsu.edu/library/thelibraries/units/ill/) in place for users to request materials not available at the Libraries electronically. Ariel software helped speed up the process of sending and receiving requests. When the School of Nursing launched its Internet programs, ILL agreed to supply distance learners with materials owned by the University Libraries. That service is not available to on-campus students. The Interlibrary Loan librarian investigated options to electronically deliver requested materials to the requestor's desk top (Calvert, 2001). After some initial difficulties, procedures are now in place for delivering documents electronically, using Adobe Acrobat to send documents in PDF format.

Nursing faculty utilize the University Libraries' Electronic Reserve service to place materials on reserve for their Internet courses. This allows on-campus and distance education students access to course reserve materials seven days a week, 24 hours a day from the convenience of their home or from their place of work (Calvert, 2001). A website (http://www.bsu.edu/library/servicesnew/distanceed/index.html) specifically designed for distance education students lists additional services available, such as reference assistance and individual research sessions and includes links to ILL, electronic course reserves, electronic journals and online databases.

In collaboration with nursing faculty, Instructional Services librarians developed tutorial modules for the Web-based nursing courses. Their goal was to ensure that the same information they teach in the on-site instruction sessions was available to distance learners. The content of the modules is closely tied to class assignments, and individual modules are inserted into the course at the point of need. This method proved to be highly successful, and Instructional Services librarians continue to collaborate with School of Nursing faculty in their quest to provide quality instruction and to improve the information literacy skills of their students. They continuously work on updating and improving the modules and plan to develop more for other programs. Two Instructional Services Librarians and a School of Nursing professor describe their efforts in detail in a 2001 article (Dorner, Hodson-Carlton, & Taylor, 2001).

The cooperation between Collections Development and the School of Nursing that began with the search for a suitable online database for out-of-state distance learners continues to date. One of the responsibilities of the Head of Collections Development is to ensure that the Libraries provide students and faculty with the resources they need to succeed in their studies and to negotiate off-campus access with the vendor. This task is becoming ever more difficult in the face of prohibitive perennial price increases that outpace increases in budget allocations on a regular basis, especially for serials, periodicals and online resources. Database vendors are making this effort more difficult by bundling aggregated packages without a clear explanation of their collection policy. In addition, some vendors pursue publishers with the goal of obtaining preferred agreements that give them exclusive rights to certain journals. A consequence of this practice is that titles disappear from one aggregated bundle and later reappear in a different one, often without prior notice to libraries. This pursuit of exclusive titles is harmful to libraries and puts added strain on already limited budgets. Because of this and in order to gain access to specific titles, libraries may be forced to pay for subscriptions to several aggregators. In many cases, other titles that come bundled with the exclusives overlap among packages. For that reason, librarians must be extremely vigilant when they select aggregations. They should examine bundled titles carefully to determine overlap and avoid duplication before signing licensing agreements.

CASE STUDY OF ILL REQUESTS

To obtain a better picture of the usefulness of Journals@Ovid, the Head of Collections Development conducted a study of interlibrary loan requests submitted by distance education students enrolled in nursing Internet courses. During the Fall Semester of 2000 and the Spring Semester of 2001, between August 1, 2000 and May 4, 2001, students submitted 823 ILL requests for journal articles. The journal titles were checked in Jake, Yale University's Jointly Administered Knowledge Environment, http://jake.med.yale.edu/, to determine whether any full-text coverage was available. A total of 47 articles were available in Ovid's Nursing Collection I to which the Libraries subscribe. Further research is needed to determine why students submitted ILL requests instead of retrieving the articles themselves. Possible reasons are that students were not able to access Ovid because it was busy or that they lacked the information literacy skills needed to succeed. An additional 230 articles were available in other Ovid databases for which no current subscription exists. These results could be an indication that the time has come for librarians and nursing faculty to review current subscriptions and consider selecting different titles for full text coverage. Jake indicated full-text for 81 more articles in various other aggregators to which the Libraries subscribe. Currently ILL does not check whether requests can be filled in-house prior to filling them. This decision is based on a study conducted in the fall of 1998 and spring of 1999 (Calvert, 2000). The in-house fill rate at that time was so low that ILL staff time required to verify could not be justified. Based on the results of the recent case study of ILL requests, it was recommended that ILL staff check borrowing requests from distance learners in Jake. Requests that can be filled online are returned to the patron with instructions for retrieving the article.

Additional research and follow up studies are needed before a definitive conclusion with regard to the appropriateness of Journals@Ovid for the Internet nursing programs can be reached. However, based on preliminary results it appears that for now Ovid remains the resource of choice for nursing. Full text in databases other than Ovid was found for only 93 of the 823 requests examined. Of these 93, 81 were available in aggregator databases to which the Libraries subscribe. It appears that OVID's quest for exclusive titles remains successful albeit at the expense of libraries.

REVIEW OF COPYRIGHT COMPLIANCE REPORT

At the end of each academic year ILL supplies a copyright compliance report to the Head of Collections Development. That report includes journal titles, ISSN numbers, publication year and the number of articles for which the Libraries paid a fee to the Copyright Clearance Center. The report for the 00/01 academic year, covering the period of August 1, 2000 and May 4, 2001, lists 74 journal titles and 201 articles for which a copyright compliance fee was paid. The author checked these journal titles in Jake and determined that 42 requests could have been filled from electronic resources available in the Libraries. These findings are significant and deserve attention. They demonstrate how the lack of clear access can cost the Libraries money, create extra work for staff and cause delays for our users. A recommendation went forward to ILL asking to check Jake before ordering articles for which copyright must be paid.

CONCLUSION

Feedback from distance education students enrolled in Nursing Internet courses has been extremely positive. Students were satisfied with Ovid and only occasionally complained about the database being busy when they needed to do research. They continually praise ILL for their fast turn around time, and remark positively on the competence of the reference librarians who assist with quick answer type questions, and on the dedication of the Libraries' Liaison for Distance Education who assists with queries that require more research. Close cooperation between faculty and librarians deserves at least part of the credit for the success of the two Internet nursing programs. While not all potential problems could be anticipated or prevented, procedures for dealing with emergencies were established, and avenues were put in place for students to request assistance at the time they need it.

The Head of Collections Development continues to monitor and evaluate on-line resources, keeping the special needs of distance learners in mind. The task is challenging and time-consuming, particularly in light of shrinking library budgets and ever-increasing journal prices for print as well as for online products. Guenther expands Katz's original evaluative criteria and presents a model for evaluating digital resources that should prove helpful in this task (Guenther, 2000). Terry addresses the impact technology has on libraries' collection choices and presents both librarians' and publishers' perspectives. Common concerns among librarians she surveyed include the desire for fair and practical access and licensing, ILL rights and open systems. She advises all parties involved to communicate better and work together toward a common understanding (Terry, 2000). Librarians will remain hesitant to rely exclusively on aggregator packages until current technical instabilities and content uncertainties have been resolved. Much work remains to be done to ensure secure archiving, to increase coverage for back files and to convince publishers that the practice of placing embargoes on titles by delaying availability of full text is contrary to the intended purpose of making information available online.

The appointment to participate with faculty and administrators in the development of a University Strategic Plan for Distance Education was a valuable experience. It provided the opportunity to dispel an often held belief that all online information is free and readily available. Librarians on the committee were able to apprise the university community of the high cost and the convoluted pricing structures associated with electronic resources, and to inform them of the many and varied restrictions vendors place on licensing their products. The final version of the Plan asks faculty and administrators to include the Libraries when they plan new programs, and asks for increases in library funding for acquiring full-text online resources, licensed for off-campus access.

REFERENCES

Association of College and Research Libraries. (1998). ACRL guidelines for distance learning library services. *College & Research Libraries News, 59,* 689-694. Also available at http://www.ala.org/acrl/guides/distlrng.html.

Association of College and Research Libraries. (2000). *Guidelines for distance learning library services.* Retrieved February 15, 2001 from Association of College and Research Libraries Web site: http://www.ala.org/acrl/guides/distlrng.html.

Baldwin, V. (2000). Collection development in the new millennium-evaluating, selecting, annotating, organizing for ease of access, reevaluating, and updating electronic resources. *Collection Management, 21*(1/2), 67-96.

Calvert, H. M. (2000). The impact of electronic journals and aggregate databases on interlibrary loan: A case study at Ball State University Libraries. *New Library World, 101*(1153), 28-31.

Calvert, H. M. (2001). Document delivery options for distance education students and electronic reserve service at Ball State University Libraries. *Journal of Library Administration, 31*, (3/4), 109-125.

Carrigan, D. P. (1996). Collection development-evaluation. *The Journal of Academic Librarianship, 22* (4), July 1996, 273-278.

Dorner, J. L., Hodson-Carlton, K., and Taylor, S. E. (2001). Faculty-librarian collaboration for nursing information literacy: A tiered approach. *Reference Services Review, 29*(2), 132-140.

Ferguson, A. W. (2000). Digital library selection: maximum access, not buying the best titles: libraries should become full-text Amazon.com's. *Journal of Library Administration, 31*(2), 27-39.

Guenther, K. (2000). Making smart licensing decisions. *Computers in Libraries*, June 2000, 58-60.

Newman, G. L. (2000). Collection development and organization of electronic resources. *Collection Management, 21*(1/2), 97-113.

Peters, T. (2000). Some issues for collection developers and content managers. *Collection Management, 25*(1/2), 137-153.

Quinn, B., (2001). The impact of aggregator packages on collection management. *Collection Management, 25*(3), 53-74.

Tenopir, C., Baker, G., and Robinson, W. (2001). Racing at full speed. *Library Journal, 126*(9), May 15, 45-58.

Terry, A. A. (2000). How today's technology affects libraries' collection choices. *Computers in Libraries*, June 2000, 51-55.

Delivering Library Services
with Centra Symposium

Margaret Casado

University of Tennessee, Knoxville

SUMMARY. The University of Tennessee's Distance Education unit is always looking for new and effective ways to deliver courses. One recent experiment has been using a course management system known as Centra Symposium for course delivery and, as a natural outgrowth of that, to deliver library services to the students.

KEYWORDS. Technology, library services, distance education, design

The University of Tennessee is a land-grant institution in the eastern part of Tennessee close to the Great Smoky Mountains. It has an enrollment of 26,000 students and a faculty of approximately 1,200 in fifteen colleges and schools and over 400 academic programs. As a land-grant institution, a considerable part of the university's mission is to provide continuing education opportunities to the state's population.

The Division of Outreach and Continuing Education at the University of Tennessee has been sponsoring continuing education opportunities for nontraditional students for over 75 years. The division has struggled over those years, as have all parts of society, with the changes that have affected the entire approach to lifelong learning. The division consists of several units that handle different aspects of the continuing education initiative at UT, including the

[Haworth co-indexing entry note]: "Delivering Library Services with Centra Symposium." Casado, Margaret. Co-published simultaneously in *Journal of Library Administration* (The Haworth Information Press, an imprint of The Haworth Press, Inc.) Vol. 37, No. 1/2, 2002, pp. 127-135; and: *Distance Learning Library Services: The Tenth Off-Campus Library Services Conference* (ed: Patrick B. Mahoney) The Haworth Information Press, an imprint of The Haworth Press, Inc., 2002, pp. 127-135.

http://www.haworthpress.com/store/product.asp?sku=J111
10.1300/J111v37n01_12

Non-Credit Programs, Summer School, Independent Study, the Evening School, and Distance Education. They have all worked with a variety of modes for delivery of instruction in programs that have included degree-earning programs, certificate programs, partnering with industry, and many other varieties of offerings in order to provide quality programs and educational opportunities statewide.

Because the Evening School and the Distance Education programs are the units that usually provide degree programs, most of the requirements for library services arise within these units. The Evening School component consists primarily of classes that involve face-to-face classroom teaching, on campus and at sites away from the Knoxville campus (traditional off-campus satellite program). Some of the faculty of the Evening School use a course management system, CourseInfo by BlackBoard, in their classes to supplement the weekly face-to-face meetings and to facilitate communication, presentation, and organization of the course materials. Because it is the course management system supported by the campus computing center, most of the faculty use BlackBoard if they use any type of course management system. But overall, the Evening School usually employs the format of the faculty traveling to off-campus sites and minimal use of computers and technology.

The Independent Study unit has always relied on the U.S. mail and UPS or FedEx for delivery and return of coursework, a very low-tech but usually reliable method of communication and transmission of materials.

The Distance Education classes, on the other hand, are the ones that use more advanced and more expensive technology in the delivery of their courses. Part of their mission is to keep exploring new modes of delivery of course work, always focusing on the convenience of the learners and the quality of the interaction. They often vary the methods of course delivery, working for the perfect match between the delivery of course content and the needs of the students and faculty.

Current program offerings through the Distance Education unit at the University of Tennessee include several MBA programs–the Executive MBA, the Physician Executive MBA, and the Professional MBA. Distance Education is also helping to make it possible for the School of Information Sciences to offer a master's degree program to people across the states of Tennessee and Virginia, of course using distance education technologies and techniques. Other programs offered include nursing, communications, physics, nuclear engineering, mechanical engineering, industrial engineering, environmental engineering, civil engineering, and chemical engineering. Students from all over the world are involved in these programs, thanks to the advances in technology that have helped make education available to more people in more locations.

On our campus, the Distance Education unit has historically been the unit to explore technologies and test implementations for feasibility of projects on a large scale. Many years ago, the hot technology was videotape. Lectures and demonstrations were taped, and the videotapes were mailed to students or the programs were broadcast. While not abandoning the use of mail and the videotapes, the Distance Education unit decided to offer classes in telecommunications classrooms using the EDNET network, a statewide network for compressed video transmission. Students have appreciated the features of the two-way interactive video classes. They can see and hear their counterparts in other cities and states, and they can see and hear their teacher. Human contact and interaction are still very much a part of the class. There are glitches in the transmissions and some other problems, but overall, it is a fairly satisfying mode of interaction and satisfactory way to learn. However, the compressed video scenario is an expensive undertaking. The break-even point is, of course, an important aspect of any venture, even in the academic world, and while we know that the state will benefit in the long run with a better-educated population, the legislature wants to see more immediate return on investment and revenue generation.

In recent years, with the demand for distance education classes growing and not showing signs of slowing down, we have also encountered the problem of scheduling courses in our telecommunications classrooms. As more and more departments are making agreements with various organizations to provide more and more learning opportunities at a distance, scheduling the electronic classrooms has gotten more difficult. The rooms are very quickly booked for all available time slots, partly because everyone wants to meet after the traditional end of the workday so that working students can attend classes. Expansion of facilities and adding more classrooms is not considered an option in Tennessee at this time with the state budget troubles and the current economic downturn we have been experiencing. So it is quite obvious that we have to explore other methods and media for course delivery, hopefully finding the perfect mix to show that continuing education and lifelong learning can be interactive and, at the same time, be profitable enterprises for the state to be involved in, not only for the benefits of an educated populace, but also for some revenue generation–or at least not a site of massive hemorrhaging of funds.

Recently the trend has been to move everything online and use the Internet (ubiquitous and relatively cheap) for delivery of coursework. With the Internet, one can have synchronous or asynchronous class meetings, or a combination of both. Some departments are mounting syllabi, assignments, and other course-related materials on a static Web site. These can add to the class, but do not handle the problem of synchronous learning, which allows for discussion and sharing and interacting.

UT's Distance Education and some of the Independent Study units have been using Centra Symposium for their class presentations. It has full audio so that students can log into the virtual classroom from anywhere and listen to the professor lecture in real time. Students can raise their hands to ask or answer questions and show laughter and applause responses. They can also interact with the people in the class by talking to them or by using the text chat. Collaboration is facilitated because the teacher can divide the students into groups (breakout feature), and they can work together easily, being able to talk to each other and using the whiteboard and the file-sharing features. Symposium is compatible with many kinds of software, so that the teacher can upload a PowerPoint slide show and use it to help illustrate the lecture, or use almost any other file type, including audio, video, html, Flash, and Java. Do you have materials you want the students to see? They probably can.

Symposium is designed not to be a bandwidth hog, as many videoconferencing programs and video and audio streaming products are. It is able to work well over ordinary telephone/modem connections. And you incur no telephone conference call charges.

There is also a feature that will allow for asynchronous learning. A tape of the session can be recorded and saved for students to go back and review the material later. There can be more than one teacher or presenter in a session, and they are the ones who control who has the microphone for speaking. The names of the members of the class in attendance are listed so that everyone knows who else is in class. Students can have private chats while the class is being conducted, and they do not interfere with the rest of the class.

The Symposium software has a lot of other neat features, including automatic upgrades, which cut down on tech support the IT people have to provide. It can also run a self-check to make sure that the users' systems are set up properly.

But my favorite feature of all is the Web Safari. With it, the teacher can take the students on a controlled Web tour. The Web Safari option is a great opportunity for exploring sites as a class. With some software you have to let the class visit a Web site without escort. You give them the URL of a site to visit and some ideas of things to look for and tell them you will meet them back at the course site in a certain number of minutes. When they all arrive back at the class site, you can discuss what they saw while at the assigned site, but you have to trust that they did visit the site and used their time constructively.

The Web Safari option in Centra lets the teacher retain control of what sites the students visit. The teacher can escort all of the students in attendance to a particular site and click where appropriate, and the students follow along (without a choice). The teacher can also be narrating the trip, thereby ensuring that the students have seen what was intended by the trip. We can search the catalog, look at databases together, answer "what if" questions, and just about anything we could do if we were face-to-face in a lab environment with the images being projected onto the screen.

I have used the Symposium software for instruction purposes with the distance education MBA programs. It works great. We do not all have to be in the same place, but they can still hear me talk, and I can explain things as we go through the materials. When they get confused, they can stop and ask questions right then. Because the human presence is still intact here, this is a much better solution than wandering dazed and confused through an online tutorial without guidance.

The Library Services class is permanently posted in the schedules of all enrolled students so that students can revisit the slides at any time. We are also posting hours for a librarian to be available to talk to students, similar to holding office hours on campus.

The better the connections, the better the transmission, of course, but Centra is able to work well over phone modems. There is no special equipment required, just a browser (Explorer preferred) and a connection. The student must download a 1 megabyte file from Centra onto his or her machine before the class starts, and the software will check the setup for a current browser, run an audio check, and make sure the student has the most recent version of the software needed.

Some people are more comfortable with the computers and the technology than others; there may always be that segment who take a little longer to adapt to a new piece of software and to become comfortable using it. But even for those people, Centra Symposium is a big help because it keeps a human connection readily available.

In Figure 1, we see the introductory page of Centra Symposium. You see all of the classes you have on your schedule, and on the left, you see the place to click for doing the system check.

In Figure 2, we see the screen the students or participants see. You can see along the top row the icons that the students see to raise their hand, to vote yes (check mark) or no (x mark) on a poll, laugh, or applaud. The other icons along the top include a keyboard as a signal to participate in a text chat, the exclamation mark where one goes to read feedback (submitted anonymously), and the door to click if you would like to leave the classroom for a while. On the left of the screen, you can see the list of participants (right now, I am the only one listed) and the agenda that shows the list of slides we will look at and talk about in this class session. You can also see in the main part of the screen the notice what Distance Education wants to show up first when students first log in–in this case, reminders about some of the most popular features to remember.

In Figure 3, we see the first slide of the session that we are presenting. In Figure 4, the whiteboard has been opened and we can see the task bar for the whiteboard commands.

In Figure 5, we are now in the presenter's interface, and we can see the button to click on to manage the agenda items (the one with the folders in it), the one to share an application (a hand offering a folder), the button to create a survey (the question mark), the globe to open a Web Safari, the button to open the whiteboard, the button to break out into groups, and the red button to stop the session.

In Figure 6, we have opened the Web Safari and are visiting the UT Libraries' home page. Notice that the screen that was showing the PowerPoint slides has reduced to show only the leaders, the participants, the agenda and a few basic commands. But it does have the ability with the drop-down lists to change the size of the screen.

The students are now able to see everything I click on, making a fabulous way to show catalog features, database searches, and many other things we would not be able to picture as well without the benefit of this software.

APPENDIX

FIGURE 1

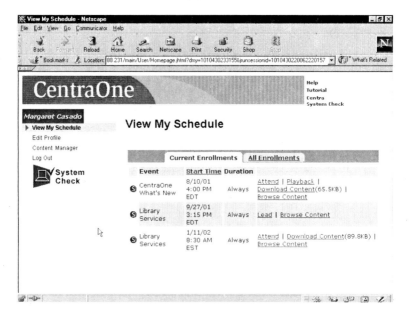

FIGURE 2

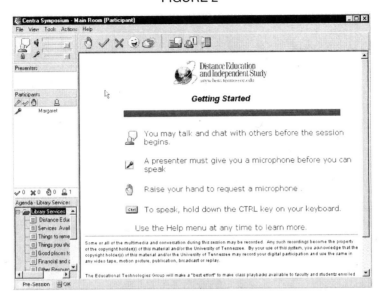

FIGURE 3

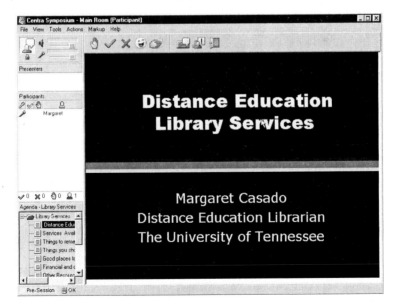

APPENDIX (continued)

FIGURE 4

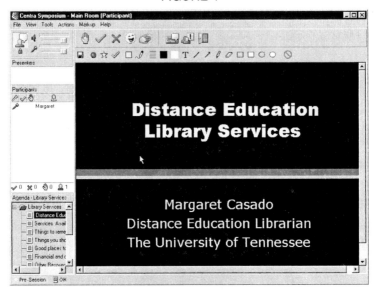

FIGURE 5

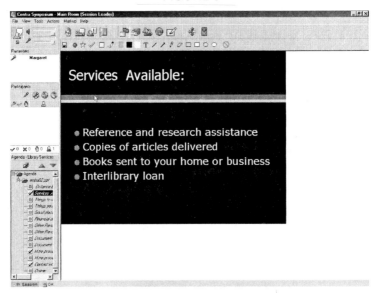

FIGURE 6

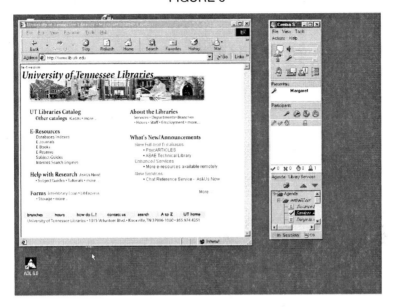

Increasing Document Delivery
to Off-Campus Students
Through an Interdepartmental Partnership

Anne Marie Casey
Pamela A. Grudzien

Central Michigan University

SUMMARY. At Central Michigan University, two separate departments in the Libraries have historically handled library services to distance learning and on-campus students. In 1999, Off-Campus Library Services and Interlibrary Loan (ILL) partnered to provide additional services to off-campus students through the on-campus ILL department. In this paper, the authors discuss the procedures, budget, successes and challenges of this interdepartmental cooperation.

KEYWORDS. Distance learners, library services, document delivery, cooperation

Central Michigan University (CMU) has been providing courses and degree programs to off-campus students throughout North America for over 30 years. Early on, a separate library department was formed to deliver library services to off-campus students and faculty. This resulted in the CMU Libraries having two distinct and exclusive public service areas. Over the years, these areas worked independently and were funded out of different budgets.

[Haworth co-indexing entry note]: "Increasing Document Delivery to Off-Campus Students Through an Interdepartmental Partnership." Casey, Anne Marie, and Pamela A. Grudzien. Co-published simultaneously in *Journal of Library Administration* (The Haworth Information Press, an imprint of The Haworth Press, Inc.) Vol. 37, No. 1/2, 2002, pp. 137-145; and: *Distance Learning Library Services: The Tenth Off-Campus Library Services Conference* (ed: Patrick B. Mahoney) The Haworth Information Press, an imprint of The Haworth Press, Inc., 2002, pp. 137-145.

http://www.haworthpress.com/store/product.asp?sku=J111
10.1300/J111v37n01_13

Unlike many academic libraries that provide services to distance learners and local learners out of the same public services departments, there was little or no service cooperation between the on and off-campus departments at CMU, although the staffs of both services have always cooperated in collection development. Students in the off-campus programs have been viewed as a separate constituency at CMU and have been served by a library program that evolved to fit their unique needs.

Off-Campus Library Services (OCLS) was formed in 1976 to serve the library needs of students and faculty in courses taught off-campus through CMU's College of Extended Learning (CEL). Since 1971, CEL has been delivering degree programs, certificate programs and professional development courses to approximately 12,000 students in over 60 locations throughout the U.S., Canada, and Mexico. Outside Michigan the two major degrees are a Master of Science in Administration (MSA) and a Master of Arts in Education (MAE). Within the state, in addition to those degrees, over 50% of the students are enrolled in undergraduate programs. Through the Distance and Distributed Learning (DDL) department, Web-based courses are offered to students worldwide and include a Doctor of Audiology degree and a Doctor of Health Services Administration degree (scheduled to begin in 2002) in addition to the other degree programs mentioned. Courses taught through CEL are primarily offered in a concentrated format. Most classes meet on alternate weekends for six weeks or on weeknights for six, eight or nine weeks.

CEL offers degree programs at centers in metropolitan areas, most notably, Detroit, Washington, D.C., Atlanta and Kansas City. Students in cities have the option of using local academic and public libraries that are open to local users. However, many of the CEL programs are offered in remote areas and on military bases where the students might have to travel for more than an hour to a library with collections sufficient enough to support the needs of the programs. Because of the variety and number of locations where CEL delivers programs, it would be difficult for CMU to contract with local libraries to provide services for the off-campus students as many other academic institutions have done for their distance learners. OCLS was designed to provide all library services to CMU off-campus learners.

OCLS is made up of three separate departments—reference and instruction, document delivery, and copyright services. All services are accessed through a toll-free phone number, a toll-free fax number, email, or forms on the OCLS Web site.

Six reference librarians travel to the required research classes of all of the MSA and MAE students and to classes in the other degree programs, which require research, to conduct library instruction classes. These classes include instruction on all OCLS services. For online classes, instruction is done by chat.

The librarians also provide reference assistance 52 hours a week by telephone, email, and chat.

The copyright office works with faculty members to obtain copyright permission on all print materials that are required for classes. The required items are reproduced in coursepacks that are sold to students through the bookstore used by CEL.

The Document Delivery Office (DDO) is responsible for taking requests for library materials from off-campus students and faculty and shipping them out within 24-48 hours of the request. The DDO staff loan books from the CMU Libraries to students for 30 or 42 days depending on their location within or outside the continental U.S. They also retrieve articles from the Libraries' collections and send them by mail, fax or electronically to students. Telephones are open 71 hours a week and students can also make requests through fax, email and forms on the OCLS web site.

The Interlibrary Loan Office (ILL) is a part of the Libraries' Collection Development department. ILL has two service sections. One part is responsible for filling borrowing requests for on-campus students, faculty and staff as well as for off-campus students. The other part responds to lending requests from other libraries in Michigan, the United States, and worldwide. CMU Libraries' material has been lent to libraries as far away as Australia and Indonesia. The office uses the latest electronic advances in ILL service–ARIEL and Prospero software–to send and receive digitized images via the Internet and to make these images accessible for each user at a World Wide Web address. Using these transmission methods in conjunction with a sophisticated ILL management system called CLIO has reduced ILL turn-around time.

In recent years with the advent of electronic full-text, all academic libraries have wrestled with the issue of "access versus ownership." The Dean of the CMU Libraries responded to this issue by actively promoting ILL service. ILL's move into electronic transmission was enthusiastically supported. In 1994, the Dean mandated that a portion of the acquisitions budget underwrite the cost of purchasing documents from commercial vendors who provide fast turn-around. As a result of this, ILL has a document-purchasing budget of about $100,000 each year.

Off-campus students make requests for library materials by toll-free phone, toll-free fax, email or request forms on the OCLS Web site. As they are received, the requests are entered into a database under the student's name and coded for the date and hour in which they are entered. Students are allowed to request up to 50 items per week. Each request is printed onto a form as soon as it is entered into the database. Each request is checked by a DDO student assistant or staff member to see if the item is in the CMU Libraries' print collections. Student assistants gather those that appear in CENTRA, the Libraries' online catalog. Book requests, which generally average approximately 15% of the overall requests, are routed to one DDO staff member who checks out the books to the students and processes them for shipping. Articles are photocopied by student assistants and processed for mailing or electronic sending by a staff member.

Up until 1999, the process ended at this point. Students were informed of requests that were not filled and were advised by OCLS librarians that they had the option of requesting items not owned by CMU through ILL. However, this was generally not a viable alternative for students whose classes were held in a compressed format and who required materials in two to three weeks. Traditional ILL processes through the U.S. mail or UPS could take sometimes up to six weeks to be filled. Most students chose not to try ILL. The best solutions for them were to look for other sources or try to locate the materials they needed at local libraries in their own communities. The exceptions to this were the off-campus students enrolled in MSA 685, the research and analysis course, in which students have up to one year to complete a final integrative project. They generally did not have the time constraints of the compressed courses and could take advantage of ILL service for their research.

Document delivery has been an important and busy OCLS service since the beginning. Off-campus students often take courses in remote locations with little access to other library services. CMU serves these students with library resources from the campus library collections and ships the items directly to any address the students provide. The first six months that OCLS was in existence, the DDO processed 545 requests for library materials. The number of requests from students grew yearly until they peaked in the 1993-94 fiscal year, when the department processed 110,046 requests. The number of requests began to fall off steadily as the CMU Libraries made full-text articles available to students through the Internet. As more online journals were made available, the number of requests continued to decline yearly. In FY 2000-2001, the number of DDO requests was 46,274.

Along with the decreasing requests, OCLS began to see an increase in the number of requests that were unfilled. In FY1993-94, the fill rate was 75%. (The fill rate is the percentage of requests that are sent to the student or faculty member within the stipulated timeframe.) By FY 1998-99, it had decreased to 60.44%. Most of this increase in unfilled requests has been attributed to the fact that many of the periodicals that were in the CMU Libraries' print collections were now accessible in electronic format through the OCLS Web site. Students were able to retrieve many of the articles they needed from the OCLS Web site and turned to OCLS only for the articles that were not readily available.

Throughout its history, one of the largest challenges that the DDO faced in filling requests was a gap in the Libraries' collections corresponding to courses taught off-campus. The degree programs that are taken off-campus by CEL normally are also taught on campus. The CMU Libraries' bibliographers ensure that the collections in the Libraries support the courses being taught on campus. In addition, OCLS has historically had an acquisitions budget with which they have maintained subscriptions to a variety of periodicals most requested by off-campus students and have added to the monograph collections whenever possible.

However, there are areas in which students off-campus have a need for specific publications that would not be collected by the Libraries because they do not support the on-campus curricula. In particular, health care and nursing journals especially are in high demand by off-campus students who are pursuing the MSA degree with a concentration in health services administration. Over the years, there arose significant subject areas, which the CMU Libraries did not ever anticipate growing, but which received substantial numbers of requests from students. In addition, the OCLS acquisitions budget was never large enough to maintain periodical subscriptions in all of these areas. For requests that OCLS could not fill, students were referred to local libraries in their areas or to Interlibrary Loan (ILL) if they had six weeks or more to wait for the articles. (Until 1998, OCLS librarians compiled lists of local libraries open to the public near most of the program centers so students would be aware of libraries they could use if OCLS could not supply the materials.)

From October 1993 to February 1995, OCLS partnered with ILL to pilot a project that would raise the OCLS fill rate by 1.16% over the trial period. Requests for articles that could not be supplied from the CMU Libraries' collections were submitted to ILL to be obtained from the CARL UNCOVER database where a deposit account for OCLS had been set up. The project ended in 1995 when its funding allocation had been expended and could not be replenished due to budget constraints (Grudzien and Jones, 1995). Although the positive results for students were short-lived, the trial opened the door to partnerships with other library departments that OCLS had not considered before.

In 1999, an OCLS survey of the electronic journals that the CMU Libraries subscribed to or licensed revealed that a significant number were available that were not in the print periodical collections, which OCLS had always searched exclusively to fill student requests. A new position in OCLS was proposed and approved. In March 1999 a staff member was hired for the DDO who was responsible for searching the electronic collections for article requests that were not in the print collection. This resulted in an average increase in the monthly fill rate of about 4%.

In the spring of 1999 another significant change was made in the department. The DDO had tracked requests on a proprietary database that had been developed by a former student assistant. By the end of 1998, the database was starting to fail and no one in the library was able to correct the problems. The person who had done the original programming was no longer available. In late 1998, the position of Director of OCLS became vacant and during the period of the search process for a new director, the Head of Collection Development and one of the OCLS librarians were appointed interim co-supervisors of the department. The Head of Collection Development supervised the DDO. Rather than create a new proprietary database, which may have been the decision of the Director of OCLS, she suggested that OCLS move the request-taking database to CLIO software, which was being used by ILL. OCLS agreed to this change and began a closer working relationship with ILL during the training process for the new database. ILL staff worked with DDO staff to assist them with their new procedures both during the transition and in the first few months working with CLIO. This close contact enabled the two staffs to understand better what services the other provided.

Shortly after the new Director of OCLS began in the summer of 1999, the manager of ILL suggested a new trial partnership with OCLS to assist off-campus students to retrieve articles from periodicals not owned in any of CMU's collections. She had collected statistics that showed that over 90% of articles requested through ILL were received within a three-week time period. This represented a significant change over the past when articles could take four to six weeks to come in through ILL. Most articles were now received within the tight timeframe that off-campus students needed to do research for their compressed classes.

The two departments decided to set up a trial period beginning on November 15, 1999 that would be assessed near the end of the fiscal year in May or June of 2000. OCLS would monitor the "not-needed after date" (the last date a students determined that the requested material could be mailed in time for their use) of every unfilled request. Those that had a window of three weeks or more were sent to ILL to be filled. ILL offered to pay any costs that resulted from the OCLS requests for the trial period.

A new step was added to the DDO request processing procedure. After the print and electronic collections are checked for periodical requests, all of those not filled that have a "not needed after date" of three weeks or more are photocopied and carried to ILL. The students are sent a copy of the request that has a note explaining that the DDO will attempt to retrieve the article through ILL within their specified timeframe. One DDO staff member is designated to have the responsibility of carrying the requests to ILL daily and checking for articles that have been received.

No new steps in the ILL request processing procedure were needed. Off-campus requests are handled in the same manner as all other borrowing requests. However, the number of requests the ILL office processes has increased significantly in large part due to this partnership. In 1999 the total number of borrowing requests was 19,476. In 2000, ILL borrowing requests increased to 23,846–a 22% increase. While ILL staff has noticed the increase in demand, new ILL technologies and a highly responsive and sophisticated software system have helped them efficiently manage this increase.

Although they no longer needed to request articles be obtained through ILL if the CMU Libraries did not own them, OCLS advertised the new procedure widely to off-campus students. Students had a tendency to give small timeframes for requests to be processed because they were under the mistaken impression that the longer timeframe they gave OCLS to send out the items, the longer it would take OCLS to process them. The OCLS staff embarked on a marketing campaign to convince students that it would be in their best interest to be honest about the length of time that they had to receive materials in a timely manner. OCLS always processes requests within a 24-48 hour time period and sends all requests they find in the libraries' collections out immediately. The DDO started sending flyers out with every envelope of filled requests announcing the new partnership with ILL. Information on the new procedure was available on the OCLS Web site and sent out to the CEL program administrators who worked directly with the students. The OCLS librarians explained the new process to students in instruction classes and in the first few months of the new partnership, received a great deal of feedback from students in those classes who were very pleased with the positive changes in the number of articles they were receiving. In particular, the health services administration students spoke out in classes about the significant increases in the number of requests they were receiving. Their success helped to convince fellow students to give lengthier "not needed after dates."

In the spring of 2000 representatives of OCLS and ILL met again to assess the program's success. From the point of view of OCLS, it was an unqualified success. The fill rate had increased by 12% in FY 1999-2000 over FY 1998-1999. The statistics showed that 63.7% of the requests were received within 7 days and 93.1% were received within 15 days by ILL. The ILL department had processed 1,499 requests for OCLS in 1999 and 6,334 in 2000. Students and CEL staff were so pleased with the increased fill rate that OCLS saw no way to discontinue the program. The greatest challenge that OCLS had was to find money in the budget to fund the program if ILL were not able to continue the funding. At the meeting, the Head of Collection Development agreed to commit ILL funds to the OCLS program for the next fiscal year.

In the spring of 2001, representatives of both departments met again to assess the program. The fill rate at the end of FY 2000-2001 was up an additional 2% to 74.39% from the start in November 1999. This was almost back to the fill rate of FY 1993-1994. The time that it takes to receive ILL requests had decreased significantly so the representatives of both departments decided to change the "not needed after date" window for ILL requests to two weeks from three. The Head of Collection Development agreed to fund the OCLS program for one more fiscal year.

It is a possibility that in the future, the funding of the OCLS/ILL program will no longer be able to come from the ILL budget. OCLS is unlikely to discontinue the partnership because it has added so significantly to service to CMU's off-campus students. If OCLS does take over the funding in FY 2002-2003, it is likely that some changes will take place. The most obvious may be to establish a budget for the ILL requests out of the OCLS acquisitions budget and to put a limit on the cost OCLS is willing to pay per article. These changes will limit the requests filled through ILL to a small degree while still maintaining the service for most of the requests.

There are a few challenges for this partnership in the near future. The ILL office has been moving toward paperless ILL. This will mean that requests submitted on paper forms soon will be the exception rather than the rule. DDO and ILL will be investigating ways to transmit off-campus students' requests electronically to ILL. The two services use request management software from the same company (CLIO). Although DDO uses a version that is adapted for a document fulfillment service rather than both lending and borrowing services as ILL does, it may be possible that the basic software functions existing in the two versions may be able to communicate and transmit requests between one another. A perennial challenge is budgeting. Changes in the state and national economies may cause a reordering of acquisitions budget priorities. It is unlikely that the enhanced service involving ILL will be stopped. The statistics show it is much too important and popular. It will be a challenge to determine the best ways to support equitable access for all CMU students, on and off campus.

The benefits of this partnership have been many. The most obvious is the increase in service to off-campus students. Additional advantages are the closer working relationship of the DDO and ILL and improved communication between OCLS and other departments in the Libraries. DDO and ILL staffs feel they are filling a large gap by meeting the information needs of a significant CMU student population. Historically OCLS had been isolated from other Libraries' departments. Since 1999, the DDO staff has worked with the ILL staff to learn and adapt the CLIO database to OCLS request taking and to establish electronic sending of articles to students. In December 2001, the DDO and ILL departments moved into adjoining offices in the renovated library building. This proximity should lead to future partnerships that will benefit both students and staff at CMU.

The success of this partnership has also opened the door to other partnerships between OCLS and other Libraries' departments. In the spring of 2001 a joint library committee decided to purchase chat software that would be used for reference and library instruction by librarians in OCLS, the Reference Services Department, and the Clarke Historical Library. Funds for the chat software came from the Libraries and the OCLS budgets. Later that year, OCLS and Reference Services began a discussion on services to students who took classes off-campus that were not delivered through CEL and reached some decisions on new and better ways to serve these students as a joint reference group.

As the distinctions between traditional on- and off-campus students become smaller, OCLS will most likely move closer to the other CMU Libraries' departments in its provision of services to CMU students. The success of the partnership with ILL makes this a welcome new chapter in the history of OCLS.

REFERENCE

Grudzien, P., and Jones, M. (1995). Internal partnerships for external sourcing: Interlibrary loan as supplier-provider for off-campus students. In C. Jacob (Comp.), *Proceedings of the 7th Off-Campus Library Services Conference*. Mt. Pleasant: Central Michigan University.

Fair Is Fair, or Is It?
Library Services to Distance Learners

Anne Marie Casey

Central Michigan University

Sheri Sochrin

Springfield College

Stephanie Fazenbaker Race

Northeast Florida Library Information Network

SUMMARY. Librarians from the Florida Distance Learning Reference and Referral Center, a statewide reference service, Central Michigan University, a public university, and Springfield College, a private college, discuss the issues surrounding the provision of library services to distance learners. The panel shares the challenges and success of serving a distant clientele within their different institutional settings.

KEYWORDS. Distance learners, library services, integration, issues

Serving the needs of distance students has been a growing concern of libraries for many years. The ACRL *Guidelines for Distance Learning Library Services* state that "institutions of higher education must meet the needs of all their faculty, students, and academic support staff, wherever these individuals are located" (Association of College & Research Libraries, 2000). Libraries have approached this in a variety of ways depending on their resources. This paper explores the way three different types of institutions–a state-sponsored, refer-

[Haworth co-indexing entry note]: "Fair Is Fair, or Is It? Library Services to Distance Learners." Casey, Anne Marie, Sheri Sochrin, and Stephanie Fazenbaker Race. Co-published simultaneously in *Journal of Library Administration* (The Haworth Information Press, an imprint of The Haworth Press, Inc.) Vol. 37, No. 1/2, 2002, pp. 147-161; and: *Distance Learning Library Services: The Tenth Off-Campus Library Services Conference* (ed: Patrick B. Mahoney) The Haworth Information Press, an imprint of The Haworth Press, Inc., 2002, pp. 147-161.

http://www.haworthpress.com/store/product.asp?sku=J111
10.1300/J111v37n01_14

ral center, a medium-sized public university and a small private college–have approached these challenges.

FLORIDA DISTANCE LEARNING REFERENCE & REFERRAL CENTER

The Florida Distance Learning Reference & Referral Center (RRC) was created in the fall of 1997 as a part of the Florida Distance Learning Library Initiative (DLLI). DLLI has received funding from the state of Florida to provide library support to distance learners at Florida's ten state universities and 28 community colleges using a five-tiered approach. The five components of the Initiative are provision of electronic resources which have included approximately 50 FirstSearch databases which are available to distance learners from remote locations; a reciprocal borrowing that allows Community College System (CCS) and State University System (SUS) students access to CCS and SUS library collections; a courier which provides delivery of print materials to libraries across Florida; and centralized research assistance and library instruction.

The University of South Florida (USF) received the grant to operate the RRC and the services were located in the USF Tampa Campus Library. The RRC's services were designed to complement, but not replace, the services provided by the distance learner's home institution.

Distance learning courses in Florida are taught via a variety of methods, including face-to-face at off-campus locations, online via the Internet, live satellite broadcasts to remote sites, audio- and videotape, and traditional correspondence. Though the Florida Virtual Campus exists to assist in providing affordable access to quality distance learning opportunities and services in a cooperative atmosphere, Florida has not yet created a comprehensive master listing of distance learning courses or faculty.

Service Strategies–How We Provide Reference, Instruction, Document Delivery, etc.

Florida's Reference & Referral Center was charged with providing reference and instruction. Initially, reference service was provided using a toll-free phone, email, fax, and a Webform. In April of 2000, the RRC initiated an online chat service, RRC*hat*, which was used for both reference and instruction. Librarians assisted distance learners with every aspect of the research question, from technical issues relating to off-site access of electronic resources to creating successful search strategies, to obtaining the materials located during the search process.

The RRC was not funded or staffed to provide document delivery. RRC staff directed students needing interlibrary loan or document delivery to either their home library or a local public or academic library that was able to fulfill these needs. ILL and document delivery was enhanced by DLLI's courier component. Florida negotiated a contract for a statewide courier system that moves print materials among over 250 participating libraries.

Staffing

The RRC was staffed by five full-time librarians and three part-time graduate assistants from the University of South Florida School of Library and Information Science (USF SLIS). Librarians were responsible for providing research assistance, instruction, creating pathfinders, maintaining the RRC website, and promotion of the RRC's services.

The RRC was open the same hours as its host, the USF Tampa Campus Library, Monday-Thursday from 7:30 a.m. until 1:00 a.m., Friday from 7:30 a.m. until 9:00 p.m., Saturday, 10:00 a.m. until 8:00 p.m., and Sunday from 12:00 p.m. until 1:00 a.m. Distance learners could request assistance 24 hours a day, seven days per week by leaving either a voicemail message if the RRC was closed or submitting an email or Webform. RR*Chat* was open from 8:00 a.m. until 8:00 p.m., Monday-Friday.

Funding

Funding for the reference and referral and instruction components of DLLI originally came as grants of $100,000 and $30,000 respectively from the state in 1997-98. In 1998-99 funding for DLLI was appropriated strictly for electronic resources with no mention of the Reference & Referral Center. Savings from vacated positions and a $70,000 grant from the Florida Public Post-secondary Distance Learning Institute covered most expenses until a grant of $245,800 was received from the Florida Distance Learning Network.

In 2001-2002, funding for the DLLI project was dispersed directly to the community colleges and they made the decision not to fund all aspects of the DLLI project. Because of limited funds available, it was determined that each institution would be responsible for serving their distance learners and that the RRC would operate until December 2001 on funds remaining from the 2000-2001 fiscal year. During the final months of operation, the RRC's hours were reduced monthly as staff found employment elsewhere.

Library Instruction

Instruction is critical to distance learners. Because many of them never actually have the opportunity to visit their home institution campus, much less the library, frequently they have no idea of the multitude of resources and services that are available to them. The RRC offered distance learning faculty a variety of instructional opportunities, including: face-to-face instruction wherever they met, online instruction in either RR*Chat* or their courseware chat room, broadcast instruction, online pathfinders designed to meet the needs of individual course requirements, brochures, handbooks, and user-aids for individual resources.

Instruction led by an RRC librarian covered a variety of topics, depending on the research needs of the group. All workshops covered services available from the RRC but also included information about services available from the student's home institution.

Early on the RRC decided that the best way to publicize its services to students was to conduct face-to-face instruction, either at their off-campus class meeting or during an orientation. Because time is so valuable for many instructors, the RRC was willing to take whatever time was allowed, from 20 minutes to 2 hours. Any time the RRC conducted an instruction session students received a brochure describing how they could get library services from both the RRC and their home institution.

Advocacy

The unfortunate thing for many distance learners is that they are unaware of the services guaranteed them by ACRL DLS Guidelines. The Reference & Referral Center worked with a variety of groups to advocate for needed services for distance learners. These included the ability to obtain a library card without coming to campus. Access to many services hinge on having a library card number that validates a student. Other access issues included the need for remote access to databases, which for the state university libraries meant the need for a proxy server. Also essential to research needs were reciprocal borrowing arrangements and document delivery, preferably direct to the student's home.

Challenges

One of the RRC's biggest challenges was promotion of services to distance learners. Florida does not maintain a list of distance learning classes, faculty or students so the RRC was forced to create a list each semester. This list was then used to send promotional material to distance learning faculty. Because the RRC did not belong to one specific institution, it was also harder to "sell" the service. Precariousness of funding was always an issue for the RRC and made it difficult to plan for future services.

Successes

Though the RRC was closed in December 2001, the project saw many successes that are evidenced by the national recognition the RRC received during its operation. Several projects undergone by the RRC, but most notably the use of RR*Chat* for instruction, have served as models for libraries and students enrolled in library schools around the country.

Each year distance learners' use of the RRC for research assistance steadily increased, as did the number of faculty responding to mailings for instructional support for their courses. The response to the User Satisfaction Survey administered by the RRC was always very favorable and indicated the need for increased awareness of library services available to distance learners.

CENTRAL MICHIGAN UNIVERSITY

Overview

Central Michigan University (CMU) is a public university in Michigan that serves approximately 19,000 students on-campus and an additional 12,000 off-campus annually. CMU is a doctoral/research university located in Mt. Pleasant at the center of the lower peninsula of Michigan.

CMU has been offering degrees at a distance through the Extended Degree Programs of the College of Extended Learning (CEL) since 1971. Degree programs are available at over 60 centers and cohort locations throughout the United States, Canada, and Mexico. In addition, online and print-based learning package courses and degrees are available nationally and internationally through the Distance and Distributed Learning (DDL) division of CEL.

Courses offered at program centers and in cohorts are taught in classrooms by campus or adjunct faculty. All of the classroom courses are offered in a compressed format. Many are taught on weekends over a six-week period. Others are taught on weeknights over six, eight or nine weeks. DDL courses are taught through the World Wide Web and through print-based learning packages.

Master's degrees in administration and education make up the bulk of degree offerings in the classroom programs outside Michigan. Within the state, more than 50% of the students are enrolled in undergraduate completion programs, with most of the remainder enrolled in the master's in administration or education. DDL offers all of these programs as well as an online doctoral degree in audiology.

In 1976, CEL instituted a library service to work exclusively with students taking courses off-campus. The department, Off-Campus Library Services (OCLS), resides in the CMU Libraries but has a reporting and strong working relationship with CEL.

Service Strategies and Staffing

OCLS is a centralized library service designed to provide all library services to CMU students enrolled through the College of Extended Learning at CMU. It is a separate unit within the CMU Libraries and is responsible only for services to off-campus students.

Reference is provided by telephone, email, fax, and chat. Librarians alternate shifts on call for any requests that come in by telephone, email or fax during the assigned period. Chat reference is handled in separate reference shifts. Librarians assist students with research by discussing search strategy and suggesting appropriate databases and search terminology, as well as trouble-shooting technical problems that occur during students' use of the OCLS Web site. Librarians also answer ready reference questions and do database searches for students and faculty on request. Most questions are answered within 24 hours of the request.

The Document Delivery Office (DDO) processes requests for library materials for off-campus students. Students may request up to 50 items per week by toll-free phone, toll-free fax, email, or by using forms on the OCLS Website. Most items are processed for sending within 24 hours.

OCLS also has a copyright staff that obtains permissions to use any materials required by faculty that are copyrighted. In addition, OCLS maintains a web site that was designed by the OCLS staff and is constantly improved to provide more materials and better access for the students.

Staffing

OCLS has a staff of seven librarians, six and one-half FTE support staff, and 12-15 student assistants. Three librarians, five and one-half of the support staff members and all of the student assistants are based in the CMU campus library. One librarian is located in CEL Detroit regional office, the Washington regional office, the Atlanta regional office and the Kansas City program center. In addition, half-time reference assistants are located with the librarians in the Detroit and Atlanta offices.

In the fall of 2001, reference assistance was available on Mondays from 8:00 a.m. to 9:00 p.m., Tuesdays through Thursdays from 8:00 a.m. to 6:00 p.m., and Fridays from 8:00 a.m. to 5:00 p.m. The DDO was open Mondays through Thursdays from 8:00 a.m. to 9:00 p.m., Fridays from 8:00 a.m. to 5:00 p.m., Saturdays from 9:00 a.m., to 6:00 p.m., and Sundays from noon to 9:00 p.m. The copyright service was available from 7:30 a.m. to 4:00 p.m., Monday through Friday. All hours are in Eastern Time.

Historically, the primary means of contact with OCLS has been by telephone. In 1977, the first toll-free number was set up for students in Ohio. Over the years, one toll-free number was available for all student contact to the OCLS departments in the main library. Students contacted librarians in other offices through separate toll-free numbers or by calling collect. In January 2000, all calls began to be routed into one toll-free number that rings into the DDO. Reference calls are transferred to librarians on duty, regardless of the office in which they are working.

In 1997, OCLS launched its first Web site, <www.lib.cmich.edu/ocls>, which included forms for ordering library materials as well as an "ask a librarian" form for reference questions. In 2001, OCLS introduced a new Web site, <ocls.cmich.edu>, in which the "ask a librarian" link was moved to the home page. Both forms generate requests for assistance on a daily basis. All document delivery requests go into one departmental email address, which is monitored by a designated document delivery staff member. Reference requests go into a departmental email account, which is monitored by the librarian on reference duty. In addition, the email addresses to both departmental accounts are freely available to students and requests are frequently sent directly to them.

OCLS encourages the students to send document delivery requests in by fax. Fax cover sheets, which include spaces for all of the necessary contact information are given out in all packets that go to students. In addition, OCLS has a toll-free fax number for the students' use. Since students are allowed to make up to 50 requests per week, fax is often the most efficient way to send and receive a large number of requests.

Funding

The College of Extended Learning funds OCLS. CEL is a self-supporting unit within Central Michigan University. CEL has been generous with the OCLS budget throughout the library service's 25-year history. Money has been available for librarians to travel to each program center at least once a year and to every cohort group once in order to do library instruction. In addition, OCLS has generally had the funds necessary to upgrade equipment on a regular basis and to purchase laptop computers and projectors for all of the librarians to use for their instruction classes.

Since November 1999, OCLS has also received financial assistance from the Libraries' budget. OCLS submits a large number of requests to the Inter-Library Loan (ILL) department daily. All fees are paid out of the ILL account.

Instruction

At CMU, students enrolled through CEL rarely live close to Mt. Pleasant, Michigan, so almost no instruction is given in the campus library. The majority of library instruction is done face-to-face in the off-campus classrooms. Students enrolled in the Master of Science in Administration (MSA) degree and the Master of Arts in Education (MAE) degree all take a required research class. Off-campus librarians travel to the classroom locations to teach a library instruction class that lasts from one to three hours, depending on the availability of computer labs. At the time of the research class instruction sessions, librarians also visit any other classes being offered at the CEL center at the same time to give a 20-minute library update. In addition, librarians conduct instruction classes during the first course of a graduate cohort in other disciplines and in many of the undergraduate classes with specific research assignments.

In some locations, librarians have conducted library instruction classes in the military libraries on bases where classes are held. In addition, some cohorts, who are affiliated with businesses that have in-house libraries, such as hospitals, have opened their libraries for instruction or tours.

In 2000, the librarian responsible for instruction to DDL students began to offer library instruction via chat to students in the research classes and in other classes with research assignments.

Advocacy

As electronic databases and journals became more accessible, OCLS librarians worked with colleagues in the main library to identify database providers that would ensure equal access to on- and off-campus students. Off-campus students were initially provided with passwords to gain access to the licensed databases. As new vendors were added, a remote authentication script was created that would verify a unique student PIN number to give students access to the databases. In the summer of 1999, a commercial proxy server was mounted on the OCLS Web site in an effort to make remote authentication simpler. The opposite occurred because many major Internet access providers were not compatible with proxy servers. In 2001, OCLS in cooperation with the CMU Libraries agreed to test a new proxy server created by the commercial vendor.

Because OCLS was originally created to offer complete library services to off-campus students, it has not set up reciprocal borrowing arrangements or outsourced any of its services. However, the librarians have historically developed relationships with librarians on the military bases where CMU offers courses. This has provided venues for library instruction on many occasions and also afforded students access to collections of military publications that were not available through the CMU Libraries.

In late 1999, OCLS partnered with ILL in the main library to increase the fill rate for document delivery by sending requests for items not owned to ILL. By July of 2001, the fill rate for document delivery had increased by 14%.

Challenges

In recent years, one of the greatest challenges has been providing remote access through a proxy server that is difficult for many students to set up. The difficulties have caused the librarians to believe they were working at a help desk rather than as part of a reference service. These difficulties have also intimidated students who began to look elsewhere for library assistance.

A significant challenge over the years has been to reach the students to teach them about the library services. OCLS has been in a better position than many library services because it provides library instruction in one class required of most master's degree students. Ideally, students are expected to take the required course among their first three. However, many defer it to the end of their programs so have little exposure to OCLS, other than a welcome letter from the librarian when they register. Different ideas have been posed and tried over the years to reach students in a timelier manner. These include orientation sessions in the metropolitan areas, packets distributed to new students, as well as online presentations and handouts given to students by CEL staff members. They have all succeeded to some degree but have not allowed for a system-wide change in alerting students about library services at the beginning of their programs.

Another perennial challenge has been the hours that reference assistance is available. All but one OCLS staff member works in the Eastern Time Zone. The West Regional Librarian is located in the Central Time Zone. CEL has program centers and cohorts operating from Boston to Honolulu and from Vancouver, Canada to Guadalajara, Mexico. This creates up to a six-hour time difference between OCLS and many of the students it serves.

Until the summer of 2000, OCLS reference hours were Monday to Friday from 8:00 to 5:00. Since then, there have been increases to 9:00 p.m. on Mondays and to 6:00 p.m. from Tuesday through Thursday. Further increases with current staffing levels are difficult because most of the OCLS librarians travel for instruction on the weekend and several also conduct instructional sessions on weeknights.

Communication has been a minor challenge because of the decentralized reference unit. In the early 1990s an electronic list was created for OCLS. It has always been one of the busiest lists at CMU. OCLS staff uses it to conduct business, discuss issues, make decisions, share information and questions about current work for students, and provide a social forum to some degree. In addition, the department has staff meetings by conference call every two weeks and an annual staff meeting in Mt. Pleasant for several days.

Successes

The major success of OCLS has been its ability to provide quality library services to students all over North America for the past 25 years. Many of the CEL program centers and cohorts have been located in remote parts of North America with little access to research collections. OCLS has responded to student needs by being flexible with services and using any means at the staff's disposal to ensure that students received the research assistance and materials they needed in the fastest possible manner. One of the hallmarks of OCLS has been to listen to the complaints and suggestions of CEL students, faculty, and staff in order to continuously improve.

SPRINGFIELD COLLEGE

Overview

Springfield College is a small private college with the main campus located in Springfield, Massachusetts. Besides the main campus there are eight other campuses, known as the remote campuses, each of which has some administrative space, some classroom space and at least a few terminals linked into the campus network. All students at these campuses (plus some at the main campus) are part of the School of Human Services (SHS), an adult education program offering both undergraduate and graduate degrees in human services. With the exception of one campus that is experimenting with evening classes, all SHS classes are on the weekends and most classes run all day. Individual courses generally meet four times, one weekend day a month for four consecutive months. In between class sessions students may not be on campus at all and many may live quite far away. Of the College's approximately 5,000 students approximately 1,500 are in the School of Human Services at the remote campuses.

Service Strategies and Staffing

Babson Library, the College's library, is located at the main campus in Springfield, MA. Remote students can do their research using the network of databases that the Library maintains. All databases are accessible while on each campus through the Library's Web pages and, wherever possible, they are also accessible from off-campus. Since the Library does not have a proxy server, some databases whose vendors restrict access by IP range are only available on campus. Students needing help with their research can contact the Library by phone (800 number or regular number), by fax, by e-mail or via a special Reference Question Web form. The Library's Web pages also provide a few Web tutorials and some answers to technical questions to help them get started. Once the students know what items they want, they can submit their requests via an Electronic Interlibrary Loan form–which they may use for items within our collection as well as for items from other libraries. They may also submit their requests via mail, fax, phone or e-mail. Items are sent to them at the address of their choice. These services provide effective ways to make information resources available to our students at the times and places of their choosing.

Springfield College integrates services throughout the Library. One librarian, the Reference and Distance Learning Librarian, has half her time committed to serving the distance students. Besides working on developing new services, she acts as an advocate for, and coordinator of, services for the students at the other campuses. However, the actual services may be provided by other Library staff. For example, all requests for items are sent to the Interlibrary Loan Assistant who fills them from the Library's collection or through Interlibrary Loan, as appropriate. She reports back any issues or problems to Reference and Distance Learning Librarian. Reference services to the remote students work in a similar way. Students contact the Library through phone numbers, e-mail accounts and web forms that go directly to the reference desk. Whichever reference librarian is available handles the question. This method of integrating the services throughout the Library serves to ease the overall workload and maximize the use of limited resources. It also keeps the needs of our remote students alive in the minds of our staff when evaluating, revising or planning services.

Babson Library has seven librarians, nine support staff and forty student assistants. The Library is open 108.5 hours a week, Monday-Thursday 7:30 a.m.-midnight, Friday 7:30 a.m.-10:00 p.m., Saturday 9:00 a.m.-10:00 p.m. and Sunday 9:00 a.m.-midnight. All hours are Eastern Time. The reference desk is staffed all but 2.5 of these hours. The Interlibrary Loan department is staffed from 8-4 Monday to Friday but students can leave messages with their requests at any time, as they can also do with reference questions.

Funding

There is no separate budget or funding for services to remote students. Instead all resources come out of other Library funds. Database subscriptions, which serve our distance students, also serve students at the main campus and come out of the library technology budget line. Salaries for student employees who fill item requests fall under the student employee budget, and those students fill requests from both remote and local students. Like the provision of services, this method of spreading the financial demands throughout the Library eases the burden on any one part of the Library's budget. However it does make it harder to respond to any specific needs of distance students which require separate or special funding.

Another concern is the lack of financial support from the college for services to distance students. In 1994 there were two campuses besides the main campus, both were in New England and they had approximately 400-450 students. In the fall of 2001 there were eight remote campuses, they were spread across the country and they had 1,500 students. In that same time the number of Librarians and support staff has remained the same (although the number of student employee hours has increased) and the budget has, in most years, been level funded or raised by the cost of living. Also, in that time, we (the Library) have increased our hours, reorganized many services and created new services such as a Library Web site, a Web-accessible database network, off-campus access to most databases, e-mail reference, Web forms for reference and interlibrary loan, online tutorials and others. Much of this we did by reorganizing our resources and taking advantage of consortial offerings. While we have done well with the resources available, there have been problems which have been difficult to address because of lack of resources.

Instruction–Our Major Challenge

One key area, and the area of service where we are weakest, is in providing library instruction to the remote students. At one point some of the limited travel/professional development budget was used to allow occasional traveling to another campus for library instruction, but as the numbers of campuses grew and they began to be farther away, this was no longer a possibility. Since we could not get funds to allow for travel and instruction we have spent the intervening years searching for alternative instructional methods. The major methods we have explored are a video, courseware programs, instruction by phone and videoconferencing.

We are looking for two elements in our instruction. One is the actual instruction in using library resources. The other is some sort of face-to-face or live interaction to help build a connection to the Library. (This second point is very important with adult students who may be nervous about research and uncomfortable with computers.) Early on, the Reference and Distance Learning Librarian looked at assorted computer conferencing software. Since financial issues were a concern she looked at free programs. One she considered was NetMeeting but she realized that the reference staff could not depend on public servers while doing instruction, and that the Library was unlikely to be able to get its own a server to support it.

She did create a video that could be used for library instruction, although it lacked the ability to interact with students. Unfortunately the College did not have the best equipment for capturing computer screen images. The video, which took almost a year to make because of the need to edit the video and re-shoot computer images several different ways, ended up with images of computer screens that were fuzzy, if somewhat readable. It was distributed to the campuses with some support from the School of Human Services administration and was accompanied by a letter from the Reference and Distance Learning Librarian suggesting ways to use it, offering to speak with classes via conference phone for follow-up questions and requests for feedback. The offer of speaking with a class via phone was never taken up but we did receive feedback from one class. The major comment was the lack of readability of computer screens. The campuses have not found the video useful and it is now out of date because of changes in the Library's Web pages and updated versions of the database interfaces shown.

The offer of speaking to a class via phone was not new to the video project. The Reference and Distance Learning Librarian had offered this before and still offers it to the remote faculty at least once a year in the letter they receive at the beginning of the academic year. The offer was finally taken up by one adjunct faculty member during the summer semester of 2001. Several classes have now been taught by that method. Feedback from the professor indicated that the students (who take the class in a computer lab), appreciate it very much. However, it is hard to do. The reference librarians instruct from the phone and computer terminals in their offices, and cannot see the class to judge if they are following the discussion/demonstration. The faculty member must routinely provide feedback as to whether the students' terminals have loaded a page and it is difficult to hear any questions asked by the students. Still, it is the first effective instruction we have been able to routinely provide to the campuses in years.

Within the last year the college has acquired a courseware program called Manhattan. The Reference and Distance Learning Librarian looked into it as a possible way to provide instruction from the beginning of the pilot project, which brought it to campus. There are ways we could do a tutorial composed of screen shots (which are already being done more effectively through Web pages), and ways to run asynchronous discussions or chats. However, these functions cannot be used simultaneously. So a class could chat, but not see images or they could see the images but then have to close them and open a different module to ask a question. As such, the software will not solve the problem of providing instruction, although we are still looking at it as a supplementary tool.

What we would like to move into is videoconferencing. A good system should allow us to see and hear the students, let them see and hear us, and also let us do a live demonstration of library resources. It would also allow us to either teach students at multiple campuses simultaneously or teach different classes at geographically separated campuses in a single day. Once again this is something the Library lacks the resources to do on its own. However, we have been advocating to other departments for it for several years. The School of Human Services in particular sees many ways it can be useful to them, and departments that need to interact with the School of Human Services remote campuses may also find it useful. Although not a Library project, the development of videoconferencing facilities are currently in progress and the Library expects to have some use of the facilities for instruction to the remote students when it is completed.

Advocacy and Successes

Other positive developments over the years include the better recognition of the existence and needs of the remote students by the college as a whole. The Library has played some part in this by advocating for the needs of the remote students and by remembering their existence when interacting with the members of other departments. We have also worked with members of the School of Human Services to try to find better ways of providing Library services to their students. One success, which sounds minor but had important implications, was encouraging them to provide student ID cards to all of their students. Once the students had their ID cards they also had their full student ID number, necessary for off-campus access to some databases and for submitting some requests. Both the advocacy of the Library and of the School of Human Services contributed to the current move toward developing videoconferencing. SHS is one of the leaders in this, but the School recognizes how it would help the Library provide better services to its students. Another issue the Library is currently advocating is the acquisition of some method of off-campus authentication so that students would have a simpler way of connecting to the Library's databases. It would also allow us to increase the number of databases available off-campus, would help us get meaningful statistics about who is using them, and could potentially allow us to revamp and expand our E-Reserve system. We are trying to tie it in to the College's current interest in Outcome Assessment. Having statistics about who is using what resources would greatly increase our ability to judge the effectiveness of our instruction and our network. The growing interest in Information Literacy is also giving us a platform to advocate for the regular inclusion of Library instruction in the curriculum of the distance students, as the ability to provide it develops.

CONCLUSION

Libraries that provide service to distance learners face many of the same issues regardless of their organization and funding levels. A common challenge that distance learning library services has is to reach students who may never come to the library and may not understand how essential these services are.

Each library service finds ways to advocate for the off-campus students it serves and to provide the services recommended by the ACRL Guidelines. These differ according to the amount of funding and staff available, the type of support from the parent institution, and the regulations of accrediting bodies, states and parent institutions. But in the end, each library service, in its own way, provides the services it can to its distant learners.

REFERENCE

Association of College and Research Libraries. (2000). *Guidelines for distance learning library services.* Retrieved November 16th, 2001 from Association of College and Research Libraries Web site: http://www.ala.org/acrl/guides/distlrng.html.

Taking the Distance Out of Library Services Offered to International Graduate Students: Considerations, Challenges, and Concerns

Mou Chakraborty
Johanna Tuñón

Nova Southeastern University

SUMMARY. Providing quality library services to distance students is always a challenge, but the advent of an increasing number of international site-based programs and online programs accessed by students around the world raises new considerations, challenges, and concerns about how libraries should be providing services to international students. This presentation will consider the issues and variety of solutions offered by programs at Nova Southeastern University. The library services being discussed in this presentation are for international students in six graduate programs offering site-based instruction in ten countries in Latin America and Europe and three doctoral programs offering online degree programs at Nova Southeastern University. The relative merits of the library solutions implemented for the various types of programs will be evaluated. Issues discussed include (1) setting up local library resource centers and local library agreements, (2) the usefulness of document delivery services such as those offered by the British Library and package courier services such as DHL, (3) providing new technology solutions such as Prospero and ILLiad, (4) telecommunications infrastructure problems in both develop-

[Haworth co-indexing entry note]: "Taking the Distance Out of Library Services Offered to International Graduate Students: Considerations, Challenges, and Concerns." Chakraborty, Mou, and Johanna Tuñón. Co-published simultaneously in *Journal of Library Administration* (The Haworth Information Press, an imprint of The Haworth Press, Inc.) Vol. 37, No. 1/2, 2002, pp. 163-176; and: *Distance Learning Library Services: The Tenth Off-Campus Library Services Conference* (ed: Patrick B. Mahoney) The Haworth Information Press, an imprint of The Haworth Press, Inc., 2002, pp. 163-176.

http://www.haworthpress.com/store/product.asp?sku=J111
10.1300/J111v37n01_15

ing countries and Europe that impact the delivery of library services via the Web, (5) finding cost-effective solutions for bibliographic instruction, (6) ensuring that international students who receive instruction in a language other than English are provided with equivalent library services for reference, instruction, and access to appropriate materials, and (7) understanding and working effectively with other peoples' cultural and political sensibilities. The one challenge for libraries is to work to ensure that international students are provided with equal or equivalent library service solutions to those offered to on-campus students and distance students who live within the United States, particularly when it comes to access to print resources.

KEYWORDS. Library services, international students, distance learners, issues

Nova Southeastern University (NSU) has been a pioneer in distance education since the 1970s, long before distance education had become popularly accepted. Providing quality library services to distance students has always been a challenge for the Library, Research, and Information Technology Center (LRITC) which has been NSU's main library, but the advent of an increasing number of international site-based programs and programs offered online that are accessed by students anywhere in the world raises new considerations, challenges, and concerns about how the NSU main library and libraries in general should provide library services to international students. The challenge is for libraries that provide services for distance students to ensure that the international students receive equivalent services to those offered distance students in the United States and to students attending classes at the main campus. The greater research needs of graduate students makes providing them with equal or equivalent services that are recommended by ACRL (Association of College and Research Libraries) become even more of a challenge when they also happen to live abroad. (See the *Association of College and Research Libraries Guidelines for Distance Learning Library Services* at <http://www.ala.org/acrl/guides/distlrng.html>.) Because NSU's main library provides library services for international students in six graduate site-based programs in ten countries in Latin America and Europe and three doctoral programs offering online degree programs, the issues and solutions developed for NSU programs can serve as a useful case study for others.

BACKGROUND

NSU has extensive experience with delivering graduate programs at international sites. NSU currently offers graduate site-based programs in the Bahamas, Brazil, Canada, China, Dominican Republic, France, Germany, Greece, Jamaica, Panama, and Venezuela and is exploring the possibilities of starting programs in Poland, Trinidad, and Korea. NSU offers these international students a variety of site-based master's and doctoral programs in business and education as well as online graduate degree programs in business, education, computer science, and social sciences.

DOCUMENT DELIVERY

Finding cost-effective methods for providing international students with document delivery services equivalent to services provided to distance students within the United States presents some thorny problems. At NSU, the Library, Research, and Information Technology Center has decided that it will be responsible for ensuring that distance students are provided with the resources to meet students' research needs rather than trying to negotiate contracts with local libraries where site-based classes are offered. In order to meet the research needs of distance students, the library provides all distance students with free document delivery for up to 25 documents per week. These include free photocopying and mailing or faxing of journal articles as well as the mailing of books and free microfiche copies of ERIC ED documents, NSU Major Applied Research Projects (MARPs) and practicums. Doctoral students are also provided with two free copies of non-NSU dissertations. If NSU does not have the requested materials in the university's library collection, these materials are obtained through interlibrary loan, commercial document delivery services, and host agreements with Wayne State University and the University of Michigan at no cost.

Delivering library materials to distance students across international boundaries presents special challenges. The time it takes to get materials via the postal system causes major frustrations for waiting students, particularly in developing countries. Problems getting mailed books through customs in some countries have also raised major difficulties on occasion. To address this problem, NSU uses DHL and FedEx to speed up the delivery of books overseas and provide the books with more security, but this solution has been a costly proposition for the library.

Sending library materials via delivery services like DHL to international sites may sound like an answer to the problem of speed and security, but there was one major problem that NSU had with this solution. NSU is a relatively young institution that has only been in existence for 35 years. As a result, the library collection does not have the retrospective depth that major research libraries normally have to support doctoral programs. In fact, the main library's collection only contains about 300,000 volume book equivalents. NSU negotiated agreements with Wayne State and the University of Michigan in order to provide students with access to these in-depth research collections of millions of books. Moreover, these host libraries had agreed to mail requested books directly to distance students, thereby providing distance students with access to more than 3,000,000 books. The problem was that the host libraries mailed books only to distance students if they lived within the United States and not to NSU's international students. Similarly, NSU could not send books obtained through interlibrary loan to third locations. The result was that the main library could only send books from within its 300,000-volume collection to international students.

In order to address this issue, NSU's main library explored using the British Library as a document delivery supplier for students at international sites, particularly in Europe. The British Library has a very impressive department known as the Document Supply Centre (BLDSC) that provides a rapid document delivery service to individuals and organizations worldwide. (See <http://www.bl.uk/services/bsds/dsc>.) On a trip to London, Paris, and Athens last year, the former Assistant Head of Distance Library Services visited the document delivery department in York and concluded that the British Library's document delivery service might prove very useful in Europe. She learned that NSU had an account through SOLINET (Southeastern Library Network) and could obtain materials from the British Library via that account. The librarian quickly discovered, however, that the problem was that U.S. libraries get charged much higher copyright fees than those in Europe. The British Library suggested that NSU partner with local European academic libraries to get document delivery at more reasonable prices. As a result, the librarian explored the possibilities for getting document delivery for new sites in England, France, and Greece through local partnerships. She was able to easily arrange for students at the Richmond site in England to get document delivery service since British students were eligible to get direct library services from the British Library without any difficulties. Arranging for document delivery in France proved more challenging, however. The partnering library for the Paris site, the American University of Paris (AUP), had limited library resources, and the AUP librarian was concerned about NSU students using the AUP library because the databases were not password protected. After being reassured that NSU students would have their own access to more than 200 online databases, the librarian agreed to allow NSU students to "piggyback" on the AUP account for document delivery from the British Library. The librarian was not able to find a library to partner with in the suburb of Kifissia, but it would have been possible to arrange a deposit account at the British Consul's library in downtown Athens. Ironically, after working out the logistics, this solution never needed to be implemented. The NSU program in the London area never materialized, the one in Paris only started in the fall of 2001, a month before the writing of this paper, and student requests in Athens never necessitated activating an account in Athens, perhaps due in part to the transportation challenges to get from the outskirts of Athens to the downtown area.

In order to better serve the research needs of distance students, NSU's main library began exploring new technologies for less expensive and timelier solutions for delivering research materials online. The library considered scanning documents and sending them to students as attachments but decided against this high-tech solution because of copyright considerations. Instead, the library looked for technology solutions that permitted the library to scan documents but house the documents on the university's server and have students come to retrieve the documents from the NSU site. One solution that was tested in 2001 was Prospero, a freeware program designed to complement ARIEL. Prospero delivers ARIEL documents to end-users by posting them on a Web server. The Document Delivery Librarian decided to test this software since the department was already using ARIEL, the Prospero software was free, and the software was designed so that NSU students could come to an NSU site to retrieve their documents. The documents were scanned into PDF (Portable Document Format) files and uploaded to Web sites. The Prospero software generated email for participating students that provided the URL where the document resided and a PIN number for accessing the site. Students were given a specific time limit for accessing the document using Adobe Acrobat and a specific limit on the number of times the document could be accessed as a security measure to ensure that only the appropriate user was making use of the service. The decision was made to test the feasibility of delivering scanned documents via Prospero first with international students because of the cost of sending documents internationally via DHL or FedEx.

Thus far, the library has had mixed responses to document delivery via Prospero. A number of students liked accessing scanned documents online because of the timeliness of the delivery. On the other hand, others had a number of problems with this approach to document delivery. Some students preferred to have the documents shipped to them because the cost and problems with obtaining printing cartridges was an issue in some countries like Germany and Korea. Also, the infrastructure for accessing the Internet in a timely manner was a problem in countries like Greece and Jamaica. The charges for connect time were often costly. Still other students lacked technology skills and/or up-to-date equipment. Even in Western Europe, students who do not own their own computers do not have the ease of access to the Internet in libraries and universities that students in the United States enjoy. The result of these various problems is that some students prefer to have the library provide traditional document delivery via mail or DHL. These students are willing to wait for their documents to be delivered by traditional means in spite of the timeliness offered by technological solutions that are made possible by Prospero and ILLiad.

A second solution was also tested during the 2001/2002 academic year. ILLiad is an automated interlibrary loan resource sharing management software from OCLC that automates manual tasks performed by the interlibrary loan staff with software modules that scan and post documents for document delivery. As a member of the Southeast Florida Library Information Network (SEFLIN), the NSU Libraries were selected as one of the ILLiad testing sites, but at the time that this paper was completed, the software had not yet been installed and implemented, so the relative merits of the two software packages cannot be addressed at this time.

ACCESS TO ONLINE RESOURCES

Online databases provide a great solution for document delivery for international students. The main library provides NSU students with access to over 200 online databases. Students are able to access full-text online journal articles, dissertations, and reference resources including online encyclopedias. Graduate students in education have access to full-text education journal articles in Wilson Web Education Full Test and ProQuest Research Library Periodicals, as well as ERIC ED documents in ERIC E*Subscribe. Graduate business students have access to full-text journal articles in ABI/Inform, Wilson Web Business, and InfoTrac's General Business File, as well as company information in FIS Online and international information in several EIU databases. Computer science graduate students have access to full-text journal articles and conference proceedings in IEEE and ACM. The problem with online databases is that the level of online coverage varies substantially between the various disciplines. Business students can find as much as 75% of what they need online, but students in the social sciences can only find about 25-30% of the indexed materials full-text online.

Because of the problems with providing international students with the document delivery of books, online access to electronic books via NetLibrary has been an important addition to the online resources offered by the library. NSU is part of the SOLINET consortium and can access all books that are part of the consortium. In addition NSU bought some unique titles to support specific disciplines such as education. The library staff works with faculty to get books that support the curriculum, particularly for distance students. The fact is, however, that the 20,000 titles for e-books are not sufficient by themselves to meet the research needs of graduate students who happen to live in other countries. There was also some concern at the time that this paper was being written about whether NetLibrary would remain financially viable or perhaps merge with OCLC.

Distance students express a high level of satisfaction when they are instructed on the access and use of these full-text databases. On the other hand, some students are unaware of the availability of the full-text articles or are unwilling to print the documents themselves because of the cost and/or availability of printing cartridges, as mentioned previously.

Although many students have expressed a high level of satisfaction with accessing research materials online, there have also been a number of problems and issues. Students have to be aware of the availability of the full-text articles, so ensuring that international students receive appropriate training is important. Because of a scarcity of computer materials such as computer cartridges, some students have been unwilling to print the documents themselves. Another problem has been that students in some countries are handicapped by the quality of Internet services available in their countries. The telecommunication system in places like the Bahamas, Jamaica, Panama, and Greece still present problems with providing reliable and high-speed services. The infrastructure for communications between continents and countries has improved markedly over the last five years but still can be a bottleneck that impedes access that students can depend on. As a result, online solutions for document delivery to international students are not yet foolproof.

FORMAL AGREEMENTS WITH LOCAL LIBRARIES

Formal agreements with local libraries have been a traditional solution for providing library services to students at distance sites, and NSU has certainly explored this option. The library has negotiated a number of formal library agreements with local academic libraries in Panama, Jamaica, the Bahamas, Venezuela, the Dominican Republic, France, and Greece, with less than a satisfactory solution in most cases. First of all, in many cases, the libraries at local sites, particularly in developing countries, are inadequate, at least by U.S. standards. A second problem is that many of the libraries located in other countries do not have library collections that support the academic programs offered at the NSU sites. When one thinks about it, this is not surprising. After all, if the local academic institutions were offering academic programs in these areas, there would not be a market for an outside institution like NSU to come in and offer the same program. A third problem relates to the cost of negotiating an agreement with a local academic library. Some large local academic libraries see this as an opportunity to demand exorbitant fees. Certain NSU programs have been willing to pay a fee per student to guarantee that the students in that program have access to a local library collection, but other graduate programs have only been willing to reimburse students for fees for a borrowing card at a local library, or have refused to provide students with this alternative at all. The biggest challenge to formal agreements with local libraries, however, has been that most academic institutions will not negotiate library agreements because the local academic institutions see NSU as competition that threatens their welfare. As a result, even when the local library would be willing to negotiate a formal agreement, the parent institution would refuse to approve such agreements.

BUILDING LOCAL RESEARCH RESOURCES

When local institutions refuse to negotiate library agreements, the question then is, what other options are there? One alternative that a number of institutions have adopted has been to start their own branch libraries ("Distance learning abroad," 2000). NSU decided to take this approach in Panama, Jamaica, and the Bahamas in response to recommendations made by the Southern Association of Colleges and Schools (SACS) during the 1997 reaccreditation visit. The library set up research rooms in all three countries, hired professional librarians to staff the libraries, and arranged for a budget of approximately $40,000 per site for print resources including books, reference resources, and journals. The library also arranged for the librarians at these sites to come to campus once or twice a year for training on how to use online resources, and to iron out administrative and technology problems that had arisen during the year. These research rooms were set up in 1998 and are all still operating.

Providing local research rooms at international sites, however, has not proven to be a "silver bullet" that solved all the library access problems for the institution, at least in NSU's case. First of all, at the time these research rooms were planned and implemented, the infrastructure for international communications was still unreliable. This situation, however, has improved markedly in the past four years. As students in Panama, Jamaica, and the Bahamas were able to access the Internet more rapidly and more dependably, the students began relying on print resources less and less. Secondly, these research rooms did not have large enough budgets to build local research collections that were really adequate to support the research needs of students at those sites, particularly at the graduate level. Last but not least, providing local research rooms for international students might address the needs of site-based students at those particular sites, but it did not provide a workable solution for international students who happened to take classes online and were located in locations throughout the world.

As the library has grappled with the question of how to ensure that international students have adequate support for their research needs, the library has concluded that it is the responsibility of the library on the main campus to support the research of students wherever they may be located. After all, why should some international students have library access provided through local libraries or university-subsidized research rooms while other students who live in more far-flung locations are not provided with a comparable level of service? If the library on the main campus provides document delivery for all students, on and off campus, then all students are being provided with the same level of service. This argument also has a couple of fallacies, however. It is true that the off-campus students do have access to the same resources, but they cannot access the materials in the same timeframe. In addition, international students face particularly high hurdles when it comes to getting print resources to overseas sites. In order to help address this concern, the library has depended on services by companies like DHL and FedEx to ensure the timely delivery of print resources to international sites, or on new technologies like Prospero and ILLiad.

In spite of the fact that rationale for local library branches may seem to have diminished, the demise of NSU's research rooms is not imminent. As with anything else, politics can muddy the equation that measures whether and how to provide local library access at international sites. The political reality is that once the research rooms exist, the accrediting agencies in those countries see the continued existence of these resources as a necessity, and would view the demise of such facilities with disfavor. This has certainly been the case with NSU's research rooms in Jamaica.

REFERENCE AND BIBLIOGRAPHIC INSTRUCTION SERVICES

It is not enough to provide distance students with document delivery and/or online databases. If students do not know these services exist, the resources do little good. As a result, reference and bibliographic instruction are also important considerations for distance students. At NSU, providing equal reference services for distance students in the United States and abroad has been problematic for a couple of reasons. First of all, distance students in the United States, Canada, and the Caribbean have access to a toll-free number, but international students in other parts of the world do not. Students call the reference desk using the toll-free number and the reference librarians sometimes spend 30-45 minutes walking students step-by-step through the search strategy and browser configuration. Secondly, reference service hours are offered by the main library from 8 a.m. to 10 p.m. ET. These hours of phone and email reference services may meet the needs of students in the western hemisphere, but these synchronous services are not offered at times convenient for students in Asia, Africa, the Middle East, and Europe. The only solution that the library has offered students on the other side of the world has been to provide them with the asynchronous option of using email to send reference questions. Although this alternative may not suit the learning styles of all students, most students not located in the Caribbean area are online students anyway so the solution has worked reasonably well.

Bibliographic instruction also presents real challenges when students attend class at international sites. Because NSU delivers distance education in a variety of formats and a variety of different program designs, no one solution has worked for the whole university. As a result, there have been a number of solutions: MBA students get training via online tutorials that are integrated into the curriculum (Tuñón, 1999). Several doctoral programs including students in the Doctorate of Business Administration, the Humanities and Social Sciences, and Computer and Information Sciences come to campus for orientation at the beginning of their programs. Still other programs that have students meet at sites have librarians go to the sites to provide the training. As a result, NSU librarians have been to Jamaica, Panama, Venezuela, Puerto Rico, Greece, Sweden, and France to provide library instruction. For yet another program where students interact online and receive videos of lectures, the library (1) has provided students with a video of library services and (2) collaborates with faculty to provide students with virtual instruction. The rule of thumb has been that if instruction is delivered to students in a face-to-face format, the students receive their library training that way. If the students receive their instruction in some type of online or asynchronous format, the library provides the training using those technologies (Pival & Tuñón, 2000).

PROVIDING LIBRARY SERVICES
IN THE LANGUAGES OF INSTRUCTION

As universities have increasingly met the educational needs for distance education in English-speaking counties, the institutions are beginning to consider offering distance programs in other languages. For example, a librarian at a Florida state university participating in an ALA panel discussed how his institution provided simultaneous instruction in French, Spanish, and Portuguese to students in Latin America by satellite ("Distance learning abroad," 2000). He also acknowledged that those students were not required to have reading competency in English and that they were not provided research resources in the language in which the instruction was delivered. Even more troubling, he indicated that the regional accrediting agency had done nothing about the lack of library support offered to these students in the language that they received their instruction. Just as problematic, the library did not provide reference services and bibliographic instruction to the students in the language being used to deliver the course.

NSU has started offering classes in other languages and is grappling with these issues. The first foray into this arena involved two graduate education clusters started in Venezuela. Classes at the beginning of the program were offered in Spanish, but the plan was that students would take intensive classes in English and transition over to English by the second year. Unfortunately, this plan proved to be overly optimistic. The library did have a bilingual librarian who was able to offer bibliographic training for the students in these clusters in Spanish, first in Venezuela, and later at a summer institute in Florida. Students were supplied, however, with materials to support their graduate research only in English. This was justified by the fact that the students were supposed to have a reading competency in English.

The next foray into site-based instruction offered in other languages occurred when the same program began to consider starting a cluster in Brazil. The courses were to be taught completely in Portuguese, and students were not going to be required to have a reading competency in English. The library tried to find solutions that would provide library materials for the students in Portuguese, or even in Spanish, without much success. There were no commercial online databases in Portuguese, and the library was unable to locate a local academic library with adequate holdings to support a graduate education program offered in Portuguese. Fortunately, the issue became mote when the project eventually died a quiet death.

The problem with providing library support for programs offered in other languages, however, has not gone away. Still another program has started a cluster, this time in the Dominican Republic. Fortunately, in this case the library was able to send a bilingual librarian to do the initial library training in Spanish and to negotiate an agreement with a local library.

The underlying question, however still remains: How should libraries handle the situation when they cannot adequately support the research needs of students because instruction is being offered in another language? Until accrediting agencies address this question, libraries will continue to be pressured by their academic institutions to be "team players" and go along with offering library services that do not adequately meet the needs of the students who do not speak English.

CULTURAL AND POLITICAL SENSIBILITIES

Students living in the other parts of the world do not always view the library the same way as people do in the U.S. Language and differing cultural experiences often pose problems as well. International students encounter library procedures, resources, and systems that are quite different from what they have used up until that time. There are discrepancies in the practice and application of library services to distance learners. Slade and Kascus (1998) identify four models of library services to distance students: (1) online collections and resources at the remote sites, (2) cooperative agreement and resource sharing among libraries, (3) document delivery from the parent institution and (4) remote access to online resources. These models are not mutually exclusive and many institutions, like NSU, have adopted a combination of the different models. Moreover, the educational systems of other countries may view of the role of the library differently. International students do not always have extensive experience doing library research to write research papers or locate information in traditional print formats, much less online. Even international students who have taken online classes from a number of institutions have often experienced very limited library support services. It is not because the libraries at the institutions are unaware of or unwilling to provide the services, but more so because of the political and the socio-economic infrastructure. As a result, students do not always fully comprehend how libraries and online resources can help them.

The students' perceptions present problems. In some parts of the world, in previous years, distance education was viewed as a remedial education for students to obtain a degree when it was not otherwise possible in a regular educational system. However, this notion is changing rapidly, and the dramatic advancement of technology has made distance education a viable and a popular alternative. The students enrolled in distance courses are often older and may feel left out, in some sense, being away from a physical campus. They often lack the self-confidence to approach the librarian and use the library effectively. This is a significant problem for even traditional libraries, but the problem is compounded when the students' library happens to be located in another country. Trying to communicate and reassure students who are uncomfortable with the library and using library services only gets compounded when there are language and cultural barriers as well.

In order to address these issues, NSU has employed or contracted bilingual librarians, when possible, to do the library training. The library, for example, has sent Spanish-speaking librarians to do the library training sessions in Venezuela, Panama, and the Dominican Republic. The library was prepared to contract to send a Portuguese-speaking librarian to Brazil as well, but the site never got started. It is true that one-shot training sessions in Spanish or Portuguese are not enough to overcome all student fears and apprehensions, but they can go a long way in mitigating some of these problems.

CONCLUSIONS

The goal of providing international students with the same kinds of library services as those offered to distance students is a laudable goal that ACRL encourages all libraries to work toward, but the harsh reality is that it is a goal that is not easily attained for international students. The advent of online journal articles, e-books, and other resources have made the jobs of libraries much easier, but many print resources, particularly in the humanities and social sciences, are simply not yet available online. This issue becomes even more important as academic institutions begin offering more and more online and site-based training for graduate students overseas. The sad fact is that many universities in the United States and abroad are not even making the attempt to provide the delivery of books to their international students. Even when libraries do try to provide these services, there are often serious limitations and problems that need to be addressed. If libraries truly believe that all students–on or off campus, in the United States and abroad–are entitled to equal or equivalent access to library resources and services, then more attention needs to be provided to improve the level of these resources and services for international students. Even with the best efforts, this objective will serve more as a purpose to be strived toward rather than an attainable goal.

REFERENCES

Association of College and Research Libraries. (2001). *Association of College and Research Libraries guidelines for distance learning library services.* Retrieved November 27, 2001, from the American Library Association Web site: http://www.ala.org/acrl/guides/distlrng.html.

Distance learning abroad: Challenges and solutions to D.L. library services to foreign countries. (2000, July 9). Panel discussion for LITA Distance Learning Interest Group, International Relations Committee, American Library Association Annual Conference, Chicago.

Pival, P., & Tuñón, J. (2000). Innovative methods for providing instruction to distance students using technology. In P. S. Thomas & M. Jones (Comps.), *The Ninth Off-Campus Library Services Conference Proceedings: Portland, OR, April 26-28, 2000* (pp. 221-230). Mount Pleasant, MI: Central Michigan University Press.

Slade, A., & Kascus, M. (1998). An international comparison of library services for distance learning. In P. S. Thomas & M. Jones (Comps.), *The Eighth Off-Campus Library Services Conference Proceedings: Providence, RI, April 22-24, 1998* (pp. 280-281). Mount Pleasant, MI: Central Michigan University Press.

Tuñón, J. (1999, June 7). *Asynchronous/distance instruction: A case study of the MBA at NSU.* Special Library Association Conference in Minneapolis, MN, on June 7, 1999.

Tuñón, J., & Pival, P. (2000). Reaccreditation at Nova Southeastern University: How reaccreditation can create opportunities for improving library services to distance students. In P. S. Thomas & M. Jones (Comps.), *The Ninth Off-Campus Library Services Conference Proceedings: Portland, OR, April 26-28, 2000* (pp. 273-282). Mount Pleasant, MI: Central Michigan University Press.

Ship to Shore:
An Online Information Literacy Tutorial
Using BlackBoard
Distance Education Software

Douglas L. Cook

Shippensburg University of Pennsylvania

SUMMARY. Shippensburg University Library has created an online Information Literacy skills tutorial for freshman College Writing students, called Ship to Shore. This tutorial makes use of the distance education software BlackBoard. The primary areas addressed in the planning and creation of the tutorial were the past experiences of Shippensburg University and other universities in creating such tutorials, ACRL Information Literacy Standards, the input of Ship's College Writing faculty, and the BlackBoard software itself.

KEYWORDS. Technology, Internet, distance education, distance learners

Shippensburg University is a medium-sized liberal arts college in south-central PA. Ship has approximately 7,000 students and is a member of the PA State System of Higher Education (SSHE). Although Ship is not usually described as a "distance education" campus, faculty members and administrators have made efforts to attract off-campus students. Several member institutions of the SSHE recently mounted a pilot grant program called the "Virtual University." This

[Haworth co-indexing entry note]: "Ship to Shore: An Online Information Literacy Tutorial Using Black-Board Distance Education Software." Cook, Douglas L. Co-published simultaneously in *Journal of Library Administration* (The Haworth Information Press, an imprint of The Haworth Press, Inc.) Vol. 37, No. 1/2, 2002, pp. 177-187; and: *Distance Learning Library Services: The Tenth Off-Campus Library Services Conference* (ed: Patrick B. Mahoney) The Haworth Information Press, an imprint of The Haworth Press, Inc., 2002, pp. 177-187.

http://www.haworthpress.com/store/product.asp?sku=J111
10.1300/J111v37n01_16

program allowed the SSHE to purchase a license to BlackBoard. Training sessions were then provided for interested faculty. A number of Ship faculty members have either partially or completely incorporated distance education technologies into their classrooms as a result of this grant.

The Library at Ship, as have most other academic libraries in the country, has made use of the WWW as the gateway to its resources. Students can now accomplish much of their searching and accessing of library holdings from outside the building. Students living on or near campus often act much like the typical profile of the traditional distance education student. As one faculty member recently related to me, "If they can't get it from their computers in their dorm rooms, they feel that they aren't responsible for it." As a result, Ship's Library has begun to embrace distance education practices and technology for its on-campus students.

The impetus for the beginning of the Ship to Shore project was an administrative-level discussion of information literacy directed by Madelyn Valunas, Dean of Library and Media Services at Ship. The concept of information literacy brought a number of informational and technological literacy issues to the forefront. Ship's President, Anthony Ceddia, was excited enough by the concept that he asked Dean Valunas to present a pilot information literacy tutorial to the administration. Besides addressing information literacy needs, the pilot was to address technological issues as well. President Ceddia also asked that the pilot use a distance education vehicle. The resulting program, then, was to address information and technological issues as well as provide a "distance education experience." The library tutorial is part of a campus-wide initiative to make better use of technology.

OTHER TUTORIALS

A team of librarians was appointed to plan the pilot. The team included Douglas Cook, Berkley Laite and later Karen Daniel–all Reference and Instruction Librarians. Library Skills have been a part of the General Education requirements at Ship for many years. During the 1980s this requirement was met by students attending a short library presentation. Later a paper-based and then a Web-based tutorial were instituted. In the late 1990s we worked with the College Writing faculty to make a library skills component part of the required Freshman College Writing course. Experiences with this previous instruction helped us to understand the basic pedagogical and institutional issues, which guide the creation of a computer-aided, individualized instructional package.

Our experience with tutorials taught us that the program should be easy for students to navigate. Information should be presented to students in "chunks"– short bits of information–so that students can feel success as they work through the program. We had discovered that the more context which can be provided with the tutorial the more successful it is. Students often attend only to what they need to know. If information literacy skills are included in a required course, such as College Writing, students deem them more valuable.

We also looked at the online tutorials instituted by other universities. We found that a good place to begin looking was the ALA Library Instruction Round Table page, "Library Instruction Tutorials." There are a great many excellent tutorials in use. Some are very simple Web presentations while others are much more complex, using the latest Web technology. Most tutorials consist of a presentation of some sort with an accompanying quiz and/or activity. The presentations usually provide very short "chunks" of information. Many tutorials center on some sort of an information literacy test. Most include general literacy topics as well as topics specific to the sponsoring institution. Some are contained within other courses, such as College Writing, and the like.

We felt that based upon our past experience and our overview of the other tutorials in use that we were on the right track. We decided to keep the tutorial as part of the College Writing program so as to retain the context that we had used with our previous Web tutorial. We decided to structure the tutorial in a "presentation followed by an activity" format. We decided to make each presentation approximately five minutes long. This short length is easier to structure for the course designer. It is also more palatable for the students as they work through the tutorial.

ACRL STANDARDS AND OBJECTIVES

One of our sub-goals was to make use of the recent ACRL Information Literacy Standards. A subcommittee of the Instruction Section of ACRL in 2001 created performance indicators for these Standards, entitled "Objectives for Information Literacy Instruction." Briefly, these standards encompass five broad areas related to research:

1. Standard One–Pre-search
2. Standard Two–Actual search
3. Standard Three–Post-search
4. Standard Four–Using information acquired in the search
5. Standard Five–Economic, legal, and social issues regarding information

Using these standards as a guideline we decided to formulate a content plan. We knew that we could not cover all standards in one introductory tutorial, so we choose the performance indicators which had the most relevance to a college student just beginning to explore information literacy as a concept. Table 1 matches the ACRL objectives to our content outline.

Traditionally at Ship our Library Skills programs have focused on our library resources. ACRL's Information Literacy Objectives propose the expansion of this coverage beyond accessing library resources. We decided to start at the searching level of typical college freshmen so we could activate their prior knowledge of searching. Thus we started with the World Wide Web. We

TABLE 1. ACRL Standards and Objectives as Related to the Content of Ship to Shore

ACRL Objectives	Ship to Shore Content
1. Pre-Search–The information literate student determines the extent of the information needed.	
1.1e. Identifies key concepts and terms that describe the information needed.	Unit 1.2. Searching the Web. Unit 1.3. Keywords and Search Strategies.
1.2a. Knows how information is formally and informally produced, organized, and disseminated.	Unit 1.1. What Is the World Wide Web?
1.4b. Describes criteria used to make information decisions and choices.	Unit 3.1. Evaluating Digital Resources.
2. Search–The information literate student accesses needed information effectively and efficiently.	
2.1c. Investigates the scope, content, and organization of information retrieval systems.	Unit 2.2. Types of Electronic Databases.
2.2b. Identifies keywords, synonyms and related terms for the information needed.	Unit 1.3. Keywords and Search Strategies.
2.2d. Constructs a search strategy using appropriate commands for the information retrieval system.	Unit 1.3. Keywords and Search Strategies.
2.3a. Uses various search systems to retrieve information in a variety of formats.	Unit 2.2. Types of Electronic Databases.
3. Post-Search–The information literate student evaluates information and its sources critically and incorporates selected information into his or her knowledge base and value system.	
3.2a. Examines and compares information from various sources in order to evaluate reliability.	Unit 3.1. Evaluating Digital Resources. Unit 3.2. Ethical Use of Digital Resources.
3.2c. Recognizes prejudice, deception, or manipulation.	Unit 3.1. Evaluating Digital Resources.
3.7b. Reviews search strategy and incorporates additional concepts as necessary.	Unit 1.2. Searching the Web. Unit 2.3. Shippensburg U. Library Resources.
5. Economic, legal, and social issues regarding information–The information literate student understands many of the economic, legal and social issues surrounding the use of information and accesses and uses information ethically and legally.	
5.1b. Identifies and discusses issues related to free vs. fee-based access to information.	Unit 2.1. Electronic Databases and the Free Web.
5.3a. Selects an appropriate documentation style and uses it consistently to cite sources.	Unit 3.3. MLA Style.

wanted to expand their knowledge by making them better Web searchers. We then used the Web to lead into resources, which they could access, via the Library's Web page. ACRL Standard Five also proposes broader issues of literacy that we had never attempted to address before.

Our final content outline (see Table 2) begins with a general overview of the concept of Information Literacy, followed by an explanation of the tutorial itself. We tried to be as specific as possible in our "Getting Started" instructions. Since students feel that all of their research needs can be solved with the WWW, we started there. Unit 1 moves from a general definition of the Web to an explanation of the different types of Web search engines. Unit 1, Lesson 3 introduces the concepts of keywords and advanced searching.

Unit 2 begins by comparing the resources of the WWW to the resources, which can be found on a Library Web page. Lesson 2 focuses on article databases and reviews the search strategies covered in Unit One. Lesson 3 spotlights Ship's Library resources and our full-text article databases.

Unit 3, Lesson 1 covers completely new territory for us. We realized that the evaluation of resources, particularly those found on the Web, was an important skill for students to learn. Lesson 2, as well, was something we had never included in our library skills tutorials before. We focused on plagiarism, which seems to be the place where students have the most difficulty when beginning to think about the ethical use of resources in the research process. We finished

TABLE 2. Ship to Shore Tutorial Content Outline

1. Read this first–What is Information Literacy?
2. Getting Started
3. UNIT 1–The Digital Information Environment
Lesson 1: What Is the World Wide Web?
Lesson 2: Searching the Web
Lesson 3: Keywords and Search Strategies
4. UNIT 2–Electronic Databases
Lesson 1: Electronic Databases and the Free Web
Lesson 2: Types of Electronic Databases
Lesson 3: Shippensburg University Library Resources
5. UNIT 3–Critically Thinking about Digital Resources
Lesson 1: Evaluating Digital Resources
Lesson 2: Ethical Use of Digital Resources
Lesson 3: MLA Style
6. Conclusion for College Writing Students–Your Final Project

the tutorial with a brief introduction to MLA Style, which is the style preferred by our College Writing faculty members.

COLLEGE WRITING FACULTY

Besides looking at other tutorials, studying the ACRL objectives, and reflecting on past experience, we also talked at length with the faculty in our freshman College Writing program. Since the College Writing course had been providing the context for our previous tutorial we knew that their opinions would be of great value. We invited a core of interested College Writing faculty to meet with us in a focus group setting. We reviewed previous practice and displayed a sample of how the new BlackBoard tutorial might look. Among other things we discovered that the College Writing faculty in the focus group were very willing to work with us on a new pilot project. We discussed the research and information literacy needs of the College Writing students. Interestingly enough their perceptions of the students' needs coincided with the ACRL Literacy Standards. This further reaffirmed our use of these Standards as a framework for the tutorial. We also discussed protocols and procedures for delivering the new tutorial. Many of their questions related to BlackBoard. Since this was the first time that many of them would see BlackBoard in action, we assured the professors that librarians would train the students in the technical skills needed to complete the tutorial.

BlackBoard

The final vital piece in the creation of the initial version of Ship to Shore was BlackBoard. As often happens, instructional content is influenced by its delivery vehicle. As with all distance education programs, BlackBoard does some things very well and others not so well. For example, BlackBoard is very easy for students to use. At its most basic, it allows students to access content and activities on the Web. It also provides tracking and grading functions to faculty. We quickly became adept at BlackBoard.

We found that the Quiz creation module of BlackBoard caused us difficulties. We used an off-line assessment product called Respondus, which allowed us to easily create and then upload quizzes. Quizzes in BlackBoard may only reside in a "Quiz Folder" which must be titled "Quizzes." In BlackBoard 5.0.2 it was not possible to mix "Presentations" and "Quizzes" in the same folder. Also it was not possible to call "Quizzes" anything but "Quizzes." I would have preferred "Review Activities." It was not possible to have a "Help" button or a "Frequently Asked Questions" button. I had to settle for an "Information" button. We also had some troubles with disappearing URLs in quizzes, which we realized was attributable to the fact that the SSHE upgraded the version of the software we were using during the creation of the prototype.

PILOT TESTING

We began the actual creation of the tutorial by putting together short PowerPoint presentations for each of the topics we were to cover. We used PowerPoint as a presentation creation tool, as we were familiar with the software. We had also tried MS Word and basic .HTML, but rejected those because we could not control the pace of the presentation. MS PowerPoint creates a "screen by screen" presentation that we felt would lend itself to our instructional design. PowerPoint also allows the students to control the pace of the presentation. We created a very simple design template to provide all the presentations with a common look. We named the tutorial Ship to Shore. Shore stands for Ship Online Resource Education (see Figure 1).

Quiz writing provided us with a challenge. BlackBoard lends itself best to multiple-choice and true/false type questions, since it has a built in quiz grader. We found, however, that it was much easier to write open-ended and essay type quizzes. We compromised by including a Pre-test, a Post-test, and three

FIGURE 1

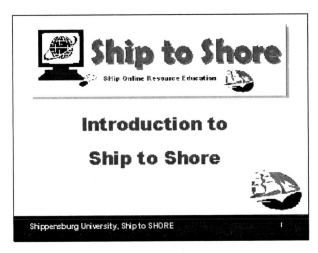

Unit Quizzes in multiple-choice format, and by including nine open-ended essay activities.

We pilot tested Ship to Shore in a number of ways. We created the tutorial section by section and asked library student workers to navigate each lesson by keeping a log of their problems and suggestions. One of our workers was a graduate student in psychology, who was extremely astute at working through the modules with a fine-tooth comb. She eventually became a large part of the initial piloting and troubleshooting effort.

One of our College Writing focus group faculty was teaching College Writing during the summer of 2001. She agreed to allow us to use her students for the first actual pilot test in a classroom setting. As you can imagine we found a number of difficulties, primarily with delivery. For example, students wondered why we talked about "Review Activities," but when they entered Black-Board they saw only "Quizzes." We finally gave up and called them "Quizzes." We had to create a paper handout which allowed students to track their way through the presentations and activities, since the presentations were in one folder and quizzes were in another (see Table 3). This paper handout helped them to understand the flow of the tutorial. And of course, we fixed typos, repaired illogical sequencing, tweaked URLs, and the like.

We decided to use four of our College Writing focus group faculty (two sections per faculty) to run a larger pilot in the fall of 2001. We created a separate BlackBoard course for each of the eight sections. This allowed us to easily track and report students' progress in each section. Eventually the tutorials were ready for each section. In consultation with the Writing faculty we decided to give students a block of two weeks to finish the tutorial. Students would still be able to work at their own pace; however, they would have a time deadline which would help to motivate them.

Between the summer 2001 pilot and the fall 2001 pilot, our version of BlackBoard was upgraded to 5.0.2. We found that the quizzes would not copy properly to the new version. For lack of any other choice we had to go back and rebuild the quizzes in each of our pilot sections one at a time. This rebuilding was also acerbated by the fact that we were having response slowness difficulties with the BlackBoard server.

PowerPoint presentations (saved as .PPT files) could not be downloaded by many students. Although we had instructions for downloading the PowerPoint Viewer plug-in, this was enough of a deterrent that some students refused to view the presentations. Also we found that students using Macs could not easily download the presentations. Our short-term solution was to ask students to finish the tutorial in a campus lab, since all campus labs were able to read .PPT files. We will be using PowerPoint to convert the presentations to .HTML presentations to overcome this difficulty.

TABLE 3. Paper Checklist for Keeping Track of Student Progress

Presentations are in the 'Presentation' folder in BlackBoard. Pre-Test, Post-Test, Activities, and Quizzes are in the 'Quizzes' folder. When you finish a presentation, review activity, or quiz, place a check beside it on this sheet.
___ QUIZ–Pre-test–(Take the pre-test before viewing any presentations)
___ Presentation–Everybody READ THIS FIRST ___ Presentation–Introduction–Choosing a topic
Unit 1, Lesson 1–What Is the WWW? ___ Presentation ___ QUIZ–Review Activity Unit 1, Lesson 2–Searching the WWW ___ Presentation ___ QUIZ–Review Activity Unit 1, Lesson 3–Keywords and Search Strategies ___ Presentation ___ QUIZ–Review Activity ___ Unit 1 Quiz
Unit 2, Lesson 1–Electronic Databases Are Different from the Free Web ___ Presentation ___ QUIZ–Review Activity Unit 2, Lesson 2–Types of Electronic Databases ___ Presentation ___ QUIZ–Review Activity Unit 2, Lesson 3–Shippensburg University Library Resources ___ Presentation ___ QUIZ–Review Activity ___ Unit 2 Quiz
Unit 3, Lesson 1–Evaluating Digital Resources ___ Presentation ___ QUIZ–Review Activity Unit 3, Lesson 2–Ethical Use of Digital Resources ___ Presentation ___ QUIZ–Review Activity Unit 3, Lesson 3–MLA Resource Citation ___ Presentation ___ QUIZ–Review Activity ___ Unit 3 Quiz
___ Presentation–Conclusion for College Writing Students
___ QUIZ–Post-test

Another major problem was caused by needing to update and maintain eight different sections of Ship to Shore. If all files had copied perfectly from the template, this may have been a more viable option. However, it was amazingly tedious and frustrating to make the same changes eight times. Temporary server slowness during the beginning of the semester made this worse. This would have become a major problem if we were to use multiple sections when we implemented the tutorial officially with 30+ sections of College Writing per semester. We are now looking into the possibility of putting a large number of students into one "course." This would allow us to maintain one version of the tutorial. We may have problems, however, with grade reporting, since there will be such a large class list.

We used a number of open-ended quiz questions in the pilot. Essay quizzes are much easier to write, but of course, someone needs to grade them. Grading essay questions for each of 200 students became quite tedious. My colleagues threatened to go on strike if we used essay questions in the next version. We are now in the processing of converting essay type quizzes into multiple-choice, which can be scored by the BlackBoard software. Assessment authenticity is still being addressed. We will be using this as an opportunity to collaborate with faculty members in the Teacher Education department who are experts at assessment. We are hoping to barter our hard-won knowledge of BlackBoard for some help with assessment validation. Over the 2001 holiday break the SSHE is upgrading BlackBoard to version 5.5.1. I am sure that this will make next semester an interesting one.

As of December 2001, we had decided that we had had enough problems that we would run another, larger pilot before we instituted the tutorial as a requirement for all freshmen. Dean Valunas aptly observed that since this would likely be students' first experience with distance education, we want to make sure that it is a pleasant one.

FUTURE PLANS

Looking beyond this first tutorial, we would like to create other such online tutorials to address subject-related research. Our College of Business has expressed interest in working with us on such a project. Our Extended Studies Program has expressed interest in reworking this basic tutorial so that it can be used with "true" distance education students. We also will be using the results of our Pre-test and Post-test to work toward the identification of a set of skills which Ship students ought to possess if they are truly information literate. A committee on campus is in the midst of creating a Web-based program that could be used for Freshman Orientation. The Library is a part of this committee. We will be including the Ship to Shore tutorial as a part of this effort. Also, we presented the tutorial to a local consortium of school librarians and discovered that middle and high school librarians are struggling with the same issues. This presentation led to discussion about mutual goals. Many asked for copies of the PowerPoint lessons from the tutorial. Finally, Ship to Shore has sparked the interest of several other Pennsylvania SSHE universities who are working with the creation of online tutorials. It is hoped that we will be able to combine efforts in some fashion.

Both the use of BlackBoard and the contextualization of library skills in the larger arena of information literacy have allowed us to collaborate or begin to collaborate with campus and community constituencies. We feel that it is vital to the success of such projects to be open and sensitive to the needs of the larger community.

CONCLUSION

As often happens, this project has taken twice as long as we expected. We were hoping to have a final tutorial in place by the spring of 2002. We are now aiming for the fall of 2002. We were very fortunate in that the project began with the blessing of the University administration. We were given the resources and the time that we needed to bring this project to life.

In conclusion, we feel that we have made a solid beginning to the creation of a viable and palatable tutorial for the online instruction of Information Literacy skills. We feel that Ship to Shore via BlackBoard is one piece of Shippensburg University's collaborative effort to use technology to its greatest advantage at the university level. Ship to Shore is not a final masterpiece. Instead it is a part of an ever-changing collage of campus-wide pedagogical procedures. Our goal is to help our students reach their potential as citizens of the information universe.

AUTHOR NOTE

Information about BlackBoard distance education software can be obtained on the WWW at http://www.blackboard.com.

Information about Respondus assessment software can be obtained on the WWW at http://www.respondus.com.

MS PowerPoint Viewer can be downloaded at http://office.microsoft.com/downloads/9798/Ppview97.aspx.

You can preview the Ship to Shore tutorial at http://library.ship.edu. Click on "Ship to Shore tutorial" and login as Username: Ezra and Password: Lehman. (Ezra Lehman is a former University president after whom our library was named. His legacy lives on as he has become the "demonstration student" in our Ship to Shore tutorial.)

You may contact the author at dlcook@ship.edu.

REFERENCES

Association of College and Research Libraries, Instruction Section. (2001). *Objectives for information literacy instruction: A model statement for academic libraries.* Available: http://www.ala.org/acrl/guides/objinfolit.html (November 18, 2001).

Library Instruction Round Table. (2001). *Library instruction tutorials.* Available: http://www.baylor.edu/LIRT/lirtproj.html (November 18, 2001).

Quality Assurance and Models of Service in an Environment of Change

Christine Cother
Stephen Parnell

University of South Australia

SUMMARY. This paper considers how changes in the information environment and increasing requirements for accountability within the higher education sector impact upon the provision of distance education library services. Emphasis is upon pedagogical and quality assurance issues at the University of South Australia Library, a library that has contractual obligations to deliver a nationwide service to students of Open Learning Australia.

KEYWORDS. Library service, change, distance education, issues

INTRODUCTION

The issues facing higher education that help determine both the nature of library services and the need for quality assurance guidelines are numerous and diverse. In this paper, distance education library services and guidelines are considered against a background of the issues faced by most off-campus education providers. These include developments in online education, the growing volume of accessible information and the needs of students enrolled in higher degrees, and increased demand for accountability. This is all within an environment where institutions compete for students. Behind all of this lies the

[Haworth co-indexing entry note]: "Quality Assurance and Models of Service in an Environment of Change." Cother, Christine, and Stephen Parnell. Co-published simultaneously in *Journal of Library Administration* (The Haworth Information Press, an imprint of The Haworth Press, Inc.) Vol. 37, No. 1/2, 2002, pp. 189-206; and: *Distance Learning Library Services: The Tenth Off-Campus Library Services Conference* (ed: Patrick B. Mahoney) The Haworth Information Press, an imprint of The Haworth Press, Inc., 2002, pp. 189-206.

http://www.haworthpress.com/store/product.asp?sku=J111
10.1300/J111v37n01_17

lifelong learning debate, information literacy as a component of graduate qualities, recognition of the limitations of technology for many students, and reconciling the needs of students as information consumers with developing their information finding skills as part of the education process. At the University of South Australia where the Library supports two distinct student groups, the sometime competing needs of different user groups provide an interesting variation on a theme. The challenge is to predict and balance workloads and levels of service while promoting organisational knowledge and learning. The University has over 25,000 students, Open Learning Australia approximately 13,500.

The Open Learning Agency of Australia was formed in 1991 as a private company with funding initially provided by the Commonwealth of Australia. The broad objective for the company was to identify, develop and deliver learning and tertiary educational opportunities to all Australians when, where and how they may require it, at a reasonable cost. The company currently trades under the name Open Learning Australia (OLA) as a broker of quality distance education for students across Australia and beyond.

During the latter part of the year 2000, staff within the Distance Education Library Service at the University of South Australia worked together to produce a set of agreed quality assurance measures and indicators for services to students, including those unable to access the Library in either its physical or virtual manifestations. The process was undertaken in recognition that quality service requires that libraries know what quality means to its clients and have in place measures that ensure that clients can be confident that this quality is met. The purpose of the resulting quality assurance measures and indicators for service is to indicate precisely what aspects and goals of quality are guaranteed and the ways in which libraries ensure these are attained. It is intended to extend formal quality assurance measures and indicators to other parts of the Library's Flexible Delivery Service during 2002.

DEFINING QUALITY

Libraries typically operate within the administrative and pedagogic framework of their parent institution and the University of South Australia Library is no exception. Although the Library developed the first draft of its quality assurance guidelines in advance of the public expression of quality assurance by the University, it has of course needed to review and re-evaluate these in the light of corporate and sector initiatives. The University's statement on quality defines its approach to quality as encompassing quality assurance, quality improvement and strategic innovation. As such, its quality management system includes processes and activities designed to assure its communities about the quality of its activities. It also provides mechanisms to enable and facilitate continuous improvement, as well as provide the opportunity to systematically identify areas where new directions and innovation are required (University of South Australia, 1999).

The Library has adopted a definition of quality assurance of, "All the planned and systematic activities which are required to provide adequate confidence that a product or service will fulfil specified requirements for quality" (International Organization for Standardization, 1994). It views the process of setting standards, collecting statistics, monitoring performance and analysing these to establish causes of deviations as a means of ensuring service standards and a way to stimulate gradual quality improvements. The underlying principle for the Library is that the same level of service should be available to all eligible students wishing to take advantage of flexible learning. Although requests from distance education students are generally processed in the order in which they are received, preference may be given to students unable to access the Library's physical or virtual services and resources. In most cases multiple requests for document delivery from individual requestors are batched and processed over several days in order to balance the needs of all clients. Services and indicators apply to University of South Australia, Open Learning Australia and Global University Alliance students.

The government established the Australian Universities Quality Agency (AUQA) in response to growing consumer demand for quality and value-for-money in education. This body has as its core task, the conduct of quality audits of Australia's universities and other self-accrediting institutions. Even before AUQA was established, however, universities had recognised the need and value of more open and rigorous quality assurance in education. The University of South Australia and other members of the Australian Technology Network (ATN), for example, agreed to adopt a common quality statement that encompasses principles within it that can be applied to each individual institution's own approach to quality. For the Australian university sector as a whole there is also an agreed code of ethical practice in the provision of education to international students (Australian Vice-Chancellors Committee, 1998). This applies to international students whether studying on campus or through distance education. There are several sections of the code such as physical infrastructure and student support that could be taken to include library services, although this is not specifically mentioned. The code refers to a supportive environment to assist students gain an understanding of their discipline and associated studies, and to provide additional assistance with study skills, including assistance in developing computer literacy. All of these are appropriately the concern of libraries.

Although this code of practice does not directly address library services to distance education students per se, it is indicative of the sort of issues the sector is looking at to ensure quality education. It is illuminating that the Board of Directors of the Australian Library and Information Association, in its deliberations of guidelines for distance education library services, has considered the benefits of integrating library services into the overall mission and function of universities and the means by which this might be achieved (Kirk, personal communication, 2000).

Existing quality guidelines for online education show student access to support services, including library access, to be a central theme, although some commentators suggest that most institutions continue to make available only a fraction of the library resources and other advantages of on-campus students to those studying off campus. The conclusion that must be drawn from this is that as long as the most important resources are available online in some form, institutions are likely to deem that standards for off-campus support have been met (Garson, 1999). There is evidence that this is changing. Two of the quality measures at the centre of the commissioned study Quality on the Line, for example, relate directly to libraries. These require access for students to sufficient library resources and the provision of hands-on training and information to enable students to secure material through electronic databases, inter-library loans and other sources (Institute for Higher Education Policy, 2001).

SERVICES PROVIDED BY LIBRARIES

Experience at the University of South Australia indicates that not only do students appreciate a quality and timely service that provides access to a range of resources and services, but they are also willing to pay for this. This is also the case elsewhere. Market research conducted by the information provider Questia in the United States, for example, suggests that the average student has $150 of discretionary income per month that could be used to purchase information (Hughes, 2000). For some students the library is a significant point of contact between students and their university, and this suggests that in a competitive market, it makes sense for universities to provide high quality library support. This provides a means of enriching the learning environment and at the same time provides security for those who see libraries as one of the features of 'real' universities. There is a happy coincidence here for marketing and relationship building. For this to be successful, however, measurement of quality service provision (including student-centricity) is essential.

As a minimum, attractive service levels and response times need to be identified and promoted to students. The major services for students identified during contract negotiations with Open Learning Australia broadly correspond to those available to students of the University of South Australia. These include:

- 7×24 hour access to online library and information resources including library catalogues, citation and other indexes and full-text databases
- books and other resources to support OLA teaching programs
- information services, including person-to-person contact with library staff via e-mail, telephone and fax
- delivery of books and articles on request by courier or via electronic medium

For OLA as a corporate client the Library uses recognised standard student satisfaction surveys and provides regular transaction and other library usage reports. It supports OLA academic programs in a way that recognises individual student needs for a variety of resources and services delivered flexibly. It has also developed an OLA specific Website and printed guides. Importantly, Open Learning Australia also specified that service to their students be included under the Library's quality assurance guidelines.

THE IMPORTANCE OF QUALITY ASSURANCE IN LIBRARIES

Libraries are one of the indicators used in Australia's annual Good Universities Guide and have a section devoted to them in the government's benchmarking manual for Australian universities (DETYA, 2000). Along with similar works, however, these pay little attention to library services for distance education students. For many mixed-mode institutions the percentage of distance education users is low compared to the total student population. Furthermore, the evidence to date is that, by and large, students who study via distance education do not access the services of the home institution at the same rate as local students. At the University of South Australia, something less than thirty percent of distance education students request assistance from the Flexible Delivery Service, and discussions with colleagues from other Australian university libraries suggest rates of active use seldom approach fifty percent. Given that the dropout rate for undergraduate distance education students is generally higher than for those studying on campus, and can double those for internal students (Thompson, 1997), research is needed to establish whether better library support would help redress this imbalance. Certainly anecdotal evidence from at least one discipline within the University of South Australia suggests that those taking advantage of the Library's distance education search service achieve better results in assignments than those who do not. Of course this is a simplistic measure of use of library services. We know that many students enrolled in "distance" programs live close enough to their own university to use the library in person and that much of this activity is not captured by existing statistics.

Quality assurance is about meeting standards and defining, measuring and maintaining the quality of services and products rather than determining the value of those services and products. However, there is clearly little merit in having high quality services that do not meet the needs of your clients, the objectives of your institution or the aspirations of your staff. You must therefore measure the cost and the quality of an activity in order to derive an understanding of its value. For libraries, instituting quality assurance provides the opportunity and incentive to:

- review activities
- improve staff morale
- promote organisational learning
- reassure staff that they are taking steps to meet client needs
- provide more accurate data that may serve to justify the investment or to identify the need to withdraw or modify certain services
- provide data that can assist in decisions related to transferring of resources across services
- highlight efficiencies and inefficiencies
- establish costing data that will assist in negotiations for support
- assist in decision making relating to the protection of core versus non-core activities
- ensure that expenditure of activities is consistent with organisational goals, objectives and strategies
- provide opportunities for benchmarking

Reviewing the activities carried out will inevitably raise other questions, including how the value of these can be measured. The Library believes that its services contribute toward meeting the University's objectives in teaching, learning and research. While it is difficult to measure the actual value of this contribution, and even harder to balance the cost of an activity against the intellectual benefit (knowledge) that the activity delivers, libraries can take steps to ensure that the services provided are timely and appropriate.

THE QUALITY ASSURANCE MATRIX

Within the Library, quality is evaluated in a number of different ways and at three different levels. At the micro-level, individual users of the service assess the quality of information provided to them. At the unit level, quality is monitored through reference to the Flexible Delivery Service's quality measures and indicators. At the Library level, different aspects of service are evaluated through use of sector wide performance indicators and inclusion of the Library in the University's annual student satisfaction survey. An additional instrument is used by the Library to determine the needs of offshore students. Quality assurance within our Flexible Delivery Service is viewed as an essential element in improving quality and developing knowledge of our own operations rather than as a means of exercising control. This requires that the quality measures and indicators not be seen as a once-off exercise but rather as a tool and process that will need to be monitored and changed constantly if it is to remain effective and appropriate.

For the Library, quality assurance starts with a general statement for all students in the Library's Client Charter. This identifies the distance education library service as one of the services that has set standards for it services and staff. At the national level, benchmark 9.1 addresses the effectiveness of information planning processes (DETYA, 2000). Amongst the elements enumerated as good practice within the national benchmark are:

- clearly articulated vision, goals and objectives
- costed and evaluated services
- monitoring performance against objectives and client needs
- involving staff and clients in the evaluation of services and activities and
- undertaking calculated risk and innovation.

Since library services for off-campus students are both numerous and varied, quality assurance measures must not only be multidimensional, they must be complemented by other measures and mechanisms that allow libraries to determine how well they meet the needs and expectations of their users. The Library has identified six areas for the initial formal application of quality assurance:

- planning and risk-taking
- subject request evaluation
- collection and evaluation of statistics
- document delivery
- item availability study
- general survey of customer satisfaction

The last three of these are performance indicators developed by the Council of Australian University Librarians (CAUL) and are used across the university sector. Responses to requests from students are evaluated in part as a component of quality assurance, and in part in recognition that providing misinformation is more than a quality issue. It can result in a legal challenge if the receiver holds the provider to be liable (Hannabuss, 1998). The possibility of such action must be considered more likely as the number of full fee-paying students increases, particularly when so many students are enrolled in business courses. Indeed many are often in business themselves.

Just as quality assurance should not be viewed as one dimensional, nor can it be confined to just one section of the Library. Services to off-campus students are not provided in a vacuum. Many students enrolled as off-campus students visit or contact their home library or the libraries of other institutions and use exactly the same services as those available to fulltime on-campus students. Not all requests received at the University of South Australia come through the Flexible Delivery Service. A high proportion of distance education students are able to visit a library in person and many more contact whichever library staff member they find listed on a Web page, mentioned in a publication or referred to in course notes or lectures. The Library provides for this diversity in approach through the reporting mechanisms used by all librarians with a direct teaching and learning role. With a standardised format and review by supervisors, the reports are themselves a tool for quality assurance. Policies and services must also recognise that requests from distance education students can find their way to many different parts of an organisation. This requires that all library staff need to adopt a client focus that, while recognising that off-campus students may have particular needs, also sees them as part of the larger group of library clients entitled to good service. This can be a challenge for libraries at a time of increasing pressure on services and staff.

Amongst the features of quality assurance identified by AUQA there are three that are seen as of particular relevance for the Library's Flexible Delivery Service. The first of these is to recognise that feedback is essential. Quality assurance is a continuous, active and responsive process. Critical evaluation of performance and the actions that flow from this should be a regular and progressive feature of library services. Secondly, the core components of a quality system must include effective processes, and clear and precise descriptions of these must be widely available. Outcomes should make reference to standards and performance indicators. Finally, it is necessary to avoid focusing on how activities are currently performed. Effective quality assurance requires the use of external academic and professional points of reference. In recognition of this last requirement the Flexible Delivery Service engaged an external consultant to review all of its operations and services, including those offered to Open Learning Australia. A separate consultancy considered quality of the Unit's telephone service.

RISK MANAGEMENT AND QUALITY ASSURANCE

Another element in quality assurance in the Library is risk management. This is consistent with Australian standards for risk management and includes feedback through a monitoring and review process. The process is applied at both the level of strategic planning for the Library and as part of the University-wide risk registers. It is also used as a guideline for reviewing risks at a project or team level.

To establish the context for both risk management and quality assurance within the Flexible Delivery Service it was necessary to examine both the external and organisational environment. This led the library to consider three key questions: who its stakeholders are, where each activity fits within the stated objectives of the Library and University, and what constitutes an acceptable level of risk. The next step was to identify and generate a comprehensive list of all potential risk exposures and possible outcomes and investigate options to manage these risks. The risk treatment options considered were accepting risk, reducing risk, transferring risk or avoiding risk.

One of the significant risks identified for the Library as a whole was disruption to communication networks that might adversely affect access to databases. This is viewed as a particular issue for those studying off campus where alternative information sources are likely to be less readily available. The Library has addressed this risk by providing access to databases and electronic journals from a range of vendors and mounting some key services locally. This reduces the likelihood that any single failure to power, network or supplier will result in loss of access to all services.

QUALITY ASSURANCE IN COURSE APPROVAL AND DELIVERY

While the introduction of quality assurance into the Library's Flexible Delivery Service has benefits for both students and the Library, it is not sufficient in itself. The challenge remains how to better integrate library services and resources into the curriculum. As part of the University's course approval process, academic Schools must advise the Library of new initiatives and their likely resources implications. For its part, the Library works with program developers to establish and cost the most appropriate resources. The costed Library Impact Statement forms part of documentation submitted for approval by the University's Academic Board. It includes an indication of what the Library sees as the likely implications for its support of existing courses. For off-campus students this may depend in part upon what library services are available locally.

As is the case elsewhere, the University of South Australia is increasingly offering programs in other countries in partnership with local education institutions. Sadly, few of the agreements signed between strategic alliance partners contain clauses covering library access. Even when they do have such clauses, these frequently lack detail. This raises issues of a pedagogical and practical nature, particularly relating to desired graduate qualities such as information literacy. In order to better assess the actual and potential demand for library and information services of students enrolled in off-campus courses, the University Library initiated visits of librarians to those countries that are home to the greatest number of its offshore students. The purpose of these visits is to place our own library provision to offshore students in its local context.

While these visits have a primary focus on providing training in search strategy and the use of databases for higher degree students, they also review actual and potential use of local libraries and other information agencies by staff and students of the University. During discussions with students we are able to determine the extent of awareness of our library services amongst our offshore students as well as promote awareness of library services available from us. This assists the Library in determining an appropriate level of resource allocation to support the needs of offshore students and provides an opportunity to determine the adequacy of existing services at first hand. The training sessions provided are subject to the same evaluation instrument used on campus.

The University does not currently require faculty to demonstrate or document that arrangements for the provision of library resources and services are adequate and appropriate to support the educational programs they offer. It is our contention that those who initiate academic programs should be required to demonstrate the availability and adequacy of local library resources and service arrangements before these can be considered as a replacement for our Library. Hours of access and the extent and nature of resources available, for example, should be of a standard appropriate for the efficient provision of educational programs. It is University policy that those who develop programs of study must negotiate with the Library for the provision of these services prior to the submission of the proposal for approval. The Library has been a strong advocate of this to the academic governors of the University, believing that to accept a wide variation in access to information resources and education opportunities leading to the same academic award is a pedagogical and quality contradiction.

One area where off-campus students may miss out compared to their on-campus colleagues is in information literacy, particularly instruction in use of libraries and information. Since the library believes that the assistance and resources it knows are needed for on-campus students are also needed for those studying off campus, it follows that information literacy resources and services will need to be developed that meet the particular needs of those off campus. Costs include travel, accommodation, booking training facilities and backfilling the "on campus" duties of those librarians conducting the training. These costs are regarded as more than offset by being able to provide the same educational experience to offshore students as to students in Australia. Although expensive, the training provided by the University of South Australia to its students in Hong Kong, Singapore, Thailand, Taipei and Malaysia has evoked very favourable responses from both local agents and students.

The Library's first survey of its students in Hong Kong and Singapore showed that there was a discrepancy in the information provided to them in regard to access to university libraries. The survey also indicated that students do not believe that resources available to them are adequate to support their learning, and many are unsure how to obtain references located during their database searching. Although many students are required to use Internet search engines they displayed little confidence in conducting such searches effectively. Comments made by students during information sessions offered offshore, and supported by returned survey forms, included lack of access to local libraries, difficulties in locating material and a need for searching and related skills such as how to save search results (Parnell & Stevens, 1999).

Using our own staff to conduct training sessions offshore provides a clear indication of our commitment to providing a comprehensive range of services to students regardless of mode of study or location. This is part of a commitment to the belief that the same services and resources that are necessary for on-campus students should also be available to those studying off campus if they are to receive the same award.

LIMITATIONS OF QUALITY ASSURANCE

We mentioned earlier that quality assurance is seen by the Library as a dynamic process. This is essential in an environment of great change and increasing accountability for universities. It is very apparent that the Web is altering the current balance between library and teaching faculty as information providers. Already faculty involved in online education incorporate direct links to "library" resources within individual courses. These are often unacknowledged, and frequently included without the knowledge of the library. The quality assurance already part of internal operations within the Library needs to be extended to those activities where librarians work with faculty. With surveys of our students showing the Internet to be a primary information resource even for higher degree students, there is clearly a need for libraries to develop quality subject gateways to online resources as well. This can only be achieved by critically evaluating the resources provided for our students and ensuring that faculty direct students to these.

While it is not surprising that universities and their libraries currently appear to be focusing on the online environment, it is important not to overlook the value of the substantial print collections held by libraries–especially books. Loan figures for the year 2000 for library services for both the University of South Australia's own distance education students and those of Open Learning Australia show requests for books continue to match those for articles. This is particularly the case for postgraduate students where much specialised research material is only available in print, which their closest university may not necessarily hold. Surveys of university students in Hong Kong, Malaysia and elsewhere confirm the need for printed resources and the difficulties experienced in locating and gaining access to items (Vassie & Woodhead, 1998). The extent to which libraries are able to meet these needs will determine the costs of their service and their value to students.

Once you embark on quality assurance the number of services and operational areas that require attention rapidly expands. Other library services that value-add to the learning process such as reference and instructional services should not be overlooked. As part of the quality assurance process at the University of South Australia, for example, the Library found it necessary to undertake a review of patron statistical categories in its automated systems to ensure that it will be able to establish whether different equity groups are using the library and with what success. Categories able to be separated out for the first time in 2002 include Aboriginal and Torrens Strait Islanders and offshore students.

While the quality guidelines adopted at the University of South Australia Library cover most of its key services, they cannot of themselves ensure that students use only quality resources. Many off-campus students use other libraries to meet their information needs. What is of interest here is that 'host' libraries are likely to provide assistance to students without an underlying awareness or appreciation of course requirements of the parent institution. While this reduces the cost of information provision by the distance education provider, it does raise interesting questions as to how far institutional teaching programs and assessment can be quarantined from the external information environment. Clearly there are limits to the reach of individual quality assurance measures.

The University as a whole has not yet sought to implement the ISO 9000 quality management system requirements, but the Library has considered the way in which the five main areas covered in this are reflected in Library policy and practice. The area most easily associated with library activities under the International Organization for Standardizations' term 'product realization' can be equated in our case to acquiring and delivering resources to support distance education programs. The other elements necessary for certification have not been overlooked. In implementing quality assurance in the Library we have also paid attention to the overall quality of the system, management responsibility, people and resource management and measurement, analysis and improvement of systems.

QUALITY IN INFORMATION SERVICES

One of the concerns within the Library that led to the introduction of both offshore visits and quality assurance guidelines relates to the level and nature of assistance that can and should be provided to students. In this context, there is concern not just with the Library's ability to deal with an increase in demand from off-campus students, but over who has responsibility for the intellectual content of literature searches for higher degree students lacking ready access to research collections. There is also concern for those students who lack the opportunity to acquire adequate search skills, and for those who appear to lack an appreciation of the relationship between library service and personal responsibility. A report for the University into library support for offshore courses concluded that these need to conform to the quality assurance processes of the University, including access to scholarly information and support programs of a range and quality comparable to that for onshore students (Parnell & Stevens 1999).

Liaison librarians and the Distance Education Librarian receive requests for assistance that suggest a reliance not just on their information seeking skills, but on their evaluative skills as well. In some instances, the nature of requests received, the volume of information sought and the frequency of follow-up requests for assistance in refining literature search results raises questions of the place of the literature search in a student's course. Some students without access to major libraries believe that the University of South Australia has an obligation to provide a complete literature search service to them if they are accepted into higher degree programmes offered offshore. In a similar vein, the Library has received offers of payment from offshore students seeking an 'enhanced' information service.

At present there is a tendency amongst Library staff at this university to be generous in meeting the needs of off-campus students, particularly if there is doubt over their ability to access suitable resources themselves. This is balanced by concern that increased numbers of students undertaking higher degrees, and their significantly greater demands upon Library services, will exceed the Library's capacity to respond to distance education students as a whole in an effective and timely manner. It is to help address just this sort of issue that the Flexible Delivery Service began work on quality assurance.

A related issue facing the Library is how to achieve its objective of fostering information literacy and lifelong learning amongst off-campus students. This is not just a quality assurance issue; it raises ethical and pedagogical questions that need to be addressed by librarians and faculty. These include the appropriateness of librarians making a value judgment on the level of assistance requested by individual students to meet desired educational outcomes. The relationship between distance education, the Library and the literature research process cannot be considered in isolation; it needs to be looked at in the context of the content, presentation and timing of online tutorials and information literacy sessions offered. Most information searches for on-campus students are carried out in close consultation with the requestor, and may in fact be regarded as much guidance encounters as reference enquiries. They merge inevitably into reader education. The distance education service's quality assurance guidelines do not specifically address information literacy for off-campus students. Rather, the service operates within the Library-wide framework of the standards endorsed by the Australian higher education sector in the belief that these are independent of the student's mode of study (Council of Australian University Librarians, 2001).

STAFF–THE KEY TO PROVIDING QUALITY ASSURED SERVICE

The first step in implementing quality assurance is training staff. While the University of South Australia Library has always endeavoured to provide a "good" service to its off-campus students, it was an audit of the University's international activities, based on the OECD report Quality and Internationalisation of Higher Education (De Wit & Knight, 1999), that provided the impetus to move beyond surveys of customer satisfaction. The audit included a review by an external expert, and one of the recommendations called for more effort to be directed to preparing staff to be culturally aware and sensitive. The Library builds upon the basic reference skills of those in the Flexible Delivery Service, concentrating on developing email and counselling skills. Staff development sessions include those on internationalisation and cultural sensitivity. Participation in sessions on improving client relationships is a requirement for staff in Flexible Delivery Services. The current program is intended to raise awareness of the importance of always providing high quality and professional client relations. It aims to build confidence, and extend and fine tune existing skills when dealing with difficult people or situations. The University's International Student Advisory Service also conducts short interactive presentation and discussion sessions on how to effectively communicate with people for whom English is not a first language; this includes general cross-cultural communication protocols.

As part of the Library's recognition of the special needs of this group of users, one of our distance education librarians created practical guidelines in written communication with Chinese students for whom English is a second language. It is designed to provide practical tips and promote an understanding of the cultural distinctions that should be observed by staff that provide library services. Guides to information on communication styles of other Asian cultures are also available. We have also found it desirable to develop telephone counselling skills for those working in the distance education library service, particularly how to direct (control) those time-consuming calls from students looking for someone to talk to rather than seeking specific course related information. Quality assurance does not just mean giving a few individual requestors good service; it means managing service response and delivery to ensure that staff resources are equitably shared.

It is important to remember that the Library has introduced quality assurance guidelines, not rules. In putting these in place we are not seeking rigid adherence to standard practices and response times where these are not in the best interest of our clients. We do not wish to cramp spontaneity on the part of our librarians or unduly constrain requestors. We are very aware of the counselling role they play and this, by its very nature, must be flexible and responsive to the different needs and learning styles of our students. Change management is a key element in quality assurance and is covered in more detail in our accompanying presentation.

THE PLACE OF STATISTICS IN QUALITY ASSURANCE

Quality assurance is impossible without quantitative data. Bundy (2000) sees library statistics as having two essential purposes. These are for effective management and benchmarking and for advocacy for investment in libraries. Douglas (1990) observed that the basic point in a library collecting statistics is to assist in the running of that library. He continues on to identify the four aspects of collecting statistics that should be paramount. These are that data collected should bear on important problems, that it should be useful in determining courses of action, that it should be reliably collectable and that it should be unambiguous. We would add that the statistics collected need to be regularly reviewed.

Statistical data collection for libraries in a quality assurance environment has to be focused strongly towards an end benefit. At the University of South Australia the Flexible Delivery Service has taken the lead in the identification and collection of statistics within the Library. The statistics collected were decided only after careful review and only where these could be related directly to the attainment of its service philosophy and objectives. In addition to the uses identified above, the statistics collected help the library and the University perform and demonstrate performance and are used to advance the case for better funding. Within the Flexible Delivery Service statistics are seen as part of the quality assurance process and are collected (and analysed) to reflect and predict workloads and demands upon collections and services. Statistics should assist us in answering basic questions such as:

- Who uses the service–numbers of users by category, location and level. This helps to determine market penetration. It is also seen variously as providing political advantage–or just survival. It also provides a measure against which services can be costed and evaluated.
- What services are used and by whom. Without this information it is not possible to establish trends and changes in demand. Such statistics inform decisions on developing or reducing services and collections. This determines workloads and staffing levels within the Library and provides a measure to correlate with client satisfaction.
- What does it cost to provide a service–by user group and service. This is an essential element for marketing, service expansion or continuation and product differentiation.

We need objective measures to back up our claims that we really do offer a good service. Towards this end, the key question is what quality standards do we meet? The answers provide a basis for quality assurance and improvement. Examples include response and delivery turnaround times and the number of items not held. Both inform collection development decisions. Of course statistics are not sufficient on their own. They need to be supplemented with qualitative data. We also need to ask what our clients think and correlate client satisfaction with quality guidelines. Both offer opportunities for promoting Library services. Those questions most clearly articulated by Dervin (1977) still require research and are even more important today as higher education focuses more on graduate qualities and value for money. As librarians serving distance education students we must also consider what effect libraries have on our users. A quality assured service will help in the education process if the information it provides helps students in their understanding of concepts. Timely provision of access to information saves time for students, time that can be better utilised in other activities. It remains to be seen if friendly and appropriate assistance lowers attrition rates.

CONCLUSION

We began this paper with an indication that the environment for off-campus education is changing. As more academic programs are offered online or in conjunction with other educational institutions, the need for libraries to re-evaluate the nature and quality of their services becomes ever more urgent. There is pressure from funding authorities in Australia, Britain and elsewhere to see quality assurance as a control mechanism, part of a move to performance indicators that can be used to judge the comparative efficiency of higher education. This is not our view. We see quality assurance as a means of evaluating our services and promoting organizational knowledge with a view to improving them to the benefit of students. While just having quality assurance guidelines in place demonstrates a commitment to quality service, such guidelines can scarcely be considered effective or worthwhile unless they are monitored, altered and improved to meet changing conditions and demands. Like Thorpe (1993, p. 207) we believe that we need to move beyond what are currently minimum standards towards best practice. The challenge will be to do this at a time when there are such pressing demands upon all library services. To fail in the current competitive environment is to disadvantage not just our students, but also our institutions.

Gale (2001) reported of higher education in Australia that, "The excitement has largely gone and been replaced by endless measures of accountability and highly intrusive audit processes." Although staff within the Flexible Delivery Service put much time into producing a set of agreed quality assurance measures and indicators, this was done with both energy and commitment. The process was undertaken in recognition that quality service requires that the library knows what quality means to its clients and has in place measures that ensure that clients can be confident that this quality is met. The end result of this exercise was a set of guidelines rather grandly titled, Quality Assurance Measures and Indicators for Services Available Through Flexible Delivery Services. These indicate precisely what aspects and goals of quality are guaranteed and the ways in which the Library ensures these are attained.

Confidence amongst clients requires that a library be able to demonstrate its capability to deliver wanted services in a timely and convenient manner every time. The process of setting standards, collecting statistics, monitoring performance and analysing these to establish causes of deviations is seen as the basis for ensuring service standards and a way to stimulate gradual quality improvements.

REFERENCES

Australian Vice-Chancellors Committee (1998). *Code of ethical practice in the provision of education to international students by Australian Universities.* Retrieved November 27, 2001 from http://www.avcc.edu.au/news/public_statements/publications/code.htm.

Bundy, A. (2000). *Best value: Libraries.* Paper presented at a panel session library industry statistics for the 21st century during the Australian Library and Information

Association Conference Capitalising on Knowledge. *Canberra 23-27 October 2000.* Retrieved November 17, 2001 from http://www.library.unisa.edu.au/papers/value.htm.

Council of Australian University Librarians. (2001). *Information Literacy Standards.* Canberra: CAUL.

Dervin, B. (1977). Useful theory for librarianship: Communication not information *Drexel Library Quarterly, 13,* 16-32.

DETYA (2000). *Benchmarking: A manual for Australian universities.* Canberra: Dept. of Education, Training and Youth Affairs.

De Wit, H. & Knight, J. (1999). *Quality and internationalisation of higher education.* Paris, OECD.

Douglas, I. (1990). The library statist. In Exon, F., & Smith, K. (Eds.), *National Think Tank on library statistics.* Papers presented at a meeting held 29 September 1990, Perth, Western Australia. Perth: Liswa.

The good universities guide: Universities, TAFE & private colleges in Australia (1999). Subiaco, Western Australia: Hobsons.

Hannabuss, S. (1998) Information ethics: A contemporary challenge for professional and the community. *Library Review, 47,* 91-98.

Gale, F. (2001) Key issues close to the heart. *Campus Review,* Oct 3-9, 9-11.

Garson, G. D. (1999) *The role of technology in quality education: Thought & action, 15*(2). Retrieved November 11, 2001 from http://hcl.chass.ncsu.edu/sscore/garson2.htm.

Hughes, C. A. (2000). Information services for higher education: A new competitive space. *D-Lib Magazine, 6.* Retrieved November 22, 2001 from http://www.dlib.org/dlib/december00/hughes/12hughes.html.

International Organization for Standardization. (1994). *Quality management and quality assurance–vocabulary ISO 8042.* Geneva: International Organization for Standardization.

Institute for Higher Education Policy (2001). *Quality on the line: Benchmarks for success in Internet-based distance education.* Washington: National Education Association / BlackBoard. Retrieved September 18, 2001 from http://www.nea.org/he/abouthe/Quality.pdf.

Parnell, S. & Stevens, A. (1999). *Report on library services for students and staff of the University of South Australia*: Singapore & Hong Kong. University of South Australia.

Thompson, E. (1997). Distance education dropout: What can we do? In R. Pospisil & L. Willcoxson, *Learning through teaching: Proceedings of the 6th Annual Teaching Learning Forum,* Murdoch University. Retrieved 30 August 2001 from http://cleo.murdoch.edu.au/asu/pubs/tlf/tlf97/thom324.html.

Thorpe, M. (1993) *Evaluating open and distance education* (2nd ed.). Harlow, Essex: Longmans.

University of South Australia, (1999). *It's all about quality.* Retrieved 11, November from http://www.unisa.edu.au/quality/introduction.htm.

Vassie, R. & Woodhead, M. (1998). *Access to library resources: A blindspot in distance learning?* Report on the proceedings of a one-day seminar on ILL for distance learning held at the British Library Document Supply Centre. Boston Spa.

Information Literacy Modules
as an Integral Component
of a K-12 Teacher Preparation Program:
A Librarian/Faculty Partnership

Hazel M. Davis

Rio Salado College

SUMMARY. Rio Salado College is a non-traditional community college specializing in customized programs and distance education. The Faculty Chair for Library Science, who is also the Library Director, collaborated with the Faculty Chair for Education to develop an integrated series of information literacy modules for inclusion in an online distance post-baccalaureate teacher preparation program. The creation and development of the modules, as well as possible future applications, are discussed.

KEYWORDS. Information literacy, library instruction, elementary students, secondary students

BACKGROUND

Rio Salado College has always been a non-traditional institution. Founded in 1978 as a "College Without Walls," the college is one of ten comprising the Maricopa Community College District in Arizona, the second largest community college district in the United States. While the other nine colleges feature traditional campuses, services and infrastructure, Rio Salado has, since its in-

[Haworth co-indexing entry note]: "Information Literacy Modules as an Integral Component of a K-12 Teacher Preparation Program: A Librarian/Faculty Partnership." Davis, Hazel M. Co-published simultaneously in *Journal of Library Administration* (The Haworth Information Press, an imprint of The Haworth Press, Inc.) Vol. 37, No. 1/2, 2002, pp. 207-216; and: *Distance Learning Library Services: The Tenth Off-Campus Library Services Conference* (ed: Patrick B. Mahoney) The Haworth Information Press, an imprint of The Haworth Press, Inc., 2002, pp. 207-216.

http://www.haworthpress.com/store/product.asp?sku=J111
10.1300/J111v37n01_18

ception, operated without a campus under the philosophy of "Let the College come to you." Over the years, Rio Salado has provided educational services to students through a variety of modalities, including print, mixed-media (a combination of print and video or audio materials), television, videotape, CD-ROM, in-person instruction at selected sites such as service centers, schools and shopping malls, and since 1996, online. The College was the first to provide instruction via the Internet in Arizona, and by 2001 offered well over 200 online courses.

Twenty-three years after its inception, the College mission statement focuses on creating convenient, high quality learning opportunities, specifically targeted towards three areas of specialization. These are customized and unique programs and partnerships with business and industry leaders, accelerated formats, and distance delivery. The teacher preparation program that will be highlighted in this article is an example of the way in which the College constantly develops new initiatives on the leading edge of educational opportunity.

In 2000-2001, Rio Salado's unduplicated, annual credit headcount numbered 34,198 students, translating into 9,400 full-time student equivalencies. In keeping with its non-traditional structure, this student body is served by 26 permanent faculty members, along with over 700 adjunct faculty who are drawn from educators, practitioners and content experts in the disciplines taught. Most of the 26 permanent faculty members serve as department heads, or Faculty Chairs, including the Library Director who is also the Faculty Chair for Library Science.

This model of a small permanent faculty cohort, all housed in the same building (and most on the same floor), results in extremely close interaction and cooperation between Faculty Chairs of different disciplines. There is continual personal and professional communication between the Chairs, and inter-disciplinary teamwork is common, resulting in considerable opportunity for developing inter-disciplinary cooperative instructional initiatives; in fact, teamwork is one of the College's core values. Because the primary instructional decision-makers work closely together, unencumbered by large academic departments, cooperative programs can be developed with considerable speed and flexibility.

LIBRARIAN/FACULTY COOPERATION

The literature contains many discussions of the issues involved in relationships between librarians and instructional faculty. Kotter (1999) provides an excellent overview, and comments also that a great deal of the published discussion regarding the quality of interactions between librarians and their teaching faculty colleagues is anecdotal, with much of it providing a negative impression. However, as Kotter (1999) states: " . . . if librarians truly believe that it is their right and obligation to become partners in the processes of education and scholarship, effective collaboration is essential" (p. 1).

Terms used to define these cooperative ventures vary, and may include "cooperation," "coordination" and "collaboration," with the latter indicating a more intensive and integrated working relationship between librarians and their instructional faculty colleagues (Gallegos & Wright, 2000, p. 98).

Whichever of these terms is preferred, there is no doubt that partnership projects between librarians and instructional faculty are increasing. Raspa and Ward (2000) postulate that collaboration has become the educational imperative of our times, and that changes in the information universe along with advantages in technology make it essential. They foresee in the future an increase in partnerships and teams wherein librarians and teaching faculty will work together to provide information to students in a variety of forms, including electronic and distance learning formats (p. 2). This latter is already a reality at Rio Salado.

The faculty librarian at Rio works closely with faculty in other disciplines on many different initiatives, usually in the role of information disseminator and integrator, and is also the president-elect of the college faculty association. Some examples of cross-disciplinary initiatives in which the faculty librarian has been involved at the college include leading a team that completely redesigned the information architecture of the college Web site (where all information was carefully organized and cross-referenced to make most content no more than two clicks deep), designing research assignments with colleagues for use in their courses, working with faculty in all disciplines to secure copyright clearance for materials incorporated in distance learning courses, and serving as the competency coordinator for information literacy, which has been identified as one of the College's core student competencies that is measured across all disciplines.

The balance of this article will address the development of a comprehensive set of information literacy modules as part of a distance learning teacher preparation program, providing an example of the type of collaboration between the faculty librarian and instructional faculty made possible at Rio Salado by the College's infrastructure and culture.

THE TEACHER PREPARATION PROGRAM

In 1998, the State of Arizona passed legislation allowing community colleges to offer post-baccalaureate teacher certification programs. Previously, this had been the exclusive purview of the universities. In light of this change, in 2001, the College decided to develop a completely online post baccalaureate teacher preparation program, designed for working adults who have already received a baccalaureate degree and wish to enter the teaching profession. The Faculty Chair for Education was responsible for the development of three versions of the program, including Elementary, Secondary, and Special Education. As best as could be determined, this was the first complete online teacher preparation program offered in the United States.

The Education Chair had previously attended a workshop offered by the Library Chair, in which electronic resources provided via the College library Web site were highlighted. She approached the Library Chair with the idea of developing a lesson incorporating instruction in electronic resources for the Teacher Prep students. Rio Salado has a centralized course development system. Thus, any course developed in a discipline and taught via distance learning has identical content and course materials for all sections of that course. This would mean that content could be offered that would be a part of every student's learning experience. The Library Chair proposed expanding the concept to include a series of six information literacy modules rather than just one lesson. A core group of five common courses is taught in all three versions of the program, and one module would be inserted in each course, which would ensure that all students would receive all content. In this way, any student proceeding through the certification program would be required to take the five information literacy modules as part of their coursework, with a sixth module for Secondary Education students only.

INFORMATION LITERACY SKILLS FOR EDUCATORS

The advantage to this approach is that the information literacy skills incorporated as part of the learning for students preparing to become K-12 teachers would then become a skill set that they, in turn, could impart to their students. This is particularly significant because of a widely held belief that a part of the problem with students who lack information literacy skills is that their teachers also lack these skills, or fail to realize their importance. Indeed, the 1989 Final Report of the American Library Association Presidential Committee on Information Literacy recommended, "Teacher education and performance expectations should be modified to include information literacy concerns" (1989, Committee Recommendations section, para. 5). However, in the progress report on information literacy published in 1998, this was the only recommendation from the original report on which no progress had been made. Accordingly, the progress report recommended encouraging leaders in existing school reform movements to incorporate information literacy skills into their efforts, and also a more aggressive partnership with national teacher education organizations to get information literacy on their agendas. As the report noted: "Key to success in this area will be the integration of information literacy efforts throughout the curriculum" (1998, Challenges section, recommendation 2). The report also specifically recommended "a plan for working with teacher education programs and the National Council for Accreditation of Teacher Education to infuse information literacy requirements into undergraduate and graduate programs of teacher education" (1998, Recommendations for further progress section).

In light of this status quo and these recommendations from authors of the progress report, the enormous importance of imbuing a teacher preparation program with integral information literacy content becomes even more evident, and is directly in line with the national information literacy initiatives.

A review of the literature conducted by Moore and Ivory (2000) indicated that college faculty are the key to whether or not students develop information literacy skills, because they control the class content, assignments and learning objectives, while also serving as role models and mentors for the students (p. 4). The review also found that while many faculty members recognize the value of information literacy assignments, they might not update these assignments regularly, nor consult with librarians to ensure their relevancy and accuracy. Furthermore, although faculty might realize the importance of these skills, they might not feel that it was their responsibility to see that their students acquired them.

The review further notes that faculty members who received their degrees before the current explosion of online information might not be comfortable with electronic modalities, nor adept at handling the ever-increasing availability of electronic information. By providing student teachers with information literacy modules in an electronic environment, and exposing them to a large variety of electronic resources in the modules, Rio Salado College's initiative addresses this issue.

INFORMATION LITERACY STANDARDS

Most definitions of information literacy developed by members of the academic library community stem from that provided in the ALA Final Report of 1989 referenced above. "To be information literate, a person must be able to recognize when information is needed and have the ability to locate, evaluate and use effectively the needed information" (1989, para. 3). Information is understood to encompass more than just the printed word, and might include visual and computer literacies as well. The *Information Literacy Competency Standards for Higher Education*, published by the Association of College and

Research Libraries in January 2000, provided standards, performance indicators and outcomes whereby to measure competency in information literacy.

The modules for the teacher preparation program were based on these standards, which had previously been modified for use at Rio Salado for the information literacy core competency initiative. According to the ACRL standards, the information literate student:

- determines the nature and extent of the information needed.
- accesses needed information effectively and efficiently.
- evaluates information and its sources critically and incorporates selected information into his or her knowledge base and value system.
- individually or as a member of a group, uses information effectively to accomplish a specific purpose.
- understands many of the economic, legal, and social issues surrounding the use of information and accesses and uses information ethically and legally.

Rio Salado's information literacy competencies and performance indicators were adapted by the Faculty Librarian from the ACRL standards. The Rio competencies and performance indicators, used to underpin the information literacy modules, are these:

A. Identify the kind of information needed for a specific research purpose
   Performance Indicators
      a. Formulates questions based on the information need (e.g., types of sources needed, current vs. historical information, scholarly vs. popular)
      b. Explores general information sources to increase familiarity with topic
      c. Defines or modifies the topic to achieve a manageable focus
      d. Clarifies and revises the initial information need as necessary

B. Develop a successful search strategy to locate specific sources that meet the research purpose
   Performance Indicators
      a. Selects appropriate retrieval systems (books, periodicals, newspapers, electronic resources)
      b. Identifies keywords and search terms
      c. Constructs and implements a search strategy appropriate to the retrieval system (Boolean for electronic, or indexes for books)
      d. Retrieves information online or in person as appropriate
      e. Refines the search terms and search strategy as needed

C. Given specific criteria, evaluate the information content of the sources by using critical thinking skills

Performance Indicators
   a. Summarizes main ideas extracted from sources
   b. Evaluates sources using such criteria as reliability, authority, accuracy, validity, timeliness, bias
   c. Revises initial query as needed if additional information is required

D. Apply the information appropriately in a research task

Performance Indicators
   a. Organizes the content (e.g., outline, draft)
   b. Communicates the product effectively to others, clearly and with a style appropriate to the intended audience
   c. Attributes directly quoted information appropriately
   d. Cites sources accurately and correctly

THE MODULES

The six core teacher preparation courses into which the modules were inserted included the Education Seminar (an orientation and overview of the entire teacher preparation program), Classroom Management, Educational Psychology, Introduction to the Exceptional Learner, Learning and the Brain, and Curriculum Development (Secondary Methods). The modules were inserted into the courses in different ways so as to provide variety and interest for the students. They appeared variously as complete lessons, as tutorials within the course content, as tutorials linked to assignments, or as mini-tutorials where the content was chunked into several sections and inserted into several different lessons within a course. In this way, the students received their information literacy skills training as an integral part of their course content, rather than as a separate "library" piece. Apart from the Education Seminar, which all students take first as a prerequisite for the program, students can take courses in any order they choose. Accordingly, the modules could not build upon one another and needed to stand alone. Because of this, basic concepts were reintroduced and reinforced in all the modules, as students might or might not have encountered them before.

As developed, the modules require students to acquire skills using the resources offered on the College's virtual library Web site, as well as Web searching techniques. It was decided to use a variety of databases that would provide instruction in different formats and media. Accordingly, the modules were structured as follows:

- An Introduction to Information Literacy, Online Catalogs and E-Books

    This module explained the concepts of information literacy and introduced the expectation that the students would cover these concepts throughout the teacher preparation program. Elements of searching OPACs were explained, specifically the OPAC at the College, and the NetLibrary E-book collection was also taught.

- Features of Electronic Databases
  EBSCO MasterFile Premier and InfoTrac Web

    This module covered the elements common to most electronic databases, and the basics of database searching, including Boolean search techniques. Two popular magazine and journal databases, EBSCO MasterFile Premier and InfoTrac Expanded Academic ASAP, were then covered in detail.

- Electronic Newspaper Databases
  ProQuest National Newspapers Five and Ethnic Newswatch

    Two very different newspaper databases were taught in this module. ProQuest's National Newspapers Five includes five major U.S. newspapers, including the *New York Times* and *Wall Street Journal*. Ethnic Newswatch is a database of the periodical literature published for various ethnic groups in the United States.

- ERIC and AP Photo Archive

    Features of ERIC E-subscribe, which contains the full-text of most ERIC documents since 1996, were taught. Knowledge of this product was considered essential for these student teachers. The AP Photo Archive is a product licensed to educational institutions by the Associated Press, containing approximately 700,000 photographs, and a smaller file of graphic images. Thus, student teachers become familiar with the enormous range of pictorial material available for classroom projects.

- Searching and Evaluating Web Sites

    The basics of searching the Web were taught in this module, along with detailed techniques to evaluate electronic content of all kinds. Additionally, citation of online resources was covered.

• Copyright and Plagiarism

> This module taught students the concepts of Fair Use and the issues relating to copyright in the educational environment. Additionally, issues relating to plagiarism were discussed, and some techniques for detecting plagiarism were covered, including the availability of commercial products for this purpose.

In each case, the students were required to proceed through online instruction, which taught the information literacy concepts and then the specifics behind each process or database, and then to perform structured searches, which were designed to mesh with content covered in the particular course in which the module appeared. Assignments that required students to perform searches and find articles relating to the content of the modules were embedded in each course and formed part of the requirement for their grade.

At the time of this writing the program has been in existence for three months. Since the initial start date, students have had the opportunity to enroll every two weeks, in accordance with Rio Salado's model, which offers course starts every two weeks for most courses. Enrollments are robust, and 360 students have enrolled in the program since its inception. Because of the recency of this application, it is too early to evaluate the impact or success of the information literacy modules. Anecdotal data show students fulfilling the requirements of the modules successfully. Once the program is well established, a survey will be conducted to explore this further. Additionally, the possibility of pre- and post-testing using an information literacy assessment instrument will be considered.

As structured, these modules could be used to infuse information literacy within several other programs taught at Rio Salado College. Because of the "one course, many instructors" model, adapting these modules to suit course content in several other disciplines would be a relatively simple task. The Faculty Librarian plans to work with Faculty Chair colleagues in other disciplines to explore this further. Also, because the modules are not sequential, individual units could be used in different courses or programs if that is more appropriate.

As Caspers and Lenn (2000) note " . . . students . . . in distance-delivered courses . . . may complete their programs without benefit of the library. . . . The most effective way for librarians to reach distance learners . . . is through cooperation (at least) and collaboration (at best) with teaching faculty" (p. 150). The Rio Salado initiative has proven to be enormously exciting and rewarding, exemplifying as it does the concepts of both Faculty/Librarian collaboration, and the infusion of information literacy as an integral part of, rather than an adjunct to, course instruction for distance learners.

REFERENCES

American Library Association. *Presidential Committee on Information Literacy.* (1989). *Final report.* Retrieved November 21, 2001 from http://www.ala.org/acrl/nili/ilit1st. html.

Association of College & Research Libraries. (2000). *Information literacy competency standards for higher education.* Retrieved November 21, 2001 from http://www.ala. org/acrl/ilcomstan.html.

Association of College & Research Libraries. National Forum on Information Literacy. (1998). *A progress report on information literacy: An update on the American Library Association Presidential Committee on Information Literacy Final Report.* Retrieved November 21, 2001 from http://www.ala.org/acrl/nili/nili.html.

Caspers, J., & Lenn, K. (2000). The future of collaboration between librarians and teaching faculty. In C. Raspa & D. Ward (Eds.), *The collaborative imperative: Librarians and faculty working together in the information universe* (pp. 1-18). Chicago, IL: Association of College and Research Libraries.

Gallegos, B., & Wright, T. (2000). Collaborations in the field: Examples from a survey. In C. Raspa & D. Ward (Eds.), *The collaborative imperative: Librarians and faculty working together in the information universe* (pp. 97-109). Chicago, IL: Association of College and Research Libraries.

Kotter, Wade R. (1999). Bridging the great divide: Improving relations between librarians and classroom faculty. *Journal of Academic Librarianship*, 25(4), 294-303. Retrieved October 22, 2001 from WilsonSelectPlus database.

Moore, A.C., & Ivory, G. (2000). *Investigating and improving the information literacy of college faculty.* East Lansing, MI: National Center for Research on Teacher Learning. (ERIC Document Reproduction Service No. ED449783).

Raspa, D., & Ward, D. (2000). Listening for collaboration: Faculty and librarians working together. In C. Raspa & D. Ward (Eds.), *The collaborative imperative: Librarians and faculty working together in the information universe* (pp. 148-154). Chicago: Association of College and Research Libraries.

Documenting Priorities, Progress, and Potential: Planning Library Services for Distance Education

Stephen H. Dew

University of Iowa

SUMMARY. The *ACRL Guidelines for Distance Learning Library Services* recommends that every library develop a written profile and a written statement addressing the needs and outlining the methods by which progress can be measured. Many libraries do not have a written plan, and occasionally at such institutions, services for distance-education students suffer as a consequence. In 1998, the University of Iowa Libraries instituted a written plan for developing library services for its off-campus students, and the plan has been an effective tool. Highlighting the University of Iowa Libraries' plan, this article discusses a variety of subjects that should be addressed when preparing, writing, and implementing a plan for distance-education services.

KEYWORDS. Distance education, library services, planning, assessment

The *ACRL Guidelines for Distance Learning Library Services* (2000) recommends that every library develop a written profile of its distance learning community and a "written statement . . . (that) addresses the needs and outlines the methods by which progress can be measured" (p. 1026). Many libraries,

[Haworth co-indexing entry note]: "Documenting Priorities, Progress, and Potential: Planning Library Services for Distance Education." Dew, Stephen H. Co-published simultaneously in *Journal of Library Administration* (The Haworth Information Press, an imprint of The Haworth Press, Inc.) Vol. 37, No. 1/2, 2002, pp. 217-242; and: *Distance Learning Library Services: The Tenth Off-Campus Library Services Conference* (ed: Patrick B. Mahoney) The Haworth Information Press, an imprint of The Haworth Press, Inc., 2002, pp. 217-242.

http://www.haworthpress.com/store/product.asp?sku=J111
10.1300/J111v37n01_19

however, do not have a written plan, and occasionally at such institutions, services for distance-education students are lost in the shuffle of day-to-day work routines. In 1998, the University of Iowa Libraries instituted a written plan for developing library services for its off-campus students, and the plan has been an effective tool, allowing librarians and other university staff to focus their efforts on priorities, progress, and potential improvements in service. The objective of this article is to inform readers about a variety of issues and subjects that should be addressed when preparing, writing, and implementing a plan for distance-education library services.

First of all, however, some background information about distance education at the University of Iowa is in order. I began work at the University of Iowa Libraries in September 1998. I was the first librarian at Iowa whose job responsibilities were devoted entirely to distance education. The University of Iowa Libraries cooperated with the Division of Continuing Education to create a new professional position–Coordinator of Library Services for Distance Education. Prior to my employment, the University Libraries had been attempting to address concerns about services for off-campus students, but since responsibilities were divided among different staff members spread about in a very large library system, some details concerning distance education always seemed to fall between the cracks. Library staff had prepared a few outlines of some distance-education services, and a couple of brief handouts had also been developed. There was, however, no overall description of library services for distance-education students, and there was no plan for developing services. As the new Coordinator of Library Services for Distance Education, I was assigned the responsibility of writing and developing a plan. It became one of my first priorities.

My first order of business was to educate myself about the variety of distance-education programs at Iowa and to immediately begin promoting library service to support those programs. I believed that I could develop a plan soon enough, but in order to be prepared to write the plan, I needed to immerse myself in the details of distance-education library services at the University of Iowa. I read all of the material concerning distance-education programs and library services at the University. I talked with all library staff who worked in some fashion with off-campus programs. I traveled to a number of off-campus sites, visiting with faculty, students, and staff. I lectured to several distance-education classes. I began developing a library Web site to support distance-education students. I met with the staff in the Center for Credit Programs and other administrators who managed distance-education programs and courses. I supervised a survey of distance-education students, a survey that proved most valuable in helping me understand my most important clients. I learned important details about the University of Iowa's off-campus programs, and eventually, I was able to start outlining a plan.

I gathered together several documents to help me prepare the plan. The documents included copies of the *ACRL Guidelines for Distance Learning Library Services*, the *University of Iowa Libraries Strategic Plan*, the *University of Iowa Center for Credit Programs Strategic Plan for Distance Education*, my job description, my written annual goals, and a few other documents related to library services or distance education at the University of Iowa.

In addition, I also did a literature review on the subject of library planning related to distance education. I found very little published on the subject, and most of what had been done related to the narrow subject of electronic services. Although a few articles provided interesting examples of the issues that distance librarians need to consider, no article or book provided a specific example of a planning document. I did, however, find a few examples of planning documents for distance-education library services on the Web (University of Minnesota, 1999; Cornell University, 1998; Florida Distance Learning, 1999). Although these documents were either much more detailed or different in focus than what I had in mind, they did inform me about some of the issues and subjects that I would need to address.

Using a wide variety of documents and on-the-job knowledge that I had gained over the previous six months, I began fleshing out my plan. By March 1999, I finally had a first draft ready to reveal to my supervisor and the staff in the Center for Credit Programs. I was very pleased that both the library administrators and the Center for Credit Programs accepted the plan. Soon afterward, copies of the plan were distributed to appropriate library staff and managers in the various distance-education programs.

Heeding Publilius Syrus' warning in his *Maxim 469*, "It is a bad plan that admits to no modification" (as cited in Bartlett, 1980), I wrote *The University of Iowa Libraries Plan for Distance-Education Services* with the understanding that it would be revised many times. One of the most important qualities of the plan is that it can be, and should be, easily revised. As our resources or services changed, as new programs or services were initiated, and as I occasionally discovered new information, I found a need to revise the plan. Over the three years since the plan was first drafted, it has been revised approximately a half-a-dozen times. Easily adaptable and regularly reviewed plans such as this are often referred to as "rolling plans" (Evans, Ward, and Rugaas, 2000). *The University of Iowa Libraries Plan for Distance-Education Services* has proved to be an essential tool for me in my work. It helped me develop an overall conception of what is involved in the University's distance-education programs; it helped me understand where my priorities should be; and it helped me focus on areas needing improvement. In addition, an extremely important point is that the plan has not only helped "me" understand all of that–the plan also has served as an informational tool and guide for many of my colleagues, especially other library and University staff members involved in distance-education services and, very importantly, my supervisors in library administration.

This article will now turn to a brief review of *The University of Iowa Libraries Plan for Distance-Education Services* (see Appendix A). The plan is organized into eleven broad sections. On the front page, following the title and author, is a date indicating when this version of the plan was revised. I would advise anyone working on such a plan to put the revision date on the front of the document, not on the back or off the front page–put the date up front where it can be seen immediately. If a plan is revised fairly frequently, then no doubt multiple versions will be in use or lying around the office at any given time, and if the revision date is on the front of the document, users can quickly identify the version in hand.

Section I of the plan is an "Introduction" that summarizes distance education at the University of Iowa, emphasizing the wide variety of teaching methodologies and the increasing use of new technologies. The "Introduction" is followed by the "Objectives," which speak to the heart and purpose of the plan–to document and summarize current library services, to identify library service priorities, to identify aspects of services that can be improved, and to suggest methods and solutions for improvements.

Section III, "Programs & Subject Priorities," presents a list of all of thirteen distance-education degree-granting programs offered through the University of Iowa. The first paragraph in the section declares that priorities will be given to library services and subject resources that support the programs listed. Section IV, "Student ID Card or Borrower's Permit Required," details the ID and permit requirements demanded by the Registrar and the Libraries. In order to be able to access library resources and services from off-campus, students must have either an ID card or a permit.

Following the Introduction, Objectives, Priorities, and ID Requirements, the plan turns to a discussion of various library services. The first service is, I think, the most important service for students being served at a distance–"Electronic & Web-based Services." For anyone involved in distance education, electronic and Web-based services are extremely important now–and they will, of course, continually increase in importance. The Internet has revolutionized the way all libraries provide services, but the Internet has been especially revolutionary for academic libraries serving distance-education programs. Clearly, the Internet will continue its profound influence during our lifetimes, and those libraries that best serve their distance-education students will most likely be those libraries that best use the power of the Internet to provide access to electronic resources and services. In this section, the plan describes the Coordinator's responsibility for developing, maintaining, updating, and improving the "Distance-Education Library Services" Web site (Dew, 2001a). By developing Web sites to support off-campus students, distance-education librarians can succeed in overcoming the challenge of location and remoteness. We should seize the opportunity and exploit this powerful tool by developing useful and functional Web sites that are designed to serve from a distance.

After the section on Electronic and Web-based Services, the plan next turns to an outline of the Libraries' "Document Delivery Services." A reflection of how important document delivery services are can be found in the fact that three pages of the plan are devoted to the subject. In this section, various options that students have for obtaining documents are listed, beginning with the most popular method of delivery–Electronic Access to Full-Text. The plan notes that in 1998-99, the Libraries conducted a survey of distance-education students, and the survey revealed that two-thirds of the students felt that providing online full-text resources was one of the most important services that the Libraries could offer, ranking second among twelve library services listed (Dew, 2001b). Over the three years since the plan was first drafted, the University of Iowa has added a number of important full-text files to its list of resources, and the Libraries will continue, of course, to add appropriate full-text resources. This portion of the plan ends with the important declaration that the Libraries should consider for acquisition any full-text file that supports one or more of the University's distance-education programs.

Since interlibrary loan services are generally free, I discuss that document-delivery option next in the plan, and then immediately following, I discuss in some detail the Libraries' special "Distance-Education Document-Delivery Service." When the first version of the plan was completed in March 1999, this service was not available, but the first version of the plan called upon the Coordinator to investigate the possibility of developing such a fee-based service. The survey of distance-education students completed by the Libraries in 1998-99 showed that over sixty-percent of the students felt that, despite the fee, providing such a document-delivery option was one of the most important services that the Libraries could offer, ranking third among twelve library services listed. As the current version of the plan notes, the Distance-Education Document-Delivery Service began in the fall of 1999, and it offers students fast delivery of articles and books for a basic fee of three dollars for each item. Students may request that articles be either faxed or mailed, while UPS delivers books. Web-based request forms provide quick and easy access to the service, and faxable request forms can be used, if a student prefers. The plan also notes that social work students receive the document-delivery service free through financing by a special endowment–the Laura L. Davis Fund. Importantly, following a discussion about the responsibility for collecting statistics, the plan reinforces the Libraries' *Strategic*

Plan, noting that statistics should be reviewed as an indicator of distance learners making greater use of library services.

Following the discussion of the document-delivery service, the plan briefly outlines circulation and library-use privileges that University of Iowa distance-education students enjoy at a variety of institutions, and then, the plan turns to a discussion of "Reserve Book Collections" and "Electronic Reserves." When the original version of the plan was drafted, the Libraries did not support either book reserves or electronic reserves for off-campus students. Soon afterward, however, I opened a discussion among library staff members about developing these services, and later versions of the plan directed the Coordinator (me) to investigate the possibility of developing these services. Finally, after working out procedural details and financing, during the fall semester 2000, both book reserve and electronic reserve services were instituted on a limited basis. The current version of the plan directs the Coordinator to investigate the possibility of expanding the electronic reserve service to distance-education programs other than just social work, noting that library and information science will most likely be the next program included.

Following the section on document delivery, the plan next turns to "User Education." This section is divided into five subdivisions–Classroom Instruction, Web-based and Computer-Assisted Instruction, Handouts (see Appendix B) and Other Print Material, UI Information Initiative, and Teaching with Innovative Style & Technology. Significantly in this section, the plan again reinforces the Libraries' *Strategic Plan*, as it directs the Coordinator to develop library education components for all graduate and professional programs involved in distance education. In addition, this section also notes that the Coordinator is responsible for maintaining appropriate statistics, and the plan directs the Coordinator to develop skills in using appropriate user-education technologies (interactive television, Web-based instructional tools, etc.). The Coordinator is also directed to work with interested faculty members to incorporate information literacy skills into distance-education classes.

After User Education, the plan next turns to a discussion of "Reference Assistance & Consultation" services. Highlighting the importance of reference assistance, the plan declares that reference questions always take priority over regular tasks and should be answered as quickly as possible. This section also reinforces the Libraries' *Strategic Plan*, noting the Coordinator's responsibility to maintain statistics, as an indicator of distance learners making greater use of library services. When the original version of the plan was completed in March 1999, only e-mail and non-toll-free telephone reference was offered. As the plan evolved, however, a toll-free telephone service was added, and an electronic consultation-request form was added to the Web site. Also notable in this section, the plan directs the Coordinator to work with the Virtual Reference Working Group to establish a digital-reference pilot project during the spring semester 2002.

In Section IX, "Communication with Faculty," the plan directs the Coordinator to send letters each semester to faculty members involved in distance-education programs, summarizing library services and offering classroom instruction and other user-education services. The plan again reinforces the Libraries' *Strategic Plan*, highlighting the fact that the letters support two Goals in the *Strategic Plan*. This section also urges the Coordinator to visit regularly with faculty members, students, and librarians at each off-campus site.

In a large academic system like the University of Iowa, the Coordinator of Library Services for Distance Education must work with a wide variety of people located in a wide variety of places. Section X, "Cooperation & Collaboration," provides a summary of the various education centers, universities, colleges, community colleges, hospitals, public libraries, private corporations, and other groups that are connected to or associated with the University's distance-education programs. The plan directs the Coordinator to communicate with personnel located at each site, keeping them up-to-date on library services and visiting the site when appropriate.

Review and evaluation are both necessary to accurately judge the quality of library service, and both are also key factors in determining aspects of library service that might be improved. In that vein, Section XI addresses the key issues of "Review & Evaluation." The plan directs the Coordinator to supervise regular student surveys for formal evaluation of library services and to develop Web-based forms for individual feedback. *The University of Iowa Libraries Plan for Distance-Education Services* ends by noting that, although the plan is subject to review and revision at any time, at least once each year the Coordinator and the Director of Central Public Services review the document. As mentioned earlier, over the three years since the plan was first drafted, it has been revised approximately half-a-dozen times, and no doubt, it will be revised many more times. One of the great qualities of a "rolling plan" like the one at the University of Iowa is that it can be easily revised. As Marilyn Gell Mason (1999) has concluded, "As change inevitably occurs, we must adapt our plan accordingly. . . . the plan is never really completed. It just continues to evolve" (p. 4). In addition, librarians attempting to write a rolling plan for distance-education library services should also keep in mind Douglas Zweizig's observation (1996), "Planning is a series of successive approximations to a moving target. . . . a process of continuous consideration of what the library is and where it is going" (p. 5).

The University of Iowa Libraries Plan for Distance-Education Services is just one example of what can be done in order to plan library services for off-campus students. Since distance-education programs vary widely across the nation and around the world, plans for library services should also differ according to each peculiar situation. Planning documents should be as unique as the individuals and institutions creating them, but certainly librarians can share ideas about ways to approach the planning process. For librarians interested in planning distance-education services, the University of Iowa welcomes the use of its plan as a source for ideas.

Librarians should also keep in mind that, although the written plan is the final goal of the writing process, the process itself could be quite rewarding, as well. From the writing process, I learned a great deal about the details of distance-education services at the University of Iowa, and that knowledge, I think, helped me address and perform my responsibilities better. As Donald Riggs (1997) once observed about the planning process, if it is done properly, "participants may find the process . . . as useful as the document itself" (p. 401).

The document itself, however, is also vitally important, of course. In addition to the learning experience gained from the writing process, I have found my plan to be extremely valuable as well. The plan is an essential tool for me in my work. It helped me develop an overall conception of what is involved in the University's distance-education programs; it helped me understand where my priorities should be; and it helped me focus on areas needing improvement. In addition, the plan also has served as an informational guide for many other library and University staff members involved in distance education. It has helped them understand the small details, as well as the broader picture, of library services for distance education. *The University of Iowa Libraries Plan for Distance-Education Services* has empowered librarians and other university staff members, providing them a tool through which they can focus their efforts on priorities, progress, and potential improvements in service.

REFERENCES

ACRL Guidelines for Distance Learning Library Services. (2000). *College & Research Libraries News 61*, 1023-1029. Also retrieved November 19, 2001, from the Association of College and Research Libraries Web site: http://www.ala.org/acrl/guides/distlrng.html.

Bartlett, John. (1980). *Familiar quotations.* Boston: Little, Brown & Company.

Clougherty, L., Forys, J., & Lyles, T. (1998). The University of Iowa Libraries' Undergraduate User Needs Assessment. *College & Research Libraries 59*, 572-584.

Cornell University Library. (1998). *Cornell University Library Distance Learning White Paper.* Retrieved October 26, 2001, from Cornell University Library Web site: http://www.library.cornell.edu/staffweb/Distance.html.

Council of Prairie and Pacific University Libraries. (n.d.). *Council of Prairie and Pacific University Libraries Distance Education Forum, Action Plan for 2001-2002.*

Retrieved October 26, 2001, from the Council of Prairie and Pacific University Libraries Web site: http://library.athabascau.ca/copdlforum/index.htm.

Dew, Stephen H. (2001). Designed to serve from a distance: Developing library Web pages to support distance education. In Barbara I. Dewey, ed., *Library User Education: Powerful learning, Powerful Partnerships* (pp. 240-245). Lanham, MD: Scarecrow Press.

Dew, Stephen H. (2001). Knowing your users and what they want: Surveying off-campus students about library services. *Journal of Library Administration 31*, 177-193. Simultaneously published in Anne Marie Casey, ed., (2001) *Off-Campus Library Services* (177-193). New York: The Haworth Press, Inc. First published in P. Steven Thomas, comp., (2000) *Ninth Off-Campus Library Services Conference Proceedings* (pp. 119-132). Mount Pleasant, MI: Central Michigan University.

Evans, G. E., Ward, L. P., & Rugaas, B. (2000). *Management basics for information professionals.* New York: Neal-Schuman.

Florida Distance Learning Library Initiative. (1999). *Final report of the Library Subcommittee of the Florida Institute on Public Postsecondary Distance Learning.* Retrieved October 26, 2001, from the Florida Distance Learning Library Initiative Web site: http://dlis.dos.state.fl.us/dlli/report.html.

Haricombe, Lorraine. (1998). Users: Their impact on planning the agile library. In Lorraine Haricombe and T. J. Lusher, eds., *Creating the Agile Library: A Management Guide for Librarians* (pp. 81-93). Westport, CT: Greenwood Press.

Hufford, Jon R. (2001). Planning for distance learning: Support services and the library's role. *Journal of Library Administration 31*, 259-266. Simultaneously published in Anne Marie Casey, ed., (2001) *Off-Campus Library Services* (259-266). New York: The Haworth Press, Inc. First published in P. Steven Thomas, comp., (2000) *Ninth Off-Campus Library Services Conference Proceedings* (175-179). Mount Pleasant, MI: Central Michigan University.

Hufford, Jon R. (2000). The university library's role in planning a successful distance education program. *The Reference Librarian 69/70*, 193-203.

Mason, Marilyn Gell. (1999). *Strategic management for today's libraries.* Chicago: American Library Association.

Morrisey, George L. (1996). *A guide to tactical planning: Producing your short-term results.* San Francisco: Jossey-Bass.

Riggs, Donald E. (1997). Plan or be planned for: The growing significance of strategic planning. *College & Research Libraries 58*, 400-401.

Slade, Alexander L. (1988). Establishing an off-campus library service for remote educational centers: Variables and potentials. In Barton M. Lessin, ed., *The Off-Campus Library Services Conference Proceedings* (pp. 374-393). Mount Pleasant, MI: Central Michigan University.

University of Iowa Libraries. (2000). *University of Iowa Libraries Strategic Plan 2000-2004.* Retrieved November 12, 2001 from The University of Iowa Libraries Web site: http://www.lib.uiowa.edu/admin/strategicplan.pdf.

University of Massachusetts Amherst Libraries. (2000). *Umass Amherst Libraries Off-Campus Outreach Situation and Plan, August 2000.* Retrieved October 26, 2001 from The University of Massachusetts Amherst Libraries Web site: http://umass.edu/outreach/or_libraries_stratplan_00.htm.

University of Minnesota Library, Twin Cities Campus. (1999). *Distance Learning Development Project, 1999-2000 Plan.* Retrieved October 25, 2001, from The University of Minnesota Library, Twin Cities Campus, Web site: http://www.lib.umn.edu/dist/99-00 plan.phtml.

Zweizig, Douglas . (1996). Overview of TELL IT. In Zweizig, Douglas; Debra Wilcox Johnson; Jane Robbins; and Michele Besant, eds., *The TELL IT! Manual: The Complete Program for Evaluating Library Performance* (pp. 3-13). Chicago: American Library Association.

APPENDIX A

The University of Iowa Libraries
Plan for Distance-Education Services

Stephen Dew, Coordinator
Library Services for Distance Education

DRAFT 11-28-01

I. INTRODUCTION

Increasingly, Iowa citizens are pursuing educational opportunities that are close to their homes and jobs, and they are more inclined to enroll in courses that are not tied to the conventional constraints normally associated with a traditional university experience. To meet this growing demand for distance education, the University of Iowa has increased its course and degree offerings by utilizing a wide variety of teaching methods, formats, and technologies. Although some distance-education classes continue to conform to the traditional correspondence-course format, others are conducted entirely over the Internet or entirely by videotape. Most distance-education classes, however, involve some level of live interaction between faculty and students. For some courses, faculty members travel to classrooms located at various sites throughout the state, where they lecture, hold class, and interact with students. In an ever-increasing number of situations, faculty members use the interactive capabilities of television, especially the Iowa Communications Network (ICN), and they conduct their classes while communicating simultaneously with students who are located at several different sites around the state.

The University of Iowa Libraries support the informational, research, and instructional needs of UI students and faculty participating in distance-education programs regardless of course format or location. In addition, the Libraries strive to adhere to the standards established in the "ACRL Guidelines for Distance Learning Library Services." Currently, for students involved in distance education, the Libraries provide a number of services, including access to electronic and Web-based resources, document delivery services, user-education services, and reference assistance. Library staff members are constantly seeking ways to improve or expand distance-education library services, and a planning document can be a powerful tool to employ. A properly developed plan enables staff members to focus on the current extent of library services and the potential for improvements.

II. OBJECTIVES

The objectives of this plan are as follows:

- To document and summarize current library services for UI students and faculty involved in distance education.
- To identify library service priorities.
- To identify aspects of service that can be improved.
- To suggest methods and solutions for improvements.

III. PROGRAMS & SUBJECT PRIORITIES

Design and development of library services for distance education will focus on the off-campus credit programs that are offered by the University of Iowa. Priorities will be given to library services and subject resources that support the following degree programs:

The Center for Credit Programs in the Division of Continuing Education currently supervises the following distance-education programs:

- Bachelor of Liberal Studies
- Bachelor of Science in Nursing
- Master of Science in Nursing
- Master of Public Health
- Master of Social Work
- Master of Arts in Library and Information Science
- Master of Science in Computer Science
- Master of Science in Electrical & Computer Engineering
- Master of Science in Science Education
- Master of Arts in Higher Education
- Graduate Endorsement in Behavioral Disorders
- Doctor of Pharmacy

The School of Management in the Henry B. Tippie College of Business Administration currently supervises the following distance-education program:

- Master of Business Administration

IV. STUDENT ID CARD OR BORROWER'S PERMIT REQUIRED

A. University of Iowa No-Picture ID Card

The University of Iowa Libraries offers services to all distance education students enrolled in the degree-granting programs directed by the Center for Credit Programs and the School of Management. In order to gain access to library services, however, students must obtain a "**University of Iowa No-Picture ID Card.**" As students register for classes, the Center for Credit Programs and the School of Management distribute ID application forms, and in addition, they send copies of the form to students who request it. The Coordinator of Library Services for Distance Education will also maintain a supply of application forms to give to students as needed. Completed forms are returned to the Registrar's Office. The Registrar produces the ID cards, sends them to the students, and adds the students' records to the Libraries' patron database.

B. Library Borrower's Permit

Students taking Guided Correspondence classes are not eligible for library services unless they are also enrolled in the Bachelor of Liberal Studies (BLS) program. In order to gain access to library services, BLS students must obtain a **Library Borrower's Permit.**

The process is as follows: The Coordinator is responsible for writing a letter that explains the availability of library services–the letter accompanies the application form for the Library Borrower's Permit. The Center for Credit Programs distributes the letter and the application form to BLS students as they register for class. Completed application forms are returned to the Center, and the Center then forwards the forms to the Coordinator. With the assistance of the Access Services staff, the Coordinator adds the new records to the patron database. The Coordinator then mails each student a Borrower's Permit, accompanied by appropriate user-education handouts.

Service would probably be improved by making the ID process for BLS students the same as that for all other distance-education students. To reach that end, the Coordinator has requested that the library programmer develop a program that will query the ID Card, BLS, and Guided Correspondence databases to automatically activate library privileges for BLS students.

V. ELECTRONIC & WEB-BASED SERVICES

The Coordinator of Library Services for Distance Education will work with the Library Webmaster, the Hardin Electronic Services Team, the Information Systems Support Team, and other library staff to ensure functionality and accessibility for all electronic and Web-based services that support distance education. All of the Libraries' electronic resources that can be accessible from remote locations will be identified, and appropriate links will be made from library Web pages. The Coordinator will work with subject specialists on the library staff to identify electronic and Web-based resources that can be useful to students and faculty involved in the University's distance-education programs. Currently, the Libraries use Ezproxy software to provide off-campus students access to restricted databases–in order to gain access, students just enter their ID numbers when prompted.

The Coordinator will develop an expertise in using Web-editing tools (such as *CLARIS HOME PAGE, DREAMWEAVER*, etc.), and he/she will maintain, update, and improve the "Distance-Education Library Services" Web site: **http://www.lib.uiowa.edu/disted/index.html**

The Web site became fully functional in September 1999, and currently, the Coordinator maintains twenty-six Web pages related to the site. The site provides general information and instruction useful to all distance-education students, as well as a list of the best electronic resources for each program. Web pages concerning electronic reference, consultation, telephone reference, and document-delivery services have also been developed (see Sections VI and VIII).

VI. DOCUMENT DELIVERY SERVICES
A. Student Options for Obtaining Documents

Students enrolled in distance-education classes have the following options when they need books, articles, and other documents.

1. Electronic Access to Full-Text

A significant and growing number of electronic resources provide access to full-text copies of books, journal articles, and other documents. Resources that provide full-text material include, among others, *EBSCOhost, Elsevier Science Direct, LEXIS-NEXIS Academic Universe, netLibrary, Books 24x7, Project Muse, JSTOR, WilsonWeb, Electric Library*, and several databases available through Hardin Library's *HealthNet*. Other full-text documents (especially ready reference sources and government publications) are available through the Libraries' *"Gateway to Online Resources,"* and in addition, the *InfoHawk* catalog provides links to full-text journals, books, and other documents. In 1998-99, the Libraries conducted a survey of its distance-education students, and the survey revealed that two-thirds of the students felt that providing online full-text resources was one of the most important services that the Libraries could offer, ranking second among the twelve library services listed. Any full-text file that supports one or more of the distance education programs should be considered for acquisition.

2. Interlibrary Loan (ILL)–Free delivery of books and articles

Since ILL services are generally free, distance-education students are encouraged to use regular interlibrary loan services when possible. All students should be able to use the services of their local public libraries, but for those involved in certain programs, students can also use their affiliated college or university libraries (see Sections X-B, X-C, & X-D). ILL services can take just a few days, or they can take up to three weeks. Students are encouraged to place requests as soon as possible.

3. Distance-Education Document Delivery Service–$3 per request

Beginning in the fall semester 1999, the Libraries began offering the Distance-Education Document-Delivery Service. For students who would like to have books or articles sent directly to their homes or offices, especially those who need material quickly, the UI Libraries provides this special service that will deliver material to students usually within 24-to-48 hours of each request. There is a fee, however.

- **Articles:** Distance-education students have the option of having articles mailed to any address that they provide or faxed to any fax number that they provide. For articles of ten pages or less, the charge is **three dollars** ($3) for each article. For articles over ten pages, there is an additional charge of **ten-cents-per-page (for pages eleven and higher)**.
- **Books:** Students also have the ability to request that books be sent by UPS to any address that they provide. The charge is **three dollars** ($3) for each book. Students are responsible for returning books to the Main Library or Hardin Library before the due date, and they may use any delivery method that they prefer (mail, UPS, hand-delivery, etc.). Renewals are possible.

Requests can be submitted electronically through the Internet or by fax. Electronic forms are available from a link on the Distance-Education Library Services Homepage, and in addition, printed forms that can be faxed are provided upon request. The Coordinator is responsible for maintaining the Web pages and all printed documents relating to this service.

For students enrolled in programs that have made financial arrangements with the Libraries (such as Social Work), total costs will be charged to the program account. Otherwise, total costs will be charged to the student's University Bill. For **social work students**, however, this service is provided **FREE** through financing by the **Laura L. Davis Fund.**

The Main Library and Hardin Library interlibrary-loan staffs will maintain monthly statistics on the distance-education document-delivery service. Statistics will be maintained on the number of requests received by program, the number of requests filled/unfilled, whether a request was mailed/faxed, and which UI library supplied the material. In addition to other uses, these statistics will be used as an Indicator (4) of Goal 1, Strategic Direction 1, in the Libraries' Strategic Plan–"UI distance learners make greater use of library services as indicated by increases in statistics for document delivery, telephone, and electronic reference services."

4. On-Campus Circulation Privileges

Student records are included in the Libraries' patron database for all distance-education students who have a **University of Iowa No-Picture ID Card** or a **Library Borrower's Permit**. Distance education students have the same circulation privileges as on-campus students, and therefore, whenever they visit campus, distance-education students may use their IDs or permits to check out books and use all other library services that are available to on-campus students.

5. Circulation Privileges at Other Schools

A number of UI credit programs are operated with the cooperation of another university, college, or community college (see Sections X-B and X-C). In those cases, UI students also have circulation privileges at libraries connected to those institutions. In addition, UI students have circulation privileges at the other Regents Universities–Iowa State University and the University of Northern Iowa.

6. Public Libraries and Other Academic Libraries

A survey conducted in 1998-99 revealed that over sixty-percent of UI distance-education students used their local public libraries on some occasions to support their research. Although resources at public libraries vary widely by location and tend to be limited, many libraries provide basic books, journals, and electronic resources, and importantly, most also provide interlibrary loan services. Public libraries in cities where UI programs are also located are especially useful to our students (see Section X-E).

B. Reserve Book Collections

During the fall semester 2000, the Libraries began supporting reserve book collections for the distance-education programs in nursing and social work. These programs are connected with several colleges, community colleges, and universities around the state (see Section X-A, X-B, & X-C), and therefore, since the programs are located at permanent sites, reserve book collections can be established in the cooperating libraries or in the offices of the local program. The process for developing the reserve collections follows. Faculty members at the off-campus sites notify the Coordinator about books they wish to place on reserve. The Coordinator notifies the appropriate Bibliographer, who reviews the requests and orders the books. When the books are received, records are added to the *InfoHawk* catalog, but the records are masked so that the information is only accessible by library staff (the information is blocked from the public catalog). The books are then sent by UPS to the off-campus site. Books for the social work program are purchased through the Laura L. Davis Fund. Purchases for the nursing program are made through the General Fund.

C. Electronic Reserves

During the fall semester 2000, the Libraries began supporting electronic reserve modules for classes in the social work distance-education program. Through the Laura L. Davis Fund, the Libraries purchased a computer, scanner, and other equipment needed to set up electronic reserves, and the fund also financed the hiring of a part-time graduate assistant (now at one-quarter-time). In addition to working on electronic reserves, the graduate assistant also works on the *Library Explorer* online tutorial (see Section VII-B). The process for developing electronic reserves follows. Prior to each semester, faculty members at the off-campus sites send the Coordinator a list of the articles that they wish to place on electronic reserve. The Coordinator reviews the list, determining which articles the Libraries own (only University-owned articles can be used in the electronic reserve collection). If any of the articles are not owned, the Coordinator notifies the off-campus faculty about articles that will not be in the electronic reserve module due to non-ownership. The Coordinator then sends the list of articles owned by the Libraries to the staff in the Interlibrary-Loan/Document-Delivery Department, who find and photocopy the articles. The Davis Fund pays for the photocopying. The Graduate Assistant scans the articles into PDF format, using *Adobe Acrobat*. In order to keep the files manageable for off-campus users (especially those using telephone lines), files are kept to a maximum size of five megabytes. A link to the electronic reserves module is maintained on the appropriate "Short Cut to Electronic Resources" Web page. A University ID is required to access the articles through the proxy server, thus limiting access to University students and faculty only.

The Coordinator will investigate the possibility of expanding the electronic reserve service to include the distance-education program in library and information science, with a goal to begin service in the spring of 2002. For other departments and programs, the Libraries will provide technical and professional advice about establishing electronic reserves. The Coordinator will be responsible for maintaining a working knowledge of the general provisions of the Digital Millennium Copyright Act and other issues related to electronic reserves.

VII. USER EDUCATION

The University Libraries supports user-education services that are designed to meet the current and changing information needs of a diverse community. The University Libraries encourages collaboration between teaching faculty and library staff, especially when that collaboration leads to a better learning experience for students and includes the acquisition of information and technology skills. Instruction is delivered using a variety of methodologies and formats, and emphasis is placed on integrating information literacy skills into the student learning experience. In addition, in accordance with the Libraries' Strategic Plan (Goal 1, Strategic Direction 2, Indicator 2), the Coordinator will work to develop a library education component for all graduate and professional programs in distance education. The five primary categories of user-education services for distance education follow:

A. Classroom Instruction

Each semester, the Coordinator will send a letter to all faculty members involved in distance education offering formal classroom instruction as well as other user education services (see Section IX-A). The Coordinator will work with appropriate library staff to develop and present classroom instruction for distance-education classes. Such instruction will include traditional classroom settings as well as interactive television, such as with the ICN. The Coordinator will report all formal classroom instruction using the Web-based "User Education Report Form," and in addition, the Coordinator will maintain statistics of all formal instruction given to distance-education students by other library staff.

Also, in order to be able to demonstrate electronic resources and services while visiting off-campus sites, especially sites without a direct Internet connection, the Coordinator will open and maintain an account with the University's ITS Remote Access Service. When necessary, ISST staff will be consulted to ensure that the Coordinator's laptop is properly configured to access the Internet from off-campus.

B. Web-Based and Computer-Assisted Instruction

Through the Distance-Education Library Services Web site, the Coordinator will provide instruction to distance-education students on the use of relevant library resources and services (see Section V). He/she will maintain and develop the "Frequently Asked Question" Web page and other general instructional Web pages as needed.

The Coordinator will also work with the User-Education Working Group and other appropriate library staff in updating, refining, and promoting the *Library Explorer* tutorial. The Coordinator shares supervisory responsibilities over the part-time Graduate Assistant with another librarian (the Coordinator of User Education), and in that vein, the Graduate Assistant is assigned duties working on **Library Explorer**. Work related to **Library Explorer** supports Initiative C of Goal 1, Strategic Direction 1, in the Libraries' Strategic Plan.

In addition, the Coordinator will work with distance-education faculty who are interested in Web-based instructional tools such as *Web-CT, BlackBoard, MOO*, etc. (see Sections V & IX-A).

C. Handouts and Other Print Material

In cooperation with appropriate library staff, the Coordinator will be responsible for writing, producing, updating, and distributing a variety of print materials for user-education. Included in that material will be a series of handouts that summarize library services. A general handout has been produced that is used for all students enrolled in distance-education programs through the Center for Credit Programs, and the Center mails the handout to all students as they register for class. Another handout has been produced for students enrolled in the MBA program, and the School of Management distributes it as an attachment to the MBA students' listserv. Due to the special nature of the free document-delivery service offered to social work students (see Section VI-A-3), a special handout for social work students has also been produced. Other user handouts will be produced as needed.

D. UI Information Initiative (UIII)

The University Libraries and the College of Liberal Arts have joined in a partnership that is called UI Information Initiative (UIII). The goal of UIII is to integrate the acquisition of information literacy skills into the fabric of the undergraduate curriculum. The Coordinator will work with appropriate library staff and interested faculty members to incorporate information literacy skills into distance-education classes. Initial efforts should focus on classes in the Bachelor of Liberal Studies program (see Section IX).

E. Teaching With Innovative Style & Technology (TWIST)

The University Libraries TWIST Project was developed to integrate networked information into the teaching and learning process. The Coordinator will work with the TWIST staff and interested faculty members to learn Web-teaching tools (such as *Web-CT*), in order to incorporate information and technology skills into the distance-education class experience (see Section IX).

VIII. REFERENCE ASSISTANCE & CONSULTATION

The Coordinator will be responsible for providing reference assistance to UI students involved in distance education, but when necessary, the Coordinator may seek the help of appropriate library staff (Reference, Branch Librarians, Bibliographers, etc.). Reference questions always take priority over regular tasks and job duties. Responses to reference questions should be delivered as soon as possible.

The Coordinator will maintain monthly statistics on all reference and consultation services supporting distance-education. In addition to other uses, these statistics will be used as an Indicator (4) of Goal 1, Strategic Direction 1, in the Libraries' Strategic Plan–"UI distance learners make greater use of library services as indicated by increases in statistics for document delivery, telephone, and electronic reference services." The four categories of reference assistance for distance education follow:

A. Toll-Free Telephone Assistance

During the summer of 1999, the UI Libraries began offering a toll-free telephone reference service to all distance-education students. The Coordinator is responsible for marketing and promoting the use of the toll-free number through Web pages, user handouts, and other methods. The number is as follows: **1-877-807-9587**.

B. E-Mail Reference Assistance

Using the Coordinator's regular UI e-mail account, an e-mail reference service will be maintained for distance-education students and faculty. The Coordinator is responsible for developing and maintaining a Web page that explains the electronic reference service and provides a link to the Coordinator's e-mail account (see Section V).

C. Consultation Service

The Coordinator is responsible for developing and maintaining a Web page that explains the in-depth nature of consultation service and provides a link to the Coordinator's e-mail account (see Section V).

D. Interactive Digital Reference

The Coordinator will work with the Virtual Reference Working Group to establish a digital-reference pilot project, with a goal of initiating the service during the spring semester 2002.

IX. COMMUNICATION WITH FACULTY

The Coordinator will promote regular and open communication with all faculty involved in distance education.

A. Letters

Each semester, from the Center for Credit Programs and the School of Management, the Coordinator will obtain a list of all faculty involved in distance education. The Coordinator will write a letter that summarizes and markets library services, and in the letter, each faculty member will be offered the option of formal classroom instruction as well as other user-education services (see Section VI). A letter will be sent to each faculty member, accompanied by a copy of the student handout and other appropriate material. In addition to other uses, these letters will be used as Indicator 2 of Goal 1, Strategic Direction 1, in the Libraries' Strategic Plan–"Library staff annually offer services to all faculty teaching undergraduate off-campus courses." The letters also support Indicator 2 of Goal 1, Strategic Direction 2–"All faculty teaching distance education graduate programs are aware of library instruction that can be developed to support their courses."

B. Off-Campus Visits

In order to develop and maintain proper communication about library services and resources, the Coordinator will attempt to visit with faculty members, librarians, and students at each off-campus site at least once each year (see Section X-A, X-B, & X-C).

X. COOPERATION & COLLABORATION

The Coordinator of Library Services for Distance Education must work with a wide variety of people. In order to succeed in any effort to provide the best possible service to UI students involved in distance education, the Coordinator must cooperate with and collaborate with a variety of individuals connected to off-campus education centers and other institutions. The following is a list of the most important off-campus centers and institutions connected to UI distance-education programs. The Coordinator will communicate with personnel at each site, keeping them up-to-date on library services for UI students connected to their institutions. When appropriate, the Coordinator will arrange for personal visits to the various sites listed below (see Section IX-B).

A. Education Centers

In some of the larger metropolitan areas of the state, some credit programs have established education centers where classes are held and, in most cases, computer labs are also available. The Coordinator will work with the staff at the education centers to ensure that UI students receive the best possible service. A list of the programs with education centers follows:

Master of Social Work
  • Des Moines Education Center
    Des Moines

  • Quad-Cities Graduate Study Center
    Rock Island, IL

Master of Business Administration
  • Cedar Rapids Area Education & Conference Center
    Cedar Rapids
  • W. A. Krause Center
    Des Moines

B. Colleges & Universities

Some of the university's credit programs have special cooperative arrangements with other colleges or universities. A list of those programs and schools follows:

  • Bachelor of Liberal Studies
    Pennsylvania State University (University Park, PA)
    The University of Iowa and Pennsylvania State University have combined forces to create an undergraduate program referred to as *LionHawk*. Students have the option of taking a wide variety of correspondence courses through either school, leading ultimately to the award of the BLS degree from Iowa or the Extended-Access Letters, Arts and Sciences Associate Degree (ELAS) from Penn State.

  • Bachelor of Liberal Studies
    Iowa Regents Institutions
    The *Bachelor of Liberal Studies Across Iowa* program allows our students the option of taking a limited number of courses through the other two Regents Universities (at least 32 hours must be taken of the U of I), leading ultimately to the award of the BLS from Iowa.

  • Master of Social Work
    Drake University (Des Moines)
    Through an arrangement worked out by the Center for Credit Programs, all University of Iowa students enrolled in the Des Moines social work program have general library privileges with Drake.

  • Master of Social Work
    Augustana College (Rock Island, IL)
    The Quad-Cities social work program is operated out of the Graduate Study Center, located on the Augustana campus, and through that arrangement, all University of Iowa students enrolled in the social work program have general library privileges with Augustana College.

- Master of Social Work
  Briar Cliff College (Sioux City)
    The Sioux City program is operated through the cooperation of Briar Cliff College, and all UI students enrolled in the Sioux City social work program have general library privileges with the college.

C. Community Colleges

Several of the credit programs are connected with community colleges, and in such cases, University of Iowa students have full access and circulation privileges at the library. The various credit programs that have community college connections are listed below. The Coordinator will communicate with and cooperate with all of the community college libraries to ensure that UI students receive the best possible service.

Bachelor of Science in Nursing
- Iowa Central Community College
    Fort Dodge
- Iowa Lakes Community College
    Emmetsburg & Spencer
- North Iowa Area Community College
    Mason City
- Northeast Iowa Community College
    Calmar
- Northwest Iowa Community College
    Sheldon & Orange City

Master of Business Administration
- Des Moines Area Community College
    Newton and Ankeny
- Muscatine Community College
    Muscatine
- Scott Community College, Kahl Education Center
    Davenport

D. Veterans Administration Hospitals

The Bachelor of Science in Nursing program has established off-campus sites at two Veterans Administration hospitals. The Coordinator will communicate with and cooperate with the hospitals to ensure that UI students receive the best possible service.
- Veterans Administration Hospital (Des Moines)
- Veterans Administration Hospital (Knoxville)

E. Public Libraries

Currently, there are no special relationships or contracts between the University Libraries and local public libraries; however, in order to ensure that UI students receive the best possible service, the Coordinator will cooperate with all public libraries where UI students seek information. Cooperation will be especially important for those public libraries located in cities where UI credit programs are also centered. Those cities include, but are not limited to: Ankeny, Bettendorf, Burlington, Calmar, Cedar Rapids, Council Bluffs, Davenport, Des Moines, Dubuque, Emmetsburg, Fort Dodge, Knoxville, Mason City, Muscatine, Newton, Orange City, Rock Island (IL), Sheldon, Sioux City, and Spencer.

F. Private Corporations

Two of the credit programs have special arrangements with private corporations (Rockwell Collins, Inc. and KGAN-TV). Although the programs are open to all qualified applicants, most students are employed by one of the two companies. To support the programs, KGAN-TV provides classroom facilities, and it also uses a satellite system to broadcast television images of classes held simultaneously in Cedar Rapids and Iowa City. Rockwell Collins provides classrooms, computer facilities, and a special library for its distance-education students. The Coordinator will work with the staff at Rockwell Collins and KGAN-TV to ensure that UI students receive the best possible service. The programs connected to Rockwell Collins and KGAN-TV are as follows:

- Master of Science in Computer Science
    Cedar Rapids
- Master of Science in Electrical & Computer Engineering
    Cedar Rapids

G. Inter-institutional Library Committee on Distance Education

The University Libraries cooperates with the other Regents institutions (Iowa State University and the University of Northern Iowa) through a variety of Inter-institutional Library Committees (ILC), including one related specifically to distance education. The Coordinator and other library staff will work with ILC committees, as well as librarians at the other Regents institutions, to ensure that cooperative efforts succeed.

H. Committee on Institutional Cooperation

The University Libraries cooperates with the other Big Ten universities through the Committee on Institutional Cooperation (CIC). The CIC-VEL project, providing uniform access to all of the online catalogs of the Big Ten University Libraries is but one of the cooperative projects involved. Other

CIC projects involving distance education concern such subjects as interlibrary loan and electronic reserves. The Coordinator and other library staff will work with CIC committees and librarians at the other CIC institutions to ensure that cooperative efforts succeed.

I. Association of Research Libraries
The Association of Research Libraries (ARL) is frequently involved with issues relevant to distance education, especially copyright concerns and electronic reserves. The Coordinator and other library staff will work with ARL committees and librarians at the other ARL institutions to ensure cooperative efforts succeed.

XI. REVIEW & EVALUATION
Continuous evaluation is necessary in order to adequately judge the quality of library service, and it is also a key factor in determining aspects of service that might be improved. The Coordinator will be responsible for supervising a variety of methods to review and evaluate distance-education services, and his/her activities will include writing, producing, and distributing evaluation forms and surveys. In addition, the Coordinator will become familiar with statistical packages (SPSS, SAS, etc.) so that data from evaluations and surveys can be fully analyzed.

A. Formal Surveys
The Coordinator will work with the Center for Credit Programs and the School of Management to formally evaluate distance-education library services every three years. The first formal survey of distance-education library services occurred during the 1998-99 academic year, and the next formal survey is tentatively scheduled for the spring semester 2002. Results from the surveys will be shared with staff members at the Center for Credit Programs and the School of Management, as well as with appropriate librarians, administrators, and faculty members.

B. Electronic & Web-Based Feedback
A Web-based "Suggestions" form has been developed and is accessible from the Distance-Education Library Services homepage. In addition, the Coordinator will investigate the possibility of developing a more formal method of online feedback.

C. Review of the "Plan for Distance-Education Services"
Although this plan is subject to review and revision at anytime, at least once each year the document will be reviewed formally. During the Coordinator's annual review meeting with the Director of Central Public Services, he/she will review the status of the plan, making suggestions for revision as needed.

APPENDIX B

University of Iowa Libraries, Handout for Distance Education Students

LIBRARY SERVICES FOR DISTANCE-EDUCATION STUDENTS

Student ID Card Required

The University of Iowa Libraries offers services to all distance education students enrolled in the degree-granting programs directed by the Center for Credit Programs. In order to qualify for these services, Bachelor of Liberal Studies students must obtain a **Library Borrower's Permit**. All other students must obtain a "**University of Iowa No-Picture ID Card**." The application forms can be obtained by contacting the Center at the following:
    1-800-272-6430 credit-programs@uiowa.edu

Distance-Education Library Services Homepage.
This Homepage provides access to library resources and services that support distance education. The Homepage is located at the following URL:
http://www.lib.uiowa.edu/disted

Short-Cuts to Electronic Resources by Subject.

For each degree-granting program (business, computer science, education, electrical engineering, liberal studies, library science, nursing, pharmacy, and social work), the Homepage provides a link to a list of the most useful electronic resources and databases. Some databases provide lists of articles and books by subject, keyword, author, etc., while other files provide information, such as full-text articles, statistics, or business information.

In January 2001, the Libraries instituted a new proxy server that allows students to access electronic resources from off-campus. There are two important changes. First, with the new proxy server, users no longer have to worry about firewalls. (Many libraries and companies set up firewalls to protect their computer systems.) Under the new proxy server, students can access the Libraries' electronic resources using computers protected by firewalls. The second important development is that, with the new proxy server, users no longer have to re-configure their Web browsers. With the new proxy server, students need only type in their ID number when prompted.

Access to InfoHawk.

The Distance-Education Library Services Homepage includes a link to *InfoHawk*, a Web-based library system that replaces OASIS. *InfoHawk* provides students with access to the online catalog of the UI Libraries and the Law Library, as well as other online catalogs concerning such subjects as government publications, the Curriculum Laboratory, and the Dada Archives. Students can use a wide variety of techniques to search the system.

Document-Delivery Services (Articles and Books)

1. Interlibrary Loan (ILL)–Free delivery of books and articles

Since ILL services are generally free, distance-education students are encouraged to use regular interlibrary loan services when possible. All students should be able to use the services of their local public libraries, but for those involved in certain programs, students can also use their affiliated college or university libraries. ILL services can take just a few days, or they can take up to two-to-three weeks. Students are encouraged to place requests as soon as possible.

2. Distance-Education Document Delivery Service–$3 per request

For students who would like to have books or articles sent directly to their homes or offices, especially those who need material quickly, the UI Libraries provides a special service that delivers material to students usually within 24-to-48 hours of each request. There is a fee, however.

- **Articles:** Distance-education students have the option of having articles mailed to any address that they provide or faxed to any fax number that they provide. For articles of ten pages or less, the charge is **three dollars** ($3) for each article. For articles over ten pages, there is an additional charge of **ten-cents-per-page (for pages eleven and higher).**
- **Books:** Students also have the ability to request that books be sent by UPS to any address that they provide. The charge is **three dollars** ($3) for each book. Students are responsible for returning books to the Main Library or Hardin Library before the due date, and they may use any delivery method that they prefer (mail, UPS, hand-delivery, etc.). Renewals are possible.

Requests can be submitted electronically. Forms are available from a link on the Distance-Education Library Services Homepage. For students enrolled in programs that have made financial arrangements with the Libraries, total costs will be charged to the program account. Otherwise, total costs will be charged to the student's University bill.

Reference Services
Email and Toll-Free Telephone

Without leaving home or office, students can ask for help or advice from library staff. Any student who needs help finding information for a class project or help with research strategies should contact Stephen Dew, the Coordinator of Library Services for Distance Education. Web-based email forms are available on the Homepage. Otherwise, Dr. Dew can be contacted at the following:

1-877-807-9587

stephen-dew@uiowa.edu

Digital Document Delivery to the Desktop: Distance Is No Longer an Issue

Ulrike Dieterle

University of Wisconsin

SUMMARY. The Health Sciences Libraries, University of Wisconsin-Madison, are offering faculty, staff and graduate students an attractive alternative to traditional forms of document delivery. Based on high-speed transfer, Web-based access and reliable service, Library Express is the first phase of a larger continuum to provide easy and convenient access to local and worldwide collections. This successful program is a direct result of strong administrative support, careful planning, a staged implementation, continued attention to quality control, an emphasis on customer satisfaction and, above all, a well-trained and dedicated staff.

KEYWORDS. Technology, library services, digitization, document delivery

On a Big Ten campus with 45 libraries spread out over 933 square acres, distance can pose a significant barrier to information retrieval. For those working off campus in the many research stations and clinics, students completing rotations and clerkships in other parts of the state or the nation, the challenges of access to health sciences materials become even more daunting. At the University of Wisconsin-Madison, a new document delivery service, Library Express, is bridging the distances and providing easy and affordable access to articles, book chapters and tables of contents from local collections and beyond.

[Haworth co-indexing entry note]: "Digital Document Delivery to the Desktop: Distance Is No Longer an Issue." Dieterle, Ulrike. Co-published simultaneously in *Journal of Library Administration* (The Haworth Information Press, an imprint of The Haworth Press, Inc.) Vol. 37, No. 1/2, 2002, pp. 243-250; and: *Distance Learning Library Services: The Tenth Off-Campus Library Services Conference* (ed: Patrick B. Mahoney) The Haworth Information Press, an imprint of The Haworth Press, Inc., 2002, pp. 243-250.

http://www.haworthpress.com/store/product.asp?sku=J111
10.1300/J111v37n01_20

243

Library Express users can initiate their requests through a Web-based interface, track the status of their requests online and receive digital documents delivered to their desktop of choice anywhere in the world in PDF format. Four campus libraries currently provide this service to a potential combined user population of approximately 24,000 faculty, staff and graduate students. While the service is currently not open to undergraduates, exceptions are made for distance learning situations. Libraries and their Library Express users are matched by subject area affiliation, major and, when necessary, by manual entry into the system. Authentication and access are determined by an active 11-digit campus ID. Within the Health Sciences Libraries (HSL) Library Express development occurred in three basic phases–an extensive planning phase, a carefully staged implementation phase and going live with second generation software to open the service to all faculty, staff and graduate students at the University of Wisconsin-Madison.

The HSL consist of three separate library facilities (main health sciences, pharmacy and hospital collections) which serve a diverse campus population including the Medical School, School of Pharmacy, School of Nursing, basic sciences, History of Medicine and other health sciences and related fields. User groups are very mobile, crisscrossing not only a large campus but also traveling the state, the nation and beyond.

The HSL have a long tradition of making library materials readily accessible to its primary users. For many years library users have had access to a shuttle that stops twice a day at each of the three libraries to pick up and deliver library materials. Requested items are shuttled for convenient pick up at the site chosen by the user. This service provides one-day turnaround and is, for some, still the document delivery method of choice. While very efficient in getting the materials to the users in a timely fashion, the service has one major disadvantage. Physical items being transported are out of circulation and not available to others at the home library. With an increasing number of electronic journals available and readily accessible from our Web pages, HSL users are quickly adopting the idea of digital retrieval as a viable option. To broaden the scope of easy access to print-only titles/volumes, digital delivery to the desktop seemed the next logical step and a welcome replacement for other more manual and cumbersome methods of document delivery of the past. Library Express also offers the opportunity to provide one point of access for multiple types of delivery services running in the background. When fully implemented, users will no longer have to ponder where to go and what to fill out for intra-campus or inter-campus services.

With the advent of appropriate and easy to use technologies, more comfort with computers and an articulated commitment to serving the information needs of our users in a timely and convenient manner, the implementation of digital delivery to the desktop seemed appropriate and attainable. The current manifestation of Library Express is viewed as a bridge to the electronic library of the future, as a road to the next generation of technology-enabled library services.

PROJECT PLANNING PHASE

Heeding lessons learned earlier in 1999 from a premature start and a quick retraction of the service in the spring of that year, the HSL put the smooth implementation of Library Express high on the list of the HSL priorities. The newly hired Head of Access Services was given the mandate to bring up a new digital delivery program in a timely and organized manner. The general components of the service would be based on an existing document delivery pilot already in place at another campus library. Early in the first planning process, Ophthalmology, a department of approximately 60-plus members, had expressed a desire and need for electronic desktop delivery. Members of this department are widely dispersed and have a broad range of information needs, including clinical, instructional and research support. They had also agreed to work with HSL to get the kinks out of the system during the beta phase. The challenges posed by this department made it an ideal test group for distance delivery services.

At this point, the project management team consisted of a newly hired .5 FTE dedicated to the Library Express planning process, the Head of Access Services and coordinator of the hospital library who had experience with the first roll-out.

Clearly defining service parameters and setting service standards early in the planning phase kept us on track, outlined basic expectations, reduced misunderstandings and streamlined staff training. HSL Library Express staff agreed to do everything within our power to make access to the service easy and effortless for our user groups, who repeatedly listed a lack of time as one of their most pressing dilemmas to information retrieval. The goal was to deliver articles from the health sciences collections within 1-2 working days. Articles would be ordered through a Web-based interface, received by processing staff in email format and delivered to the user with a link pointing to the PDF document. Adobe Acrobat would be used for scanning materials. Data storage and report generation would be MS Access-based. The main health sciences library, which has the largest collection, would serve as the sole recipient and screener of all incoming requests. Requests for articles from materials located at either of the other health sciences facilities would be electronically forwarded for processing and delivered directly to users. Requests for items from non-HSL libraries would be retrieved manually from other campus libraries whenever possible, returned and scanned for delivery to the user. Requests not found on campus would be sent to our HSL interlibrary loan staff for processing and then returned to Library Express staff for scanning and digital delivery. All requests would be delivered electronically. No paper delivery options would be available through Library Express. Links to scanned materials would be available on our server for two weeks, then automatically deleted. Color images would be delivered whenever possible. Status of requests throughout the processing queue would be posted to the users email box using canned messages manually initiated by staff. No fees would be charged during the beta phase in exchange for input from, and extended patience of, our users. In summary, it was a very labor-intensive process.

Setting a realistic implementation timeline was of paramount importance to the project management team. Keeping a vigilant eye on the details helped us stay grounded and focused on the ultimate goal, namely to provide a smooth and speedy experience for the user. A loose timeline was set at "as soon as possible, but not before we are truly ready." After one false start and a project cessation of 6 months, we needed a successful outcome to restore confidence and sustain momentum. A successful jumpstart was perceived as imperative to the extended well-being of the program.

During the fall and winter of 1999/2000, staffing and equipment demands were closely reevaluated. The library director made it clear that staffing as well as other forms of program support such as space requirements and equipment would be provided. The .5 FTE hired in the fall to assist with initial project planning was no longer sufficient to handle projected development activities, staff training, setup, promotional and processing duties. The .5 was converted to a full-time position with a robust position description. Identical scanners (Fujitsu ScanPartner 600C) and software (Adobe Acrobat 3.0) were purchased and set up at each of the three health sciences libraries to assure uniform processing and training at each site when demand picked up.

Since one Library Express shop (Wendt Engineering Library) was already functional on the campus, the first few months of planning were devoted to familiarizing ourselves with the successful processes already in place and how we could adapt these to our HSL environment. We were able to emulate much of the workflow and "borrow" the home-grown software that allowed us to scan, mount and deliver image files with less effort. Library Express staff was trained to verify citations in a number of databases, and work with existing email clients, MS Access and Adobe Acrobat. Student assistants were hired to retrieve, scan and mount articles to the server. Trouble-shooting and communication with users was limited to LX staff and closely monitored.

During this time a procedures manual was designed to support training and to communicate acceptable practices. A Web page was developed to provide a point of access and source of service information for our users. Promotional materials and other aids, such as a letters of introduction and a brochure were also developed. Other functions and practices of the first generation system were worked out piece by piece in countless meetings and discussions throughout the 16-month beta phase.

BETA PHASE

Starting out small afforded the project management team time to assess, tweak and fine-tune the service before moving on to serve a larger and more complex user group. We introduced the initial version of Library Express to members of the Ophthalmology Department (clinicians, faculty, residents, fellows and support staff) during February 2000 and opened the service to them March 1. Library Express staff conducted on-site demos, circulated letters of introduction, trained Ophthalmology staff in the efficient use of the service and closely monitored their progress. A Web-based tutorial was designed for the existing splash page to aid new users and refresh the memories of the occasional visitor. Technical issues were addressed immediately, often with an on-site visit to see first-hand what obstacles the users were encountering. Starting with a small group (approximately 60) with varying needs and varying degrees of computer comfort levels allowed for more control, better communication and more immediate resolution of problems as they surfaced.

After working with Ophthalmology for two months, we added the School of Pharmacy to the Library Express test pool. The pharmacy graduate students doing clerkships throughout the state gave us another challenge–how to deliver large PDF files to users with minimal hardware configurations through firewalls and slow modem connections. Additional user groups were added incrementally throughout the year by invitation only. Promotion was very focused and controlled to keep activity levels in line with our ability to provide a high level of service. Staggered additions to the Library Express service roster included the Department of Surgery, Student Health Services, Psychiatry, and the School of Nursing, each bringing with them unique demands and service challenges.

Although Library Express staff had been meeting often, we now felt a need to formalize the meeting calendar in order to include staff from all three libraries that were now processing more requests. Staff hours during this time tripled as requests increased ten-fold. The first month of the beta period with only Ophthalmology on board, we received 129 requests. Sixteen months later during the last month of the free beta phase, we received 1,881 requests. Business was booming.

The Library Express working group had now grown to include the Head of Access services, the coordinator of the hospital library and front-line Library

Express staff (1.5 FTE). Regular weekly meetings were helpful in keeping us on track, addressing problems quickly, making corrections immediately and communicating any changes in policies and procedures to all Library Express staff at all three processing locations. Regular meetings continue to this day, but on a bi-weekly basis.

Throughout the beta phase the Library Express team remained flexible yet focused, smoothing out the bumps in the road as they came up, willing to make changes, if needed, to improve the quality of service. Nothing was set in stone. Everything was up for evaluation. Attention to detail became our mantra. Staff scrutinized, assessed and evaluated each step of the process. We conducted a time study, which tied staffing needs to volume levels. Daily, weekly and monthly statistical reports generated from MS Access were helpful in identifying trends (or the lack of them), aided with scheduling, equipment and space needs, as well as planning for future service enhancements.

During the beta phase we also listened carefully to our users. Two questionnaires were sent out, one in May 2000 to approximately 100 users and the second in February 2001 to 350 users of Library Express. Beyond a high degree of satisfaction with the service, responses to the early survey also revealed a desire for color images, that faculty were doing their own requesting and that we needed to do a better job informing non-users of the service. Responses to the February 2001survey indicated that the suggested fee of $1 per delivered article would substantially reduce the number of requests. A majority of respondents clearly stated that they would exercise more caution when ordering to avoid the $1 fee. This was very useful in planning for short-term staffing needs. Other information uncovered from this survey was a perceived need for 24-hour service, a desire to have tables of contents delivered and a confirmation that most Library Express users loved the service and found it extremely helpful in conducting both research and their daily business.

One of the most rewarding experiences during the beta phase was working with colleagues across campus to design the generation two software, which would be offered to all faculty, staff and graduate students by four different libraries each with its own specific user group. During this time of collaborative development, the group made a wish list of Library Express features that each site wanted in place in the new version, both on the public/user side and on the processing/staff side. Out of these meetings came an end product that had a common look and feel, yet one that was able to retain some of the site-specific features and functions. For example, HSL had, for most of the beta, offered the option of color images. This was an important feature for our Ophthalmology group and others who needed the color variations of photos. Blacks, whites and grays were not always as useful. This feature choice was incorporated into the design for the HSL Web-pages, but not for other shops. The new software would be totally Web-based, eliminating the awkward interactions between email clients, homegrown programming, MS Access, and other bits and pieces that had been cobbled together.

Working together with campus-wide Library Express staff also allowed us to share general document delivery experiences and philosophies. It strengthened our understanding of current practices in other document delivery areas on campus and created opportunities for further collaboration and partnerships beyond Library Express.

GO LIVE PHASE

After testing the new software with a small sampling of current users, the second generation of Library Express software was activated July 2001. Bugs and potential enhancements were identified and scheduled for resolution. None prevented requesting or delivery, but did add to confusion on the staff side. Reports were not in place when the new system was activated, resulting in continued data entry with MS Access. User and transaction data, now collected by a Web-based system, could not be harvested without considerable programming that, at this writing, is still in progress.

In anticipation of the $1 per article fee, users swamped us in May and June resulting in our highest productivity to date–1,513 and 1,881 respectively. During the month of July, our activity level fell to less than half, confirming what we had learned from our survey earlier in the year. Since July the number of monthly requests has continued to climb, albeit slowly, leveling out at approximately 1,000.

The new Library Express software provides a total Web-based environment for both users and processing staff. The only remnants of the previous system are the manual scanning process, which we have found no way to streamline, and the initial citation verification and location procedures. Users now have the ability to track the progress of their requests online, limiting the amount of email generated in communicating request status with users. A built-in request forwarding feature allows requests to be moved to other Library Express shops for retrieval and processing. We no longer send students to other campus libraries to copy articles found there. This significantly reduces the turnaround time for those deliveries.

Library Express has proven to be a time-saver and a tool of convenience for many affiliated users who choose to pay $1 per article rather than travel across campus. It is a life-saver for faculty, staff and students who are off campus without access to needed information resources. As we near the second year of operation, HSL will increase promotional efforts to communicate the advantages and features of Library Express to a wider audience. We will continue to watch activity levels to determine staff, monitor the quality of the service and listen to our users.

As Library Express has grown to four processing shops, to a common software with common attributes, our autonomy and, therefore, flexibility have decreased. We can no longer make quick adjustments to our services and practices without consulting others and without generating considerable programming efforts and costs. The campus is also looking at Library Express as a model for digital document delivery between UW System campuses across the state. At this writing it appears that the local success of this service may eventually lead to the purchase of a standards-compliant system that has more stability and more interconnectivity with existing products. Until libraries can offer their users a truly complete menu of electronic resources from which to choose, Library Express, and similar systems will continue to build bridges to the future. The Health Sciences Libraries, University of Wisconsin-Madison, will continue to serve its affiliated groups with fast, easy-to-use document delivery to the desktop, taking the obstacles of distance out of the equation.

Library Express at a Glance:

Statistics:

Average requests per month:	approx 1,000
Average per day:	39
Highest month (June 2001):	1,881
Total requests to date:	17,619 (Oct 2001)

Software during beta:

Web-based user interface

Staff side local email
Article sent in PDF via email

Adobe Acrobat
Locally programmed software
MS Access for data storage
and reports

New software since July 2001:

Locally programmed Web-based user and staff interface
Request tracking
Staff side request forwarding to other filling libraries on campus
Adobe Acrobat

Statistical reports still being designed

User Authentication:

Campus ID

Method of payment:

Electronic fund transfer (monthly)
Campus debit card (monthly withdrawals)

Total staff devoted to processing Library Express at three sites:

4 FTE plus student hours

At the Crossroads:
Library and Classroom

Mollie Dinwiddie
Linda L. Lillard

Central Missouri State University

SUMMARY. What do distance learners expect regarding library reference service? Will they respond to a personalized customer service offered by a librarian in an online course? Is there a place for this type of interaction in online courses? Data was collected in several online courses that included results of a survey of distance learners, discussion board interaction, and individual e-mail comments and questions from students to the librarian.

KEYWORDS. Distance learners, library services, library instruction, reference service

Every day a growing number of universities are restructuring courses to offer via distance education. Though universities have been in the business of providing distance education since the late 1800s via correspondence courses involving text-based course materials and instructor-student communication by postal mail, technology is rapidly changing the methods by which these courses can be offered (University of Texas, October 25, 2000). Course offerings are made available to distance learners by such methods as video conferencing, instructional television or other methods (Palloff & Pratt, 1999). Between 1994-95 and 1997-98, the use of video-based technology as a medium for distance delivery did not grow. Most of the growth was in courses

[Haworth co-indexing entry note]: "At the Crossroads: Library and Classroom." Dinwiddie, Mollie, and Linda L. Lillard. Co-published simultaneously in *Journal of Library Administration* (The Haworth Information Press, an imprint of The Haworth Press, Inc.) Vol. 37, No. 1/2, 2002, pp. 251-267; and: *Distance Learning Library Services: The Tenth Off-Campus Library Services Conference* (ed: Patrick B. Mahoney) The Haworth Information Press, an imprint of The Haworth Press, Inc., 2002, pp. 251-267.

http://www.haworthpress.com/store/product.asp?sku=J111
10.1300/J111v37n01_21

that use asynchronous computer-based technology (primarily the Internet) rather than two-way or one-way video.

Especially popular are the Web-based course software packages such as WebCT and Blackboard with which the instructor can almost duplicate the traditional classroom experience. Interactive video/audio feeds, discussion lists, chat rooms, and the like provide the dialogue needed between the instructor and the students. At the same time, students determine when to do much of the course work and where, limited only by access to the Internet. The techniques for the best teaching are still in the experimental stages, but quality instruction is available for students who are self-directed and self-motivated.

Learning, however, occurs in other areas outside the classroom. Students are expected to explore independently and to develop critical thinking skills. In the traditional classroom, students leave the class and assume responsibilities for reading assignments, conducting research on topics relevant to the course, synthesizing knowledge as demonstrated in research papers, reports, group and individual presentations, and other learning activities. These "out of class" learning expectations exist in a distance education course as well.

On a university campus, students have ready access to libraries, laboratories, and study partners. Distance education instructors must find ways to make these sources equally accessible to students who are not physically convenient to one another or to campus academic support mechanisms. Fowell and Levy (1995) assert that information professionals are critical players in the distance learning environment, as they are likely to be the prime developers of learning support mechanisms as well as the providers, thus moving them into the role of culture change agents within their institutions. In this role, the burning question for information professionals then becomes, how can we make a level playing field for our distance students?

THE CHALLENGE OF PROVIDING LIBRARY SERVICES
FOR DISTANCE LEARNERS

Regardless of what method is used to deliver a distance course, a common problem with all distance courses is the fact that the student may not have physical access to campus and consequently does not have access to certain amenities such as library services. Librarians everywhere are facing the problem of finding creative ways to meet guidelines set forth by the Association of College and Research Libraries (ACRL) that support the premise that members of the distance learning community are entitled to services that are equivalent to those provided to their campus-based constituents (Gover, 1999). In the *Guidelines for Distance*

Learning Library Services approved in July of 1998, the Association of College and Research Libraries (ACRL) asserted that:

> Access to adequate library services and resources is essential for the attainment of superior academic skills in post-secondary education, regardless of where students, faculty, and programs are located. Members of the distance learning community are entitled to library services and resources equivalent to those provided for students and faculty in traditional campus settings. (Gover, 1999, Philosophy section, para. 1)

Realizing that traditional methods of providing research assistance to students must be altered to fit the online course environment, librarians are utilizing various methods of meeting what they perceive as the needs of these online students, such as e-mail and technology enhanced reference (Barsun, 2000; University of Minnesota, 1998; Gray, 2000; Pernat, 1999), a toll-free line (Blair, 2000), a distance learning library services Web page (Buckstead, 2000; Diaz, 1998), document delivery (Calvert, 2000), improved remote access to electronic resources (University of Minnesota, 1998), online tutorials (University of Minnesota, 1998), and electronic reserve (Calvert, 2000; Pernat, 1999; Diaz, 1999).

In many cases it is easier to provide remote access to the physical resources such as online catalogs and online databases than it is to provide access to the human resources that are a critical aspect of superior library services. ACRL believes that "traditional on-campus library services themselves cannot be stretched to meet the library needs of distance learning students and faculty who face distinct and different challenges involving library access and information delivery." In order to compensate for this lack of access to the full range of library services that would provide equivalent services for the distance learning community, the services offered to this group are often a more personalized kind of service than that available on campus.

BACKGROUND OF THE STUDY

At Central Missouri State University several librarians are attempting to help students meet information needs in an online course environment by not only providing them with access to full-text databases, document delivery, and state-wide library cards, but by actively engaging a librarian to assist with course instruction. This practice is consistent with the idea of more personalized service and becomes the kind of proactive role that is promoted by contemporary library schools (Grover & Hale, 1988) for librarians moving into the 21st century information environment with all of its new and exciting roles (Callahan, 1991; Medhurst, 1995). Caspers (1999) believes that librarians must be proactive in their efforts to make the library visible and accessible to distance learners because they can't simply look at the campus map and go there, as traditional students are able to do. She asserts that "it is crucial for the distance education librarian to actively become part of the distance education community, especially as related to programs emanating from the home campus" (pp. 301-302).

Traditionally, librarians have attempted to forge alliances with faculty members to provide enhanced library services for classes by soliciting faculty input for collection development, meeting with faculty members to discuss the information needs for individual courses, examining course syllabi to get a feel so that the applicable library resources can be easily integrated, and producing pathfinders and specialized instruction sessions for classes. In addition, during the past several years, librarians have been creating Web pages that provide links to Web sites they have examined and deemed useful for certain subject areas and individual classes.

In the project at Central Missouri State University, librarians are going beyond these traditional partnerships and becoming co-instructors of online courses offered using Blackboard's Web-based course software. The software allows for more than one instructor in a course; consequently, the librarian can be added to the course as a co-instructor, thus giving the librarian access to students that is identical to the access available to the content instructor. A librarian in the role of co-instructor in an online course is a new approach to providing library services for distance learners. Not only does this approach make mediation into the research process a possibility, it also allows for mediation into the entire student learning experience. In the face-to-face learning environment, one would never expect to find a librarian in the traditional classroom with the content instructor during every class meeting. In the virtual learning environment, however, this presence is a viable option.

In addition, this project gives the student virtually 24/7 access to the librarian, which is something difficult to achieve in the traditional library setting. This 24/7 access to a librarian does not mean that there is a real librarian available to answer questions 24-hours a day every day of the week. What it means is that the student has a library advisor and can send e-mails, faxes, or phone messages to this librarian at any time of the day or night when working on a project and expect a timely response. The librarian might also be contacted through the course discussion board, where a student can leave a question and the librarian can answer, giving all students in class the opportunity to benefit from the answer to a particular question. This personalized service also allows the student to work with this librarian throughout the entire life of a research project or a course, providing greater continuity in the project and alleviating the need to constantly re-define the project each time assistance is requested, as happens when the student spontaneously asks for help when conducting research in the library and must ask for assistance from whoever is manning the reference desk at that particular time.

THE ONLINE LIBRARIAN/INSTRUCTOR PROJECT– THE FIRST ROUND

In the fall semester of 1999, a faculty member who had initiated the first distance education (DE) course for the Nursing Department asked the library liaison to the department to participate in the DE course, Nursing 4010, Nursing Research. The librarian readily agreed and was duly added as a co-instructor of this online course through the Blackboard online course software. Clearly this invitation provided an opportunity for the librarian to participate in course instruction to a greater extent than the traditional instruction sessions provided when the classroom teacher brings a class to the library.

The nursing librarian provided a Web page of useful information resources related to nursing and medical information. The distance learning librarian prepared a Web page for distance students with information related to interlibrary loan, access to library catalogs and general Web resources, off-campus access to online databases, how to use the cooperative borrower card at partner libraries across the state, and other services available to students. After learning the rudiments of the Blackboard software, the nursing librarian was able to communicate with students in the class. This consisted primarily of an offer to provide research assistance via e-mail to assist the students in the completion of course assignments. At first the students were a bit reluctant to contact the librarian/instructor. There was also some confusion among students regarding what was appropriate to ask. The first exposure to the distance students proved to be mainly a learning experience for the librarian.

THE ONLINE LIBRARIAN/INSTRUCTOR PROJECT– THE SECOND ROUND

During the spring 2000 semester, the nursing librarian acted as a co-instructor for two distance learning courses, Nursing 4010, Nursing Research and Nursing 5010, Nursing Theory. She had direct access to the entire course as presented by the course content instructor and as received by the students. The course syllabus, calendar, assignments, and lectures were readily accessible. After reading the objectives and assignments of the course, the librarian/instructor was able to identify Web links that were relevant and post direct links in a "Library Corner" folder in the Web-based course.

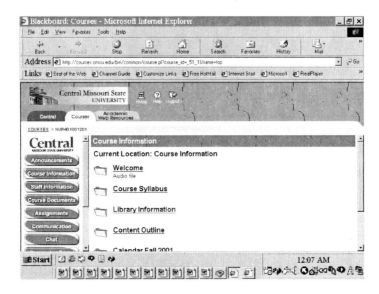

She posted announcements to the students' discussion board and e-mailed an introductory message to each of them. Her goal was to provide them with instructions on how to access Web resources and databases that might be useful, and to serve as a reference resource for individual research projects related to the course. She sought to provide the same kind of assistance students might have experienced in a face-to-face reference desk exchange.

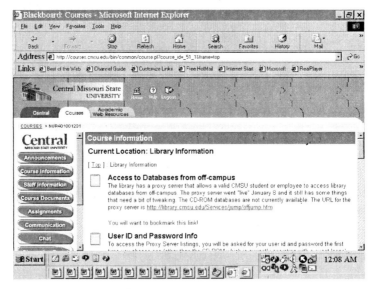

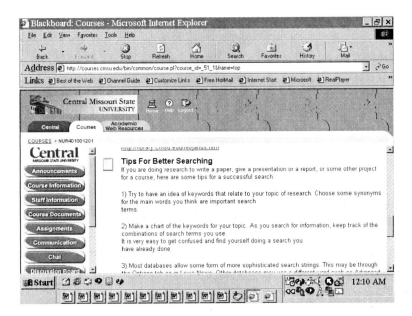

The librarian in the key role of co-instructor in an online course is a very different approach to providing library services for students, and one that would be rarely, if at all, found in the face-to-face learning environment. Will the students take advantage of this new role for the librarian in such close proximity and request more mediation into their research process? If so, what type of services will they request?

Several questions guided this project:

1. How will students utilize the librarian's expertise given 24/7 access?
2. What kind of library services and research assistance do distance learners really want from a librarian?
3. Do distance students feel that the librarian is helpful to their research process?
4. Is librarian mediation throughout their entire research process something that distance learners will embrace enthusiastically?
5. Will the students take advantage of this new role for the librarian in such close proximity and request more mediation into their research process?

STUDY DESIGN

A case study design was chosen with the unit of analysis by students who were enrolled in Criminal Justice and Nursing classes that were conducted with an online element using the Blackboard Web-based course software during the spring 2001 semester at Central Missouri State University. All students enrolled in these classes had 24/7 access to the librarian through e-mail and the discussion board area of the Blackboard course software. While the students were able to access online resources of the library from any location and were enrolled in an online course, many of them were actually on campus and therefore, had access to the physical library. In the study there was no differentiation between those students who were entirely online and those who were on campus. Future study is planned to examine how use varies depending upon easy availability of the physical library.

Data Collection

Several methods of data collection were used by the researchers in this project. One method was the use of anonymous survey questions, administered through the Blackboard software. Students were asked to respond to 15 questions in a Likert scaled survey. Out of 170 students, 115 responded to the survey questions, which resulted in an approximately 68 percent response rate. As a part of this survey, students were also asked to respond to three open-ended questions that provided qualitative data. In addition, students were asked to respond to a question posted in the discussion board. They were asked if they thought having a librarian in the online classroom was useful to them. A small sample of nursing students was asked to describe their online search experiences, as well. In addition, there were unsolicited e-mails from students who asked for assistance.

DATA ANALYSIS

Survey Results

Data analysis consisted of presenting the data collected from the Likert scaled survey questions in tabular format to allow for visual comparison and analysis. Answers to the questions are presented for the overall group of respondents from online criminal justice and nursing classes and presented for each particular group.

Question 1: The information provided about access to library databases from off campus helped me locate materials for my course research.

Response	Criminal Justice n = 87		Nursing n = 28		Overall N = 115	
	Frequency	Percent	Frequency	Percent	Frequency	Percent
Strongly Agree	26	29.9	14	50.0	40	34.8
Agree Somewhat	44	50.6	12	42.9	56	48.7
Disagree Somewhat	3	3.4	0	0	3	2.6
Strongly Disagree	5	5.7	0	0	5	4.3
No Opinion	9	10.3	2	7.1	11	9.6
Totals	87	99.9	28	100.0	115	100.0

The librarian made sure that information about access to library databases from off-campus was clearly explained to students. The response of the students about the usefulness of this information shows that approximately 84 percent of them found this helpful.

Question 2: I used the links to Kirkpatrick Library's Distance Education Web page to get additional information to help me with my research.

Response	Criminal Justice		Nursing		Overall	
	Frequency	Percent	Frequency	Percent	Frequency	Percent
Strongly Agree	19	21.8	13	46.4	32	27.8
Agree Somewhat	36	41.4	7	25.0	43	37.4
Disagree Somewhat	8	9.2	6	21.4	14	12.2
Strongly Disagree	10	11.5	0	0	10	8.7
No Opinion	14	16.1	2	7.1	16	13.9
	87	100.0	28	99.9	115	100.0

While not an overwhelmingly popular source, almost two-thirds of the students did use the Distance Education Web page to gain additional library and research information. Without the librarian's ability to make this known to all class members through her access to the online course as an instructor, the students might have missed knowing about this resource.

Question 3: I was aware of the ability to obtain a MIX card to allow me charge-out privileges at participating libraries in Missouri.

Response	Criminal Justice		Nursing		Overall	
	Frequency	Percent	Frequency	Percent	Frequency	Percent
Strongly Agree	10	11.5	10	35.7	20	17.4
Agree Somewhat	10	11.5	5	17.9	15	13.0
Disagree Somewhat	18	20.7	4	14.3	22	19.1
Strongly Disagree	40	46.0	7	25.0	47	40.9
No Opinion	9	10.3	2	7.1	11	9.6
	87	100.0	28	100.0	115	100.0

Unfortunately students still miss out on critical pieces of information that they are given, as only about 30 percent were aware of the MIX card. This may simply indicate that the librarian must be more aggressive about reminding these students of the various services.

Question 4: The announcements provided by the library liaison at Kirkpatrick Library were timely and useful in helping me conduct my research.

Response	Criminal Justice		Nursing		Overall	
	Frequency	Percent	Frequency	Percent	Frequency	Percent
Strongly Agree	18	20.7	10	35.7	28	24.3
Agree Somewhat	37	42.5	13	46.4	50	43.5
Disagree Somewhat	10	11.5	1	3.6	11	9.6
Strongly Disagree	8	9.2	2	7.1	10	8.7
No Opinion	14	16.1	2	7.1	16	13.9
	87	100.0	28	99.9	115	100.0

In the experimental study almost 68 percent of the students responded that they found the documents posted by the librarian were useful. While a number of students obviously ignored the information provided, the librarian is assured that 100 percent of the students had some communication from the librarian. Most of us have had the experience of walking into a department store and having no sales assistance offered and we have been annoyed by this! Occasionally we are offered more assistance than we really want, but most of us would agree that it is preferable to have the offer made than not. We can always choose to say "no, thank you" if we do not require help.

Question 5: Having a librarian available to assist in my research via e-mail or telephone is a service I would like to have for other classes.

Response	Criminal Justice		Nursing		Overall	
	Frequency	Percent	Frequency	Percent	Frequency	Percent
Strongly Agree	53	61.0	19	67.9	72	62.6
Agree Somewhat	26	29.9	6	21.4	32	27.8
Disagree Somewhat	2	2.3	0	0	.2	1.7
Strongly Disagree	1	1.1	0	0	1	.9
No Opinion	5	5.7	3	10.7	8	7.0
	87	100.0	28	100.0	115	100.0

Perhaps this response is the one we would expect most students to make when asked if they would like assistance. What is interesting is that students indicate they want the potential assistance, over 90 percent, whether it is evident that they ever made use of the service in this course.

Question 6: Questions I directed to the librarian working with this course were answered in a timely manner.

Response	Criminal Justice		Nursing		Overall	
	Frequency	Percent	Frequency	Percent	Frequency	Percent
Strongly Agree	27	31.0	10	35.7	37	32.2
Agree Somewhat	19	21.8	4	14.3	23	20.0
Disagree Somewhat	5	5.7	0	0	5	4.3
Strongly Disagree	0	0	1	3.6	1	.9
No Opinion	36	41.4	13	46.4	49	42.6
	87	99.9	28	100.0	115	100.0

Since most questions that were asked were via e-mail, there was at least a short delay in response time. The librarian made every effort to reply to all e-mail questions within a two-day time period. Perhaps the students expected a more instantaneous response. In reality, students would prefer to have someone available 24 hours a day, whenever the question occurs. But on the whole, students were satisfied with the response time of the librarian.

Question 7: I was able to complete my research for this course without making an actual visit to Kirkpatrick Library.

Response	Criminal Justice		Nursing		Overall	
	Frequency	Percent	Frequency	Percent	Frequency	Percent
Strongly Agree	25	28.7	5	17.9	30	26.1
Agree Somewhat	24	27.6	5	17.9	29	25.2
Disagree Somewhat	17	19.5	2	7.1	19	16.5
Strongly Disagree	14	16.1	14	50.0	28	24.3
No Opinion	7	8.0	2	7.1	9	7.8
	87	99.9	28	100.0	115	99.9

The response to this question clearly shows that 100 percent access is not yet available in the online environment. A distance learner may still need to go to a physical library to obtain information for his/her research. There are problems posed for distance learners who are not within reasonable distance of a good library. It may be unrealistic to expect to have all one's research needs available via the Internet. However, this is what students are likely to think should be the case.

Question 8: I could not complete my research for this course without making an actual visit to the Kirkpatrick Library.

Response	Criminal Justice		Nursing		Overall	
	Frequency	Percent	Frequency	Percent	Frequency	Percent
Strongly Agree	20	23.0	12	42.9	32	27.8
Agree Somewhat	23	26.4	6	21.4	29	25.2
Disagree Somewhat	17	19.5	4	14.3	21	18.2
Strongly Disagree	18	20.7	6	21.4	24	20.9
No Opinion	9	10.3	0	0	9	7.8
	87	99.9	28	100.0	115	100.0

Soliciting the same response in two opposite statements was designed to ascertain if students were actually thinking about their responses. With a few exceptions, the students appeared to be reading the question accurately and were accurate with their responses.

Question 9: I utilized Interlibrary Loan services from Kirkpatrick Library to get access to materials I needed for my research.

Response	Criminal Justice		Nursing		Overall	
	Frequency	Percent	Frequency	Percent	Frequency	Percent
Strongly Agree	9	10.3	7	25.0	16	13.9
Agree Somewhat	14	16.1	1	3.6	15	13.0
Disagree Somewhat	6	6.9	2	7.1	8	7.0
Strongly Disagree	22	25.3	10	35.7	32	27.8
No Opinion	36	41.4	8	28.6	44	38.3
	87	100.0	28	100.0	115	100.0

We rely heavily on Interlibrary Loan to provide resources to distance learners. They may request materials in the library and have them mailed to them or we will borrow what they request from other libraries and mail it to them. Unfortunately, the students surveyed did not seem to use Interlibrary Loan or mail delivery from the library as much as one would hope.

Question 10: I felt comfortable asking for assistance from the librarian working with this course.

Response	Criminal Justice		Nursing		Overall	
	Frequency	Percent	Frequency	Percent	Frequency	Percent
Strongly Agree	31	35.6	15	53.6	46	40.0
Agree Somewhat	27	31.0	6	21.4	33	28.7
Disagree Somewhat	4	4.6	0	0	4	3.5
Strongly Disagree	7	8.0	0	0	7	6.1
No Opinion	18	20.7	7	25.0	25	21.7
	87	99.9	28	100.0	115	100.0

Certainly it is imperative that the students be willing to ask for help. Ideally, the librarian would convey a willingness to help that provides a comfort level for 100 percent of the students. The responses indicate that quite a few students were still unwilling to ask for help or did not choose to commit themselves to a position on the statement. This remains a challenge for the librarian–how to encourage students to ask for the help they do need.

Question 11: I would like to have an online tutorial available that explains use of the electronic library resources in detail.

Response	Criminal Justice		Nursing		Overall	
	Frequency	Percent	Frequency	Percent	Frequency	Percent
Strongly Agree	41	47.1	14	50.0	55	47.8
Agree Somewhat	32	36.8	6	21.4	38	33.0
Disagree Somewhat	6	6.9	5	17.9	11	9.6
Strongly Disagree	2	2.3	0	0	2	1.7
No Opinion	6	6.9	3	10.7	9	7.8
	87	100.0	28	100.0	115	99.9

Students reacted positively to the idea of online tutorials, however it seems a bit odd that 100 percent of the responses were not in the affirmative.

Question 12: I would benefit from an interactive "real time" tutoring session presented by the librarian working with this course.

Response	Criminal Justice		Nursing		Overall	
	Frequency	Percent	Frequency	Percent	Frequency	Percent
Strongly Agree	19	21.8	12	42.9	31	27.0
Agree Somewhat	44	50.6	6	21.4	50	43.5
Disagree Somewhat	10	11.5	8	28.6	18	15.7
Strongly Disagree	5	5.7	0	0	5	4.3
No Opinion	9	10.3	2	7.1	11	9.6
	87	100.0	28	100.0	115	100.1

Interestingly, a large number would like a "real time" session to occur with the librarian. Whether all 72 percent of these students would actually "be there" during a real time session, however, is questionable.

Question 13: My expectations regarding the assistance provided by the librarian were met.

Response	Criminal Justice		Nursing		Overall	
	Frequency	Percent	Frequency	Percent	Frequency	Percent
Strongly Agree	30	34.5	14	50.0	44	38.2
Agree Somewhat	28	32.2	6	21.4	34	29.6
Disagree Somewhat	4	4.6	1	3.6	5	4.3
Strongly Disagree	0	0	0	0	0	0
No Opinion	25	28.7	7	25.0	32	27.8
	87	100.0	28	100.0	115	99.9

On the whole, students appeared to get what they thought was appropriate from the librarian involvement. Knowing precisely what their expectations were would be enlightening.

Question 14: Because of her involvement with this course, I will ask for assistance from the Blackboard librarian for future research needs while I am continuing my degree program at Central.

Response	Criminal Justice		Nursing		Overall	
	Frequency	Percent	Frequency	Percent	Frequency	Percent
Strongly Agree	35	40.2	18	64.3	53	46.0
Agree Somewhat	33	37.9	7	25.0	40	34.8
Disagree Somewhat	3	3.4	0	0	3	2.6
Strongly Disagree	3	3.4	0	0	3	2.6
No Opinion	13	14.9	3	10.7	16	13.9
	87	99.8	28	100.0	115	99.9

Our hope would be that students who are exposed to some assistance from a librarian in their online courses would have an improved "comfort level" for future research needs. Knowing that a real person is offering assistance should encourage students to feel less apprehensive about asking questions. Many students at the reference desk preface a question with the words "I'm sorry to bother you." One goal of this involvement with online courses was to try to encourage students not to feel as though they were intruding when they asked for help.

Question 15: I found that access to the library resources from off campus worked very well from my remote site.

Response	Criminal Justice		Nursing		Overall	
	Frequency	Percent	Frequency	Percent	Frequency	Percent
Strongly Agree	29	33.3	12	42.9	41	35.7
Agree Somewhat	34	39.1	10	35.7	44	38.3
Disagree Somewhat	5	5.7	1	3.6	6	5.2
Strongly Disagree	6	6.9	1	3.6	7	6.1
No Opinion	13	14.9	4	14.3	17	14.8
	87	99.9	28	100.1	115	100.1

This last survey question illustrates a concern that we still have regarding the reliability of access to resources. The resources that students need will exist only if reliable and quick access is the norm. Technical problems compound the frustrations that students have with locating the information they seek. On the whole it appears that students did not experience several technical malfunctions.

Forty-two responses were posted from students in the discussion board. They were all positive comments indicating that students thought the idea of having a librarian available in this manner is a good thing. Comments generally were along the lines of "I think it is a great idea." However, some students put more thought into their responses. One student stated, "I'm new to the online world of classes so I'm not yet sure of exactly what I do need. I had begun my research without utilizing the available resources you had gathered for us. I'm anxious to use these resources since I think it will greatly aid in my search for information." Another said, "Most people do their research now at home with their computers so to have someone at your fingertips to help with projects would be very helpful." One student's comment will find favor among librarians: "I know that a librarian assisting is very helpful. Mollie has helped me out in my other online class. She has helped me when looking for information–where to look, what topics to look for, etc. I think this is a great idea as long as the librarian has the time and will get paid for the extra work." Another student had a similar thought: "I think that this would be very helpful, however, I don't think that the librarians would be able to keep up with the requests."

CONCLUSIONS

Despite the efforts of the librarian to encourage students to ask for help, the discouraging truth is that few took advantage of the opportunity. One may speculate that the research demands of the courses were not substantive enough to stimulate a need for research assistance or that students were able to navigate without assistance using the tools and information provided already by the librarian. There has been an increase in face-to-face requests for assistance from students enrolled on campus and also taking an online course. However, the number of individual e-mail requests from students is still very low. One conclusion is that students on campus, who are in the library and have a research problem, are more likely to seek out the librarian with whom they are familiar in the online course. Positive comments from students far outnumbered negative input. The students are grateful for a library presence within the online course. Clearly, there is a place within online course software for librarian intervention. Additional experimentation is needed to determine how a library can best meet the needs of its online students.

REFERENCES

Barsun, R. (2000). Computer mediated conferencing, e-mail, telephone: A holistic approach to meeting students' needs. In P. S. Thomas (Ed.), *The Ninth Off-Campus Library Services Proceedings* (pp. 19-28). Mount Pleasant, MI: Central Michigan University.
Blair, A. (2000). . . . And a free 800 line! Managing technical and information support for distance education. In P. S. Thomas (Ed.), *The Ninth Off-Campus Library Services Proceedings* (pp. 19-28). Mount Pleasant, MI: Central Michigan University.
Buckstead, J.R. (2000). Developing an effective off-campus library services web page: Don't worry, be happy! In P. S. Thomas (Ed.), *The Ninth Off-Campus Library Services Proceedings* (pp. 19-28). Mount Pleasant, MI: Central Michigan University.
Callahan, D.R. (1991, February). The librarian as change agent in the diffusion of technological innovation. *Electronic Library, 9*(1), 13-15.
Calvert, H.M. (2000). Document delivery options for distance education students an electronic reserve service at Ball State University Libraries. In P. S. Thomas (Ed.), *The Ninth Off-Campus Library Services Proceedings* (19-28). Mount Pleasant, MI: Central Michigan University.
Caspers, J.S. (1999). Outreach to distance learners: When the distance education instructor sends students to the library, where do they go? *The Reference Librarian 67/68*, 299-311.
Caspers, J., Fritts, J. & Gover, H. (2000). Beyond the rhetoric: A study of the impact of the ACRL guidelines for distance learning library services on selected distance learning programs in higher education. In P. S. Thomas (Ed.), *The Ninth Off-Campus Library Services Proceedings* (pp. 19-28). Mount Pleasant, MI: Central Michigan University.
Diaz, K. (1998, Fall). The role of the library web site. *Reference & User Services Quarterly, 38*(1). Retrieved October 25, 2000, from Infotrac on the World Wide Web: http://infotrac.galegroup.com.
Dow, S.H. (2000). Knowing your users and what they want: Surveying off-campus students about library services. In P. S. Thomas (Ed.), *The Ninth Off-Campus Library Services Proceedings* (pp. 19-28). Mount Pleasant, MI: Central Michigan University.

Fowell, S. and Levy, P. (1995). Developing a new professional practice: A model for networked learner support in higher education. *Journal of Documentation, 51*(3), 271-280.

Gover, H. (July 13, 1999) *ACRL guidelines for distance learning library services.* Retrieved May 24, 2000 from http://caspian.switchinc.org/~distlearn/guidelines/.

Gray, S.M. (2000, Summer). Virtual reference services directions and agendas. *Reference & User Services Quarterly, 39*(4). Retrieved October 25, 2000, from Infotrac on the World Wide Web: http://infotrac.galegroup.com.

Grover, R. & Hale, M.L. (1988, January). The role of the librarian in faculty research. *College & Research Libraries, 49*(1), 9-15.

Medhurst, J. (1995, September). Do or die: The librarian in the 21st century. *Managing Information, 2*(9), 30-31.

Palloff, R.M. & Pratt, K. (1999). *Building learning communities in cyberspace: Effective strategies for the online classroom.* San Francisco: Jossey-Bass Publishers.

Pernat, M. (1999, September). Widening the net: Monash University Library's flexible, student-centered information services. *Australian Academic & Research Libraries, 30*(3). Retrieved October 25, 2000, from Infotrac on the World Wide Web: http://infotrac.galegroup.com.

University of Minnesota (1998, November). Library uses innovative technology to enhance resources and services for distance learners: Making being there as good as being here. *Information Technology Newsletter,* (8). [Online] Available: http://www1.umn.edu/oit/newsletter/1198-itn/innovative.html.

University of Texas. *Distance education: A primer.* Retrieved October 25, 2000 from the University of Texas Web site: http://www.utexas.edu/cc/cit/de/deprimer/overview.html.

Community Connections
in Off-Campus Outreach Services

Ann Duesing

University of Virginia

SUMMARY. Integration of outreach information services directly into community health projects provides the opportunity to make a more definitive contribution to the health services and outcomes for community members. This paper describes four community connection projects undertaken in a rural health information outreach program in southwestern Virginia.

KEYWORDS. Collaboration, cooperation, outreach, library services

Primary audiences for the University of Virginia Health Sciences Library off-campus outreach program include affiliated preceptors, medical students and medical residents. The secondary audience includes unaffiliated health care providers, students, and regional health institutions. While services for these groups continue to be the focus of the outreach program, the target audience is expanding. Regional health organizations, community health coalitions, consumer/patient groups, and public and school librarians who need health information services and resource access have led to the development of many effective and rewarding community connections.

Why is this significant? Health care education, especially that by a state higher education institution, looks to produce effective health care providers, a portion of whom will perhaps locate in or near their area of training. Clerk-

[Haworth co-indexing entry note]: "Community Connections in Off-Campus Outreach Services." Duesing, Ann. Co-published simultaneously in *Journal of Library Administration* (The Haworth Information Press, an imprint of The Haworth Press, Inc.) Vol. 37, No. 1/2, 2002, pp. 269-278; and: *Distance Learning Library Services: The Tenth Off-Campus Library Services Conference* (ed: Patrick B. Mahoney) The Haworth Information Press, an imprint of The Haworth Press, Inc., 2002, pp. 269-278.

http://www.haworthpress.com/store/product.asp?sku=J111
10.1300/J111v37n01_22

ships, internships and residencies within the community are a part of their training and early service. Health information services for the local community health providers, regional health organizations, coalitions, patients and consumers is a complimentary and supportive continuum of the health education center focus on excellence in community and regional health care provision. Well-informed health professionals, local health organizations, patients and consumers can only increase the opportunities for better health care and better health.

This off-campus library outreach program is based at the University of Virginia's College at Wise that is approximately 300 miles from the main health sciences center and health sciences library in Charlottesville. The outreach librarian provides information services working from an office at the affiliated college library and by traveling throughout the region. The community connections have developed through work with the regional Area Health Education Center, local hospitals, residency programs, the affiliated college library programs and faculty, and individual contacts.

While many off-campus library programs are designed to deliver information services from remote sites directly to student populations, the lack of community connectivity often disallows a sense of personal integration for the learning experience. This model not only integrates the information delivery directly into the community, it makes the community a part of the information services system.

The community connection programs selected for discussion include a diabetes coalition, a cancer coalition, health fairs, and a regional health expedition. Program development and implementation will be described as well as key players' roles and program impact on community health and health information access.

DIABETES COALITION

Virginia's Department of Health received a grant from the Centers for Disease Control and Prevention in 1994. Through this grant the state of Virginia began to address diabetes as part of a multi-state diabetes control program. The Virginia Diabetes Control Project includes partnerships with diabetes care health agencies. Some of these partners are the American Diabetes Association, the Virginia Center for Diabetes Professional Education and the Department of Health Evaluation Sciences at the University of Virginia, and the Survey ad Evaluation Research Laboratory at the Virginia Commonwealth

University. One of the community projects to deal with the burden of diabetes has been developed in the LENOWISCO (Lee, Scott, and Wise Counties and the City of Norton) Health District in southwestern Virginia. There is a local plan of action for implementing interventions based on community needs assessments using CDC guidelines (Turf, 1997, p. 1).

In early 1997 the Outreach Librarian attended a board meeting of the Southwest Virginia Area Health Education Center. One of the board members was also the Director of the LENOWISCO Public Health Departments and Project Director for the LENOWISCO Diabetes Coalition. After the Outreach Librarian's presentation and update on outreach health information services, the Director of the Health Departments discussed the Diabetes Coalition and suggested that the Outreach Librarian attend the meetings and get involved.

Early contributions by the Outreach Librarian to the coalition included providing background research on questions that arose as educational program offerings were developed. These would range from information on the latest developments in diabetes treatments to what the contact address was for speakers who were being sought for presentations at seminars. The Coalition developed a series of seminars for health care providers through cooperative efforts with the University of Virginia's diabetes outreach team. As a member of the coalition, and a coalition professional education committee member, the Outreach Librarian worked on planning for the educational series. She also attended the diabetes seminars and gave a presentation at the beginning of each new seminar about health information services, resources and access in SWVA. When local health professionals participated in the educational series, literature searches and assistance with document delivery were provided.

Another component of the diabetes coalition is the educational services provided directly to persons with diabetes who live in the region. Classes entitled IN CONTROL were developed for spring and fall sessions. When presenters for these classes needed assistance with research, the Outreach Librarian was frequently able to provide that assistance. As interest developed in learning more about the resources directly available to persons with diabetes, the Outreach Librarian created and presented classes on locating, evaluating and using diabetes resources on the Web. Another Coalition project was a partnership for developing and providing a summer camp for children with diabetes. The second year, 2001 Diabetes Summer Camp was held at a state park in SWVA. The Outreach Librarian provided a program for the parents and their children with diabetes. Web sites and resources for diabetes information were discussed and reviewed online; hands-on access was made available so that families could search together.

A separate, but related project that addressed health care professional information needs about diabetes was also provided through the Outreach Program. An NNLM (National Network of Libraries of Medicine) subcontract for 1999-2000 provided funding for specialty Internet classes on diabetes resources, among others, on the Web. Contacts from the Diabetes Coalition brought these classes to the attention of both primary care and specialty physicians in the southwestern Virginia region.

HEALTH FAIRS

Health Fairs are an excellent avenue of awareness for outreach services as well as provision of access to health information resources for students, health care professionals and consumers. As indicated earlier, the Area Health Education Center (AHEC) has been a consistent connection to regional health events for the Health Sciences Outreach Library program in southwest Virginia. The local AHEC coordinator located in Norton, Virginia, and reporting to the AHEC Executive Director currently based at the UVA College at Wise is one of the regional contact persons for health fair planning. Since Outreach and AHEC have worked together on many projects, the Outreach Librarian is included as a community resource person for health fair planning and participation. A major partner in many of the health fairs is the East Tennessee State Medical School Family Practice Residency and Medical Student Program. Since the ETSU program is located in Johnson City, Tennessee, just over the state border from southwestern Virginia, many of their students participate in the health fairs and their program is the focus of medical services and exams at the fairs. Health fairs are planned in cooperation with local health service systems and/or local service organizations. The fairs are held at small hospitals, fire departments, housing projects, senior centers, public schools, etc. Outreach health information services promotions at the fairs range from a display featuring types of services, partnerships and projects; handouts including brochures about Outreach Information services, recommended Web site addresses for health information, and flyers about local public library access and consumer health information resources, as well as library hours and Internet access so that health consumers know how to locate information locally after the event; and, sometimes, Internet connection and projection of health information sites and searching technique.

The health fairs provide excellent opportunities to meet the physicians and students who are donating services. This promotes the awareness that even though these are remote rural communities, access to current health information resources is readily available along with assistance from a health sciences librarian. It also allows opportunities for the Outreach Librarian to discuss what preceptors and students see as types of information needs and how they wish to be able to access information. Nursing instructors and students who are supporting the medical services, and those who provide screening services, also have opportunities to learn about outreach information services as well as professional, consumer, and patient Internet health information resources. Because so many health agencies are represented at the fairs there is a great deal of interaction among the health professionals from those agencies. It also gives the Outreach Librarian an opportunity to make new contacts and discuss services that may be of interest. Outreach classes, presentations, and consultations have all resulted from these health fair interactions. There have also been instances when being part of another coalition, such as the one on diabetes, has allowed the Outreach Librarian to discuss this program and its services with consumers who were attending the health fairs and looking for information on a related topic, such as meal planning for persons with diabetes.

The health fairs are usually collaborative efforts that include medical students and residents from a larger more urban community. They are working with local health department physicians, nurses and staff, local hospital staff and many area agencies and services. In southwestern Virginia there is a small hospital, St. Mary's, which has a health services outreach mobile unit called St. Mary's Health Wagon. The sister who is a nurse practitioner and directs the outreach services is Sister Bernie. She is an institution in herself and highly revered and respected not only for her good works but also her tenacity in developing and providing programs such as the health fairs. Her target population is the poor and medically underserved, of which there are many in these rural mountain areas. Not only does she help organize the ETSU medical student health fairs, she provides smaller ones with her own staff and drives the mobile unit herself on often-treacherous back mountain roads.

REGIONAL HEALTH EXPEDITION

In 1999 Sister Bernie learned of a Remote Area Medical (RAM) Expedition in Mountain City, Tennessee, just across the border from southwest Virginia. RAM is an organization created by Stan Brock, formerly of Marlin Perkins' Wild Kingdom television series. For many years RAM has provided medical services in remote areas all over the world. It was found that many areas of the U.S., including northeast Tennessee and southwest Virginia have as great a need for these services as anywhere. Although there are significant numbers of health care providers currently, this has long been a medically underserved area and some sections are still so designated. There remain many people with no health insurance and especially no coverage for dental or eye care. The focus of the RAM services is to provide those specific services, dental and eye care.

Sister Bernie, of course, decided to organize a Remote Area Expedition for Southwest Virginia. Having been part of the previous health fair planning committees and also providing information services, the Outreach Information program was included in Sister Bernie's plans. One particular Outreach service, a CancerHelp touch screen computer system, was of considerable appeal for this program. It would be available as an educational and information resource for many people who would not necessarily be computer literate, but who would, with a touch screen, be able to locate cancer information with some assistance. Also, many regional health professionals would be providing services at the RAM. An Outreach display as well as the cancer information system would also allow many opportunities to update those participants about these resources.

It proved to be an amazing opportunity to meet many health care providers and community volunteers, and community members with health information needs. These opportunities are invaluable as a way to become more completely aware of and integrated into the community. The first year of the RAM, over 1,800 people were served, the second year over 2,000. Medical services included eye exams, with glasses being provided immediately through services and support of the Lions Clubs of Virginia, as well as referrals to and support for services from local eye care and lens providers. Even more demand was seen for dental care, with services ranging from cleaning, fillings, many extractions and some oral surgery. Mammograms were provided and some physical exams. During the second year expedition, more state and regional providers were involved. The event organization was tremendously improved and more educational and support services, such as those for mental health, were introduced.

CANCER COALITION

Cancer is the second leading cause of death in this region. In the early 1990s a regional cancer coalition, the LENOWISCO chapter of CHALIC (Central Highlands Appalachian Leadership Initiative on Cancer) was formed under the umbrella of the wider Appalachian Leadership Initiative on Cancer (ALIC). Funding for this program came from a National Cancer Institute grant to the Markey Cancer Institute (MCI) at the University of Kentucky. The reasoning was that local organizations would be more effective in determining what their needs and resources were, and could better implement efforts to address cancer issues in their own communities. Support for leadership development of these community coalitions was provided by MCI. One of the local workshops held in southwest Virginia in 1996 utilized storytelling as the tool for presenting cancer experiences and discussing cancer issues. The stories were recorded and developed into a dramatic reading format for presentation by the members of this workshop who eventually became a group called Life's Circle. Members change and stories are refined and new stories incorporated, but the Life's Circle continues. They perform at local events to promote awareness of CHALIC and the ongoing need for support for cancer patients and survivors who live in this region.

From the Life's Circle members' stories and those of other CHALIC members came a recurring theme. When someone is diagnosed with cancer, it is devastating. As people begin to realize what an effort it will be to fight this disease, they are desperate for information about therapy options and research findings that might help them. Every person and family had to struggle with this task and found it daunting. They did not want to leave the region to use academic libraries or major hospital libraries. They did not want to be in a clinical setting at all. They wanted to have a cancer information resource center in their own community. But they also wanted a center that provided a warm and welcoming atmosphere with caring people to assist them in locating information, giving them support during this time of crisis and throughout the ongoing struggle.

The LENOWISCO CHALIC organization met monthly and was provided a team leader, through funding from the larger CHALIC organization, to assist with project development, organization and direction. Supporting and expanding the role of Life's Circle activities, working with the Breast and Cervical Cancer Detection program operated through the local Health Department, and a continued interest in establishing a resource and information center were the major focuses of the group. In 1998 CHALIC invited the Outreach Librarian to attend their meetings and discuss ways in which she might be able to assist with the information center project. This invitation came after a recommendation by the AHEC Executive Director to the CHALIC team leader that they contact the Outreach Librarian for assistance. Community connections again brought about the initiation of what would become an exciting and fulfilling relationship for information support and organizational development.

During the first meeting of CHALIC and the Outreach Librarian, two projects were identified. The first project was to determine what information was available locally through public and academic libraries that could be tapped immediately for cancer information resources. This would require visits to those libraries and, if possible, a printout of the cataloged cancer information in the regional public library system would be requested. The second project was to locate what CHALIC members had identified as a computer with cancer information, which they had heard about and thought was in one of the regional hospitals, perhaps one in Tennessee. During the next several weeks, those projects were undertaken. The regional public library was willing to provide a printout of cancer related holdings. Community colleges and the UVA College at Wise were willing to have the general public utilize resources of interest for cancer information research.

Through calls to local Virginia hospitals and northeastern Tennessee hospitals, the cancer computer was located at a hospital in Kingsport, Tennessee, where many southwestern Virginia patients went for diagnosis and treatment. A visit was arranged by the Outreach Librarian to see the system and discuss it with the nurse manager of the cancer treatment unit where the computer was located. The cancer information resource is known as the CancerHelp System and is produced by the CancerHelp Institute located in Wilmette, Illinois. It is available through a grant, which requires local matching funds and an ongoing subscription for cancer information updates through an annual subscription fee. The Oncology Nurse Manager at the hospital provided copies of grant request forms and contact information. She also described how the system was used there at the hospital.

Armed with this information, the Outreach Librarian contacted the CancerHelp Institute to learn more about the system and the grant process. The system was originally designed and created by a cancer patient, with help from her oncology professional team, other cancer patients and their families and the National Cancer Institute (NCI). Much of the cancer description, therapy, prevention, and support information included in the system comes directly from NCI. Also included are various regional and national oncology hospital system resource center contact information, national and regional support groups, organizational hotlines, and contact information for all CancerHelp system locations in hospitals and institutes throughout the country.

Upon contacting the CancerHelp Institute, it was determined that not only was CHALIC eligible for the grant, but there was also great interest in having a grassroots coalition become involved with utilization of the system. All of this information was presented to the next CHALIC coalition meeting. There was genuine interest in obtaining this system because of the content and the possibility of having such a resource available as the first concrete step toward establishing the cancer resource center. The CHALIC members discussed ways to raise the needed funds and how to support the ongoing costs of the subscription fees. It was determined that there were some funds available and fund raising would be used, if necessary, to meet future costs. The Outreach Librarian offered to write the grant and submit it to the Institute. The proposal was completed and readied for submission; however, funding did become an issue and the proposal was held for submission until later in 1999. It was funded in early 2000.

The CancerHelp System was demonstrated by the Outreach Librarian for the CHALIC organization at a meeting held at the College at Wise Library. Following this meeting the Outreach Librarian developed an agenda for recruiting volunteers who would learn to use the CancerHelp System. These volunteers would then take the system to health fairs and community events to publicize its availability and the efforts toward establishing a cancer resource center. CHALIC volunteers and local community college nursing students received training that spring and summer. The system was housed at the College at Wise Library and from there taken to events either by the Outreach Librarian or trained volunteers. Some of these events included the ETSU health fairs, community craft days, hospital health fairs, the Remote Area Medical Expedition, regional health services community awareness events, the Virginia/Kentucky Fair and regional CHALIC organizational meetings.

From all of these activities and projects it became evident that an information center and a program coordinator for that center were needed to fulfill the dream as envisioned by the Life's Circle participants. When the University of Virginia Health Sciences Library received a request for proposals for funding from the National Network of Libraries of Medicine for consumer health information services, the Outreach Librarian was asked to submit ideas. It was a perfect opportunity to describe the Cancer Center project and the need for a program coordinator. The grant (called a subcontract because of funding structure through the Regional Network system) proposal was focused on funds for hiring the program coordinator, who would develop the training program for volunteers who would then work directly with cancer patients and families as well as interested health professionals in the region. Volunteers would assist with access to cancer description, treatment and prevention information resources in a welcoming and caring environment. The current CHALIC Team Leader, who is also the Executive Director of the Mountain Empire Older Citizen (MEOC) Agency in southwestern Virginia and a two-time cancer survivor, volunteered to provide space in her office building for the Cancer Information Center as a local contribution in the grant process.

The proposal was submitted in March 2000 and funded for $50,000 in July of 2001. The first stages of the program are underway. A Program Coordinator is being hired and should be in place by January 2002. The subcontract period is for eighteen months. During this time the training program will be created, volunteers selected and trained, publicity for the program developed and implemented, office furnished and services made available to cancer patients, families, health providers and interested members of the community.

A grant submitted by the CHALIC Team Leader to the Appalachian Regional Commission to begin planning for the larger Cancer Resource Center, of which the Information Center is a segment, was funded for $50,000. The funding for that grant is being administered by MEOC. The director for that project will work with the Outreach Librarian, the Information Center Program Coordinator and other CHALIC members to organize, plan and to seek ongoing funds to make the CHALIC dream a reality.

All of these projects have provided significant opportunities for growth in health information outreach services. The diabetes coalition and the cancer coalition are ongoing projects. The RAM Expeditions will be annual events as the need continues. Health fairs remain a regional tool for reaching underserved populations and providing opportunities for medical student training and community health service contributions. The University of Virginia Health Sciences Library Outreach Program will strive to remain active in and contribute to all of these programs as well as look for new challenges for partnership in health services programs for this region.

REFERENCE

Turf, E. E. (1997). Diabetes surveillance in Virginia. *Virginia Epidemiology Bulletin,* *97*(1), 1-3.

Watch for the Little Red Light: Delivery of Bibliographic Instruction by Unconventional Means

Steven Dunlap

Golden Gate University

SUMMARY. Higher education has started using broadcast and video conferencing technology as well as Web-based software specifically designed for teaching classes online. Librarians can participate in classes and deliver "bibliographic instruction" presentations as part of the class. But how similar the presentation may be to the traditional in-person class varies depending on the technology employed. This paper describes the principle differences between bibliographic instruction in a closed circuit broadcast, ISDN videoconference, Web-based class and traditional in-person class visits.

KEYWORDS. Library instruction, technology, Internet, distance learners

Golden Gate University is a private institution with a college, graduate school and law school located in San Francisco, California. The University Library serves the college and the graduate school. A separate law library serves the law students. The economic boom in the Bay Area turned to bust by about the year 2000. In the spring of 2001 the curriculum which the University Library supports changed drastically after the President announced that the University would phase out half of its programs. In addition, the President of Golden Gate University remains committed to consolidating classes formerly

[Haworth co-indexing entry note]: "Watch for the Little Red Light: Delivery of Bibliographic Instruction by Unconventional Means." Dunlap, Steven. Co-published simultaneously in *Journal of Library Administration* (The Haworth Information Press, an imprint of The Haworth Press, Inc.) Vol. 37, No. 1/2, 2002, pp. 279-285; and: *Distance Learning Library Services: The Tenth Off-Campus Library Services Conference* (ed: Patrick B. Mahoney) The Haworth Information Press, an imprint of The Haworth Press, Inc., 2002, pp. 279-285.

http://www.haworthpress.com/store/product.asp?sku=J111
10.1300/J111v37n01_23

taught simultaneously on several different campuses into a single Cyber-class. These two trends indicate that the librarians will have to make use of the new technology in order to reach the students at all, and in a timely fashion.

The library first started performing "non-traditional" bibliographic instruction for CyberCampus starting in 1998. First of all, we had to drop the term "bibliographic instruction" in favor of "research instruction" since we predicted that most students and many faculty would misunderstand the term "bibliographic." We continue to have the cyber age image problem that places librarians with paper and "information technologists" with computers. The term "bibliographic instruction" only has meaning to other librarians.

CyberCampus at Golden Gate University is an asynchronous environment. Typically, a faculty member contacts the library and requests a librarian to "visit" the Cyber-class. This visit consists of the professor creating a "conference" on the class entitled something like "Research Help," or "Librarian Q&A," as one of the conferences on his/her class Web page. All participants (students, professor, librarian) must log in using a secure password to enter the class. When someone responds to your message you receive an e-mail notification to that effect. The librarian posts some general information and then responds to the students' questions in the designated conference. At least in theory, that should teach the students the same basic information as an in-person presentation.

Actual practice taught me two important lessons about how to handle the new medium. First, surfing the Web differs greatly from using the Web as a tool for one's education. Second, having flexibility and even rudimentary skills in graphic design will make you very effective. I am sure there are many more lessons I have yet to learn.

I had the good fortune to do a "cyber-visit" for a "mixed-mode" class in the spring of '01. Faculty has the option of making their class half in-person and half CyberCampus. The class meets in person for half of the usual visits of a traditional class and "meets" in a CyberCampus class for the rest of the time. I posted the informational messages to an E-Commerce class including links to sources or library pages I wanted the students to look at (the CyberCampus software allows the post to contain HTML code and links). The next week I happened to be working at the regional campus where the E-Commerce class met for its in-person sessions on a day that it met in person. The professor asked me to meet with the class in person, since some of them had questions for me. Much to my dismay, I had already answered all of their questions in my messages to the class conference. I asked the class if they read my posts. Most (but not all) said yes. I asked if anyone who had read my posts had followed any of the links. They all said no. I proceeded to lecture them about the importance of following the links in the messages that faculty or librarians hack into the messages they post to Cyber-classes.

This illustrates the greatest challenge we have in utilizing the Web as an educational tool. Most (if not all) people quickly grow accustomed to "surfing" the Web. What do you do when you get bored while surfing the Web? Click on something and leave the page. The students think of the links in a message as optional. This experience makes clear that the professor and the librarian must communicate to students, perhaps repeatedly, that following the link is not an option, but a requirement. Students need to have explained to them that their use of the Web as a tool in their education must differ from the usual surfing that one does for recreation, or casual research. They have to read the words on the Web page, not just skim them. If the education the students receive teaches them to use the Internet more effectively, and even perceive it differently, then we have won a major victory.

In another Cyber-class, I faced a different challenge. The Public Administration program has changed over the last two years into an EMPA (Executive Master's in Public Administration) Cyber-program. This master's program takes people already working in public service and teaches them entirely through Web-based instruction. Many of the students are municipal administrators such as chiefs of police and managers in public agencies. In the research methods class, many found themselves lost and confused. The professor told me in a phone conversation that the students did not know how to obtain peer-review journal articles and asked me to contribute something in the conference he created for me in his Cyber-class to explain this to his students. In between questions while sitting at the reference desk one evening, I did several screen captures and worked with them on Photoshop to created a single Web page tutorial on what constituted a peer-review article and how to find them on ProQuest. I created a link to the page in a message to the course conference. This put the confusion over peer-review journals to rest. (You can view this page at http://internet.ggu.edu/university_library/ustudy/peer.html.)

The librarian cannot predict all of the possible questions or problems that students will have. In the traditional in-person exchange the librarian can demonstrate the appropriate database as needed. But when students live scattered throughout the country or the world, a degree of flexibility becomes essential. An overly bureaucratic management of the library's Web site would kill this capability. I have the authority and ability to put up Web pages first and improve them or remove them later. If I had to bring a given page before a committee, the class would end before the page became available to view. The ability to create and load a Web page in an evening without having to seek approval or delegate the task to another made the "cyber" exchange as fast and effective as an in-person demonstration.

The School of Technology and Industry runs a workplace cohort program at Pacific Bell utilizing closed circuit television. (In a cohort program, all the students take the same class at the same time in lockstep.) The professor (or librarian) works from a small studio in the basement without any students physically present. The students sit in classrooms specially made for the purpose with huge T.V. screens on the wall at the head of the room and small, simple control boxes at each seat for communicating with the instructor and also creating an attendance record. In the studio, the station at which the instructor sits looks very much like the ones on commercial television news and includes two kinds of phone consoles, an "Elmo" device, similar to an overhead projector, and a laptop computer. Two cameras fixed in place and without human operators stand about a dozen feet from the presenter's station. A technician operates the cameras from a control room out of sight of the person teaching. You must wear a small microphone on your shirt or tie. While broadcasting, a red light lit up on one of the cameras tells you which one is operating.

My first experience with this system did not take place smoothly. I did not have a clear idea what capabilities the technology had for me to work with until I arrived. A bureaucratic snafu held me at the guard desk for nearly 40 minutes before I could get anyone to escort me to the studio. And then instead of the studio, I found myself in the classroom! A mad dash to the studio (with one of the students acting as my native guide) left me with barely a minute to receive a briefing on what would happen and how to work with the phone consoles. I found the lack of any students in front of me a bit disconcerting. Although not nervous or suffering from stage fright, I did have a few lapses. I forgot to look into the camera that had the red light lit. Then I realized my mistake and turned suddenly toward the operating camera. I also froze at the phone console a couple of times. Despite these setbacks, I did manage to communicate the essential information about the library, its services and how to contact us.

I made plans to make sure that the next time would be better. I created two PowerPoint presentations—one called "Web Browsing Essentials" and the other "Advanced Database Searching" (both available from my home page: http://internet.ggu.edu/university_library/reg/). While helping students over the phone from the earlier cohort, I noticed I had a hard time making myself understood when describing almost anything on a Web page.

Question: "Do you see the radio buttons on the right?"
Answer: "What's a radio button?"

Question: "Please tell me the URL or address of the page you're looking at now."
Answer: "What's a URL? What do you mean by address?"

In my experience, most of these students did not know any terms for most of the graphics useful in using and navigating through Web-based databases. This led to my creating the "Web Browsing Essentials" PowerPoint Presentation. I distilled the online searching tutorials I had already made for the Web into a shorter PowerPoint version and called it "Advanced Database Searching." This one explained Boolean logic and had an example database search.

I found that my presentation to the next two cohorts in this program came off without a hitch. I arrived in plenty of time and had made numerous calls the day before to make sure my name would appear on the approved list and that an escort to the studio would be available. For the next cohort I spent a half-hour with the Pacific Bell person in charge of the control room and the professor before the class. By the time of the third cohort group address I had become an "old hand" at running the console and presenting the slides. In each visit I had plenty of time to load the PowerPoint Presentations on the laptop (which fed the images directly to the TV screens in the various locations) and to make sure all the slides displayed properly. I repeated important information several times.

I thought the presentation accomplished its intended task. All students in this particular program need to make a request for a barcode sticker by sending me e-mail with specific information about themselves. The fact that all the requests I received had all the required information gave me some indirect feedback that at least part of my presentation had gotten through to the audience. But assessment tools for measuring effectiveness remain limited. Students do not have to take a quiz or do any assignment directly related to the librarian's presentation. The faculty member's assessment of the quality of the students' research papers gives us the best indication of our effectiveness, but we do not always receive such feedback and have not established any formalized system for receiving this assessment from faculty. Unfortunately, my personal opinion that I had done well had no empirical evidence behind it.

Thus far the only such feedback I have received from the faculty indicates that I "took too long." I may have attempted to communicate too much, especially given the intensive format of the program. Furthermore, I must admit the possibility that the "Web Browsing Essentials" presentation did not prove necessary for most of the students. This illustrates the danger of teaching to the lowest common denominator. If you lose most of the rest of the class, you have defeated the purpose of your presentation. On the one hand, every slide in the "Web Browsing Essentials" resulted from numerous exchanges I had had over the telephone with students. Between my presentations to the last two Pacific Bell cohorts, I tried this presentation on an in-person class. The facial expressions and body language indicated a rather profound lack of interest. Only one student told me she liked that part of my presentation.

The peculiar nature of the Web technology makes the task of communication and education a very precarious balancing act for the person teaching how to do research in this medium. You can have students who do not know the difference between the Internet and the World Wide Web, ones who do not know the difference between a browser and AOL, ones who do not know how to go to a Web page given its URL, and ones who know all of this but do not understand Boolean logic. And they are all in the same class. If you try to teach everything mentioned above, the students who know the basics but nothing about Boolean logic get bored and leave the room, thus missing the parts of the presentation they actually need to hear. If you assume the students know the simple elements of the Internet and computers, your lecture will lose the ones who do not have this knowledge. If you ask up front if the students need you to go over the essentials of how to use the Web, of course they will all say no–no one who needs the "Web Browsing Essentials" presentation thinks they need it. Almost every student who has surfed the Web at all thinks they have learned all they need to about the Web already. Using closed circuit television to broadcast a lecture removes the valuable visual feedback one gets from viewing the students. A presentation in this medium must go quickly through the simpler concepts (if at all) and repeat only when absolutely necessary the more complex and important ones.

In the summer of 2001 I had the experience of using video conferencing. Unlike the Pacific Bell cohort program, the video conferencing took place in the buildings of the San Francisco campus and three of the regional campuses. An ISDN line transmitted the signal to the other campuses and a "bridge" allowed multiple sites to connect with each other. Video conferencing also allowed me to see the students in the other campuses. The television monitor in front of the instructor shows one of the other sites and a small "box" in the corner of the image shows the instructor (what the students at the other sites see). A voice activation device on each video conferencing unit triggers the system to display the classroom on the other campuses' monitors when someone at a given location speaks.

I used this equipment to deliver my usual "beginning of the term" visits to three different regional campuses. Most of my in-person class visits last about 10 minutes during which I have the students follow along with me on two handouts. One handout lists all of the University Library's URLs that they need in order to do their research. The other one lists all of the commercial databases with a brief description of each one. I go over the list of URLs one by one but I only mention examples from the longer "list of databases" handout, picking out the databases most relevant to the subject matter of the class I am addressing. The use of the video conferencing equipment saved the University the expense of having me visit three different campuses over the course of three weeks.

Prior to my use of the video conferencing equipment I tested it with the help of another librarian. While I visited one of the regional campuses, my colleague in San Francisco broadcast to the video conferencing unit where I could see how the handouts, computer screens and words on the white board would look. I realized that no one would be able to follow along with the handouts, given how small the print appeared on the television screen. In preparation for my presentation I hacked the "list of URLs" handout into HTML and increased the font size to display clearly on the television screens. My assistant mailed copies of both handouts to the regional campuses, and volunteers at those campuses ushered students from the various classes into the one room with the video conferencing unit and distributed my handouts for me.

The advanced planning paid off, but I did learn some more aspects of the technology and adjusted my plans accordingly. The program director informed me that bridging more than two locations cost over $50 an hour per location (with a half-hour minimum). But just San Francisco and one regional campus only cost about $10 per hour. Since my presentation was the quick 10-minute variety, it made more sense to do "three shows a night" at a cost of about $10 or so, rather than bridge all three campuses with San Francisco at a cost of about $80.

The use of these three different technologies has allowed education to reach more students. But in order for the librarian to make the best use of the technology, flexibility, planning, at least intermediate computer skills and a good working relationship with the faculty are required. The willingness to make changes to one's original "in-person" presentations as well as solicit and accept criticism, makes our entrance into the new medium far more effective and rewarding for all parties—student, faculty and librarian. Sometimes we find ourselves "dropped into the deep end of the pool." But when we have the opportunity to test our equipment, make the most of it. When possible, test presentations created for the distance education medium on an "in-person" class in order to obtain the sort of feedback one can observe in the behavior, body language and facial expression of the audience. Even very simple graphics, such as screen captures with circles and arrows, can substitute for an "in-person" demonstration to communicate the necessary and important lessons about research and library services effectively. Beware of teaching to the lowest common denominator since this has limited effectiveness. In the absence of a student audience in front of you, dwelling too long on basics can cause you to "lose" the other students in the class. And a good working relationship with your faculty can help you with valuable feedback, as well as future invitations to address their classes.

Here, There and Everywhere:
A Virtual Library
for Access to Business Information

Wes Edens

Micaela Agyare

Carol Hammond

Thunderbird: The American Graduate School
of International Management

SUMMARY. Thunderbird, The American Graduate School of International Management, offers a graduate business program and serves a student population scattered across the globe. This population is highly educated, culturally diverse, and often demanding when it comes to service. To meet the information needs of students and faculty, the International Business Information Centre (IBIC), Thunderbird's library, takes advantage of the School's intranet, My Thunderbird (MTB), in order to provide library services and resources around the world, 24/7. My Thunderbird is integrated with the School's management system, Datatel. This integration permits authentication and screening of users, and the ability to target specific user groups with information resources. The IBIC leverages the capabilities of MTB to serve patrons with remote access to databases, paperless services, electronic reserves, online reference and enhanced bibliographic instruction.

KEYWORDS. Distance learners, library services, technology, instruction

[Haworth co-indexing entry note]: "Here, There and Everywhere: A Virtual Library for Access to Business Information." Edens, Wes, Micaela Agyare, and Carol Hammond. Co-published simultaneously in *Journal of Library Administration* (The Haworth Information Press, an imprint of The Haworth Press, Inc.) Vol. 37, No. 1/2, 2002, pp. 287-303; and: *Distance Learning Library Services: The Tenth Off-Campus Library Services Conference* (ed: Patrick B. Mahoney) The Haworth Information Press, an imprint of The Haworth Press, Inc., 2002, pp. 287-303.

http://www.haworthpress.com/store/product.asp?sku=J111
10.1300/J111v37n01_24

INTRODUCTION

Graduate programs today are conducted in a variety of ways to meet the needs of diverse and dispersed student populations: on-campus full-time, part-time, via satellite, via the World Wide Web, or through a combination of the aforementioned. In graduate business programs especially, schools operating from a single campus often offer programs worldwide. This not only has great implications for classroom instruction, but also for faculty and program planners, and for library services. Today, business school students may boast of never visiting the library, but what they do not realize are the myriad of ways in which library services have become seamlessly integrated into the curriculum through technology, and the ways that remote access developed by the library and featuring its resources have made that boast possible. At Thunderbird, The American Graduate School of International Management, a graduate business school, the library uses the campus Intranet to deliver many of its resources and services to its dispersed student population. The International Business Information Centre (IBIC), Thunderbird's library, provides resources to students and faculty who may be anywhere in the world. This paper will cover how the IBIC has created a virtual library that delivers both traditional library services to students across the globe, and uses the technology to add value to many of its products.

BACKGROUND AND DESCRIPTION OF THUNDERBIRD

Thunderbird, The American Graduate School of International Management, is located in Glendale, Arizona, a suburb of Phoenix. Its mission is to educate high potential individuals for roles in the global economy. Long a leader in developing individuals for management in international enterprises, Thunderbird is the world's oldest and largest school of international management. In fact, *U.S. News & World Report* has ranked Thunderbird number one in international business for five straight years. Founded at the close of World War II, Thunderbird was established on the principle that business on a global scale requires managers who can speak different languages, understand the customs and cultures of different peoples, and have international business skills. The Master of International Management (MIM), Thunderbird's flagship degree, provides a three-part curriculum that provides training in one of nine modern languages, courses in international studies and world business.

Thunderbird recruits globally for its students, and is well-known for its international mix of business scholars. Some eighty nations are represented among those who are enrolled, and currently more than sixty percent of the students are foreign. The faculty is equally diverse; a large majority is bilingual and forty-five percent are from countries outside of the United States. The exposure to the rich mix of cultures and languages represented in the students themselves is just one way Thunderbirds gain an international background. Many other options are also available to broaden a student's international experience. In addition to its Glendale campus, Thunderbird operates two centers, one in Geneva and one in Tokyo, where students can spend a summer or semester taking courses for credit toward their degree. With the aim to explore the regional business environment and issues in that area related to international business, Thunderbird also sponsors learning opportunities that take place all over the world including Australia, South America, Africa, the Middle East, Europe and Asia. Students also may earn academic credit through projects they carry out for companies seeking expertise in opening their business in another country, or selling their product internationally. Internships provide another avenue for gaining business experience abroad.

A major new direction for the School is in distance education, and that is also taking place on an international level. A large expansion and investment has been made in technology for the delivery of instruction to an international market. Currently, Thunderbird presents its degree program in Latin America through distance education to students in Mexico, Panama, Ecuador and Peru in a partnership with a Mexican university, using a satellite network. This program is growing in other countries in Latin America, and is a model for delivery of degrees in other parts of the world. Executive Education is also a growing area at Thunderbird and one that is looking abroad for students. Currently the school has initiatives offering business development skills in China and Russia and is offering a MIM for Executives program in Brazil and Taiwan.

Operating in a truly global environment presents special challenges for the library, which provides resources and services for faculty and students that support teaching, learning and research. To handle this demand, the IBIC has built collections that are specialized and very focused. IBIC acquires materials on International business, cross-cultural management, foreign languages and industry-specific materials along with reference tools relating to topics such as emerging markets, competitive intelligence, political risk, international business ethics, electronic commerce, finance, and other areas related to international business. Its collection includes about 70,000 volumes, 1,200 periodicals, newspapers from around the world, 900 videos in more than nine languages, and nearly fifty databases, almost all of which are Internet-based. Access to this collection is through its SIRSI-based gateway, THOR (Thunderbird Online Resources). However, access to the databases via THOR is IP controlled and therefore only works for those students who are on campus. All students are required to have a laptop computer. With that as a given, the IBIC has been able to take advantage of the School's unique Intranet to provide its resources, especially commercial databases, to users worldwide, as long as they have an Internet connection.

The IBIC has also experimented with electronic books. For part of 2000, Thunderbird students worldwide had access to NetLibrary as part of a business school trial. This trial was popular with some of the students; however, the number of e-books relevant to graduate business education is limited, and the trial was not followed up with a subscription. The IBIC also has a Gemstar electronic book (formerly called RocketBook), a handheld device for reading materials published in Gemstar format. So far, circulation of this device has been mostly by people who are merely curious about the emerging technology of e-books, or by students who are researching the field of electronic publishing.

MY THUNDERBIRD

Launched in the fall semester of 1998, MTB provides a secure, Web-based intranet for faculty, staff, and students. The MTB instructional portal is database-driven, and access is automatically controlled via Datatel, the School's management software. Datatel keeps track of prospective students, current students, alumni, faculty, and staff. The integration of Datatel allows MTB to generate individualized pages for instructors, students, departments, and courses. Students have access to course pages for only those courses in which they are enrolled, and faculty have access to photos and biographies of their students. Individuals can add content to their pages and specify which MTB groups can see that content. Students, faculty, staff, and courses all have pages generated for them, and they are free to personalize them. The IBIC uses MTB to deliver electronic course reserves (mostly through durable link technology) and other library services to users around the globe. MTB can be delivered to any authorized user's desktop, regardless of hardware or software, providing the user has a browser and an Internet connection.

The IBIC uses MTB to reach students difficult to serve because of geography. The intranet is used to support all of our students in a variety of widely dispersed distance education programs from Europe to Asia, which have been described earlier. Besides Web access from anywhere in the world, students at Thunderbird's Glendale campus can plug into MTB with their laptops via hundreds of network ports located all over campus. The IBIC has 222 MTB ports, plus 40 desktop computers that also allow access. This same system delivers remote access to students working in dorms, apartments, and wherever they live in the Phoenix area.

The original My Thunderbird was developed over a two-month period, and cost $100,000 to design and develop a prototype. A six-month, $400,000 follow-up development period followed the initial launch of the product. MTB 2.0 was released in the summer of 2001.

MTB was not originally designed as a distance learning tool. It was a matter of Thunderbird's Information Technology department evaluating existing Internet technologies and deciding how to leverage those technologies to support instruction. The original MTB concentrated on file sharing, and for the first time, allowed instructors to have a course page automatically generated for them, limited to enrolled students. Faculty members were able to share syllabi, course notes, old exams, and other documents with students in a secure environment without knowing even the most basic HTML. Everything was a matter of pointing and clicking.

Later enhancements to MTB included online discussion groups where students, faculty, and administration could share information on a variety of topics in a bulletin-board system (BBS) format; live chat; drop boxes where students could submit assignments online and have those assignments time-stamped; a course evaluation tool; and the ability to target very specific audiences. This last feature allows the IBIC to publish information for a subset of the MTB universe–for example, students taking classes at the Thunderbird Europe Center in Archamps, France.

INTERNATIONAL BUSINESS INFORMATION CENTRE (IBIC)

The IBIC found that it could successfully operate in a truly global environment by utilizing Thunderbird's Intranet, My Thunderbird (MTB). MTB could enhance many of the IBIC's programs and services, including reference services. Through its department Web page on MTB and faculty course pages, the IBIC provides access to a major part of its resources and services to users anywhere in the world. This includes access to library databases, reserve readings, forms and policies, the online catalog, resource guides, the schedule of library instruction classes, hours, directions for using specific databases, and other information. These resources are available to any student, staff or faculty member with a connection to the World Wide Web. Each IBIC staff member's photo and personal page is also found here. What follows are some of the uses the IBIC has made of MTB to become a virtual library available to its users worldwide.

Access to Databases

The IBIC uses a program called EZ Proxy, together with MTB's authentication capability, to provide access to licensed databases from off-campus. Authorized users (faculty, staff, and current students) see a "Remote Access to IBIC Databases" page in MTB, where the IBIC maintains links to 28 IP-authenticated databases. These links actually go to the EZ Proxy server. EZ Proxy accesses the databases via IP on the library's behalf, via IP authentication, and brings those pages to the patron. Authorized users can use any dialup or broadband Internet service provider. My Thunderbird provides the necessary authentication and screening of users; EZ Proxy provides the access.

Before implementation of EZ Proxy, the IBIC could only provide remote access to 18 database vendors. This was accomplished by a variety of means, including referring HTTP, ID/password combinations, and scripts. Some vendors were unwilling or unable to provide passwords. Some were also reluctant to allow access by referring HTTP, a method by which the host system checks the last page visited by the user. Implementation of EZ Proxy meant that any IP-authenticated database could be provided to remote users, subject to license terms. EZ Proxy has an advantage in that it works for cable modem users, whereas hardware proxy servers do not. Patrons behind corporate firewalls (such as students on internships) sometimes encounter difficulties, but these can be overcome by simply using a dialup ISP or by accessing from home. Detailed information about EZ Proxy can be found at: http://www.ezproxy.com.

AskIBIC

MTB has also enhanced the way the IBIC provides reference services. In addition to traditional reference services offered in the library from the reference desk, reference service is also available 24/7 to students around the world via an electronic bulletin board called AskIBIC. Here students can post a question and get an answer without having to come into the library. Librarians provide assistance and suggestions for finding information and doing research as they would in a face-to-face consultation. Oftentimes students benefit from the consultation of more than one of the IBIC's librarians and sometimes students themselves post advice and suggest resources. The site is checked at least once a day, including weekends. Students can also search an archive of AskIBIC questions to see if a similar question has been asked before.

The kind of assignments students have at Thunderbird contributes to the usability and success of AskIBIC. Questions are very specific, and follow-up exchange with a librarian to clarify what is needed is rare. In a single week via AskIBIC, librarians may hear from a student in Mexico enrolled in the degree program in Latin America seeking information on environmental issues related to a business enterprise, a group of students in Poland working on a marketing project for an American clothing store seeking to open a franchise in Warsaw, a student at the Archamps center doing research on the German automotive industry, or a faculty member on sabbatical and doing research in Shanghai. Some actual questions posted on AskIBIC have been:

> I am looking for automotive demand and production figures for Russia from 1997 and forecast through 2008. Can you give me a path to follow or database information to locate?

> How do I find qualitative data for Japanese consumer behavior for interactive TV, Internet, mobile phones, etc.?

> I'm looking into the Hyundai Group's competitive environment. Any suggestions on a good database or site that shows comparisons of multi-industry conglomerates such as Hyundai?

> Could you help me locate information on the size of the U.S. Hispanic market in respect to DVD sales figures for future years?

Interlibrary Loan (ILL)

Interlibrary loan requests can still be submitted by visiting the IBIC and filling out a paper form, however, most faculty and students prefer to submit requests electronically. After a check of the online catalog via THOR and/or a check of the IBIC's full-text journal holdings online, if an interlibrary loan is needed, a form is available online through MTB. In most cases, it is more convenient for users to fill out the form online because they do not have to make a special trip to the IBIC, and they spend less time filling out the form due to the auto-fill feature on MTB. Because users are logged onto MTB, the system recognizes who they are and it automatically fills in their name and e-mail address. Clicking the "send" button connects the completed form to the campus e-mail system, and it is automatically transmitted to the interlibrary loan staff for processing. Accuracy and readability of the requests is improved. Computers with MTB access are readily available in the IBIC, in every office, and across the campus. Faculty make requests from their offices, and students overseas make particular use of this feature.

Fine Appeals

Because Thunderbird provides an e-mail account for all students, the library long ago switched to electronic reminders sent by the circulation system three days before books are due. This reduced overdue fines enormously. When something still becomes overdue, students receive overdue notices through the campus e-mail system as well. Should they wish to file an appeal and begin the process of challenging a fine, a form is available on IBIC's department page on My Thunderbird. This is also designed with a question box, and once it is electronically completed, is automatically sent by e-mail.

Electronic Reserves

My Thunderbird was introduced at almost exactly the same time that UMI (now Bell & Howell) released a major option for use with ProQuest. ProQuest is a database of over 1,600 business and management journals. It provides indexing and full text for 900 of those titles. The feature, known as SiteBuilder, allows users to create durable links to individual articles within ProQuest. SiteBuilder also allows faculty members and librarians to create powerful, complex Boolean searches on a given topic. An HTML link is created that is placed on a course page or a library guide. To execute the search, all the student has to do is click, and the most recent articles are presented. EbscoHost, another popular database providing access to full-text of many academic and business publications, soon offered the same type of functionality through its Save Manager. As with SiteBuilder, it allows users to create durable links to individual articles in its database. Copyright is not an issue, as Bell & Howell and EbscoHost own the rights to the articles and explicitly give permission to create the links.

Among instructors, the synthesis of MTB with ProQuest and EbscoHost created unprecedented interest in the library. Faculty could provide students with electronic readings on course pages, available to them anywhere and anytime. Current bibliographies of articles on topics related to the course could be posted and automatically updated. Courses are offered every semester to show faculty members how to integrate ProQuest and EbscoHost with MTB. It is not uncommon for these workshops, conducted jointly by the library and the Instructional Services department, to be completely booked within hours of announcement. Since it can be used both on the campus and for distance education, it solves both goals of using technology to enhance teaching, and providing resources to dispersed, international users.

The term "electronic reserves" conjures images of workers feverishly scanning paper documents and uploading them to a course page. With electronic publishing now coming into its own, however, paper-to-byte conversion is less and less necessary. With some publications, scanning and uploading is still required, but MTB facilitates that, as well. The library is able to accommodate both the needs of the instructor and the requirements of copyright law, by observing some simple guidelines regarding intellectual property. While discussion of copyright is beyond the scope of this paper, it should be noted that the automatic restrictions in effect on MTB help insure compliance with the doctrine of Fair Use.

IBIC Guides

The IBIC has created a series of electronic resource guides, or pathfinders, to help students identify resources for their research needs. These are only intended as a jumping off point for student research, and are not designed as exhaustive bibliographies. For this reason, the guides cover broad topic areas such as company information, industry and market research, countries and cultures and emerging markets, to name a few. These guides point to a full range of resources including the online catalog, dynamic links to articles in full-text using ProQuest's SiteBuilder and EbscoHost's Save Manager, suggested databases, and World Wide Web sites. As with electronic reserves, the synthesis of ProQuest's SiteBuilder and EbscoHost's Save Manager with MTB has enabled the library to add value to its products. The guides are consistent in content, format, and organization to facilitate ease of use and, more importantly, to serve as an instructional tool on how to conduct further research.

Global Gateway

An added information resource, available not only to students through the Web, but to anyone with Internet access, is the Global Gateway, created by IBIC librarians with the help from our many international students. Global Gateway is a live, Web-based database of over 3,500 links for the international business researcher. Each link is carefully evaluated, rated, described, and categorized. Users can either browse through the categories or find the sites they need by keyword searching. The database is updated continually, and users may submit sites for inclusion. The section on Countries and Regions is an area of particular focus. This section includes subcategories on government, education, culture and language, companies and markets, and travel. The URL for the Global Gateway is www.T-bird.edu/ibic/links/.

Other

The IBIC Department page on MTB also provides the opportunity to provide other information regarding the library. Students can check hours, announcements and take a virtual tour of the library created with a digital camera via the department page. In addition, each term the IBIC gives a series of workshops on how to find information about companies, industries, countries, competitive intelligence, and also how to find information once students become alumni. Although the schedule is handed out to students during orientation, is available at the reference desk, and is posted in the library, the schedule is also available electronically via the IBIC department page. For students who are unable to attend the workshops either due to scheduling conflicts or distance, after each workshop the PowerPoint presentations are posted on the Web. This also allows students to review the material at their convenience. Links to sources are embedded in the slides, which is an additional enhancement and time-saver.

DISTANCE LEARNING AND LIBRARY INSTRUCTION

The Master's of International Management-Latin America (MIMLA) program was the first actual distance education program at Thunderbird. The executive education-style program is a partnership between Thunderbird and the Instituto Tecnológico de Estudios Superiores de Monterrey (ITESM). Modeled after Thunderbird's tripartite MIM program, including courses in international business, international studies, and English Business Communications, the program can be completed in 24 months. Begun in 1998, there are now approximately 240 students enrolled in the program. These students take classes in their home cities at selected ITESM campuses in Mexico and at ITESM sites in Peru, Ecuador, and Panama. Students work toward a joint Thunderbird-ITESM degree via satellite courses broadcast from both Thunderbird and ITESM. Students are required to have access to a computer and an Internet connection, and the majority of them own laptops. They utilize MTB to share files and resources and communicate among themselves.

In October 2000, Thunderbird launched its first Executive Degree Program for Executives in Asia. This program is conducted in collaboration with the Acer Group's Aspire Academy in Taiwan. Thunderbird professors and Asian experts teach all of the courses, and the curriculum is drawn from Thunderbird's MIM degree program. The curriculum includes eight sessions of classroom work plus eight e-learning sessions of individualized, Internet-based study delivered over seventeen months. The first and last modules are conducted on the Thunderbird campus and the remaining modules are conducted at Aspire Academy in Taipei. Each module consists of in-class meetings supplemented by e-learning sessions.

A similar program will be launched in October of 2001 in São Paulo, Brazil. Delivered in partnership with Amcham, the American Chamber of Commerce-São Paulo, the Master of International Management for Executives-São Paulo program consists of ten six-day modules of in-class instruction, preceded and followed by a six-week period of individualized Web-based learning. Nine modules are held at the American Chamber of Commerce in São Paulo and one module is held at the Thunderbird Campus. The program's timeline enables participants to graduate in only 15 months, while maintaining job and personal responsibilities.

The IBIC librarians are challenged by how to teach theses distance education students how to access and use the resources they need to complete their graduate-level research. In response to the format of these programs and technological tools such as MTB, various methods have been devised to communicate with these students throughout the course of their program. They represent two different models that have been used for our instruction program. In the first, the students begin the program by physically coming to campus, where they receive orientation, and then rely on virtual support and remote access, using many of the services just as other students do. The second model is one in which everything, including orientation to using databases and services, is provided by distance learning to students who do not physically come to campus until the very end of their program of study.

The MIMLA program is an example of the first model. During an initial ten-day on-campus orientation held in Arizona at the Glendale campus, librarians hold sessions with all MIMLA students to introduce them to the primary databases and Web sites that they will use. These sessions include a lecture-style presentation and a series of workshops in the computer lab where students ask questions as they learn to access the IBIC resources via MTB. In addition to receiving instruction on remote access and database usage while on campus for orientation, MIMLA students engage in ongoing communication with librarians via e-mail or AskIBIC. To provide students with more face-to-face follow-up, librarians appear in classes broadcast via satellite to answer students' questions about their research projects and information needs. This interaction virtually emulates face-to-face contact, as it would be in a classroom with an instructor.

The kinds of assignments the distance education students are given are similar to those on-campus students might also have. For example, a professor of cross-cultural communication asked his MIMLA students to do group research projects on the cultural issues of doing business in several different countries. Since the members of each group lived in different cities, they conducted all research and communication via the Internet, specifically through MTB and e-mail. The faculty member reported that students felt apprehensive at first but that an IBIC presentation made during one of the satellite broadcasts helped allay their fears. The librarian who made the presentation demonstrated how to access and effectively search the databases most useful for this particular project. Additional feedback from faculty indicates that as with students generally, the quality of the research received from students varied based on the amount of effort that they put in to the project.

For those students who do not have the opportunity to attend IBIC workshops or an orientation on campus, which is the second model we use, MTB has allowed the IBIC to bring instructional modules to their desktop in a couple of ways. During the first two modules of the Executive Degree Program for Executives in Asia, the IBIC took advantage of the built-in instructional features of MTB that are used by faculty for their course Web pages. These tools include electronic bulletin boards, chat, assignment drop boxes that can be time stamped, a class broadcast feature that allows the instructor to send an e-mail to all students enrolled in the course, and an Excel spreadsheet for grades. All of the tools and resources are available from a single course page on MTB. Using this system, the IBIC developed an online module called "Information Skills for Business Executives" that consisted of four sections: Using Secondary Sources of Information for Business Research, Using IBIC Databases for Business Research, Using the World Wide Web to Find Business Information, and How to Cite Sources for Research Papers. Links to relevant Web sites, IBIC databases and full-text articles from ProQuest and EbscoHost were also provided as required readings. The course aimed to teach participants how to leverage the power of the Internet to efficiently and effectively find business information, and skills in finding, evaluating and using business information resources were emphasized.

The IBIC has also begun to use an exciting new technology called Tegrity. This technology uses software to turn a PC, projector, video cameras, and ordinary whiteboard into a self-recording presentation system. This technology captures annotated PowerPoint and video into one short, easy presentation. The IBIC is using this system to create short three to five-minute modules that instruct students on how to use IBIC resources. Students can view the media-rich content using software on any browser, PC or Mac, at speeds as low as 28.8Kbps. The executable files are then uploaded onto MTB so that only students who are enrolled in overseas programs can download and view the presentations. Instructions and hardware and software recommendations for the Tegrity presentations are also provided to the students via MTB. For more information on the Tegrity system, visit www.tegrity.com.

CONCLUSION

The campus intranet, MTB, has allowed the IBIC to offer its patrons a virtual library, complete with reference services, ILL, research guides, and worldwide access to rich third-party content. It took a large investment in technology at Thunderbird to bring the intranet into existence, a step that was necessitated by the global needs of the School's students and faculty. The IBIC's virtual library is just one part of the overall result from that commitment. Access to an intranet has facilitated improved services for the IBIC's patrons, and has allowed it to interact more fully with its users around the globe.

The following Appendix shows some examples from My Thunderbird of the services and systems used to deliver library support in a virtual environment.

APPENDIX

FIGURE 1. IBIC Home Page on My Thunderbird. Every department in the School has a department page. This is where the library posts its schedule and provides links to its catalog, databases, AskIBIC, all of the interactive guides, online forms, and other services and resources.

APPENDIX (continued)

FIGURE 2. A screen from AskIBIC, the virtual reference service. Provided as a BBS, questions are posted as well as answers, which are open to the whole School community to view. Often students and additional librarians will add to answers.

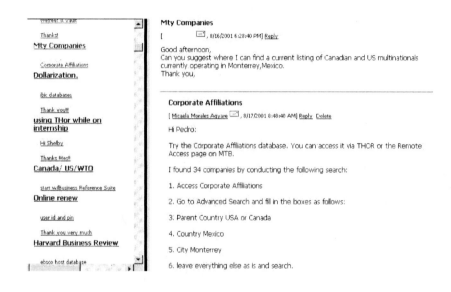

FIGURE 3. Sample of online Interlibrary Loan form. The form will auto-fill information about the user and it is sent directly to interlibrary loan staff for processing.

IBIC INTERLIBRARY LOAN ONLINE BOOK REQUEST FORM

Please read the IBIC Interlibrary Loan policies and copyright notice.
(* means required info)

*NAME John Doe   *BOX #   *PHONE #

*STATUS Select one   ▼ *DATE   *EMAIL doej@t-bird.edu

Item Request

Please check THOR (Thunderbird Online Resources catalog) first.

Item is Select one ▼ Material needed by   (request will be cancelled after this time)

*BOOK TITLE

AUTHOR

PUBLISHER

EDITION   Need this edition only? select one ▼

ISBN

FIGURE 4. Gateway page for access to remote databases. My Thunderbird is the "home" for the EZ Proxy server.

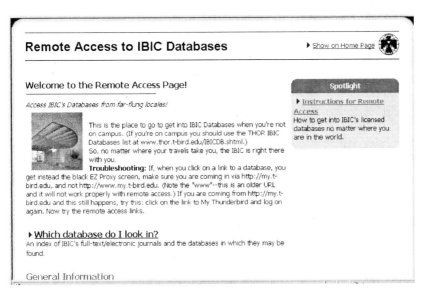

Remote Access to IBIC Databases   ▶ Show on Home Page

Welcome to the Remote Access Page!

Access IBIC's Databases from far-flung locales!

This is the place to go to get into IBIC Databases when you're not on campus. (If you're on campus you should use the THOR IBIC Databases list at www.thor.t-bird.edu/IBICDB.shtml.)
So, no matter where your travels take you, the IBIC is right there with you.
Troubleshooting: If, when you click on a link to a database, you get instead the black EZ Proxy screen, make sure you are coming in via http://my.t-bird.edu, and not http://www.my.t-bird.edu. (Note the "www"--this is an older URL and it will not work properly with remote access.) If you are coming from http://my.t-bird.edu and this still happens, try this: click on the link to My Thunderbird and log on again. Now try the remote access links.

▶ **Which database do I look in?**
An index of IBIC's full-text/electronic journals and the databases in which they may be found.

General Information

Spotlight

▶ Instructions for Remote Access
How to get into IBIC's licensed databases no matter where you are in the world.

APPENDIX (continued)

FIGURE 5. Sample online interactive Resource Guide. Links take users directly into programmed searches in databases and the online catalog.

Professional & Career Resources

This guide is organized to help you find information on career/employment resources. It covers print resources in the IBIC & CMC, online databases, and sources that are freely available on the World Wide Web. For a printable version click here.

Directories & Guides

This section of the guide includes resources that help identify and locate information about careers. It includes resources that are in the IBIC as well as the Career Management Center.

The Almanac of American employers
(REF HF5549.5 .C67 A5X 2000-2001)

America's Top Internships
(LC1072 .I58 A54 2000 - CAREER CTR)

CareerXroads : career(cross)roads
(HF5382.7 .C75 2000 - CAREER CTR)

Current jobs international : the national employment bulletin for the foreign language professional
(Periodical - CAREER CTR)

Cyberspace job search kit : the complete guide to online job seeking and career information
(HF5382.7 .J36 2000 - CAREER CTR)

Article Search via ProQuest

Retrieve the 25 most recent articles by using the following search terms:
> Career advancement
> Career changes
> Career development planning
> Employment interviews
> Job hunting
> Resumes

Selected Periodicals via ProQuest

Access the table of contents and full-text of the following journals:
> HRMagazine
> Inc.
> Workforce

FIGURE 6. Page from online instruction course for executive education program in Taiwan.

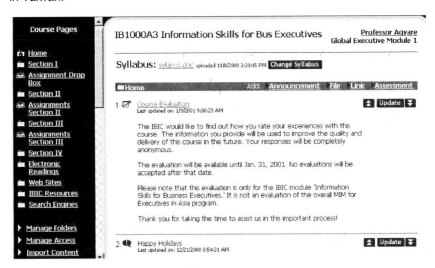

FIGURE 7. Global Gateway, IBIC's Web site with links to over two thousand sites for business and country information. This page shows the links for France.

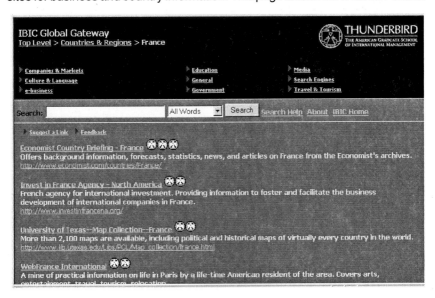

Never Having to Say You're Sorry: An Integrated, WWW-Based Software Solution for Providing Comprehensive Access to Journal Literature

John W. Felts, Jr.

University of North Carolina at Greensboro

SUMMARY. One of the persistent problems in finding journal literature is that there are so many places to locate such information. UNCG's Jackson Library has simplified the process with Journal Finder, a locally developed software solution that seamlessly integrates electronic journal content, pay-per-view content, local print holdings, unmediated document delivery (fully funded by the Library), and interlibrary loan, for comprehensive, unmediated, "one stop shop" access to journal articles. Also integrated into this solution are remote authentication options, title-level access to journals wherever possible, and the development of cross-linking between vendored database products for both title-level and even article-level access.

KEYWORDS. Technology, integration, distance learners, Internet

INTRODUCTION

The importance of journal literature in teaching, learning, research, and scholarly activities cannot be understated. In recent years, with the advent of

[Haworth co-indexing entry note]: "Never Having to Say You're Sorry: An Integrated, WWW-Based Software Solution for Providing Comprehensive Access to Journal Literature." Felts, John W., Jr. Co-published simultaneously in *Journal of Library Administration* (The Haworth Information Press, an imprint of The Haworth Press, Inc.) Vol. 37, No. 3/4, 2002, pp. 305-316; and: *Distance Learning Library Services: The Tenth Off-Campus Library Services Conference* (ed: Patrick B. Mahoney) The Haworth Information Press, an imprint of The Haworth Press, Inc., 2002, pp. 305-316.

http://www.haworthpress.com/store/product.asp?sku=J111
10.1300/J111v37n03_25

the World Wide Web, one of the persistent problems in locating journal literature is that there are simply so many places from which it may be obtained. How do we acquire, organize, and make available the vast amount of resources available to our communities in a sophisticated and robust, yet clean, user-friendly environment? Factor in real-time, online access to electronic journals, traditional access to print materials, interlibrary loan and document delivery services, and the issue is even further complicated.

Jackson Library has remedied this situation by creating Journal Finder, an all-inclusive World Wide Web (WWW)-based product that offers patrons access to virtually any journal article through one simple WWW form. Journal Finder provides access and direct links wherever possible to over 9,000 electronic journals available through publishers, aggregators, direct subscriptions, free WWW sites, pay-per-view sites or any other reliable source. If real-time online access is unavailable, Journal Finder also integrates the Library's print holdings by providing a "look back" feature that locates and provides title-level information as to whether the Library has a specific title in its print collection. Also, if no immediate access is available via these two methods, Journal Finder seamlessly integrates access to unmediated document delivery and interlibrary loan services, as well as access information to regional libraries, thereby creating an environment where the inability to acquire a journal article is indeed a rarity.

In 1998, Jackson Library realized the importance of providing access to this world of electronic journal information by creating an electronic journals database, which provided users a dynamically created means of ascertaining whether Jackson Library had access to an electronic journal title, provided dates of coverage, real-time access, and remote authentication to any of over 7,000 electronic journal titles. However, the Library wanted to create an environment in which other means of access and other formats were integrated, as opposed to excluded, and in which users weren't turned away without their desired information with no solution for acquiring this information. Building upon the popularity of the ejournals database, Jackson Library launched Journal Finder in August of 2001.

OVERVIEW

The University of North Carolina at Greensboro's Jackson Library supports a clientele of approximately 13,000 students, who are enrolled in both traditional and off-campus programs at the undergraduate, graduate, and doctoral levels, as well as to nearly 3,000 faculty and staff. The Library employs over eighty librarians and staff members, and the development department for the Journal Finder product, Electronic Resources and Information Technology

(ERIT), has nine employees. The Library features access to over 9,000 unique electronic journal titles from over sixty distinct sources, 4,000 print publications, and several unmediated table of contents and document delivery services. Clearly, a solution was needed to bring these disparate resources into one comprehensive, user-friendly WWW-based environment.

FEATURES AND FUNCTIONALITY

Ultimately the most valuable feature of the Journal Finder product is its ability to offer a means of access to journal literature without ever having to turn away a patron without a solution for obtaining this information. Due in some part to the lack of a comprehensive, customizable vendor-provided solution, and also in part to the popularity of Jackson Library's ejournals database, Journal Finder's predecessor, the Library made the decision to invest its resources into a product ultimately called Journal Finder. It was developed in-house over a three-month period, with a series of six librarians and staff involved in various aspects of the development process in both the technical areas and content development. The Journal Finder interface is very clean, featuring one field in which to enter the publication title for which you are looking (see Figure 1).

It was initially decided to provide one option for searching using a search with automatic right truncation ("begins with" search) to reduce false returns and to offer the user more titles to access. Upon execution of the journal title search, the user is provided with a series of icons, which represent various points of access to the desired publication. For example, if one were to enter "Journal of Accounting," a list of all journals that begin with the words "journal of accounting" appears in the search results list, and to the left of each title are a series of icons which represent various points of access to this material.

FIGURE 1. Journal Finder Interface

Enter the name of the journal:

SEARCH

In Figure 2, seven titles appeared that begin with the phrase "journal of accounting." A legend that appears at the bottom of each search results page explains precisely what each icon represents:

- The computer icon represents electronic, immediately available access
- The book icon represents that the Library maintains print holdings
- The mail icon represents that document delivery and/or interlibrary loan options are available
- The car icon represents holdings that are available at several regional colleges.

Essentially, any title with the computer icon is part of our ejournals collection, meaning that the user can access the material online twenty-four hours a day, seven days a week, which of course, represents the most desirable means of access to the average user. As seen in Figure 2, if there is no computer icon present, this indicates that no online access is available for that given title. This is true of the book icon as well, which represents our print holdings, and is essentially a catalog "look back" feature.

As shown in Figure 3, only one point of online access is available for this title, through Science Direct. Notice that the title is in a hypertext format, which provides title-level access, and the source is listed, as are the beginning and ending dates of coverage. Our development team came to the conclusion that

FIGURE 2. Search Results Page

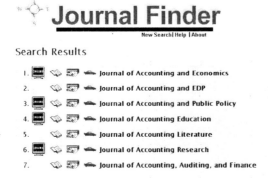

other information such as ISSN, description of the item, modes of access, etc., was superfluous and of little value to the patron, and was therefore not displayed as part of the search results information.

At this point in the electronic access procedure, each link to online access is scripted, so that:

1. If the user is on-campus, no validation process is necessary as long as the vendor supports IP-based access; the user goes directly to the desired title.
2. If the patron is accessing this information from off-campus, the same script detects this, and invokes a very simple routine for remote authentication, where the user simply enters their student ID number one time per session, and is then granted access to our online journal collection regardless of their geographic location.

For remote authentication and access, the Library has been very pleased with a product called EZproxy, which essentially acts as a URL rewriter. It operates between the user's Web browser and the restricted service, intercepting both the Web browser's requests and the pages returned by the Web server. From the perspective of the restricted Web service, the requests come from an authorized IP address and are accepted as valid. All the URLs on the Web pages that returned from the restricted service are rewritten as they are displayed on the user's Web browser with the base address of the EZproxy server.

Since the book icon was present in the search results screen in Figure 2 for "Journal of Accounting & Economics," the user also has the option of performing a catalog look-back which presents holdings information about this publication in its print format (see Figure 4).

Not only is this of interest to on-site users, but our technical services team enjoys the fact that each MARC record in our catalog has a hypertext 856 field dynamically created by Journal Finder and displayed in the "Journal Finder:" field of the record. This link runs a script that captures the DBCN number of the par-

FIGURE 3. Online Access

Journal Finder

New Search| Help | About

Online Access

Journal Title	Source	Full-Text Begins	Full-Text Ends
Journal of Accounting and Economics	Science Direct	2/1/95	

Need help? 336-334-5419 or journalfinder@uncg.edu

UNCG

FIGURE 4. Print Access

Record # 1

Title : Journal of accounting & economics.

Portion of title : Journal of accounting and economics

Holdings :

Location	Call Number
Periodicals Desk	v. 29:no. 1 (02/2000) - v. 31:no. 1/3 (09/2001)
Book Stacks	CALL NUMBER: HF5601 .J730 -- Bound -- v. 2 (01/1980) - v. 28 (12/1999)

Journal Finder : Find all methods of accessing this title

INTERNET Link : Available online (1995 to present)
Available online.

Publisher : Amsterdam, North-Holland Pub. Co.

Subject Heading(s) : Accounting--Periodicals
Economics--Periodicals
Electronic journal.

Description : v. ill. 24 cm.

Notes : Restricted to institutions with a site license to ScienceDirect; access limited to the UNCG community
Also available on WWW: http://www.elsevier.nl:80/homepage/sae/econbase/jae

Other Name : ScienceDirect (Online service)

ISSN : 0165-4101

ticular item, which maintains the title-level integrity, and provides a link back to Journal Finder should a patron have begun their search in the Library catalog, thereby providing added points of access to the journal title at hand.

At this point, the ERIT development team decided to add more flexibility for the user, giving them options based on their particular needs. Should the student be on-campus, physically accessing a journal in the Library is usually not a problem; however, should the user be off-campus, and not in urgent need of a particular journal article, Journal Finder also integrates a document delivery solution to the user which is financially underwritten by the Library. This is represented by the mail icon, and is present for every title in Journal Finder (and could also be utilized for obtaining any available title, not just those in the Journal Finder database, if the patron has the necessary bibliographic information). In other words, the Library provides unmediated document delivery service to its entire community of faculty, students, and staff, for each of the 14,000+ unique titles in the Journal Finder database as well as any title a user requests. Given the Library's commitment to distance education, document delivery service is not based on or limited to whether the library happens to have access to a title either in its online or print formats (see Figure 5).

After researching various prospective vendors, the Library chose Infotrieve as its document delivery provider. Not only do they boast a 98% fill rate, which has proven to be true to date, but it was discovered that should other document delivery suppliers such as the Information for Scientific Information's (ISI) Document Solution service not be able to supply a particular document re-

FIGURE 5. Document Delivery and Interlibrary Loan Services

Journal Finder

New Search| Help | About

Mail, E-Mail, or Web Delivery

Service	Available To	Typical Delivery Time	
		Mail	Web
Mail Delivery via Infotrieve More Info	Current UNCG Faculty, Students, and Staff	7-10 days	Not available
Mail or Web Delivery via Interlibrary Loan More Info	Current UNCG Graduate Students and Faculty	2-10 days	2-10 days

Need help? 336-334-5419 or journalfinder@uncg.edu

quest, they turn to Infotrieve to fill this request. Interestingly, as of this writing, it appears that ISI has outsourced their document delivery service to Infotrieve. The development team also found that an additional benefit to using Infotrieve was their ability to handle any personal customizations to form and function as requested. Also, they allowed implementation of an HTTP referrer method for remote authentication, which, after the user has authenticated locally, greatly simplifies access to Infotrieve by allowing access into Infotrieve without first having to go through the process of setting up a customer profile, thus precluding the need for some type of intermediary WWW page which queries the user as to whether they have yet to create an account before they can access the Infotrieve order form. If the user has created a profile, they enter their username and password; if not, they can create their profile at any point before submitting the order.

Traditional interlibrary loan services are also available to graduate students and faculty, but the Library emphasizes our document delivery arrangement through Infotrieve, since through informal analysis it was found that it costs the Library slightly less for users to use unmediated document delivery services than to use interlibrary loan. Additionally, interlibrary loan is restricted only to graduate students and faculty (see Figure 6).

Last, the car icon indicates which of any local libraries might have a particular title available for access, essentially creating a regional electronic union catalog. Since Greensboro is in the somewhat unusual position of having five colleges and universities within a very close driving radius, it was felt that if the user needed a particular journal article quickly, driving to a nearby library was certainly a reasonable means for gaining needed access (see Figure 7).

FIGURE 6. Infotrieve Document Delivery Interface

ADMINISTRATION

The administrative functionality of the Journal Finder product features a very robust WWW Administration Module, complete with the ability to add/delete/edit titles, search for specific titles by title name, vendor, ISSN, print-only or electronic-only titles, maintain subject-related information and access points, and create real-time reports on a variety of information such as overall database statistics, cataloging statistics, usage reports, etc. Since all the data is counted in the same way, as opposed to relying on disparate database vendors for usage information, the need to attempt to reconcile these types of data is no longer necessary (see Figure 8).

Since the actual content maintenance of the product is by far the most labor-intensive Journal Finder activity, having this WWW-based Administrative Module has allowed ERIT to give access rights to many librarians and staff to help maintain content information without having to go directly into the

FIGURE 7. Other Libraries Interface

Journal Finder
New Search| Help | About

In Other Libraries

These libraries in Greensboro have some printed issues of **Journal of Accounting and Economics**. Follow the link for more information.

- North Carolina A&T State University

You can use these resources to find out what libraries outside Greensboro have some printed issues of **Journal of Accounting and Economics**.

- Academic Libraries in North Carolina and South-Central Virginia
- Libraries Around the World

Need help? 336-334-5419 or journalfinder@uncg.edu

FIGURE 8. WWW Administration Module

Journal Finder Administration

Administrative Tasks

- Search for Access Points
- Search for Titles to Delete or Edit (including subject associations and access points)
- Add Titles (not including access points)
- Add or Edit/Delete Subjects
- Add or Edit/Delete Electronic Sources

Queries and Views

- cataloging information for all titles
- titles without a catalog date, web-only titles without a catalog date
- titles with no hard copy
- title, source, and ISSN for all e-journal titles
- recently-deleted titles or access points
- titles accessed via a particular source (tblAccessE) or in Jackson Library (tblAccessJac)
- titles associated with a particular subject

Database Statistics

actual database, thus eliminating the department's fear that the relational integrity of the database or the scripts therein might be broken by those less-informed on the inner workings of relational database management systems.

THE TECHNOLOGY

Having realized the success of Journal Finder's predecessor, Jackson Library's ejournals database, and monitoring usage trends over a period of approximately eighteen months, it was noticed that, as usage increased to relatively high levels, the current database product, Microsoft Access, was starting to show signs of slower performance, plus a seeming inability to share memory and server resources well with other applications. For these reasons, Journal Finder's development team opted to scale up to a more robust product, Microsoft's SQL Server, which has been widely touted as a more "industrial strength" database solution, with the ability to handle more transactions faster, even with heavier server loads.

Although in theory similar to Access, SQL Server requires a more extensive knowledge of Structured Query Language (SQL), which is embedded in all of our scripts for querying the database. Using the Windows NT 4.0 server platform, with Internet Information Server (IIS) as the WWW server software, a natural extension of these technologies was to write our scripts using Active Server Pages (ASP). ASP pages were developed exclusively to work within the Microsoft server environment. More of our development team had familiarity with this scripting language, which was personally found to be less complicated than creating PERL scripts for a UNIX environment, and proved to be very flexible and robust in their ability to search, retrieve, and manipulate data into a variety of formats. The server software, database, and scripts all run on a Dell PowerEdge 2300 Server with 256 MB of RAM and an eight GB hard disk, which is partitioned into a two GB system drive, and a six GB application/data drive. The database proper is approximately 35 MB, which fluctuates slightly as records are added or deleted.

IN DEVELOPMENT

After the first iteration of Journal Finder went into production in August 2001, many changes and developments, some subtle and others quite exciting, have occurred or are currently in development. First, in addition to the automatically right-truncated search option, several other search strategies are being added as an advanced search interface, which will include keyword searching, support of Boolean operators, and perhaps subject searching and "date added" searching. Also, there is always the issue of title authority. For example, if a user searches for the journal title "Journal of the American Medical Association" as opposed to "JAMA: Journal of the American Medical Association," no retrievals would be evident. How does one handle the plethora of title permutations, ampersands vs. the word "and," abbreviations, articles such as "the," "la," "die," etc.? Our development team decided to add a hidden field in one of the database tables that now includes all permutations of a particular title, as well as automated data entry correction options that will drop certain stop words and scour the added title field for any permutations, thereby retrieving titles that otherwise may have been overlooked by a right-truncated search. As many title variants as necessary can be added to better enable the user to find their journal title.

Another exciting capability currently being developed in Journal Finder is linking between distinct journal titles among different vendored databases. Using a series of ASP scripts, Journal Finder can link at the title level between vendored databases such as InfoTrac, ProQuest, Project Muse, JSTOR, Ovid, IDEAL, Emerald, Ingenta, Catchword, Blackwell, Cambridge University Press, SIAM, AMS, Wiley, and dozens of other vendors. Journal Finder acts as the middleman between these databases, and by clicking on the Journal Finder link in one database, a search is dynamically created, retrieving and displaying other access options to the title in a hypertext format through Journal Finder.

Perhaps an even more intriguing venture in which Journal Finder is being developed is linking at the journal *article* level. In those databases that are currently utilizing the OpenURL Standard, it has been possible to capture enough bibliographic data about an article from within the source code of a given record in the vendored database, retrieve and reformat this data through Journal Finder, then display an actual hypertext link to the exact article for which one was looking in another database. For example, if a user searches InfoTrac's OneFile database, but finds no full-text availability for a particular journal article, one click of the mouse will run this search in the Journal Finder database and retrieve another resource that contains that specific full-text article, which is then displayed as a hypertext link in Journal Finder. *Journal Finder brings the user from the citation in one database to the full-text article in another.* Of course, this feature is currently limited to those vendors embracing the OpenURL Standard, and there is uncertainty as to whether this will continue to emerge. However, the National Information Standards Organization (NISO) has recently announced the formation of a committee to develop the Open URL Standard, which hopefully portends a greater acceptance and implementation of this standard.

CONCLUSION

Although relatively still in its infancy, Journal Finder has already evolved as new standards and new technologies emerge and mature, and more usability information is analyzed. To date, student, faculty, and staff feedback to this product have been almost unanimously positive, and more thorough usability studies are being planned to further enhance Journal Finder's look, feel, and functionality. Providing a resource where easy access to journal literature, or perhaps more directly, *any* journal article, is almost always a reality, from one convenient, integrated, user-friendly WWW page clearly has made Journal Finder a very beneficial addition to the resources and services Jackson Library makes available to its community. The future should prove to only enhance Journal Finder's features and functionality as it evolves and grows within the ever-changing fields of technology and librarianship.

REFERENCES

Additional information on Active Server Pages (ASP) can be found at http://msdn. microsoft.com/asp/, as well as and many other Websites such as http://www.asp101. com/, http://www.learnasp.com/, and http://www.aspfaqs.com/.

Breeding, M. (2001). Offering remote access to restricted resources. *Information Today*, *18*(5), 52-53.

Felts, J.W., Jr. (2001). Now you can get there from here: Creating an interactive web application for accessing full-text journal articles from any location. *Library Collections, Acquisitions, & Technical Services*, *25*(3), 281-90.

NISO issues report on statistics forum, Forms Committee to develop open URL standard. (2001, May 1). *Information Today*, p. 62.

Stern, D. (2001). Automating enhanced discovery and delivery: The open URL possibilities. *Online*, *25*(2), 42-47.

Yager, T. (2000). SQL server takes aim at high end. *InfoWorld*, *22*(20), 69-74.

Building a Digital Library
in Support of Distance Learning

Jessame Ferguson
Joel Fowler
Marilyn Hanley
Jay Schafer

University of Massachusetts

SUMMARY. In this paper we will describe the University of Massachusetts System libraries' efforts to offer services and information to our students and broader user communities through the creation of a shared digital library. The digital library delivers a library and its services anytime, anyplace, and in any medium. The new UMass Digital Library complements the existing bricks-and-mortar libraries, by maximizing the provision of services and resources through collaborative measures to our growing distance learning community. Each of the major components that went into the development of the digital library are detailed, including extended reference service, developing shared collections, Web site development, and the technical aspects necessary to make everything work together.

KEYWORDS. Technology, distance education, distance learners, information resources

BACKGROUND INFORMATION

The UMass Digital Library (www.UMassDigitalLibrary.net) evolved out of years of preliminary work and planning, and came to fruition in a flurry of

[Haworth co-indexing entry note]: "Building a Digital Library in Support of Distance Learning." Ferguson, Jessame et al. Co-published simultaneously in *Journal of Library Administration* (The Haworth Information Press, an imprint of The Haworth Press, Inc.) Vol. 37, No. 3/4, 2002, pp. 317-331; and: *Distance Learning Library Services: The Tenth Off-Campus Library Services Conference* (ed: Patrick B. Mahoney) The Haworth Information Press, an imprint of The Haworth Press, Inc., 2002, pp. 317-331.

http://www.haworthpress.com/store/product.asp?sku=J111
10.1300/J111v37n03_26

activity over the past year. The libraries of the five University of Massachusetts campuses–which are in Amherst, Boston, Dartmouth, Lowell and
Worcester–have a history of putting together proposals to share resources or
services. In 1999, the UMass Libraries were successful in securing funding as
a group through state Information Technology Bond opportunities. Over the
next two years the libraries laid the foundation necessary to make a combined
digital library possible by purchasing or upgrading integrated library systems,
enhancing network and information technology infrastructures, working on
digitization projects with other campus entities, and creating a specialized digital library called MassBedrock (www.MassBedrock.org) to support outreach
to members of business and economic development communities throughout
the Commonwealth. After these initial projects were complete, all five of the
campus libraries' staff met in August 2000 for an active meeting that outlined
the UMass Digital Library concept and plans for development.

Soon after this meeting, task forces were formed under the general guidance
of the five campus library directors/deans to plan and implement specific goals
of the digital library. Each task force contained representatives from each of
the five campus libraries and members were assigned based on their relation to
the individual mission of that group. The Collection Development Task Force
met almost immediately to make decisions about potential resources to purchase jointly. The Extended Reference Task Force worked together to develop
live online reference service. The Information Literacy Task Force provided
help guides and documentation for the Web site. The Digitization Task Force
worked on developing standards and obtaining equipment for digitization of
special collections. The Web Site Development Task Force was charged with
creation of the Web site itself. And the overall governance was provided by the
five campus library directors/deans who met regularly throughout the process.

A major impetus for the development of the UMass Digital Library, aside
from the desire of the five campus libraries to work together and combine
resources, was the development of UMassOnline (www.umassonline.net). Distance education has become a greater focus for the University of Massachusetts over the past year with the creation of UMassOnline, and the libraries
have a keen desire to assure they are part of this future focus. UMassOnline
combines online course, degree and certificate offerings of all five campuses
in order to reach a broader audience of potential students. Our distance education offerings do not end there; we also have several remote locations offering
specific areas of study needed in that community, such as the I-495 Center for
Professional Education (www.umass-i495.net/). The libraries realized these
developments would create increasing numbers of students seemingly discon-
nected from our five main campuses and uncertain where to go for their information needs. The UMass Digital Library had to be created immediately to

provide a starting place for our students to find access to library materials from anywhere in the state.

EXTENDED REFERENCE SERVICE

Prior to the five campuses meeting in August 2000, many of the reference librarians prepared in various ways for this momentous day of planning. Two librarians had attended the First Annual Digital Reference Conference at Harvard University. Some had done extensive research in order to update their knowledge on the subject. Others had been long thinking of ways to make the reference experience a more viable one for the apparently retreating patron. Although there had been some contact with fellow librarians in other consortia, this was an opportunity to quickly see common concerns and to propose to the directors a list of priorities for our shared future.

Here is what we proposed:

1. *Live Reference Pilot Project.* At least two of the five campuses should engage in a live reference pilot project that will explore the efficacy of launching a full service. Suggested vendors include LivePerson (http://www. liveperson.com/), Webline (http://www.webline.com/products/web.htm), and Remedy (http://www.remedy.com/solutions/index.html).
2. *800 Telephone Lines for In-State Calls.* Distance education and off-campus use means that more of our patrons are outside our local calling areas. Establishing 800 numbers for each of the reference departments that can be called from any Massachusetts area code will eliminate the cost and inconvenience of toll calls and encourage patrons to call for reference assistance.
3. *Full-Text Virtual Reference Desk.* In conjunction with the Shared Electronic Resources group, consideration should be given to acquiring full-text standard Reference resources that could be offered to users from a single Web page.
4. *Joint Subject Web Pages.* Campuses should seek specialized assistance in creating shared subject Web pages, both to extend reference and collections services. This and the above suggestion imply that the five libraries create a shared homepage.
5. *Shared Libraries Homepage.* A 5-campus library homepage should be constructed to better effect the previous two suggestions.

The first steps:

1. *Form Intercampus Committee or Task Force.* This committee should be made up of reference, and other appropriate library staff (i.e., Systems

personnel), representing the campuses. Their charge would be to investigate and bring to fruition the above and other relevant services. This committee could be called the Extended, or Digital Reference Committee.

2. *Send Representatives to the 2nd Annual Digital Reference Conference.*
Based on the experience of the first conference, this one was likely to
offer more presentations and demonstrations on digital reference services that would be useful to our Extended Reference Committee. This
conference was held October 16-17, 2000, Seattle, WA (http://vrd.
org/conferences/VRD2000/index.shtml).

3. *Initiate Intercampus Digital Reference Listserv.* This suggestion would
not only enhance the work of the committee, but also help to maximize
personal interaction between librarians. Stronger relationships are required, particularly if we are to know each other's collections and areas
of expertise.

4. *Assessment of Services.* While it is important to consider new services,
and while it might be fine to just begin such a service and see how it
grows, it is also important to examine issues such as support, where the
payoff is, and whether people will or are using the service.

Most of the above proposals were accepted and steps were taken to begin
work. The librarians appointed to the Extended Reference Task Force represented a range of experience and interest in the mission to remake reference. The
group realized it should be a service that both spoke to our local practices, needs
and resources, and responded to a larger goal of cooperation with the other campuses to create a resource for the remote user of a university attempting to evolve
into an amalgam of undifferentiated campuses. Up to this point we had functioned as fairly discrete and rooted entities. The act of collaboration then became
as significant as the building of a newer and more responsive service.

The group's charge was to choose a "live" reference product, learn to use it,
teach other reference librarians to provide the service, and plan to offer
real-time online reference, first to their own campus users and then to the University as a whole. They looked at several products, such as LivePerson which
was originally created as commercial call center software to offer customers
assistance in shopping from Web sites, as well as LSSI's Virtual Reference
Software (http://www.lssi.com/), one of the only products developed for library reference services. The version of LSSI that the group saw demonstrated
was more complicated and more expensive than the libraries were ready to implement at the time. LivePerson had been adopted by a number of university libraries, including Carnegie Mellon, Virginia Polytechnic Institution,
Georgetown, and the Wharton School of the University of Pennsylvania, some
having been in service for more than a year. It was also relatively inexpensive
and easy to use. The decision to select LivePerson for a two-year subscription

was based on price, ease of use, availability of support and the assumption that by the end of the subscription period other choices would be available.

The LivePerson customizable product is essentially chat room software. It allows the reference librarian to see the URL of visitors, put up a busy sign, end the conversation, or provide a default e-mail function when offline. Web pages can be pushed to the visitor. Canned answers can be created, which are especially helpful for greetings, salutations, and recurring questions. And, those who visit the page on which the LivePerson button has been loaded can be invited in for a chat session. The operator sees visitors approaching when they enter the page, and the visitor soon sees a balloon drifting across their screen inviting them in to chat.

The remaining part of this group's funding was used to purchase laptop computers for the installation of the operator software, so that the librarians would not be limited to offering the service from fixed locations. In addition to the five operational accounts purchased for each of the campuses, each account is also allowed numerous downloads and operators. One of the limitations found with LivePerson is that there is no function for the reporting of statistics. But, there is a log of the activity, which can be manually transcribed into a report. While the librarians were able to work out most of the idiosyncrasies of this system, they learned that it was essential to have a practice period before offering the service "live."

The multi-campus approach to this service required one more technical issue to be worked out. How was the LivePerson icon going to "know" which campus was responsible for answering questions at a given time? The group had decided that each campus would be responsible for one four-hour period each day. But, there was nothing inherent in the software that would be able to switch traffic between the campuses. With help from the UMass libraries technical staff, a script was written to automatically change the link associated with the LivePerson button to the campus providing the service at that time of the day.

Finally, there were the issues associated with serving each other's patrons, including differences in library policy, authentication methods, and learning about each other's databases and basic campus information. The many meetings this group had and their listserv, e-mail, telephone and chat room communications helped to clear away uncertainty that librarians may have felt about the other campus libraries. They also developed a standard FAQ at each library that would help librarians answer questions related to another campus. This has proved to be an extremely useful exercise, and resulted in each library creating a page of links that will answer most of the basic questions one gets at a reference desk, virtual or not.

The librarians are excited about extending reference service to online patrons, and have had positive responses, such as one from the student who said at the end of an exchange, "By the way, this is a cool service."

COLLECTION DEVELOPMENT

The Collection Development Task Force was made up of one acquisitions librarian and one collection development librarian from each campus. The group's initial charge was to develop recommendations for the library directors regarding titles to be acquired under the Information Technology (IT) Bond funding. The five libraries had no previous history of cooperating as a system to make joint purchases. Each library belongs to the Boston Library Consortium, and that had been a common source for obtaining discounted database licensing.

The target spending for shared resources was $200,000 from funds already released, with the possibility of an additional $250,000 if more funding at the same level was released at mid-year (which did not happen). These amounts were to be spread over two years (i.e., $100,000/$125,000 per year). Using one-time "capital" funding for ongoing database expenses is a risky route to take, but there was no other financial source available with which to purchase content for the UMass Digital Library. To accomplish this task, members of the group met twice and corresponded electronically on a regular basis.

Rather than simply provide a list of desired resources, the group based its recommendations on the concept of a system-wide virtual library that can be developed over time as demand grows and resources become available. The underlying philosophy of this system-wide virtual library is based on these understandings:

- Full-text resources are the first priority for the system-wide virtual library because they will best support the information needs of the growing numbers of distance education and non-residential students.
- Since funding is seen as "one time," the new resources of the system-wide virtual library are seen as supplementing those already offered by the individual libraries. In some cases, one or two individual libraries may already provide access to selected resources, but the general principle is to add new resources, not to off-load the expense of current resources.
- The system-wide virtual library will support programs across the disciplines. Every attempt will be made to add resources that support the greatest numbers of programs. The specialized nature of the Worcester

medical campus will obviously limit the usefulness of some resources commonly used by the other four campuses.
- Five-campus purchases will be partnered with other consortia when it offers advantages of broader resources, better pricing, or easier vendor negotiations.
- The group assumes issues of access and user authentication will be successfully addressed so that the selected products will be available to appropriate constituents across the University system.

Suggested Online Resources

The following prioritized list of recommendations for resources was developed using a process of nominating products for consideration, exploring the availability, usefulness and pricing of those products, and, finally, working on a consensus basis to select and prioritize desired products. The total cost of the recommendations knowingly far exceeds the current anticipated allocations. This serves to demonstrate the common need for resources across the five campuses and may be useful in justifying additional funds.

- ABI/INFORM–Global
- Electronic Reference Books (NetLibrary)
- Mental Measurements Yearbook
- Oxford English Dictionary
- ScienceDirect®
- OVID Package
- ProQuest Package (*Criminal Justice Periodical Index, Computing, Education Complete*)
- ProQuest Psychology Collection
- CQ Library (Congressional Quarterly)
- New Grove's Dictionary of Music and Musicians, 2nd Edition
- UMI Digital Dissertations
- ProQuest Nursing Collection
- American Periodical Series (APS) OnlineOr PCI Full Text (Periodicals Contents Index)

Now and the Future

The initial $200,000 has funded the first four databases on the list for two years. The Extended Reference Task Force recommended a list of NetLibrary reference titles that were purchased with "perpetual access." Additional funding has not materialized, but the five campuses have pursued other database licenses as a system by using institutional funding. The major hope for the future is that this model will encourage support from the UMass President's Office and the Massachusetts Board of Higher Education for a common state-wide cooperative of public and private higher education library resources similar to VIVA (The Virtual Library of Virginia) or GALILEO (Georgia).

WEB SITE DEVELOPMENT

The first meeting of the Web Site Development Task Force took place on December 18, 2000. The group's charge was to create a visible and accessible Web site portal for the shared presence of the UMass Digital Library. More specifically they were expected to:

- Make decisions about what it should look like.
- Create or gather content that includes the UMass libraries shared services and resources, and also that which is available from each individual campus.
- Decide what functionality and technology are needed for the site.
- Decide how the content will be maintained.
- Identify the costs necessary for development of the site.
- Develop a timeline that shows how the work can be completed by June 30th.

During the conceptual planning of the project, strategic principles were formed. They outlined exactly what the new digital library needed to do and helped to provide the purpose and focus for the Web site. These principles were used to guide the decision making process:

- Remove geographical, time, and physical access barriers to the collections and services of the UMass libraries.
- Meet the needs of distance education students and remote users by providing resources and instruction over a robust network.
- Enhance access to information for users on our campuses, across the Commonwealth and beyond, from the 67,000 enrolled UMass students to the countless citizens in business, government, and other organizations around the state.
- Link the library and information resources of the five campuses with those of UMassOnline, the I-495 Center for Professional Education, and promote the ease of access, time savings, and cost-effectiveness of this collaboration.

Project funding allowed the use of contracted services for the design and creation of the Web site. The task force was allocated roughly $50,000, which also had to include the purchase of the server and any software needs. But the group realized that before they could bring in an outside party to work on the project, they had to make some decisions about how the site should function. At the same time, the group wanted to make sure that all campuses were contributing as equally as possible so that in the end, each would be invested in the digital library's success. Fortunately this group included members from each of the other task forces developing components for the digital library, which kept them informed about how those individual services were being created and fit into the overall digital library development.

To decide what functionality and general organization the Web site should have, the task force began by looking at other digital libraries or statewide consortia Web sites which had already developed similar projects. After comparing the benefits of sites such as VIVA, GALILEO, the California Digital Library, and the University of Alberta, the group put together a list of possible components for the UMass digital library. The group also took the time to discuss and identify the specialized needs of the digital library audience. The group decided that one of the main purposes for the site was that it should satisfy user needs by including a mechanism for identifying individual electronic resources for the off-campus researcher. When the UMass libraries' resources are combined within the digital library, hundreds of online databases and electronic journals will be accessible. Therefore, it was necessary to provide off-campus users with the ability to search for a specific topic of interest to locate the right resource. Ultimately the task force would like to implement a content (or meta) search inside the resources, so that individual articles would be listed on the digital library site, but this implementation wasn't possible with such a short timeline. Instead, the group decided to provide a searchable database of the online resources, both those subscribed to by individual libraries, and also those purchased jointly. It was also desirable to use a database for the combined resources so that the records each campus maintained could be easily and automatically updated. A menu of broad subject areas became the main search function for querying this database because there was a realization that users might type anything into an open search, not understanding what they were searching. An additional piece of functionality the task force was very attracted to was a "My Library" design allowing students to customize a personalized interface, but the group decided to put this off because of time constraints.

With all of these preliminary decisions made, the task force wrote a proposal and requested bids from Massachusetts Web site developers. The budget for Web site development was roughly $25,000 after subtracting the cost of other purchases. The decision to use a contractor was not solely based on having funding; it was also to assure a final design that reflected the UMass identity but looked different from any of the individual libraries. There was also clear direction from the start that this large duty not be added to someone's existing workload, and without dedicated staff for the project during the development phase, contracting out was the only possibility. Gravity Switch of Northampton, MA won the contract because of their thorough proposal, which demonstrated their ability to address our digital library's needs clearly, as well as their quick response and eagerness to work with the UMass libraries. Other companies were difficult to reach by phone or were slow to respond to requests for information and some only provided a flat fee without clear details. Gravity Switch also indicated that they were willing and able to develop the Web site so that a "My Library" structure would already be a part of the underlying design and more easy to implement in the future using the scalable technologies the group had decided upon–ColdFusion programming and Oracle for the database.

The contractor led the task force through a process of "design inspiration" which helped define the look and feel of the Web site. Questions were asked that helped to provide an image of what the Web design outcome should be, such as–If the site had a musical score what type of music would it be? Or what brand of car would this Web site be? The group discussed other forms of brand association and the contractor explained how each of the words "UMass," "Digital" and "Library" have pre-existing associations attached to them. The group was also led through a discussion of words they would most like associated with the Web site and came up with this list: expert, engaging, welcoming, responsive, functional, and dynamic/active. Lastly, the contractor explained how colors and fonts used in site design project a feeling to the user; based on this information the group narrowed down what they wanted to use to project our image. Soon after gathering results of this discussion, the contractor provided the group with a timeline which showed how the work could be completed by the deadline, four examples of site design, several logo graphics to choose from, and a site map. The task force then formed a smaller group to make final decisions about design features, but all examples were shared with the entire group for feedback so that all opinions would be included. Based on the information gathered from members, the smaller group took bits and pieces from the design and logo examples to come up with the final design.

Librarians were responsible for the textual content of the Web site, and it was the task force's responsibility to assure that the contractor had all the content necessary for the site. The group mapped out the content needs for the site and assigned each group member, or other groups as appropriate, to provide this content. For efficiency, the group appointed one member to act as the content editor in order to provide a necessary single point of contact for all content needs. The content editor was responsible for maintaining a consistent vocabulary throughout the site, clarifying content needs for content providers, enforcing deadlines, and editing final content before sending to the contractor.

TECHNICAL ASPECTS

There were numerous technical aspects of the project that needed to be addressed before the UMass Digital Library could move forward as planned. These included identifying the hosting location, deciding who would provide technical assistance for the project, and solving the authentication issues associated with shared resources. Prior to the meeting in August 2000, the UMass System Library IT directors met to discuss these issues, and assigned their staff to serve as members on each task force to provide technical support.

Hosting

The library IT directors then worked with members of the UMass Amherst Library Information Systems and Technology Services (LISTS) Department to determine the best approach for the hosting of the UMass Digital Library. There were two viable options to consider: (1) offer to host the site at UMass Amherst in the LISTS computer room, (2) contract the hosting to an outside vendor. Given the tight timeframe, the simplest solution was to host the digital library Web server in the LISTS computer room. Since LISTS had the expertise, experience and facilities to do this, it did not make sense to contract with an outside agency that might not understand or be responsive to library concerns, or treat them with the highest priority.

An additional benefit to housing the server in the LISTS computer room was the ready access to a high-speed Internet connection. The LISTS server room has a Cisco 2900 switch serving 100MB/FDX to every server. This switch has a 100MB/FDX fiber connection straight to the Cisco router at the border of the library. From the library border router (a Cisco 7507), the campus is running a Gigabit Ethernet mesh among border routers. The Internet access from the campus consists of one DS3 to the Internet and one DS3 to Internet 2 (each DS3 is 45MB and is approximately equivalent to 24 T1s). Within the library, traffic from the desktop computers runs on separate fibers, and there are more available if these become saturated.

The next step was to decide whether to do virtual hosting or purchase a separate server. The cleaner solution was to purchase an independent SUN Enterprise 250 server to host the site so that the project could migrate to a new location at some point in the future. Another decision was to use the operating systems and software with which the LISTS staff was already familiar, to speed the project along. Shortly after the arrival of the server, LISTS staff installed and configured the Web server with Solaris 8 and Apache 1.39 and provided access accounts for those who needed to work on it. The additional work of registering the server in the Internet domain was done with the assistance of the University's IT department. After the Web server software was installed and configured, the next step was to install ORACLE 8 and ColdFusion for database and Web functionality, and NetTracker software to provide statistics on Web page usage.

Authentication

The next major hurdle was finding a combined solution to the process of authentication and authorization of valid UMass system faculty, staff, and students. Each of the UMass five campus libraries had some sort of authentication system in place for remote access. However, integrating these five systems to form a single authentication system, or creating a single, system-wide authentication system that didn't create more problems than it solved, seemed daunting. Although the long-term solution could potentially be an integrated solution with the PeopleSoft project, its possibility as a solution was not available during the tight timeline of this project. The UMass libraries needed a simple, short-term solution that could serve our target audience without creating additional inconveniences or jeopardize the potential to transition to PeopleSoft when that becomes available.

The LISTS staff had experience implementing authentication solutions with EZproxy, and put forward a proposal to the library directors (subsequently approved) that all libraries utilize that software. It was suggested that a relatively straightforward modification of existing Perl cgi scripts used by the LISTS Web and proxy servers would provide a reasonable solution for the current situation. These scripts would be implemented on the UMass Digital Library Web server. The result would be that a patron who chose a database from this Web server would be passed straight through to that database if they were coming in from any of the five campuses. If they were coming in from off-campus, they would be presented with a dialog window for their affiliated campus that requires a user name and password from a computer account with one of the five campuses. They would then be passed through the proxy server for that campus. A session cookie from the UMass Digital Library Web server with a 30-minute timeout would remember their campus affiliation so that they would not be repeatedly faced with that dialog. Since the electronic resources being purchased for the digital library are available to all five campuses, each campus library would add the appropriate entries to their ezproxy.cfg files to serve these resources. Patrons affiliated with a given campus would get passed back to their campus and would need to provide their login information just as though they had clicked through from their own library's Web page.

Advantages and disadvantages to this short-term solution to authentication:

- No additional hardware or commercial software, aside from the EZproxy purchase required.
- No additional accounts required.
- No additional ongoing maintenance required to keep a centralized patron database up to date.
- It leverages existing accounts and authentication systems at each of the five UMass campuses.
- It utilizes existing library personnel and expertise.
- Easy to get up and running in time for the end of fiscal year deadline.
- It does not achieve a single point of authentication for the UMass Digital Library.
- It requires patrons to obtain an affiliation and an account with a specific campus.

Database Development

After the Web server hosting and patron authentication issues were resolved, the next major task was the creation of the database. From a data perspective, the goal of the UMass Digital Library project is to take data from the five separate campuses, which is stored in different systems and in different formats, and present this data in a unified manner via the Internet. These three characteristics–separate location, different storage systems, and different formats–present unique and difficult challenges toward achieving the end goal–unified presentation. Added to these challenges is the additional characteristic that some of the data is repeated across locations, duplication that would need to be automatically eliminated in order to achieve a unified presentation. After deciding that it made the most sense for each campus to be responsible for delivering the data in a common format, and only data that complied to this common format would be included in the UMass Digital Library project, the next task was to develop a standard for delivering the data. This standard would have to accomplish several goals in order to be an effective solution: (1) it had to be achievable by all campuses, (2) it had to contain enough information to be useful for the end user, and (3) it had to have a minimum set of data elements that would allow for classification and the removal of duplicate information. Working with library catalogers, the most common storage format for library records, MARC, was used as a model. A process then had to be developed that would take this data from a flat file format and manipulate it so that it could be stored and used in a single relational database. A three-stage process was developed to achieve this end goal:

1. The first step is to take the data contained in flat ASCII text files and load it into an Oracle database. Each campus has its own separate loading area so there is no mixing of data at this point. During the process of loading the data from the flat ASCII text files into Oracle, the data is checked for compliance with the standard.
2. Moving records from the Load area to the Stage area during the second part of the process is a lengthy and complicated process. As with the Load area, each campus has its own separate Stage area. However, for each record that gets moved from the Load area to the Stage area, two important questions are asked:

   • Does this record already exist for that campus in the Stage area?
   • Does another campus have the same or similar record as well?

   Additionally, each record in the Load areas for the other four campuses is examined in an attempt to find duplicate records. If duplicates are found, then the records from each campus are compared to each other to determine which record is richer, the winning record becoming the parent and the other its children, and all records are simultaneously moved to their respective Staging area. Once records are safely placed in the Stage area, additional operations are performed on them. These operations include, among others, the removal of the proxy prefix to the resource URL, the normalization of the title field, and the removal of additional unwanted characters and anomalies from character delimiters.
3. The final Production area looks vastly different from both the Load and the Stage area. Whereas each campus had its own Load and Stage area, the Production area consists of only one central location for data storage and several dependant and related tables. The only records that are moved from the Stage area into the Production area, regardless of which campus they originated from, are those records that have no children and those records that are the parent records for one or more child records. Certain data elements are moved into the main storage area while other data elements are expanded and moved into the related tables. In essence, when moving records from the Stage area to the Load area, we are only selecting either unique, or rich, flat records and moving and expanding them into a relational database model. We have now achieved the end goal of storing the records from five different locations into a single, unified relational database.

FUTURE DEVELOPMENT

Before completing the first phase of the UMass Digital Library development, we knew where we wanted to go in the future. The largest factor in our ability to move forward on our "Phase 2" plans will be whether or not we receive further funding as promised. Most importantly we have requested funding for 2.5 FTE staff dedicated to the UMass Digital Library project. We realize we cannot continue developing a comprehensive digital library on the good nature of existing staff who are already dedicated to other duties. So far we have managed to develop our collaborative "proof of concept" and present it as a success worthy of continued funding. At the time of submitting this paper, future funding of the UMass Digital Library remains uncertain. If we do manage to secure adequate funding, our desire is to continue developing the following initiatives:

- System-wide authentication to provide seamless access to licensed electronic resources to students affiliated with any of the five campuses.
- Continue digitizing resources and developing methods to provide access to licensed material in special collections and unique UMass archives.
- Further development of information literacy and online instruction tools.
- Simultaneous searching of all UMass catalogs by users, and user-initiated borrowing by joining the Boston Library Consortium's Virtual Union Catalog.
- A delivery system for "hard copy" collections.
- Implementing a "My Library" component to the Web site design.
- Develop a meta search function to query multiple database content and return results in a uniform format.

Although the UMass Digital Library may have been developed under extremely tight deadlines and without many of the resources that existing consortia and statewide digital libraries have available, we believe we have the beginnings of an excellent resource for our distance learning community. Our fundamental guiding principals for the development of the site pinpoint exactly what we believe will make this resource undeniably necessary for the education and continuing education of our students. We hope that the strong foundation we have laid for supporting distance learning in our state will continue to expand, and that our progress will provide a model for similar projects in development elsewhere.

Grading Ourselves:
Using the ACRL Guidelines
for Distance Learning Library Services
to Develop Assessment Strategies

Linda Frederiksen

Washington State University Vancouver

SUMMARY. While the need for a plan to evaluate distance library services is clear, the means by which this work should be done is less obvious. Faced with a variety of measurement tools, it can be difficult to decide not only what to evaluate but also how to do it. With the goal of providing information on how to develop appropriate assessment instruments to document performance and service quality, this paper gives an overview of the assessment movement. As a lens through which librarians, administrators, accrediting bodies and other stakeholders might view the effectiveness and value of distance library services, the Distance Learning Library Services (DLS) Guidelines serve as a framework that can be used to build an assessment strategy, as well as a gateway to other measurement tools and accreditation standards.

KEYWORDS. Guidelines, evaluation, assessment, strategies

INTRODUCTION

While there is general acknowledgement throughout the higher education community that assessment must and will be done, agreement on how, what

[Haworth co-indexing entry note]: "Grading Ourselves: Using the ACRL Guidelines for Distance Learning Library Services to Develop Assessment Strategies." Frederiksen, Linda. Co-published simultaneously in *Journal of Library Administration* (The Haworth Information Press, an imprint of The Haworth Press, Inc.) Vol. 37, No. 3/4, 2002, pp. 333-339; and: *Distance Learning Library Services: The Tenth Off-Campus Library Services Conference* (ed: Patrick B. Mahoney) The Haworth Information Press, an imprint of The Haworth Press, Inc., 2002, pp. 333-339.

http://www.haworthpress.com/store/product.asp?sku=J111
10.1300/J111v37n03_27

and when to assess is not as widespread. Faced by questions from governing and accrediting bodies, as well as taxpayers, senior administrators, and students about the value, worth and purpose of academia, faculty struggle to design data collection tools that will provide timely and meaningful answers.

Academic librarians face the same challenges. What is the business and mission of the institution? What products, services, and long-term benefits are being delivered? Are expectations of quality, effectiveness, and performance being satisfied? Add to these questions those having specifically to do with distance education and it isn't difficult to imagine the state of turmoil currently experienced on American college and university campuses.

Although this landscape is without a doubt unsettled, it is also one where well-planned strategies and tools can do much for increasing the visibility and viability of distance library services. By developing an assessment strategy, distance librarians will have the means not only to demonstrate value to parent organizations and various constituencies, but also to improve operations and services. One method for creating a framework for assessment that leads to "a set of guideposts for evaluation" (Wallace & Van Fleet, 2001) is by examining the ACRL Guidelines for Distance Learning Library Services.

DEFINITIONS AND MODELS

The literature of higher education and academic librarianship discusses assessment in both broad and narrow terms. Some view it as applying to the undergraduate experience (Lambrecht, 2000, p. 25) or only to student achievement and development (Davis, 1989, p. 7).

Performance measurement, a subset of assessment, is often used interchangeably with assessment but more specifically refers to how an institution will use data. That is, performance indicators are often used to "provide evidence of what students have learned and how much, sometimes along with the cost of doing so" (Lindauer, 1998, p. 548).

Broadly defined, assessment is a mechanism that both improves accountability and learning (Ratcliff, 1996, p. 1). According to Banta, Lund, Black, and Oblander (1996), assessment is an institution's ability to "provide tangible, systematic evidence of what students know and can do as a result of the collective college experience" (p. xxii).

Most recently, assessment, particularly in the academic library setting, has come to mean how well the library supports the mission of the parent institution and how well the library achieves its own goals and objectives not only for student learning but also for organizational effectiveness, cost-efficiency, and service quality (Standards Committee, 2000).

By also identifying the various stakeholders in this enterprise, libraries are coming to terms with ways in which previously unmeasured activities can be measured. Assessment, then, can be defined as a multivariate process and product whereby goals and objectives are systematically identified, measured and evaluated for future use.

Guidelines are, in general, explanatory statements that often accompany or link to professional standards or criteria (Garten, p. 274) and can be used as a vehicle leading to coordinated effort in service delivery (Kingston, Krumberger and Peruzzi, 2000, p. 364). In the academic library setting, guidelines can often be used to help identify important institutional outcomes to which the library contributes, describe specific performance measures, and offer a conceptual framework of the assessment domains in a teaching-learning library (Lindauer, 1998, p. 546).

A model taken from business education literature shows intended learning outcomes interacting with student characteristics and the educational environment to produce actual outcomes and client satisfaction (Lambrecht, 2000, p. 27). Borrowing from management and organizational effectiveness literature and narrowing Wallace's seven models of effectiveness (Wallace & Van Fleet, p. 14), Cullen and Calvert (1995, p. 439) list four measurement models that also apply to higher education. In the goal attainment model, goals and objectives are defined and then measured to determine a fulfillment rate. The system resources model looks at how well or poorly an organization secures resources for staffing, budget and facilities. Using an internal processes model, inputs are measured for internal control purposes. Of greatest interest to service agencies is the customer satisfaction model that measures satisfaction rates. The LibQual instrument developed by the Association of Research Libraries in collaboration with Texas A&M University and with financial support from the U.S. Department of Education's Fund for the Improvement of Postsecondary Education (FIPSE) fits into this model. This spring, it will be used by Washington State University and 169 other libraries to measure library users' ideas about service quality.

STRATEGIES AND TOOLS

Critical to the success of any assessment plan are decisions made about how it will be constructed. At the most basic level, mission statements and goals are identified or written, followed by selection of measurable objectives. Once objectives are stated, data-gathering tools are chosen. After evidence is gathered, it is analyzed, interpreted, distributed and acted upon.

Tools used in assessment may be qualitative or quantitative (McClure & Lopata, 1996, p. 11), formative or summative (Weingard, 1999, pp. 148-152), and must be reliable and valid (Williams, 1994, p. 28). Examples of tools used most frequently in academic libraries to gather data include: surveys, focus groups, user panels, directed conversations, list-checking, usability studies, interviews, portfolios, statistics, observed behaviors, workflow analysis, citation or syllabi reviews, and benchmarking or best practices comparisons. A multifaceted approach is indicated (Ratcliff, 1996, p. 37), whereby all stakeholders may be included (Banta et al., p. 35; Cullen & Calvert, p. 440; and Lindauer, p. 550).

While knowledge, skills, attitudes, behaviors and values can all, in theory, be measured (Davis, 1989, p. 11), in practice the process of choosing what to assess is far from simplistic. Librarians, recognizing that reporting circulation statistics and other data to a state agency or professional organization is not in and of itself an assessment activity (Wallace & Van Fleet, 2001, p. 216), have not had experience unbundling the influence of the library from other influences on student growth (Davis, 15), including teaching and learning. At the same time, accreditation bodies although including standards, guidelines and criteria dealing with libraries, face their own set of problems in dealing with the functions of academic libraries (Williams, 1994, p. 24).

The networked environment that is distance education brings with it a new set of complexities for libraries, parent institutions and accreditors. No longer is the university a "black box where well-qualified faculty and staff and a certain number of library books magically turn out fit and educated college graduates" (Abbott, 1994, p. 82). At the same time, it is not yet known exactly what assumptions will guide decision and policy-making processes in regards to distance learning (Budd, 1998, p. 19).

Teaching, learning and research remain major functions of academia. What has changed is how the results or outcomes of those activities will be measured and demonstrated. In developing assessment strategies for their own institutions, librarians may do well to become more familiar with teaching and learning indicators, as well as faculty productivity (Lindauer, 1998, pp. 555-557) and development measurement tools around those functions.

Information literacy is an area where librarians, both distance and on-campus, can begin to make connections with the larger academic community. Often left out of campus-wide discussions on how library services and resources affect institutional goals and outcomes, librarians have often collected data and results that were not meaningful to administrators or accrediting teams (Lindauer, 1998, p. 546). Rather than being seen as just one subset of the entire network of information resources available both on and off-campus (Wolff, p. 130), information literacy training is often "viewed as directly affecting student outcomes because these skills support such general/liberal education outcomes as critical thinking, computer literacy, problem-solving and lifelong learning" (Lindauer, 1998, p. 549).

Herndon and Whitman (2001) summarize an effective strategy by stating that "the assessment process links the mission statement to the setting of service priorities, the gathering of evidence, the interpretation of that evidence (in the context of outcomes and appropriate questions or measures), and a determination of the extent to which the priorities are attained" (p. 62).

ACRL DISTANCE LEARNING LIBRARY SERVICES GUIDELINES

Written in 1967, the ACRL Guidelines for Library Services to Extension Students have evolved into the present document, most recently approved by the ACRL Board of Directors and the American Library Association Standards Committee in the fall of 2000. The intent of the guidelines has remained as providing a set of principles that libraries can draw upon to create adequate and equitable library services for students and faculty removed from a traditional campus library (Caspers, Fitts and Grover, 2000, p. 90). The document is a relevant, credible tool to use in decision-making as it is a relevant and credible tool that has been well developed, implemented, evaluated and disseminated (Kingston, p. 368; Caspers, pp. 91-92).

The guidelines may be used as a gateway to other performance or collection review measures, such as those in the standards for the College Libraries Section, the University Libraries Section, and the Community and Junior College Libraries Section, not to mention those for bibliographic instruction, information literacy and performance assessment. Some distance librarians may choose to develop assessment objectives based on these more prescriptive documents.

The DLS Guidelines can also be used as a starting point for determining what kinds of activities, services, and resources should be measured in an assessment plan. In addition to calling for access to adequate library services and resources and links between computing facilities, instructional media and telecommunication centers, the guidelines also list as a primary outcome for distance learning library services the establishment of "lifelong learning skills through bibliographic instruction and information literacy" (Guidelines Committee, 2000, p. 1025). The guidelines also give a partial list of assessment tools as well as identifying some of the stakeholders in the distance learning community.

Unlike statistical reporting of inputs and outputs that give too much data in such detail without any framework for interpreting its meaning or significance (Davis, 1989, p. 10), an assessment strategy that uses the DLS Guidelines as a starting point may help synthesize information into a recognizable structure that translates activities into knowledge and best practices (Kingston et al., p. 365) and in such a way that it can be understood by administrators and accreditors.

Whether the mission of the parent institution is to provide an experience that will "free its students from ignorance to take up responsible citizenship in the world" (Budd, 1998, p. 171), to simply provide a down-payment on a career (p. 353), or more realistically, to produce 21st century quality graduates and relevant research (Williams, 1994, p. 24), distance librarians can also use the guidelines to begin constructing objectives that correlate to institutional mission statements and coincide with national goals for critical thinking (Lindauer, 1998, p. 555).

From a range of possible objectives, distance librarians can use the guidelines to choose what activities, functions, competencies, or resources should be measured. Since what is measured is often what is valued (Ruppert, 1995, p. 17), using the guidelines to determine those measurements may be an effective strategy in the distance librarian's assessment plan.

REFERENCES

Abbott, T.E. (1994). Distance education and off-campus services: Challenges for the accreditation process and librarians. In E.D. Garten, (Ed.). *The challenge and practice of academic accreditation: A sourcebook for library administrators* (pp. 77-89). Westport, CT: Greenwood Press.

Banta, T.W., Lund, J.P., Black, K.E., and Oblander, F.W. (1996). *Assessment in practice*. San Francisco, CA: Jossey Bass.

Budd, J.M. (1998). *The Academic library: Its context, its purpose, and its operation*. Englewood, CO: Libraries Unlimited.

Caspers, J, Fritts, J., and Gover, H. Beyond the rhetoric: A study of the impact of the ACRL Guidelines for Distance Learning Services on Selected Distance Learning Programs in Higher Education. In P.S. Thomas & M. Jones (Comps.), *The Off-Campus Library Services Proceedings: Portland, OR, April 26-28, 2000* (pp. 83-97).

Cullen, R.J., and Calvert, P.J. (1995). Stakeholder perceptions of university library effectiveness. *Journal of Academic Librarianship, 21*(6), 438-448.

Davis, B.G. (1989). Demystifying assessment: Learning from the field of evaluation. In P.J. Gray (Ed.). *Achieving assessment goals using evaluation techniques* (pp. 5-20). San Francisco, CA: Jossey Bass.

Garten, E.D. (ed.). (1994). *The challenge and practice of academic accreditation*. Westport, CT: Greenwood Press.

Guidelines Committee. ACRL Distance Learning Section. (2000). ACRL guidelines for distance learning library services. *College & Research Libraries News, 61*(11), 1023-1029.

Hernon, P., and Whitman, J.R. (2001). *Delivering satisfaction and service quality: A customer-based approach for libraries*. Chicago: American Library Association.

Kingston, M.E., Krumberger, J.M., and Peruzzi, W.T. (2000). Enhancing outcomes: Guidelines, standards, and protocols. *AACN Clinical Issues, 11*(3), 363-374.

Lambrecht, J.L. (2000). Characteristics of good assessment. In J.D. Rucker and R.J. Schoenrock (Eds.). *Assessment in business education* (pp. 25-38). Reston, VA: National Business Education Association.

Lindauer, B.G. (1998). Defining and measuring the library's impact on campuswide outcomes. *College & Research Libraries, 59*(6), 546-70.

McClure, C.R., and Lopata, C.L. (1996). *Assessing the academic networked environment: Strategies and options.* Washington, DC: Coalition for Networked Information.

Ruppert, S.S. (1995). Roots and realities of state-level performance indicator systems. In G.H. Gaither (Ed.). *Assessing performance in an age of accountability: Case studies* (pp. 11-23). San Francisco, CA: Jossey Bass.

Ratcliff, J.L. (1996). *Realizing the potential: Improving postsecondary teaching, learning, and assessment.* University Park, PA: National Center on Postsecondary Teaching, Learning, and Assessment.

Standards Committee. ACRL College Libraries Section (2000). Standards for college libraries. *College & Research Libraries News, 61*(3), 175-82.

Wallace, D.P., and Van Fleet, C. (2001). *Library evaluation: A casebook and can-do guide.* Englewood, CO: Libraries Unlimited.

Weingand, D.E. (1999). *Marketing/planning library and information services.* Englewood, CO: Libraries Unlimited.

Williams, D.E. (1994). Challenges to accreditation from the new academic library environment. In E.D. Garten (Ed.). *The challenge and practice of academic accreditation: A sourcebook for library administrators* (pp. 23-31). Westport, CT: Greenwood Press.

Wolff, R.A. (1994). Rethinking library self-studies and accreditation visits. In E.D. Garten (Ed.). *The challenge and practice of academic accreditation: A sourcebook for library administrators* (pp. 23-31). Westport, CT: Greenwood Press.

Managing Thesis Anxiety: A Faculty-Librarian Partnership to Guide Off-Campus Graduate Education Students Through the Thesis Process

Rosemary Green
Mary Bowser

Shenandoah University

SUMMARY. This paper describes a pilot study, which investigates the faculty-librarian collaboration formed in a graduate education program. The levels of anxiety experienced by off-campus graduate students are examined to determine whether the partnership has had any effect. Quality of the thesis literature reviews produced by these students is also studied. Trends suggested by the data are reported.

KEYWORDS. Collaboration, faculty, graduate education, distance learners

INTRODUCTION

The off-campus graduate student must become acclimated to the requirements of an academic program in an environment apart from the traditional campus. When a master's research thesis is required for completion of the graduate program, the off-campus graduate student may undergo the entire thesis process without the benefit of interaction with faculty advisors and with mentor-peers

[Haworth co-indexing entry note]: "Managing Thesis Anxiety: A Faculty-Librarian Partnership to Guide Off-Campus Graduate Education Students Through the Thesis Process." Green, Rosemary, and Mary Bowser. Co-published simultaneously in *Journal of Library Administration* (The Haworth Information Press, an imprint of The Haworth Press, Inc.) Vol. 37, No. 3/4, 2002, pp. 341-354; and: *Distance Learning Library Services: The Tenth Off-Campus Library Services Conference* (ed: Patrick B. Mahoney) The Haworth Information Press, an imprint of The Haworth Press, Inc., 2002, pp. 341-354.

http://www.haworthpress.com/store/product.asp?sku=J111
10.1300/J111v37n03_28

who have completed the process. The student may also lack immediate access to research resources. Despite geographical limitations, these students must manage the complex process of gaining topic approval, identifying research sources, evaluating the sources, developing a comprehensive and scholarly review of the literature, and applying the research literature to their own thesis projects.

The Division of Education of the School of Arts and Sciences at Shenandoah University offers both on-campus and off-campus Master of Science in Education programs. Nearly two-thirds of the students enrolled in these programs participate as members of off-campus cohorts and complete all coursework at off-campus sites. Program courses are typically delivered by University faculty traveling to these sites; delivery format is face-to-face. Responding to a perceived need identified in evaluations of the program, a librarian began to participate more directly in the final thesis process. A teaching partnership between a graduate education professor and graduate instruction librarian was formed in 1999, and a faculty-librarian team now collaborates in teaching the four-course thesis research and composition process.

This teaching partnership has given the graduate instruction librarian an enhanced opportunity to interact directly and consistently with graduate students throughout the stages of the thesis process, from proposal to final defense. The graduate librarian instructs students in the research and evaluation strategies necessary for building a literature review during an introductory research methodology course. Typically the thesis course falls two semesters later, and, at that point, the graduate librarian instructs the students in more sophisticated strategies for identifying and analyzing research literature. Faculty and librarian guide students in determining appropriate subtopics, organizing the literature review, and establishing relationships within the body of literature.

In the interest of examining the effects that the faculty-librarian collaboration might have upon the graduate thesis process, we designed a pilot study to be undertaken in the fall 2001 term. We examined both student perception of the collaboration and quality of thesis literature reviews produced under the guidance of the faculty-librarian team.

REVIEW OF THE RELATED LITERATURE

The focus of the current study is to investigate whether the faculty-librarian collaboration affects anxiety experienced by off-campus graduate education students during the process of researching and producing the thesis literature review. The current study also includes an investigation of whether the faculty-librarian collaboration has affected the quality of the final literature reviews authored by those students. With these topics under consideration, the published literature in three areas was considered: the nature of faculty-librarian collaborations, types of anxiety among graduate students, and the scholarly literature review.

Faculty-Librarian Collaboration

During the last twenty years, academic libraries have undergone a dramatic shift in emphasis from traditional printed sources to sources presented in the electronic format. Consequently, students and faculty engaged in research continue to adjust their research strategies. Building upon the trend in bibliographic instruction that has evolved during the same twenty-year span, strong relationships between academic departments and the librarians who have supported these departments have developed (D'Amicantonio & Scepanski, 1997; Robertson & Sullivan, 2000).

The literature regarding faculty-librarian collaborations can be divided into two categories. A greater number of examples regarding faculty-librarian collaborations concentrates on the collegial model formed by teaching faculty and library staff (D'Amicantonio & Scepanski, 1997; Heller-Ross, 1996; Wright, 2000). In this model, responsibilities such as library collection development, bibliographic instruction, and academic curricula development are shared by teaching faculty and by librarians. Heller-Ross (1996) and Wright (2000) both suggest that working partnerships between academic and library units would ensure academic quality for students of the institution. A second and smaller group of publications describes the team approach to course instruction in which a member of the teaching faculty and an instruction librarian collaborate to teach a significant portion or all of an academic course (Caspers & Lenn, 2000; Isbell, 1995; Stein & Lamb, 1998). While many examples of faculty-librarian collaborations have been identified, few describe partnerships developed to the same degree as the graduate thesis course described in our study. Furthermore, the majority of team-taught courses thus identified in the current literature have been formed during the instruction of undergraduate courses.

In describing a team-taught undergraduate writing course, Isbell (1995) reports that students perceive both the librarian and faculty member as facilitators, resource providers, consultants, and experts–roles that are often assigned separately to one or the other but not to both. Stein and Lamb (1998) describe an upper level undergraduate social psychology class in which the teaching faculty and librarian collaborate extensively in designing course objectives, guiding the students through the literature review process, and assessing final projects. The teaching format allows repetitive introduction of research concepts and facilitates the advancement of student skills to a more sophisticated level. Stein and Lamb report that quality of student projects has improved as a result of the close faculty-librarian collaboration. Caspers and Lenn (2000) indicate that this collaboration model is "exciting because it is so unique. Because few librarians are working collaboratively with teaching faculty, the opportunity to do so seems unusual" (p. 151).

Of particular interest to our study is the 1985 article by Bailey entitled "Thesis Practicum and the Librarian's Role." Bailey recommends a three-way partnership formed among the graduate thesis student, the thesis advisor, and the librarian. Macauley and Cavanagh (2000) draw upon that recommendation and, in describing the same partnership, state that the benefit to be gained "combines the various talents and strengths that only disparate experts can achieve" (p. 228).

Anxiety Among Graduate Students

The literature identifies several contributors to anxiety among graduate students. Among these factors are anxieties associated with library research, writing apprehension, and a sense of isolation experienced by graduate students in general (Gottlieb, 1994; Onwuegbuzie, 1998; Onwuegbuzie & Jiao, 1998). The off-campus graduate student engaged in thesis preparation may experience additional factors, such as social and geographic isolation and concern about use of technology (Jegede & Kirkwood, 1994; Kerka, 1996), which may contribute to heightened levels of anxiety.

The production of the graduate thesis literature review requires both the ability to search for literature and the writing skills to present that literature (Bruce, 1994). As such, the process of developing and composing a literature review presents a source of anxiety for many graduate students. The identification and retrieval of research materials necessitates the use of library resource tools and materials. Preparation for library use may induce a situation-specific anxiety known as library anxiety (Onwuegbuzie & Jiao, 1998). Graduate students in particular have been found to "become anxious when undertaking library research" (Onwuegbuzie, 1997, p. 6). The anxiety is related to factors such as confidence in one's library research skills, perception of library staff responsiveness, and difficulties with using technology (Bostick, 1992). Furthermore, when the task is complex, such as the research and completion of the literature review, the level of anxiety among graduate students may be maximized (Onwuegbuzie, 1997). Library anxiety may be addressed by both the teaching faculty and collaborating librarian with classroom and instructional techniques.

Graduate students often have little or no experience writing in a technical style; that style is necessary for composition of the literature review and clear documentation of sources (Oliver, 1995). Consequently, the thesis candidate may experience writing difficulties which in turn lead to writing anxiety or writing apprehension. At the graduate level, writing anxiety appears to be widespread. Nevertheless, thesis completion requires competence in writing

(Onwuegbuzie, 1998). Bloom (1981) recommends that graduate schools incorporate thesis research through the entire graduate program, thereby providing students with opportunities to practice scholarly writing. Instruction in research methodology and writing as an integral component of the graduate curriculum should also be included. Students should be encouraged to seek exemplars of form, style, methodology, and bibliographic format in the expert professional literature of their disciplines.

Distance education students experience isolation to some extent (Jegede & Kirkwood, 1994; Kerka, 1996; Macauley & Cavanaugh, 2000). Coupled with the sense of isolation often experienced by graduate students in general (Gottlieb, 1994), the off-campus graduate student may view the thesis process as a difficult task. The general profile of the distance learner is an adult, one who has elected to return to the academic environment following some period of absence (Heller-Ross, 1996; Jegede & Kirkwood, 1994). As such, these students may lack current library skills, recent experience with academic libraries, and experience using electronic research sources. Distance learning requires a format in which technology is necessary for the delivery of course materials and for the facilitation of communication with faculty, librarian, and fellow students. Some students are not comfortable with such a format (Kerka, 1996; Piotrowski & Vodanovich, 2000).

The off-campus graduate student is required to undertake a dual education (Haythornwaite, Kazmer, Robins & Shoemaker, 2000). This student must acquire technological skills while learning the concepts, literature, and methodology of the subject discipline. The off-campus student considers distance from an academic library as well as an overall feeling of isolation to be problems (Jegede & Kirkwood, 1994). Students surveyed about their feelings regarding learning at a distance used descriptors such as "afraid," "panicky," "nervous," and "worried" (p. 290).

The Scholarly Literature Review

The production of the scholarly literature review requires skills in planning, information retrieval and evaluation, and composition. According to Cooper (1989), social science methods texts have typically failed to give adequate attention to the literature review. While methods of identifying and accessing information are addressed, "little is available on the crucial process of preparation of the review" (Libutti & Kopala, 1995, p. 15).

The literature review is both process and product. The novice graduate researcher initially views the literature review as a list of sources. Eventually the literature review evolves into a vehicle for shaping research, then a final integrated report (Cole, 1993). The extent to which supervisory intervention by teaching faculty, graduate advisor, or librarian might be needed is unclear. Nevertheless, as the literature review process requires transition to a sophisticated product (Bruce, 1994), the interaction of student, faculty, and librarian is important. Both librarian and teaching faculty should participate in instructing graduate students in developing useful strategies for development of the literature review and in critically examining the literature review (Gottlieb, 1994).

METHOD

Recognizing that off-campus graduate students experience anxiety produced by several factors associated with completing the thesis process while coping with geographical limitations, we have first examined levels of anxiety among these students. In a second part of the study, we have evaluated quality of thesis literature reviews. We consider this to be a pilot study; as such, the sample size is small and the instruments under preliminary development. Collection of data for determining validity and reliability is ongoing.

The population for our study was drawn from off-campus cohorts of Master of Science in Education students. Eighteen participants were selected from among six cohorts, and those participants were surveyed for levels of anxiety. Eight of the participants were selected from cohorts that had received little or no instruction from the graduate instruction librarian during their graduate program (pre-collaboration). Ten participants were selected from cohorts in which the collaborative model was used, and the graduate thesis and research courses were team-taught by the graduate faculty member and the graduate instruction librarian (post-collaboration).

An eighteen-question survey was mailed to the participants with a cover letter describing the pilot study and specifically inviting their participation; a self-addressed stamped envelope was enclosed. Two weeks later, another copy of the survey was mailed with a second cover letter and stamped return envelope. A total of thirteen responses or 72% of the surveys were completed and returned. Twelve surveys were included in the data analysis.

The survey questionnaire consisted of eighteen affective items (see Appendix). The first twelve questions were designed to identify the degree to which tasks or factors relative to the development and composition of the thesis produced anxiety. Using a five-point Likert scale, respondents were asked to rate tasks such as library research (Bostick, 1992; Onwuegbuzie & Jiao, 1998), and writing (Bloom, 1981; Onwuegbuzie, 1998) and factors such as the use of technology (Bostick, 1992) and engagement as an off-campus student (Jegede & Kirkwood, 1994; Kerka, 1996). Two questions rating the anxiety produced by the process surrounding the thesis defense were also included. The remaining six questions asked students to identify with which of the aforementioned tasks the faculty member, librarian, and cohort members were most helpful and least helpful.

A two-sample, one-tail *t* test was performed for each of the twelve items rating anxiety, and scores from pre-collaboration and post-collaboration respondents were compared. A frequency distribution was used to analyze the results on the last six survey questions rating helpfulness.

In a second part of this pilot study, ten thesis literature reviews were evaluated. The sample was drawn from theses authored by graduate student participants who had received the survey questionnaire: five from pre-collaboration participants and five from post-collaboration participants. A seven-item, three-category rubric sample was used as the foundation (ED690: Assessment Rubric, 2000). Our pilot rubric included the following criteria: historical/theoretical background, seminal studies, breadth, depth, quality, relatedness, organization, transitions, rationale, clarity, and bibliographic quality.

The ten thesis literature reviews were distributed among four faculty readers. Each literature review was rated by two separate readers. The faculty readers were drawn from the University health professions, music education, communications, and library faculty. They were chosen for individual strengths such as experience in directing graduate research writing, experience with thesis or dissertation writing, professional writing expertise, and professional expertise as a reader/evaluator.

The faculty readers were initially trained using a sample literature review, and their inter-rater reliability was established in a session in which they rated a thesis taken from another department in the master's program. Because this part of the study is one of several phases of development of the literature review rubric, we asked the raters to record specific concerns with the rubric as they were using it. We are using this collateral feedback to revise the rubric for the next implementation. We are considering their expressed concerns in relationship to their various strengths as readers as we make our recommendations for revision of the rubric and the process under consideration. Also, four literature reviews received widely varying ratings and were removed from the analysis because they represented extremes that could have been caused by our reader selection or training process. Six remaining literature reviews, three from the pre-collaboration group and three from the post-collaboration group, were analyzed by performing two-sample, one-tail *t* tests on each of the twelve items in the rubric.

FINDINGS AND DISCUSSION

Results obtained by analyzing the eighteen-question survey are inconclusive. As a pilot, the sample was too small to establish defensible decisions.

Nevertheless, preliminary findings have demonstrated trends in the relationship between anxiety and tasks or factors related to thesis production, pre-collaboration and post-collaboration.

Table 1 summarizes the findings for Questions 1, 5, 6, and 11, questions related to library research, technology use for writing, status as distance learners, and post-defense writing revisions. The two-sample *t* tests indicated that each had significant positive results ($p < 0.05$), indicative of a trend toward reduction of anxiety in the post-collaboration students.

Question 12, related to the process of post-defense bibliographic revisions, was indicated to be significant positive ($p < 0.001$). (See Table 2.) This finding pointed toward a greater reduction of anxiety in the post-collaboration students during the post-defense stage.

The analysis of Questions 2, 4, and 8 did not reveal statistical significance. Thus, no shift in anxiety trends were noticed for these three questions pertaining to literature review composition, technology use for research, and thesis writing. Questions 9 and 10, which were related to the thesis defense, showed no significant gain in anxiety. However, these two questions had a positive trend related to less anxiety concerning the thesis defense in the post-collaboration respondents.

A negative *t* was obtained in the analysis of Question 3, writing the literature review, and Question 7, composing the thesis. Thus a trend for post-collaboration students to feel greater anxiety during these tasks was indicated.

We then sought to identify connections among the trends in these limited findings. Students may tend to sense greater anxiety in writing the literature re-

TABLE 1. Results Obtained from t Tests, Graduate Survey Questions 1, 5, 6, 11

	Question 1. Library research		Question 5. Technology for writing	
	Post-Collaboration	Pre-Collaboration	Post-Collaboration	Pre-Collaboration
M	3.33	2.17	2.83	1.17
t	1.83		2.17	
p	0.05		0.03	
t Critical	1.81		1.81	

	Question 6. Off-campus student		Question 11. Post-defense writing revisions	
	Post-Collaboration	Pre-Collaboration	Post-Collaboration	Pre-Collaboration
M	4.17	2.67	3.17	1.83
t	2.18		1.98	
p	0.03		0.04	
t Critical	1.81		1.81	

TABLE 2. Results Obtained from t Tests, Graduate Survey Question 12

| | Question 12. Post-defense APA revisions | |
	Post-Collaboration	Pre-Collaboration
M	3.33	1.83
t	3.31	
p	< 0.001	
t Critical	1.81	

view and in overall thesis development and construction that takes place during the collaboration period. The opportunity for managing anxiety is offered at that time by the faculty-librarian team. This reported anxiety is experienced within the supportive context of the graduate thesis class, where writing the literature review and thesis composition are repeatedly addressed. Trends derived from the findings indicate that anxieties generated by the tasks of performing library research, using technology for writing, and completing bibliographic and other post-defense revisions were reduced among post-collaboration students. The process and product of library research receive heavy concentration in the graduate thesis class, and, because of the nature of this emphasis as well as the timing of the additional support, students tend to feel less anxious about library research. The use of technological tools for writing is promoted and instruction offered in the thesis class, possibly affecting student anxiety. We have also observed that student skills in using technology continue to improve, and that improvement most likely contributes to this trend as well.

The findings also indicate a trend toward reduced anxiety among post-collaboration students in completing the structural, bibliographic, and editorial revisions required after thesis defense. The frequency data support the trends indicating the benefits of the librarian-faculty team approach. We have concluded that, as a team, we have used the benefits of our partnership and increased oversight to guide the students in producing better constructed theses to take to defense. In particular, our partnership may also affect the trend toward a reduction in anxiety among post-collaboration respondents engaging in the thesis process as off-campus students. These students may be responding as well to an overall increase in library support for off-campus students, support which includes enhanced availability of electronic resources as well as document delivery.

In analyzing the frequency distribution of the data from the last six questions on the survey, we found that the numbers are indicative of possible trends. We identified clusters of supportive feedback for the faculty advisor for Questions 2 and 3 (composing and writing the literature review), and again for Questions 6 through

11 (off-campus students, composing and writing the thesis, and preparing/conducting the thesis defense). The librarian's cluster of positive feedback is centered on Questions 1 through 4 (library research, composing and writing the literature review, and research technology), and then Question 12 (APA format revisions). These frequency data support the trends which indicate benefits of the librarian-faculty team approach. Each individual's strengths counterbalance the other's limitations and produce effective teaching throughout the thesis process.

At the present time, results from analyzing the twelve-item rubric are also inconclusive. We have determined that the rubric is a valuable instrument, and we are continuing to adjust instrument design and application. In the next stage of development, we will obtain a larger, random sample with $N = 30$, which will allow for higher frequency of paired raters. On the instrument itself, we are expanding the three-category rating scale to a five-category scale in order to establish a range of response, giving a more precise separation of student report for each category. We will conduct a more extensive rater training, thereby gaining higher inter-rater reliability. We have established two criteria for rater selection: experience with thesis research writing and familiarity with topics in education.

It would appear that we are creating trends in the research classroom. One notable trend among post-collaboration students is the reduction of the anxiety related to thesis tasks and factors. A second trend is the shift of anxiety perception toward the earlier phases of the thesis process; during the pre-defense phase, the faculty-librarian partnership can engage intervention techniques. We are continuing to follow up on this pilot study. We are interested in determining whether the follow up is consistent with the trends indicated thus far and whether the trends continue to hold true.

Development of instruments and data gathering are ongoing. Any results gained since the preparation of this paper will be reported in the authors' presentation at the Cincinnati Conference.

CONCLUSION

Graduate students often present highly individualized needs (Cole, 1996), particularly as they advance through the thesis process. Guidance by a team of two experts provides greater response to those individual needs and fosters a range of skills (Gottlieb, 1994; Libutti & Kopala, 1995). Recently, one of our thesis class members said, "The collaboration allows for a broader view of the thesis writing process. Each has a separate expertise that allows me to make better decisions."

Various course- and program-related strategies are useful in alleviating the sense of anxiety and isolation often experienced by the off-campus graduate student (Haythornwaite et al., 2000). An individual's participation within a cohort of similar students, such as the cohorts studied here, helps in moving the student from the position of an isolated learner to becoming a member of a learning community. Private communication in person-to-person contact, such as private conferencing with faculty or librarian, which we are able to provide in the face-to-face environment, is also important. Because the graduate librarian attends the thesis class on an ongoing basis, group and individual research questions can be personally addressed as they arise in the thesis process. Another of our graduate students recently commented, "I feel as if I have more than one faculty member to guide me in the process."

We have found that weekly contact with class members facilitates regular submission of written drafts of the thesis, including cumulative drafts of the literature review (Gottlieb, 1994). Consequently, the students receive regular, timely, and appropriate feedback from faculty and librarian readers (Aspland, Edwards, O'Leary & Ryan, 1999; Gottlieb, 1994). Such feedback can help reduce writing anxiety and can be provided by both members of the faculty-librarian team. Our students have noted that they get assistance quickly, and one student said, "The collaboration allows for quick feedback for both research and format questions as well as for content questions."

Library anxiety can be reduced by interaction with a librarian (Mellon, 1986), a trend to which our study points. When the graduate student is encouraged to become comfortable in consulting with a librarian, particularly during the earlier stages of thesis development, the student gains additional support in research and writing. To that point, we received the student comment, "I can't imagine going through this process without the librarian."

As we continue to develop this project, we look forward to gaining stronger evidence that the faculty-librarian collaboration model can be of benefit to the off-campus graduate education student.

REFERENCES

Aspland, T., Edwards, H., O'Leary, J., & Ryan, Y. (1999). Tracking new directions in the evaluation of postgraduate supervision. *Innovative Higher Education, 24,* 127-147.

Bailey, B. (1985). Thesis practicum and the librarian's role. *Journal of Academic Librarianship, 11,* 79-81.

Bloom, L. Z. (1981, March). *Why graduate students can't write: Implications of research on writing anxiety for graduate education.* Paper presented at the annual meeting of the Conference of College Composition and Communication, Dallas, TX. (ERIC Document Reproduction Service ED199710).

Bostick, S. L. (1992). *The development and validation of the Library Anxiety Scale.* Unpublished doctoral dissertation, Wayne State University, Detroit, MI.

Bruce, C. (1994). Supervising literature reviews. In O. Zuber-Skerritt & Y. Ryan (Eds.), *Quality in postgraduate education* (pp. 143-155). London: Kogan Page.

Caspers, J., & Lenn, K. (2000). The future of collaboration between librarians and teaching faculty. In D. Raspa & D. Ward (Eds.), *The collaborative imperative: Librarians and faculty working together in the information universe* (pp. 148-154). Chicago: American Library Association.

Cole, K. (1993). *Doctoral students in education and factors related to the literature review process.* Unpublished master's thesis, Fort Hays State University, Fort Hays, KS. (ERIC Document Reproduction Service ED349892).

Cooper, H. M. (1989). *Integrating research: A guide for literature reviews* (2nd ed.). Newbury Park, CA: Sage.

D'Amicantonio, J., & Scepanski, J. M. (1997). Strengthening teacher preparation through a library program. *Education Libraries, 21*(1/2), 11-16.

ED 690: Assessment Rubric/Criteria for Literature Review. (2000). Retrieved March 1, 2001, from San Diego State University, College of Education site: http://edweb. sdsu.edu/Courses/Ed690DR/grading/literaturereviewrubrique.html.

Gottlieb, N. (1994). Supervising the writing of a thesis. In O. Zuber-Skerritt & Y. Ryan (Eds.), *Quality in postgraduate education* (pp. 110-119). London: Kogan Page.

Haythornwaite, C., Kazmer, M. M., Robins, J., & Shoemaker, S. (2000). Community development among distance learners: Temporal and technological implications. *Journal of Computer-Mediated Communication, 6*(1), 1-25.

Heller-Ross, H. (1996). Librarian and faculty partnerships for distance education. *MC Journal; The Journal of Academic Media Librarianship, 41*(1), 1-8.

Isbell, D. (1995). Teaching writing and research as inseparable: A faculty-librarian teaching team. *Reference Services Review, 23*(4), 51-62.

Jegede, O. J., & Kirkwood, J. (1994). Students' anxiety in learning through distance education. *Distance Education, 15*, 279-290.

Kerka, S. (1996). *Distance learning, the Internet, and the World Wide Web.* Columbus, OH: ERIC Clearinghouse on Adult, Career, and Vocational Education. (ERIC Document Reproduction Service ED395214).

Libutti, P., & Kopala, M. (1995). The doctoral student, the dissertation, and the library: A review of the literature. *The Reference Librarian, 48*, 5-25.

Macauley, P., & Cavanagh, A. K. (2000, April). *Doctoral dissertations at a distance; A novel approach from downunder.* Paper presented at the Ninth Off-Campus Library Services Conference, Portland, OR.

Mellon, C. A. (1986). Library anxiety: A grounded theory and its development. *College and Research Libraries, 47*, 160-165.

Oliver, P. V. (1995). *Learning to write, writing to learn: A study on process-oriented writing in graduate education.* Hartford, CT: University of Hartford. (ERIC Document Reproduction Service ED401850).

Onwuegbuzie, A. J. (1997). Writing a research proposal: The role of library anxiety, statistics anxiety, and composition anxiety. *Library and Information Science Research, 19*, 5-33.

Onwuegbuzie, A. J. (1998). The relationship between writing anxiety and learning styles among graduate students. *Journal of College Student Development, 39*, 589-598.

Onwuegbuzie, A. J., & Jiao, Q. G. (1998). Understanding library-anxious graduate students. *Library Review, 47,* 217-224.

Piotrowski, C., & Vodanovich, S. J. (2000). Are the reported barriers to internet-based instruction warranted? A synthesis of recent research. *Education, 121*(1), 48-54.

Robertson, S., & Sullivan, S. (2000, October). *The rediscovered agents of change: Librarians working with academics to close the information gap.* Paper presented at ALIA 2000: Capitalizing on Knowledge; The Information Profession in the 21st Century, Canberra, Australia. (ERIC Document Reproduction Service ED452877).

Stein, L. L., & Lamb, J. M. (1998). Not just another BI: Faculty-librarian collaboration to guide students through the research process. *Research Strategies, 16*(1), 29-39.

Wright, C. A. (2000). Information literacy within the general education program: Implications for distance education. *JGE: Journal of General Education, 49*(1), 23-33.

APPENDIX

Graduate Survey
Shenandoah University, Division of Education

Using a 1-5 scale where **1 is lowest** and **5 is highest**, rate the level of anxiety you experienced when undertaking each task. Circle your answer.

	Low			High	
1. Library research	1	2	3	4	5
2. Composing the literature review	1	2	3	4	5
3. Writing the literature review	1	2	3	4	5
4. Using technology for research	1	2	3	4	5
5. Using technology for writing	1	2	3	4	5
6. Engaging in the thesis process as an off-campus student	1	2	3	4	5
7. Composing your thesis	1	2	3	4	5
8. Writing your thesis	1	2	3	4	5
9. Preparing for your thesis defense	1	2	3	4	5
10. Your thesis defense	1	2	3	4	5
11. Completing the final thesis revisions recommended at your thesis defense	1	2	3	4	5
12. Completing the final APA and literature review revisions	1	2	3	4	5

APPENDIX (continued)

Select one or more appropriate responses from the preceding 12 tasks. Write the number of the task(s) beside the question.

13. In which of the preceding 12 tasks was your primary faculty advisor most helpful?

14. In which of the preceding 12 tasks was your primary faculty advisor least helpful?

15. In which of the preceding 12 tasks was the graduate librarian most helpful?

16. In which of the preceding 12 tasks was the graduate librarian least helpful?

17. In which of the preceding 12 tasks was your cohort most helpful?

18. In which of the preceding 12 tasks was your cohort least helpful?

Reducing High Anxiety:
Responsive Library Services
to Off-Campus Nontraditional Students

Karen J. Harrell

Mercer University

SUMMARY. Reentry, adult, and nontraditional students attending classes at off-campus sites have special needs and situations that require responsive programming. The average student attending classes at Mercer University's Extended Education Centers is female and 33 years-old. Many students have full-time jobs and child care responsibilities. Fear of failure, lack of confidence, commitments to family and job, lack of technological knowledge and geographical barriers all contribute to the high anxiety level of many off-campus adult students. This paper presents demographic data on adult students, describes the andragogy model of adult education, summarizes library literature on serving adult students, and outlines responsive library programs for off-campus adult and nontraditional students.

KEYWORDS. Distance learners, nontraditional learners, library services, distance education

Reentry, adult, and nontraditional students attending classes at off-campus sites have special needs and situations that require responsive programming. While the students who attend classes at Mercer University's Extended Education Centers are a diverse group, most of them share some common character-

[Haworth co-indexing entry note]: "Reducing High Anxiety: Responsive Library Services to Off-Campus Nontraditional Students." Harrell, Karen J. Co-published simultaneously in *Journal of Library Administration* (The Haworth Information Press, an imprint of The Haworth Press, Inc.) Vol. 37, No. 3/4, 2002, pp. 355-365; and: *Distance Learning Library Services: The Tenth Off-Campus Library Services Conference* (ed: Patrick B. Mahoney) The Haworth Information Press, an imprint of The Haworth Press, Inc., 2002, pp. 355-365.

http://www.haworthpress.com/store/product.asp?sku=J111
10.1300/J111v37n03_29

istics. The majority of our students are female; they have children at home; they are full-time students; and they work full-time. All of these factors contribute to a high level of stress and anxiety.

Mercer University considered these factors when designing library services for students at the Extended Education Centers. The key ingredient was to provide for individualized and in-person services, including bibliographic instruction sessions at a center and rapid response to telephone and e-mail inquiries. Essential in the design of these programs is knowledge of the students' demographics and awareness of adult student characteristics.

MERCER UNIVERSITY'S DIVISION OF EXTENDED EDUCATION

Mercer University is a church-related institution of higher learning that seeks to achieve excellence and scholarly discipline in the fields of liberal learning and professional knowledge. Mercer has an undergraduate population of 4,700 located on two campuses and four off-campus sites in the state of Georgia. The centers are located in Griffin, south metro Atlanta; Douglas County, west metro Atlanta; Covington, east metro Atlanta; and Eastman, south central Georgia. Recent enrollment figures revealed that 39% of the undergraduates take classes at one of the four off-campus Extended Education Centers.

Mercer University Extended Education programs offer seven bachelor degrees and two Teacher Certifications. Classes are taught at night and on Saturdays during eight-week sessions. Most students take two classes each eight-week session or four classes per semester, which is considered a full load.

MERCER UNIVERSITY EXTENDED EDUCATION
LIBRARY SERVICES

Mercer University Libraries include the Jack Tarver Library (Tarver) on the Macon Campus, the Monroe F. Swilley, Jr. Library (Swilley) on the Atlanta Campus, and the Libraries at our four off-campus Extended Education Centers. The Swilley Library serves Mercer University's graduate and professional school campus. Most of these library materials support graduate-level students in education, business, pharmacy, theology, engineering, and recently nursing with the addition of the Georgia Baptist College of Nursing. The Tarver Library serves Mercer University's undergraduate campus and supports the four undergraduate colleges and schools on that campus. Separate libraries, not under the Dean of the University Libraries, serve the medical and law schools.

Extended Education Library Services is an extension of the Tarver Library. The Extended Education Library Services Coordinator, who is based at the Extended Education Center in Griffin, administers library services and programs. The only other staff member is a part-time Library Assistant who operates the library at the largest center in Douglas County. Circulating material housed at any Mercer Library can be checked out and sent to any other Mercer Library via an intra-university courier system. This includes government documents, since the Tarver Library is a Federal Depository. Searches can be conducted on the online catalog and titles can be requested for delivery through the same system.

The primary online source is GALILEO, GeorgiA LIbrary LEarning Online, which provides access to over 100 databases indexing thousands of periodicals and scholarly journals and e-books. Individual subscriptions are held for databases that meet the unique needs of Mercer Extended Education students and faculty. Reference services are provided by reference librarians at both the Swilley and Tarver libraries and include telephone, e-mail, and in-person assistance. In addition to traveling to each metro Atlanta site once a week, the Extended Education Library Services Coordinator teaches Library Instruction Sessions to classes at the four centers to assist the students in identifying, locating, and procuring materials.

STUDENT DEMOGRAPHICS

It is no secret that the numbers of adult students in academia have greatly increased in the last 30 years. The biggest jump was in the 30 and over group, 1,310,000 or 15% of all college students in 1971 and 3,973,000 or 27% in 1998 (Digest of Education Statistics, 1999). In 1986, there were 2,384,000 students 24 years of age and over or 40% of all college students. By 1998 this age group remained at 40% yet had increased to 5,947,000 (NCES 2000, Table 11A). The U.S. Department of Education projects that in the year 2011, there will be almost seven million students aged 24 or over enrolled in degree granting institutions (NCES 2000, Table 11B).

The number of adult women students has risen significantly as well. In 1970, there were 879,000 adult women students or 10% of all students. In 1997, there were 3,868,000 adult women students or 27% of all students (Digest of Education Statistics, 1999). Adult female students have many of the same motivations, barriers and stresses as adult male students. The stress factors do not seem to be related to gender, but rather to which roles the student has outside of class. A male student with children who does not have a spouse assisting with child care or other home responsibilities will be just as anxious

and stressed as his female counterparts. A single adult student with no children
or marital responsibilities, but in a 60 hour a week job, will have a different set
of stress factors.

According to the most recent statistics, 79% of Mercer University's off-campus students are female and 21% are male. Fifty-one percent are white, 38% are
African-American, 4% are Hispanic, 4% are International, and 5% are unknown
or other. The mean age of our students is 33 (Term Enrollment Profiles, 2001).
Comparing current numbers with the data from past years, the Mercer University's Department of Extended Education has predicted the "minority" adult students will become the majority in the next 2-4 years (Johnson, 2001).

FALL 2001 LIBRARY SURVEY

An informal survey was administered in the fall of 2001 at the three largest
Extended Education Centers. The survey was administered to determine
non-academic responsibilities, access to technology, and library usage. A total
of 142 surveys were completed.

The survey revealed the following potential stress factors for Mercer University students taking courses at one of the Extended Education Centers: 67%
have full-time jobs, 17% have part-time jobs, 68% have children living at
home, and 95% are full-time students taking 12 hours or more per semester
(Table 1).

Technology is another potential stress factor, so survey respondents were
asked about their access to a computer, including computer ownership. The
vast majority, 90%, have a home computer they use for their university classes.
The respondents also use the computers located at the Extended Education
Centers' computer labs and libraries. These numbers assist us in planning for
technology expansion and online subscriptions (Table 2).

We also asked students to indicate their use of the computer, including
searching the Internet for research purposes. Of 119 total respondents, 110,
92%, indicated that they do conduct research using the Internet (Table 3).

Finally, to determine the best use of Library resources, respondents were
asked to indicate their level of Center Library usage. Weekly or occasional use

TABLE 1. Stress Factors for Mercer University Extended Education Students

Married	Single	FT Job	PT Job	Unemployed	Children	FT Student	PT Student
59%	41%	67%	17%	15%	68%	95%	5%

of the Center Library was the response of 78%, while 40% indicated weekly or occasional use of print resources, and 63% indicated weekly or occasional use of the Library computer (Table 4).

The survey confirmed anecdotal information that most of our students are using their home computers to complete their university assignments. To a lesser degree, they are also using the computers at the Center Libraries. They are using the print resources at the Center Libraries even less. We also learned that 95% of the respondents use another area library on an occasional or weekly basis.

A review of the demographic and survey information reveals that the average Mercer Extended Education student is a 33 year-old female. She may be married or single and probably has young children at home. She works full-time, attends classes full-time, and has a home computer with Internet access. She is also stressed.

TABLE 2. Computer Ownership by Mercer University Extended Education Students

Own a PC	Do not own a PC	Home and Mercer PCs	Mercer PCs only
90%	10%	68%	93%

TABLE 3. Computer Usage by Mercer University Extended Education Students

Conduct assignment-related research on the Internet	92%
Write papers using word processing software	92%
Other applications, such as presentation or spreadsheet software	75%
E-mail	86%

TABLE 4. Center Library Use by Mercer University Extended Education Students

Usage	Weekly	Occasional	Never	Some
General library	26%	78%	36%	78%
Print resources	10%	46%	83%	40%
Library PC	29%	58%	52%	63%
Other library	31%	98%	7%	95%

ADULT LEARNING THEORY

Adult educators are still in the process of defining and codifying differences between adult learners and other types of learners. There is disagreement among some adult educators as to whether or not adults learn differently from children. There is also more than one model or theory of adult education. The best known of these theories is andragogy. The term andragogy is from the Greek word "andros" which means, "man" or "grown person." Malcolm Knowles first introduced the concept of andragogy to this country in 1968. He contrasted pedagogy, the art and science of teaching children, with andragogy, "the art and science of helping adults learn" (Knowles, 1998). Simply put, andragogy implies that adults learn best in a more collaborative environment than in the traditional "sage on the stage" model.

Knowles' Assumptions About the Adult Learner (as summarized by Merriam and Cafferella, 1999):

- As a person matures, his or her self-concept moves from that of a dependent personality toward one of a self-directing human being.
- An adult accumulates a growing reservoir of experience, which is a rich resource of learning.
- The readiness of an adult to learn is closely related to the developmental tasks of his or her social role.
- There is a change in time perspective as people mature–from future application of knowledge to immediacy of application. Thus, an adult is more problem-centered than subject-centered in learning.
- Adults are motivated to learn by internal factors rather than external ones.

Using Knowles' model, Stephen Lieb (2001) has developed a list of characteristics of adults as learners:

- autonomous and self-directed
- accumulated a foundation of life experiences and knowledge that may include work-related activities, family responsibilities, and previous education
- goal-oriented
- relevancy-oriented
- practical, focusing on the aspects of a lesson most useful to them in their work
- need to be shown respect–as do all learners.

Based on his own model, Knowles lists the elements for designing instruction for adults (Ingram, 2000):

- climate of openness and respect
- learner involvement in planning
- learner involvement in diagnosis of needs
- learner collaboration in formulation of objectives
- sequenced design of instruction
- experiential learning activities
- mutual evaluation.

Other common characteristics of adult and nontraditional students:

- They are motivated by hope for a better job, career, or standard of living.
- The roles of employee, spouse, and parent are perceived as fundamental to self-image. The role of student may be considered secondary.
- Most adult or nontraditional students are in transition. Changes in marital or employment status and children leaving home are among the reasons given for starting an educational program.
- They are highly motivated and achievement oriented.
- They usually make better grades than younger counterparts, but may take longer to complete their programs.
- They are not usually interested in extracurricular activities.
- They tend to be more tied "to career culture than to academic culture" (Kerka, 1995).

Many off-campus adult and nontraditional students experience barriers to services and programs. Some of these barriers are:

- Geographic barriers. Traditional college students attend classes and live on campus within driving and walking distance of campus resources. Mercer's Extended Education students live and work in the same community as the off-campus center, but they often do not have access to many resources available on the main campus. Classes are taught at night and on Saturdays. Most campus support offices close at 5:00 p.m. The Tarver Library, location of many resources, is 50 miles from the closest Extended Education Center.
- Time constraints. Due to their work schedules or family responsibilities, they may not have access to administrative and support services during business hours.
- Psychological or mental barriers. Nontraditional students are more likely to be "at-risk," coming from a background without role models. They may also suffer from a fear of failure and lack of confidence.

LIBRARY LITERATURE REVIEW

Much that has been published about adult learners and library services has been in the areas of reference and bibliographic instruction. Librarians at community-based institutions like community, vocational, and technical colleges seem to produce more literature in this area than those at more traditional, four-year institutions. The following is a short list of valuable resources.

Starting with Sheridan's 1986 article "Andragogy: A New Concept for Academic Librarians," we have been steadily increasing our knowledge of adult learners as library patrons. Sheridan outlines the history of andragogy and applies its principles to library instruction.

Witucke's article "Off-Campus Library Services: Leading the Way" (1990) examines the adjustments off-campus library programs have made in creating services to nontraditional students and how those could be adapted to on-campus library programs.

Hammond's "Nontraditional Students and the Library: Opinions, Preferences, and Behaviors" (1994) is a report on a survey conducted at Arizona State University West. In it, both traditional and nontraditional students were asked to give their status (full or part-time), gender, age, and library usage habits. One significant finding was nontraditional students were actually more comfortable with using electronic resources than previously published literature had indicated.

Niemi and Ehrhard's "Off-Campus Library Support for Distance Adult Learners" (1998) is aimed specifically at those librarians who provide off-campus library services. This article demonstrates how combining knowledge of adult student characteristics with available technological delivery methods can produce a successful distance library program.

Reference Services for the Adult Learner: Challenging Issues for the Traditional and Technological Era (2000), which was also published as issue 69/70 of *The Reference Librarian*, is a wonderful resource. It is a collection of 34 articles with sections on "Information Explosion, Technophobia, and Technostress," "Understanding the Characteristics, Needs and Expectations of Adult Learners," "Theories of Adult Learning: Implications for Reference and Instructional Services," and most welcome, "From a Distance: Providing Reference and Instructional Services For the Adult Learner."

In "Can We Still Do Business as Usual?" an excellent paper delivered at the 8th Annual ACRL National Conference, Fidishun (1997) states,

> In summary, we need to make libraries more user-friendly for adults. We need to be aware of how adult students work and study as well as characteristics of adult learners. We should be cognizant of adult learning the-

ory and understand andragogy as opposed to pedagogy. We need to ask ourselves some important questions: Do we have hours before and after classes so the students can stop in and do quick research or pick up books? Can students access the online catalog and other services from off-campus? Are we aware of the diverse abilities that students have with regard to technology and are we doing something about it? Finally, are we marketing our services and seeking feedback? For it is only by listening to adult students that we can know how best to serve their current needs as well as how their demands will change in the future.

RESPONSIVE LIBRARY SERVICES

Law Four in Ranganathan's Five Laws of Librarianship states that we should "Save the time of the reader." We need to save our adult students' time without compromising the educational process. Any responsive library services program should incorporate:

- Librarian awareness of lifestyles, pressures, and characteristics of adult and nontraditional students. We also need to consider that returning adult or nontraditional students may have a high level of anxiety and specifically anxiety about using the library and technology.
- Ongoing assessment activities to determine needs. These include the following:
    - Surveys of computer (especially off-campus) usage.
    - Using off-campus computers to test accessibility of the library's materials and services.
    - Bibliographic instruction satisfaction surveys.
    - Focus groups.
    - Compiling circulation statistics to determine usage levels of collections by off-campus students.
- Aggressive marketing. Off-campus, adult students have difficulty receiving information about campus-based services. It is also true that "Adult students are consumers, making it important for the library to market their services and to be responsive to patron feedback" (Fidishun 1997).
- Bibliographic instructions services. Provide training and instruction at convenient times on how to use our services and resources. Our situation allows me to visit each site and instruct the students. I have also incorporated remote access training into library instruction to meet the needs of the home PC user as well as on-site users. Knowing what I now know about adult learners, I tailor each session to a specific assignment the class is to complete in the near future. Face-to-face bibliographic instruc-

tion is not possible for every situation. Telephone tutorials, printed materials, and electronic delivery of bibliographic instruction sessions are other ways of reaching the adult off-campus student.

- Formalized agreements with community public libraries. Community-based adult learners will use the library that is most familiar and with convenient hours. Many, if not most, off-campus programs have agreements with local public libraries to provide services to their students. Three of our centers have on-site libraries and hope these agreements will enhance our existing services. Students at our smallest center will soon be served exclusively through the public library. Mercer will provide document delivery to the public library from our collections and an annual stipend for materials.
- Provision of services and materials at the hours and places our patrons need. This includes electronic, 24/7 delivery, and training on how to access these resources.

Finally, in our interactions with adult students, whether in a telephone reference interview or a face-to-face instruction session, we need to practice patience, flexibility, and compassion. We need to become aware of adult students' unique needs, strengths, and characteristics. We may not be able to cure their "high anxiety" about the conflicting roles in their lives and the pressures caused by pursuing an education, but with responsive, proactive library services, we can help alleviate some of the symptoms.

REFERENCES

Ely, E. E. (1997). *The non-traditional student*. Paper presented at the 77th American Association of Community Colleges Conference, Anaheim, CA. (ERIC Document Reproduction Service No. 411906).

Fidishun, D. (1997). *Can we still do business as usual? Adult students and the new paradigm of library service*. Paper presented at the 8th annual ACRL National Conference, Nashville, Tennessee. Retrieved November 14, 2001, from http://www.ala.org/acrl/paperhtm/c25.html.

Golian, L. M. (1996). Helping re-entry women develop library technical skills and research strategies. *Feminist Collections, 17*, 44-46. Retrieved August 5, 2001 from Contemporary Women's Issues database.

Hammond, C. (1994, July). Nontraditional students and the library: Opinions, preferences, and behaviors. *College and Research Libraries*, 323-341.

Ingram, D. S. (2000). The andragogical librarian. In K. Sarkodie-Mensah (Ed.), *Reference services for the adult learner* (pp. 141-150). New York: The Haworth Information Press, Inc.

Johnson, G. (2001, December). Presentation given at the Mercer University Extended Education Enrollment Summit, Covington, GA.

Johnson, L. G., Schwartz, R. A. & Bower, B. L. (2000). Managing stress among adult women students in community colleges. *Community College Journal of Research and Practice, 24,* 289-300.

Kaplan, P. L. & Saltiel, I. M. (1997, May/June). Adults who do it all: Balancing work, family, and schooling. *Adult Learning,* 17-18, 31.

Kerke, S. (1995). *Adult learner retention revisited.* (ERIC Digest No. 166). Columbus OH: ERIC Clearinghouse on Adult Career and Vocational Education.

Knowles, M. S. (1984). *Andragogy in action: Applying modern principles to adult learning.* San Francisco: Jossey-Bass.

Knowles, M. S., Holton, E. F. & Swanson, R. A. (1998). *The adult learner: The definitive classic in adult education.* Woburn, MA: Butterworth-Heinemann.

Lieb, S. (2001). *Principles of adult learning.* Retrieved November 22, 2001, from Honolulu Community College, Faculty Guidebook: http://www.hcc.hawaii.

Mercer University, Office of Planning, Budgeting, and Institutional Research (2001-2002). *Term enrollment profiles.* Retrieved November 15, 2001 from http://www.mercer.edu/pbir/PAGES/IR/profile/top.htm.

Merriam, S. B. & Cafferella, R. S. (1999). *Learning in adulthood: A comprehensive guide.* San Francisco: Jossey-Bass.

Miller, P.(1999). The hurried student: NHCTC Library finds many ways to "help" their busy users. *Community & Junior College Libraries, 8,* 63-69.

Neimi, J. A. & Ehrhard, B. J. (1998). Off-campus library support for distance adult learners. *Library Trends, 47,* 65-74.

Sarkodie-Mensah, K. (Ed.). (2000). *Reference services for the adult learner: Challenging issues for the traditional and technological era.* Binghamton, NY: The Haworth Press, Inc.

Sheridan, J. (1986). Andragogy: A new concept for academic librarians. *Research Strategies: A Journal of Library Concepts and Instruction, 4,* 156-167.

U.S. Department of Education, National Center for Education Statistics (2000) *The encyclopedia of education statistics, Education statistics at a glance, Projections of education statistics, Tables 11A & 11B.* Retrieved November 14, 2001 from http://nces.ed.gov/pubs2001/proj01/tables.asp.

U.S. Department of Education, National Center for Education Statistics (1999). *Digest of education statistics, Table 177.* Retrieved November 14, 2001 from http://nces.ed.gov/pubs2000/Digest99/d99t177.html.

Witucke, V. (1990, March). Off-campus library services: Leading the way. *College & Research Libraries News,* 252-256.

A Kaleidoscope of Learning Styles:
Instructional Supports
That Meet the Diverse Needs
of Distant Learners

Katherine E. Holmes

Lesley University

SUMMARY. Our library intends to create a tutorial to assist students in library research. In preparation, we need to understand the diverse learning needs of students. Some students seem to thrive in the online environment while others feel at a loss. A review of learning styles literature reveals that many adult learners require personalized, interactive learning environments. The author reviewed library tutorials to identify models of library instruction that meet the needs of such students. This paper serves as background and literature review for an interactive workshop on learning styles and the Internet, which was presented at the conference.

KEYWORDS. Learning styles, library instruction, distance learners, technology

At our university library, we need to build a library tutorial that links all the resources of our Web site, and supports all students in their research efforts, whether on-campus or off-campus. In recent years, we have worked hard to create instructional supports for off-campus students and distant learners. The library Web site first came online in 1996, and was redesigned in 1999, with pathfinders and research guides as well as abundant full-text resources. We

[Haworth co-indexing entry note]: "A Kaleidoscope of Learning Styles: Instructional Supports That Meet the Diverse Needs of Distant Learners." Holmes, Katherine E. Co-published simultaneously in *Journal of Library Administration* (The Haworth Information Press, an imprint of The Haworth Press, Inc.) Vol. 37, No. 3/4, 2002, pp. 367-378; and: *Distance Learning Library Services: The Tenth Off-Campus Library Services Conference* (ed: Patrick B. Mahoney) The Haworth Information Press, an imprint of The Haworth Press, Inc., 2002, pp. 367-378.

http://www.haworthpress.com/store/product.asp?sku=J111
10.1300/J111v37n03_30

have created instructional videos and PowerPoint presentations for faculty to use in off-campus classes. We have worked with faculty to integrate information literacy concepts in the curriculum (Holmes & Brown, 2000). Librarians offer individual instruction by e-mail and toll-free telephone. The library receives positive feedback on these instructional tools from students and faculty.

Unfortunately, despite our best efforts, some students still fail to find the research information they need. They are unable to navigate through our Web site to uncover the treasures contained within, or to use the resources effectively. The pieces do not fit together into a whole image that is visible and comprehensible to all students. It feels important to create a library tutorial that will serve all students, regardless of ability or learning style.

First, some background about Lesley University. Located in Cambridge, MA, Lesley is best known for its School of Education, which offers bachelor's, master's and Ph.D. degrees. Other areas of strength are the arts, counseling psychology, expressive arts therapies, management and human services. Although traditional-age undergraduate students attend classes on campus, the largest population of Lesley's students are adult learners, taking courses on and off-campus or through distance learning programs. In a population of 7,500 students, well over half are taking courses off-campus or online. Eighty percent are female students, of whom most are teaching or preparing to teach in elementary schools. Lesley programs emphasize the blend of theory and practice–the real-world application of knowledge through service learning, pre-professional or professional development. Classes are small and most professors take pride in innovative teaching styles that minimize lectures. Off-campus courses are generally delivered in intensive weekend format at sites in 16 states, to cohort groups of about 24 students who proceed together through their degree program (Lesley University, 2001). These non-traditional programs attract adult learners with a wide variety of backgrounds and goals. Though they may be drawn to Lesley because of small classes and personalized instruction, students must navigate the World Wide Web to access library resources and services–an environment in which many students are not comfortable.

LEARNING STYLE THEORY

Although a literature search reveals several theoretical models of learning styles, I have chosen to address two here–the theories of David A. Kolb (1984) and Nishikant Sonwalkar (2001, December). Kolb's work is the basis of several studies that relate directly to our concerns at Lesley. Sonwalkar's three-dimensional "Learning Cube" is a stunning new model for designing online education. Kolb speaks of learning as based in personal experience, "shared and interpreted through dialogue with one another" (Kolb, 1984, p. 2). In other words, the experience and the dialogue are equally important aspects of learning. Dialogue and experience form a feedback loop that completes the learning cycle. Dialogue is informed by experiences, ideas, opinions, and feelings, according to the individual's particular learning styles.

Kolb describes four different learning styles:

- *Convergent learning* relies on abstract thinking and active experimentation. Convergent learners prefer dealing with technical tasks and problems rather than social and interpersonal issues. They are good at problem solving, decision making and the practical application of ideas (Kolb, 1984, p. 77). They are not fond of open-ended discussions or working in small groups (Kolb & Fry, as cited in Jonassen & Grabowski, 1993).
- *Divergent Learning* emphasizes concrete experience and reflective observation. Divergent learners prefer observation to experimentation, and enjoy brainstorming multiple perspectives. They are imaginative, and are interested in people and feelings (Kolb, 1984, p. 78). "They are often paralyzed by their inability to make a decision and, in many instances, prefer to observe rather than participate" (Terrell & Dringus, 1999/2000, p. 234). Divergers value self-diagnostic activities, open-ended assignments, and minimal course structure (Kolb & Fry, as cited in Jonassen & Grabowski, 1993).
- *Assimilation* merges abstract thinking and reflective observation. Assimilative learners enjoy inductive reasoning and theoretical models. They are more interested in ideas than people, in theory rather than its application (Kolb, 1984, p. 78). They are "good at taking in a wide range of information and reducing it to a more logical form" (Terrell & Dringus, 1999/2000, p. 233). "Assimilators value conforming to directions or rules, assigned readings, . . . role playing and lectures" (Kolb & Fry, as cited in Jonassen & Grabowski, 1993, p. 255).
- *Accommodative* learning is both active and concrete. Accommodators enjoy diving into new experiences. They thrive on change, and tend to look to other people for information. If the theory does not seem to fit facts, they may disregard the theory (Kolb, 1984, p. 78). They tend to get involved quickly through a "hands-on" or trial and error method of learning (Terrell & Dringus, 1999/2000, p. 233). "Accommodators value a lack of structure, a high amount of peer interaction, and a lack of authority figures in the classroom" (Kolb & Fry, as cited in Jonassen & Grabowski, 1993, p. 255).

[Note: Kolb's *Learning Style Inventory* (Kolb, 1976) is a self-assessment tool that enables individuals to identify their learning styles. Now available online (http://trgmcber.haygroup.com/Products/learning/lsius.html), the Inventory (LSI) is easy to administer, with immediate feedback, and costs only $10. Readers are invited to complete the assessment for a deeper understanding of the learning styles described above.]

Of the four learning styles described by Kolb, Accommodators seem to be the most at risk in online learning environments. Liam M. Rourke (2000) found that Accommodators were the least likely to succeed in a hypertext learning environment that is abstract and reflective. "The Accommodators have an intuitive, active approach to perceiving and processing information. They perform best in environments in which concrete, practical information is presented through interaction with peers and instructors. They process information best when they can actively apply this information to authentic situations" (Rourke, 2000, p. 9). Such situations are not easy to replicate online.

Steven R. Terrell and Laurie Dringus (1999/2000) tracked 98 information science students in an online master's program at Nova Southeastern University. Divergers, Convergers and Assimilators all completed the program at roughly an 80% rate; whereas, only 60% of Accommodators completed the program. This "is far less than might be anticipated since the students in the other categories maintained graduation rates" at 80% or higher (Terrell & Dringus, 1999/2000, p. 235). They concluded that Divergers, Convergers and Assimilators are better able to succeed in online learning environments, thanks to particular attributes. Divergers are able to assimilate knowledge by observation. Convergers prefer information presented in structured ways. Assimilators enjoy structure as well as theory. Observation, structure, and theory tend to be easy to build into Internet-based learning environments (Terrell & Dringus, 1999/2000).

In studies for his 1997 master's thesis, Jonathan L. Ross concluded that "computer assisted instruction may alienate certain learners. In particular, students who desire social interaction as part of the learning process, and [students who] think in a multidimensional, random-like fashion have difficulty adapting to computer instruction" (Ross, 1998, para. 5). Once more, Accommodators fit this description. [Note: Ross's article "On-Line but Off Course: A Wish List for Distance Educators" (Ross, 1998) offers an excellent checklist of diverse teaching practices and media for the online environment.]

The concern for Accommodators is heightened by Jean Moeller's finding that "the most dominant learning style in the non-traditional learning environment was the accommodator style" (Moeller, 2000, p. 177). This finding underscores my own experience of eight years working with students at Lesley University–many of our students need personalized, hands-on support. Although students may be drawn to Lesley's small classes and personalized instruction, all Lesley students become online learners the minute they attempt to access library resources and services on the World Wide Web. For libraries serving adult learners, it is critical to create learning environments that meet the needs of Accommodators–personalized learning with hands-on experiences.

CULTURE AND GENDER DIFFERENCES

Rita Dunn has reviewed dozens of studies of major cultural groups in the United States, to assess preferred learning styles. Although she found that individuals in these groups reflect a diverse array of learning style preferences, she also concluded that certain learning preferences are characteristic of the majority of members of each group. For example, European Americans prefer learning alone, whereas Native Americans enjoy learning with peers. Asian-Americans prefer highly structured learning activities, whereas African-Americans are more comfortable with minimal structure. African-Americans prefer kinesthetic or experiential learning activities more than do Asian-Americans or European Americans (Dunn, 2000).

Maureen Lage, Glenn J. Platt and Michael Treglia reviewed the literature of gender differences and learning styles. In contrast to male students, who often thrive on competition, the authors found that female students generally prefer collaborative environments with concrete learning experiences that relate directly to their own lives. In their "Inverted Classroom" at Miami University, the authors empowered students to choose from a variety of learning media to obtain the content outside of class that was normally delivered through lectures. Class time was reserved for students to complete assignments individually and in small groups, with the support of instructors. The female students appreciated the opportunity to choose from a variety of media instead of listening to a lecture, to work in small groups and receive personalized instruction from the professors (Lage, Platt & Treglia, 2000).

These findings underscore the need to provide diverse learning experiences in order to support the learning preferences of female students, as well as diverse cultural groups. Lesley University's large proportions of female students and adult learners, and increasing cultural diversity, make it essential for us to be responsive to their needs in designing our library tutorial.

LUDCKE LIBRARY HOME PAGE

In light of Kolb's Learning Styles, an examination of the Ludcke Library Home Page (http://www.lesley.edu/library/home.html) reveals a pattern that strongly supports Convergers, Divergers and Assimilators. The site is logically organized, with a table of choices on the opening page, leading the learner on a linear descent through sections of services and resources. Inner pages were designed to facilitate printing as a handout. They offer an overview to an issue, process or subject area, with links to resources. Pages offer instruction that is clear, often in step-by-step format. However, instruction is passive, inviting students to read and click, but not necessarily to interact. Accommodators may find this an alien learning environment. For true interaction to take place, students should be challenged to think about an issue, respond to a question, and get immediate feedback. There is very little theory provided, so Assimilators may also feel a bit short-changed.

In order to personalize the site, we have added "personal" touches to pages and services wherever possible. Our new Ask-A-Librarian page (http://www.lesley.edu/library/guides/asklib.html) displays a photo of the librarians who deliver this service, in order to give students a sense of personal connection, even though they are completing a Web form (Holmes, 2001). Carol Goodson has complimented us on the "evident warmth" of our online Off-Campus Handbook (http://www.lesley.edu/library/guides/offcampus.html), where a "Welcome" note and "A Note to Students with Disabilities," as well as a "cheery" tone greet students (Goodson, 2001, p. 96). We have inserted photos of students and faculty on pages where relevant. We will continue to find ways to help students feel a personal connection to our services, particularly Accommodators, who prefer to learn from people rather than objects.

LIBRARY TUTORIALS

In the search for library tutorials that might serve as models, I have viewed the tutorials linked by the LOEX Clearinghouse for Library Instruction (LOEX, n.d.). Many sites offer excellent text-based instruction, with clear text and images to illustrate concepts, but no true interactivity. A number of tutorials found creative ways to engage students in interaction, either through a quiz with a feedback loop, or instructions that resulted in immediate action from a library resource. Only a few tutorials manage to personalize the work with students–with humor and illustrations, a personal login name that continues through the tutorial, or the opportunity for students to choose a topic of personal interest for their tutorial. Tutorials that require pre-approved login or special software (BlackBoard, WebCT, or AuthorWare) are not included, nor are tutorials that become interactive by virtue of a printed activity sheet that is handed in to the instructor for correction and feedback.

Three library tutorials are exceptional examples of interactive learning opportunities with a personalized approach:

Blais Tutorial–Libraries of Claremont Colleges
http://voxlibris.claremont.edu/research/tutorials.html

Cartoon figures of students lead users through the tutorial, providing expert guidance from a potential "peer." An interactive quiz is imbedded throughout the modules, giving immediate feedback for both right and wrong answers, with explanations.

MAGS (Magician) Tutorial (University of California Riverside)
http://library.ucr.edu/MAGS/Welcome.html

A delightful magician personalizes the tutorial, with humor and emotion. Frames show instructions on the left, the magician on the right. Periodic quizzes reinforce learning. During the quiz, if the student chooses the right answer, the Magician looks elated and says, "Correct." If the student chooses the wrong answer, the magician looks dejected, explains why the answer is wrong and says, "Try again."

TILT (University of Texas)
http://tilt.lib.utsystem.edu/

This tutorial actually manages to engage the user in an online brainstorming session for keywords. Cartoons, with a good sense of humor, illustrate the non-library meanings of words such as "citation" (traffic ticket). Explanatory text is revealed as the user sweeps the mouse over a database record. This masterful tutorial is especially thorough on Information Literacy concepts, and personalizes the instruction through student selection of topics and keywords.

These tutorials are enjoyable, sometimes even fun, and extremely interactive, requiring that users think, click or enter a search, and think again. They offer immediate feedback in a friendly, supportive manner that reinforces learning and motivates one to continue. Text and images are clear and relevant to each other. Screens load quickly and offer student control of the modules–where to start, when to stop. Kudos to the designers of these outstanding library tutorials!

INSTRUCTIONAL DESIGN

Developing online tutorials such as the above requires creative attention to instructional design principles. Two writers have addressed these concerns especially well.

Nishikant Sonwalkar, an "educational architect" at the Massachusetts Institute of Technology, proposes a three-dimensional "Learning Cube" to represent the student's learning style, the varied instructional media, and the relative student control or teacher control of the activity. His learning style definitions are different from Kolb's, but include similar concerns. The Letter/Number designations in parentheses (L_1 to L_5) correlate with the horizontal axis on Sonwalkar's Learning Cube (see diagram which follows).

- Apprentice learners (L_1) prefer a step-by-step learning approach.
- Incidental learners (L_2) take information from events or stories.
- Inductive learners (L_3) prefer to be presented with a concept and examples (Sonwalkar, 2001, p. 13).
- Deductive learners (L_4) infer concepts from experiments, simulations, and data.
- Discovery learners (L_5) learn by doing, through an interactive exercise, simulation or quiz (Sonwalkar, 2001, p. 14).

According to Sonwalkar, students may develop through each of these learning styles, but individuals may ultimately prefer one particular style. In any group of students, all of these learning styles are likely to be represented. By creating learning activities that meet the needs of all five styles, instructional designers provide appropriate learning experiences for all students. Sonwalkar asserts that "distributing . . . content in the form of online textbooks (e.g., in PDF or HTML formats) is not sufficient" to meet the needs of students learning in the online environment (Sonwalkar, 2001 December, p. 13). "The pedagogy must allow for flexibility, interactivity, and media-rich and adaptive environments that both provide individualized learning and are also accessible to large numbers of learners" (Sonwalkar, 2001 November, para. 7).

Sonwalkar's model for online learning is best illustrated by his graphical Learning Cube. The image illustrates a dynamic view of online instruction, where student control of the information-seeking process is an important element of instructional design. On the vertical axis, are the learning media: text, graphics, audio, video, animation, and simulation. On the horizontal axis, are the learning styles, from L_1 (Apprentice) to L_5 (Discovery Learner). As one reads the cube starting in the lower left corner, both the text-based media and Apprentice learning style tend to reflect a teacher-centered environment. As one progresses diagonally outward from that corner, increasingly complex media and learning styles facilitate progressively more student-centered learning experiences. Thus Sonwalkar describes a dynamic learning environment in which a variety of learning tools are designed to meet a complex diversity of learning needs, placing control over the learning experience in the hands of the student (Sonwalkar, 2001 December).

Sonwalkar's principles have obvious application to the design of library instruction tools. For example, an instructional module on Boolean Searching could enable students to choose how they will receive information, by way of step-by-step instructions, graphic illustrations, audio or video clips, animations, or through hands-on simulations. Students could choose to practice creating search statements through simultaneous chats or self-correcting quizzes. They could be led to test their search statements in a database, and evaluate the results. As Sonwalkar's articles were just recently published, there has been no opportunity to see the online environments he has created. It is my goal before the conference to contact him and see if it is possible to view any of the online courses that display these concepts.

2D Pedagogical Model for Online Education (Sonwalkar, 2001 December, p. 13)

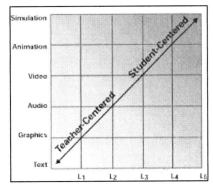

Reprinted with permission from *Syllabus Magazine*.

Catherine McLoughlin expresses concern that, rather than address individual student needs, "instructional material often remains fixed, unvaried and static, adaptive to individual needs in only minor ways, if at all. Students are expected to fit into the system and to cope as best they can, . . . [resulting in] high rates of attrition in distance learning settings" (McLoughlin, 1999, p. 1).

McLoughlin proposes the following principles for the design of online tasks to benefit all learners:

- A self-directed, active approach where learners are given the choice of selecting life events and experiences as the basis of learning;
- Inquiry and reflection;
- Multiple and varied learning experiences;
- Ongoing feedback (McLoughlin, 1999, p. 9).

Thus, in a library tutorial, students might be empowered to select a sample research topic from a suggested list, enabling them to relate the tutorial exercises most closely to their subject area or life experiences. New library technologies such as databases and search engines may be compared to old familiar technologies such as the telephone book, in which white pages are indexed by name and yellow pages are indexed by category, or a television programming guide, which is indexed by time. Varied learning opportunities can be provided through demonstrations, text, outlines, charts, video clips and audio tracks. Reflection is stimulated with thought-provoking questions. Online quizzes provide instant feedback for right and wrong answers, with the opportunity for self-correction.

CONCLUSION

As librarians design online library tutorials, it is more important to understand the variety of learning styles in our student populations than it is to be knowledgeable of any one learning style theory. All learning styles are valid, yet each learner feels more comfortable and successful in particular learning environments. Unfortunately, regardless of their relative comfort or discomfort in online learning, all students must navigate the World Wide Web in order to access library catalogs and databases. Although we do not have the luxury of ascertaining which students prefer which learning style when they come into our library home pages, we do have the obligation to make our online resources accessible to the largest number of students possible. Most online situations best serve the students who function well in a logical, text-based, passive environment. But many students require more personalized attention in an interactive environment. If we are to provide equivalent services to all our students, it is essential that special attention be paid to developing resources that support students who require this more personalized, interactive learning environment. When we offer a diversity of learning approaches, we enable all students to choose the best environment (possibly multiple environments) for their learning.

A KALEIDOSCOPE FOR LESLEY UNIVERSITY

Lesley University libraries are in the process of applying for a state grant through the Massachusetts Board of Library Commissioners. If we are successful, this grant will enable us to obtain the expertise and release time necessary to build a library tutorial with many of the features described above. We are currently engaged in refining the Library Web site to meet accessibility needs of patrons with disabilities. The tutorial will build on that effort, linking all library Web pages and resources in an information literacy environment where students control the learning process, where options are available to meet diverse learning styles, and where personalized interactions stimulate immediate feedback. We hope to build a kaleidoscope through which students can bring into focus the multiple options for their library research.

REFERENCES

Dunn, R. (2000). Capitalizing on college students' learning styles: Theory, practice and research. In R. Dunn and S.A. Griggs (Eds.), *Practical approaches to using learning styles in higher education* (pp. 3-18). Westport, CT: Bergin & Garvey.

Goodson, C. (2001). *Providing library services for distance education students: A how-to-do-it manual.* New York: Neal-Schuman.

Holmes, K. (2001, Fall). Asking for answers on digital reference: From "personal" to "personalized." *DLS Newsletter, 11*(1), p. 7.

Holmes, K. & Brown, C. (2000). Meeting adult learners, wherever they may be: If it's Thursday, it must be Thermopolis. In T.E. Jacobson & H.C. Williams (Eds.), *Teaching the new library to today's users: Reaching international, minority, senior citizens, gay/lesbian, first-generation, at-risk, graduate and returning students, and distance learners.* New York: Neal-Schuman.

Jonassen, D.H. & Grabowski, B.L. (1993). *Handbook of individual differences, learning, and instruction.* Hillsdale, NJ: Lawrence Erlbaum.

Kolb, D.A. (1984). *Experiential learning.* Englewood Cliffs, NJ: Prentice-Hall.

Lage, M.L., Platt, G.J., & Treglia, M. (2000, Winter). Inverting the classroom: A gateway to creating an inclusive learning environment. *The Journal of Economic Education, 31*(1), pp. 30-43. Retrieved December 1, 2001, from Wilson OmniFile Database.

Lesley University. (2001). *Off-campus programs.* Retrieved December 28, 2001, from http://www.lesley.edu/offcampus/map.html.

LOEX Clearinghouse for Library Instruction. (n.d.) *Instruction links: Tutorials.* Retrieved December 28, 2001, from http://www.emich.edu/public/loex/islinks/tutlinks.htm.

McLoughlin, C. (1999). The implications of the research literature on learning styles for the design of instructional material. *Australian Journal of Educational Technology, 15*(3), 222-241. Retrieved November 23, 2001, from http://cleo.murdoch.edu.au/ajet/ajet15/mcloughlin.html.

Moeller, J.S. (2000, September 27). A research study to discover temperament types, communication styles, and learning styles of adult learners in non-traditional and online learning environments. In M. Glowacki-Dudka (Ed.), *Honoring our roots and branches . . . our history and future.* Proceedings of the Annual Midwest Research to Practice Conference in Adult, Continuing, and Community Education (19th, Madison, Wisconsin, September 27-29, 2000). (ERIC Document Reproduction Service No. ED445203).

Ross, J.L. (1998, May 12). On-line but off course: A wish list for distance educators. *International Electronic Journal for Leadership in Learning, 2*(3), 19 pages. Retrieved November 25, 2001, from http://www.acs.ucalgary.ca/~iejll/volume2/Ross2_3.html.

Rourke, L.M. (2000, April 26). *The influence of learning style on achievement in hypertext.* Paper prepared for the Annual Meeting of the American Educational Research Association in New Orleans. (ERIC Document Reproduction Service No. ED466102).

Sonwalkar, N. (2001, November). Changing the interface of education with revolution-ary learning technologies. *Syllabus Magazine, 15*(4), para. 7. Retrieved December 28, 2001, from http://www.syllabus.com/syllabusmagazine/article.asp?id=5663.

Sonwalkar, N. (2001, December). The sharp edge of the cube: Pedagogically driven in-structional design for online education. *Syllabus Magazine, 15*(5), p. 12-16.

Terrell, S.T. & Dringus, L. (1999/2000). An investigation of the effect of learning style on student success in an online learning environment. *Journal of Educational Tech-nology Systems, 28*(3), 231-8.

Using the Invisible Web
to Teach Information Literacy

Mary Hricko

Kent State University

SUMMARY. In an age where it is crucial that students have an understanding of how to locate, evaluate, and use information appropriately, it
is important that instructors engage their students in research activities
that provide opportunities to develop information literacy competencies.
By introducing the use of the Invisible Web in information literacy instruction, novice researchers gain a better understanding of the organization of information on the Internet. The Invisible Web serves as a
gateway to provide direct access to information not easily retrieved by
the popular search engines. It is much more structured than traditional
search engines to offer students a sense of organization in their research.
A review of various Invisible Web Search Sites is provided along with
discussion of how to integrate the use of the Invisible Web into information literacy instruction.

KEYWORDS. Internet, literacy, library instruction, distance learners

In January 2000, the Association of College and Research Libraries (ACRL,
2000) published the guide *Information Literacy Competency Standards for
Higher Education* that outlines the standards for information literacy that offer a
"framework for assessing the information literate individual" and identify the
range of competencies students should master to meet the objectives of each

[Haworth co-indexing entry note]: "Using the Invisible Web to Teach Information Literacy." Hricko,
Mary. Co-published simultaneously in *Journal of Library Administration* (The Haworth Information Press, an
imprint of The Haworth Press, Inc.) Vol. 37, No. 3/4, 2002, pp. 379-386; and: *Distance Learning Library Services: The Tenth Off-Campus Library Services Conference* (ed: Patrick B. Mahoney) The Haworth Information Press, an imprint of The Haworth Press, Inc., 2002, pp. 379-386.

http://www.haworthpress.com/store/product.asp?sku=J111
10.1300/J111v37n03_31

standard (p. 4). In an age when it is crucial that students have an understanding of how to locate, evaluate, and use information appropriately, it is important that instructors engage their students in research activities that provide opportunities to develop information literacy competencies. Information literacy "enables learners to master content, and extend their investigations, become more self-directed, and assure greater control in their learning" (p. 5).

Since information literacy forms the basis for lifelong learning, it is important to develop a framework of instruction that extends one's learning beyond the classroom. In order to improve the way in which our students access information, librarians have taught students how to formulate search strategies, use specialized search engines, and then evaluate the Web sites that they have retrieved. However, by introducing alternative means of Web searching such as the use of the Invisible Web, novice researchers gain a better understanding of the organization of information on the Internet. In 1994, Dr. Jill Ellsworth coined the phrase "Invisible Web" to refer to the information retrieved from content specific search engines. Currently, the Invisible Web has become the fastest growing research tool for subject specific information primarily because it serves as a gateway to provide direct access to information not easily retrieved by the popular search engines. The Invisible Web also provides access to more current information and offers more structure for novice researchers in locating information.

Although most librarians make use of traditional search engines and directories to teach students how to use the Internet for research, it is important to also include instruction in the use of the Invisible Web search sites because as Web developers begin to use more dynamically charged content in the design of their Web documents, it will be harder to create Web indexes to retrieve these pages. Web pages made up of data types such as graphics, CGI scripts, Macromedia Flash, or PDF files cannot always be accessed through traditional search engines. Sites that include specialized databases may also be difficult to retrieve because they are not easily indexed. In most cases, researchers using search engines to retrieve links have difficulty locating material from what is considered the "deep Web" and often end up sifting through a number of interfaces just to obtain high quality information. For the average student user, this process can lead to a frustrating experience. If we only teach students to use general search engines and directories to locate information from the Internet, then we are limiting the range of material they will be able to access for their research.

To understand ways in which the Invisible Web can be used to teach information literacy, it is first necessary to provide a general overview of the five standards of information literacy.

STANDARD ONE:
THE INFORMATION LITERATE STUDENT
DETERMINES THE NATURE AND EXTENT
OF THE INFORMATION NEEDED

Students who have mastered this skill are able to define the need for information, identify a variety of information sources, determine the costs associated with obtaining information, and reevaluate the extent of the information need. Educators can evaluate the way in which students have mastered this skill by creating assignments that involve comprehensive library research that includes the use of both print and electronic resources. Assignments should engage students in the process of acquiring materials through interlibrary loan and research through automated library catalogs and electronic databases. Many libraries also have subject-specific Web pages designed to assist students with research. Some of these sites include access to online databases that provide citations to retrieve full-text articles from scholarly journals. The goal is to demonstrate to students that the Internet also includes specialized databases that can be accessed through the Invisible Web. Students need to understand that there are varying levels of locating information through the use of the Internet. Students should come to understand that research involves much more than using simple search engines.

The best way to begin review of the Invisible Web search sites is to provide students with an activity that requires them to compare and contrast a search query using their favorite search engine and an Invisible Web search site such as Direct Search (http://gwis2.circ.gwu.edu/~gprice/direct.htm). Direct Search is a Web archive maintained by librarian Gary Price. It indexes a wide range of specialized resources and reference materials that traditional search engines have difficulty retrieving. Many of these Web sites are from educational and government Web pages. Students will be able to note the difference in the quality of material that is retrieved. Infomine (http://www.infomine.ucr.edu/Main.html), from the University of California, focuses primarily on archiving hard-to-find academic Web sites. The Scout Report signpost (http://www.signpost.org) also includes gateways to Web sites that have been reviewed for rigorous standards of quality. By introducing these sites to students, students realize that there are different types of indexing used in search engines. All too often, novice researchers tend to rely on one search engine for all of their information needs. Introducing them to the Invisible Web search sites provides them a better understanding of the limits of traditional search engines.

STANDARD TWO:
THE INFORMATION LITERATE STUDENT
ACCESSES NEEDED INFORMATION
EFFECTIVELY AND EFFICIENTLY

All too often students have difficulty locating material for their assignments because they do not know how to form search strategies. It is important for instructors to realize that some students may not know the subject vocabulary that will generate the best retrieval for information. For novice researchers, concepts such as truncation, Boolean operators, and other search strategy protocols are not easily understood. Since online students may not have access to traditional bibliographic instruction, it is the responsibility of the instructors to provide students with the general background information that will assist them with beginning a search. Furthermore, unless the library staff has access to the Web assignment, providing reference assistance to students' online queries may be difficult if the student fails to provide all details of the assignment to the librarian. As a result, it is crucial that online instructors teach students how to develop and refine their search strategies. If the instructors are unable to provide this assistance, then they must find a way to include an element of Web-based bibliographic instruction in their course.

By using the Invisible Web, novice researchers can learn about "targeted Web crawlers." A targeted Web crawler is a search tool that guides the researcher to specific sites to find more detailed and relevant material. An example of a targeted Web crawler is Lawcrawler (http://lawcrawler.findlaw.com). Lawcrawler serves as a search portal for information specifically related to legal topics and information. There are specific legal databases easily accessible on this page. A similar targeted crawler is Psychcrawler (http://www.psychcrawler.com). Like Lawcrawler, Psychcrawler serves as a portal for specific subject-oriented information. Teaching novice researchers to use more specialized Web search engines enables them to be much more efficient in their information gathering. A Web-based bibliographic instruction module can lead students through the process of a search in much the same manner as traditional bibliographic instruction engages students to use print resources. In many ways, the Invisible Web can be compared to an encyclopedia reference tool; it assists students with developing preliminary ideas about the topic they are researching and provides an overview of the topic to help students narrow the focus of their proposed ideas.

STANDARD THREE:
THE INFORMATION LITERATE STUDENT
EVALUATES INFORMATION AND ITS SOURCES CRITICALLY
AND INCORPORATES SELECTED INFORMATION
INTO HIS OR HER KNOWLEDGE BASE AND VALUE SYSTEM

Students who master this standard are able to cite information and restate it in such a way that it supports their arguments. Students must be taught how to cite electronic information and instructors should not accept e-mail attachments of papers or other written projects if there is question regarding citation. Some instructors may not choose to impose standards for materials submitted in electronic format, but they need to be aware and proactive about identifying Internet plagiarism. Instructors who do not check their students' assignments for plagiarism are only perpetuating further academic misconduct. If instructors limit students to using materials retrieved from specialized Invisible Web search engines, it is easier to determine citations and references. Granted, some students may sidestep this requirement, but most instructors will be able to determine that the material retrieved was not from the Invisible Web search sites. In many cases, the Invisible Web search engines monitor the status of their links to ensure that "dead" links are not retrieved. Students who use traditional search engines may cite from a link that no longer exists and an instructor may not be able to check the link to determine if plagiarism had occurred.

Students who master this standard should also be able to evaluate the information they locate to determine its validity. There are numerous Web sites that provide discussion and sample forms for Web evaluation. Students are taught how to compare information, identify cultural biases, and recognize the strengths and weaknesses of given information within its context. All too often, students equate technology with accuracy; some students believe that visually appealing Web sites are more accurate than ones just listing text. Instructors need to remind students that accuracy, authority, point of view, and the timeliness of the site's data are all key factors in differentiating the reliability of information retrieved from the site. Almost all of the Invisible Web search sites have what I deem to be a librarian's perspective: the sites retrieve the most concise and resourceful information available. The links retrieved are not ranked in the order of the highest bidder for the placement, but rather for the relevance to the query that was posted. Some sites, such as Direct Search, were created by librarians who understand the complexities novice researchers have in using the Internet to locate information.

STANDARD FOUR:
THE INFORMATION LITERATE STUDENT,
INDIVIDUALLY OR AS A MEMBER OF A GROUP,
USES INFORMATION EFFECTIVELY
TO ACCOMPLISH A SPECIFIC PURPOSE

Information retrieved for an assignment may mean little to other students or the instructor of the course if it is not communicated effectively. The fourth standard suggests that students need to know how to prepare the information they retrieve so that it communicates clearly to its intended audience what it is supposed to communicate. This skill is crucial in an online setting where students do not have the face-to-face opportunities to clarify what is written in their assignments. Since the menu-driven structure of the Invisible Web search sites offers students a visual of information organization of broad to narrow, narrow to broad search hierarchies, students are directed to follow this sequencing when they are locating material. This practice, although an indirect method, helps students understand the importance of placing information into a logical sequence. To illustrate this idea, let's suppose a student went to the LibrarySpot site at http://www.libraryspot.com to begin a search looking for full-text articles in scholarly journals. Students would then be instructed to follow the menu choices that link to where they can search for full-text articles: http://www.libraryspot. com/ask/askfulltext.htm. Upon selection of this link, they are directed to another menu that organizes the type of electronic publication available. It is here that the instructor can explain the difference between scholarly and popular culture articles that can be found online, but more importantly, the student sees how the menu organizes the subject to accomplish a specific purpose, in this case, to find articles in scholarly journals.

STANDARD FIVE:
THE INFORMATION LITERATE STUDENT
UNDERSTANDS MANY OF THE ECONOMIC, LEGAL,
AND SOCIAL ISSUES SURROUNDING THE USE OF INFORMATION
AND ACCESSES AND USES INFORMATION
ETHICALLY AND LEGALLY

This standard involves an understanding of copyright, privacy, and security in both the traditional and electronic environments. As students share resources over the Internet, issues of intellectual property need to be discussed. Students need to be made aware of the institution's policies regarding the use and access of materials. Net-etiquette, campus acceptable use policies, and academic misconduct must be discussed in all classrooms. All instructors should obtain a copy of the standards from ACRL at http://www.ala.org/acrl.html to have for use in creating course assignments. Assignments should be modified to address the objectives and competencies of the guidelines.

Students enrolled in Web-based courses should be given library research assignments. If online instructors would simply place a link to the library home page on their Web site (a very simple task), it would at the very least suggest to the students that the instructors hold some value for the library. Instructors who fail to provide their students with opportunities to develop their "information literacy" skills are only creating courses below the standards comparable to traditional courses. Hence, instructors involved in online course development have a responsibility to review the resources available to their students in the online environment. If student success is an objective for online instruction, then it is crucial to create an environment that provides the same level of academic support. "Courses structured in such a way create student centered learning environments where inquiry is the norm, problem solving becomes the focus, and thinking critically is part of the process" (ACRL, 2000, p. 5).

Librarians involved in bibliographic instruction should use different Internet tools to teach students which electronic resources are best to consult for the best information. The same methods of differentiating the strengths and weaknesses of traditional print resources can be applied to the electronic and online resources available. Even though librarians engage in the evaluation of these Internet tools, we need to teach our students to do the same. Bibliographic instruction assignments should require students to gain practice in using directories and specialized databases from the Invisible Web. Directories and specialized databases for the Invisible Web are much more effective in categorizing Web pages because they are indexed by people, and not software tools. Directories are organized in hierarchal formats that enable students to analyze subject trees of information. If our objective is to show students how to find more specific and focused results, we should teach them how to use more specific and focused Internet tools.

Using the Invisible Web over traditional search engines is much more practical for novice researchers who are not so much concerned with the quantity of the Web pages their keyword search has generated, but rather the quality of the Web pages they have found. Most students tend to look through the first two pages of links for their research rather than filter through the millions of links that popular search engines generate. Michael Bergman (2000) published a white paper entitled "The Deep Web: Surfacing Hidden Value" that investigates the structure and content of the "hidden" Web. Bergman argues that the term "Invisible Web" is an inaccurate description for the hidden content on the Web so he refers to this material as the "Deep Web." Among the findings that Bergman and his colleagues discovered in their research is the following:

- The Deep Web has grown 400 to 500 times larger than the content found on the "visible" Web.
- More than 200,00 Deep Web sites presently exist.

- The Deep Web is the largest growing category of new information on the Internet.
- Total quality content of the Deep Web is 1000 to 2000 times greater than conventional surface sites. (Surface sites are those that are retrieved from traditional search engines.)
- More than half of the Deep Web content resides in topic-specific databases.

Bergman's findings further demonstrate to us why information literacy instruction is so important.

While librarians and other scholars may be aware of the vast material available on the Web, novice researchers have no sense that they have yet to "scratch the surface." Teaching these individuals to go beyond the general practices of Web searching forces them to recognize this fact first hand. Furthermore, as librarians we want our novice researchers to use the best tools for their information seeking. In the Bergman analysis, three of the most common categories of Deep Web sites included searchable databases for archived articles, subject-specific aggregations of information, and library portals. Hence, by teaching our students about the Invisible Web or Deep Web search tools, we demonstrate to them that there is much more to the Web than the latest gimmick-directed search engine that always promises to generate the most hits.

REFERENCES

Association of College and Research Libraries. (2000). *Information literacy competency standards for higher education.* Chicago: ACRL.

Bergman, M. (2000). The Deep Web: Surfacing hidden value. *BrightPlanet.* Available: http://www.brightplanet.com/deepcontent/tutorials/DeepWeb/index.asp. Retrieved: December 15, 2001.

Ellsworth, J. (1994). Retrieved: December 15, 2001 from http://www.tcp.ca/Jan96/Busand Mark.html.

The Answer You Get
Depends on Who (and What) You Ask:
Involving Stakeholders
in Needs Assessments

Judy Ann Jerabek

Lynn M. McMain

Sam Houston State University

SUMMARY. This paper focuses on identifying and involving various distance-learning stakeholders in a needs assessment for library services. Topics covered include "Why who you ask matters" (rationale for including stakeholders), "Who you ask" (identifying stakeholders), "What you ask" (developing questions that ask what you need to know), and "How to involve those you have identified" (ways to increase stakeholder participation and, thereby, investment in the needs assessment process and library services related to distance learning programs).

KEYWORDS. Assessment, distance learners, stakeholders, distance education

INTRODUCTION

A waiter asks four diners, "What may I bring you for dessert?" The first diner enthusiastically orders the double chocolate fudge cheesecake; the sec-

---

[Haworth co-indexing entry note]: "The Answer You Get Depends on Who (and What) You Ask: Involving Stakeholders in Needs Assessments." Jerabek, Judy Ann, and Lynn M. McMain. Co-published simultaneously in *Journal of Library Administration* (The Haworth Information Press, an imprint of The Haworth Press, Inc.) Vol. 37, No. 3/4, 2002, pp. 387-395; and: *Distance Learning Library Services: The Tenth Off-Campus Library Services Conference* (ed: Patrick B. Mahoney) The Haworth Information Press, an imprint of The Haworth Press, Inc., 2002, pp. 387-395.

http://www.haworthpress.com/store/product.asp?sku=J111
10.1300/J111v37n03_32

ond responds with, "No thank you, I'm a diabetic"; the third states, "Something light–the raspberry sorbet"; and the fourth says, "No dessert for me. I'm too full, just coffee, thanks." Each person has a unique answer based on particular wants and needs. If the waiter had asked, "Do you *want* dessert?" the answers may have been different. The answer the waiter receives depends on which question is asked and the person who responds. This whimsical, tongue-in-cheek example illustrates our initial point–the answer you get depends on who and what you ask. The relationship between question, respondent, and response illustrated in the restaurant scenario applies to needs assessment as well.

That relationship is examined here with a particular focus on identifying and involving various distance-learning stakeholders in a needs assessment for library services. Topics covered include "Who you ask?" (identifying stakeholders), "Why who you ask matters" (rationale for including stakeholders), "What you ask?" (developing questions that ask what you need to know), and "How to involve stakeholders you have identified" (ways to increase stakeholder participation and, thereby, investment in the needs assessment process and library services related to distance-learning programs).

OVERVIEW OF THE LITERATURE

As emphasis on distance learning programs by many colleges and universities has increased, academic librarians face the challenge of meeting the needs of those involved in distance learning programs. Many distance learners may never enter the library itself or have a face-to-face encounter with a librarian. Responding to the challenge of providing library services in support of distance learning programs may involve continuing and/or adapting present library programs and services, establishing new delivery modes, and/or creating entirely new services. Effectively meeting the needs of the various participants in distance learning programs first requires identifying those needs. A valuable tool available for identifying these needs is the needs assessment.

Library services for distance learners (Cooper, Dempsey, Menon, & Millson-Martula, 1998; Gasaway, 1999; Kascus & Aguilar 1988; Niemi, Ehrhard, Neeley, 1998; O'Leary, 2000), as well as needs assessment related to library services (Cloughtery, Forys, Lyles, Persson, Walters, & Washington-Hoagland, 1998; Ellern & Kimble, 1997; Lawton, 1989) have been the subject of research and publication. Authors discussing needs assessments have noted the importance of identifying and involving those groups who have come to be known as "stakeholders."

The concept of stakeholders originated in the areas of business (Wimer & Nowack, 1998) and management (Freeman, 1984; Mitchell, Agle, & Wood, 1997; Cummings & Doh, 2000). This concept has also been applied to education (Burrows, 1999; Barrick & Cogliano, 1993), and more specifically to libraries ("Identify Your Library's Stakeholders," 1994).

"WHO YOU ASK"–
HOW WE DEFINE AND IDENTIFY STAKEHOLDERS

A number of researchers have defined "stakeholder" or "stakeholders" in various ways. Freeman and Reed (1983) note that the word "stakeholder" was "coined in an internal memorandum at the Stanford Research Institute in 1963. . . . " In that context it referred to "those groups without whose support the organization would cease to exist" (p. 89). A chronology compiled by Mitchell, Agle, and Wood (1997) charts the development of responses to the question "Who is a stakeholder?" beginning with that 1963 memo and continuing through the following thirty-two years. They note that these definitions generally fall into one of two categories, broad or narrow. Those two categories in turn derive from two definitions proposed by Freeman and Reed (1983):

> *The wide sense of stakeholder.* [italics added] Any identifiable group or individual who can affect the achievement of an organization's objectives or who is affected by the achievement of an organization's objectives. (Public interest groups, protest groups, government agencies, trade associations, competitors, unions, as well as employees, customer segments, shareowners and others are stakeholders in this sense.)

> *The narrow sense of stakeholder.* [italics added] Any identifiable group or individual on which the organization is dependent for its continued survival. (Employees, customer segments, certain suppliers, key government agencies, shareowners, certain financial institutions, as well as others are all stakeholders in the narrow sense of the term.) (p. 90)

It is worth noting that "wide" and "narrow," as just defined, form what may be considered the ends of a continuum, along which most definitions of stakeholder fall. Westbrook's (2001) definition of stakeholders as "those groups or individuals (whether or not they are library patrons), who have a strong interest in the library and its services" (p. 45), falls near the narrower end of the continuum. For the purpose of library needs assessment a more narrow definition of "stakeholder" is preferable. While a broad definition may be useful in determining a library's service area or potential patron base, a narrow definition facilitates identifying and targeting those individuals and groups to be involved in a needs assessment project. The more specifically stakeholder groups are defined, the more readily assessors will be able to target members of those groups, thus making the assessment process more manageable.

Accurately identifying stakeholders can be a difficult task. It is crucial to the needs assessment process to have the perspective of everyone involved. There are several different criteria proposed for identifying stakeholders. Mitchell, Agle, and Wood identify stakeholders in terms of what they call attributes: power, legitimacy and urgency. Burrows (1999) has created her own categories and groups to identify stakeholders, external vs. internal, active vs. passive, potential for cooperation and threat, and types of stakes and influence (pp. 6-7). Westbrook (2001) advocates the identification of stakeholders by "systems," as well as by traditional groupings, both demographic and organizational. Initial identification of stakeholders in a structured and highly bureaucratic organization, such as a university, is best accomplished by organizational groupings. By its very nature, the academic organization distinguishes which individuals belong to which groups, and provides pathways to access these groups, such as directories and e-mail. In the case of the academic library, such groups include students, faculty, university administrators, and library personnel.

The primary group of stakeholders that comes to mind when thinking of library needs and distance-learning is the students; however, the faculty who will be designing the courses, determining the content, and creating the assignments warrant consideration as well. Additional stakeholders may include administrators of distance-learning programs, and of computer services, as well as teaching faculty who have already integrated Internet support in their classes, and those in specific departments who in the future may want to develop and design distance-learning programs. Librarians and library staff in reference, interlibrary loan, government documents, reserves and library administrators, as well as from any other area supporting distance learning programs, should all be included as stakeholders.

In connection with identifying stakeholders, it may be useful to determine the particular stake each group holds. While Freeman (1984) considers stakes in a business context, Burrows (1999) applies that work to an academic setting and considers a number of possible stakes which various individuals or groups may hold. These include institutional, economic, social, scholarship, moral, and personal. Knowing the type of stake involved provides clues to the way a particular stakeholder or stakeholders may be approached. For example, to those who hold an institutional stake, the needs assessment and its results can be presented as a way to improve the institution's distance-learning programs and recruit additional students to those courses (also a plus to those with an economic stake). Improved library programs will appeal to those with a scholarship stake. Thus discerning the stake is a valuable part of stakeholder identification.

"WHY WHO YOU ASK MATTERS"–
RATIONALE FOR INCLUDING STAKEHOLDERS

Given the thought, time and energy required to define then identify stakeholders in a particular setting, it is valid to ask why. Why make this effort? The answer, in a word, is success. Essential to a valuable and relevant needs assessment is "broad-based participation by stakeholders" (Witkin & Altschuld, 1995). Three more detailed reasons for involving stakeholders in needs assessment will be given here.

One reason for involving stakeholders right from the beginning of a needs assessment project is the pool of resources they offer for planning and conducting the needs assessment. For example, the inclusion of teaching faculty and those directly responsible for the university's distance learning program provides a more balanced and complete foundation for the project. Including past or present distance learners will add valuable insights.

Increased support of and participation in the needs assessment itself constitutes a second reason for involving stakeholders. Whether by taking part in focus groups, encouraging response to questionnaires or providing funding, widespread support of the people who will be affected by the outcome has significant impact. Including the full spectrum of identified stakeholders leads to more accurate, useful results.

The third reason for involving stakeholders relates to post-assessment activities. Involvement of stakeholders leads to greater commitment, again of time, skills and other resources, to implementing any changes or new services developed as a result of the assessment findings.

It should be noted here that involving stakeholders places what may be considered a responsibility on the assessment group. That is, the assessors will be accountable for attending to the data and other information given by stakeholders who have been asked to be involved. Stakeholders by virtue of that involvement will have expectations of the assessment and its results. Nevertheless, the variety of perspectives, skills and resources members of stakeholder groups have to offer warrants their inclusion in the needs assessment process from the initial stage through implementation of any resulting changes.

"WHAT YOU ASK"–
DEVELOPING QUESTIONS THAT ASK WHAT YOU NEED TO KNOW

Having determined who will be involved in the needs assessment, the next step is to develop the what–that is, to frame the questions that will be asked.

Although treatment of specific data collection methods (interview, focus group, questionnaire, etc.) is outside the scope of this discussion, all of them incorporate questions to some degree. Before constructing questions, consider the type of data or information to be gathered. Questions asking "How much?" "How many?" and "How often?" yield numeric data. Items asking if the stakeholder agrees/disagrees or likes/dislikes probe opinions. Inquiring about specific resources or titles provides narrative information.

Each question used as a part of any needs assessment tool should be ". . . a very special construct with a clearly focused purpose" (Czaja & Blair, 1996, p. 63). General rules for creating questions for any needs assessment tool are: each question should be concise, unequivocal, contain a single thought, avoid double negatives, and for a survey, be close-ended (Hayes, 1997; Reviere, Berkowitz, Carter, & Ferguson, 1996). Converse and Presser (1986) recommend using simple language, and short questions, avoiding implicit negatives, overlong lists and dangling alternatives (pp. 10-15). Fink (1995) offers these guidelines for using conventional language in questions: use complete sentences, but avoid the use of abbreviations, slang and colloquial expressions, jargon and technical expressions, dual issue questions and negative questions (pp. 22-29).

Questions should also be as bias-free as possible and ". . . sound natural if administered by an interviewer or . . . read smoothly if self-administered. . . ." (Czaja & Blair, p. 62), and as Westbrook (2001) states, " . . . not be 'loaded' to elicit a particular reaction or response" (p. 81). Westbrook (2001) also emphasizes that questions should be reliable and valid. She defines reliable questions as those worded in such a way so the answers are consistent, providing quantifiable data; examples are age, address, and education level. Valid questions provide more subjective information, such as preferences, and feelings.

Different sets of questions will be more appropriate for different stakeholder groups. Querying frequency of library use among administrators would not yield profitable data for assessing needs of students in distance learning programs. However, the attitudes of administrators toward distance learning programs, electronic library resources, and the Internet in general might prove very insightful. Faculty also would require a unique set of questions. The nature and number of assignments in traditionally based courses, compared to both Internet supported courses and Internet based courses would be useful. Questions for students might inquire as to their area of residence, study habits, previous use and experience in the academic library, comfort in using the Internet, and familiarity with electronic library resources, such as databases, electronic journals and electronic books. Each stakeholder group can provide a valuable parcel of information that will complete the picture of the needs assessment.

Obviously the purpose of constructing the questions is to generate usable responses and gather the answers for meaningful analysis. While stakeholder involvement throughout the needs assessment process has been a major point of this discussion, nowhere is such involvement more crucial than in their response to whatever assessment methods and processes are used.

"HOW TO INVOLVE THOSE YOU HAVE IDENTIFIED"–WAYS TO INCREASE STAKEHOLDER PARTICIPATION

The most difficult feature of the needs assessment process is involving stakeholders. It is crucial to the success of a needs assessment process. Yet, it is often the one thing that is overlooked or ignored. There are four important points related to involving stakeholders: acknowledging their importance, communicating with them, treating them with consistency and honesty, and identifying to them the advantages of participation.

Firstly, the importance of the stakeholders has to be acknowledged. The needs assessment process is a hollow, empty vehicle if there are no stakeholders involved. It is only in the cooperation and participation of stakeholders that the needs assessment will have any meaningful results. Let the stakeholders know how important their opinions and needs are to the entire process. Involving representative stakeholders, even in the planning phase, acknowledges their importance to the entire process.

The second step is communicating with stakeholders. Communication with participants may be initiated by a pre-assessment promotion. Promotion may take the form of publicizing the upcoming assessment in terms of the new distance learning program being offered, and possible new library services which may attract the attention of potential student and faculty groups. This promotion can also serve to inform potential participants by supplying details about who is sponsoring/conducting the assessment, what the assessment process will be, and how the data collected will be used. An article in a local or student newspaper may be a good starting point. Additionally a library display, flyers, posters or paper bookmarks may attract the attention of potential stakeholders. E-mail and voice mail announcements to distribution lists associated with the library or campus may also be helpful. Sending stakeholders written confirmation of their agreement to participate, reminders of interview times, or of the date survey forms will be available may increase involvement.

The third step is to be consistent and honest with stakeholders. It seems this should go without saying, but too often assessors overlook being consistent in what they say and do. If a deadline is stated, stick with it; if copies of the findings of the needs assessment are promised to faculty, deliver them. The opposite is also true: refrain from making promises that cannot be kept. Do not imply that a coveted and expensive database will be subscribed to, or that library hours will be extended simply because certain individuals have endorsed or participated in the assessment. Each group of stakeholders has their own agenda and it is unethical to use that agenda to manipulate their participation.

Fourthly, demonstrate to stakeholders the advantages of participation. The ultimate goal of the needs assessment is the enhancement of library resources and services available to students in a distance-learning program. Involvement by stakeholders provides them with a chance to help shape and customize library services. Also, this is an opportunity for stakeholders to make their voice heard through giving honest input, which will remain confidential. In addition, stakeholders may be provided with an opportunity to earn a bonus or reward as an incentive.

Other general methods for increasing participation by stakeholders include repeated contacts with participants, providing information regarding the use of the results, identifying the sponsor, and the use of rewards or monetary incentives (Hayes, 1997). The use of rewards or monetary incentives is expensive and generally out of reach for many libraries, especially academic libraries. As noted previously, different stakeholder groups have different stakes, and therefore will be motivated by different incentives. For example, students might respond to a willing professor allowing a few "extra points" for participation. Perhaps the managers of the university bookstore could be persuaded to donate low cost items such as pens, pencils, or stickers for distribution as a thank you (incentive) for participation. Additionally, libraries fortunate enough to have an active library volunteer group might ask the volunteers to make flyers, or bookmarks, or bake cookies for promotion or as incentives for participation in the needs assessment process.

In conclusion, it is essential to remember the importance of defining, identifying and involving stakeholders in any needs assessment for library services, particularly in a distance-learning environment. Though such involvement may seem like trying to please all the diners in the introductory scenario, with careful consideration all may leave satisfied and, perhaps, even with a smile.

REFERENCES

Barrick, C.B., & Cogliano, J.F. (1993). Stakeholder involvement: mythology or methodology? *Evaluation Practice, 14*, 33-37.

Burrows, J. (1999). Going beyond labels: A framework for profiling institutional stakeholders. *Contemporary Education, 70*, 5-8.

Clougherty, L., Forys, J., Lyles, T., Persson, D., Walters, C., & Washington-Hoagland, C. (1998). The University of Iowa libraries' undergraduate user needs assessment. *College & Research Libraries, 59*, 572-584.

Converse, J. M., & Presser, S. (1986). *Survey questions: Handcrafting the standardized questionnaire.* Beverly Hills, CA: Sage Publications.

Cooper, R., Dempsey, P.R., Menon, V., & Millson-Martula, C. (1998). Remote library users–Needs and expectations. *Library Trends, 47,* 42-64.

Cummings, J.L., & Doh, J.P. (2000). Identifying who matters: Mapping key players in multiple environments. *California Management Review, XLII,* 83-104.

Czaja, R. & Blair, J. (1996). *Designing surveys: A guide to decisions and procedures.* Thousand Oaks, CA: Pine Forge Press.

Ellern, J., Kimble, S. (1997). H.E.L.P.: A needs assessment. *North Carolina Libraries, 55,* 170-171.

Fink, A. (1995). *How to ask survey questions.* Thousand Oaks, CA: Sage Publications.

Freeman, R.E. (1984). *Strategic management: A stakeholder approach.* Boston: Pitman.

Freeman, R. E., & Reed, D.L. (1983). Stockholders and stakeholders: A new perspective on corporate governance. *California Management Review, XXV,* 88-106.

Gasaway, L.N. (1999). Guidelines for distance learning and interlibrary loan: doomed and more doomed. *Journal of the American Society for Information Science, 50,* 1337-1341.

Hayes, B. E. (1997). *Measuring customer satisfaction: Survey design, use, and statistical analysis methods* (2nd. ed.). Milwaukee, WI: ASQ Quality Press.

Identify your library's stakeholders, tell them your story. (1994). *The U*n*a*b*a*s*h*e*d Librarian, 92,* 8-10.

Kascus, M., & Aguilar, W. (1988). Providing library support to off-campus programs. *College & Research Libraries, 49,* 29-37.

Lawton, B. (1989). Library instruction needs assessment: Designing survey instruments. *Research Strategies, 7,* 119-129.

Mitchell, R.K., Agle, B.R., & Wood, D.J. (1997). Toward a theory of stakeholder identification and salience: Defining the principle of who and what really counts. *Academy of Management Review, 22,* 853-886.

Niemi, J. A., Ehrhard, B.J., Neeley, L. (1998). Off-campus library support for distance adult learners. *Library Trends, 47,* 65-74.

O'Leary, M. (2000). Distance learning and libraries. *Online, 24,* 94-96.

Reviere, R., Berkowitz, S., Carter, C. C., and Ferguson, C. G. (1996). *Needs assessment: A creative and practical guide for social scientists.* Washington, D.C.: Taylor & Francis.

Westbrook, L. (2001). *Identifying and analyzing user needs: A complete handbook and ready-to-use assessment workbook with disk.* New York: Neal-Schuman.

Wimer, S., & Nowack, K.M. (1998). 13 common mistakes using 360-degree feedback. *Training & Development, 52,* 69-77.

Witkin, B.R., & Altschuld, J.W. (1995). *Planning and conducting needs assessments: A practical guide.* Thousand Oaks, CA: Sage Publications.

Help!
I'm the New Distance Librarian–
Where Do I Begin?

Marie F. Jones

East Tennessee State University

SUMMARY. This paper informally presents the results of a study using a combined survey/interview technique that asked experienced extended, distance and/or distributed library services librarians for their advice to novice librarians in the field. The primary recommendation is to build relationships. Other strategies are offered in the areas of marketing, gathering information, evaluating policies, remaining flexible, keeping up with technology, and using the *ACRL Guidelines for Distance Library Services*.

KEYWORDS. Distance education, library services, guidelines, study

INTRODUCTION

When I applied for my current position as Extended Campus Services Librarian at East Tennessee State University, I had over a decade's experience in libraries, but little with serving off-campus library users. Before I began the job, I read everything I could get my hands on related to the topic, and as I hit the ground running, I tapped into the expertise of veteran colleagues in the field.

Realizing what a valuable asset the advice of others was to me, I decided to gather some of that advice and expertise and present it for others new to the

[Haworth co-indexing entry note]: "Help! I'm the New Distance Librarian–Where Do I Begin?" Jones, Marie F. Co-published simultaneously in *Journal of Library Administration* (The Haworth Information Press, an imprint of The Haworth Press, Inc.) Vol. 37, No. 3/4, 2002, pp. 397-410; and: *Distance Learning Library Services: The Tenth Off-Campus Library Services Conference* (ed: Patrick B. Mahoney) The Haworth Information Press, an imprint of The Haworth Press, Inc., 2002, pp. 397-410.

http://www.haworthpress.com/store/product.asp?sku=J111
10.1300/J111v37n03_33

field. I present, here, the result of that information-gathering, salted a bit with my own experience, hoping that it will save some other "newbies" some time as they begin to serve our off-campus clientele. Perhaps it might even give more experienced librarians a bit of food for thought.

DEFINITIONS

I use the terms distance education (DE), off-campus and extended campus interchangeably to encompass all programs that are offered away from a main campus, or in programs that have no traditional campus. While there are different problems and solutions associated with different kinds of extended campus situations, many of the topics covered in this paper will be applicable to most kinds of programs.

METHODOLOGY

Quite simply, I asked librarians on two different extended campus services librarianship e-mail listservs to share with me the answer to the following question: "If you were to offer advice to a brand new distance education/extended campus services librarian, what would that advice be?" I then followed up with telephone interviews with some of the respondents, asking for clarification or expansion of their answers. The 27 respondents came from around the world, but primarily from the U.S. and Canada. Once I gathered the responses, I separated the different ideas ("meaning units")[1] from each person's answers, and then took the resulting list of responses, and organized them by theme under broad headings. Most of what you will read below is given in the words of the librarians as they responded to my query. You'll find the raw data in the Appendix of this document.

RESULTS

The main ideas that arose in the responses were:

1. Networking and communication
    a. With librarians at your institution
    b. With faculty and administrators
    c. With other DE librarians
    d. With librarians at libraries your students use
2. Marketing
3. Gathering information

  a. Identify user needs
  b. Identify funding sources
  c. Document use patterns
4. Evaluating policies
5. Being flexible
6. Keeping up with technology
7. Using *ACRL Guidelines for Distance Library Services*
8. Encouraging words

Networking and Communication: "Don't Try to Do It All Yourself"

Overwhelmingly the most common response to my question was that new Distance Education Librarians need to communicate with and get to know people: fellow librarians in their institution, distance education faculty and administration on campus, and colleagues in D.E. around the world. A piece of advice offered by various respondents, referring to different categories of this theme was, "Don't try to do it all yourself." Basically, this means that you don't need to start from scratch, and you don't need to do everything alone; work as part of a team with your colleagues, and learn from the experiences of other librarians.

Build Relationships with the Librarians at Your Institution

In some institutions, the distance education librarians are isolated from socializing or participating in regular library events. If you're based at a branch library, spend a lot of time traveling to off-campus sites, or even have an office in a secluded part of the library, it's easy to be out of touch with your colleagues. You need to establish relationships with all departments of the library and form collegial relationships within the library. Volunteering for non-distance education activities can help build these relationships, as can serving on library committees. Many emphasize the advocacy role of a DE librarian, and serving on library committees can allow you to bring DE issues to the forefront of committee discussions, while building relationships with your colleagues. Part of your job, if you work in a bricks-and-mortar campus, is to sensitize on-campus colleagues to the needs of the off-campus community. In most libraries, it's also important to build relationships with other librarians in order to integrate services into on-campus library operations. Unless you have a separate budget, staff and collection, distance learners will be served by the entire library, and you need the entire library staff's support in that service. In a similar vein, one respondent suggested that you form a committee to oversee services rather than trying to do it yourself. Depending on the organizational structure of your library–mine detests committees and would rather function informally–this may be a wise way to get others to feel responsible for off-campus services.

Build Relationships with Faculty, Administrators, and Support Staff

Become as visible as possible to distance education colleagues. You must contact faculty and administrators and keep contacting them. As with your library colleagues, these people need to become your friends and allies. Call them up and make appointments to talk about their courses and your services. Contact them by whatever means possible: e-mail, snail-mail, telephone, in person. Use informal networking to get to know them, also. Attend campus social events; eat lunch in the faculty dining room; introduce yourself to people, and have your library colleagues introduce you. Get yourself onto committees and work groups. You can best advocate for the library and for your off-campus users by being a part of teams that do campus planning. Individuals I spoke to each make these connections in different ways, but they all emphasize that it's important. Do the things that best fit your style, but be sure that you get out there somehow.

You also need to become well acquainted with the people who administer the academic programs that you are supporting. Find out from them how courses are being delivered, where, and by whom, and how they are funded. Establish relationships with all of the people in these departments. You'll need their help and they'll need yours. Making these contacts is one of the very first things you'll need to do.

From my own experience, making these contacts with administrators and faculty might not be as easy as it sounds. What I thought of as one set of programs is administered in any number of different offices. Faculty who teach off-campus courses are often listed as "staff" in the course listing. When meeting administrators, I started by asking within the library who it is that administers these programs. I was given a couple of names. I called those people, met with them, asked them what they needed from me and told them what I had to offer. Then I asked them for more contact names. I met with them and had the same type of conversations. It took me months to meet with people, and I still haven't met everyone that I should. Eventually, I figured out the organizational structure, but in the meantime, I was able to get my name out there on campus, and give some key people an idea of what my role is in serving their programs. Keep reminding yourself that building relationships is an ongoing process that never ends, and that there's no way to do it all in your first year. It's easier if you begin right away, though, because early on people excuse your "stupid questions"; later, they will assume that you know more than you actually might.

You also need to find out what support and administrative services are available on campus and develop relationships with those people. Some areas to think about include: instructional design services, media, computing support, publications office, departmental secretaries, and the registrar's office. Each one of these areas can be important, but make absolutely certain that you meet the secretaries. They hold a vast amount of information (and power) that can make your operations run much more smoothly.

Tap into the Expertise Available Around the Globe from Other Librarians

I have found the people in this field to be incredibly helpful to newcomers. Just as they have been willing to respond to this study, they are willing to help individuals in the field. In many institutions, there is only one librarian dedicated to serving off-campus populations. Most of us don't have colleagues with expertise in DE and librarianship to brainstorm with, or ask advice of. Even within a region, there may only be a handful of people doing jobs like ours. That is where tapping into the expertise of national and international groups can be a godsend.

The responses of people who recommended these resources were remarkably uniform. Most said:

- Join the Distance Learning Section of ACRL[2] and attend the ALA Midwinter and Annual conferences. Be an active member and serve on committees. If you can't attend meetings, become a virtual member of committees. AND
- Attend the biennial Off-Campus Library Services Conference sponsored by CMU and/or read the proceedings (which, of course, you are)
- Join OFFCAMP, the Off-campus Library Services list[3]
- It appears that since the preponderance of librarians who responded to this survey did so from the OFFCAMP list, there may be some bias toward American organizations and listservs. If you are in a library outside of the United States, you will want to look for your own regional and national organizations to join, also.

Get to Know Other Librarians Who Work with Your Students

Besides being a great collegial support network, librarians in the regions where your users live can help provide services. You will need these connections to make borrowing agreements for your students to use other libraries. You will also find that you learn a lot about your students by talking to the librarians who meet them "live." Having friendly, informal and formal relationships with these librarians will benefit your students and help you better serve them.

I've found that librarians at other libraries are amazingly helpful. I have groups of students in cohorts that are as much as five or six hours drive away from my location. This year, librarians at two different community colleges that house our cohort classes conducted library instruction sessions for our students. They have no real stake in these students and their research, but they were more than willing to offer them instruction, including instruction on our databases and off-campus access protocols. I had tried to make arrangements with the faculty at those sites, but they had been unwilling to give up class time for me to come and give instruction. The students contacted the librarians on their own, and the librarians set up group sessions to give them the information they needed. Not only did the students get needed instruction on our resources, they received information on local resources that I couldn't have provided, and it saved me two very long road trips.

Marketing: "Publicize Everything You Do"

Almost inextricably intertwined with networking and communication is marketing. Yet it's such an important aspect of our jobs that I thought it deserved a separate heading. Repeatedly, respondents said that you must be proactive in reaching out to the off-campus learning community. No one is going to come to your doorstep asking for services, so you can never do enough publicizing of those services. You have to reach out and promote services and resources to which off-campus users are entitled but do not know. Contact students and faculty by whatever means possible: e-mail, snail-mail, telephone, print advertising, Web sites (for more on Web sites, see "Technology," which follows).

In order to distribute this publicity, you have to find out about the communication infrastructure of your campus as soon as possible. Ask both inside and outside the library, because sometimes your internal colleagues won't know everything that's available. Are there e-mail distribution lists for the whole campus? For students? For faculty? For off-campus students? Off-campus faculty? Particular departments or cohorts? Can you get funding for postage and mailing of PR materials by regular mail? If your library can't fund it, can some other administrative unit? (Wherever DE is administered, Continuing Studies, for example, might be able to help; this is where your connections with the administrators in those departments can come in handy.) Put the telephone to good use, too. Does your campus have a voice mail system that allows for distribution lists? Set up distributions for your faculty and administrators. Call and make appointments to meet in person with faculty and administrators to tell them about your services and learn about their courses. Call departmental secretaries. They can help you track down the elusive adjunct faculty or the invisible cohort. They can also tell you who coordinates a particular program, and give you the contact names of people who will actually get back to you.

Some suggestions arose on useful materials to include in your marketing materials. You can make use of any mandate from a campus president/chancellor that supports distance education. Referring to accreditation standards also gets faculty attention and provides credibility. The *ACRL Guidelines for Distance Learning Library Services* might be able to be used in a similar way.

The question then becomes, what exactly is it that I'm marketing? One respondent said that in contacting faculty, "You need to be sure that [they] understand the instructional function of libraries (you'd be surprised at how many don't) and how they and their students can tap into that expertise online." From this response, I realized an important thing–although I've been marketing library instruction services for years, my handouts for faculty at my extended campus sites say only that I offer library instruction in flexible formats, but they do not say *what* library instruction *is*. I'm sure that many of my faculty members have no idea that instruction has broader information literacy implications, and doesn't just mean an orientation to the tools. Many may think of library instruction as a synonym for "library tour" and have little idea how that is adapted to a virtual environment.

Gathering Information

Focus on User Needs: "Don't Sweat the Details"

You need to get to know the library users and find out what their needs and problems are. Design your services around that. "Don't sweat the details," says one librarian, "what students want most is easy-to-find information (how do I do this/get this) and quick delivery." Make sure students can contact you in a variety of ways: e-mail, a toll-free number, and a good Web site are all good ways of doing this. Then, when they're in touch with you, keep track of what it is they've asked for.

It's important that you know who your users are. Use both formal and informal methods of gathering this information. When you are first meeting the administrators of your distance education programs, you can use this information gathering as an opening for the conversation. It's important to identify the characteristics of the population you're serving and what's already in place to serve them. How many are enrolled in what programs? What are the patterns of enrollment? What are the methods of course delivery? What are the service expectations of your clientele?

You can use a variety of methods for gathering those service expectations. I was lucky enough to be invited within my first months of work to be a part of some standard yearly surveys that are sent to off-campus students. I used that opportunity to find out what kinds of technology our students are using at home, how often they use library resources, and how satisfied they've been with services. Just plain talking with students is a good way of gathering information, also. In library instruction sessions I try to talk to individuals and to draw them out on the problems they've had accessing library materials. As noted above, I keep track of reference questions that come by e-mail, phone, or in person, and I use those questions to develop collections, services, and training resources. We've also had some campus focus groups that have brought up distance library issues that have helped me identify some needs I hadn't recognized in other venues.

Funding: "The Great Elusive Budget"

You also need to know about how programs are funded and what funding is available. If you have no control over your own funding and all services are funneled through your main library, then that means you must put even more effort into building relationships with the staff in your library. Regardless of where the money comes from, you need to know the funding sources and the process for getting and maintaining funding. In some settings, this may be one of the most frustrating challenges of your job. One person I interviewed also emphasized that before you take a job in this field, you should verify that funding and support really are in place and that they're not just paying lip service to support issues. You should get those promises in writing early on, so that you know exactly what is in place before you accept a position.

Documentation: "Prove that What You're Doing Is Valuable"

Be ready to justify your work to the outside world. No matter what situation you're in, part of the job is keeping meaningful statistics. If you're starting a program from scratch, you need to figure out right away what documentation you need. The *Guidelines for Distance Learning Library Services* lists 18 different types of documentation that you should keep. It doesn't, however, identify the specific statistics you should count, nor did the respondents to this survey.

Policies: "Don't Promise More Than You Can Deliver"

As you work your way through the process of identifying student needs, you should be using those identified needs to evaluate or create policies for your program. While you want to do everything you can for as many people as you can, you also need to set some boundaries so that you can provide your promised level of service. It is also very important to set up policies if you come into an institution where there are none in place. Remember that policies aren't set in stone. They can be changed when need or staffing changes, but when you're providing a premium service, you can't serve all populations all of the time. It's also easier to add a service than it is to take it away. You might consider beginning with a fairly conservative agenda and then branch out when you have a feel for what you can do with the resources available. It's important that when you advertise services, you promise only what you can actually deliver, or you will lose credibility among your users. Setting guidelines helps you keep your promises.

Also, make sure that your policies fit the programs you are serving. Don't try to use a cookie-cutter approach to apply policies across all programs or to borrow policies from other institutions. While borrowing ideas that seem to fit your situation is a good idea, taking someone else's policy statements wholesale is a particularly bad idea. Also, applying the same rules to all programs can hamper your attempts to provide equivalent services. For example, technology access in some countries is much different than in the United States. If you plan to deliver everything through Web-based full-text, you may rapidly discover that your international students aren't able to access the material. You need to have policies that allow for document delivery to those students in a medium they can access–most probably in paper. On the other hand, if you have a site-based program where you know what computers and software are available to the students in labs or library spaces, or you have an online program where there are minimum software and hardware requirements in order to take classes, then you have a built-in technological infrastructure on which you can base electronic document delivery.

Technology: "Don't Wait for Newer/Better Technology"

Technology skills are so basic to our work that not many people mentioned them in their advice. They are, nonetheless, vital. Says one respondent, "Develop as fast as you can and as far as you can your automated library skills." I would add to that the need for instructional technology skills. You can build amazing tutorials relatively easily these days, and making online instructional resources available benefits all library users, regardless of location. Another respondent says to get to know whatever courseware your campus has adopted (Blackboard, WebCT, etc.) because it will help you work with faculty if you know the teaching environment in which they are working. Other basic skills like spreadsheet use, e-mail management (especially distribution lists), and of course, word processing, are essential to the job. If you can fine-tune your skills in these areas, you will find that it streamlines your work.

It is vital, however, that your Web pages are "very good, interesting, workable and updatable." That's hard to do if you have to rely on someone else to make your updates, although as I talk to people, I discover that many of us are in situations where making our own updates is not possible. In this case, it comes back to that primary theme of relationships: in a situation where others make the updates, you have to rely on your relationships with them and your team-building skills to make sure that the pages get updated in a timely and accurate fashion. If you are lucky enough to have control over your own Web space, make sure that your Web design skills are as strong as possible, or work closely with the support services your campus may offer. In addition to general information about your programs and services, your Web pages should offer good tutorials and "how-to" information. Keep in mind bandwidth limitations as you design your pages, also.

Finally, while it's important to make use of new technologies as they emerge as viable options, it's equally important to "make do" with what you have at any given time. As another person wisely advised, "Don't wait for newer/better technology. Use what is available and go out and do it."

Flexibility: "Always Expect Change"

Changes in program offerings, policies, database interfaces, and technology tools always happen at the moment you least expect it. Try to anticipate whatever changes might come along by keeping up with trends. Ask those people you've connected with across campus "if anything new is in the wind." Don't wait for them to get around to telling you.

But when changes do catch you by surprise, don't get stressed over it. Be open to new approaches that might seem impossible to manage at first. Two people advised, "Think outside the box," and another noted that instead of thinking about the rules first, you should think about how to get the materials/information to the patron.

Taking risks may seem a bit scary, but it's also what makes our jobs so exciting. We're carving new ground here, and the old rules need to be re-examined and adjusted so that we can best fit the needs of our clientele. As one respondent said, "To give the best service, you must be open to new possibilities."

Use the ACRL/DLS Guidelines and Other Standards

I could easily have subsumed this theme into the one on tapping into national DLS resources, but I think that it's important enough to stand on its own, and a good point on which to conclude this discussion. Three respondents mentioned the guidelines (http://www.ala.org/acrl/guides/distlrng.html). Study them carefully, and you'll find that they can provide an outline for your work agenda and goals for your program. The main areas that the guidelines cover in relation to programs are: philosophy, management, finances, personnel, facilities, resources, services, and documentation. Some parts of the guidelines are useful in justifying to administration the need for funding or other resources. Other parts outline the kinds of services a good distance education program should offer, the kinds of documentation you should keep, and the functions of a manager in this kind of program.

Other standards that were mentioned were "Best Practices for Electronically Offered Degree and Certificate Programs," (http://www.wgu.edu/wgu/about/Best Practices.pdf), "Principles of Good Practice site for Library and Learning Resources" (http://www.wascweb.org/senior/guide/pgpc.htm) and "The Statement of Commitment" by the eight regional accrediting commissions (http://www.wascweb.org/senior/guide/pgpc.htm). It was pointed out that you may be the individual responsible for pulling together materials for accreditations teams. If so, the documentation you have gathered will be a key component in making your case for accreditation, and the standards can be used as a tool to help you gather the most meaningful statistics.

CONCLUSIONS AND ENCOURAGING WORDS

This advice, taken in its totality, might seem overwhelming. One respondent wisely said, "Don't expect to understand all the distance programs at once." While you need to get a sense of the scope of your programs and to begin to build relationships across campus, remember that it's a process. "Be patient," said one respondent, and "Don't be discouraged." You can't do everything at once, and your priorities need to be set with the size of your programs and staff in mind. Break everything down into manageable pieces, but keep your eye on the big picture. One of the things I've found is that the longer I'm in my job, the more I am bogged down in details. I have to keep reminding myself of my larger goals in order to keep myself from spending too much time on things that really don't contribute to those goals.

While you're thinking of this job as a process that won't happen overnight, remember, too, that you need to watch for opportunities and capitalize on them as they occur. You never know where those opportunities may arise, but if you're always looking for an "in" for your program and your students, you will recognize and jump at the chances as they arise.

I think that the main piece of advice I gleaned from this study is to become involved. It's the best way to build relationships, establish credibility, informally market and advocate your services. Remember that there are others doing the same thing you are in other places. Learn from their experience and don't be shy about e-mailing or calling others for advice. One thing I've found is that I loved chatting with fellow DE librarians on the phone. It was sometimes hard to focus on the study once I got them on the phone because we started comparing notes and sharing ideas, and it felt like some of them were as starved for that kind of conversation as I was.

Looking broadly over the feedback I received as I talked to these experienced librarians, I find a few things very heartening. Most of these people seem as enthusiastic about their jobs after serving in them for years as I feel after being here only one year. They care about the students. The service ethic is alive and well. They enjoy serving library users and they enjoy exploring new ways of using technology to improve service. They seem satisfied by the work they do, and they expect that we will be satisfied, too.

I close with the words of one final respondent who reminds us that, if we're patient, we will see the payoffs for the work we do: "You will find great satisfaction in seeing an off-campus student receive a degree knowing that you played a part in his or her educational success." Aren't we lucky to be able to have that kind of satisfaction from our work?

NOTES

1. The language of this paper is consciously informal. While I could have framed these findings in the language of qualitative research, I choose to approach it in a more accessible format in order to encourage the broadest possible readership.

2. See http://caspian.switchinc.org/~distlearn/ for more information.

3. To subscribe send an e-mail to listserv@cwis-20.wayne.edu and in the body of your message type: subscribe offcamp [YOUR NAME].

APPENDIX

The following responses are those given to both written and telephone inquiries. Numbers following phrases indicate the number of times the theme was suggested. Note that, for the purpose of brevity, some of the larger themes were condensed into broader topics. These are marked with an asterisk.

Learn from other off-campus librarians 4
Attend Off-Campus Library Services Conference (or at least read proceedings) 4
Join DLS/ACRL and be active 2
Join ACRL/LITA 1
Join OFFCAMP 3
Establish relationships* with librarians at institution 6
Form a library committee to oversee services 1
Don't try to do it all yourself 2
Integrate services into the on-campus Library operations; unless you have a separate budget, staff and collection, distance learners will be served by the entire library 1
Establish relationships* with DE faculty 6
Establish relationships* with DE administration 10
Have support of senior management on policy issues 2
Establish relationships* with support staff/services 4
Get to know departmental secretaries 3
Become as visible as possible 2
"Insinuate yourself" into groups 2
Emphasize liaison/advocate role 2
Sensitize on-campus colleagues to needs of off-campus 1
Marketing 4
Promote services and resources to which off-campus users are entitled but might not know 1
Communicate by whatever means possible 3
　e-mail

　snail mail
　telephone
Find out about campus information infrastructure (e-mail lists, campus mail, voice mail system, etc.)
Make use of any mandate from any president in publicity 1
Refer to accreditation in P.R.1
Don't promise more than you can deliver 3
Make the first move 1
Contact instructors 1
Keep contacting instructors 2
Let instructors know what you provide 2
Be flexible 2
Think outside the box 2
Be open to new approaches 2
Take risks 1
Anticipate change 2
Don't sweat the details 1

Find out about the characteristics of the population you are serving:
　Number enrolled 1
　Patterns of enrollment 1
　Methods of course delivery 2
　Service expectations 2
　Funding 3
　Get to know students 3

Pay attention to technological limits of some international programs 2
Have a clear policy on who is included, excluded from services 2
Set reasonable limits 1
Communicate the need for sufficient budgeting 2

APPENDIX (continued)

Make sure funding will increase and numbers of students increase 1

Make sure institution has a commitment to ongoing funding before you accept job 1

Good Web site 4

Tutorials on Web site 1

Interesting, workable, updateable 1

Keep bandwidth limitations in mind 1

Develop as far as you can and as fast as you can your automated library skills 1

Don't wait for newer/better technology 1

Become familiar with course authoring software 1

Many access options for users to get info 1

e-mail

toll-free number

Web site

Live online reference

Paper handouts/mailings

Study the ACRL Guidelines for DLLS 2

Convince staff, administrators and institution to adopt the guidelines 2

Work with a university that cares about the guidelines & accreditation standards–get it in writing 1

Be familiar with accreditations standards and guidelines 1

"Best Practices for Electronically Offered degree and Certificate Programs"

Principles of Good Practice site for Library and Learning Resources: http://www.wascweb.org/senior/guide/pgpc.htm

The Statement of Commitment by the eight regional accrediting commissions http://www.wascweb.org/senior/guide/pgpc.htm

Don't expect to understand all the distance programs at once 1

Be patient 1

Capitalize on opportunities as they occur 1

Don't be discouraged

Distilling
the Information Literacy Standards:
Less Is More

Jamie P. Kearley
Lori Phillips

University of Wyoming

SUMMARY. This paper describes the history and rationale for an interactive multimedia Web tutorial that was created by librarians at the University of Wyoming to serve the needs of distance learners and on-campus students. The tutorial is called *TIP, Tutorial for Information Power*, and it moves beyond standard library instruction in its focus on the broader concepts of information literacy. Also discussed is the creative process of developing *TIP*, including how the authors determined which information literacy standards were most appropriate for inclusion. The initial evaluation of *TIP* is described, as well as future possibilities.

KEYWORDS. Literacy, standards, library instruction, distance learners

INTRODUCTION

In today's society, it is imperative that college students acquire the ability to locate, evaluate, and use information successfully. While electronic information sources have become easily available through a desktop computer, the abundance of choices, sources, and search engines make the task of locating

[Haworth co-indexing entry note]: "Distilling the Information Literacy Standards: Less Is More." Kearley, Jamie P., and Lori Phillips. Co-published simultaneously in *Journal of Library Administration* (The Haworth Information Press, an imprint of The Haworth Press, Inc.) Vol. 37, No. 3/4, 2002, pp. 411-424; and: *Distance Learning Library Services: The Tenth Off-Campus Library Services Conference* (ed: Patrick B. Mahoney) The Haworth Information Press, an imprint of The Haworth Press, Inc., 2002, pp. 411-424.

http://www.haworthpress.com/store/product.asp?sku=J111
10.1300/J111v37n03_34

reliable and accurate information more complex. It is essential that individuals know how to use computers, databases, Web search engines, and other information technologies to achieve a variety of educational, occupational, and personal goals.

Currently some of these skills are addressed in a library component of a required course for freshman students at the University of Wyoming. However, off-campus students are not required to take this course. Consequently, distance learners only receive instruction when their professor requests it for a particular class. To address this discrepancy and to incorporate innovations in information technology, librarians at the University of Wyoming have developed an interactive multimedia Web tutorial call *TIP: Tutorial for Information Power*. The addition of *TIP* to the Libraries' Web menu offers instructional materials to users at point of use. Furthermore, *TIP* is readily available for all students, including off-campus, online, and transfer students; in other words, students who in the past might not have received education in information literacy.

This paper will describe how our project grew from a text-only tutorial, based on a traditional bibliographic instruction model, to an interactive multimedia Web tutorial focused on information literacy standards and indicators. The project was funded by a small university grant and was created by librarians who were assisted by a graphic designer and a student computer programmer. We will describe the process of how we created and tested the tutorial and implemented it in a required freshman course.

HISTORY AND RATIONALE

By the late 1990s the University of Wyoming Libraries, like most libraries, had migrated to the Web to deliver library catalogs, databases, and other information resources. The UW Libraries were also distributing instructional handouts and subject specific guides via the Web because it was easy to keep instructional materials current and avoided the expense of printing as well as the postage costs for off-campus students. This practice reflects a national trend in the use of instructional technology and has been a boon to distance education students.

Concurrently, in the past five years there has been a substantial decline in the number of library instructional sessions requested for distance classes. We surmise the decrease in requests for instruction is related to a rise in computer proficiency and increased familiarity with the Web. Increasingly, professors assume that students have the expertise to seek out and evaluate information. In contrast, librarians believe that familiarity with the Web does not create expert searchers or critical researchers.

To ameliorate this situation, our distance librarian was eager to offer bibliographic instruction via the Web so that off-campus students would have instruction available at point of need. Consequently, a group of reference librarians, including the distance librarian, began work on a Web tutorial in 1998. The result was *ORT, Online Research Tutorial*. Interactivity and graphics were considered ideal, but because librarians were limited in time and financial resources, *ORT* necessarily was a text only tutorial. It was based on a typical bibliographic instruction model and included information on database searching, finding books, articles, and full-text articles online, and evaluating Web resources. The Web design was created in-house and was limited to a simple menu of buttons that functioned as entry points to each module. *ORT* went live in 1999 but was not a required assignment for students. It was used on a voluntary basis or when the distance education librarian referred students to it. There was no counter on *ORT*, so no use statistics were gathered. The only evaluative information came from two people who contacted us: one requested permission to link to a section of *ORT*, and the other to say she had attention deficit disorder and had found it very useful. These comments indicated the tutorial had potential.

Nevertheless, librarians were never satisfied with the appearance, content, or use of *ORT*. In part this dissatisfaction was due to the incomplete nature of *ORT*, but more importantly, without interactivity and graphics *ORT* was dull and boring. Librarians knew that additional expertise in programming and graphic design was needed before further improvement to the tutorial would be made. Librarians had also heard reports of Web tutorials taking a year to develop and costing as much as $20,000 (Adams, 1998), a daunting sum of money. As a result, *ORT* was just a link on the Libraries' desktop that was not used frequently.

Fortuitously, the University's Ellbogen Center for Teaching and Learning issued a request for proposals (RFP) for collaborative projects that would enhance student learning and address issues in the University of Wyoming's Academic Plan. This RFP was issued shortly after a campus-wide evaluation of the University Studies first-year program, a required freshman course, which concluded that information literacy should be a goal of the course. Librarians promptly submitted a proposal to develop an interactive multimedia Web tutorial focused on information literacy for students enrolled in University Studies. The proposal requested $5,000 to purchase a server, zip drive, and salaries for a programmer and graphic designer. The grant was awarded in December 2000 with serious work on the tutorial beginning in January 2001. The expectation was the tutorial would be live by Fall 2001. This gave us exactly eight months to create a completely functional tutorial.

EXISTING WEB TUTORIALS AND PREPARATORY WORK

In preparation for our creative work, librarians reassessed the existing text tutorial, closely examined other tutorials, and attended ACRL workshops on online tutorials and information literacy standards. We quickly concluded that our text-only tutorial could not be used as a basis for the new one, since it did not focus on information literacy. This will be explained more fully in the discussion on the design process. On the other hand, two innovative library Web tutorials that intrigued us were: *The Data Game* (2000) created by Colorado State University librarians and *TILT: Texas Information Literacy Tutorial* (1998) created by University of Texas librarians.

The visual animations, graphics, sound, and game show concept of *The Data Game* were highly original. *The Data Game* was entertaining, engaging, and humorous; in fact Coach Locknut, the host of the finding books module, made us laugh out loud. In contrast, we found Gloria Gownwell, hostess of the finding articles module, a bit distracting. *The Data Game* had interactive activities and a quiz, features we wanted to incorporate. The most significant drawback from our point of view was the standard bibliographic model of how to find books and articles, and how to search the Web.

In comparison, the focus of *TILT* was information literacy, which grabbed our attention. It also had graphics, sound effects, novel interactive quizzes, and learning exercises. *TILT's* three modules (selecting, searching, and evaluating) were very comprehensive. In fact, participants must choose one of six topics and the selected topic is then used for illustrations throughout the tutorial. The depth of *TILT*, while admirable, also made it quite lengthy. The introduction states one and a half hours are needed to complete the modules but it took us longer. We concluded that *TILT* was longer and more comprehensive than what was necessary for our one hour University Studies course, in which the library component is only one assignment.

Finally, we took advantage of two pre-conference sessions at the 10th National ACRL Conference in Denver. The workshop, "Reaching Students and Faculty: Putting the Information Literacy Competency Standards to Work," provided a solid framework for thinking about the curriculum design that would most effectively teach information literacy outcomes. The discussions about the assessment of student learning were also meaningful at this juncture since we intended to include a graded quiz as part of our tutorial.

In contrast, the workshop "Online Tutorials, Virtual Tours, and Cyber Assignments: Exploring the New Frontiers of Library Instruction" presented guidelines for the functionality and design of Web instructional materials. It was instrumental in getting us to think differently about instructional design for Web media.

OBJECTIVES FOR THE WEB TUTORIAL

Based on this preparatory process and extensive discussions we developed broad objectives for the tutorial. The tutorial should be:

- Focused on information literacy skills rather than standard bibliographic instruction tasks.
- Designed so that concepts are presented in a text and graphic format and then practiced using interactive games and questions. (Students should pause and think rather than click through.)
- Graphically appealing to keep the content interesting and novel.
- Organized in short pieces of text whenever possible to avoid scrolling and excessive reading. (Information should be kept above the scroll.)
- Easy and transparent to navigate. (You should always know where you are.)
- No longer than one hour in length so only a basic introduction to information literacy would be included.
- Universal in content and thus relevant to distance students.

We also wanted to include a final quiz that would be scored automatically and be submitted to professors. The quiz needed to generate a database of raw scores and evaluative comments that could be used to analyze the content for use in future revisions.

INFLUENTIAL INFORMATION LITERACY DOCUMENTS

Three separate documents also shaped the direction and content of our tutorial. These included the University of Wyoming's *University Studies Program (USP) Review Committee Report* (2000), *Information Power: Building Partnerships for Learning* (American Association of School Libraries, 1998), and the ACRL *Information Literacy Standards* (2000).

The University of Wyoming has a University Studies first-year program designed to introduce freshmen and transfer students to various services and agencies on campus. The Libraries have been an integral part of this course since its inception in 1990. The library assignment was composed of a chapter describing the Libraries, a walking tour, and a paper and pencil exercise designed to teach use of the online catalog.

In 1999, under the direction of the Associate Vice-President for Academic Affairs, the entire University Studies first-year program was reviewed. Goals and strategies were re-examined and a more holistic profile of a well-educated undergraduate emerged. The USP Review Committee issued its final report in

March 2000. Of the eleven measurable objectives articulated in the report, three had a direct connection to information literacy. It was against this backdrop of interest and support that two other sources were examined.

Information Power was the second source of influence early in the planning process. It outlines nine standards that are grouped by threes under the broad headings of information literacy, independent learning, and social responsibility. The group agreed that standards relating to independent learning and social responsibility were best dealt with by classroom instructors because they have prolonged contact with students and thus more opportunity to develop these themes.

The final, and most influential source of inspiration for the group was the ARCL *Information Literacy Competency Standards*. These standards, adopted by ACRL and endorsed by the American Association of Higher Education, are complex and inter-related. According to ACRL, the information literate student:

- Determines the nature and extent of information needed
- Accesses needed information effectively and efficiently
- Evaluates information and its sources critically
- Uses information effectively to accomplish a specific purpose
- Uses information ethically and legally.

Most useful to us were the performance indicators that accompanied the standards. We combed through them carefully, targeting specific behaviors that we wanted to elicit from students.

THE DESIGN PROCESS

Having armed ourselves with knowledge, we moved into the phase of actually designing the tutorial. It is possible to liken what we did to the process of distillation, which is defined as the purification of a substance by successive activity. We were faced with the daunting task of extracting the essential nature of the information literacy goals and translating them into a teaching tool.

Early meetings of the tutorial group did little to move the project forward. All along, we had assumed that the text-only tutorial, *ORT*, would provide the basis of the new online product. That was not to be the case, however. Initially, the existing tutorial was divided into sections and each group member assumed responsibility for re-working the content. Each person made a valiant attempt to dress the old content up with suggestions for graphics and interactivity, but it remained just that, old content. It was only at this point that we faced the reality that *ORT* taught library skills, not information literacy.

Each person involved had their own vision of what the final project was to look like, but very little understanding of how to get there. We patiently listened to each other pontificate, stressing what concepts we thought were most important and what the finished product might look like. Some of us spoke in sweeping terms about the big picture, while others wanted to focus on the smallest details. It was a frustrating process. Since the group had no initial agreement about how to organize and proceed, valuable time was lost.

Finally, desperate for some common ground, we took what appeared to be a step backward, and went back to the documents that we had studied (*USP Review Committee Report, Information Power*, and the ACRL *Information Literacy Standards*) and thought we understood. In doing so, we began to ground our vision in reality and to move forward. Slowly we moved through the standards and performance indicators. We examined each one with an eye toward how we would teach it and how students would demonstrate understanding. Our group included several library instruction veterans; therefore framing our discussion in this practical way immediately improved not only the atmosphere within the group, but also the flow of productive ideas. We realized that we had already incorporated information literacy into our instruction and, thus were able to bring tactics and strategies already in use to the discussion.

In order to organize our work and keep track of where we were, we decided to assemble a loose framework that roughly approximated a logical progression of information seeking behavior. The framework we developed also reflects the goals of the five ACRL *Information Literacy Standards*. In keeping with our emphasis on outcomes, we used action verbs to name the steps in our progression:

- Investigate
- Search
- Locate
- Evaluate
- Utilize.

These action verbs eventually came to be the names of the five different modules of our tutorial.

Creating a topical outline also assisted us as we communicated with our computer programmer and graphic designer. Neither was a librarian, but it was essential that they understood the overall direction and objectives of the project. Another decision that had to be made early in the creative process to assist the designer and the programmer, was a title, theme, and other identifiable images for the tutorial. The title, *Tutorial for Info Power*, and the more memorable acronym, *TIP*, emerged after several brainstorming sessions.

Once we had established a system of organization, we began to move the various pieces into place. From the *USP Review Report*, the book *Information Power*, and the ACRL *Information Literacy Standards*, we began to group things logically. At this juncture, we decided that student ability to perform requested tasks would be the measure of our success. Consequently, we were able to discard ideas that, while important, could not be practiced through interactive activities or be successfully measured by the quiz that would accompany *TIP*. For example, we concluded it would be difficult to construct a task that would measure the ability to organize information chronologically, hierarchically, and topically, so that piece of Standard 3 in *Information Power* was not addressed.

Our instructional design strategy was to teach selected concepts and then immediately challenge the students with some kind of interactivity that asks them to apply what they have learned. The interactivity is a second line of teaching within the tutorial. The interactive questions reinforce the message conveyed by the textual information. Although the questions asked within the body of the tutorial are not graded, they come with feedback for each possible answer. If students choose incorrectly, they are provided with the correct answer and a rationale for it. Even correct answers are reinforced with comments. For example, in the Investigate module, we use flash animations to visually depict different formats of materials. We use actual magazine covers, journal covers, and front pages of newspapers to create colorful images to accompany the text that explain each type of information and describe its most appropriate uses. Following this section, we ask students to play a game entitled "The Source is Right," where they consider information sources in response to specific research questions such as: Would gun control reduce school violence? Students then rank the usefulness of each type of material (books, journals, or the Web) for researching the topic.

Most online tutorials use interactivity to teach and engage student interest. Interactivity within the body of the teaching tool requires students to be alert, and if it is correctly constructed, then the interactivity reinforces the point being taught. We felt it important to avoid too much repetition in asking questions and expecting a student response, and subsequently decided that for each concept a limit of three or fewer questions would be used.

The next step in the design process involved adapting the information literacy standards and indicators for the actual tutorial content. Standard Two, from the ACRL Standards (2000) is a case in point. It states, "The information literate student accesses information effectively and efficiently." Included is the Performance Indicator 2 " . . . the student constructs and implements effectively-designed search strategies." We began casting about for ways to express what a "successful strategy" might be. Initially, we discussed listing the steps in the process, but discarded that idea as uninteresting. Then one member of the group suggested profiling two different students' information seeking behavior. A scenario comparing their processes and relative success or failure could then be used to teach the strategy. Another member of the group picked up the idea and created personalities for students, assigned them names, and wrote a text that described their information odysseys. Another group member took this text and roughed out a cartoon strip that told the story of Sisqo and Shania, two University of Wyoming students with an assignment to write a research paper about e-commerce. Finally, the entire sequence was turned over to the graphic designer for his professional implementation. This synergistic process repeated itself time and again in the creation of *TIP*.

The virtual tour of the library is another example of how we moved from standards and indicators to actual content. The ACRL standards discuss location in terms of the ability to use various classification schemes, i.e., call number systems, to locate resources within the library. However, our experience at the University of Wyoming indicates a physical orientation to the building is also important for freshman students. Therefore, as the focal point of the virtual tour, we employed the process of using a library catalog to find a call number, riding an elevator to the appropriate stack level, and finally using the call number to locate the item on a library shelf. The tour begins when the student enters the building and concludes with the student exiting, having checked out the book. The location of other pertinent services and collections are noted along the journey, thus giving a physical orientation to the building. Streaming video was a natural choice to present this virtual tour. The technology allowed us to suspend the linear progression through physical space that occurs in a physical tour.

Collaboration was a hallmark of the design process. It occurred as we developed the logo, theme, navigation features, and images with the graphic designer. It also occurred with the programmer as we created interactive games and the quiz database. In developing the quiz database, librarians described the desired features: to register users, to grade electronically, to post results by instructor, to provide opportunity for feedback. Based on our description, the programmer designed a database structure that met our requirements and that enables us to easily modify the content. For instance, we can add or delete questions, names of instructors, and students. We can also examine the breakdown of answers for each question to determine the frequency of each response. The final database was the product of several discussions between librarians and the programmer.

TESTING THE PROTOTYPE

Once *TIP* was complete, we needed to test the prototype before going live. The purpose of testing the model was three-fold. First, we wanted to identify technical problems, second to elicit constructive criticism so we could make improvements, and finally to gain students' reaction to *TIP*. Ultimately, we wanted to know if we had succeeded in meeting our objectives of creating an instructive and interesting Web tutorial.

Seven student employees of the UW Science Library took *TIP* while librarians recorded their comments and reactions. Included in this group were five females and two males. There was one high school graduate, one freshman, one sophomore, one junior, two seniors, and one graduate student. Two were African-Americans and the other five were Anglo-Americans. They ranged in age from 17 to 30. Students were compensated for their participation.

At the conclusion of the session, students were asked two questions: do you think students will learn anything from *TIP* and what suggestions do you have for improvement? Comments were similar and informed us that we were on the right track:

> I knew a lot of this, but it refreshed my memory. I expected it to be boring but it wasn't. Freshman

> It is good that you put in the (university) code for the infraction (of academic dishonesty). Freshman

> You learn a lot more than the previous (library instruction) assignment. This has explanations and is more complete. It takes you through more steps. You can go at your own pace. I had a session in this room (Libraries' electronic classroom) with a librarian but missed most of what was said. Junior

> (I) like it a lot better than what we did. I was a sophomore before I really understood what I was doing. Senior

> I think students will learn a lot. I learned a lot. You are giving out a bunch of information and covering all the bases. Senior

> I picked up some things I didn't know. Senior

As a result of other comments the speed of the flash animations was altered, bullets were added for emphasis, the instructions for one interactive exercise were improved, and the call number ordering exercise was expanded.

IMPLEMENTATION OF TIP

We began using *TIP* in conjunction with the required first-year course in Fall 2001, and approximately 1,300 students have completed the tutorial for credit. As students electronically submit their quiz, they are invited to make evaluative comments and approximately 500 have done so. These comments will be used to make revisions to the tutorial. Instructors in the first-year course have been encouraged to use *TIP* in their other classes, if appropriate. The Outreach Librarian is also making faculty of off-campus courses aware of *TIP*, and we expect them to make use of the tutorial as word spreads.

FUTURE POTENTIAL

At the time of writing, the benefit of *TIP* to distance learners has not been realized. *TIP* was completed just prior to the beginning of the fall semester, which left no time to promote it to off-campus students and faculty. Nevertheless, we are convinced *TIP* has considerable potential to benefit distance learners in our rural state. Wyoming has a population of less than a half million distributed over 98,000 square miles. Distances are great and library collections are modest. The University of Wyoming is the only four-year institution in Wyoming. It is our experience that students who have limited access to library resources and databases in their home communities are easily overwhelmed with the large number and selection of UW Libraries' resources and databases. Consequently, students are apt to use the Web, which they view as an uncomplicated source of information, as their primary resource unless convinced otherwise. *TIP* emphasizes the need to critically evaluate sources of information, especially the Web. A promotional campaign is planned for spring of 2002.

In addition to the feedback received from the 1,300 freshman students, instructors of the University Studies course will be sent an e-mail survey that asks for their overall impressions. This information will be invaluable as we contemplate the shape the tutorial will take in the future.

It is possible that an advanced version of the tutorial will be created or a module added that examines some concepts more in depth. On the other hand, we might consider constructing some kind of pre-test that measures information literacy. Subsequently, students scoring above a certain threshold might be excused from the requirement to take *TIP*.

We have no evaluative data about the impact of *TIP* on our instruction program, and we have not seen a decline in requests for instruction in the first semester of use. We expect requests to work with students on an advanced level of writing and research assignments as they become more information literate. Another possibility is to develop an advanced research course that would be offered for credit.

Creators shared the tutorial with other librarians at the annual meeting of the Wyoming Library Association in September 2001 and received an enthusiastic response. Audience members included school, public, and academic librarians from around the state. To our surprise, librarians requested permission to link to *TIP* and incorporate it into their instruction program. To date, one Wyoming public library has put a link to *TIP* on its homepage, a Wyoming community college librarian is using *TIP* in a research methods course, and a school librarian has introduced her teachers to *TIP*. We see the intersection of goals between the different libraries in our state as positive. We would like to do all that we can to insure that Wyoming students are information literate and prepared to function in the working world that awaits them.

CONCLUSIONS

The creation of *TIP* took eight months of hard work and extensive collaboration. The project entailed an incredible amount of time. Our group met weekly for two hours, and between meetings individual members worked frantically to write content. The content was written in a storyboard format and then turned over to the graphic designer and programmer to implement. The team approach worked well for us. The time we allowed for extensive brainstorming of objectives, format, content, appearance, and interactivity created a synergy that stimulated the creative process.

In our opinion, a graphic designer and programmer are indispensable for a project of this magnitude. They were instrumental in implementing the vision of librarians and were ultimately key to the success of *TIP*. We also took advantage of the expertise of the staff of the University of Wyoming Ellbogen Center for Teaching and Learning. They offered invaluable skills in creating the virtual tour and offered design suggestions.

We discovered that deciding which information literacy standards and indicators are most appropriate was an art, not a science. We had to take into account our diverse audience of on and off-campus students and our instructional goals. We also had to identify which standards were appropriate for inclusion in a library tutorial and which were best left to university faculty to address in their courses.

Finally, we experienced resistance from faculty and staff. While people tout the merit of change, actually changing the way things are done is more difficult to accept. Our advice is to inform all parties with a vested interest in the final product about the objectives early in the process. We also suggest providing opportunities for them to voice concerns. However, external involvement may cause considerable distraction from work on the project. Unwarranted interference late in the process caused us anxiety about the acceptance and success of *TIP*. Our recommendation is to wait until a complete and polished product is ready before unveiling it. Once the tutorial is fully functional it will win support on its merit and originality.

REFERENCES

Adams, C. (1998). A web handbook for library research. In P. S. Thomas & M. Jones (Comp.). *The Eighth Off-Campus Library Services Conference Proceedings: Providence, R.I., April 22-24, 1998* (pp. 1-16). Mount Pleasant, MI: Central Michigan University.

American Association of School Libraries. (1998). *Information power: Building partnerships for learning.* Chicago: American Library Association.

Association of College & Research Libraries. (2000). *Information literacy competency standards for higher education.* Available: http://www.ala.org/acrl/ilcomstan.html.

Association of College & Research Libraries. (2001). *Objectives for information literacy instruction: A model statement for academic librarians*, approved by the ACRL Board January 2001. [Online]. Available: http://www.ala.org/acrl/guides/objinfolit.html.

Breivik, P. S. (2000). Information literacy and the engaged campus. [Electronic version]. *AAHEBulletin.* Retrieved November 12, 2001 from: http://www.aahe.org/Bulletin/nov2000_1.html.

Colorado State University Libraries. (2000). *The data game.* Available: http://manta.colostate.edu/datagame/.

Fowler, C. S., Dupuis, E. A. (2000). What have we done? TILT's impact on our instruction program. *Reference Services Review 28*(4), 343-348.

Kelley, K., Orr, G. J., Houck, J., & SchWeber, C. (2001). Library instruction for the next millennium: Two web-based courses to teach distance students information literacy. Co-published simultaneously in *Journal of Library Administration, 32* (1/2), 281-294 and *Off-Campus Library Services* (ed. by Anne Marie Casey), 2001, 281-294.

University of Texas System Digital Library. (1998). *TILT: Texas information literacy tutorial.* Available: http://tilt.lib.utsystem.edu/.

University of Wyoming. (2000). *University studies program review committee report.* Retrieved November 12, 2001 from University of Wyoming Web site: http://uwadmnweb.uwyo.edu/unst/university_studies_program_revie.htm.

University of Wyoming Libraries. (2001). *TIP: Tutorial for info power.* Available: http://tip.uwyo.edu.

APPENDIX

Timeline

January

- Review existing Web Tutorials
- Brainstorm name, logo, and theme
- Write objectives for tutorial
- Discuss technical issues and software selection

February

- Hire programmer and graphic designer
- Study information literacy standards and objectives

March

- Identify modules/organization framework of tutorial and begin writing
- Discuss objectives with programmer and graphic designer
- Gather information on recommended tutorial instruction and design characteristics
- Finalize details of name, logo, and navigation features
- Write content
- Collaborate with graphic designer to develop images to match content

April

- Write content
- Collaborate with programmer to develop interactive activities

May

- Write and revise content
- Order server
- Create virtual tour
- Create quiz database in collaboration with programmer

June-August

- Review and revise completed work
- Test prototype and make final revisions

September

- Implement tutorial
- Promote tutorial to faculty and distance learners

All Aboard the eTrain:
Developing and Designing
Online Library Instruction Modules

Melissa H. Koenig
Martin J. Brennan

University of Illinois at Chicago

SUMMARY. As more and more library resources become available through the Internet, and as libraries move to 24/7 access to their collections and services, library instruction must move to this environment. The question is how to best move instruction to the Web while continuing to provide quality interactive sessions that are meaningful to the patron. While much of the literature dealing with developing online instruction focuses on for-credit courses, most librarians still reach the majority of their patrons through one-time instruction sessions. This paper looks at how one large urban university began moving its one-time instruction onto the Web, exploring the main developmental efforts in this area, including dedication to process, content quality, faculty input, and student feedback.

KEYWORDS. Library instruction, distance learners, technology, design

THE PROBLEM

The number of electronic resources available through library homepages continues to increase at an astonishing rate. It is not uncommon for libraries to

---

[Haworth co-indexing entry note]: "All Aboard the eTrain: Developing and Designing Online Library Instruction Modules." Koenig, Melissa H., and Martin J. Brennan. Co-published simultaneously in *Journal of Library Administration* (The Haworth Information Press, an imprint of The Haworth Press, Inc.) Vol. 37, No. 3/4, 2002, pp. 425-435; and: *Distance Learning Library Services: The Tenth Off-Campus Library Services Conference* (ed: Patrick B. Mahoney) The Haworth Information Press, an imprint of The Haworth Press, Inc., 2002, pp. 425-435.

http://www.haworthpress.com/store/product.asp?sku=J111
10.1300/J111v37n03_35

double the number of subscriptions to electronic journal and databases within one or two years. Additionally students have, in ever increasing numbers, looked to the Web to conduct their research. The Pew Internet & American Life Project recently reported that "94% of youth ages 12-17 who have Internet access say they use the Internet for school research and 78% say they believe the Internet helps them with their schoolwork" (Lenhart, Simon, and Graziano, 2001). As more users look to the Web as a source of information instruction librarians need to make their presence on the Internet known.

The proliferation of online resources has also proved challenging for librarians who need to train and retrain hundreds if not thousands of library patrons each year. While these patrons need training, they are less available for face-to-face (F2F) instruction. There are many reasons these users may be unable and/or unwilling to attend a traditional library workshop. These reasons may include: distance (they are not located geographically in the same place as the library); time (they are accessing resources in the evening or other hours that librarians are not available or the physical library is not open); or comfort (users may be unwilling to admit their ignorance to their peers or others). Additionally, constraints on library staff time often make it impossible to reach all users during the "teachable moment."

A recent study of early adopters of electronic journals and other electronic resources among faculty of the hard and life sciences found that they are extremely resistant to F2F instruction on new resources. These same faculty are aware that they need to be informed, but find that time constraints are a problem. They appreciate the advantages of accessing library resources through their desktop, and are growing accustomed to avoiding the library (Brennan, Hurd, Blecic, & Weller, 2001). This attitude from early adopters will likely spread to other faculty and/or their students with time.

Given the current environment, instruction librarians are increasingly looking to online instruction both to fulfill a user need and promote the use of library resources. The question of how to move F2F instruction into the Web environment becomes paramount. This paper will look at how one large urban university chose to tackle the problem.

BACKGROUND OF THE UIC PROGRAM

Like other libraries, the University of Illinois at Chicago (UIC) began facing these issues on its own campuses. The composition of the UIC student body provides some additional challenges not faced by all universities. UIC is an urban campus with a largely commuter population. Additionally, according to surveys done by the American Council on Education, the students at UIC are "more likely to be first-generation college students and from families with moderate incomes than the average U.S. student" ("UIC–About UIC," 2001). Many of these students hold down full-time jobs and raise families in addition to attending school.

Add to this mix the UIC Medical campus, which has regional sites in Rockford, Peoria, and Urbana as well as in Chicago. The University's Library of the Health Sciences also serves as one of the National Network of Libraries of Medicine, a program of the National Libraries of Medicine. As part of this contract, the library provides health information and outreach to patrons in the greater Midwest region including Illinois, Indiana, Iowa, Kentucky, Michigan, Minnesota, North Dakota, Ohio, South Dakota, and Wisconsin. With such a distributed population, the focus on easy access to library resources from locations other than the physical library became an important focus.

While providing access to the Library's electronic resources was a relatively easy task, instructing these distributed users on how to access, search, and retrieve library materials was much more difficult. The growth of online courses and Internet use at home and work further complicated the issue. Users could now access and use library resources on their time, but still needed to adhere to the library's schedule to get assistance. Add to this environment those users, like the previously mentioned early adopters, who were unable or unwilling to attend in-person library workshops or classes. Recognizing these changing user expectations, the librarians at UIC decided to begin investigating the use of online tutorials to provide instruction to our patrons when and where they needed it.

In 1993, the University Library began its first experiment with Computer Assisted Instruction (CAI) via the Internet. In November of 1993 a taskforce was formed and charged with "developing and offering an online Internet course to be administered over the University's computer network via the Internet" (Vishwanatham, Wilkins, & Jevec, 1997, p. 435). The course was called "Ride the eTrain: An Introduction to the Internet at UIC" and was offered during the fall semester of 1994. Training was delivered to patron desktops via e-mail messages. The course contained 16 lessons and included such topics as "What is the Internet," "Electronic Mail," "Using FTP," and an "Introduction to GOPHER at UICVM." With more than 450 people subscribed to the course, this training program was considered a success.

Given the success of the e-mail training program, and the substantive growth of the Internet, the librarians envisioned online tutorials as the next logical step. Additionally, the growth of online courses at UIC suggested that students were becoming increasingly comfortable with the Internet as an instructional medium. Accordingly, in the spring of 1999, the library conducted a second pilot to investigate using CAI. This pilot used the Internet, instead of e-mail, as its delivery method. While the population in the first pilot included a cross section of UIC community members, the second pilot was restricted to students enrolled in two Communication 100 sections offered during the summer of 1999 (Koenig & Novotny, 2001).

The goal of this pilot was two-fold. First, the librarians wanted to test the assumption that the students would not only be open to this type of instruction, but that they would also learn from it. Second, the librarians needed to begin creating a course so that they could test software, both for development and delivery, and determine the best instructional design model. It was decided that starting with a small course and testing the modules during the summer session when the classes were smaller and the librarians had more time to write the content and troubleshoot would be ideal.

These first CAI modules were developed using PowerPoint with the addition of Macromedia Dreamweaver Attain (the precursor to Coursebuilder) quizzes and CGI scripts. Students enrolled in Communication 100 were randomly assigned to participate either by taking a series of five online modules or attending a 50-minute F2F workshop. The students' performances on a pretest/posttest instrument were compared to assess the effectiveness of the delivery method. Although the pilot only provided usable pretest/posttest data for a limited number of students, the results revealed two things. First, students who took the online tutorials did significantly better on the posttest than their F2F counterparts. This finding fits with previous studies that found that overall students completing library CAI tutorials performed as well, if not better, than their F2F counterparts on posttest evaluations (Germain, Jacobson, & Kaczor 2000; Kaplowitz & Contini, 1998; Vander Meer, 1996; Lawson, 1984). Second, and paradoxically, the students who attended the F2F workshop were significantly more confident in their abilities (Koenig & Novotny, 2001).

These paradoxical findings–more confidence among less competent users and vice versa–may be explained in part, the investigators speculate, by the lack of feedback or real interaction in the modules. In a 1999 article, Marvin Wiggins discussed the importance of adding a "human element" to "canned" instruction sessions (1994, pg. 225). Other researchers have also talked about the importance of feedback in creating a learning environment that motivates and stimulates learning (Smith, 2001; Cyboran, 1995). Vince Cyboran goes on to emphasize that feedback is crucial in computer based training systems since "there is only one place for the student to get feedback about his performance–from the computer" (1995, p. 18).

It was also observed that many of the participants were simply clicking through to the end of the module and completing the short test. Successful completion of the test produced a form that students filled in to earn credit for the module. The developers felt the addition of simulated events and other interactions within the module content would not only slow the user down, but would also aid in reinforcing the material being taught. Authors of online instruction and Web-based instruction how-to books stress that both interactivity and feedback are essential elements of successful courses (Smith, 2001; Kearsley, 2000).

Feedback and interaction are also two components of active learning. During active learning, the student becomes a "participant in the instructional process" (Smith, 2001, p.136). Active learning has become an important element in classroom instruction, and it is becoming increasingly evident that it is also important in the online environment. While many believe that clicking a mouse or pushing buttons on a keyboard are active learning, it has been found that these actions cannot always be considered active on the part of the student. In 1994 Roger Schank advocated moving away from what he calls "page-turning architecture" (p. 69). Robin Starr goes further, noting that "true interactivity goes beyond static Web pages and page linking, and creates truly interactive pages with information exchange between the user and the server" (1997, p. 8).

Given the need for creating truly interactive exercises and the need to track user behavior, the librarians investigated a number of Web development products and chose Macromedia's Dreamweaver with Coursebuilder. This choice was made for a variety of reasons, but the flexibility of the Coursebuilder extension to assist the developers in the creation of a variety of quizzing interactions, without needing to learn advanced programming languages, was paramount.

THE SEARCH FOR COURSEWARE

Early in the process, it became evident that a course management system was necessary. Not only would such a tool eliminate the need to manually record module completion–if the instructor needed validation–but it would also provide the content developers with feedback about the course. The librarians investigated a number of courseware products on the market at the time and found that while there were many available, none addressed the unique needs and characteristics of the target library user population.

It was important that the software not require the library to register users (registration should be user initiated) since the goal was for users to have access to the modules when they needed it. If patrons had to first contact the library to register, this goal would be defeated. Additionally, the library modules did not require many of the features common to most courseware packages. Since the library was not planning on using the management system to conduct a semester-long class, these features, like threaded discussions, group chat rooms, and instructor mailboxes, would go unused and would only serve to confuse the user. Because of the size of the expected user population, it was also important that the system be able to support at least 100 simultaneous users. Tracking of user activities within the database and the ability to record module completion were also important considerations.

After extensive investigation, the librarians found that there was no existing solution for their needs and decided to contract with a company to co-develop a system that would be built to the local library's specifications. To facilitate development and future maintenance, it was proposed that the system would run on a server housed in the library. Upon completion, local systems staff would be responsible for updating, maintaining, and modifying the software.

The vendor chosen had an extensive history of building similar course management databases for corporate applications, such as human resources development, and had a track record for creating custom products. As an added benefit, the company also provided training in Dreamweaver and Coursebuilder for the Content Developers (CDs), with particular emphasis on instructional design for the Web and other pedagogical concerns.

DEVELOPING THE COURSEWARE PRODUCT

Once the vendor was chosen, the CDs began the development process in conjunction with the library's systems division and the vendor. The CDs scheduled a focus group with the first intended users of the courseware product–a group of school media librarians from the Chicago area. This target group was chosen because of their interest in taking a course on using Internet resources that would be delivered using the new courseware product. It was anticipated that this course would be one of the first offered through this system. Based on feedback from these focus group participants and responses from the posttest questionnaire from the second pilot, a list of desired functionality was developed and discussed with the vendor.

Because the librarians envisioned the CAI modules as a way to reach patrons unable or unwilling to contact the library, it was important that patrons be able to login and use the system with little or no intervention on the part of the library. To this end, it was proposed that the courseware product be linked to the campus proxy server and that patrons be required to use their NetIDs (campus e-mail address) and password for access. Not only would this make it easy for patrons to use (they only need to know one password), but it would also eliminate asking patrons personal questions upon creating their account. All of this information could be culled as needed from the campus phone book using the NetID. Additionally, the librarians would not be responsible for setting or resetting passwords, a taxing task. This function would remain under the purview of the campus computer center.

Verification of tutorial completion was necessary to support ongoing face-to-face teaching efforts. For example, a librarian may require that before teaching an F2F class in advanced searching, all students complete the basic tutorial online. In another scenario, an instructor may encourage their students to attend a library workshop for extra credit and would need some documentation from either the student or the library that the workshop was successfully completed. To aid in the verification process, it would be necessary for students to be able to print verification of module completion. Since students may be required to show verification of completion beyond the current semester, it was also deemed necessary that their records be able to be stored in the system for a longer period of time.

As mentioned earlier, feedback is an essential element for online modules. To make the tutorials more akin to F2F instruction, immediate feedback for the users was necessary. Additionally, qualitative and quantitative feedback are important elements in most instructional design models. Therefore, detailed user statistics that provided information about answers students gave most often and the amount of time they spent in any given module were needed to assess the effectiveness of the course content. In addition, the ability to track student performance would allow for assessment of long-term effects on student performance and confidence.

Student concerns were crucial. Ease of access and a simple identification process already common among UIC systems were vital components. Additionally the courses needed to be cross-platform and, if possible, cross-browser compatible. It was anticipated that these considerations would allow access from anywhere and entry with minimal technical expertise. It was also important that the management system remember the student when he/she reenters the course. This would allow students to track their own progress. It would also allow the student, regardless of the reason they left the module, to resume a module not completed where they left off. The CDs believed that the latter feature was a crucial component that would make the system less frustrating and more user-friendly.

Finally, since the UIC libraries also provide service to the general public, accommodations had to be made to provide instruction to those users. Because verification of completion and user tracking were less important for these users, it was decided guest access should be an option. Since these users would not log in, tracking data on them would be collected and expressed in aggregate terms. In addition, those users with guest access would see some, but not all, of the CAI components. For example, instruction on accessing resources remotely and using proprietary databases would not be included for guest login.

Once the functionality requirements were listed and discussed, the vendor moved forward with these considerations in mind. Weekly meetings and a closed listserv were set up for interested parties to use for communication during the development phase.

It should be noted that another key component of the database is still under development, an additional functionality called prescriptive pretesting. This optional user-initiated test of questions, developed using the module objectives, is designed to test user understanding of the material before prescribing a set of modules. New users could opt to take this test to determine just how much they really know about library resources. The database will then automatically score the test and, based on the user's performance, provide a list of suggested tutorials that will fill in gaps in their skill set. Since this component was not included in the original contract with the vendor, it was set aside for completion at a later date.

CONTENT DEVELOPMENT

While the functionality of the courseware was an important component to the CAI modules, the content of the modules was paramount. Concurrent with the development of the courseware product, the CDs began the systematic development of the database content. From the beginning, it was understood that the database would provide introductory and basic training in the understanding of essential library skills that span the disciplines. It was also envisioned that the scope would grow to include specific training modules on every database for which UIC maintains access, and eventually provide training for discipline-specific library skills.

Eventually it was hoped that many public service librarians in the UIC system would be able to contribute to the content. Since this was still a pilot project it was decided that the number of people involved in creating the initial content be kept to the authors of this article. Limiting the number of people developing content in the beginning allowed for the creation of a more comprehensive design document, and it allowed the authors to become comfortable with the development tools, before having to train others.

It was, however, clear that no two librarians could adequately assess the content needs for a database that would serve the needs of library patrons at a variety of different locations, each location having a wide variety of service needs and expectations. To account for all of these different perspectives, an advisory group of public service librarians, representing a cross section of the different types of libraries within the system, was formed to help the CDs determine the scope of the initial content, and prioritize the further stages of content development. The Group's focus was to first envision the scope of the ideal, complete database. That scope was then dissected into discrete chunks of content: skill sets that could be delivered in distinct training modules with clear sets of objectives.

From the beginning it was anticipated that the Library's CAI tutorial would be modular in design. This would allow the components to be rearranged based on feedback from users, which eased the pressure on the initial design plan–if the structure and order of the tutorials didn't work, the group knew that the modules could be easily rearranged. In addition, the modular construction would also be flexible enough to be easily updated. This was important considering the frequency in which interfaces, vendors, and databases change.

While it was understood that the modules could be rearranged, it became clear that initially organizing the modules into a cohesive unit was not an easy task. The group first made a list of the most important things that library patrons needed to know about the library. These skills were then arranged and rearranged into one of four chapters–Library Overview, An Introduction to Library Resources, Doing Research I and Doing Research II. These four categories would form the top layer of the CAI tutorial. Under each of these chapters, modules on different topics would exist.

In addition, the modular design would also be versatile enough to take into consideration the needs of the teaching faculty. Faculty could, with the assistance of a librarian, have a tutorial constructed specifically for a course or to teach a skill set relevant to a group of courses. Because of the modular nature of the core CAI modules, the librarian would be able to easily pick and choose from the core course, modify those pages to make them relevant to the class focus, and remount the new course modules in a separate part of the server. This approach would allow limited staff to maintain, update, and customize the CAI tutorials.

From a pedagogical perspective, the modules are designed to take anywhere from five to fifteen minutes to complete. Research has shown that a person's attention tends to diminish over time (Horton, 1994; Richardson, 1994). Any longer, and it was feared that users would not retain the information or even worse lose interest. Webpage design principles, like those found in Yale's Web Style Guide (Lynch & Horton, 1997), provided additional guidelines on page layout, use of graphics, and typography.

CONCLUSION AND CURRENT STATUS

The development of the eTrain database at UIC is simply the latest chapter in the gradual transition to comprehensive online services. Many developmental steps led to its inception, and it is likely this database will lead to more sophisticated products yet to be envisioned. The strength of this project depends upon dedication to process, content quality, faculty input, and student feedback. The CDs have kept these principles in mind while moving forward, and believe that these strengths provide a strong basis for success.

Problems common to custom-built endeavors such as ours have unfortunately slowed this process. Typical of the development of such products, there were many functional issues and bugs that arose during the database installation at UIC, which have disrupted the timeline of the project. Moreover, in the midst of the meltdown of the technological sector over the last two years, a larger corporation bought out the vendor. The new parent company shifted the focus of the vendor, and they were no longer doing custom development work like the work done for UIC.

Concurrently, many of the major players contributing to the development of the database left the company, leaving few of the original development team to help iron out the bugs in the system. With continuing problems in the installation process and a vendor newly uninterested in the development of such products, and no one at UIC with the skills and/or time available to resolve such issues, it became apparent that another vendor had to be contracted to resolve the stalemate. The new vendor has been contracted to fix the problems in the database, and there is a new delivery estimate of January 2002.

Careful attention paid thus far has insured that the project retains strong administrative support. Since few libraries have the resources to build the type of software infrastructure needed, many librarians find themselves using products that don't meet their needs. For those that decide to co-develop or build a custom-built solution, problems like these are to be expected. For this reason it is important to plan for a long-term process. Flexibility to adapt to changing environments and timelines are also important considerations.

REFERENCES

Brennan, M. J., Hurd, J., Blecic, D., and Weller, A. (2001). *Digital collections: Acceptance and use by early adopters among university faculty.* Paper presented at the annual meeting of the American Society for Information Science and Technology, Washington, D.C., November, 2001.

Cyboran, V. (1995). Designing feedback for computer-based training. *Performance & Instruction, 34*(5), 18-23.

Germain, C. A., Jacobson, T.E., and Kaczor, S.A. (2000). A Comparison of the Effectiveness of Presentation Formats for Instruction. *College and Research Libraries, 61*(1), 65-72.

Horton, W. (1994). *Designing and writing on-line documentation: Hypermedia for self- supporting products.* New York, NY: Wiley.

Kaplowitz, J. and Contini, J. (1998). Computer -assisted instruction: Is it an option for bibliographic instruction in large undergraduate survey classes? *College & Research Libraries, 59*(1), 19-27.

Kearsley, G. (2000). *Online education: Learning and teaching in cyberspace.* Belmont, CA: Wadsworth Thompson Learning.

Koenig, M. and Novotny, E. (2001). On-line course integrated library instruction modules as an alternative delivery methods. In Barbara I. Dewey (Ed.), *Library User Education: Powerful Learning, Powerful Partnerships* (pp. 200-208). Lanham, MD: Scarecrow Press.

Lawson, V.L. (1984). Using a computer-assisted instruction program to replace the traditional library tour: An experimental study. *RQ, 29*(1), 71-79.

Lenhart, A., Simon, M., and Graziano, M. (2001), *The internet and education: Findings of the Pew Internet & American Life Project.* Retrieved November 18, 2001 from http://www.pewinternet.org/reports/toc.asp?Report=39.

Lynch, P.J. and Horton, S. (1997). *Web style manual.* Retrieved October 25, 2001 from http://info.med.yale.edu/caim/manual/.

Richardson, G. (1994). Computer-assisted library instruction? Consider your resource, commitment, and needs. *Research Strategies, 12*(1), 45-55.

Schank, R. (1994). Active learning through multimedia. *Ieee MultiMedia, 1*(1), 69-78.

Smith, S.S. (2001). *Web-based instruction: A guide for libraries.* Chicago, IL: American Library Association.

Starr, R.M. (1997). Delivering instruction on the World Wide Web: Overview and basic design principles. *Educational Technology, 37*(3), 7-15.

UIC–About UIC–Teaching mission (n.d.) Retrieved November 18, 2001 from http://www.engl.uic.edu/homeindex.2001.12.5/about_uic/mission_teach.html.

Vander Meer, P.F. (1996). Multimedia: Meeting the demand for user education with a self-instructional tutorial. *Research Strategies, 14*(3), 145-158.

Viswanatham, R., Wilkins, W. and Jevec, T. (1997). The internet as a medium for on-line instruction. *College and Research Libraries, 58*(5), 433-444.

Wiggins, M.E. (1999). Instructional design and student learning. *Reference Services Review, 27*(3), 225-228.

Going Virtual:
A Non-Traditional Approach
to a Pharmacy Degree

Natalie Kupferberg

Ohio State University

SUMMARY. In January 2001 Ohio State University admitted its first class of non-traditional Doctor of Pharmacy students. The impetus for offering a complete distance education program in Pharmacy came from the decision of the American Council on Pharmaceutical Education that by 2004 all practicing pharmacists would need the PharmD degree for entry into practice. The first class consisted of 30 students all who already had a Bachelor of Science in Pharmacy and were licensed practicing pharmacists. The paper describes the steps the library took to assure that off-campus students would have access to the same sources and services as traditional students, describes what services the students used and how satisfied they were with what the library offered. Tips are given for librarians who may be involved in setting up their institution's distance education program.

KEYWORDS. Distance education, information resources, nontraditional students, program development

MY BACKGROUND

When I interviewed for a job as Pharmacy Librarian at OSU in 1999, there was some talk that the College of Pharmacy would be the first program at Ohio

[Haworth co-indexing entry note]: "Going Virtual: A Non-Traditional Approach to a Pharmacy Degree." Kupferberg, Natalie. Co-published simultaneously in *Journal of Library Administration* (The Haworth Information Press, an imprint of The Haworth Press, Inc.) Vol. 37, No. 3/4, 2002, pp. 437-449; and: *Distance Learning Library Services: The Tenth Off-Campus Library Services Conference* (ed: Patrick B. Mahoney) The Haworth Information Press, an imprint of The Haworth Press, Inc., 2002, pp. 437-449.

http://www.haworthpress.com/store/product.asp?sku=J111
10.1300/J111v37n03_36

State to offer a distance education degree, and I was asked if I thought I was up to the challenge. As anyone who wants a new job would say, I answered "of course." When I actually started at OSU in January 2000, I asked how the planning for the program was going. One of the assistant deans of Pharmacy told me the program was on hold but not to worry, they would give me 48 hours notice before it would begin.

I had other things to worry about in starting a new job than the fact that there might be some new program someday. After all it was my impression after almost 15 years in several academic libraries that nothing happened very quickly. So I was surprised in May 2000 when the head of public services told me that the pharmacy college had been targeted to begin their distance education program and that I'd better get ready fast.

The college was going to begin a program where students could obtain a Doctorate of Pharmacy (PharmD) degree without ever setting foot on campus. Students would be admitted to the program if they already had a B.S. in pharmacy and were licensed pharmacists. The program was to begin in January 2001. I had a lot of doubts about offering an entire degree online, and although not exactly a Luddite, I was never a person who went rah rah about the wonders of the digital library. Instead of digitizing the library I thought they should go and digitize the football team. I also had some doubts about students not meeting in classes face to face, and thought of my own experience in graduate school. I had been one of the few who actually enjoyed library school, and I think a large part of the enjoyment was because I enjoyed meeting and socializing with my new classmates, many of whom I remain in contact with twenty-one years later. Now after one year of the non-traditional program and after admission of the second class, I still believe more than ever that they should digitize the football team. However, I now also believe that distance education can work both in terms of library services and from an academic viewpoint.

Distance education is growing quickly in this country and internationally in three different ways: more individual courses are being offered online, there are more full-degree programs where students can get their entire degree online and there are even some colleges that offer nothing but distance education degrees. I am going to speak about how the librarian can contribute to a successful program right from the start of the degree program and mention certain problems that the librarian may anticipate. I am going to conclude by offering some tips for librarians who may find that they are their institutions "distance education" contact person.

THE RATIONALE FOR DISTANCE EDUCATION

The impetus for offering a complete distance education program in Pharmacy came from the decision of the American Council on Pharmaceutical Education

(ACPE) in June 1997 that by June 30, 2004 all practicing pharmacists would need the PharmD degree (American Association of Colleges of Pharmacy, 2000). Licensed pharmacists with a B.S. degree could continue practicing but a survey found that 43% of these working pharmacists also wanted to get the higher degree (Kelly, Chrymko, and Bender, 1994). Talking about surveys reminds me that Gallop polls have found that over the past few years pharmacists have become the first or second most trusted profession. Last year nurses came out ahead of pharmacists. They even came out ahead of librarians who were not even chosen to be one of the twenty-eight professions evaluated. If they had been considered, I am sure they would have come out ahead of everyone else.

The AACP recognized that the pharmacy profession has evolved from dispensing drugs prescribed by physicians to the provision of patient-focused pharmaceutical care that includes patient counseling, monitoring the patient to see if the drug has worked and if there are adverse effects, and advising other health professionals on the interactions and side effects of drugs. Pharmacists are often the most accessible members of a health care team, the first person patients will confer with regarding a health question and the last person patients consult with about their medication and its use (American Association of Colleges of Pharmacy). Today there is a shortage of pharmacists while there is an increased need of them, partly because the FDA is approving more drugs faster, and because there is a larger aging population. Pharmacist growth is expected to increase 5.4% from 2000-2005 while prescription growth is expected to increase by 46 percent in that same time period (Where Have All the Pharmacists Gone, 2001). There are also changes in the health care system that have a direct effect on the pharmacists. Patients are being discharged from the hospital "quicker and sicker" which gives the pharmacists more responsibility.

B.S. pharmacists wanted to get the PharmD degree to stay competitive in their profession; when they would be going up against the new PharmD graduates they did not want to be left behind. They also wanted to increase their knowledge and clinical skills to provide better patient care. Finally there is always the convenience factor. As one Pharmacy educator put it: We built our program on the basis of trying to develop something that would enable someone with a one-person store in some small town to have access to a program without selling the store, divorcing the mate, and moving to Little Rock (Conlan, 1999).

Non-traditional programs in pharmacy have been offered in various forms since the late 1980s. By 2001 there were 54 non-traditional PharmD programs available in the 82 Pharmacy schools in the United States (American Association of Colleges of Pharmacy). This August, Creighton University became the first school to offer an online PharmD degree for undergraduates; other non-traditional programs are similar to Ohio State's, designed for B.S. pharmacists looking to upgrade their degree (Ukens, 2001). The Creighton program is interesting because students will spend only a few weeks together in the summer doing hands-on lab courses. I guess when it comes to certain things like compounding medications and patient counseling you still cannot totally rely on the computer.

OHIO STATE'S PHARMACY DEGREE

Ohio State University, a public institution, is one of the largest in the country with an enrollment of 55,043 (Office of the University Registrar, 2001). The School of Pharmacy was founded in 1885 and became a college in 1895. Today the College of Pharmacy, with an enrollment of 307 students, grants a four-year graduate PharmD degree, an M.S. and a Ph.D. degree. The last two are research-oriented and do not prepare the students to become licensed pharmacists. In 1999 the college began offering a B.S. in Pharmaceutical Sciences, which also does not lead to a license. The school no longer offers a B.S. in Pharmacy.

Serious planning for the non-traditional program began in 1999 and the non-traditional team was in place by August 2000. "The mission of the Non-Traditional Doctor of Pharmacy Program at the Ohio State University College of Pharmacy is to provide the opportunity for practicing pharmacists at the baccalaureate level to enhance their ability to provide high quality pharmaceutical care and obtain the PharmD degree" (College of Pharmacy at the Ohio State University, NTPD Program section, para. 2). It may be too soon to tell if employers will give the same value to a non-traditional PharmD degree as the traditional on-campus one, but the goal is that the outcomes of both the on-campus and off-campus programs will be the same. The OSU College of Business did a survey after students in the non-traditional program completed their first course in the Spring of 2000 and 94% thought their degree would be perceived as being equivalent to an on-campus degree.

As already noted, to be admitted to the program the students had to have a B.S. in Pharmacy and be licensed practicing pharmacists. They also had to have access to computers that met certain technological requirements, both minimum and recommended. The applicants did not have to demonstrate any level of computer proficiency, which proved to cause problems later on. Students would need to complete forty-two (42) credit hours of didactic course work in 3 years and then have eight months of professional experience rotations. Courses are offered on a trimester basis to give these full-time professionals enough time to complete their work, rather than on a quarterly basis, which the rest of the university follows. The first course offered would be "drug information which would include biostatistics and literature evaluation" followed by "clinical pharmacokinetics." Throughout the program students would also be enrolled in a Pharmaceutical Care Longitudinal course where they would have to pick a disease, create a strategy for implementing a pharmaceutical care program, create a strategy to implement the pharmaceutical care program, identify a population to benefit from the program, intervene in the population and then measure the outcome of the intervention (College of Pharmacy of the Ohio State University).

Ohio State chose to use WebCT as their Web-based course management system. The classes would use a mix of assigned readings, audio lectures using RealPlayer, QuickTime, PowerPoint, required chat room participation and bulletin board discussions.

OHIO STATE'S LIBRARIES

Ohio State University libraries contain 5.2 million volumes and regularly receive approximately 36,000 serial titles (Ohio State University Libraries, 2000). Affiliated users can connect to almost all of the library resources from home. The libraries consist of a main library, law and health science libraries and ten department libraries of which the Biological Sciences/Pharmacy Library (BPL) is one. In addition to access to Ohio State's library holdings, students have access to OhioLink, a consortium of the libraries of 78 Ohio colleges and universities. Usually a book can be borrowed using OhioLink within 3-5 working days. BPL contains over 150,000 volumes and 1,500 periodicals. The staff of this library consists of the Biological Sciences Librarian who is the head of the library, the Pharmacy librarian, the circulation supervisor and three other library assistants and from 12-15 student assistants. Pharmacy students are also heavy users of the health sciences library, which has approximately 2,500 journal subscriptions, and a book collection of approximately 58,000 (Ohio State University Libraries). Although students sometimes complain that they must use two different libraries, fortunately the buildings are not far from each other.

LIBRARY SERVICES FOR DISTANCE USERS

At present there is no distance education librarian (and no plans to hire one) so it was up to the staff of the Biological Sciences/Pharmacy library to set up initial policies and procedures regarding distance education. Fortunately many other libraries have set up distance education programs, and I found that joining the Off-Campus Library Services Listserv was a great help. All of our staff members welcomed the additional responsibilities and challenges. One plus was that we were a small group of six who worked well together and could "agree to disagree."

In designing new services we reviewed the Guidelines for Distance Learning Library Services prepared by the American College of Research Libraries Distance Learning Section Guidelines Committee printed in *C & R L News* December, 2000. A tenet of the guidelines is "members of the distance learning community are entitled to library services and resources equivalent to those provided for students and faculty in traditional campus settings" (ACRL Distance Learning Section Guidelines Committee, 2000). There was agreement that everyone would get the same level of services as on-campus students. However, there was less agreement among the staff whether they should get additional services. For example, one of the earliest things we considered was mailing articles from our libraries to students' homes until the desktop delivery mechanism could be put in place. On-campus students do not get a service like that. Several of us had to compromise. Now that the program is in operation, I believe that the non-traditional students do get a higher level of services than on-campus students. I will talk more about that later.

The library realized that working collaboratively with the Pharmacy College team would be essential to the program's success, and good communication between the faculty and librarians was essential. Since the first course was drug information sources, we also knew that students would be using the library immediately. The Biological Sciences and Pharmacy librarians met often with the Non-Traditional Pharmacy Degree (NTPD) team, and we also had to bring in the head of electronic resources to discuss copyright issues, the interlibrary loan librarian and the assistant director of public services from OSU's main library. The Biological Sciences/Pharmacy Library was involved in planning the program with the Pharmacy College from the start, and I now believe that I have close rapport with the Pharmacy faculty members who are involved in the NTPD program.

Hard core planning of library services actually got underway in September 2000. In an e-mail to the assistant director I wrote, "The Biological Sciences/Pharmacy Library's goal is to provide all information resources to off-campus students. This includes:

- Access to all electronic based information resources. (Databases, full text electronic journals) and instructional assistance in using these tools.
- Electronic reserves.
- Access to document delivery and interlibrary loan.
- Library reference-users should be able to e-mail questions and receive an answer.

- A Web page for off-campus students listing resources and explaining the services."

The NTPD faculty agreed with us on all the goals except the first. They not only wanted the students to have access to all electronic-based information resources, but also immediate access to at least the 1,500 journals and 150,000 books in the Biological Sciences/Pharmacy Library, as well as the 2,500 journals that the health sciences library received and their 58,000 books. Best of all would be if they could have access to all 5.2 million volumes at OSU. We said we would try.

Our first concern was to make sure students could access all the electronic-based information services that we subscribe to. At Ohio State students must configure their browsers for the proxy server to access electronic resources. Authentication problems were common and students sometimes had difficulty with the process. To help with the problem, we obtained a list of the students' names and social security numbers to make sure they were in the database. Since the first class had only 30 students this was manageable.

There was obviously no way we could provide full-text access to 4,000 journals and textbooks, but we had to decide what full-text databases in medicine we were going to consider adding to our collection. This would be the first expense that the new program entailed. After doing research on full-text databases in medicine I found there was really only one that the faculty and librarians could recommend–MD Consult–which contains the full text of 40 medical reference books and 50 medical journals. It also has MEDLINE and the drug database Mosby's Drug Consult. I cannot reveal how much the Biological Sciences/Pharmacy Library paid for MD Consult (in fact, I do not even know what we ended up paying for it since the price negotiations were done by the collection development librarian at the health sciences library), but we had to get money from several departments to purchase it. In addition to the Biological Sciences/Pharmacy and health sciences library, the college of Pharmacy, and the departments of internal medicine and pediatrics all chipped in. We made the argument that having the database would benefit a lot more than the NTPD students. We also purchased the full-text drug database Micromedex with funding from the health sciences library. This gave the students access to four different drug databases since we already had Facts and Comparisons, the Physicians' Desk Reference (PDR) and with the purchase of MD Consult, Mosby's Drug Consult.

Document delivery was the area that gave the students more services than the on-campus students. OSU does not photocopy and deliver articles from one of its 13 libraries to another. Patrons must go to the different libraries and pick them up themselves. However, the health sciences library had developed the document delivery system Prospero where digitized journal articles were sent directly to students' computers. We decided to use this software, which meant purchasing a scanner and working out some bugs in the software with the systems librarian. Student assistants would page articles from the health sciences library.

Deciding what to do with books became a little more difficult. The head of interlibrary loan was not happy with the idea of mailing out books. We decided that the BPL staff would be the ones responsible for keeping track of the students and we would try to photocopy chapters instead of mailing books. We developed a dummy library card and the Pharmacy librarian would keep track of lost books. The library would pay the expense of mailing out books to the students, and we provided a prepaid return envelope for them to return it as well as a letter explaining our policies. This took some negotiating with the mailroom, which insisted on knowing how many books we would be mailing out. This is where I had to say I don't know.

Having worked out the above I now felt the NTPD students would have a good portion of the OSU libraries in their living room at least within 48 hours. However, they were still missing access to Pharmacy textbooks. As of today, I do not know of any Pharmacy textbooks online. MD Consult has several internal medicine textbooks and medical specialty books online but no Pharmacy books. This fall students took the course therapeutics and were required to purchase the classic textbook *Pharmacotherapy: a pathophysiologic approach* for $150 since that book is kept on reserve and I could not send a 2,440 page book via desktop delivery. Fortunately, *Gray's Anatomy* is online.

The system of electronic reserve was already in place at OSU but was not heavily used. Once we told the two Pharmacy faculty members involved in the first course about electronic reserve, they were very happy to use it, although there were several questions concerning copyright. I did not become an expert on copyright nor did the Pharmacy faculty members. I did learn, though, whom to refer the faculty members to at Ohio State.

None of the above library services would be of any use to the students if traditional reference services were not also available. We realized that in addition to reference questions, there would be "bugs" with the new services and we wanted the students to know that they could count on help from live librarians and library assistants. It was not quite 24/7 service that we aimed for, but we wanted to let them get in touch with us anyway they wanted. In addition to the 800 number, we set up an e-mail cluster account. The first person that read their e-mail would see the question and forward it to the appropriate person. Students would still have the options of e-mailing the Pharmacy or Biological Sciences librarian individually, but they would not have to wait until they opened their own mail.

Developing a Web page for the NTPD students seemed like a simple matter. We would have links to Pharmacy databases, Internet sites, links to electronic course reserves, and provide forms for interlibrary loan and to answer reference questions. The problem was where to put this Web page. I originally thought there could be a link from the Biological Sciences/Pharmacy library Web page. However, then the "traditional" on-campus Pharmacy students would see that the non-traditional students were getting more services than they were getting. The decision was made to make this Web page available to the NTPD students through WebCT.

THE FIRST NTPD CLASS

The first class admitted in 2001 had 30 in-state students with a third of them actually from the Columbus area. (Two of the 30 dropped out during the first course saying they would continue at a later date and one transferred in during the summer.) Ohio State had decided to limit its first class to in-state students but at first we were surprised that students living in the city actually chose a non-traditional program. However, why attend classes at a set time when you could do your work when you wanted? One student wrote "This program gives me the opportunity to be a full-time working professional while at the same time, I earn an advanced degree. Traditional programs do not have that kind of flexibility." Although I am sure this thought did not occur to the students, why settle for traditional library services when you could get books and articles mailed to you?

Twenty of the students were OSU alumni; the other students had earned their undergraduate Pharmacy degrees from the University of Cincinnati, Ohio Northern University, University of Toledo, University of Pittsburgh and Seoul University. Two of the students had a master's degree and one had a Ph.D. The students ranged from having graduated last year to having graduated 20 years ago. They represented all disciplines of Pharmacy, including retail, hospital, home care and pharmaceutical companies. One person who enrolled was OSU's Medical Center's senior director of pharmaceutical services, who was actually an adjunct faculty member in Pharmacy school.

The first class did have a required on-campus orientation that lasted two days. Several of the activities were social and included press attendance as well as a speech by the President of OSU. The Biological Sciences librarian and I gave the students a 45 minute orientation stressing that we were there to serve them and adding that they were in a sense guinea pigs of distance education at OSU (their words not ours). We wanted to let them know that, although there might be bugs in offering our services, we would do all we could to make life in the library (virtual or not) as easy for them as possible. We also covered some traditional aspects of library orientations such as an introduction to full-text databases, MEDLINE and a review of Boolean searching. The orientation was well received. In talking to the students at several of the social events I realized that they had a wide range of computer expertise. Several of the students had graduated from the Bachelor of Science in Pharmacy program from Ohio State a few years ago and were very familiar with the library and its services, while one student told me that the reason he had enrolled in the program was because he knew he needed to learn more about computers.

After the first course, *Drug Information and Literature Evaluation*, the library conducted a survey on library use and student satisfaction. Twenty-eight students returned the survey. During the first course in drug information, 23 students requested articles, 17 students requested articles 1-5 times while 5 students made 5-10 requests. One student made more than 10 requests.

The second course, *Pharmacokinetics*, did not require use of the library, yet we had 28 requests for articles. However, 22 came from one patron we have labeled our biggest fan. We did not ask the users the reason for their request because we do not ask that of our on-campus users. However, I did gently ask the student with the 22 requests whether the requests were course-related or if they were for a special project she was doing. (They were for a special project.) Most of the articles were not surprisingly held at the health sciences library but, with the exception of one day, our student workers were happy to make the trip to that library. The one exception was when the thermometer hit 95 degrees and the student who was our biggest fan made five requests. About 80% of the requests were either held in our library or the health sciences library and we did fill all of those within 24 hours. We had three book requests.

The library received about 10 actual reference questions, which were mostly for information on diseases. In several cases we photocopied pages from textbooks and sent them via desktop delivery or fax. We do not keep statistics on reference questions asked at the library, but this is pretty close to the pattern of our traditional students. Most Pharmacy students prefer to do their own searches. We did receive a lot of questions that involved technological problems when students needed to connect to databases. This is when I realized that there was a wide range in computer knowledge among the students. Although we did solve most of the students' problems, it usually took several phone calls and consultation with the Pharmacy faculty, and in some cases, the information technology departments.

The databases the students used were MD Consult with 26 of the 28 respondents having used it, followed closely by MEDLINE and Micromedex. We certainly got our money's worth with MD Consult, which shows that full text is what patrons want.

The results of the survey on student satisfaction were most satisfactory. Fourteen of the 28 respondents indicated that they were very satisfied with our service, 10 were somewhat satisfied and 6 were "neutral." All but one had requested journal articles and used online databases. All but 2 had contacted the library for help. Some of the other findings of interest were:

- 26 of the students found the Web page very useful or useful.
- The most popular time to conduct library research was during the weekdays in the evening while not a single student did research on a weekend evening.
- 21 of the library students found the on-site library orientation very useful or useful.
- 1/3 of the respondents used other libraries besides OSU because they were more convenient.
- E-mail was the preferred method of contacting the library followed by the phone.

I was glad the Web page was helpful since a lot of work goes into creating one. It's nice to know that students do not devote their weekend evenings to academic pursuits since, although it sometimes seems that all life consists of is studying, there are other aspects to living. In terms of using other libraries, if a student lives in Cincinnati they would want to use the library there.

However, not all was smooth sailing for this first class. Here are some comments that the students wrote on how we could improve.

- I have never been able to access MD Consult or several of the other databases from the computer–in spite of hours spent trying to work with the proxy server.
- If there is any way we can access databases without going through the proxy server that would be great.
- I wish there were clearer directions on how to access the proxy server.
- Easier access to MD Consult.

From the students' comments, I learned that we should offer better instructions on the use of the proxy server, and more print information about the library before the next NTPD class starts in January. We are also working with our information technology department on a software program which will allow students to get access to the journals and databases they are most likely to use without going through the proxy server.

SOME TIPS

If you have the chance to be involved in a distance education program from the start here are some tips I would recommend from my experience at Ohio State:

- Join the off Campus Library Services Mailing List–The OFFCAMP (Off-Campus Library Services) Listserv OFFCAMP has been established for the purpose of "discussion about all aspects of service to remote users" (Central Michigan University Off-Campus Library Services).
- Consult Association of College and Research Libraries Guidelines for Distance Learning Library Services.
- Collaborate with teaching faculty members–If you do not already work in an environment where there is active collaboration with subject faculty and librarians then the beginning of a distance education program is a great time to start.
- Work closely with other library departments. This depends on the size and structure of your university but some of the departments you may have to work with include interlibrary loan, electronic reserve, information technology and even the mailroom.
- Prepare for technological problems. While all students have a wide range of technological abilities this is especially true for students who have been out of school for several years.
- Make arrangements with other university departments and libraries to chip in for new electronic resources to help defray costs.
- Understand copyright issues or know who the experts are.
- Last, but not least, enjoy the challenge and celebrate your success.

In conclusion the program has started, the students are satisfied, the Pharmacy faculty members involved are satisfied and our library staff all contributed to making the first course work. After all the B.S. in Pharmacy graduates have received their PharmD degrees will distance education still continue for Pharmacy students? It is probably safe to conclude yes.

REFERENCES

ACRL Distance Learning Section Guidelines Committee. (2000, December) Guidelines for distance learning library services. *C & RL News.* 1023-1029.
American Association of Colleges of Pharmacy. (2000). *Pharmacy school admission requirements 2001-2002*, Alexandria, VA.
College of Pharmacy at the Ohio State University. *Non-traditional PharmD*. Retrieved December 11, 2001. http://www.osuntpd.com/.
Conlan, M.F. (1999, January 18) Back to school. *Drug Topics, 143*(2), 34.
Kelly, W. N., Chrymko, M.M., & Bender, F.H. (1994). Interest and resources for non-traditional PharmD programs in Pennsylvania. *American Journal of Pharmaceutical Education.* 58, 171-176.

Office of the University Registrar. (1994-2001). *Admission and enrollment for the total university during the autumn quarters 1999-2000.* http://www.ureg.ohio-state.edu/ourweb/srs/AnnStatsSummary/AnStSumm0001/Table01.html.

Ohio State University Libraries. (2000 April 28). *About the libraries: General information.* http://www.lib.ohio-state.edu/Lib_Info/geninfo.html.

Ukens, Carol. (2001, April 2) Creighton pioneers web-based Pharm. D. program. *Drug Topics.* 145, 31.

Where Have All the Pharmacists Gone? (2001, Winter) *Scripting Success From Pharmacy Deans From Walgrens, 3,* 1-2.

Collaboration
Between Distance Education Faculty
and the Library:
One Size Does Not Fit All

Jill S. Markgraf

University of Wisconsin-Eau Claire

SUMMARY. At a university with no centrally administered distance education (DE) program, the library is faced with the challenge of not only identifying but also supporting a rapidly increasing number of disparate DE initiatives. In this environment, a one-size-fits-all approach to inviting and encouraging faculty collaboration in the integration of library research into the DE curriculum was not sufficient. This presentation will discuss various methods used at one university to increase the level of collaboration between the library and distance education (DE) faculty.

KEYWORDS. Collaboration, faculty, distance learners, distance education

INTRODUCTION

Librarians have been discussing the issue of collaboration with faculty for decades. We have learned through the years that effective collaboration requires librarians to build and nurture relationships with faculty, to promote and market services, and to provide reliable, timely responses to requests and demonstrated need for service. It is beginning to look like a very one-sided rela-

[Haworth co-indexing entry note]: "Collaboration Between Distance Education Faculty and the Library: One Size Does Not Fit All." Markgraf, Jill S. Co-published simultaneously in *Journal of Library Administration* (The Haworth Information Press, an imprint of The Haworth Press, Inc.) Vol. 37, No. 3/4, 2002, pp. 451-464; and: *Distance Learning Library Services: The Tenth Off-Campus Library Services Conference* (ed: Patrick B. Mahoney) The Haworth Information Press, an imprint of The Haworth Press, Inc., 2002, pp. 451-464.

http://www.haworthpress.com/store/product.asp?sku=J111
10.1300/J111v37n03_37

tionship. Why do we stay in it? Because the teaching faculty has something we need: direct, consistent and assured access to the students we are trying to reach. We are committed to teaching library research and information literacy skills, and we have long known that such skills are most effectively learned when they are integrated into the curriculum (e.g., Kohl, 1986). We know that such integration requires support from and collaborative efforts with the faculty responsible for course content.

This paper discusses various methods one library employed in its efforts to build collaborative arrangements with distance education (DE) faculty. In an administrative environment with no centralized DE unit or coordinating entity, the library faced challenges in identifying–as well as supporting–disparate DE courses, programs, students and faculty. Efforts to reach, and ultimately collaborate with, the DE faculty included identifying their needs and presenting library services in terms of how the library could assist faculty in meeting those needs. In order to get what it needs, a library has to figure out what faculty need and how to provide it. With a mutually beneficial and satisfactory relationship, collaboration can take flight.

BACKGROUND

The University of Wisconsin-Eau Claire is a comprehensive university comprising three colleges: the College of Arts and Sciences, the College of Business, and the College of Professional Studies, which includes the School of Education, the School of Human Sciences and Services, and the School of Nursing. Enrollment of 10,549 includes 10,101 undergraduates and 448 graduate students. UW-Eau Claire's McIntyre Library has a library faculty of 16, including a faculty member from the Initiative in Curricular Software and Support (ICSS), an instructional technology support center that falls under the auspices of the library.

Approximately 540 students enrolled in distance education courses during the fall 2001 semester. UW-Eau Claire has no centralized office coordinating its distance education and online courses. Each of the Colleges has its own DE initiatives, including those that have existed and evolved over decades and those that emerge with each new semester. Challenges for the library, as well as for other support services on campus, have included simply identifying DE courses to be offered, understanding the several multi-institutional collaborative DE programs in which various UW-Eau Claire colleges participate, anticipating and responding to the unique and varied needs of DE students and faculty, and communicating with DE students and faculty.

In response to an observed growing need, as well as adherence to its mission of providing comparable library services to all students regardless of location, the library developed its first Web page for distance education students in 1997. The website was revised and expanded in early 1999 upon the hiring of a half-time Distance Education Librarian. Since then, the library has developed a full array of services for distance education students, similar to those that most academic libraries provide. In addition to the website specifically designed for DE students and faculty, the library offers remote access to the library catalog, databases and other research resources; reference assistance available electronically and via toll-free telephone; document delivery services; and an online research tutorial as well as an ever-increasing bank of online instructional services and tools.

While the maxim, 'If you build it, they will come,' may be true for fictitious baseball diamonds (L. Gordon, C. Gordon, and Robinson, 1989), it is not necessarily so for library services, as evidenced by relatively infrequent requests received for library assistance and resources. During the first year for which DE library statistics were kept (1999), the library counted 19 requests for journal articles, 9 for books, 16 interlibrary loan requests and 20 reference requests. These numbers represent a conservative estimate of actual use because they do not include DE students having used services without being identified. For example, questions asked at the reference desk or searches conducted in the library's catalog or online databases by DE students were not included in the DE statistics unless a student explicitly identified him or herself as a DE student. While the numbers may be more indicative than definitive, they were still sparse enough to suggest that merely having the services available was not sufficient in getting DE students to use the library.

PROMOTING LIBRARY SERVICES

The lack of a centrally coordinated DE program made it virtually impossible for the library to identify and communicate directly with DE students to promote services. Therefore, the most promising method of reaching students was through their instructors. Furthermore, studies show that students are more apt to use the library services if their professors endorse them. "Most students use library services only when they are encouraged or required to do so by their institutions" (Kotter, 1999, Rationale section, ¶ 2). As a result, the library engaged in what might be considered the underpinnings of collaborative efforts with faculty: promotion. The library needed to let faculty know about the services it was offering. Library services for DE students were promoted in a number of ways:

- *Articles in campus newsletters*

The library publishes a semi-annual newsletter, *Off the Shelf*, which is distributed to all faculty members. Each issue since November 1998 has included an article featuring DE library services in general or highlighting specific resources available for off-campus students. The library is part of the Information & Technology Management (ITM) Division at UW-Eau Claire, which distributes two newsletters each semester to faculty and staff: an *ITM Semester Welcome Back* newsletter at the beginning of each semester and an *ITM Semester WrapUp* at the end of each semester. These newsletters contain myriad brief articles and tips about using technology on campus. For example, a typical issue may include information on submitting grades electronically, setting out-of-office messages in e-mail, using classroom technology, using voicemail, obtaining copyright assistance, or protecting oneself against computer viruses. In addition, these newsletters alert faculty members to library and technology instruction services available for faculty and students, as well as other library services. Information about library services for DE students is routinely included in these newsletters.

- *Campus presentations and workshops*

The University's Center for Instructional Technology Improvement & Innovation (CITI) conducts a series of workshops each semester, as well as during the summer and winter breaks. The workshops cover a broad range of information technology topics, including training in Microsoft Office™ products, Web development, Web-based learning systems, file management, and development and use of visuals. The library plays an active role in the series, offering workshops on library research-related topics. Since 1998, workshops on DE library services have been offered at least semi-annually. While several faculty members expressed interest in the workshops, and several did indeed attend, staff members supporting DE teaching faculty rather than the teaching faculty themselves were more likely by a 3 to 1 ratio to actually attend the workshops.

- *Collaboration with support staff*

Attendance of support staff at the workshops resulted in further promotion of DE library services. For example, a staff member from the Registrar's Office who attended one of the workshops arranged to have information about library services published in the Distance Education Course catalog. Similarly, staff members who maintained departmental Web pages made links to the library DE page.

- *E-mail notices to DE faculty*

   Because it could not be assumed that faculty members actually read the newsletters sent to them, information about DE library services and related upcoming workshops was e-mailed to DE faculty members each semester. Due to the decentralized nature of DE offerings on the Eau Claire campus, the DE librarian determined who would be teaching DE courses by perusing the Class Schedule Bulletin when it became available. Faculty names were added to an e-mail distribution list maintained by the DE librarian. Anecdotal evidence indicated that the e-mailed information generated more of a response from faculty than did the newsletter articles. Supporting this observation are survey results reported by Shellie Jeffries (2000, p. 118) indicating that 80 percent of faculty members preferred e-mail to other methods of communication.

- *Promotional/informational brochures*

   Though becoming less common, some DE faculty require or recommend that their students visit the campus or attend an orientation session at least once during the semester. These on-campus visits often included a library orientation session, giving the library an opportunity to provide a traditional instruction session. A promotional brochure outlining library services available at a distance was developed to distribute to these students. The brochures were also mailed to off-campus students. Again, due to the lack of a centrally-administered DE office, mailings to students were not a routine matter; rather mailings to students were left to the discretion of each department, DE program or faculty member. Brochures were distributed to DE faculty members with notification that the library would be happy to supply brochures for their students.

   While promotion of services did increase the level of awareness of services among DE faculty, it became apparent that those DE faculty members who were most likely to follow-up on the information were those who already had some connection with the library or librarians. A nursing faculty member, for example, who invited the DE librarian to become part of an online course development team was married to a librarian and, one might conclude, more receptive to library initiatives as a result. A marketing professor and the DE librarian discussed ways in which they might work together while perched upon very small chairs and drinking apple juice at the campus daycare their children attended together. Raspa and Ward (2000) discuss the importance of relationships in collaborative efforts. They cite Mattessich and Monsey's description of collaboration as a "mutually beneficial and well-designed relationship entered into by two or more [individuals or] organizations to achieve common goals," adding that, "collaboration should be an integrated and authentically interpersonal relationship as well" (p. 4).

NETWORKING WITH FACULTY MEMBERS

Recognizing the importance of relationships in the collaborative process brought us to the next level of collaboration: networking. If faculty members with a connection to a library or librarian were more apt to work closely with the library, then those connections would have to be built.

The literature provides a wealth of ideas for networking. Among the suggestions presented by Young and Harmony are: meeting with new faculty, both at orientation sessions and one-on-one meetings; attending department meetings, lecture series and faculty retreats; and attending social and cultural events (Young & Harmony, 1999, pp. 22-24). Shellie Jeffries (2000) offers networking advice, much of which applies to nurturing any healthy relationship. For example, she suggests being friendly, courteous, respectful, a good listener, responsive to needs, interested and knowledgeable.

The DE librarian at UW-Eau Claire set out to get to know the DE faculty. She scheduled one-on-one meetings with DE faculty members. She attended the Annual Conference on Distance Teaching & Learning and scanned the program, crowd and list of conferees for UW-Eau Claire colleagues. Networking with local colleagues at a national conference underscored the common interest and agenda shared by librarians and faculty in providing distance education. She sent individual invitations to DE faculty to attend workshops devoted to DE library services. In addition to offering workshops, the librarian attended campus workshops and brown bag lunches likely to be attended by DE faculty. These sessions invariably began with brief introductions of those in attendance during which the librarian found out who faculty members were and which courses were slated to go online. These faculty members were then added to the librarian's e-mail distribution list. The introductions also provided an opportunity for the librarian to make herself, her role and her interest in working with faculty known.

While marketing and networking efforts resulted in increased interest and awareness on the part of DE faculty, as well as positive and grateful acknowledgement from DE faculty, the actual integration of information literacy and library research components into the DE course curriculum remained relatively low. It appeared that while faculty viewed the library services as good ideas, positive attitudes on the part of faculty toward the library were not enough to bring about collaboration. A survey of faculty and staff (not limited to DE) conducted in the fall of 2000 at the UW-Eau Claire indicated that 84.1% of respondents agreed or strongly agreed with the statement that library staff was helpful.

(When those who expressed no opinion were eliminated from the total, the figure climbed to 96.9%.) While the responses, as well as numerous written comments on the survey, indicated an overwhelmingly positive attitude toward librarians, when faculty were asked if librarians addressed or worked with students in their courses, only 50% indicated that they did. Eighty-five percent of respondents whose students received library instruction indicated that they were satisfied with the instruction. While the approval ratings were relatively high, the positive feelings toward the library did not necessarily translate into correlating levels of collaboration (Rose and Roraff, 2000).

IDENTIFYING FACULTY NEEDS

If faculty members liked libraries and librarians so much, why weren't they collaborating with us to ensure that their students were able to take full advantage of what we had to offer?

Ann Wolpert offered a likely explanation, "Just as libraries need their attention, faculty are themselves distracted by the challenges and demands of teaching in a new environment. . . . Faculty who must deliver educational products to students both on campus and at a distance can be expected (perhaps not unreasonable) to care more about production values, revenue sharing, time management, class control, and re-purposing of intellectual content than about the library and its problems" (Wolpert, 1998, Servicing Market Segments section, ¶ 2).

Requests to add a library research component to an online course might be viewed by faculty as yet another task that they are being asked to do. Suggestions to integrate library research skills into a course might be seen as a burden rather than as a service that would make the faculty member's task easier to accomplish. Perhaps what we needed to do was present our services in terms of how they can provide what a faculty member needed. We discussed earlier that the faculty member has something we need, i.e., access to the students. What do we have that the faculty member needs? To answer this question we need to know what faculty members need.

From our own experience on college campuses, working, living and socializing with faculty, we can quickly come up with a list of pretty good guesses as to what most faculty need. Our short list might include:

- time
- publications
- technology assistance
- and, of course, money.

The literature bears out these assumptions:

The Need for More Time

The seemingly universal need for more time is supported by several studies. A study by Milem, Berger and Dey (2000) comparing faculty time allocation in 1972 and 1992 suggests that faculty are spending an increasing amount of time teaching, preparing for teaching and engaged in research, leaving them with a decreasing amount of discretionary time.

The *American Faculty Poll* (Sanderson, Phua and Herda, 2000) reports that having time for family and personal needs is one of the career factors of most importance to faculty members. "Workload and the lack of student preparation and commitment are the most often cited negative factors impinging upon faculty members' academic work" (p. vii).

How might the library offer faculty members more time? In a brown bag discussion sharing their experiences teaching online, several Eau Claire faculty members mentioned the significantly greater amount of time spent in one-on-one e-mail communication with students in their online courses as compared to students in on-campus courses (Knesting, Oberly, Reid, and Ikuta, 2000). This sentiment was also expressed in an Arkansas State University survey, in which a faculty member described the amount of e-mail communication in an online course as "overwhelming" (Dickinson, Agnew and Gorman, 1999). If librarians were to field often time-consuming questions such as those related to library research methods and technical database access issues, the faculty member would be saved a considerable amount of time. The DE librarian offered to assist in this manner to a marketing professor. The professor accepted the offer. The first online offering of this course was fraught with problems related to the proxy server in use at the time, and the librarians spent a significant amount of time fielding these questions.

As a result, communication with the library in resolving these problems was indispensable in the students' ability to do their research. The unfortunate access problems did have the unintended effect of getting students and the faculty member in the course in the habit of consulting with the librarian. Students who had consulted with the librarian regarding access problems were encouraged to contact her again with research-related questions, and many did. The faculty member got into the habit of referring questions to the librarian, and even when the proxy server was replaced with a more seamless access solution, the faculty member referred students to the librarian with research-related questions. The success of this relationship developed when the course was offered online a second time. The faculty member and librarian worked together to develop an additional library research exercise assigned early in the course which would get the students familiar with library databases, differentiate library databases from Web searching, identify any access problems, and introduce the librarian. By the third time the course was offered, the librarian was added as a participant to the online course where she monitored a Blackboard™ discussion thread pertaining to research issues.

The Need for More Publications

In addition to the need for more time, the unrelenting pressure on faculty to publish is another well-documented and oft-cited need of faculty members. The *Chronicle of Higher Education* reported last year that, "the process of judging a tenure candidate varies widely from place to place–and from discipline to discipline–but whatever an institution expected 10 years ago, it now expects more. . . . The most significant change, people say, is the overwhelming pressure on young professors to publish early and publish frequently" (Wilson, 2001, ¶ 6).

Sheila Intner, reporting on a faculty-librarian workshop she conducted, wrote, "If faculty want to increase their publications, what partnership is more helpful than librarians trained to find the information on which any new publication must be based?" She went on to say that "faculty need endless assurance that librarians are not trying to steal their subject expertise, but only to supply their bibliographic expertise" (2001, Playing the Self-Interest Card section, ¶ 6).

The development of the collaborative relationship between the marketing professor and the DE librarian described above offered another opportunity to give a faculty member something he needed. The librarian suggested writing up their experiences and submitting them for publication. Few are the faculty members who will turn down an opportunity to publish. The resulting article was accepted for publication, and it is hoped that publicity in the campus newsletter once the article is in print will garner the attention of other faculty members (Markgraf, in press).

The Need for Technology Assistance

Faculty members teaching at a distance often have the extra burden on their time and attention of learning and managing the technology necessary to deliver a course off-campus. In focusing on the needs specific to faculty teaching online, a 1999 survey conducted at Arkansas State University suggested that faculty teaching online most needed more time, training and support. (Dickinson et al., 1999). In addition to the demands encountered by traditional classroom professors, faculty teaching online were faced with additional technological and instructional design challenges.

Attendance of campus workshops was indicative of this need at UW-Eau Claire. As attendance at traditional library workshops hovered in the single digits, attendance at Web publishing and Web-based learning systems workshops, such as Blackboard™, WebCT™ and LearningSpace™, was often full to capacity. While workshop evaluations and comments made on the library's faculty and staff survey (Rose and Roraff, 2000) indicated that library workshops were desired and useful, low attendance was the norm and lack of time often given as the reason. And yet, faculty members made time to attend workshops addressing the technical issues involved and essential in simply getting a course online. As a result, the instructional design staff took on an integral role in the online course development process. The faculty clearly needed assistance and support in developing their online courses. The library set out to become part of the team offering online course development assistance and support.

In the summer of 2000, the University launched a Summer Online pilot project. While a few courses had already gone online or were in the process of going online as a result of individual faculty or departmental initiatives, the Summer Online project was the first institutionally supported effort to develop a process for converting courses to the online environment. Four faculty members were selected to participate in the project, and with the technical assistance of an instructional design staff and a spring semester course-release, they were to develop an online course for summer. Often frustrated by an organizational structure that provided no centralized coordination for DE efforts, the library now found itself fortunate to have an organizational structure that put instructional design staff under the auspices of the library. Such an arrangement meant a heightened awareness on the part of instructional designers of the importance of library and information literacy skills in course development. During the spring of 2000, instructional designers, who had an institutionally mandated support role with online faculty, served as advocates for the library by facilitating meetings and communication between faculty and librarian. For the first time, the library was involved in a DE course during its development stages.

The project continued for a second year, and the course development process evolved. Four newly selected faculty members were again given a spring semester course release and the support of the instructional design team. This time the team included the DE librarian. Monthly meetings bringing the faculty members and the design team together were offered to cover topics of common interest and to enable faculty to meet, confer and share ideas with each other. The monthly meetings covered such topics as access to library services, copyright, courseware options, facilitating online discussions, evaluation in an online environment, and course management.

The Need for Financial Support

Who couldn't use more money? The *American Faculty Poll* revealed, not surprisingly, that low salaries were one of four main factors contributing to job dissatisfaction among faculty members, and yet over 90 percent of faculty members indicated a clear and overall satisfaction with their career choices. The survey results suggest that, in terms of what's important to them in their careers, money is not the primary consideration for most faculty members. In the same poll, however, only 8.6 percent of respondents believed that financial resources available at their institution were sufficient for the academic needs of faculty members (Sanderson, Phua and Herda, 2000). How can libraries provide faculty members with financial support when they never seem to have enough themselves? Value-added services and grant funding are two examples of areas where collaboration can make a financial difference for faculty members. Intner writes "librarians are educated and trained to help faculty succeed in being more productive, and . . . more productive faculties were likely to get more goodies–recognition, promotions, invitations, grants, you name it–as well as more money" (2001, Playing the Self Interest Card section, ¶ 5). Extra services for DE faculty to save them time, and by extension money, are ways in which a library can give faculty what they need. Current awareness services alerting faculty members to books, databases and other resources to help them in their research and teaching can translate into time and cost savings. Document delivery direct to the faculty member's office, similar to the service we provide for DE students, can save a faculty member time and money, while demonstrating some of the services their students can expect.

While examples of grant projects between librarians and faculty abound, one with which the author was involved resulted in a $1 million grant awarded to a consortium of medical colleges and organizations in Mississippi. The project was spearheaded by a librarian interested in incorporating information-seeking skills into the curricula and continuing education of healthcare professionals and students statewide. Principal investigator Ada Seltzer, Director of Rowland Medical Library, University of Mississippi Medical Center, enlisted the cooperation of faculty, colleagues and health professionals throughout Mississippi to develop a health sciences information infrastructure. The grant proposal, funded by the National Library of Medicine in 1992, tied library and information literacy objectives to the interests and activities of the other health professional organizations, thus providing all participants with the funding they needed to meet individual as well as shared goals (Seltzer, 1994).

The Need for Information Literate Students

If not necessarily motivated by money, what is most important to faculty? The *American Faculty Poll* (Sanderson et al., 2000) reports that the opportunity to educate students is the most important professional consideration for faculty members. This shared interest between librarians and faculty is ultimately our most compelling reason to collaborate.

While the Internet has changed the way we deliver course content to DE students, it has also changed the way DE students do research. The changing nature of teaching and learning offers us an opportunity to remind and redefine for faculty members the ways in which librarians can assist in educating students. When asked to estimate where their students did the majority of their research, four out of four UW-Eau Claire summer online faculty members ranked the Internet above the library. A study by Susan Davis Herring found that while most faculty members accept the Web as a suitable research resource, most are not satisfied with it as a sole source of information. In addition, "they have some serious doubts about the value, accuracy, authority, and reliability of Web-based information and about their students' ability to evaluate this information after they find it" (2001, Analysis and Conclusions section, ¶1). The *American Faculty Poll* (Sanderson et al., 2000) found that ill-prepared students were one of the most often cited negative factors affecting faculty members' work. Such findings point to openings where librarians can provide something faculty members deem valuable. In the new online environment, faculty members recognize that students need to learn how to use and evaluate the information they find on the Internet. Librarians need to let DE faculty know that they are able and willing to teach this sort of thing. Librarians can take the initiative in offering instruction by demonstrating the possibilities. Librarians at UW-Eau Claire worked with other librarians in the University of Wisconsin System to develop an online tutorial for students enrolled in collaborative DE programs (Dieterle et al., 2000). The tutorial–in addition to providing information on traditional library research–included modules on Web searching, evaluating information, plagiarism and copyright. The tutorial was presented to DE faculty as a resource available to them to use with their DE classes. Similarly, the DE librarian developed an online research guide specifically for DE students doing company and industry research and presented it to the faculty member teaching the course (University of Wisconsin-Eau Claire, 2001). Offering such resources to DE faculty reminds them of the librarian's role in the online environment, provides samples of our work and demonstrates our interest in working together toward a common goal.

CONCLUSION

Which of the many approaches to collaboration discussed here worked and which ones didn't? The answer would have to be that all approaches worked to some extent and yet no single approach was the silver bullet that would ensure a holistically collaborative effort between the DE librarian and faculty member. Development of collaborative endeavors is incremental, and like any solid relationship must be built one step at a time, taking into consideration the needs and interests of all involved parties. The DE librarian continues with the marketing, networking and collaborative efforts described herein. The instructional design team, including the librarian, has plans for strengthening collaborative efforts. Such plans include the development of a "toolbox" for faculty teaching online, which is to include examples of best practices, samples of assignments integrating library research, FAQs, and testimonials from other online instructors. Successful collaborative efforts with one faculty member can serve as examples for others. Heller-Ross suggested that "establishing a partnership with one faculty member for one course is also an effective way to create an environment in which library services can become integrated into distance learning programs. This serves to highlight the possibilities and showcase them . . . " (1996, Creating a Partnership section, ¶ 2). As faculty members become more comfortable and proficient in the online environment, they are able to shift their focus from daunting technical matters to other ways in which they can finesse and improve the online teaching experience. When their immediate and urgent needs have been met, faculty members can address what matters most to them, and to us: better educating students. And when that time comes, the continued nurturing of our relationship with faculty members will ensure that the library will be clearly in their sights.

REFERENCES

Dickinson, G., Agnew, D, & Gorman R. (1999). Are teacher training and compensation keeping up with institutional demands for distance learning? *Cause/Effect Journal* 22(3). Retrieved November 15, 2001, from http://www.educause.edu/ir/library/html/cem9939.html.

Dieterle, U., Richmond, B., Markgraf, J., Kasuboski, A., Piele, L, Cardinal, D. et al. (2000). *Research Tutorial*. Retrieved November 15, 2001, from http://www.uwec.edu/library/tutorial/index.html.

Gordon, L. (Producer), Gordon, C. (Producer) & Robinson, P.A. (Writer/Director). (1989). *Field of Dreams* [Motion picture]. United States: Universal Studios.

Heller-Ross, H. (1996). Librarian and faculty partnerships for distance education. *MC Journal, 4*. Retrieved July 21, 2001, from WilsonWeb Library Science and Information Full Text database.

Herring, S. D. (2001). Faculty acceptance of the World Wide Web for student research. *College & Research Libraries, 62*. Retrieved Nov. 15, 2001, from WilsonWeb Library Science and Information Full Text database.

Intner, S. S. (2001). Ask not what your library can do for you; ask what you can do for your library. *Technicalities 21*(3). Retrieved September 26, 2001, from WilsonWeb Library Science and Information Full Text database.

Knesting, K., Oberly, J., Reid, R. & Ikuta, J. (2000, August). *Developing and delivering online courses: Stories from the trenches*, Panel discussion presented at University of Wisconsin-Eau Claire Professional Development Workshop, Eau Claire, WI.

Kotter, W.R. (1999). Bridging the great divide: Improving relations between librarians and classroom faculty. *Journal of Academic Librarianship 25*(4). Retrieved November 11, 2001, from WilsonWeb Library Science and Information Full Text database.

Jeffries, S. (2000). The librarian as networker: Setting the standard for higher education. In D. Raspa & D. Ward (Eds.), *The Collaborative Imperative: Librarians and faculty working together in the information universe* (114-129). Chicago: Association of College and Research Libraries.

Kohl, D.F. & Wilson, L.A. (1986). Effectiveness of course-integrated bibliographic instruction in improving coursework. *RQ 26*(2), 206-211.

Markgraf, J. & Erffmeyer, R. (in press). Providing library service to off-campus business students: access, resources and instruction. *Journal of Business & Finance Librarianship*.

Milem, J.F., Berger, J.B. & Day, E.L. (2000). Faculty time allocation: a study of change over twenty years. *Journal of Higher Education, 71*, 454-475.

Raspa, D. & Ward, D. (2000). Listening for collaboration: Faculty and librarians working together. In D. Raspa & D. Ward (Eds.), *The Collaborative Imperative: Librarians and faculty working together in the information universe* (1-18). Chicago: Association of College and Research Libraries.

Rose, R., & Roraff, C. (2000). [Summary analysis of fall 2000 UWEC faculty & staff survey. Survey conducted by McIntyre Library Strategic Planning Committee]. Unpublished raw data.

Sanderson, A., Phua, V.C. & Herda, D. (2000). *The American faculty poll*. Chicago: National Opinion Research Center.

Seltzer, A.M. (1994). Delivering information anywhere in the state. *Gratefully Yours (September/October)*. Retrieved November 23, 2001, from http://www.nlm.nih.gov/pubs/gyours/gyso94.txt.

University of Wisconsin-Eau Claire, McIntyre Library. (2001). *Marketing information: The situation analysis. Guide to resources for off-campus students*. Retrieved November 15, 2001, from http://www.uwec.edu/library/Guides/sit_anal2.html.

Young, R.M. & Harmony, S. (1999). *Working with faculty to design undergraduate information literacy programs*. New York: Neal-Schuman.

Wilson, R. (2001). A higher bar for earning tenure. *Chronicle of Higher Education, 47*(17), A12. Retrieved November 15, 2001, from EbscoHost Academic Search Elite database.

Wolpert, A. (1998). Services to remote users: Marketing the library's role. *Library Trends, 47*(1), 21-42. Retrieved November 16, 2001, from EbscoHost Academic Search Elite database.

Fee or Free?
New Commercial Services
Are Changing the Equation

Brian L. Mikesell

St. John's University

SUMMARY. Online full-text research services such as Questia and Ebrary are targeting faculty and undergraduates directly, offering them library-like services for a fee. This has caused a great deal of negative response in the library community, because these companies seem to be trying to compete with and undercut freely available library services. However, rejecting them outright is probably not the best answer–if only because their marketing budgets dwarf our own. This presentation will explore the impacts these services could have on libraries, as well as the ways we might use them to extend our online collections and services. If we engage these companies in conversation, we could end up with cooperation and even partnerships. They may have an inevitable impact on libraries, but it is up to us to shape that impact by taking the initiative.

KEYWORDS. Fees, library services, Internet, information

Change has become an integral part of the librarian's working world: changing responsibilities, changing resources, changing expectations from all sides. Most of these changes involve, are accelerated by, or are exacerbated by the explosion of information that accompanied the rapid expansion of the

[Haworth co-indexing entry note]: "Fee or Free? New Commercial Services Are Changing the Equation." Mikesell, Brian L. Co-published simultaneously in *Journal of Library Administration* (The Haworth Information Press, an imprint of The Haworth Press, Inc.) Vol. 37, No. 3/4, 2002, pp. 465-475; and: *Distance Learning Library Services: The Tenth Off-Campus Library Services Conference* (ed: Patrick B. Mahoney) The Haworth Information Press, an imprint of The Haworth Press, Inc., 2002, pp. 465-475.

http://www.haworthpress.com/store/product.asp?sku=J111
10.1300/J111v37n03_38

Internet. It was, perhaps, inevitable, that libraries would develop serious competition from commercial enterprises that seek to take advantage of the buying power of the communities we serve.

Online full-text research services such as Questia and Ebrary are targeting faculty and undergraduates directly, offering them library-like services for a fee. This has caused a great deal of negative response in the library community, because these companies seem to be trying to compete with and undercut freely available library services. However, rejecting them outright is probably not the best answer–if only because their marketing budgets dwarf our own. This paper will explore the impacts these services could have on libraries, as well as the ways we might use them to extend our online collections and services. If we engage these companies in conversation, we could end up with cooperation and even partnerships. They may have an inevitable impact on libraries, but it is up to us to shape that impact by taking the initiative.

We certainly can and should take advantage of the full portfolio of skills that we, as librarians, have developed and honed when we begin to take a look at how we can take advantage of whatever opportunities these commercial, library-like services may offer us. In some sense, we can begin approaching the problem in much the same way as we would approach any potential resource. The first step is to identify the resources that we want to evaluate. We should not wait until these companies launch their products and initiate major marketing campaigns before we take stock of them. Libraries need to begin engaging in environmental scanning to equip ourselves with the competitive intelligence we need to remain vital.

The next step, of course, is to evaluate those resources and services that we have identified. Librarians are adept at evaluating the quality and usefulness of content for our constituencies, but sometimes the desire to make more content available to our patrons electronically leads us to accept less than the best interfaces. We should, then, make the interface design a significant factor of our evaluations. If, in the end, the commercial service offers our students an intuitive, easy-to-understand interface while we offer them cumbersome, restrictive interfaces, they may choose what is to us an inferior product in terms of content. We must also evaluate how well the commercial service supports their product. Librarians have a strong tradition of excellence in service and we should not lower our expectations. Rather, we should challenge both ourselves and commercial providers to meet the highest standards of service. Finally, of course, we must examine the company offering the service so that we are comfortably assured that the content and service will remain viable and affordable over time.

The final step–and this is where we may have been lacking in terms of forcefulness–is to respond. Our responses should not be limited to just "yes" or "no," but should include the possibility of a challenge to do better. Considering the size of the market for which we purchase information products, we should take advantage of whatever leverage we can build up together. If we do not find products that meet the needs of our patrons, we should begin emulating the best functionality of commercial products when creating our own information products such as Web sites and library portals.

So, are these commercial services competition for libraries? Yes. Let's face it, they are competing for the attention of our patrons and trying to create users loyal to their tools. Well, then, what is the difference between these services and licensed resources libraries already make available? The major difference is the business model. Library-focused resources license their products to libraries on behalf of their patrons, while the emerging commercial services are marketing directly to our patrons and asking them to pay an annual fee or a per-article price. But when we say free, is it really free? Of course not. Our patrons are paying indirectly for access to the online resources we make available. But since that cost is built into fees they already pay, should they have to pay again for material they need? No, but if they are deciding to pay for these commercial services, libraries have an obligation to discover why and to come up with some solutions.

IDENTIFICATION/ENVIRONMENTAL SCANNING

While some of the library-like commercial services out there spend large amounts of money on marketing and get a corresponding share of attention and ire from libraries, there are actually quite a few companies in this market. Some are quite small, some have yet to launch a working product, some seek to partner with libraries, and some are aggressively going after customers. All of these companies' products are targets of libraries' environmental scanning.

Effective environmental scanning requires us to keep our eyes open and to be a little creative. Some of these companies advertise their products as virtual library services, but others more quietly fill similar needs. The fact is that when the *New York Times* offers to sell articles online for a fee, it is competing for our patrons' attention in much the same way as Questia does–but with even better name recognition. While the following is by no means a complete list of the products and companies out there, it does provide us with good context for the continuing discussion.

Questia [http://www.questia.com]

Questia claims to have the "world's largest online library of books" with over 40,000 books and 25,000 journal articles covering the humanities and social sciences (*Questia: Explore the Library*, December 3, 2001, para. 1+). In addition to the full-text resources, Questia also offers tools to highlight, make notes, and create bibliographies and footnotes automatically. Users can subscribe for a monthly or annual fee to get unlimited access to the entire collection during the paid period of time. Questia has gotten a great deal of notice due to its aggressive marketing directly to undergraduate students, faculty, and librarians.

Ebrary [http://www.ebrary.com]

Ebrary has not yet officially launched its product, with only one implementation through Learning Network (*Ebrary: Press Release*, July 25, 2001, para. 1). No information is available about the size or content of their online collections, just that they have partnered with "more than 80 of the world's leading publishers" (*Ebrary*, para. 2). Searching, reading online, and paging through online materials is free, so payment is based on a micro payment for the specific amount of information copied or printed. Ebrary's position relative to libraries indicates a desire to form partnerships, with an incentive to libraries in the form of revenue sharing.

NetLibrary [http://www.netlibrary.com]

A familiar service to most libraries, NetLibrary provides a "comprehensive approach to eBooks that integrates with the time-honored missions and methods of libraries and librarians" (*NetLibrary: About Us*, December 3, 2001, para. 1). Libraries subscribe by choosing the books to which they would like to have access to create a unique collection for the use of their patrons. Users may "check out" those books. Only one user may access any particular book at a time. NetLibrary started as a service offered to individuals and over time switched to a library-subscriber service.

XanEdu [http://www.xanedu.com]

XanEdu is marketed primarily to faculty as "on-demand access to copyright-cleared resources from the world's most respected databases" (*XanEdu: Elearning*, December 3, 2001, para. 3). Basically, the service is an easy way to create copyright-cleared course- or topic-packs. The service is free to the faculty member and students purchase the packs based on the per-item fees assessed through XanEdu, which includes whatever copyright fees may be charged by the publisher. XanEdu has a content distribution agreement with

ProQuest, the source of their databases and copyright-clearance. There is also a ReSearch Engine targeted at students, and billed as "the most powerful research tool on the planet" (*XanEdu: Internet Research*, December 3, 2001, para. 1), to which students can subscribe for 3, 6, or 12 months at a time.

Jones e-Global Library [http://www.e-globallibrary.com/]

Of all the services described here, this is the most like a traditional library. They provide "a suite of research tools that can expand or extend the academic library, providing students with targeted, online research guidance and academically appropriate, Internet-based resources" (*Jones e-Global Library: Higher Education*, December 3, 2001, para. 2). The services include: annotated Internet resources, databases, reference services, document delivery, research guides, and online tutorials. Their services are available to institutions wishing to subscribe on behalf of students and can be customized in order to avoid paying for resources already available through the library. One important feature is that the services have been developed and are managed by a team of experienced librarians.

Authority Finder [http://www.authorityfinder.com]

Authority Finder "is a simple and intuitive querying tool that allows one to locate relevant quotations and corresponding citations from a list of authoritative academic journals" (*Authority Finder FAQ*, December 3, 2001, para. 1). The databases consists of 250 academic and business journals and covers 1998 to the present. Authority Finder claims to have a very advanced search interface that uses language pattern-matching algorithms to produce highly relevant search results. Otherwise, it appears to be an online, full-text database that is available to individuals on a two- or six-month subscription basis.

eLibrary [http://ask.elibrary.com]

Within eLibrary, users can "ask questions in plain English, and eLibrary searches a billion words and thousands of images and quickly returns the information requested" (*eLibrary: Learn More About eLibrary*, December 3, 2001, para. 1). eLibrary includes access to a variety of full-text resources, while also providing online reference works, e-mail alerts, and a personal folder. eLibrary is a service of Tucows, Inc. and is available to individuals on a monthly or annual subscription basis.

Northern Light's Special Collection [http://www.northernlight.com]

Known primarily for its unique search engine, Northern Light also has what it calls a Special Collection, "an online business library comprising 7100 trusted, full-text journals, books, magazines, newswires, and reference sources" (*Northern Light: Special Collection: Overview*, December 3, 2001, para. 1). They are constantly adding to the collection and full-text resources go back as far as 1995. Searching the database is free and an abstract is provided, but users must pay $1-4 to view the full text of most articles. Northern Light's Special Collection is just one example of the pay-per-article model of online resources.

These are just a few of the emerging library-like commercial services out there, so environmental scanning has to be a continuous process. Librarians should be doing it all the time to identify potential commercial services and resources that are of interest. Scanning on one's own, though, is not enough. Libraries must take the information gathered in scanning and turn it into competitive intelligence. Competitive intelligence involves more than just knowing that the companies and products exist; it requires analyzing them to know what they do and how they do it.

EVALUATION/COMPETITIVE INTELLIGENCE

Using evaluative methods already familiar to libraries, we can turn shallow knowledge about our competition into competitive intelligence so that we can prepare ourselves to make a move. We must start, of course, with the content. Without useful, reliable, relevant content, these commercial services have very little to recommend them.

Librarians have been evaluating content for a very long time. Electronic content, while adding new layers of evaluation, has fundamentally the same qualities. This is especially true in the case of these commercial services, since they are really just re-packaging content from publishers. The librarian's job, then, is to evaluate whether they have chosen the "right" content–from reputable publishers, written by recognized scholars, with appropriately up-to-date content. We must also decide whether they have chosen content that would be useful for our patrons–applicable to courses offered at the institution or for research in areas where students want to find information. Finally, we must be assured that there is a critical mass of high-quality information available in that product so that our patrons can find enough information on enough different topics to satisfy their needs. The best content alone, though, is not enough to make the resource truly valuable to our patrons or us.

The design of the interface must also be a significant factor in the evaluation of any online resource. We and our communities must interact via computers with the information stored on those commercial servers we want to access. If, due to an unfriendly or difficult interface, we are unable to find relevant information at the time it is needed, the resource has failed. Of particular importance is to decide whether the interface is properly targeted to the audience for which it is intended. Using library jargon or requiring special search syntax may indicate that a resource is targeted more to a library professional than an undergraduate student. An interface that places links to significant functionality in unlikely places or "buries" them under multiple layers of links is one that will probably not serve our users well. A resource that requires the user to read instructions before beginning will most likely fail. Most users, librarians included, have a particular information need at a particular time and want to proceed with a simple search that produces useful results.

Should a search not produce the desired results, does the resource offer help or does it merely respond that nothing was found? Automatically produced "suggestions" are becoming commonplace in online resources–Google [http://www.google.com] will check spelling and ask "Did you mean:" while Amazon [http://www.amazon.com] will offer you all kinds of options for finding related material. Even if suggestions are not offered automatically, is there a prominent help button? And when that button is clicked, is the help context sensitive? Most users do not want to have to figure out the "help topic" that fits their problem, but want instead to have an explanation or suggestion that is relevant to the difficulty they are experiencing. There are, of course, limitations to computer-generated help. It cannot respond in a truly intelligent way, merely make a guess based on previously programmed scenarios. So, is there anyone out there I can talk to?

Service to users of a resource is an often ignored or difficult-to-access aspect of commercial services. Libraries, of course, have a long history of providing high-quality services, often one-on-one. If these commercial competitors want to do better than libraries, how are they meeting the challenge of serving the personal, sometimes idiosyncratic, needs of the entire range of library users? With the emergence of live online reference services offered by libraries, there is no longer a significant technological argument to be made to defend the lack of excellent patron service. While this has not been substantiated, it is likely that cost is a major factor in commercial services' decision to limit the amount of live services offered to their users.

This brings up a significant difference, and perhaps the major point of contention, between commercial library-like services and libraries themselves–business model. In the climate of dot-coms gone dot-bust, an evaluation of the business model of these services is an essential part of the intelligence libraries need to gather to make informed decisions about how to respond to the competition they represent.

The first issue is the bottom line–price. We must evaluate the price, as we do with any resource, to decide not only whether it is affordable to us or to our students, but also whether the product is worth the level of investment required. This is true whether the price is paid as a monthly or annual fee for unlimited access, a micro payment for a portion of a document, or a price-per-document. Where we must work within budgets negotiated with college and university administrations, commercial services must balance what their customers are willing to pay with what they need to make their company profitable. An item related to budgets that libraries will want to evaluate is how the commercial service is marketed. Some advertise aggressively even on our campuses, while others seek to partner with libraries to promote the use of their services. The marketing presence created by these companies will inevitably affect the way libraries are able to respond.

Finally, and importantly, libraries must make a decision about the permanence of these companies. A company that is unstable and likely to fail because of poor management or inadequate cash flow will require a very different response than a company that is strong and will be a player in the market for a long time to come. This is not to say that a weak company that is likely to disappear soon deserves to be ignored by libraries. In the larger scheme, we should at least be concerned that the resources digitized by these companies remain accessible.

While libraries may not have venture capital to invest, we can have an impact on these competitors of ours in other ways. We can certainly impact them by advising our communities whether or not the service is worth the money. We could make them obsolete by discovering what they are doing that our patrons like and emulating that service or resource or quality. We could partner with one or more of these companies to improve our visibility and to serve our patrons better. We will have no impact, though, if we ignore this commercial competition. We must create competitive intelligence in our library communities and be proactive in our responses to these commercial ventures.

RESPONDING/CREATING POSITIVE STANCES

Fear of emerging competition from library-like commercial services, their budgets, their professional and widespread marketing, and their ability to appeal to users is an understandable reaction. That fear may also lead libraries to reject and even vilify these companies as services that are inappropriate for our users and cannot be models that show libraries where we may be lacking services or resources. Outright rejection without a planned response, though, neither addresses the issues that create markets for these companies, nor will it cause these companies to fail or lessen the competition they pose. Libraries should instead gather competitive intelligence and use it to create positive stances that respond to these new areas of competition appropriately and intelligently.

If, after appropriate analysis, we decide that there is nothing worthwhile about one or another of these commercial services, we can do more than just ignore the company and its services. A positive stance from the library's point of view might be to monitor the company, checking in at intervals to review the analysis to see whether the company has developed new resources or services that may be of interest. If the conclusion strongly indicates that our communities would be wasting their money by paying for the service, we could initiate a marketing campaign of our own. That marketing could be done in a variety of ways, and should not only tell our users that we advise against using the commercial service, but also indicate to them the reasons for this advice. This may seem counter-intuitive–after all, publicity may bring to notice services that our users otherwise may not have known about. On the other hand, if it is obvious to our patrons that we are not just protecting the library's territory, but are advising them and potentially saving them money, we may convince our patrons to avoid certain products. At the same time, we may be able to advertise how our own services can help them better.

Another positive response is to embrace these companies to one degree or another. After all, many of them are digitizing materials not available elsewhere electronically and others may have functionality that we find intriguing and potentially useful. Embracing one or more commercial library-like services does not have to mean unqualified acceptance. Our response can certainly be measured so that we gain the most benefit possible from any interaction.

One way of embracing the services of these companies would be to negotiate a special rate for your library. This could be done so that the library can offer an especially useful commercial resource to a particular course or for majors in a department. If the service is based on a price per item, you could decide that this is a service to which the library will subscribe and use to extend resources–for document delivery or through mediated searches. This type of response is, perhaps, much the same as for other online resources whose content libraries license. The commercial service just becomes another online resource offered through the library, although there may be slightly different requirements for users to gain access to it.

There are more involved ways of embracing these services, too, through much more extensive partnering. A number of the commercial library-like services are more than just digitized content. Rather, they offer functionality that makes them more like an online research and paper-writing environment.

Done well, such an environment could prove a great benefit to our user communities. Our response could be to contact the company and suggest that they work with us to try to bring together a variety of sources of content within their environment, so that our patrons could use their tools with the best variety of resources we can make available. This is predicated on the notion that library users would prefer to use a single resource that gives them the best possible interface, functionality, and content. It also relies on the idea that once within an online resource that has especially useful services, a user is less likely to want to use an incompatible resource. If successful, the result might be a library research portal that caters to the needs of library patrons, makes access to online resources easier and more unified, and which allows the commercial service to remain viable by licensing the portal and some content to libraries.

Perhaps, on the other hand, we find one or more parties unable or unwilling to create a partnership or there is no one product that appeals strongly enough. In such a case, we could still create a positive stance by emulating the best services and functionality of each of the commercial library-like services to create our own online service that satisfies our requirements as well as those of our patrons. It may be that few libraries have the financial and technological resources required to build such an environment, but libraries have a strong tradition of partnering with each other to meet common needs. A consortium may be able to bring together the resources necessary to create such a product. In the current academic climate where colleges and universities are becoming more entrepreneurial, there may even be an opportunity for cost-recovery by licensing the resulting product outside the consortium or institution where it is created.

The most important thing to remember is that the goal is to provide the best possible service to our patrons. Reacting negatively out of fear may be natural, especially since libraries are not accustomed to competition, but such a reaction will not produce the best situation for our patrons or even for us. If our patrons abandon us to pay for commercial services on their own, we risk becoming obsolete. Libraries need to use the strengths and traditions developed over centuries to move decisively forward into an ever-changing world of information services.

Libraries and librarians cannot control the explosion of information, but we can seek ways of working with the elements out there to improve our patrons' ability to find and access the best sources for the information they need. Through environmental scanning we can identify new resources with potential. The competitive intelligence developed by analyzing these new resources will give us the information we need to respond to the challenges that are posed by changes in our competitive environment. Measuring our response so that it is appropriate and takes advantage of new and positive developments can only put us in a stronger position. By combining our buying power and influence, we can put pressure on commercial library-like services to respond to our inquiries and proposals seriously.

Change is, perhaps, inevitable, but it does not have to be entirely chaotic. We need to begin to be not merely reactive, but take a positive role in creating and shaping change within libraries as well as in the products that are created for the use of libraries and the communities we serve. We purchase and recommend resources on behalf of our patrons, but must also be aware of and take an interest in the non-library resources our patrons may be using. The very use of fee-based resources should indicate to us that there is a gap somewhere in our services and collections. Even activities that may seem counter-intuitive, such as working to improve the services offered by our competitors, can work to our benefit. In this way, we can improve services for our patrons and at the same time make our own position in the changing world of information services more comfortable and competitive. The equation is changing and we must be active in balancing that equation to the benefit of libraries and the communities we serve.

REFERENCES

Authority Finder FAQ. (n.d.) Retrieved December 3, 2001, from http://www.authority finder.com/aboutaf2.html.

Ebrary. (n.d.) Retrieved December 3, 2001, from http://www.ebrary.com.

Ebrary: Press release. (July 25, 2001) Retrieved December 3, 2001, from http://www. ebrary.com/news/010725.jsp.

eLibrary: Learn more about eLibrary. (n.d.) Retrieved December 3, 2001, from http://ask.elibrary.com/aboutpopup.asp.

Jones e-Global Library: Higher education. (n.d.) Retrieved December 3, 2001, from http://www.e-globallibrary.com/eglobal/higher.html.

NetLibrary: About us. (n.d.) Retrieved December 3, 2001, from http://www.netlibrary. com/about_us/index.asp.

Northern Light: Special collection: Overview. (n.d.) Retrieved December 3, 2001, from http://www.northernlight.com/docs/specoll_help_overview.html.

Questia: Explore the library. (n.d.) Retrieved December 3, 2001, from http://www.questia. com/aboutQuestia/exploreLibrary.html.

XanEdu: Elearning. (n.d.) Retrieved December 3, 2001, from http://www.xanedu.com/.

XanEdu: Internet research. (n.d.) Retrieved December 3, 2001, from http://www.xanedu. com/researchengine/students/index.shtml.

Added Value, Multiple Choices: Librarian/Faculty Collaboration in Online Course Development

Tom Riedel

Regis University

SUMMARY. This paper investigates the integration of library resources, library instruction and services into the design of online courses. While many libraries embrace the ACRL guidelines for library support of distance learners, many of the Web-based resources we develop still depend upon students seeking them out. Distance learning librarian collaboration with teaching faculty and instructional designers at Regis University resulted in a proactive method of library resource delivery applicable in multiple online scenarios.

KEYWORDS. Collaboration, course development, faculty, distance education

THAT WAS THEN, THIS IS NOW

The Regis University Libraries' model of support for distance education has evolved over the past 15 years in response to advances in technology as well as to expansion of university distance learning programs. Distance education at Regis originally consisted of adult education classes offered at a number of sites remote from the main Denver campus, but a traditional model of library service, the branch established in 1985 at the Colorado Springs cam-

[Haworth co-indexing entry note]: "Added Value, Multiple Choices: Librarian/Faculty Collaboration in On-line Course Development." Riedel, Tom. Co-published simultaneously in *Journal of Library Administration* (The Haworth Information Press, an imprint of The Haworth Press, Inc.) Vol. 37, No. 3/4, 2002, pp. 477-487; and: *Distance Learning Library Services: The Tenth Off-Campus Library Services Conference* (ed: Patrick B. Mahoney) The Haworth Information Press, an imprint of The Haworth Press, Inc., 2002, pp. 477-487.

http://www.haworthpress.com/store/product.asp?sku=J111
10.1300/J111v37n03_39

pus, has not been repeated at other teaching sites. In 1990, an Outreach Librarian position was created and charged, according to ACRL guidelines for distance learning library services, with implementing, coordinating, and evaluating library resources and services provided to the distance learning community. Since then, cooperative agreements between Regis Libraries and junior college, public and university libraries have served our extended constituency, along with librarian visits to extended campuses, networked computer labs, enhancements to interlibrary loan and document delivery services, and the implementation of electronic reserves. Three years ago, the Outreach Librarian position was reconfigured as "Distance Learning Librarian," with additional responsibilities as Head of Access Services.

Currently, classroom courses are provided at six remote teaching sites from Colorado Springs, 60 miles south of Denver, to Fort Collins, 55 miles north, to Las Vegas, Nevada. Each Regis site is equipped with a computer lab on the Regis network, or RegisNet, so students have direct, IP-filtered access to the full array of library electronic resources through our Web pages. The library Web pages also provide tutorials on research strategies, database searching, finding books and articles, and other topics. A *Distance Learning Library Services* Web page details the services available to distance learners, which the libraries define as anyone taking courses at a Regis location other than the main campus, or online students living more than 10 miles away. Services we provide to our distance students include:

- Reference assistance by local call, toll-free number, and e-mail
- Databases available remotely through authorization and password access (proxy authentication will be in place by mid-2002)
- Free intercampus and interlibrary loan via a Web-based request form
- Courier service linking our Colorado campuses
- Materials such as books mailed directly to students
- Consortial agreements with libraries that see high concentrations of our students. Memoranda of understanding have been signed with public and academic libraries (Scrimgeour and Potter, 1991).

THE CHALLENGES

Even though many library resources and services are available to our distance students, our primary concern remains how to make students aware of what's available and how to use the resources, whether they are taking classes at extended campuses or online. Of course, an important part of that equation is the faculty themselves. While a reference librarian serving a student constituency face-to-face can take corrective steps and build instructional relationships with on-campus faculty, librarians charged with the support of students in online courses are often challenged to know what kind of assignments online students are required to complete, what resources they use to complete them, or even the name and location of the instructor. Since SPS has 55 full-time and over 600 affiliate faculty, the task of communication can be a daunting one.

Another challenge for Regis Libraries has been maintaining a place at the table when important planning and decision-making about the direction of distance education programs are underway. In the 1990s, Regis had classroom space strewn across Wyoming as well as in Colorado mountain towns, and often the libraries were left to play catch-up so that services, including negotiating memoranda of understanding with local libraries, could be put in place to serve our distance students. The relationship between the libraries and the School for Professional Studies has improved over the years, but the libraries have had to roll with the punches both in terms of the expansion of the distance learning enterprise and the way it has been expanding–primarily in the online arena.

The past few years have seen a dramatic increase in the number of Regis students enrolled in online courses, dictating new models of library support. Distance learning curricula are developed primarily by the Regis University School for Professional Studies (SPS). In 1995, over 80% of SPS classes were classroom-based, and just under 5% were offered over the Internet. By 2000, classroom-based enrollments had dropped over 20% as more students opted for online courses. Now, more than one-fourth of SPS credit hours are delivered online, representing nearly 10,000 class enrollments. In early 2000, 75 online courses were offered, and 75 more were slated to be converted to online format in the following eighteen months. I became concerned, based on these staggering numbers, that a whole new generation of distance students had the potential of falling through the cracks of library service. Having worked with many students at extended campuses, from orientations to student representative meetings to classroom library instruction, it was clear that many of them could be nearing the end of their studies before they became aware of the full array of resources available to them.

Knowing that instructors did not present students with the library information they needed to effectively complete their coursework was compounded by the occasional dissemination of misinformation by SPS, which has created modules that detail first night assignments and outline week by week objectives for each course offering. Although each instructor has latitude in constructing a course syllabus, the basic course content remains the same. In trying to understand what SPS faculty might be up to in terms of course assignments, I stumbled across some troubling information in the modules–attempts by faculty to suggest appropriate research resources for students in their classes. One, for an undergraduate business research class, included a section entitled "Internet Research." Under the subheading "Secondary Research," I found the following: "Often the best place to start is to search with *meta search engines.* . . ." More shocking was the list of suggested sources for competitive analysis on companies, including chamber-of-commerce.com, moodys.com, stat-usa.gov, thomasregister.com, the U.S. Census Bureau and the Library of Congress. Well, where to begin? First of all, library resources such as General BusinessFile and ABI Inform were not listed. Although Regis Libraries license Moody's (FIS Online) and Stat-USA, the URLs given were not those to our subscription databases (which, at any rate, would require additional logon information). Any student following the links given for many of the sources cited would be prompted to subscribe as individuals. All in all, students were presented with a list of potentially frustrating dead ends ranging from inappropriate to plain wrong.

A PREEMPTIVE BLOW

Rather than simply critique the resources put forth in the Business Research course module, I realized that this misinformation pointed to a bigger problem in getting the correct information about research resources where it needed to be, and just as important, its dissemination back in the hands of librarians. I contacted SPS Faculty Chairs to let them know that I would be happy to compile Web-mounted lists of library resources appropriate to the different subject areas, and suggested that they create links to these from the course modules. Then, I created a series of "Recommended Online Resources by Subject," compilations of appropriate Regis databases that would be useful to students completing assignments in the broad subject areas of Business, Communication, Computer Science, Education, English, Health Sciences, History, Humanities, Philosophy, Religious Studies and Social Sciences. Further resource lists were compiled for the master's programs in Management, Nonprofit Management and Liberal Studies. Each resource list includes step-by-step information about accessing databases, contact information for the Distance Learning Librarian, reference and circulation desks, information about library card numbers (an ever-confusing topic for our distance learners who are not issued a physical card), links to and information about Interlibrary Loan, and links to examples of electronic citation styles. Authorizations and passwords for the databases not authenticated by library card number are included in the lists, which, since they provide such proprietary information, are themselves password-protected.

The Recommended Online Resources by Subject quickly proved to be an effective way to answer many remote access and other questions received directly by my office as well as the reference desk, but they have not yet been linked directly to the SPS course modules. The modules, from 10 to 40 pages long, are in PDF format, are generally due to be revised, and still hold secondary importance to students who must adhere to a particular course syllabus. Instead, I have put links to the resource guides on the library distance learning pages, where they generate many requests for the password to access them. Rather than believe that having the guides available would be enough to guarantee their use, however, I marketed their focused use in online classes.

WHAT THE LITERATURE REVEALED

The *ACRL Guidelines for Distance Learning Library Services* set out the challenge to libraries to provide services for distance learners equivalent to those provided to on-campus students, and the literature has echoed the guidelines, with many authors detailing what their libraries provide in terms of resources and services, and others simply reiterating what many of us have known for quite some time–that content, in the form of online databases and Web resources should be made available to distance students, as well as links (and phone contacts) to services such as reference, instruction, and interlibrary loan (O'Leary, 2000). The literature abounds with suggested technologies to serve distance learners, but many focus on providing the technology while depending on the student to find it and use it. In other words, we build it, they come. One such current trend in the literature focuses on a current trend in technology: virtual reference and instruction by way of MOOs, chat and course management software (Black, 2000; Smyth, 2000; Goodson, 2001; Pival, 2001; Viggiano & Ault, 2001). The mechanics of integrating library resources into online courses has received little attention; while some libraries have succeeded in ensuring that links to library Web pages are embedded in online courses, such as at the University of Wyoming (Kearley, 2000), others, such as the University of Maryland, offer online library instruction for credit (Kelley & Lange, 2000). A more substantial, course-specific integration is suggested as an important aspect of strategic planning at DePaul University (Cervone & Brown, 2001). A crucial component of integration, marketing library services to and collaborating with faculty receives attention for its effectiveness as well as its importance in long-range planning (Hart, Coleman & Hong, 2000; Kearley & Lang, 2000; Cervone & Brown, 2001).

PLANNING MEETS SERENDIPITY

The Distance Education unit at Regis, a division within SPS, is charged with developing and maintaining online courses using WebCT software. In early 2000, I met with three instructional designers to pitch integration of library resources into online classes, specifically by creating links to the resource guides I had already compiled and by making use of the distance learning Web pages and our online research skills tutorial. I also offered to tailor resource and instructional guides to the needs of particular classes.

Two other developments coincided serendipitously at the time, helping pique faculty interest in what I was proposing–the imminent implementation of electronic reserves and the courtship of SPS by XanEdu. XanEdu, a division of Bell and Howell (ProQuest) markets itself directly to faculty, giving them a straightforward way to compile coursepacks of readings and passing along all costs to students. I was asked by SPS faculty to evaluate XanEdu, and I ultimately encouraged them instead to take advantage of the databases we already licensed–which duplicated much of XanEdu's content. I proposed better use of our collection through electronic reserves, a system slated to be up and running by late spring of 2001. Electronic Reserves (we use Docutek ERes) was an important step for Regis Libraries since instructors at extended campuses had rarely taken advantage of our relationship with other libraries to place materials on reserve for extended campuses, and as far as I knew, online instructors were not using WebCT to mount reserve materials electronically. I saw this as a good opportunity to market a service that would enhance course content at no extra cost to students who already pay substantial tuition. My initial meeting with the instructional designers resulted in work with three different teams to develop three online courses.

THE COLLABORATIVE ENTERPRISE–YOUR GOALS OR MINE?

While I was pleased with the immediate response to my offer to participate in online course development, I was also a bit wary about the time that could be required of me if I were called upon to participate in meetings to develop up to 75 classes in short order. Each design team consisted of an instructional designer, two faculty members, or Subject Matter Experts, who had taught each course before in classroom or guided independent study format, and the Distance Learning Librarian. We met in full groups face-to-face for initial planning, then conducted business primarily by e-mail and phone up until implementation. My goals going into each project were practical:

- Students should be pointed to relevant library resources for a specific assignment
- Resource lists should be pushed to students at an appropriate time rather than requiring students to seek them out
- Web pages should not require special plug-in applications or a great deal of development time on my part
- Any library course module should indeed be modular, and able to be applied to different scenarios
- The library should maintain control of library content by creating separate Web pages linked to each online course
- Library assignments for an individual course should contribute to the students' information literacy and impart skills transferable to other courses.

Generally, the instructional designers embraced incorporating library resources and instruction into online course content, sometimes to a degree beyond what I considered possible given the short timeframe for development. Working with faculty also proved to be rewarding and they were generally pleased with the added value of incorporated library resources. Even so, the process revealed that faculty were not always aware of the library resources in their own fields and that their expectations of the types of materials that could be culled from library resources were not always realistic. For example, one faculty member insisted that I should be able to identify journal articles to place on electronic reserve that defined terms and provided the sort of synopses and overviews more likely to be found in course textbooks, dictionaries or encyclopedias. Expectations were also high for recreating library tutorials to more closely fit the needs of a specific course. On the other hand, I was eager to suggest and develop library assignments that required too much work for faculty to administer and grade. I believe that in all three cases we met on philosophical middle ground, and that the results, worthwhile for faculty and students alike, do much to impart library instruction and push library resources.

THREE COURSES, THREE APPROACHES

MLS (Master of Arts in Liberal Studies) 621–The Nature of Language and Communication, broken into four subtopics, or tracks. Since courses in this program have historically been guided independent study, the conversion to online format gives students more opportunity for interaction. Among the assignments students are required to complete are (1) the comparison of a book from a suggested bibliography to a "comparable Website," (2) finding articles on relevant topics from recent journals to discuss in classroom forum, (3) finding journal articles, books and Websites for a final project, (4) a case study of an author. Faculty on the instructional design team were content with the MLS suggested source list as I had compiled it, so I initially created a duplicate Web page that did not require a password for access; since students must log in to online courses, the proprietary library information is protected at this level. Students are directed to Gale and FirstSearch databases as well as to more subject specific resources such as the Anthropological Index Online, MLA International Bibliography and Philosopher's Index. A link was also created to information on critical evaluation of Internet sites. While the first Web page design referred to assignments in each of the four tracks, I ended up creating four pages, each specific to the assignments for each track. Although there was much duplication in terms of my work, much of it was accomplished simply by cutting and pasting, and clarity was gained by providing four simplified resource lists rather than one overarching one.

MNM (Master of Nonprofit Management) 670–Financial Resource Development and Marketing. Students in this course are not required to do standard library research, but must complete a "prospect research" project, identifying and investigating potential donors. In addition to a course textbook, a list of suggested resources is provided, and it is suggested that students regularly read daily newspapers and *The Chronicle of Philanthropy* to maintain current awareness and to contribute to class forums. At the bottom of the suggested resources, the initial course syllabus for the classroom-based course stated: "The library, CARL system [our ILS] and Internet are also excellent resources." Needless to say, this information may have given students some tantalizing leads but not much in terms of substantive information. The online course now links to the MNM suggested library resource list, including giving information about access to the online version of *The Chronicle of Philanthropy* and to online newspapers. A separate section of the resource list addresses the particularities of prospect research and includes library and Internet resources for conducting it. The instructors for this course were particularly taken with the possibilities of electronic reserves, and links to ERes, along with access information, were created within the course.

BA 485–Business Research Principles and Methods. This undergraduate course in Business Administration sees enrollment of over 300 students each year, and requires them to design primary research as well as conduct secondary research. (As a reminder, this is the course mentioned earlier whose module suggested the unlikely sources for research.) While the graduate courses above were content to draw upon the Web resources I had already created, adding value to them by making them more specific and linking to them at the appropriate time, the sights were set much higher for BA 485. Since this course focuses on research, it made more sense to integrate library use from the beginning and from week to week within the course. Initial plans included producing a streaming video or compact disc orientation to the library, a project subsequently abandoned. Interest still remains in such an orientation, and we will pursue it further in 2002. Some of my considerations about preparing such a visual orientation were:

- The Regis University Web pages were slated for redesign, so would possibly not match the reality of a CD very far into the future
- Even though this orientation was proposed for a specific online class, I wanted to make sure it would be general enough to serve any student
- Streaming video would doubtlessly frustrate many of our online students due to bandwidth issues
- We are likely to implement proxy server authentication within the next several months, thus making many aspects of the current orientation obsolete
- Funding.

In BA 485, the library and library resources become a presence from the first week of the class. In week one, a WebCT page, "Using the Regis University Library for Research," encourages students to familiarize themselves with the library Web site and gives them fair warning that they will be expected to find resources using the site throughout the course. Links to library-created "Resources for Business and Economics" and to "Business Resources on the World Wide Web," a list created by the Regis Library business bibliographer, are also included. In week one and throughout the eight-week course, links to electronic reserves are provided so that students can read articles and comment on them in forum discussions. Student exposure to library resources in week one are not simply passive–one of the initial assignments is to read the "Research Strategies" tutorial, complete the ten-question quiz, identify a business encyclopedia or dictionary available in Regis Libraries and cite it in APA format. While students are not expected to retrieve this source, the concept of identifying and citing is taken into the following weeks.

In week two, one of the assignments is to complete three of the other library tutorials: Finding Books, Finding Periodical Articles, and Internet Research. The exercise requires students to retrieve articles, Web sites, and books (suggesting that students may need to use Interlibrary Loan) and to create an annotated bibliography by week seven.

FUTURE OPPORTUNITIES

The good relationships spawned by work with instructional design teams has led to more work–although the projected 75 new courses have not come down the pike, yet. I hope to work more with design teams to target and then develop the most likely courses to incorporate library instruction. My insistence on keeping library Web pages autonomous rather than incorporated wholesale into WebCT content will allow me easy access to revise all the resource lists once we have a proxy server in place. Other projects that will enhance the library piece of online courses include a scheduled redesign of our library tutorial as well as the development of a video or audio library orientation. One immediate result of library integration in online courses is that more faculty are interested in learning about our databases so that they can incorporate current literature in their courses through electronic reserves. Librarian-instructed faculty workshops now provide a soapbox as well as an instructional opportunity; faculty aware of the multiple choices of library integration in course design will doubtlessly raise the bar for their students as well as for librarians.

REFERENCES

ACRL Guidelines for Distance Learning Library Services. Association of College and Research Libraries. 30 Nov. 2001. http://www.ala.org/acrl/guides/distlrng.html.

Black, N. (2000). Emerging technologies: tools for distance education and library services. In P. Thomas (Comp.), *Ninth Off-Campus Library Services Conference Proceedings: April 26-28, 2000*, pp. 29-38. Mount Pleasant, MI: Central Michigan University.

Cervone, F., & Brown, D. (2001). Transforming library services to support distance learning: strategies used by the DePaul University Libraries. *College & Research Libraries News, 62*(2), 147-149.

Hart, J., Coleman, V., & Hong, Y. (2000). Marketing electronic resources and services: Surveying faculty use as a first step. In W. Arant & P. Mosley (Eds.), *Library Outreach, Partnerships, and Distance Education: Reference Librarians at the Gateway*, pp. 41-51. New York, NY: The Haworth Press, Inc.

Kearley, J., & Lange, K. (2000). Partners in emerging technology: Library support for web-based courses. In P. Thomas (Comp.), *Ninth Off-Campus Library Services Conference Proceedings: April 26-28, 2000*, pp. 181-189. Mount Pleasant, MI: Central Michigan University.

Kelley, K., Orr, G., Houck, J. & SchWeber, C. (2000). Library instruction for the next millennium: Two web-based courses to teach distant students information literacy. In P. Thomas (Comp.), *Ninth Off-Campus Library Services Conference Proceedings: April 26-28, 2000*, pp. 191-197. Mount Pleasant, MI: Central Michigan University.

O'Leary, M. (2000). Distance learning and libraries. *Online 24*(4), 94-96.

Pival, P., & Tuñón, J. (2000). Innovative methods for providing instruction to distance students using technology. In P. Thomas (Comp.), *Ninth Off-Campus Library Services Conference Proceedings: April 26-28, 2000*, pp. 231-238. Mount Pleasant, MI: Central Michigan University.

Scrimgeour, A., & Potter, S. (1991). The tie that binds: The role and evolution of contracts in interlibrary cooperation. In C. Jacob (Comp.), *The Fifth Off-Campus Library Services Conference Proceedings, October 30 to November 1, 1991*,
pp. 241-254. Mount Pleasant, MI: Central Michigan University.

Smyth, J. (2000). Using a web-based MOO for library instruction in distance education. In P. Thomas (Comp.), *Ninth Off-Campus Library Services Conference Proceedings: April 26-28, 2000*, pp. 253-259. Mount Pleasant, MI: Central Michigan
University.

Viggiano, R., & Ault, M. (2001). Online library instruction for online students. *Information Technology and Libraries, 20*(3), 135-138.

Surviving
a Distance Learning Accreditation Visit

Sandra K. Stratford

Columbus State University

SUMMARY. Columbus State University (CSU) was the first higher education institution in Georgia to experience an on-site distance learning program review by the regional accreditation agency, the Southern Association of Colleges and Schools (SACS). Library services and personnel are essential in the support and delivery of distance learning at CSU and were therefore critical elements in the SACS review. The role of the library, campus preparations, the on-site visit, and the review outcomes are discussed in this paper. Initiated by a "substantive change" in the quantity of distance learning offerings, CSU's accreditation experience can prove beneficial to others as there is a similarity in the review process despite differences among institutions and accreditation agencies.

KEYWORDS. Distance learners, accreditation, programs, library resources

INTRODUCTION

Columbus College was founded in Columbus, Georgia, as a two-year college within the University System of Georgia in 1958. The institution was renamed Columbus State University in the late 1990s in recognition of its mission to provide undergraduate and graduate educational opportunities to the surrounding region, which includes some of the least economically developed areas of Georgia.

[Haworth co-indexing entry note]: "Surviving a Distance Learning Accreditation Visit." Stratford, Sandra K. Co-published simultaneously in *Journal of Library Administration* (The Haworth Information Press, an imprint of The Haworth Press, Inc.) Vol. 37, No. 3/4, 2002, pp. 489-501; and: *Distance Learning Library Services: The Tenth Off-Campus Library Services Conference* (ed: Patrick B. Mahoney) The Haworth Information Press, an imprint of The Haworth Press, Inc., 2002, pp. 489-501.

http://www.haworthpress.com/store/product.asp?sku=J111
10.1300/J111v37n03_40

Located 110 miles southwest of Atlanta on the Alabama border, Columbus State University has over 5,000 students and 250 faculty. The student population is predominantly non-traditional, with the typical student being over 26, working, and having family responsibilities. Columbus State University (CSU) offers degrees ranging from associate to specialists, and participates in a collaborative doctorate in education degree with Valdosta State University. CSU has been recognized for its leadership role in educating a workforce for area computer and business firms.

By 1990, distance learning was recognized as a means of providing educational opportunities to the underserved population of the region and became an institutional goal. Experimentation with two-way interactive compressed video/audio delivered via telephone lines became possible through participation in Georgia ClassConnect, an eight-site project sponsored by BellSouth, NEC America, and two other companies in Fall, 1991. Two years later, Columbus College became one of some 100 sites (K-12, technical, higher education, and Zoo Atlanta) to be funded under the *Georgia Distance Learning and Telemedicine Act of 1992*. This project provided the equipment, infrastructure, and technical support for one of the world's largest two-way interactive distance learning networks, the Georgia Statewide Academic and Medical System (GSAMS). Within a few years, GSAMS sites numbered almost 400, with Columbus College hosting five sites–four on campus and one at the Coca Cola Space Science Center in downtown Columbus.

Surveys had indicated a particular need for graduate education courses for place-bound teachers within the service region and the two-way interactive technology offered an ideal opportunity for Columbus College to address these needs. Agreements were made to offer courses at GSAMS two-way interactive classrooms located at Georgia Southwestern College in Americus (90 miles south), at Flint River Technical Institute in Thomaston (70 miles northeast), and at Griffin Technical Institute in Griffin (90 miles northeast). The three sites served residents both in the specific communities and in outlying areas. Some students chose to drive to the Griffin site from up to fifty miles away in the Atlanta metro area, selecting Columbus College over more urban institutions.

During this same period, the demand for online computer science courses had been growing both locally and internationally. To meet this need, Columbus College entered an agreement with Real Education, Inc., to provide technical and faculty support for a 100% online master's in applied computer science.

Columbus State University (formerly Columbus College) has long been accredited by the Commission on Colleges of the Southern Association of Colleges and Schools (SACS). In 1995, at the time of a full accreditation visit, two-way distance learning was being used on an experimental basis for a small number of credit and non-credit courses. By 1998, the percentage of courses within the graduate education and computer science programs that were delivered via two-way interactive video/audio or the Internet had reached the point that a "substantive change" report was required by SACS, the regional accrediting agency. An on-site visit to examine the six graduate programs where over 50% of the courses were delivered primarily via distance learning technologies was scheduled for November 1998–providing CSU with the distinction of being the first higher education institution in Georgia to undergo a distance learning accreditation review by SACS. A visit by representatives of the National Council for Accreditation of Teacher Education (NCATE) was scheduled for the week preceding the SACS visit.

DISTANCE LEARNING RESPONSIBILITIES

In 1994, *Working Guidelines for Distance Learning* were developed to specifically address academic standards and criteria, learning resources and support services, procedures, and priorities for offering distance learning courses (Stratford, 1994). Following approval by the Council of Deans, the document was distributed across the campus and the sections made available at the school's Website (http://dl.colstate.edu/faculty/index.shtml). A key component in the guidelines was the establishment of an advisory committee to address issues related to distance learning and explore new distance learning opportunities.

The *Working Guidelines for Distance Learning* clearly confirmed that all academic matters related to distance learning courses and programs were the responsibility of the department, college, or Vice President for Academic Affairs (Stratford, 1994). Determination of courses, class size, and instructor remained the purview of the department. Admission, course, and graduation requirements were to be identical for traditional and distance learning students.

Library, bookstore, and other student services were identified as being the responsibility of the traditional agency responsible for providing these services for students on-campus. Initially, the Division of Continuing and Regional Education (DCRES) assumed responsibility for facilitating the identification and meeting of support needs at the off-campus GSAMS sites. DCRES was also responsible for arranging off-campus contact personnel, negotiating site-usage charges, and determining costs for courses. Instructional Technology Services, a department within the Simon Schwob Memorial Library, was (and is) responsible for the technical and training aspects of GSAMS and assisting the faculty teaching online courses.

A private software company (Real Education, Inc.) was contracted to provide technical and developmental support for the Computer Science master's degree. Campus support for students in this program was coordinated through links to CSU agencies' Websites established originally to serve the GSAMS off-campus students.

PREPARATIONS FOR SACS DISTANCE LEARNING REVIEW

Leadership and Teamwork

The first step in preparing for the distance learning accreditation review was the appointment of a team of faculty and staff with both experience and a vested interest in the success of distance learning at Columbus State University. Members included faculty teaching via GSAMS two-way interactive technology, Chair of the Computer Science Department, Director of Continuing and Regional Education, Coordinator of Instructional Technology Services/Library Outreach Liaison, and Director of Enrollment Services.

The Director of Institutional Research and Assessment (IR&A) provided leadership for the CSU re-affirmation efforts. In addition to bringing prior experience with SACS and NCATE accreditation activities, she was a faculty member (and former department chair in the College of Education) who taught over GSAMS in its earliest days. As a member of the Vice President for Academic Affairs office, she brought a commitment and support for the distance learning activities from the top administration and the ability to cut across departmental and agency boundaries. Her low-key, yet tenacious, style contributed greatly to her ability to obtain needed information from a variety of individuals, reduce turf issues, and to create a truly collaborative team. Of particular value was her skill in taking raw data and placing it in the appropriate format and terminology.

Meetings of the distance learning accreditation team members included brainstorming activities and gripe sessions that both cleared the air and identified solutions to problems or concerns. Additional individuals invited to meet with the team as areas of concern were identified included other distance learning faculty, the CSU Bookstore Manager and the Director of Computer and Information Network Services.

Criteria Review, Assessment, and Documentation

The first charge to the team was to review the SACS *Criteria for Accreditation* and identify the key points that would be addressed in the review process, including relevant "must" statements (Commission on Colleges of the Southern Association of Colleges and Schools [SACS Criteria], 1996). The team also carefully studied the *Planning Distance Learning Activities* publication of the Southern Association of Colleges and Schools and found it to be particularly helpful in identification of areas that should be well-documented and might be addressed during an on-site visit (1996).

Once identified, the goal of the team was to assess and document Columbus State University's compliance with each of the relevant criteria. Primary issues identified for assessment and documentation included having clear and explicit goals for distance learning programs that are consistent with the institution's purpose, faculty credentials and availability for student interaction, and provision of adequate and accessible learning and support resources (SACS Criteria 4.5, 4.8.2.4, 5.1.1, and 5.1.2).

Team members believed that one of the strengths of Columbus State University's distance learning program was the emphasis on comparable quality. Admission, course, and graduation requirements–along with faculty qualifications–were identical regardless of delivery methods. For all GSAMS courses and many of the online courses, on-campus and off-campus students were literally in the same courses. While formal comparison had not been made, anecdotal evidence indicated that the off-campus students performed at an equal or higher level than on-campus students.

As part of the assessment effort, a survey was developed and administered to students currently enrolled in GSAMS courses. The results were analyzed and areas of concern addressed. Prior technology evaluations administered and discussed with distance learning faculty by Instructional Technology Services were gathered and placed in an Exhibits Room created within the College of Education to house these and other collected materials. Additional documents in the Exhibits Room pertained to distance learning faculty qualifications; courses offered; agreements with other institutions for GSAMS facility usage and with Real Education, Inc.; and the *Working Guidelines for Distance Learning*. A computer for use by the visiting accreditation team members in accessing CSU Websites and preparing their report was available in the Exhibits Room.

LIBRARY AND OTHER LEARNING RESOURCES

The criteria for library and other learning resources are detailed very clearly in the SACS *Criteria for Accreditation* (1996). In addition to the criteria that are applicable to all college and university libraries (purpose and scope, services, collections, information technology, cooperative agreements, and staff), specific criteria address library and learning resources for distance learners:

5.1.7 Library/Learning Resources for Distance Learning Activities
For distance learning activities, an institution *must* ensure the provision of and ready access to adequate library/learning resources and services to support the courses, programs and degrees offered. The institution *must* own the library/learning resources, provide access to electronic information available through existing technologies, or provide them through formal agreements. Such agreements should include the use of books and other materials. The institution *must* assign responsibility for providing library/learning resources and services and for ensuring continued access to them at each site.

When formal agreements are established for the provision of library resources and services, they *must* ensure access to library resources pertinent to the programs offered by the institution and include provision for services and resources which support the institution's specific programs–in the field of study and at the degree level offered. (p. 59)

Library faculty at Columbus State University had been interested for many years in providing access to resources from locations across campus as well as from off-campus. This was due in large part to the non-traditional nature of the CSU student population, the growing desire of faculty for access from their offices and homes, and development of off-campus centers in Columbus. Thus, when a significant student population began taking courses at a distance–either at specific GSAMS sites or in online courses–library personnel were prepared to address their needs. The library also had an advantage in establishing a role in distance learning courses since the library's Instructional Technology Services department schedules, trains faculty and delivers welcome remarks for all GSAMS classes. The Coordinator of Instructional Technology Services, an Associate Professor of Library Science, assumed the role of Outreach Librarian.

The cornerstone of the library's philosophy of service for distant learners is that of comparable services. In seeking to accomplish this goal, analysis was made of the services and functions of the traditional library. Ways were then sought to provide students enrolled in distance learning courses with these services and functions. Service areas addressed include:

- Locating information (e.g., dictionary, encyclopedia, library catalog)
- Finding resources (e.g., books, journals)
- Obtaining resources owned by CSU or other libraries
- Reference assistance
- Bibliographic instruction

The Internet provides an access route to library services and resources at Columbus State University. Through the Simon Schwob Memorial Library

Website (*library.colstate.edu*), the GIL (GALILEO Interconnected Libraries) online catalog can be visited; e-mail reference assistance, interlibrary loan and bibliographic instruction requests can be made; and subject webliographies (online bibliographies) and library tutorials can be consulted. Most importantly, GALILEO–a virtual library initiated in 1995 by the University System of Georgia–can be accessed through the library Website or directly. GALILEO (Georgia Library Learning Online) is described at the CSU Website as follows:

- Web-based and accessible (with password) off campus;
- contains some online full-text articles and books;
- includes reference databases such as dictionaries, directories, and encyclopedias;
- includes categorized lists of World Wide Web resources;
- allows you to send reference questions to your local librarians using the "Ask A Librarian" button (2001).

A specific library Web page for distance learners offers these students the opportunity to request a book, journal article, or other materials owned by CSU or other libraries. Circulating items and copies are sent directly to the student's home. This decision was one of many based on information gathered at prior Off-Campus Library Services conferences.

Due to cost and staffing constraints, the decision was made that some services would be available only to students enrolled in distance learning courses (i.e., document and book delivery to the student's home). The only charges to distant learners are for copies and any interlibrary loan charges from the lending institutions–identical charges to those paid by students coming into the library. Evaluation is made periodically to determine the workload created by these policies and whether additional funding is needed to continue to provide these services.

Agreements were made with the institutional libraries at the remote locations where the GSAMS classes met to provide CSU students with access to the Internet, thus providing access to the CSU library and GALILEO. In addition, reserve collections could be placed at the libraries. CSU students taking classes via GSAMS in Americus at Georgia Southwestern College were automatically provided with circulation privileges at that institution's library, which includes a graduate education collection. All CSU students, faculty, and staff–regardless of location–are eligible for a borrower's card that allows them to borrow materials from any of the University System of Georgia libraries.

The Systems Librarian and Instructional Technology Services Coordinator also created Web pages for distance learners that provided access to course listings, bookstore services, and campus information as well as to library resources. Copies of the library and support services Web pages were provided to the accreditation team members.

During the "Welcome to GSAMS" by Instructional Technology Services at the first class meeting, general information about accessing the library Website is provided. GSAMS faculty are encouraged to schedule class time for bibliographic instruction. While this instruction usually takes places over the two-way technology, occasionally an instructor will make this a required visit to campus for a "hands-on" experience in a computer lab.

The Website developed by Real Education, Inc., for students in the computer science master's program provides links to the library Web pages, including GIL and GALILEO. These students, who are scattered around the world, are also eligible for document delivery.

THE ACCREDITATION VISIT

The accreditation visit began on a Monday afternoon with a welcome by the President and a brief introductory meeting with the Vice Presidents for Academic Affairs, Student Services, and Business and Finance. Also attending were the Library and Continuing Education directors, CSU's accreditation team leader, the Chief Officer of the Faculty Senate, and the Coordinator of Instructional Technology Services. Following this meeting, the visiting accreditation committee separated with several members going to off-campus GSAMS sites and one member meeting with the Computer Science Department faculty and students.

At the Griffin and Thomaston sites, the visitation team had an opportunity to meet with several current and past students in GSAMS two-way courses. They then briefly observed a GSAMS course originating from Columbus. At each site, the SACS team visited the library of the technical institute where the courses were being received. The Director of Continuing Education and a College of Education distance learning faculty member accompanied the visitors to the remote sites.

On the second day, following a meeting with the Deans and Department Chairs of the programs under review, the accreditation team members went in somewhat different directions. For example, one member met with the library director, then with the Coordinator of Instructional Technology Services/Outreach Librarian, and last with the Continuing Education director. Another met with the Vice President for Business and Finance and then with the Plant Operations Director to discuss distance learning facilities. Late in the afternoon, the SACS team visited the Georgia Southwestern campus in Americus. They again met with distance learning students, visited the library, and briefly observed a GSAMS class.

The accreditation visit concluded on the morning of the third day with an exit conference. At that time, draft recommendations and suggestions were shared with CSU faculty, staff, and administrators involved in the GSAMS and online distance learning programs under review.

THE DISTANCE LEARNING ACCREDITATION REPORT

In the exit conference, the library was cited as the "star" of the Columbus State University's distance learning activities. The *Report of the Substantive Change Committee, Columbus State University, Columbus, Georgia, November 2-4, 1998* praised the library for its "careful measures to ensure that students in its off-campus graduate programs have convenient, effective access to the library resources needed in their programs." The *Report* further stated that:

> In addition to GALILEO, library staff members have created impressive web pages that link students to source information on how to find and discriminate among electronic sources, and to directions for navigating the worldwide web. This site also encourages users to seek assistance from librarians to get help with locating and using electronic information. The Committee takes special note of the quality and scope of the Schwob Memorial Library's web site and salutes the University for this beneficial use of technology to enhance student learning. (p. 19)

The agreements with remote site libraries was also discussed in the report. Since only one of the libraries involved in other communities serves a graduate education program, electronic access to CSU library services–including bibliographic instruction–was deemed crucial. The *Report* concluded that:

> The University library has clearly accepted the responsibility for providing library/learning resources and services and for ensuring continued access to these at each DL site. Students at these sites reported a high degree of satisfaction with the library and learning resources available to them. (p. 20)

Other Columbus State University strengths noted in the final report included faculty enthusiasm and concern for student welfare, the substantial financial support provided, and the decision to provide all GSAMS two-way classes with facilitators. The report contained three recommendations and three suggestions (Appendix A). The recommendations addressed program equivalency, assessment and evaluation, and distance learning goals, while the suggestions were related to information distribution, faculty workload, and faculty development opportunities. A response was prepared by Columbus State University which included CSU's newly developed distance learning goals (Appendix B). Columbus State University's distance learning programs successfully passed the review of the Southern Association of Schools and Colleges.

SUGGESTIONS FOR FUTURE VISITS (LESSONS LEARNED)

Following the visit, a list of ideas for future distance learning visits was compiled. The primary suggestion was that the first meeting with the visitation team should include a discussion and possibly a demonstration of the distance learning technologies employed. Other topics for the introductory meeting include organizational responsibilities for distance learning and any other unique institutional features that may differ from the team member's own institution or experiences. Provision of area maps showing off-campus distance learning sites and student dispersion would be useful to the visiting accreditation committee.

Advance information and access to resources such as the GALILEO virtual library and GIL online catalog was very helpful to the accreditation team. However, not all team members had the opportunity to visit the Websites, so a brief introduction to these services should be provided at as early a point in the visit as possible. The campus team planning the institutional response should try out the remote services–the visitation team may well check them out in advance or on-site.

The concise scheduling and travel time limited observation of the content and most interactive portions of a GSAMS two-way class. The visitation team saw a typical class start-up, but only limited instruction and interaction between sites even though one class involved multiple sites. Use of the interactive capability of the technology by team members to talk to the students and faculty at other locations would have been informative and time efficient.

The visiting accreditation team split up and met with different individuals or groups simultaneously. Questions asked were not always limited to the current topic or area of expertise of the CSU attendees at a particular meeting, therefore it is important to brief the institutional personnel scheduled to participate in the visit as fully as possible. In fact, the entire campus needs to be aware of the visit as individuals who are not involved directly in distance learning may be asked questions about the institution or specifically about distance learning.

Specific library queries included questions about the awareness of library services by distant learners and the use of such services by distant students in comparison to on-campus students. The process and timeline for evaluation of cooperative library agreements was reviewed. Detailed information regarding the library collections, hours, and access at the sites where GSAMS classes were received was needed. The CSU library Website and services were clearly important to the accreditation review.

Overall, the visiting accreditation team appeared particularly interested in assessment activities, actions taken due to information collected, policies, and information specifically targeted to distance learners (i.e., a distance learning student handbook). Internet access to information and services were clearly seen as an important ingredient in serving distance learning students.

OTHER ACCREDITATION VISITS

As the first institution of higher education in Georgia to undergo a SACS distance learning program review, the experience of CSU was closely observed by others in the state. In addition to the NCATE visit of 1998 which addressed distance learning courses offered by the College of Education, the accreditation agency for Occupational Therapy has examined CSU's support and resources for distance learners. In this latter case, CSU is part of a partnership with the Medical College of Georgia (MCG) in a program delivered primarily over GSAMS, with MCG faculty at both Augusta and Columbus.

The University System of Georgia (34 institutions) voluntarily underwent a SACS distance learning program review in 2001. At that time, CSU was reviewed relative only to the institution's participation in a system-wide online course delivery program known as GLOBE (Georgia Learning Online for Business and Education, *www.georgiaglobe.org*). Columbus State University will undergo a full accreditation review by the Southern Association for Schools and Colleges in 2005.

Having survived two distance learning accreditation visits, Columbus State University faculty and staff feel confident they can survive additional reviews. Key ingredients to our past successful review included the leadership and teamwork in preparing for the reviews in a thorough manner. New areas of preparation will include ensuring that all policies related to distance learning are in writing, including those regarding class size and faculty workload, and the collection of more data comparing students in face-to-face classes with those in distance learning classes (grades, retention, and use of support services). It will continue to be very important that CSU be able to show action taken after surveys, technology evaluations, and other assessment activities are conducted. Clearly, the library will always be at the "heart" of any review of learning and support services for distance learning students.

REFERENCES

Columbus State University (2001). *Welcome to GALILEO.* Retrieved December 31, 2001, from http://library.colstate.edu/info/gal.shtml.

Commission on Colleges of the Southern Association of Colleges and Schools (1996). *Criteria for accreditation* (10th ed.). Decatur, GA.

Commission on Colleges of the Southern Association of Colleges and Schools (1996). *Planning distance learning activities.* Decatur, GA.

Commission on Colleges of the Southern Association of Colleges and Schools (1998). *Report of the Substantive Change Committee, Columbus State University, Columbus, Georgia, November 2-4, 1998.* Decatur, GA.

Georgia Distance Learning and Telemedicine Act of 1992, *Official Code of Georgia annotated,* Chapter 5, Title 50 (1992).

Stratford, S. K. (1994). *Working guidelines for distance learning.* Columbus State University, Columbus, GA.

APPENDIX A

Report of the Substantive Change Committee, Columbus State University: Recommendations and Suggestions

Recommendations:

- that the University demonstrate that it ensures appropriate levels of student achievement and equivalent quality of programs among its various methods of instruction and program locations.
- that the University demonstrate that it uses program assessment and evaluation results to improve its MS in Applied Computer Science program.
- that the University (1) formulate clear and explicit goals for its distance learning programs, (2) demonstrate that they are consistent with its stated purpose, and (3) are being achieved.

Suggestions:

- that the University use its various publications including the Web page to inform all students about the availability of instruction through its distance learning programs.
- that the University develop and implement a formal policy that allows for equitable and reasonable reassignment time for graduate faculty teaching distance learning courses.
- that the University evaluate the online instruction professional development needs of its computer science faculty and implement an ongoing plan for meeting those needs as soon as possible.

APPENDIX B

Distance Learning Goals
Columbus State University (CSU)

1. CSU will provide distance learning course offerings that are equal in quality to those offered on the campus.
   1a. Students enrolled in distance learning courses must meet the same criteria as in on-campus courses (admissions, pre-requisites, academic standards, and student outcomes).
   1b. Faculty teaching distance learning courses must meet the same criteria as faculty teaching on-campus.
2. CSU will provide library resources to students enrolled in distance learning courses that are comparable to those offered on campus.
3. CSU will provide students enrolled in distance learning courses support services comparable to those provided on campus. These will include access to admissions, registration, advising, financial aid, textbooks, and career and other student services.
4. CSU will identify market opportunities for distance learning courses and programs compatible with academic strengths.
5. CSU will insure a stable funding base for distance learning.
6. CSU will recruit, train, support, and recognize faculty who effectively design, develop, and deliver distance learning courses and programs.
7. CSU will provide the human and technical resources necessary to reliably deliver distance learning.

March 1999

Who's Out There in CyberSpace: Profiling the Remote Learner for Service Design

Terri Pedersen Summey

Emporia State University

James Fisk

Morningside College

SUMMARY. Colleges and universities are expanding their offerings through distance education courses and programs. One challenge associated with these offerings is defining the remote learner. Emporia State University offers several distance education programs with students scattered throughout the United States. Although the university moved quickly into providing remote education, the library has struggled to provide equitable access to services and resources for distance learners. This paper reports the results of a project undertaken to profile the distance learner enrolled in the School of Library and Information Management of Emporia State University.

KEYWORDS. Distance education, distance learners, library service, survey

INTRODUCTION

Distance education is becoming commonplace. Throughout the United States, colleges and universities are expanding their courses and programs to

[Haworth co-indexing entry note]: "Who's Out There in CyberSpace: Profiling the Remote Learner for Service Design." Summey, Terri Pedersen, and James Fisk. Co-published simultaneously in *Journal of Library Administration* (The Haworth Information Press, an imprint of The Haworth Press, Inc.) Vol. 37, No. 3/4, 2002, pp. 503-513; and: *Distance Learning Library Services: The Tenth Off-Campus Library Services Conference* (ed: Patrick B. Mahoney) The Haworth Information Press, an imprint of The Haworth Press, Inc., 2002, pp. 503-513.

http://www.haworthpress.com/store/product.asp?sku=J111
10.1300/J111v37n03_41

students at a distance from a traditional campus. In 1995, approximately one-third of higher education institutions in the United States offered distance education courses. The American Council on Education estimated that by 1998, eighty-five percent of "traditional" colleges and universities would either offer or be planning to offer distance education courses (Kirk and Bartelstein, 1999). Researchers in a study conducted during 1997 and 1998 by the National Center for Education Statistics (1999) found that 34 percent of post-secondary institutions offer distance education courses to over 1.6 million enrolled students. Of these schools, approximately 25 percent offer associate and bachelor degree programs that may be completed without ever entering a traditional classroom setting. At the graduate level, common program offerings are in the fields of library and information management, education, engineering, and business.

Emporia State University assumed a leadership role in providing distance education to the residents of Kansas. Distance education initiatives at Emporia State developed from the grassroots with faculty taking a leading role in the creation of online courses and programs. Distance education offerings at Emporia State are not only available to the residents of Kansas, but several programs also extend across the United States. The Office of Lifelong Learning, whose motto is "Helping Students to Go the Distance," administers these programs. On the undergraduate level, the university offers an online degree completion program, the Bachelors of Integrated Studies. There are approximately 50 students in this program; its first graduates completed their studies in May 2000. The university also offers approximately 40 online classes per semester with that number continuing to increase. In addition, several schools and departments have online programs that offer complete master's degrees. Such a school is the Teachers College at Emporia State University. Several departments within the Teachers College offering the master's degree include Health, Physical Education and Recreation, Educational Administration, and Instructional Design and Technology. Evidence of the success of these programs is the waiting lists of potential students who wish to enroll. Other schools and colleges are also developing distance education programs. The School of Business offers several online degrees along with a 2-plus-2 degree completion program in coordination with community colleges in the Kansas City metropolitan area.

The 'pioneer' in distance education at Emporia State is the School of Library and Information Management, also known as SLIM. Beginning in 1987, SLIM began offering combinations of instructional formats including classroom teaching in a weekend intensive setting, interactive video to Kansas students through the Kansas Telnet system, interactive two-way video, and most recently, Web-based instruction via the Internet. Currently, the school makes its Master of Library Science degree available to locations in the states of Kansas, Colorado, New Mexico, Oregon, North Dakota and Utah. The American Library Association fully accredits the program and it is approved by the agencies for higher education in each of the states where the program is offered. According to the SLIM Web site, more than 500 persons, living in areas where programs leading to a master's degree in Library Science were not readily available, have graduated from SLIM without ever coming to a classroom in Kansas. The administrators and faculty of SLIM have also designed the program to accommodate individuals unable to either relocate or enroll in a traditional on-campus program. During the spring of 2000, the School of Library and Information Management had an approximate enrollment of 460 students (SLIM, 2001).

Distance education offerings and remote students pose both challenges and opportunities for library services. Although the university has moved forward with distance education, the library has struggled to provide equitable access to library resources and services for off-campus students. To assist academic libraries in providing services to distant learning communities, the Association of College and Research Libraries (ACRL) has provided guidelines. Initially written in 1981, the "Guidelines for Distance Learning Library Services" were first revised in 1990 and then again in 1998. The "Guidelines" define distance learning library services as "library services in support of college, university, or other post-secondary courses and programs offered away from a main campus, or in the absence of a traditional campus, and regardless of where credit is given" (ACRL, 1998). Several recommendations are made in the "Guidelines." The first of these is that distance learners are entitled to services and resources equivalent to those provided to students and faculty in the traditional campus setting. The "Guidelines" also call for the provision of information literacy instruction to distant students, sufficient funding beyond the traditional library budget, and for the host library to provide resources and services consistent with the goals and objectives of the sponsoring institution. According to the "Guidelines," the library of the host institution also has the responsibility to identify, develop, coordinate, provide and assess library services provided to the distant learning community (ACRL, 1998). However, according to Lebowitz, "there seems to be no correlation between how innovatively an institution delivers distance courses and the way in which it provides library services to its distance learners" (1997, p. 303).

LITERATURE REVIEW

According to John Butler, the Director of Library Support for Distance Learners Project of the University of Minnesota, "distance learners are used to getting by with less, improvising and avoiding situations in which they may need library support" (Regents of the University of Minnesota, Office of Information Technology, 1998). His words summarize the findings of a survey of University of Minnesota distance learners and faculty. Survey results showed that 63 percent of distance learners planned for limited access to library resources and services. Faculty had similar perceptions of library services for distance learners. Only 30 percent of the faculty responding to the survey said that they were aware of the library resources and services available to their students. As a result, 87 percent of the faculty reported that they provide their students with little or no information about library resources and services available to them. A majority of the faculty also said that they rarely or never worked with a librarian during course delivery or its development because they were not aware of any existing library support.

Although expectations may be low, library service to distance education students is critical to the success of a distance education program. ACRL in its "Guidelines" declares "access to adequate library services and resources is essential for the attainment of superior academic skills in post-secondary education, regardless of where students, faculty, and programs are located" (1998, p. 2). In 2000, the Institute for Higher Education Policy issued a report, *Quality on the Line: Benchmarks for Success in Internet-Based Distance Education.* The goal of this study was to provide and validate benchmarks as they relate to Internet-based education. Its authors identified 24 traits of a quality distance education program, two of which describe library services: "Students are provided with hands-on training and information material through electronic databases, interlibrary loans, government archives, news services and other sources." Students also "have access to sufficient library resources that may include a 'virtual library' accessible through the World Wide Web" (Institute for Higher Education Policy, 2000, p. 3).

Much of the research reported in the literature indicates that library support is essential to the success of academic programs including distance education programs. Students that are "library less" must struggle to meet the research needs of courses. A 1993 survey at the University of Northern Colorado assessed the needs of off-campus faculty and students. Intended to design effective library support services, the survey asked faculty what services distance education students needed. As a result of the survey the following services were deemed important: library use instruction, reference and referral, and finally document delivery (Lebowitz, 1993). Starr (1998) describes the remote learner as typically older than the traditional college student and as someone who has been away from the academic environment for some time. They are generally new users of technology and not completely comfortable with electronic resources. Committed to their educational goals, these students, however, have the same information needs as traditional students. Starr goes on to identify three areas of reference services that require special attention relative to remote learners. This includes remote access to the catalog and other electronic resources, research guidance and instruction, and points of contact in the library for the distance education student (Starr, 1998).

Several studies found that although the library at the host institution may provide library services to its distance education students, many students do not use them to their fullest potential and may not even be aware of their availability. In the fall of 1997, the University of Nebraska at Lincoln surveyed its distance education students and faculty to determine if their needs were being met. The researchers discovered that remote learners did not use the services provided by the library and that faculty did not request additional library support. Students surveyed stated that they used other local libraries for their research needs. In order to improve distance services, the study's authors made several recommendations. They proposed, for example, that the university library work to expedite its document delivery process. They also suggested that students be made aware of the library services available to them and that these same students would benefit from efforts in the area of online bibliographic instruction. The study concluded that effective communication between the library and faculty teaching distance education courses can be a vital element in the success of remote library services (Cassner, 1998).

STUDY

One challenge in providing library services to the cyber-learner is defining and profiling those remote students in order to effectively design off-campus library services. The "Guidelines" state that the librarian in charge of administering remote library services should continually assess the needs of the distant learning community and "prepare a written profile of the distance learning community's information and skills needs" (ACRL, 1998). Designed by a student in the SLIM distance education program in collaboration with a librarian at Emporia State University, the focus of this study is to identify the characteristics and information needs of the students in the School of Library and Information Management. The results from the survey are being used to assist the W. A. White Library in designing its services to the remote learning community at Emporia State University.

In April 2000, 437 students of the School of Library and Information received a questionnaire containing over 30 questions soliciting information and opinions relative to a number of subjects. The survey was divided into the following sections: "About You," "Access," "Emporia State University Library Services to Distance Students," and "Proposed New Services." Students were also given the opportunity to respond to three open-ended statements. Completed surveys were received from 170 students for a 39 percent return rate.

RESULTS

Students of SLIM are members of a community, albeit spread across the western United States. The "About You" section requested information commonly found in a community analysis. Knowledge of the characteristics of community members is useful to those information professionals responsible for planning and packaging library services. It contained questions about the cohort name or place the student is receiving instruction, the amount of time that had elapsed since the student returned to school, the hours per week that are worked outside the home, whether or not the individuals work in the library, how many children do they have under the age of twelve, the size of the community that they reside in, and their perception of their research skills. In analyzing the results, it discovered that like many non-traditional adult students, SLIM students are a busy group with 69 percent reporting that they work outside the home more than thirty hours per week and 32 percent are parents of at least one child under the age of 12. Seventy percent of SLIM students live in communities larger than 25,000 people. Students of SLIM 'know their way around the library' as 64 percent of the respondents currently work in a library setting. Most students (78 percent) also report being at least reasonably comfortable conducting their course-related research. A majority of respondents are five years or less removed from college-level work. As such, they are very likely familiar with current library technology. Although many similarities exist amongst the cohorts, some significant differences do exist. Several of the cohorts are in mainly rural areas, making library services to distance students even more important.

Distance education students generally do not have physical access to their own campus library. As such, they must often rely on interlibrary loan services and access to online databases and the Internet in conducting their research activities. In addition, they may visit and use the libraries in their immediate area. The "Access" section of the survey questioned how and how well SLIM students do their work without the services of a home university library. Questions were asked about the types of libraries used by the students, the databases and services that the students could access, availability of the Internet, access to a fax machine, and the students' ability to do the research and work required by the courses. It was discovered that SLIM students regularly use other public, college and university libraries in support of their course work. Students either do not always have full access to services and resources of these facilities or may not be aware of the access available to them. Of those responding, 69 percent used interlibrary loan services at least once a semester and 94 percent had access to the Internet. A majority reported that with readily available resources, they could do their best work either most of the time or all of the time.

Marketing is a common theme in professional library literature. The "ESU Library Services to Distance Students" section assessed the familiarity with and use of available online services. Questions examined the awareness that distant students had of services currently offered by the library to remote students. Services included a Web page designed specifically for distance students, e-mail reference, remote access to the online catalog, and access to electronic databases. It was discovered that a significant number of non-Kansas students are either unaware of or rarely use services provided for distance students. Of the respondents, only a minority of SLIM students used the services frequently. A significant majority of all students are unaware of the availability of e-mail reference services. The results from this section correspond with results from other surveys of distance education students in that communication with faculty and students and extensive marketing of services and resources are needed to make library services to remote learners effective.

Any student who visits the W. A. White Library can reasonably expect to access and retrieve print resources and to receive library instruction and reference assistance from qualified and trained staff. The "Proposed New Services" section of the survey identified a number of proposed online services to address the part of the "Guidelines" that called for library services extended to distance students "to be equivalent to those provided for students and faculty in traditional settings" (ACRL, 1998). The proposed services included the following: agreements with libraries near cohort areas, a toll-free number for the W. A. White Library reference desk, extended weekend hours for those attending weekend classes at ESU, library instruction tutorials, topical pathfinders to library literature, electronic reserves, virtual office hours for professional reference staff, a Distance Education Web Page, and electronic document delivery. A majority of all respondents indicated that they would most certainly or probably use each of these proposed new services. The prospect of electronic reserves and document delivery appeared to be very popular amongst all of the students.

Probably the most beneficial findings of the survey for the White Library were those in response to three open-ended questions. These were:

1. I would use the existing remote services of the William Allen White Library if . . .
2. My major obstacles in securing information for my research are . . .

3. If I could make just one recommendation regarding remote library service to the management of William Allen White Library, I would suggest . . .

After the comments were reviewed nine reoccurring themes emerged. The first of the themes involved the hours of White Library. When students come to Emporia to attend weekend intensive classes, they attend class on Friday night, all day Saturday, and on Sunday morning. These students expressed a strong desire for extended weekend hours in support of their research and coursework. The second theme indicates that awareness of remote library services is problematic. Many students would use the library's services designed for the distance education student if they only knew of them. This finding points to a need for the William Allen White Library to aggressively market their remote services. Services that are designed and implemented have no value if they are not used. One student's comment on the survey was brief but insightful–"Better advertisement of the library services now provided to Distance Students is needed. I had not a clue!"

References to other libraries emerged as a third theme, with comments indicating that some students prefer to use other libraries to support their research efforts rather than the remote services of the W. A. White Library. This may be, because of several reasons, including familiarity with local libraries, convenience, and the fact that many of the SLIM students currently work in libraries. Personal circumstances emerged as a strong theme. Many of the comments and answers to the demographic section of the survey suggested a fourth theme. Students at SLIM lead busy and stressed lives while trying to combine full-time work and family life with the demands of graduate school studies. Respondents identified issues associated with remote access to resources as a fifth theme. Many students requested access to full-text articles. Other respondents shared comments regarding technical problems that they encountered in trying to access remote resources and the navigability of the Library's Web page. Comments relative to interlibrary loan and document delivery emerged as a sixth theme. Students count on the delivery of print resources through interlibrary loan. In many cases those needs were not being met.

A seventh theme emerged when students spoke to their own research skills. Responses suggested that they are not equal across the student population and that some individuals might be helped if they were to receive some assistance in developing online skills. Access to a library collection specializing in Library Science literature is an eighth theme that became apparent. Because of the specialized nature of Library and Information Management studies, other libraries used by SLIM students do not often have scholarly Library Science literature. The last theme involved customer service. SLIM students commented that they expect timely and knowledgeable follow-through from library personnel in response to phone or e-mail requests for services. At the time of the survey, the library did not have one point of contact for distance library services.

CONCLUSION

Grover (1993) in his model of reference service depicts it as a diagnostic process. He describes steps one and two as the diagnosis and analysis of an informational need. After completion of steps one and two, the informational professional then prescribes a remedy and implements access and retrieval. The process may occur at either the client level or, as in the case of this study, at the community level. The purpose of the survey was to build a profile of the remote SLIM student and help the library determine the needs of the students. This fulfilled the first and second steps of the diagnostic process. The next portion of the study concerns how the library will use the results to design and also market effective library services to students at a distance.

The library has already made some strides towards responding to some of the survey results. Some actions have occurred as a result of strategic planning undertaken by the library in January of 2001. The library used the results from the survey to educate participants about distance library services provided. Faculty members who teach online courses were involved in focus groups on distance library services.

Following strategic planning the library administration revised the library's organizational structure and named a librarian to the position of Coordinator of Distant Library Services. Prior to this point, the library had several individuals working on remote access issues. Jesse Shera, a noted scholar in the field of Library Science, described the function of a library in this way: "To bring together human beings and recorded knowledge in as fruitful relationships as possible" (Sloan, 1999). Electronic access does not diminish the desirability of or eliminate the need for these relationships. The Coordinator for Distance Library Services is charged with developing, implementing, and coordinating library services for remote students.

Already the William Allen White Library has developed new services in response to the survey. Many of these changes have transpired because of the survey results and the nine reoccurring themes identified. Following is a list of the changes that have occurred in the library:

- The library extended its Saturday hours to provide more access to SLIM students in Emporia for weekend intensive classes.
- The Coordinator developed a brochure to mail to students.
- The Library's Webmaster revised the library's Web page for distance students with more changes forthcoming.

- A SLIM student assisted in writing a marketing guide to assist the library in marketing its distance library services.
- The library offers proxy access to its databases through its integrated library system.
- The library is making an effort to make more resources that are full-text available electronically.
- Staff designed a form for off-campus students to use to request the delivery of items owned by White Library. Students are now able to have items sent directly to their homes.
- The library instruction team is in the process of designing online instructional modules.

Customer service was the last theme identified in the survey. The library is improving its customer service philosophy as it relates to distance education students and faculty. Appointing a Coordinator of Distance Library Services provides a point of contact for remote students and faculty. The library added a toll-free number in the fall of 2001 to help distant students be just a phone call away from assistance. The library is also adding an "instant messaging service" to the computers at the library's reference desk. The library is constantly seeking ways to improve its service to its customers, whether on campus or not, and has made great strides in improving service to the cyber-user. However, library administration and staff recognize that more improvements are necessary to get the library to the point of providing equitable access to all faculty and students. In January of 2002, library personnel will look at the strategic planning process and evaluate accomplishments in light of established goals. Assessment needs to occur for other off-campus groups and the SLIM survey administered again. The authors used traditional mail to distribute this survey. In the future, a web survey may be a better alternative for online students. In order to continue to remain viable to distance students, the library needs to assess the needs of its distant student population and develop services to meet those needs. Part of assessing the needs of the remote learner is developing a profile of the typical cyber-learner.

REFERENCES

Association of College and Research Libraries (ACRL). (1998). Guidelines for distance learning services. Retrieved November 20, 2001 from the American Library Association web site at http://www.ala.org/acrl/guides/distlrng.html.

Cassner, M., & Adams, K. (1998). Instructional support to a rural graduate population: An assessment of library services. In C. J. Jacob (Comp.), *The Eighth Off-Campus Library Services Conference Proceedings, Providence, Rhode Island, April 22-24, 1998* (pp. 117-132). Mount Pleasant, MI: Central Michigan University.

Grover, R. (1993). A proposed model for diagnosing information needs. *School Library Media Quarterly,* (Winter): 95-100.

The Institute for Higher Education Policy. (2000). Quality on line: Benchmarks for success in Internet-Based Education. Retrieved June 29, 2000 from the World Wide Web: http://www.ihep.com/Pubs/PDF/Quality.pdf.

Kirk, E. and A. Bartelstein. (1999) Libraries close in on distance education. *Library Journal,* (April 1, 1999), 40-42.

Lebowitz, G. (1993). Faculty perceptions of off-campus student library needs. In C. J. Jacob (Comp.), *The Sixth Off-Campus Library Services Conference Proceedings, Kansas City, Missouri, October 6-8, 1993* (pp. 143-154). Mount Pleasant, MI: Central Michigan University.

Lebowitz, G. (1997). Library services to distance students: An equity issue. *The Journal of Academic Librarianship, 23,* (July 1997): 303-308.

National Center for Education Statistics. (1999). Distance education at postsecondary education institutions: 1997-1998. Retrieved June 29, 2000 from the World Wide Web at http://nces.ed.gov/pubsearch/pubsinfo.asp?pubid=2000013.

Regents of the University of Minnesota, Office of Information Technology. (1998). Library uses innovative technology to enhance resources and services for distance learners: Making being there as good as being here. *Information Newsletter, 3*(8). Retrieved June 20, 2000 from the World Wide Web: http://www1.umn.edu/oit/newsletter/1198-itn/innovative.html.

School of Library and Information Management. Emporia State University. (2001). SLIM web site. Retrieved November 18, 2001 from the World Wide Web at http://slim.emporia.edu/info/distance/distance.htm.

Sloan, B. (1998). Service perspectives for the digital library: Remote reference services. *Library Trends, 47*(1): 117-235.

Starr, L. K. (1998). Reference services for off-campus students. *OLA Quarterly, 4:*3 (Fall 1998). Retrieved November 13, 2001 from Library Literature Fulltext on Wilsonweb at http://hwwilsonweb.com.

Creating a Research Literacy Course for Education Doctoral Students: Design Issues and Political Realities of Developing Online and Face-to-Face Instruction

Johanna Tuñón

Nova Southeastern University

SUMMARY. Education students are often not very information literate, and doctoral students are no exception to this "rule of thumb." The challenge of preparing doctoral students in education to use online resources as they begin the literature review process becomes even more complicated when these students are also distance students who happen to meet at various sites throughout the United States. This presentation will discuss the pros and cons of designing and delivering online and face-to-face versions of a one-credit elective course for students in Programs for Higher Education at Nova Southeastern University. The advantages and disadvantages of delivering content in synchronous and asynchronous formats are examined. Issues addressed include: (1) the relative merits of using WebCT versus using ordinary Web pages and WebBoard discussions, (2) how to incorporate active learning into both modalities for delivering the course, (3) how to pace and structure the delivery of both versions of the course to meet the needs of distance learners, (4) how to meet the needs of students with different learning styles, (5) how to assess learning outcomes, (6) how effective group work was in synchronous and asynchronous environments, (7) how

[Haworth co-indexing entry note]: "Creating a Research Literacy Course for Education Doctoral Students: Design Issues and Political Realities of Developing Online and Face-to-Face Instruction." Tuñón, Johanna. Co-published simultaneously in *Journal of Library Administration* (The Haworth Information Press, an imprint of The Haworth Press, Inc.) Vol. 37, No. 3/4, 2002, pp. 515-527; and: *Distance Learning Library Services: The Tenth Off-Campus Library Services Conference* (ed: Patrick B. Mahoney) The Haworth Information Press, an imprint of The Haworth Press, Inc., 2002, pp. 515-527.

http://www.haworthpress.com/store/product.asp?sku=J111
10.1300/J111v37n03_42

much sequential and developmental learning is necessary in the instructional process for doctoral students, and (8) how the dynamics of collaboration with an academic program can impact the political realities of the design process.

KEYWORDS. Literacy, library instruction, distance learners, course development

Education students are often not very information literate (Morner, 1993 & Morner, 1995), and doctoral students are no exception to this "rule of thumb." The challenge of preparing doctoral students in education to use online resources as they begin the literature review process becomes even more complicated when these students are also distance students who happen to meet at various sites throughout the United States. With the growing popularity of distance education, academic libraries face the challenge of finding ways to provide library instruction for distance students. This has certainly been the case for the librarians at Nova Southeastern University (NSU). This presentation discusses the pros and cons of the process of developing and implementing an online and a face-to-face version of a one-credit elective course for the doctoral education students in the Programs for Higher Education (PHE). The presentation will examine the relative merits of each approach and discuss the lessons the librarians learned in the process.

BACKGROUND

Nova Southeastern University has been a pioneer in the field of distance education since the early 1970s. NSU is a large, not-for-profit academic institution located in Ft. Lauderdale, Florida. The university's mission has always focused on providing instruction at times and places convenient for a student body consisting primarily of working professionals. In 2001, about half of the university's 19,000+ students are enrolled in distance programs. Most of these distance students attend field-based classes at 79 sites within Florida, 66 sites in other states, and 15 sites in other countries. There are, however, also a growing number of distance students at NSU who are enrolling in a variety of online courses, particularly in business, education, and the computer sciences.

Providing library services has become an important and integral part of the services offered to all NSU students. The NSU Libraries actively support the information needs of students both on and off campus, and the main academic library, the Library, Research, and Information Technology Center (LRITC), supports all but the professional programs at the university. Within the LRITC, Distance and Instructional Library Services (DILS) is the department that (1) handles accreditation and licensure issues relating to library services to distance students and (2) works with the various NSU programs to ensure that all distance students are offered some form of library instruction. An important part of Distance and Instructional Library Services' job is demonstrating to the Southern Association of Colleges and Schools (SACS) that all distance and virtual students at NSU receive some form of library instruction. Meeting this mandate is a major challenge because NSU's academic programs deliver instruction in a wide variety of ways.

Distance instruction at NSU ranges from professors traveling to field-based sites to synchronous instruction delivered via compressed video, and desktop video conferencing and asynchronous Web-based courses using a variety of course software packages including WebCT, Embanet, and Chatty. All of these methods of delivering distance education have, in turn, resulted in the need for Distance and Instructional Library Services to find new synchronous and asynchronous methods for delivering library instruction to NSU's distance students (Tuñón & Pival, 1997; Tuñón, 1999b; Tuñón & Pival, 2000). NSU librarians have experimented with everything from delivering synchronous one-shot instruction sessions using compressed video and NetMeeting (Pival & Tuñón, 1998; Pival & Tuñón, 2000) to providing entire library modules online (Tuñón, 1999) and working with academic programs to integrate library training into the curriculum (Tuñón, 1999, June).

ORIGIN OF THE PROJECT

Finding a method for providing library training to Programs for Higher Education students originally became an issue when NSU was going through its reaccreditation process. The Southern Association of Colleges and Schools (SACS) recommended that "Nova Southeastern University demonstrate that it is providing adequate and appropriate access to information technologies and systems and training for their use *at all locations* where educational programs are being provided [emphasis added]" (Southern Association of Colleges and Schools, 1997, p. 141). At the time, the university administration responded by mandating that Distance Library Services [as the department was known then] begin providing the training for NSU programs in which distance students were not already receiving training.

Students in the PHE program were directly impacted by the SACS recommendation. PHE's field-based classes presented special challenges for the library because new students might get added to each site every time a new session started, unlike other NSU cluster-based programs where the students would start as a group and go through their program together as a group. The problem was that the library could not afford to send librarians to each site every term to train new students. Waiting to offer training until students met at their summer institute was considered unacceptable by the main library because students could be more than half way through their programs before they would get the library training. Because no easy solution presented itself as an alternative, the administration in Programs for Higher Education eventually agreed to a three-pronged approach. The library would go to every site for one-shot training every year or so, offer optional sessions at PHE summer institutes, and provide a one-credit elective course entitled Information Literacy Skills for Doctoral Students in Education for students who wanted a more in-depth understanding of how to do library research for their literature reviews. This just left the "minor" issue of getting a course designed and implemented.

ANALYSIS AND ASSESSMENT
OF THE ONLINE LIBRARY COURSE

The planning process for the online course got off to a rocky start. At the time that the course was proposed, Distance Library Services was woefully understaffed with only two librarians working full-time, one working a part-time schedule after a maternity leave, and two positions unfilled. As a result, there was no staff to provide a library design "team" for assessing what the project would require or beginning the design process. As a result, one of the two librarians finally agreed to develop and implement the project in her "spare" time.

The fact that PHE had specified that they wanted the course to be offered via WebCT, instead of in either a face-to-face format or by using Web pages and a Web discussion board, presented a second challenge. This choice meant that the developer could not even start on the project until she had learned how to use WebCT. Fortunately, she already had much of the necessary content already created for an earlier project (Tuñón, 1999) so she did not have to develop all the online materials from scratch.

The first step the developer faced was to assess student skills. The librarian knew from past experience with PHE students that the students in the program worked in various types of higher education settings and had technology skills that ranged from moderate to highly proficient. Because of a lack of staff, the librarian decided to simply base the planning process on her prior working knowledge of students' technology skills rather than go through a formal needs assessment process.

THE DESIGN AND PLANNING PROCESS FOR ERD 8226

Once the needs had been assessed, the developer began the design and planning process. Her first step was to decide on the broad elements of the course. The decision made by PHE to use WebCT course software presented problems. The librarian knew that the university was transitioning to using WebCT, but she was concerned that using this courseware was going to present a technology hurdle for most PHE students. Up until ERD 8226 (as this course became known) was offered, only one course had been delivered in PHE using this software. Being required to use WebCT, however, had the advantage of consolidating all the course tools and resources in one place and providing the instructor with a variety of class management tools.

The librarian turned her attention next to the actual content for the Web-based modules. Because the administration in PHE had given the Distance and Instructional Library Services department a free hand in deciding on the content of the course, the developer decided to build on the Web-based training materials she had already prepared in 1999 as part of a practicum. Because the materials were still relevant and had already proven effective for students in that other doctoral education program, the developer used the basic course outline library module. (These Web pages can be seen at the Library Research Resources site at http://www.nova.edu/library/cysprac.) Having much of the library's course content already available made the design and planning process easier. The librarian decided to continue focusing on students learning when and how to find education information for their literature reviews. Students were to learn where and how to find (1) resources via subscription databases using electronic indices and full-text databases on the Internet, (2) free resources on the Internet, and (3) resources that were available only in print. She decided to focus primarily on ERIC as the premier index for in-depth education research, but she also planned to address ERIC E-Subscribe, ProQuest's Research Library Periodicals and Psychology Journals, Wilson's Education Full Text, Digital Dissertations, and WorldCat.

Next, the librarian had to decide how best to organize and format the content in WebCT. Recycling Web pages that she had already developed into the Course Content section of the course was easy. She "chunked" the pages into a Getting Started page and nine modules. Week 1 focused on how to select a database and the basics about ERIC, how to develop a search strategy, and how to use keyword searching and proximity searching. Week 2 included two modules. Module 2 dealt with how to locate full-text documents using ERIC E-Subscribe and an introduction to PDF (Portable Document Format) files. Module 3 focused on how to refine a search, with pages on how to use ERIC descriptors to refine a search, subject versus keyword searching, limiting by publication years, limiting by document type in ERIC, plurals, truncation, and wildcards in FirstSearch, evaluating search results, using Boolean Operators, and combining terms to refine a search. Week 3 discussed other useful databases. The module provided links to pages on ERIC versus Wilson Education Full Text, locating psychology, social science databases, and health resources for education-related research, psychological tests and measurements, and locating articles on topics ranging from leadership and management to technology resources for education-related research. Week 4 focused on how to use full-text databases to retrieve articles. Pages included information on how to locate journals, NSU's "Full Text Journal Search" search engine, and the difference between full-text articles, full-image articles, and articles with text and thumbnail pictures. Week 5 discussed (1) various types of appropriate materials for a doctoral literature review, (2) stages of the publication cycle, (3) the types of research, primary research, (4) how to distinguish between scholarly journals, trade journals, and magazines, (5) peer-reviewed or refereed journals, and (6) how to locate and obtain dissertations, theses, and practicums. Week 6 focused on print resources including books and reference resources. Pages were provided on how to locate books, reference resources in education, and education encyclopedias. Week 7 discussed how to evaluate Web sites and use Web search engines. Week 8 provided information on how to use document delivery services at NSU to obtain materials. Last but not least, there were general introductions to the content for each week that anchored and provided an overview for the week.

Once the decision about the content was finalized, the librarian had to decide on the structure of performance-based activities. Up until this time, PHE students had not been required to demonstrate their proficiency with library skills so the librarian was somewhat at a loss about where to start. She first considered breaking the assignments into a series of "bite-siże" assignments what were to build developmentally and sequentially. However, she decided that a series of small assignments would seem too "Mickey Mouse" for doctoral students. The librarian also considered including self-tests for each module using the WebCT quiz software. She had thought about requiring students to complete the self-tests even if the tests were not graded because she was determined that students would master the details. On second thought, however, she decided that the doctoral students might feel that they were being treated like undergraduates and also abandoned that idea.

As a result, the librarian/developer opted instead to require two big assignments. The first assignment, worth 20 per cent of the course grade, had students identify encyclopedias, databases, and other useful resources at local academic libraries in their areas. The second assignment, a bibliography that was worth 50 per cent of the grade, required students to create a bibliography of appropriate ERIC, theses or dissertation, NSU practicum, book, and journal article citations using APA format that would be appropriate for a literature review.

Next, the librarian considered ways to incorporate active learning in the course activities that would account for the other 30 per cent of the grade. She decided to have an online team project in which groups would analyze a case study and develop a search strategy on a topic for searching ERIC and some full-text databases. She also decided to have students participate in weekly online discussions on topics ranging from their topics of interest to issues relating to plagiarism, the relative merits of search engines, and information literacy.

IMPLEMENTATION AND ASSESSMENT OF THE ONLINE VERSION OF ERD 8226

The course was completed and submitted to PHE in 2000, and the doctoral program added the course to its offerings in the fall of 2000. There was sufficient interest for the course to actually get implemented in January of 2001. The course turned out to be quite successful with five sections of the course offered in 2001, four sections using WebCT and one section of face-to-face instruction.

A number of problems arose the first time that the course was taught. Three out of the 15 students in the Winter 2001 term had difficulties in Week 1 either logging on or understanding when to use the discussion boards and when to use WebCT e-mail. Students had difficulties using threaded discussions, using the course management feature for submitting assignments, or accessing instructor feedback. The librarian was able to help students iron out all but problems with submitting assignments. As a result, she decided to ignore the assignment submission feature in WebCT and simply have students submit assignments via e-mail using Word attachments. This decision, however, meant that the librarian had to track student participation in the discussion boards, group projects, and assignments manually. By Week 3, all the students had mastered the course software, and several students commented later that, as professionals who worked in higher education, they had appreciated having the opportunity to take a class using the WebCT courseware.

The much bigger problem with the implementation involved the bibliography for the final assignment. The instructor had expected that she would have

to provide students with a good deal of help with their topics and search strategies in the weekly discussions. However, she had not anticipated major problems at the end of the course with students not being able to correctly use the
APA (American Psychological Association) style format for their bibliographies. Although students were able to locate appropriate books, journal articles, ERIC documents, and dissertations that were timely and appropriate, they
had real difficulties understanding that published and unpublished doctoral
documents, ERIC documents that happened to be conference papers or government reports, and journal articles that had been retrieved online each had to
be formatted in very specific ways. Furthermore, the instructor had not expected to have so many students also have problems with such simple formatting issues as when to capitalize words in the title of a document and how to
correctly punctuate names of multiple authors in a citation. As a result, the instructor was forced to provide a great deal of individualized feedback for students' final projects. She realized that she should have designed a series of
small assignments that built sequentially and developmentally so that students
would have received this feedback much earlier in the course rather than be
overwhelmed at the end of the course.

The formative assessment of the course was based in part on the librarian's
personal experiences teaching the course. Based on the problems with the initial implementation of the course, the librarian revamped the assignment portion of the course. The second time the course was offered, the librarian had
students complete a series of mini-assignments in which students had to locate
specific types of citations each week and use those citations for the compiled
bibliography. Initially, many students were concerned and upset when they received the feedback on the first week's assignments, but the approach worked
out well in the long run because students had time to learn and become comfortable with using APA. Because students got feedback about the citations
earlier in the process, the final assignments were done correctly and required
much less feedback from the instructor at the end of the course.

The librarian also obtained additional feedback from students through an
anonymous online Student Satisfaction Survey that was the last activity for the
course. Two issues were raised in the student feedback. Some students thought
there was too much work for a one-credit course while other students did not
like active learning activities (the group project and the weekly discussion topics) that had been built into the course. The librarian did not reduce the workload for the course, but she did feel that students raised a valid issue about
online activities. She had come to realize that some students had work schedules that made it difficult for them to participate during the work week while
others had learning styles that preferred independent learning rather than
group activities and discussions. As a result, the author modified the assign-

ments for the spring term and allowed students to choose between participating in WebBoard discussions and writing a short essay on one of the discussion topics. She also eliminated the group project. Contrary to most recommendations for online courses (Bren, Hillenamm, & Topp, 1998; Cudiner & Harmon, 2000; Dunigan & Thompson, 1998; Germain, Jacobson, & Kaczor, 2000; Mehlenbacher, Miller, Covington, & Larsen, 2000; O'Hanlon, 2000), the result was that the course became less team-based and focused more on facilitated independent study.

REDESIGNING ERD 8226 TO BE DELIVERED IN A FACE-TO-FACE FORMAT

In contrast to most institutions that go from traditional instruction to online instruction, PHE asked if the librarian would be willing to teach the online course in a face-to-face format at the program's summer institute when PHE students would be coming to Ft. Lauderdale for eight days of classes and activities in July of 2001. The course instruction was to be offered in a one-day format, but students were to have time after they returned home to practice the skills learned to complete their assignments. The final projects would be due by the end of August. The librarian was excited about this opportunity to try teaching the course in a synchronous format but stipulated that she would only be able to teach the class if PHE could make a computer lab on the day the course was to be taught.

Redesigning the class was relatively easy. First of all, the librarian decided to eliminate any use of WebCT since most of the course would take place at the summer institute. Instead, she decided to use e-mail to communicate with students before and after the summer institute. As for the content, the librarian decided to devote the morning to learning about the ERIC database, search techniques to use to search ERIC in FirstSearch, and locating ERIC ED documents in ERIC E-Subscribe. The librarian modeled the search demonstration on the content in the online tutorial so that students could refer back to the tutorial when they returned home. Instead of having students e-mailing their topics, she had them identify topics to search that morning. She was able to take time to stop at each terminal and consult with the students on their topic and search strategies. The last part of the morning was to be devoted to how to correctly cite the search results located in ERIC. In the afternoon, she designed the course to move on to how to locate full-text articles in ProQuest's Psychology Journals and Research Library Periodicals and Wilson's Education Full Text and OmniFile. She planned to include a plagiarism activity and discussion of how to format citations of articles that had been retrieved full text online next.

The later part of the afternoon was to focus on locating primary sources like theses, practicums, and dissertations, how to identify peer-reviewed journals, and using search engines to locate Web pages. APA formatting issues for these types of materials were also discussed.

IMPLEMENTING THE FACE-TO-FACE VERSION
OF THE COURSE

The implementation went smoothly. A number of students expressed their preference for face-to-face instruction. The librarian was able to communicate more easily with students and work with them on their search topics, search strategies, and the selection of appropriate databases. She was also able to demonstrate how to format different types of citations appropriately. A comparison of the quality of the two formats revealed no significant differences in the quality of the resources cited in the final bibliographies. Perhaps more surprisingly, in spite of the concentrated one-day format, a comparison of the final projects revealed no significant differences in the problems with APA formatting between students who completed mini-assignments asynchronously and students who received instruction synchronously.

PROS AND CONS OF SYNCHRONOUS AND ASYNCHRONOUS
FORMATS OF COURSE

Both formats produced students who could research a topic, identify and locate appropriate resources, and produce bibliographies appropriate for a literature review of a doctoral student in education. It was also true that each format had some advantages and disadvantages. It was harder for the librarian to find a good formula for designing a manageable number of effective mini-assignments that she could use in an asynchronous environment. Even when she reformatted the course for a third time and began requiring that the bibliography be annotated, some students experienced some problems. The annotations were used to evaluate the appropriateness of the resource for the search topic and identify the search strategy used to locate the resource. Group activities and online discussions became an even smaller portion of the online course as she focused even more on the individual activities.

In contrast, the librarian found that the synchronous version of the class offered a different set of strengths and weaknesses. Students did not obtain the bulk of the content in print but by lecture and live demonstrations. Students liked having the opportunity to get hands-on experience and immediate feedback from the instructor. On the other hand, there were some distinct disadvantages to the face-to-face format. Because of the time constraints of 8 hours of consecutive class time, there was not time for students to complete mini homework assignments that built sequentially and developmentally. The fact that the class was held in the conference room at a hotel also meant that the instructor did not have time to focus on more traditional print resources. The librarian had had high hopes that the face-to-face format would help in communicating how to cite resources correctly using the APA format. She dedicated time in both the morning and afternoon to activities related to APA formatting, provided detailed handouts and even included a PowerPoint presentation with problem areas in various types of citations highlighted. The concentration on formatting issues alerted students to several formatting issues that they had not paid attention to before. The information was presented in a sequential and developmental manner, but students could not go home and practice one type of formatting on their own before moving on to the next learning objective. Some of the students did not seem to pay attention, so it was not surprising that they later experienced significant problems with APA formatting in their final projects. The main disadvantage of the eight-hour class, however, was that students did not have enough time to absorb all the details covered during that day of instruction. A number of students reported that they got confused and did not have time to sort through their questions before the class moved on to the next topic. A face-to-face version of the course that meets in four two-hour segments would have addressed this particular problem, but this alternative was not an option because of the format of this distance program.

CONCLUSIONS

Case studies such as the one examined here are useful in providing others with insights into the challenges and possible solution strategies that can be employed in the design of courses offered both online and face-to-face. What quickly becomes obvious, however, in this discussion is that no one format tried was a "silver bullet" offering the perfect solution for library training. Each format had strengths and weaknesses, advantages and disadvantages. Activities and delivery systems that worked for one student might not satisfy the next student. The reality is that no one approach provides the "best" pedagogical approach or solution.

Perhaps as important as the fact that there is no one instructional design solution that works in all educational situations is the need to recognize that academic politics are very important in the instructional design process. Decisions about whether to offer library training online or in a face-to-face format often are made by academic programs, and are based on the administrative and political constraints of those academic programs and curricula rather than fundamental pedagogical considerations. For example, the library at NSU did not have the final decision about the nature of the collaborative efforts with PHE. Instead, both the decision to use WebCT for the asynchronous class and the decision to have the synchronous class offered in an 8-hour block of time were made unilaterally by the PHE administration based on what would "fit in" with the curriculum and delivery structure already in place. Librarians must be willing to accommodate the realities of each situation if they want successful interactions with academic programs. A library course or training module that doesn't fit into the curriculum and delivery methods utilized by that academic program will never get implemented, no matter how well-designed or how useful. The reality is that pragmatic considerations can, and often do, play an important role in instructional design decisions. The bottom line is that collaborative efforts between librarians and academic programs must be based just as much on the flexibility needed to work with real-world constraints as on the development of effective instruction using solid instructional design principles.

REFERENCES

Bren, B., Hillenamm, B., & Topp, V. (1998). Effectiveness of hands-on instruction of electronic resources. *Research Strategies, 16*, 41-51.

Cudiner, S., & Harmon, A. R. (2000). An active learning approach to teaching effective online search strategies: a librarian/faculty collaboration. *T.H.E. Journal, 28*(5), 52-57. Retrieved November 18, 2001, from Wilson Web Education Full Text database.

Dunigan, J., & Thompson, J. C., Jr. (1998). Using technology to make a difference: Engaging student in active learning. *T.H.E. Journal, 26*(4), 30. Retrieved November 13, 2001, from ProQuest Research Library Periodicals database.

Germain, C. A., Jacobson, T. E., & Kaczor, S. A. (2000, January). A comparison of the effectiveness of presentation formats for instruction: Teaching first-year students. *College and Research Libraries*, 65-72.

Mehlenbacher, B., Miller, C. R., Covington, D., & Larsen, J. S. (2000). Active and interactive learning online: A comparison of Web-based and conventional writing classes. *IEEE Transactions on Professional Communication, 43*(2), 166-184.

Morner, C. J. (1993). A test of library research skills for education doctoral students (Doctoral dissertation, Boston College, 1993). *Dissertation Abstracts International, 54*(06), 2070A.

Morner, C. J. (1995). Measuring the library research skills of education doctoral students. In R. AmRhein (Ed.), *Continuity and transformation: The promise of confluence. Proceedings of the Seventh National Conference of the Association of College and Research Libraries, Pittsburgh, Pennsylvania, March 19-April 1, 1995* (pp. 1361-1391). Chicago: Association of College and Research Libraries.

O'Hanlon, N. (2000). Ohio State University Libraries' net.TUTOR project. *Research Strategies, 17*, 207-214.

Pival, P., & Tuñón, J. (1998). NetMeeting: A new and inexpensive alternative for delivering library instruction to distance students. *College & Research Library News, 59*, 758-760.

Pival, P., & Tuñón, J. (2000). Innovative methods for providing instruction to distance students using technology. In P. S. Thomas (Compiler), *The Ninth Off-Campus Library Services Conference proceedings* (pp. 221-230). Mount Pleasant, MI: Central Michigan University Press.

Southern Association of Colleges and Schools Commission on Colleges (1997). *SACS report*. Unpublished manuscript.

Tuñón, J. (1999). *Integrating bibliographic instruction for distance education doctoral students in the Child and Youth Studies Program at Nova Southeastern University.* Unpublished doctoral practicum, Nova Southeastern University, Fort Lauderdale, FL. (ERIC Document Reproduction No. ED440639).

Tuñón, J. (1999, June 7). *Asynchronous/distance instruction: A case study of the MBA at NSU.* Special Library Association Conference in Minneapolis, MN, on June 7, 1999.

Tuñón, J. (in press). Chapter entitled "Collaborating on Web-based instruction for MBA students at Nova Southeastern University."

Tuñón, J., & Pival, P. (1997). Library services to distance students: Nova Southeastern University's experience. *Florida Libraries, 40*, 109, 118.

Tuñón, J., & Pival, P. (2000). Reaccreditation at Nova Southeastern University: How reaccreditation can create opportunities for improving library services to distance students. In P. S. Thomas (Compiler), *The Ninth Off-Campus Library Services Conference proceedings* (pp. 273-282). Mount Pleasant, MI: Central Michigan University Press.

The Relationship Between Library Anxiety and Off-Campus Adult Learners

Robin Veal

Saint Mary's University

SUMMARY. The focus of this research is to assess the level of library anxiety of off-campus adult learners ($n = 143$) enrolled in a Master of Arts (M.A.) in Education program offered at various off-campus locations. The off-campus adult learner's level of library anxiety will be accessed using the LAS (Library Anxiety Scale, Bostick, 1992). Also examined will be the degree that the following variables impact the library anxiety level of off-campus adult learners: age, gender, previous library instruction, physical distance from an academic library, length of time available to research the topic, and access to materials. A small statistically significant relationship was found between composite library anxiety score and the variable amount of time available. Descriptive data pertaining to age and gender was consistent to the extant research.

KEYWORDS. Student relationships, distance learners, anxiety, study

The literature assessing the level of library anxiety and the degree it impacts students' feelings of competency focuses primarily on undergraduate and graduate students who are enrolled in a program at a traditional campus. Although some aspects of this research may be applied to off-campus adult learners, overall these learners have unique challenges in terms of access to library resources and instruction that significantly impact their feelings of competency regarding their academic performance. The focus of this research is to

[Haworth co-indexing entry note]: "The Relationship Between Library Anxiety and Off-Campus Adult Learners." Veal, Robin. Co-published simultaneously in *Journal of Library Administration* (The Haworth Information Press, an imprint of The Haworth Press, Inc.) Vol. 37, No. 3/4, 2002, pp. 529-536; and: *Distance Learning Library Services: The Tenth Off-Campus Library Services Conference* (ed: Patrick B. Mahoney) The Haworth Information Press, an imprint of The Haworth Press, Inc., 2002, pp. 529-536.

http://www.haworthpress.com/store/product.asp?sku=J111
10.1300/J111v37n03_43

assess the level of library anxiety of off-campus adult learners ($n = 143$) enrolled in a Master of Arts (M.A.) in Education program offered at various off-campus locations. The off-campus adult learner's level of library anxiety will be accessed using LAS (Library Anxiety Scale, Bostick, 1992). Also examined will be the degree that the following variables impact the library anxiety level of off-campus adult learners: age, gender, previous library instruction, physical distance from an academic library, length of time available to research the topic, and access to materials.

SELECTED LITERATURE REVIEW

Mellon (1986) defined library anxiety as a construct. Utilizing a qualitative analytical framework, Mellon (1986) assessed college students' perceptions regarding their initial response to the library. Results of her two-year investigation indicated that college students described their initial response to the library in terms of "fear" or a "feeling of being lost." Her analyses indicated that students' responses to the library as an instructional environment stemmed from their perceptions regarding (a) the size of the library, (b) lack of knowledge about where things were located, (c) how to begin and (d) what to do. Students' responses also indicated that they felt incompetent in utilizing library resources and felt embarrassed to ask questions that they believed would reveal their incompetence.

Bostick (1992) developed an instrument called the Library Anxiety Scale (LAS) in accordance with the work of Mellon (1986) to quantitatively measure library anxiety. Mech and Brooks (1995) utilized survey methodology, specifically the State-Trait Inventory (Spielberger, Gorsuch & Lushene, 1970) and a modified Library Anxiety Scale (Jacobson & Mark, 1995), to assess undergraduates' levels of library and trait anxiety. Their findings indicated that library anxiety is specific to the library environment and that students who experience library anxiety did not generally experience anxiety in most other areas of their lives. Mech and Brooks replicated their results in a follow-up study in 1997. More recently, Jiao and Onwuegbuzie (1999) assessed graduate students' library and trait anxiety levels. These researchers administered the State-Trait Inventory (Spielberger, Gorsuch & Lushene, 1970) and the LAS (Bostick, 1992) and also found that library anxiety was a state and not a trait anxiety.

Intrinsic variables, such as gender and age, have been identified in studies assessing college students' levels of library anxiety. For example, Jiao, Onwuegbuzie and Lichtenstein (1996) and Jiao and Onwuegbuzie (1997) found that, overall, males' responses to the LAS (Bostnick, 1992) indicated a higher degree of library anxiety in contrast to the responses of the females.

Bostick (1992) reported that students over 50 years of age had higher levels of library anxiety.

College students' perceptions of available resources and instruction pertaining to library utilization have been identified as influential variables. Using qualitative analytical techniques Onwuegbuzie (1997) found resource anxiety, defined as anxiety produced by the inability to obtain material found in a library search, was a pivotal variable influencing the overall quality of graduate students' written research proposals. Gilton (1994) advocates information literacy instruction as a method of reducing library anxiety. Jacobson and Mark (1995) found that instructional techniques that elevate students' confidence in using the library may decrease anxiety. Kuhlthau (1988, 1991) and Zahner (1993) have found that instruction that included both cognitive and affective aspects of the information search process reduced library anxiety.

Both qualitative and quantitative methods have been used to measure library anxiety in college students. It has also been demonstrated that library anxiety is specifically related to the library environment and not to overall trait anxiety. Males seem to report a higher level of library anxiety than females. Lastly, instructional interventions have been shown to reduce library anxiety.

This research originates from the premise that the majority of empirical literature relating to library anxiety has focused primarily on traditional undergraduate students and/or graduate students who have convenient physical access to the home institution's library. This study sought to extend this database by focusing on off-campus adult learners and their perceptions regarding library anxiety. In this study, off-campus adult learners have been defined as graduate students attending classes at a distance of at least 50 miles from their home institution's library.

METHOD

Adult learners ($n = 143$) participating in this study were enrolled in an M.A. program in education at a small Catholic university located in an urban midwestern city. The adult learners attended classes at one of eleven cohort locations throughout the state. These students were primarily K-12 educators who were returning to school after an absence from post-secondary education.

Instrument

Adult learners were administered the LAS (Bostick, 1992) to assess their level of library anxiety. This instrument consists of 43 questions designed to measure respondents' overall level of library anxiety according to five subscales: barriers with staff, affective barriers, comfort with the library, knowledge of the library, and mechanical barriers. Bostick (1992) defined the following factors in accordance to the work of Mellon (1986):

1. Barriers with staff–The perception that librarians or library staffs are intimidating, unapproachable and too busy to provide help.
2. Affective barriers–A student's feelings that they, alone, have inadequate library skills.
3. Comfort with the library–Refers to how safe and welcoming the students perceive the library to be.
4. Knowledge of the library–Refers to how familiar students feel they are with the library.

Factor analytical techniques used by Bostick (1992) identified mechanical barriers as a fifth factor. "Mechanical barriers" is defined as a student's level of anxiety caused by being unable to operate equipment in the library, such as copy machines and printers.

Adult learners' level of agreement with LAS questionnaire items was measured using a Likert-type scale anchored from 1 (strongly disagree) to 5 (strongly agree). A higher score indicated a higher level of anxiety. In addition, adult learners responded to eight general survey questions. These questions were designed to obtain students' perceptions regarding: (a) availability of materials, (b) time to complete research, (c) instruction received, and (d) physical distance from both an academic and public library. Demographic data were obtained pertaining to adult learners' age, gender, and their progress in the program. Because the adult learners were off-campus students and did not have physical access to the library of their home institution, they were asked to select the type of library (academic, public, or other) they used most frequently in order to complete their academic work.

RESULTS

Seventy-one percent of the adult learners were female and 29% were male. The average number of courses completed in the program was five. In response to the question measuring adult learners physical access to the library they used most frequently to complete their academic work, 48 (34%) selected the academic library, 75 (52%) selected the public library, and 20 (14%) indicated some other type of library. Ninety-three adult learners (65%) reported they were 20 miles or more from an academic library, while 101 adult learners (71%) reported they were 5 miles or less from a public library.

In this study, the overall Cronbach reliability coefficient for these scores is .95 and the individual Cronbach reliability coefficients pertaining to the subscale scores are shown in Table I. These scores are consistent with reliability scores obtained in other studies (Bostick, 1992; Jiao & Onwuegbuzie, 1997; Jiao & Onwuegbuzie, 1999; Onwuegbuzie & Jiao, 2000; Jiao et al., 1996; Onwuegbuzie, 1997). Tables I and II show overall and the individual subscale averages and the reliability analysis. Bostick (1992) indicated that a higher score overall or per subscale indicated higher anxiety. Since the averages of the Likert-type scale range from 5 (strongly agree) as a high score and 1 (strongly disagree) as a low score, we can see that this group of adult learners has average to low anxiety in regards to using the library overall and in regards to the subscales.

Table III shows the data pertaining to gender and age of the adult learners. Males reported slightly higher levels of anxiety than females and these findings support research conducted by Jiao et al. (1996) and Jiao and Onwuegbuzie (1997).

Table IV shows that 20-29 year olds reported the highest levels of library anxiety, followed by 30-39 year olds , 50-59 year olds and 40-49 year olds with the lowest reported levels of anxiety. These findings lend support to the research conducted by Jiao et al. (1996) and Jiao and Onwuegbuzie (1997) who reported a inverse relationship between age and library anxiety.

TABLE I. Overall and Per Factor Library Anxiety Averages and Reliability

	Average	Standard Deviation	Reliability
Overall	2.22	.56	.95
Affective Barriers	2.38	1.09	.85
Barriers With Staff	2.12	.98	.93
Comfort with the Library	2.19	1.00	.74
Knowledge of the Library	2.09	1.03	.66
Mechanical Barriers	2.36	1.03	.84

TABLE II. Average Anxiety Score (Range Possible 43-215)

	Average Score
Overall (n = 143)	95
Female (71%)	94.27
Male (29%)	96.24

Table V shows the impact of library instruction on adult learners' level of anxiety. Eighty-eight adult learners (61%) had received instruction from their home institution and 44 (31%) from another source.

A point-biserial correlation procedure was utilized to correlate the relationships between composite library anxiety score and (a) perception of resource availability, (b) distance from an academic library, and (c) amount of time available to conduct research. Spearman rank correlational analyses indicated no statistically significant relationships pertaining to composite library anxiety score and (a) perception of resource availability and (b) distance from an academic library. A statistically significant relationship rho = .16, p ≤ .05 was found between composite library anxiety score and amount of time available to conduct research. By Cohen's (1988) criteria, this correlation is small.

The goal of this research is to examine off-campus adult learners' level of library anxiety utilizing the LAS (Bostick, 1992) and to examine other variables such as age, gender, previous library instruction, physical distance from an academic library, length of time available to research the topic, and access to ma-

TABLE III. Gender and Library Anxiety Averages

	Mean	Standard Deviation
Overall (n = 143)	2.22	0.56
Female (71%)	2.21	0.55
Male (29%)	2.24	0.58

TABLE IV. Age and Library Anxiety Averages (Possible Range 43-215)

	Number of Students	Average Score
20-29 years	45	100.93
30-39 years	57	93.61
40-49 years	30	89.70
50-59 years	11	92.36

TABLE V. Average Anxiety Scores and Instruction

	Library Instruction	No Library Instruction
Instruction from Home Institution	93.25	97.02
Instruction from Another Source	90.59	96.88

terials as variables mediating adult learners' level of anxiety. The findings of this study are consistent with the extant literature investigating gender and age in terms of library anxiety. The results of this study are primarily descriptive and correlational. Therefore, future research should assess the causal nature of the relationship between level of library anxiety and the variables assessed in this study for this specific population of learners.

REFERENCES

Bostick, S. L. (1992). The development and validation of the Library Anxiety Scale. *Dissertation Abstracts International*, 53(12), 4116A. (UMI No. 9310624).

Cohen, J. (1988) *Statistical power analysis for the behavioral sciences* (2nd ed.). Hillsdale, NJ: Lawrence Erlbaum Associates.

Gilton, D. L. (1994). A world of difference: Preparing for information literacy instruction for diverse groups. *MultiCultural Review*, 3(3), 54-62.

Jacobson, T. E. & Mark, B. L. (1995). Teaching in the information age: Active learning techniques to empower students. *The Reference Librarian*, (51-52), 105-120.

Jiao, Q. G. & Onwuegbuzie, A. J. (1997). Antecedents of library anxiety. *Library Quarterly*, 67(4), 372-390. Retrieved March 24, 2001, from Expanded Academic ASAP database.

Jiao, Q. G. & Onwuegbuzie, A. J. (1999). Is library anxiety important? *Library Review*, 48(6), 278-282.

Jiao, Q. G., Onwuegbuzie, A. J. & Lichtenstein, A. A. (1996). Library anxiety: Characteristics of 'at-risk' college students. *Library & Information Science Research*, 18(2), 151-163.

Keefer, J. (1993). The hungry rats syndrome: Library anxiety, information literacy, and the academic reference process. *RQ*, 32(3), 333-339.

Kuhlthau, C. C. (1988). Developing a model of the library search process: Cognitive and affective aspects. *RQ*, 28(2) 232-243. Retrieved March 24, 2001, from Expanded Academic ASAP database.

Kuhlthau, C. C. (1991). Inside the search process: Information seeking from the user's perspective. *Journal of the American Society for Information Science*, 42(5), 361-371.

Mech, T. F. & Brooks, C. I. (1995). Library anxiety among college students: An exploratory study. In R. Amrhein (Ed.) *Continuity & transformation: The promise of confluence* (pp. 173-179). Chicago: American Library Association.

Mech, T. F. & Brooks, C. I. (1997). Anxiety and confidence in using a library by college freshman and seniors. *Psychological Reports (81)*, pp. 929-930.

Mellon, C. A. (1986). Library anxiety: A grounded theory and its development. *College and Research Libraries*, 47(2), 160-165.

Onwuegbuzie, A. J. (1997). Writing a research proposal: The role of library anxiety, statistics anxiety, and composition anxiety. *Library & Information Science Research*, 19(1), 5-33.

Onwuegbuzie, A. J. & Jiao, Q. G. (2000, January). I'll go to the library later: The relationship between academic procrastination and library anxiety. *College & Research Libraries*, 61(1), 45-54.

Spielberger, C., Gorsuch, R. & Lushene, R. (1970). *State-Trait Anxiety Inventory manual*. Palo Alto, CA: Consulting Psychologists Press.

Zahner, J. E. (1993). Thoughts, feelings and actions: Integrating domains in library instruction. *Proceedings of Selected Research and Presentations at the Convention of Association for Educational Communications and Technology*. (ERIC Document Reproduction Services No. ED362215).

The Ins and Outs
of Providing Electronic Reserves
for Distance Learning Classes

Pat Wilson

University of Kentucky

SUMMARY. Distance Learning Library Services at the University of Kentucky provided an electronic reserves service as a pilot project for distance learning courses in the 2000-01 academic year. Distance Learning Programs, which is a part of the Distance Learning Technology Center, funded the project. Policies and procedures were formulated, an account was set up with the Copyright Clearance Center, and the service was marketed. Our first electronic reserves were available for the Fall 2000 semester.

KEYWORDS. Library reserves, distance learners, library services, technology

WHO WE ARE AND WHO WE SERVE

The Distance Learning Library Services (DLLS) at the University of Kentucky have two hats. We are part of the library system and at the same time work with and serve the Distance Learning Technology Center (DLTC). I equate us to being the same as a branch library. In the library system we are part of the Access Services Team along with Circulation and Interlibrary Loan. In the DLTC we are one of four units. The other three are Distance Learning Programs (DLP), Media Design and Production (MDP), and Distance Learning

[Haworth co-indexing entry note]: "The Ins and Outs of Providing Electronic Reserves for Distance Learning Classes." Wilson, Pat. Co-published simultaneously in *Journal of Library Administration* (The Haworth Information Press, an imprint of The Haworth Press, Inc.) Vol. 37, No. 3/4, 2002, pp. 537-548; and: *Distance Learning Library Services: The Tenth Off-Campus Library Services Conference* (ed: Patrick B. Mahoney) The Haworth Information Press, an imprint of The Haworth Press, Inc., 2002, pp. 537-548.

http://www.haworthpress.com/store/product.asp?sku=J111
10.1300/J111v37n03_44

Networks (DLN). We work and interact with all of the units, but our closest relationship is with DLP. The Director of DLP is the one who works directly with the colleges to put in place graduate programs and a comprehensive selection of undergraduate courses, which are offered throughout Kentucky and beyond. DLP does everything in-house such as registering students, making arrangements for sites, problem solving, and more. They also support us by providing a budget line for supplies, student assistants, photocopying, travel for the librarian, and more.

Some of our graduate programs are social work, education, rehabilitation counseling, and library science. We also have an undergraduate engineering program 200 miles from campus. Our classes are offered on-site, online, via interactive video, and via satellite.

WHAT WE WERE DOING RESERVE-WISE

In January 2000 when I started working in the position of Distance Learning Librarian, we were not doing reserves in any form. There had been a prior problem of materials not being returned. In February 2000 I had a call from an instructor asking what I was going to do about reserves. My thought was "I don't know," for I had barely settled into the position. Having come from a public services background I knew the importance of reserves to the faculty and students, so I started doing some research on copyright issues and methods of delivery. Since our classes were off-campus, it made sense that we should make our readings available electronically.

SETTING UP THE SERVICE

Fortunately for us, our main library had already established an electronic reserves service, http://www.uky.edu/Libraries/Reserves/eresvinfo.html, in the fall of 1999. The Reserves unit in Circulation was already mounting some e-reserves. They had their policies and procedures in place, and they had a workstation set up to handle the process. As far as copyright was concerned, their policy was to ask instructors to secure their own permissions. They did provide a form for them to use (see above URL). In thinking about our service I decided that we should follow their model. The next step was to propose the service to the Director of DLP. I suggested that we start the service in the fall of 2000, claim fair use for the first time a reading was used, have the faculty member secure copyright permission for any subsequent use, scan the document into a PDF file, and make it available to the students via an ID/password.

Not only did she agree with me, but also she went a step beyond and suggested that we seek copyright permission for every use, and open an account with the Copyright Clearance Center (CCC) to pay for copyright fees.

We set up the account with the CCC. We didn't have to worry about the workstation because we could use the Reserves scanner and computer. We did have to market the service and to do that we had to know what our policies and procedures were going to be.

POLICIES AND PROCEDURES AND MARKETING

Our policies were fairly basic:

- The DLLS would request copyright permission from the CCC
- DLP would fund the pilot project for the fiscal year 2000-01
- If the item is "not permissioned" by the CCC, it would not be placed on reserve unless the rightsholder gave permission
- Requests must be made three weeks in advance of needed access
- Permission must be sought for each item every semester it is taught
- Access is ID/Password controlled
- Course reserve placement would depend on how the course was delivered, the individual sites, the students' access to the Internet, etc.
    ° Referred to books and paper reserves

It was decided that a brochure would best serve our marketing needs. When it was ready, we sent it to the distance-learning faculty. Other DLTC units promoted it and it was handed out in our Blackboard and CATAlyst workshops. CATAlyst was a program sponsored by DLTC and the Teaching and Learning Center to work with faculty interested in developing online courses. See Appendix A.

GETTING STARTED

Our first e-reserve consisted of 20 articles. Almost all of the articles were available through EBSCOhost's Academic Search Elite. We have access to this database through the Kentucky Virtual Library (KYVL). Even though I knew that all of our students could remotely access these articles via KYVL, I opted to go the CCC route because it was our first job and I wanted to get the process going. This particular class was a Blackboard online class, which meant that we had to decide if the Blackboard Support Tech would mount the readings on her server or if we would mount them on the library server. Our decision was to make them available on the library's server because we would have control over putting them up and taking them down. We had a link to the electronic Reserves put on our home page for easy access.

Electronic Reserves Access on the DLLS Home Page

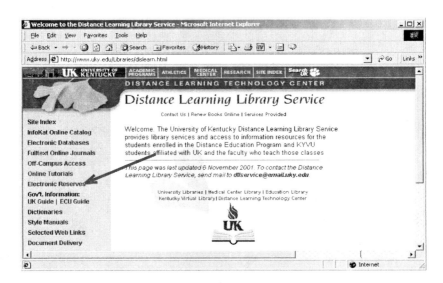

We contacted the CCC, paid the copyright fee, scanned the articles into a PDF file, made them available on the server for our Electronic Resources people who then mounted them and made them available via an ID/password. The authors retained the copyright for two of the articles so we contacted them directly for permission to use.

ELECTRONIC RESERVES SPRING 2001

In the spring of 2001, we had five classes participating in our project. One of our instructors presented us with a list of 100 class readings, which he wanted us to mount electronically. I hadn't thought about limiting the number of readings until that time. After discussing this with the Director of DLP, we felt that a limit of 50 articles and $300 per course was reasonable. The instructor didn't have a problem with the limits and willingly pared the list down.

We then started the permission process with the CCC. We quickly realized that the CCC did not cover a lot of our publications, so we started contacting the rightsholder directly when article permissions were not available through the CCC. This was a valuable lesson for us. Many times the rightsholder waived the fee entirely. Of course this didn't happen all of the time. In order to track all of these transactions and to organize the information on the rights-holders, we decided to build two databases. One database would track each class's readings and the other would contain all of our rightsholder informa-tion. We include: article information, number of pages, number of students, date of initial permission request, number of redirected requests beyond initial request, rightsholders' fee, CCC fee, whether it was a CCC or direct permis-sion, permission receipt, rightsholder, journal, comments and the number of days required to obtain permission. See Appendix B and Appendix C.

In setting up the service we didn't anticipate more than one budget line. We had the account with the CCC and thought that would take care of our ex-penses. It didn't take long for us to realize that we needed a budget line for fees paid directly to the rightsholders. Fortunately, our budget officer is in the same office with us so we took each invoice directly to her to be sure that we could pay for it. DLP has been very generous to us in this regard.

We ran into budget problems with two of the classes. One of the classes had twenty-five students, so if the rightsholder charged $1.50 per student we had a bill of $37.50. We ended up asking the instructor to choose which articles to make available when we were close to going over our $300 limit. With the other class we were so new to the process that before we knew it, we were over budget, and decided to allow it. We did send a note to all participating faculty stating how many readings we had made available and the total cost. Our "over budget" class instructor will work with us the next time the class is taught to re-duce the cost.

We ask the instructors to give us clean copies of the documents they want placed on electronic reserve. Of course this doesn't always happen. We double-check the citations, and get the articles when necessary. There may be a time when this is a problem, and if so, we will handle it at that time.

FALL 2001 SEMESTER

We took a different approach for the Fall 2001 semester. If the publication was available via a direct URL, we linked it. This was the first semester that we had this situation. If the publication was available via the EBSCOhost data-bases, we provided the link and information for the students to access it re-motely. The KYVL databases are available via ID/password for all Kentucky students and citizens. Everything else we scanned and made available as PDF files. To access the readings, all students have to do is go to our home page or directly to our copyright statement page and click on the *I have read and understood* link. They will then see a page with a list of classes with electronic readings available. The instructor's name and class number are listed. To access classes' readings you must use an ID/password. Instructions are given for accessing each type of publication at the top of the list.

Instructions for Accessing Readings

Two steps for the EBSCOhost databases will be eliminated for the Spring 2002 semester. We will link the article titles directly to the database at which point the ID/password will be required.

WORKING WITH CONSORTIA

Currently we are working with one consortial program, a Canadian Online Studies Program. Faculty members from six Kentucky institutions are teaching the classes online. Students from all of the institutions are enrolled in the program. They receive credit at their home institutions for each course they take. We are making the readings available for all students in the classes our faculty are teaching. The other institutions will do the same for their courses. I see this as a growth area. We will be working with at least one other consortium in the spring of 2002.

WORKING WITH CLASSES
GIVEN OFF-CAMPUS AND ON-CAMPUS

Other situations we have dealt with are the same class with more than one section being given off-campus and on-campus. Our money for copyright fees comes from DLP; consequently, we provide electronic readings only for those classes which are offered through our Center. We have solved this in two ways so far. The same professor is teaching both sections. We made the readings for her off-campus section available in the usual way, and then made arrangements with the Education Librarian to provide the same readings as paper reserves for the on-campus section. In the other case, all of the readings were available through KYVL and the EBSCOhost databases, and the instructors handed out the readings list with their locations. We are then available as a back up when there are access problems.

Statistics

	Fall 2000	Spring 2001	Fall 2001
Number of Classes	1	5	8
CCC Permissions	20 articles	40 articles	17
CCC Payment	$166.60	$665.30	$179.54
Direct Permissions		17 articles	10 articles
Direct Permission Fees		$276.77	$132.00
Fees Waived		35 articles	83 articles
Directly Linked to Database			10 articles
Directly Linked to Web Page			11 articles
Total Number of Articles	20	92	132
Total Cost	$166.60	$942.50	$321.54

PAPER AND BOOK RESERVES

When the need has arrived for books to be placed on reserve at our off-campus sites, we have made arrangements with the hosting site to place the item on reserve. Fortunately for us our colleagues have been more than gracious in taking care of us. If the requested book is in their collection, they put it on reserve for us. If they do not own the book, we send it if we have it and order it to send if we don't own it.

CONCLUSION

We could never have provided this service without the support of Distance Learning Programs. Not only do they underwrite the service, but they also provided a new and faster scanner for us. The faculty loves the service. They think that we are an undiscovered treasure. Our concern is that as we advertise and build our service, it might become more difficult to manage. We have also discussed the monetary limit we have set per class. This will have to be reexamined as we add more classes.

Our rightsholder database has been an invaluable asset for us. We will continue to add to it. Currently we are adding information for international rightsholders as we are dealing with foreign publications. Surprisingly, some of these permissions have only taken a day or two. We use the individual class information databases to track the fees as they come in to us because we want to make sure that we stay within budget.

When adding a new class, I have to make sure that I know all of the particulars, such as: is this a consortium, are there multiple sections, and are the classes being offered through the DLTC? When everything is up and running, we make sure that the students and faculty have our contact information in case there are problems. This is a very nice way to handle class readings especially for students at a distance. It works out well for us because we can mount and take down the readings, and they are ID/password protected.

APPENDIX A.1. DLLS Brochure

Distance Learning Library Service (DLLS)

Will Make Available

- Book Reserves
- Electronic Reserves
- Paper Reserves

Book Reserves

- Policy will vary depending on the site facilities.

- Only UK owned books can be placed on reserve.

- The library will purchase books at the faculty's request when possible.

For consultation please contact:

Pat Wilson
Distance Learning Librarian

pwilson@pop.uky.edu
1.800.829.0439 (option 6)
1.859.257.0500 x2171 (local)
1.800.257.0503 (fax)

B-67 William T. Young Library
500 South Limestone Street
University of Kentucky
Lexington, KY 40506-0456

Electronic Reserves

- DLLS staff will request copyright permission from the Copyright Clearance Center (CCC*) for materials to be placed on reserve.

- Distance Learning Technology Center (DLTC) will fund this pilot project for the fiscal year 2000-01.

- If item is "not permissioned," it will not be placed on reserve unless copyright owner gives permission.

- Requests must be made three weeks in advance of needed access (earlier is better).

- Permission must be sought for each item every semester it is taught.

- CCC does not cover every publication.

- Access is ID/Password controlled.

The Copyright Clearance Center obtains the permission to use copyrighted materials from various publishers, and handles the fees charged by the publishers.

Paper Reserves

- DLLS staff will request copyright permission from the Copyright Clearance Center (CCC*) for materials to be placed on reserve.

- Distance Learning Technology Center (DLTC) will fund this pilot project for the fiscal year 2000-01.

- If item is "not permissioned," it will not be placed on reserve unless copyright owner gives permission.

- Requests must be made three weeks in advance of needed access (earlier is better).

- Permission must be sought for each item every semester it is taught.

- CCC does not cover every publication.

- Reserve policy will depend on individual sites.

The Copyright Clearance Center obtains the permission to use copyrighted materials from various publishers, and handles the fees charged by the publishers

545

APPENDIX A.2. DLLS Brochure Verso

COURSE•RESERVES

Distance Learning
Technology Center

and

Distance Learning
Library Services

UK

Requests

A request form must be filled out for items to be placed on reserve.

Forms are available electronically at http://www.uky.edu/Libraries

Click on:
Distance Learning Library Service

-or-

Contact:
Distance Learning Library Services at
1-800-829-0329 (option 6) x2044
1-859-257-0500 x2044 *(local)*
1-859-257-0503 *(fax)*
dllservice@email.uky.edu

Distance Learning Library Service
http:www.uky.edu/Libraries/dislearn.html

**Distance Learning
Technology Center**
http://www.uky.edu/DistanceLearning

UK
UNIVERSITY OF KENTUCKY

Policies

Adequate lead-time must be provided because of processing (i.e., copyright permission, scanning, individual locations).

If an item is "not permissioned," we will need to work with you individually.

Course reserve placement will depend on how course is delivered, individual sites, students' access to the Internet, etc.

Course packets might be the answer for some classes, for example:

- Johnny Print, *(1-859-254-6139)* makes course packets
- They seek copyright permission from the CCC
- Students can order and have mailed

We would appreciate your patience and feedback as we implement this pilot project.

The success of our Distance Learning faculty and students is our first priority.

546

APPENDIX B. Course Reserves Statistics. Music 600

Article Requested for Reserve	Number of Pages in the Article	Number of Students in the Class	Date of Initial Permission Request	Number of Redirected Requests Beyond Initial Request	Rightsholders Fee	CCC Fee	CCC or Direct Permission?	Permission Received?	Date of Permission Receipt	Rightsholder	Journal	Comments	# Of Days Permission Required
Gabrielsson, Alf "Studying Emotional Expression in Musical Performance"	7	5	11/17/2000	2	$0.00	$2.50	CCC fee, Waived by Rightsholder Directly	Yes	12/5/2000	Council for Research in Music Education	Bulletin of the Council for Research in Music Education	Received e-mail granting permission for one-time use	18
LeCroy, Hoyt "Community-Based Music Education: Influences of Industrial…"	17	5	11/17/2000	0	$0.00	$3.35	CCC	Yes	11/18/2000	Music Educators National Conference	Journal of Research in Music Education	Got permission through CCC	1
Burnard, Pamela "Bodily Intention in Children's Improvisation and Composition."	16	5	11/17/2000	2	$0.00	$2.50	CCC fee, Waived by Rightsholder Directly	Yes	12/1/2000	J.W. Davidson, Editor	Psychology of Music	Received e-mail granting permission for one-time use	14
Madsen, Clifford K. "Focus of Attention and Aesthetic Response."	10	5	11/17/2000	0	$0.00	$3.01	CCC	Yes	11/18/2000	Music Educators National Conference	Journal of Research in Music Education	Got permission through CCC	1
Duke, Robert A. "The Other Mozart Effect: An Open Letter to Music Educators."	8	5	11/17/2000	4	$0.00	$2.50	CCC fee, Waived by Rightsholder Directly	Yes	12/5/2000	Robert Floyd and Robert Duke	Update	Received e-mail granting permission for one-time use	18

APPENDIX C. Rightsholders Data

Alphabetical Listing of Rightsholders	Contact Information	Most Recent Requirement
Academic Press/Harcourt	Permissions Permission queries should be directed to: Permissions Department Harcourt, Inc. 6277 Sea Harbor Drive Orlando, FL 32887-6777	Paid for permission for one-time use
Academy of Management	Copyright Clearance Center Attn: Axxx Rxxxx 222 Rosewood Drive Danvers, MA 01923 Phone 978-750-8400 Fax: 978-750-4470 http://www.copyright.com Questions about republishing material can be addressed to Axxx Rxxxx at the CCC: arxxxx@copyright.com	Received permission through the CCC
Agricultural Education	JOURNAL OF AGRICULTURAL EDUCATION EDITORIAL POLICY: The Journal of Agricultural Education is a publication of the American Association for Agricultural Education (AAAE). The Journal is published four times a year. The Journal publishes blind, peer-reviewed manuscripts addressing current trends and issues, descriptions or analyses of innovations, research, philosophical concerns, and learner/program evaluation in agricultural education … including extension and international agricultural education. The submission of empirically based manuscripts that report original quantitative or qualitative research, manuscripts based on historical or philosophical research, and reviews/synthesis of empirical or theoretical literature are encouraged. All or part of any current or previous issue may be reproduced for educational purposes only.	Received Permission through the CCC, Also waived in copyright statement.
Allyn & Bacon/Longman	All permissions requests must be faxed in writing to the Permissions Department at 781-455-7024. For printed classroom reproductions, requests must include: Allyn & Bacon author, title, ISBN, copyright date, exact page numbers of material you wish to reproduce, and number of copies you will reproduce. Also indicate the term of use. For permission to reprint in another publication, requests must include: Allyn & Bacon author, title, ISBN, copyright date, exact page numbers, description of your publication including author's name, publisher, length of publication, approximate print run and price, and a brief outline of your organization and of the content of the work in which the Allyn & Bacon material will appear. If you are requesting figures or tables, please include the pages copied from the Allyn & Bacon book itself. If you wish to adapt the material, you must include a copy of your adaptation. http://www.ablongman.com/permissions/1,2184,00.html	Paid for permission for one-time use
American Anthropological Association	4350 North Fairfax Drive, Suite 640, Arlington, VA 22203-1620	Received permission through the CCC

Being RAD:
Reference at a Distance
in a Multi-Campus Institution

Shelle Witten

Maricopa County Community College District

SUMMARY. Upon completing a Fall 1999 sabbatical studying how reference services were being provided to library patrons at a distance, the MCCCD libraries have been piloting a collaborative live reference service since Spring 2001. This paper describes the organic evolution and current state of Maricopa's Librarians Online.

KEYWORDS. Distance education, multiple sites, distance learners, reference

INTRODUCTION AND BACKGROUND

The Maricopa County Community College District in Phoenix, Arizona consists of 10 accredited colleges, two skill centers plus several education centers. Annual enrollment has topped 265,000 students. The Fall 2001 headcount was 109,770 that equated to 45,000 full-time student equivalent. The ratio of full-time to part-time students is typically one to four, whereas the ratio of day to evening students one and a quarter to one. The colleges range in size from the smallest, Estrella Mountain, at 4,000 headcount to Mesa at 23,000. Each college operates autonomously, as do the libraries.

[Haworth co-indexing entry note]: "Being RAD: Reference at a Distance in a Multi-Campus Institution." Witten, Shelle. Co-published simultaneously in *Journal of Library Administration* (The Haworth Information Press, an imprint of The Haworth Press, Inc.) Vol. 37, No. 3/4, 2002, pp. 549-567; and: *Distance Learning Library Services: The Tenth Off-Campus Library Services Conference* (ed: Patrick B. Mahoney) The Haworth Information Press, an imprint of The Haworth Press, Inc., 2002, pp. 549-567.

http://www.haworthpress.com/store/product.asp?sku=J111
10.1300/J111v37n03_45

Although each library has its own fine and circulation policies, they do share a centralized technical services as well as a union catalogue. However, the MCCCD libraries have never before offered a centralized service to students. This paper describes the organic evolution of Librarians Online, a live reference service now in its third semester of operation.

After observing students, back in 1996/97 coming into the library asking for help following frustrating Internet searches at home, I was curious whether librarians could be available to students while they were online. At Paradise Valley Community College, the MCCCD college where I work, one of my colleagues had been experimenting with CU-SeeMe videoconferencing software, and I observed my son using chat software to communicate with friends. An article appeared in the local newspaper describing the LoanMaker System that enabled a loan counselor and homebuyer or realtor to see each other while at the same time display various loan scenarios on the monitor (Doerfler, 1997).

The aforementioned technologies seemed potentially adaptable to library use. Because I wondered if libraries were already employing such technology, in October 1998, I applied for a fall 1999 sabbatical to study how libraries across the country were providing reference assistance to patrons who were conducting their research on the Internet and proprietary Web-based databases from outside the library walls. While conducting research for my sabbatical proposal, I also discovered that several libraries in California and Michigan were experimenting with videoconferencing for provision of reference services (Folger, 1997; Lessick, Kjaer, & Clancy, 1997; Morgan, 1996).

My sabbatical travels took me to some of the libraries best known for their innovative and comprehensive services for off-site library patrons, including Central Michigan University, the Internet Public Library, Walden University, Nova University, and the Florida Distance Learning Reference and Referral Center. These libraries were using phone and electronic mail technologies to provide reference services. At Austin Community College, however, Jonathan Buckstead was experimenting with NetMeeting, a free product included in the Microsoft Office suite. He had videoconferencing, scanning, whiteboard and application sharing capabilities. And finally, in Los Angeles, I visited with Susan McGlamery and Steve Coffman who had obtained a grant to develop a 24x7 reference project using Webline, a call center software product.

In addition to the fact-finding objective of the sabbatical, I also scouted out funding sources, wrote a sample grant proposal, conducted user needs surveys of students and faculty, and developed a marketing plan plus a prototype Web page. Although all these objectives were met, the process of creating a real, viable online reference service in a large multi-campus institution is cumbersome and agonizingly slow. In the year and a half since my sabbatical, there have been remarkable and far-reaching changes that impact this field.

We have seen a tremendous proliferation of Web-based proprietary databases, which allow for remote access. Carol Tenopir references Martha Williams' tally of over 12,000 databases in her "The State of Databases Today" introduction to the most recent *Gale Directory of Databases* (2001). Although at the time of this writing, the state of electronic books is uncertain, OCLC's offer to purchase netLibrary bodes well for e-books (2001). In its annual survey of information technology in higher education, the Campus Computing Project data indicate a 22% increase of full online courses in 2001 over 1999 (2001). Chat software, or instant messaging, has caught on for everyday communication, with over a billion instant messages sent on the Internet each day (Dalton, 2001). In fact, a growth rate of 140% was predicted in an October 2001 article in the corporate instant messaging market (Legard, 2000). This is mirrored by the increase in retailers' use of call center software for customer service. These changes have been noted on the Digital Reference listserv with discussion shifting from provision of electronic mail reference service to live reference technologies. The creation of the LiveRef listserv, the LiveRef(sm) Registry of Real-Time Digital Reference Services (McKiernan, 2001), and the Teaching Librarian's Digital Reference Web site (Francoeur, 2001) are all testimony to the reference revolution R. David Lankes foresaw at the second annual Virtual Reference Desk conference (Oder, 2001).

PLANNING

Upon returning from sabbatical, during Spring 2000, the district's Library Technology Group formed an ad-hoc committee, later dubbed RAD (Reference at a Distance) to form recommendations for an online reference service. In the two meetings we had before we broke for the summer, we discussed the following issues:

- Is online reference necessary?
- Goal/Mission
- Should we operate as a centralized, distributed or hybrid service?
- What should be the parameters of the service?
- How will we fund it?
- How will we staff it?
- When should we offer it? Dates? Times?

We also decided that we needed input from library staff across the district. Taking advantage of the August 24, 2000 All Library Staff meeting, we invited interested library staff to participate in a brainstorming session. With the help of a facilitator, as well as Roy Tennant, the keynote speaker for the day, we asked the following questions:

- Who are we serving?
- Which services do we want?
- What do we consider to be Reference at a Distance?
  - Telephone, Ask-A-Librarian e-mail or Web form, Chat, Fax, MOO, Videoconferencing, Document Delivery, Library Instruction, Electronic Reserves, Online Databases
- When should we offer the service?
- How should we do this?
  - Funding? Centralized?

Following these discussions, the committee went forward with a demonstration of LSSI's Virtual Reference Desk software, plus we submitted a $10,000.00 Learning Grant proposal on November 2, 2000 to the Maricopa Center for Learning and Instruction. Five thousand dollars were awarded December 14, 2000, paving the way for a Spring 2001 pilot.

SPRING 2001 PILOT

To maximize the $5,000.00 and also to test an evening service, the money was devoted to contract librarian hours. We chose AOL Instant Messenger as our chat software because of its popularity. With Steve Coffman's assistance, we secured a demonstration of the collaborative Web-browsing product, Hipbone. Our pilot shaped up as follows:

- 10 Week Operation (February 20-May 2)
- Days and Times
  - Sundays 7:00-11:00 p.m.
  - Monday-Wednesday 8:00-11:00 p.m.
- Seven librarians on contract
- AOL Instant Messenger (AIM) and Hipbone software
- Training one week prior to startup, plus practicing with each other after startup

Our main goal was simply to gain experience with the online modality.

A few simple policies were determined: we would serve people affiliated with Maricopa, but we would not be absolute sticklers; we would use only the district's shared databases, rather than being versed in all the unique databases at the individual colleges; and we would emphasize instruction.

A friendly logo/icon (Figure 1) was, and still is, the centerpiece of our marketing efforts. The logo has been used on flyers and bookmarks that have been distributed in the libraries and in some English classes. The majority of the college libraries have used the logo as a link to the service from their Web pages, as have some college departments and courses. Several student newspapers have carried articles about our new service. We have also been invited to do demonstrations at several campus and district events.

On the top half of our Web page (Figure 2) was the vehicle to connect students to the service. Though a rather homemade design, it nonetheless provided several tools to make the connection. The AIM Remote banner enabled students to open a chat window directly to our screenname, Maricopalibchat. It also provided a link to automatically add our screenname to the student's buddy list. After scrolling down to the bottom half of the page (Figure 3), students were provided with a link for downloading and installing AIM. The Frequently Asked Question link provided explicit instructions for downloading AIM, an explanation of co-browsing and a listing of Internet sites for APA and MLA citation. The most unique component of our page was the Web form toward the bottom. Once a student was provided the required ID by the librarian, a Hipbone connection was established (Figure 4). Once established, the Hipbone console and co-browsing windows opened and Web pages could be exchanged and viewed on each other's monitors. At any one time, multiple windows were open including: the AIM chat and buddy windows, the original online Web page, and the Hipbone windows, a big strain on most computers (Figure 5). AIM worked flawlessly, assuming students didn't have difficulty with the downloading. Hipbone, when it worked smoothly, gave us insight into the versatility of co-browsing. Unfortunately there were browser and platform compatibility glitches.

FIGURE 1

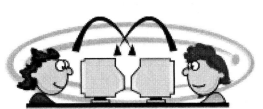

Click Here! Chat live with a librarian.

FIGURE 2

We kept statistics and also created an online evaluation/survey form we asked students to fill out following a session. During our 10 weeks a total of 30 questions were fielded. Though this was a small sample, those of us involved felt we had gained valuable experience. We also discovered that Sundays were not at all popular. One of our Sunday librarians called himself the Maytag librarian because he did not field one question. We also found that most use took place in the earlier hours offered; 10:00-11:00 was underutilized. We were most pleased by the quality of the questions posed. We had expected questions such as how to access to our databases. However, the majority of the questions were genuine reference questions, running the gamut from "how-to-cite" questions to needing the e-mail address for the Hofburg in Vienna. This gave us the opportunity to hone our online reference skills.

Through the statistics, the responses on our evaluation form and gleaning comments in the context of the chats themselves, we began to formulate plans for a phase II pilot for Fall 2001.

FIGURE 3

FALL 2001 PILOT

Given the reality that we had no new funds available, our overriding component to the Fall service relied on a daytime service, staffed by librarians volunteering one-to-two hours of their office time. I registered an account with Livehelper, which was free at the time and offered some desirable features, including Web pushing.

Then we were given a wonderful surprise. During a June meeting with two of our Vice Chancellors, three of our library directors outlined a broad funding proposal which would be submitted for the Academic Year 2002/2003. Included in that proposal was a request to purchase access to virtual reference software. Our Vice Chancellor of Information Technology gave approval to purchase the software immediately. This put us on the fast track. The library orientation of LSSI's Virtual Reference Service was our guiding reason for choosing the LSSI product. We cut a purchase order for a two-year contract with two seats by month's end.

FIGURE 4

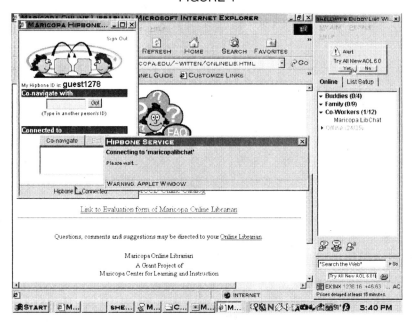

Once everyone returned from summer we solidified the parameters of our service as follows:

- Monday-Friday
- 10:00 a.m.-4:00 p.m.
- September 24-December 7
- Training by LSSI August 20 and 21 via speakerphone
- Follow-up, advanced, in-person training first week of October

Seventeen librarians representing eight MCCCD colleges stepped forward to volunteer one to four hours of their office time, with three librarians offering some additional time to serve as a backup. This backup monitoring is spotty throughout the week, but has proven to be a savior in a few cases when the librarian scheduled was having technical difficulties, had stepped away momentarily from the computer, or was overwhelmed by multiple simultaneous contacts.

Given our speedy startup, the LSSI staff agreed to train us via speakerphone for a total of three hours in August, a week before classes began. I should be forthright, here, for education's sake. Our original startup date was September 17th. As an administrator of the system software, I observed that quite a few colleagues had not had a chance to practice. As a result, we pushed our startup date back one week, with much appreciation voiced by participating librarians. Then, after one week "live," we gathered for a two-hour supplemental, face-to-face training session.

We also revamped our logo to be more inclusive (Figure 6). Marketing efforts have continued as before with one difference being that all 10 college libraries now include at least one link to Librarians Online somewhere on their

FIGURE 5

FIGURE 6

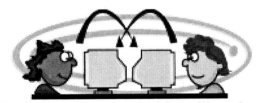

Click Here to chat with a librarian.

Web site. Figure 7 shows an example of one library that has included the icon on the first screen of their Web site. Figure 8 is an example of a text link on a secondary screen. Our entry screen into the service is depicted in Figure 9.

With one week left for this semester's operation, we have almost topped 160 questions. We're starting to get a sense of usage patterns. With the system report features, we have been able to track the number of queries, the queries themselves, the day and time of week, the referring URLs, plus a breakdown by week. Transcripts are also available to ascertain how a question was answered, and whether there were any underlying technological or policy-related problems.

Once again, we have been pleased with the quality of the questions asked. The one repetitive question we've had relates to access to the online catalog and our informational databases. Beyond that, however, we've had a healthy variety of questions. Here's a small sampling:

- Looking for articles discussing the reasons Americans are turning to religion after the September 11 attack.
- What is the psychological effect of home schooling?
- How do you find the horizontal and oblique asymptote?
- Statistics for jeans sales last year.

FIGURE 7

FIGURE 8

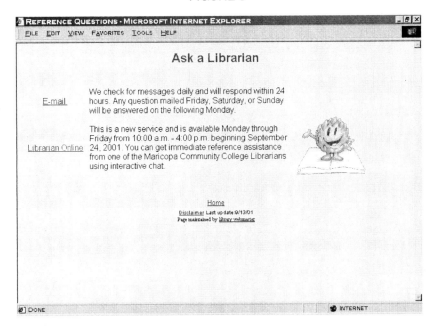

The following figures are samplings of statistics we are tracking. In Figure 10, Day of Week Minus Holiday Weeks, I determined that including the weeks with holidays would not be a true depiction of day of the week use. Thus, I removed the week with Veterans Day and Thanksgiving. Figure 11, Time of Day, should be helpful when deciding on future operational schedules. What is missing here is time of day, combined with day of week. Although this data is available, it takes some manual manipulation to extract it. I plan to do this during the Spring 2002 semester because we may find, for instance that 2-4 p.m. on Monday afternoons is underutilized, but Wednesdays at that same time may be popular. This way, if we need to change our schedule due to fewer volunteers, or some time slots being impossible to fill, we'll have data to back up our decisions.

Conclusions drawn from the referring URL statistics (Figure 12) are speculative. Though the Mesa Community College's URLs were used the most, is it because the link to Librarians Online is on their opening screen? Is it because they are using the logo for the link, rather than a text link? Is it because the librarians and faculty at Mesa are actively promoting the service? Or is it simply because Mesa has the largest enrollment? Actually it probably had a lot to do with the fact that one of our online librarians was teaching a library technician

FIGURE 9

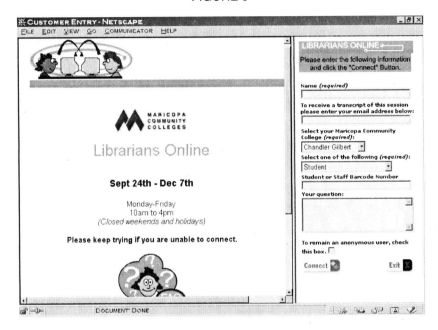

FIGURE 10

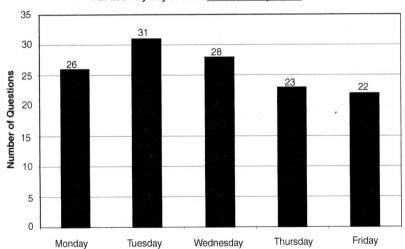

Fall 2001-By Day of Week *Minus Holiday Weeks*

FIGURE 11

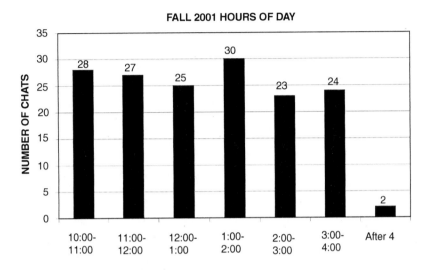

FIGURE 12

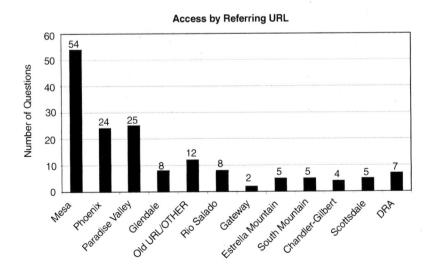

reference course at Mesa in which she encouraged her students to utilize the service by giving extra credit if they turned in a copy of a transcript.

Transcripts are somewhat controversial. After all, we are not typically privy to the details of a colleague's reference transactions. We may observe one another while we're stationed together at the reference desk, but nothing is recorded. Of course, there is also the question of privacy for the patron. We have chosen to take advantage of the patron anonymous check box available with the system, which approximately 20% of our patrons have chosen to use. This strips any identifying information at the time of the transaction and in the transcripts.

Nevertheless, the transcript is available to whomever is designated an administrator. I have trampled lightly in this realm. When I have detected a common misunderstanding or problem I have sent out e-mails to the entire group of online librarians to clarify. For example, a significant number of chats were clocking in *after* our closing time. Therefore I had to contact the librarians involved to come up with the actual time they had contacts. After some experimenting, I concluded that this problem was due to not exiting the chat session properly. Apparently this has been a common problem amongst libraries using the LSSI software because LSSI sent a message on their user listserv outlining the proper exit procedure. I was able to forward LSSI's message to emphasize the need to exit properly. I have also, at times, contacted a librarian if it looks as though he or she seems to be having difficulties picking up a customer. This may indicate a technological problem that needs follow-up. I have not, however, judged the approach any individual librarian has taken when assisting a student. We have 30-year librarian veterans volunteering their office time; I don't want to lose their participation by questioning their methods.

We've also used the transcript to our advantage for follow-up e-mails and/or phone calls. Some of our patrons were cut off due to our inexperience or technical difficulties. If they provided an e-mail address, we were able to contact them after the fact to assist. A recent example of a follow-up phone call was when the librarian saw that a student had been on hold for almost 50 minutes, yet the librarian had not seen a customer waiting. We called, apologized and asked if we could still be of help.

Additional statistics are available such as average hold time and average service time. Taking a random mid-operation sampling of 3 weeks, we averaged 31 seconds and 20 minutes service time respectively.

In addition, we developed an evaluation form which pops up upon exiting the service (Figure 13). The LSSI software compiles this data automatically. Unfortunately, as of this writing, the programming has not been put in place to access it. Hopefully we'll garner valuable information from our customers' responses. However, comments, such as the following are showing up in the transcripts giving us some indication that the service is appreciated and helpful:

- Thanks so much. This was awesome.
- This is a great tool.

It wouldn't be truthful to say that all has been smooth sailing. In addition to the technical difficulties touched on above, some of our challenges have related to what amounts to a consortium arrangement of colleges in the district. To reiterate, although the Maricopa Community College District is a single district, the autonomous operation of each college characterizes us as more of a loose network with shared students, geography, governing board and a district administration that directs an overall mission and vision.

This diversity amongst the MCCCD libraries is causing us to stretch our knowledge beyond our own library. For instance, although we have common informational databases across the district, each library has a set of its own unique databases. Even though we had developed the policy to only refer students to the shared databases, our students are unaware they may be chatting with a librarian who is not from their college. We have gotten questions such as: "What is the username and password I need to access the databases." There will often be one method from the college's Web site and a different method from the common

FIGURE 13

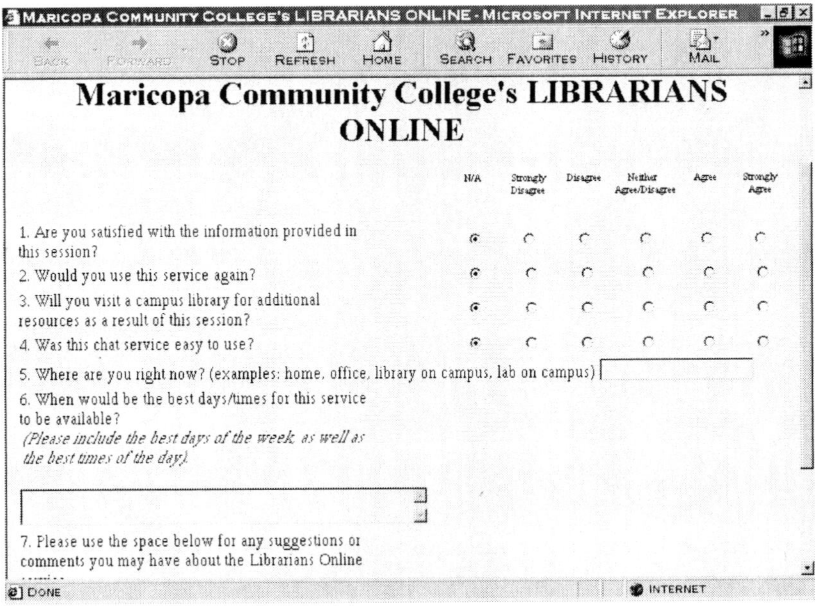

database list. This has been confusing for both the librarians and the students. Other unique resources which have surfaced are: a specialized e-mail service at one college; events and programs at each college a student may be asking about; and, of course, specialized assignments by instructors well-known at the originating college, but not at all known outside of the college.

Due to Librarians Online growing from a grassroots effort, although district administration has put some monetary support behind it, universal support across the colleges' administrations is lacking. At one college, for instance, librarians may only volunteer if they do so on their own time. Hopefully district support will be forthcoming in the future.

A related dilemma has been funding as it relates to extending the service. Were we to offer some evening and weekend hours or more personal coverage during the day, more contract hours would be required. These hours would incur additional expenses by paying for librarians' time or by outsourcing. From whence would this funding come? Would we ask for a district line item to fund the service, or contributions from each college's budget? Obviously this has yet to be solved.

A second funding-related question is the time I am devoting as the coordinator of the service. In addition to the statistical data I am maintaining, I make myself available for questions, supplemental training, backup monitoring, public relations and marketing, and the list goes on. I estimate I am spending 10 to 15 hours per week on the project. Eventually, as the usage increases, this will need to be addressed. A coordinator position will need to be created in order to sustain the service.

A final problem which has not been a huge problem yet, but could be as the service becomes mainstream, is that of sustaining our jigsaw-like schedule. Some librarians are doing two-hour stretches, some are doing one hour on two different days, and just in our nine weeks of operation, we've had at least 15 trades take place. We've also had people coming online late which affects the person ahead of them. Once, a librarian was sick and naturally didn't think of her scheduled online time slot. Although I am pleasantly surprised at how well we sustained the schedule this fall, I think the only way to be assured that we are open when we say we are, is that we have two people consistently online.

THE IMMEDIATE FUTURE

We are gearing up for our Spring 2002 operation. We know the following:

- January 21-May 3 (Second week of classes through the week prior to final exams)
- 10:00 a.m.-4:00 p.m. (We wanted a point of comparison so maintained the same hours as Fall)

- 14 of the 17 librarians have recommitted
- Continue with LSSI's software.

At this year's All Library Staff meeting, we were invited to do a demonstration of Librarians Online in front of the entire district's library staff. The online librarians will then gather for lunch to informally share their experiences online with each other. Other librarians who are toying with the idea of volunteering some hours will be encouraged to join our lunch conversation.

We plan to pursue funding for a coordinator, and we hope in the summer to apply for summer project funds in order to develop an online policy and procedures manual.

Summer staffing is a challenge. As faculty at MCCCD we are on a 9-month contract. Although some of us work in the summer, our schedules are scattered and we do not have office hours. The obvious solution is special district funding, which we will also pursue.

FUTURE PREDICTIONS

I have no doubt that digital reference at Maricopa will continue and become mainstreamed. It may continue as a centralized service, but more likely be absorbed as an extension of reference services at each college during operating hours and as a centralized, perhaps outsourced service, after hours.

Consistent, committed funding will be the mechanism that keeps Librarians Online in business, and thus will be sought as a line item in the district budget for staffing, software, office equipment and marketing.

We will develop methods to help us assist students from the diverse colleges such as an intranet whereby we will be able to lookup each other's policies and idiosyncrasies.

Our numbers will grow as links to the service are incorporated routinely in all distance learning courses, Web-enhanced courses and district department Web sites such as the learning support/tutoring departments as well as academic departments.

The software used for digital reference will improve dramatically. Once the bandwidth is no longer an obstacle, and the need to download plug-ins on one's computer is not required, we'll see videoconferencing and voice-over-IP integrated, thus making it possible to conduct a reference interview in much the same way we do now at the physical reference desk.

CONCLUSION

Ours has been a steady, if perhaps somewhat reticent, foray into the digital reference milieu. But because enough librarians in the Maricopa district believe we have embarked on an important new approach to reference services, we are experimenting, experiencing and learning.

Once we feel more comfortable with the digital modality, we must then move toward assessing its effectiveness. This will be an important next step. At this year's *Measuring & Assessing the Quality of Digital Reference Services* Virtual Reference Desk pre-conference workshop, Charles McClure asks the question, "What do we want to accomplish which we aren't accomplishing through traditional reference?" In other words, what do we want our outcomes to be? Mr. McClure, with his usual humor, also suggested that although we could continue blissfully offering these services, there will come a time when we will need to be ready to justify the personnel and monetary resources devoted to them (2001).

Until such time as we do a formal evaluation, we feel instinctively that we want to "meet the students where they are," which is an echo of Anne Lipow's keynote address at the Ninth Australasian Information Online & On Disc Conference and Exhibition (1999) in which she said:

> We have to become more convenient. You might look at it this way: rather than thinking of our users as remote, we should instead recognise that it is we who are remote from our users. We need to change how we do business in such a way as to get us back together. (Remote User or Remote Librarian section, para. 3)

REFERENCES

The Campus Computing Project. (2001, October). *The 2001 National Survey of Information Technology in U.S. higher education*. Retrieved November 25, 2001, from http://www.campuscomputing.net.

Dalton, R. (2001, January 31). I'll be with you in an instant. *Byte.com*. Retrieved November 25, 2001, from Expanded Academic ASAP database.

Doerfler, S. (1997, September 13). Instant match: LoanMaker speeds, simplifies, mortgage process. *The Arizona Republic*, pp. AH1-AH2.

Folger, K. (1997). *The virtual librarian: Using desktop videoconferencing to provide interactive reference assistance*. Paper presented at the ACRL 8th National Conference. Nashville. Retrieved September 18, 1998, from http://www.ala.org/acrl/paperhtm/a09.html.

Francoeur, S. (Comp.). (2001, July 3). Digital Reference. In *The teaching librarian: Exploring the intersection of reference services, technology and instruction*. Retrieved November 28, 2001, from http://pages.prodigy.net/tabo1/digref.htm.

Legard, D. (2000, October 24). Instant messaging to grow annual 140%. *Network World*. Retrieved November 25, 2001, from Expanded Academic ASAP database.

Lessick, S., Kjaer, K., & Clancy, S. (1997). *Interactive reference service (IRS) at UC Irvine: Expanding reference service beyond the reference desk*. Paper presented at the ACRL 8th National Conference. Nashville. Retrieved September 18, 1998, from http://www.ala.org/acrl/paperhtm/a10.html.

Lipow, Anne G. (1999, January 20) *Serving the remote user: Reference service in the digital environment.* Paper presented at the Ninth Australasian Information Online & On Disc Conference and Exhibition. Sydney, Australia. Retrieved November 12, 2001 from http://www.csu.edu.au/special/online99/proceedings99/200.htm.

McClure, Charles R. (2001, November). Digital reference evaluation basics. Presentation at the *Measuring & Assessing the Quality of Digital Reference Services* pre-conference workshop of the Third Annual Virtual Reference Desk Conference, Orlando, FL.

McKiernan, G. (Comp.). (2001, October 16) *LiveRef(sm): A registry of time digital reference services.* Retrieved November 28, 2001, from Iowa State University Homepage Server: http://www.public.iastate.edu/~CYBERSTACKS/LiveRef.htm.

Morgan, E. L. (1996). *See you see a librarian final report.* Retrieved September 18, 1998, from http://sunsite.berkeley,edu/~emorgan/see-a-librarian.

OCLC makes offer to purchase assets of netLibrary. (2001, November 15). *OCLC News.* Retrieved from http://www.oclc.org/oclc/press/20011115.shtm.

Oder, N. (2001, February 1). The shape of e-reference. *Library Journal, 126*(2), 46-50.

Tenopir, C. (2001, October 1). Database and online system usage. *Library Journal, 126*(16), 41. Retrieved November 25, 2001, from Expanded Academic ASAP database.

Contributor Index

A

B

C

D

S

Schafer, Jay
and Jessame Ferguson, Joel Fowler, Marilyn Hanley: *Building a Digital Library in Support of Distance Learning*, 317-331
Sias, Jennifer
and Judith Arnold, Jingping Zhang: *Bringing the Library to the Students: Using Technology to Deliver Instruction and Resources for Research*, 27-37
Sochrin, Sheri
and Anne Marie Casey, Stephanie Fazenbaker Race: *Fair Is Fair, or Is It? Library Services to Distance Learners*, 147-161
Stratford, Sandra K.
Surviving a Distance Learning Accreditation Visit, 489-501
Summey, Terri Pedersen
and James Fisk: *Who's Out There in Cyberspace: Profiling the Remote Learner for Service Design*, 503-513

T

Tuñón, Johanna
Creating a Research Literacy Course for Education Doctoral Students: Design Issues and Political Realities of Developing Online and Face-to-Face Instruction, 515-527
Tuñón, Johanna
and Mou Chakraborty: *Taking the Distance Out of Library Services Offered to International Graduate Students: Considerations, Challenges, and Concerns*, 163-176

V

Veal, Robin
The Relationship Between Library Anxiety and Off-Campus Adult Learners, 529-536

W

Wilson, Pat
The Ins and Outs of Providing Electronic Reserves for Distance Learning Classes, 537-548

Index

10.1300/J111v37n03_47

Access, Ownership, and Resource Sharing, edited by Sul H. Lee (Vol. 20, No. 1, 1995). *The contributing authors present a useful and informative look at the current status of information provision and some of the challenges the subject presents.*

Libraries as User-Centered Organizations: Imperatives for Organizational Change, edited by Meredith A. Butler (Vol. 19, No. 3/4, 1994). *"Presents a very timely and well-organized discussion of major trends and influences causing organizational changes." (Science Books & Films)*

Declining Acquisitions Budgets: Allocation, Collection Development and Impact Communication, edited by Sul H. Lee (Vol. 19, No. 2, 1994). *"Expert and provocative. . . . Presents many ways of looking at library budget deterioration and responses to it . . . There is much food for thought here." (Library Resources & Technical Services)*

The Role and Future of Special Collections in Research Libraries: British and American Perspectives, edited by Sul H. Lee (Vol. 19, No. 1, 1993). *"A provocative but informative read for library users, academic administrators, and private sponsors." (International Journal of Information and Library Research)*

Catalysts for Change: Managing Libraries in the 1990s, edited by Gisela M. von Dran, DPA, MLS, and Jennifer Cargill, MSLS, MSed (Vol. 18, No. 3/4, 1994). *"A useful collection of articles which focuses on the need for librarians to employ enlightened management practices in order to adapt to and thrive in the rapidly changing information environment." (Australian Library Review)*

Integrating Total Quality Management in a Library Setting, edited by Susan Jurow, MLS, and Susan B. Barnard, MLS (Vol. 18, No. 1/2, 1993). *"Especially valuable are the librarian experiences that directly relate to real concerns about TQM. Recommended for all professional reading collections." (Library Journal)*

Leadership in Academic Libraries: Proceedings of the W. Porter Kellam Conference, The University of Georgia, May 7, 1991, edited by William Gray Potter (Vol. 17, No. 4, 1993). *"Will be of interest to those concerned with the history of American academic libraries." (Australian Library Review)*

Collection Assessment and Acquisitions Budgets, edited by Sul H. Lee (Vol. 17, No. 2, 1993). *Contains timely information about the assessment of academic library collections and the relationship of collection assessment to acquisition budgets.*

Developing Library Staff for the 21st Century, edited by Maureen Sullivan (Vol. 17, No. 1, 1992). *"I found myself enthralled with this highly readable publication. It is one of those rare compilations that manages to successfully integrate current general management operational thinking in the context of academic library management." (Bimonthly Review of Law Books)*

Vendor Evaluation and Acquisition Budgets, edited by Sul H. Lee (Vol. 16, No. 3, 1992). *"The title doesn't do justice to the true scope of this excellent collection of papers delivered at the sixth annual conference on library acquisitions sponsored by the University of Oklahoma Libraries." (Kent K. Hendrickson, BS, MALS, Dean of Libraries, University of Nebraska-Lincoln) Find insightful discussions on the impact of rising costs on library budgets and management in this groundbreaking book.*

The Management of Library and Information Studies Education, edited by Herman L. Totten, PhD, MLS (Vol. 16, No. 1/2, 1992). *"Offers something of interest to everyone connected with LIS education–the undergraduate contemplating a master's degree, the doctoral student struggling with courses and career choices, the new faculty member aghast at conflicting responsibilities, the experienced but stressed LIS professor, and directors of LIS Schools." (Education Libraries)*

Library Management in the Information Technology Environment: Issues, Policies, and Practice for Administrators, edited by Brice G. Hobrock, PhD, MLS (Vol. 15, No. 3/4, 1992). *"A road map to identify some of the alternative routes to the electronic library." (Stephen Rollins, Associate Dean for Library Services, General Library, University of New Mexico)*

Managing Technical Services in the 90's, edited by Drew Racine (Vol. 15, No. 1/2, 1991). *"Presents an eclectic overview of the challenges currently facing all library technical services efforts. . . . Recommended to library administrators and interested practitioners." (Library Journal)*

Budgets for Acquisitions: Strategies for Serials, Monographs, and Electronic Formats, edited by Sul H. Lee (Vol. 14, No. 3, 1991). *"Much more than a series of handy tips for the careful shopper. This [book] is a most useful one–well-informed, thought-provoking, and authoritative." (Australian Library Review)*

Creative Planning for Library Administration: Leadership for the Future, edited by Kent Hendrickson, MALS (Vol. 14, No. 2, 1991). *"Provides some essential information on the planning process, and the mix of opinions and methodologies, as well as examples relevant to every library manager, resulting in a very readable foray into a topic too long avoided by many of us." (Canadian Library Journal)*

Strategic Planning in Higher Education: Implementing New Roles for the Academic Library, edited by James F. Williams, II, MLS (Vol. 13, No. 3/4, 1991). *"A welcome addition to the sparse literature on strategic planning in university libraries. Academic librarians considering strategic planning for their libraries will learn a great deal from this work." (Canadian Library Journal)*

Personnel Administration in an Automated Environment, edited by Philip E. Leinbach, MLS (Vol. 13, No. 1/2, 1990). *"An interesting and worthwhile volume, recommended to university library administrators and to others interested in thought-provoking discussion of the personnel implications of automation." (Canadian Library Journal)*

Library Development: A Future Imperative, edited by Dwight F. Burlingame, PhD (Vol. 12, No. 4, 1990). *"This volume provides an excellent overview of fundraising with special application to libraries. . . . A useful book that is highly recommended for all libraries." (Library Journal)*

Library Material Costs and Access to Information, edited by Sul H. Lee (Vol. 12, No. 3, 1991). *"A cohesive treatment of the issue. Although the book's contributors possess a research library perspective, the data and the ideas presented are of interest and benefit to the entire profession, especially academic librarians." (Library Resources and Technical Services)*

Training Issues and Strategies in Libraries, edited by Paul M. Gherman, MALS, and Frances O. Painter, MLS, MBA (Vol. 12, No. 2, 1990). *"There are . . . useful chapters, all by different authors, each with a preliminary summary of the content–a device that saves much time in deciding whether to read the whole chapter or merely skim through it. Many of the chapters are essentially practical without too much emphasis on theory. This book is a good investment." (Library Association Record)*

Library Education and Employer Expectations, edited by E. Dale Cluff, PhD, MLS (Vol. 11, No. 3/4, 1990). *"Useful to library-school students and faculty interested in employment problems and employer perspectives. Librarians concerned with recruitment practices will also be interested." (Information Technology and Libraries)*

Managing Public Libraries in the 21st Century, edited by Pat Woodrum, MLS (Vol. 11, No. 1/2, 1989). *"A broad-based collection of topics that explores the management problems and possibilities public libraries will be facing in the 21st century." (Robert Swisher, PhD, Director, School of Library and Information Studies, University of Oklahoma)*

Human Resources Management in Libraries, edited by Gisela M. Webb, MLS, MPA (Vol. 10, No. 4, 1989). *"Thought provoking and enjoyable reading. . . . Provides valuable insights for the effective information manager." (Special Libraries)*

Creativity, Innovation, and Entrepreneurship in Libraries, edited by Donald E. Riggs, EdD, MLS (Vol. 10, No. 2/3, 1989). *"The volume is well worth reading as a whole. . . . There is very little repetition, and it should stimulate thought." (Australian Library Review)*

The Impact of Rising Costs of Serials and Monographs on Library Services and Programs, edited by Sul H. Lee (Vol. 10, No. 1, 1989). *". . . Sul Lee hit a winner here." (Serials Review)*

Computing, Electronic Publishing, and Information Technology: Their Impact on Academic Libraries, edited by Robin N. Downes (Vol. 9, No. 4, 1989). *"For a relatively short and easily digestible discussion of these issues, this book can be recommended, not only to those in academic libraries, but also to those in similar types of library or information unit, and to academics and educators in the field." (Journal of Documentation)*

Library Management and Technical Services: The Changing Role of Technical Services in Library Organizations, edited by Jennifer Cargill, MSLS, MSed (Vol. 9, No. 1, 1988). *"As a practical and instructive guide to issues such as automation, personnel matters, education, management techniques and liaison with other services, senior library managers with a sincere interest in evaluating the role of their technical services should find this a timely publication." (Library Association Record)*

Management Issues in the Networking Environment, edited by Edward R. Johnson, PhD (Vol. 8, No. 3/4, 1989). *"Particularly useful for librarians/information specialists contemplating establishing a local network." (Australian Library Review)*

Acquisitions, Budgets, and Material Costs: Issues and Approaches, edited by Sul H. Lee (Supp. #2, 1988). *"The advice of these library practitioners is sensible and their insights illuminating for librarians in academic libraries." (American Reference Books Annual)*

Pricing and Costs of Monographs and Serials: National and International Issues, edited by Sul H. Lee (Supp. #1, 1987). *"Eminently readable. There is a good balance of chapters on serials and monographs and the perspective of suppliers, publishers, and library practitioners are presented. A book well worth reading." (Australasian College Libraries)*

Legal Issues for Library and Information Managers, edited by William Z. Nasri, JD, PhD (Vol. 7, No. 4, 1987). *"Useful to any librarian looking for protection or wondering where responsibilities end and liabilities begin. Recommended." (Academic Library Book Review)*

Archives and Library Administration: Divergent Traditions and Common Concerns, edited by Lawrence J. McCrank, PhD, MLS (Vol. 7, No. 2/3, 1986). *"A forward-looking view of archives and libraries.... Recommend[ed] to students, teachers, and practitioners alike of archival and library science. It is readable, thought-provoking, and provides a summary of the major areas of divergence and convergence." (Association of Canadian Map Libraries and Archives)*

Excellence in Library Management, edited by Charlotte Georgi, MLS, and Robert Bellanti, MLS, MBA (Vol. 6, No. 3, 1985). *"Most beneficial for library administrators . . . for anyone interested in either library/information science or management." (Special Libraries)*

Marketing and the Library, edited by Gary T. Ford (Vol. 4, No. 4, 1984). *Discover the latest methods for more effective information dissemination and learn to develop successful programs for specific target areas.*

Finance Planning for Libraries, edited by Murray S. Martin (Vol. 3, No. 3/4, 1983). *Stresses the need for libraries to weed out expenditures which do not contribute to their basic role–the collection and organization of information–when planning where and when to spend money.*

Planning for Library Services: A Guide to Utilizing Planning Methods for Library Management, edited by Charles R. McClure, PhD (Vol. 2, No. 3/4, 1982). *"Should be read by anyone who is involved in planning processes of libraries–certainly by every administrator of a library or system." (American Reference Books Annual)*